Investors' International Law

Edited by
Jean Ho
and
Mavluda Sattorova

•HART•
OXFORD • LONDON • NEW YORK • NEW DELHI • SYDNEY

HART PUBLISHING
Bloomsbury Publishing Plc
Kemp House, Chawley Park, Cumnor Hill, Oxford, OX2 9PH, UK
1385 Broadway, New York, NY 10018, USA
29 Earlsfort Terrace, Dublin 2, Ireland

HART PUBLISHING, the Hart/Stag logo, BLOOMSBURY and the Diana logo are trademarks of Bloomsbury Publishing Plc

First published in Great Britain 2021

A catalogue record for this book is available from the British Library.

Library of Congress Cataloging-in-Publication data

Names: Ho, Jean, editor. | Sattorova, Mavluda, editor.

Title: Investors' international law / edited by Jean Ho and Mavluda Sattorova.

Description: Oxford ; New York : Hart, 2021. | Series: Studies in International Trade and Investment Law ; volume 24 | "This book project is the output of a two-day closed-door workshop held at the Faculty of Law of the National University of Singapore, 18–19 January 2019"—ECIP acknowledgments. | Includes bibliographical references and index.

Identifiers: LCCN 2021017153 (print) | LCCN 2021017154 (ebook) | ISBN 9781509937912 (hardback) | ISBN 9781509951062 (paperback) | ISBN 9781509937929 (pdf) | ISBN 9781509937936 (Epub)

Subjects: LCSH: Investments, Foreign (International law)—Congresses. | Social responsibility of business—Law and legislation—Congresses. | Tort liability of corporations—Congresses.

Classification: LCC K3830 . I68485 2021 (print) | LCC K3830 (ebook) | DDC 346/.092—dc23

LC record available at https://lccn.loc.gov/2021017153

LC ebook record available at https://lccn.loc.gov/2021017154

ISBN: HB: 978-1-50993-791-2
ePDF: 978-1-50993-792-9
ePub: 978-1-50993-793-6

Typeset by Compuscript Ltd, Shannon

PREFACE

This book project started by chance, was nurtured with a chat and countless emails, and blossomed with the concerted belief and commitment of 15 other chapter contributors. We first met as invited speakers at the ICSID@50 Anniversary Conference in Xi'An, China, and again as panelists at the 6th Asian Society of International Law Biennial Conference in Seoul, South Korea. Of all the panelists in Seoul, we were the only two who discussed the challenges of securing investor accountability and, in particular, corporate investor accountability, under international law. We gravitated towards each other, as like-minded people do, and promised to explore the possibility of collaboration.

Over the next three years, from 2016 to 2018, we realised that we wanted to do more than point out why and how the substance and procedure of international law hampered the pursuit of investor accountability, and we were realistic about the dim prospect of an imminent and thorough overhaul of international law to rid it fully of its colonial and capitalist tenor. Between the familiar extremes of helpless description and ruthless iconoclasm, accompanied by invitations to *others* to solve the problem of chronic investor under-accountability for severe misconduct, lies a space to reflect on how we can make the best of the deck of cards which we have been dealt. We must stress at this juncture that we are not opposed to a fundamental rewriting of international law as it pertains to foreign investor regulation. However, until that fateful moment comes to pass, we firmly believe that it is more constructive to use and recalibrate the tools at our disposal than to dream of a better tomorrow.

By 2019, we knew that we wanted to write a book that investigates the other side of international law, the side that harbours potential for the attachment of investor accountability, the side that both the apologists and radical reformists seem to assume does not or cannot exist, and the side that we might very well be the first to study and elaborate on. In deliberately going against the grain of critical international law scholarship that is rich on reasons for change but typically thin on concrete measures for change, we saw the book as a showcase for the eclecticism, ingenuity, courage and ambition of a diverse cast of some of the most exciting, emerging international law scholars whose known research profile encompasses foreign investor regulation. We are honoured to be joined in our atypical quest by José Daniel Amado, Barnali Choudhury, Lorenzo Cotula, Martin Doe Rodriguez, Tomoko Ishikawa, Martin Jarrett, Jackson Shaw Kern, Julian Ku, Nitish Monebhurrun, Priscila Pereira de Andrade, Nicolás Perrone, Prabhash Ranjan, Lucas Roorda, Anil Yilmaz Vastardis and Jure Zrilič.

This is a book borne from cautious optimism amid the gloom of an international law skewed towards investor protection, and completed while the world was gripped by the COVID-19 pandemic. It represents our and all our contributors' endurance for unprecedented setbacks and, above all, unwavering collective confidence in the reimagined avenues to investor accountability. With the hope that you will find reading this book as rewarding and as thought-provoking as we did over five years of conceptualising, writing and refining it, we present to you: *Investors' International Law*.

JH
Duke's Road, Singapore

MS
Wirral, United Kingdom
31 December 2020

ACKNOWLEDGEMENTS

This book project is the output of a two-day closed-door workshop held at the Faculty of Law of the National University of Singapore, 18–19 January 2019. It was made possible by a generous grant from the Singapore Ministry of Education's Academic Research Fund Tier 1, WBS No. R-241-000-173-115.

We thank Roberta Bassi and Rosemarie Mearns at Hart Publishing, and Professors Gabrielle Marceau, Krista Nadakavukaren Schefer, Federico Ortino and Gregory Shaffer for believing in our project and for awarding it a spot in the Studies in International Trade and Investment Law series. Roberta and Rosemarie checked in with us constantly, and were extremely encouraging and obliging throughout the submission and the publishing process. We thank our two anonymous reviewers whose detailed and extensive comments and suggestions for improvement enabled us to put our very best foot forward.

We are grateful to Dean Simon Chesterman for his support of the project, and to Professors Antony Anghie and Wang Jiangyu for moderating the sessions during the workshop in Singapore. We also wish to thank the administrative team at NUS Law for their seamless organisation of the workshop and for overseeing all large and small logistical details. In particular, we salute the professionalism and efficiency of Senior Assistant Dean Jayagowry d/o Appalasamy, Wendy Wee Hong Mui, Finna Wong and Alexandria Chan. We are grateful to NUS Law student assistants, Melissa Heng' 19, Hong Qibin' 19, Ong Shaw Shiuan' 19 and Uma Jitendra Sharma' 19 for serving as local contact points and eloquent Singapore guides to all foreign workshop participants.

Last but not least, we thank NUS Law students Ryan Moey' 23, Seah Ding Hang' 22 and Lai Shueh Chien' 21 for assisting with the completion of the final manuscript.

TABLE OF CONTENTS

CONTRIBUTOR BIOGRAPHIES

José Daniel Amado is the founding partner of Miranda & Amado, based in Lima, Peru. José received his JD from the Pontifical Catholic University of Peru and his LLM from Harvard University. From 2015–2016, José was a member of the Lima Chamber of Commerce Arbitration Court. He served as deputy to the Prime Minister of Peru from 2000–2002 and was named Leader of the Year by Latin Lawyer in 2009. Alongside Jackson Shaw Kern and Martin Doe Rodriguez, he is co-author of *Arbitrating the Conduct of International Investors* (Cambridge University Press, 2018).

Barnali Choudhury is Professor in Law at University College London Faculty of Laws. She is the sole author of *Public Services and International Trade Liberalization: Human Rights and Gender Implications* (Cambridge University Press, 2012), co-editor of *Understanding the Modern Company: Corporate Governance and Theory* (Cambridge University Press, 2017), and co-author of *Corporate Duties to the Public* (Cambridge University Press, 2019). Barnali's research has been cited by the United Nations, the House of Commons and the House of Lords EU Select Committee, among others. Barnali has held visiting positions at Cambridge University and the Max Planck Institute for Comparative and Private Law. In 2017, Barnali was awarded a Leverhulme Research Fellowship.

Lorenzo Cotula is Principal Researcher in Law and Sustainable Development at the International Institute for Environment and Development (IIED), and a Visiting Professor at Strathclyde Law School. Lorenzo conducts research, policy engagement and field-level projects on the legal arenas where natural resource governance meets the global economy – cutting across international investment law; land and natural resource law and governance; human rights law, business and human rights, and responsible investment; political economy of natural resources and foreign investment; and legal empowerment, citizen agency and public accountability. Lorenzo leads IIED's Legal Tools for Citizen Empowerment programme, a collaborative initiative to strengthen local rights in the context of natural resource investments in the Global South.

Surya Deva is Associate Professor of Law at City University of Hong Kong. Surya is the sole author of *Regulating Corporate Human Rights Violations: Humanizing Business* (Routledge, 2012), and co-editor of *Human Rights Obligations of Business: Beyond the Corporate Responsibility to Protect* (Cambridge University Press, 2013), *Socio-Economic Rights in Emerging Free Markets: Comparative Insights from India and*

China (Routledge, 2015), and *Building a Treaty on Business and Human Rights: Context and Contours* (Cambridge University Press, 2017). In 2016, Surya was appointed to the United Nations Working Group on Business and Human Rights.

Martin Doe Rodriguez is Senior Legal Counsel at the Permanent Court of Arbitration in The Hague. At the PCA, he works closely with arbitral tribunals constituted under the auspices of the PCA to resolve investment treaty disputes, contract claims involving state entities and international organisations, and inter-state disputes arising under various international conventions and treaties. In particular, he handles matters involving Latin America and the Iberian Peninsula, or where Spanish or Portuguese is a language of the arbitration. In addition, he assists the PCA Secretary-General in carrying out his roles under the Arbitration Rules of the United Nations Commission for International Trade Law, and is also regularly called upon to assist in the diplomatic work of the PCA with its Member States and other intergovernmental organisations. He holds degrees in common law, civil law and biochemistry from McGill University and is a member of the Barreau du Québec, New York State Bar and the Chartered Institute of Arbitrators. He speaks English, Spanish, French and Portuguese. Alongside José Daniel Amado and Jackson Shaw Kern, he is co-author of *Arbitrating the Conduct of International Investors* (Cambridge University Press, 2018.

Jean Ho is Associate Professor of Law at the National University of Singapore, and a member of the Singapore and New York Bars. Prior to academia, Jean specialised in international investment disputes at Shearman & Sterling LLP, and she now acts as counsel in investor-state disputes. Jean is an Expert for the UNDROIT Working Group on Land Agricultural Investment Contracts, an elected Member of the Executive Committee of the Asian Society of International Law, as well as an Editorial Board Member and Book Review Editor of the *Journal of International Economic Law*. Jean's sole-authored monograph, *State Responsibility for Breaches of Investment Contracts* (Cambridge University Press, 2018), is synopsised in English, French and Mandarin in the United Nations Audiovisual Library on International Law Lecture Series. She is also a principal co-author of *International Investment Law and Arbitration* (Cambridge University Press, 1st edn 2018, 2nd edn 2021).

Tomoko Ishikawa is Professor of Law at the Graduate School of International Development at Nagoya University. Tomoko is an invited Member of the Investment Treaty Forum of the British Institute of International and Comparative Law, and was appointed to the ICSID Panel of Conciliators by the Chairman of the ICSID Administrative Council in 2017. Tomoko is the sole author of 'Third Party Participation in Investment Treaty Arbitration' (2010) 59 *International and Comparative Law Quarterly* 373, and co-editor of *Reshaping the Investor-State Dispute Settlement System: Journeys for the 21st Century* (Brill, 2015), *Natural Resource Grabbing: An International Law Perspective* (Brill, 2015), *International Economic Law and Governance* (Oxford University Press, 2016), *Asia's Changing*

International Investment Regime: Sustainability, Regionalization, and Arbitration (Springer, 2017) and *International Investment Treaties and Arbitration Across Asia* (Brill, 2018).

Martin Jarrett is Senior Research Fellow at the Max Planck Institute for Comparative Public Law and International Law. He was educated and qualified in Australia (BA, LLB (1:1) and Grad Dip of Legal Prac), and was previously Senior Lecturer at the University of Mannheim, Germany. His primary research interests lie in international investment law, most particularly the topic of investor misconduct. Martin graduated *summa cum laude* for his doctorate on this topic, and is the sole author of *Contributory Fault Defences in International Investment Law* (Cambridge University Press, 2019).

Jackson Shaw Kern is Of Counsel at Addis Law Group LLP and a member of the Bars of New York, Washington, DC and Montana. He has acted as counsel across Africa, Asia, Europe and the Americas, where he represents sovereign states, state entities, and state enterprises as well as private interests in a wide range of contentious matters. Jackson was a Visiting Fellow at the Lauterpacht Centre for International Law at the University of Cambridge, and is a frequent guest lecturer at institutions in Africa and beyond. Alongside José Daniel Amado and Martin Doe Rodriguez, he is co-author of *Arbitrating the Conduct of International Investors* (Cambridge University Press 2018).

Julian Ku is the Maurice A Deane Distinguished Professor of Constitutional Law at Maurice A Deane School of Law at Hofstra University. He is co-author of *Taming Globalization: International Law, the U.S. Constitution, and the New World Order* (Oxford University Press, 2012), and has sole authored more than 40 law review articles, book chapters, symposia contributions and essays on international dispute resolution, international criminal law and China's relationship with international law. Julian is co-founder of the leading international law blog *Opinio Juris*, which is read daily by thousands worldwide. His essays and op-eds have been published by major news publications such as *The Wall Street Journal*, the *Los Angeles Times*, and NYTimes.com.

Nitish Monebhurrun is Professor of Law at the University Centre of Brasília (Brazil) and Visiting Professor at the University of Sabana (Colombia). He is also the Director of the Business, Human Rights and Public Policy Clinic of the University Centre of Brasília and the Editor of the Brazilian Journal of International Law. Nitish's recent publications include a sole-authored monograph, *La fonction du développement dans le droit international des investissements* (L'Harmattan, 2016) and a string of sole-authored articles: 'Diligentia Quam in Suis as a Technique for a Contextual Application of the Full Protection and Security Standard: Considering the Level of Development of Host States in International Investment Law' (2020) 28 *African Journal of International and Comparative Law* 596; 'What would change in Brazil's practice with the adoption of an Investor-State Dispute Settlement Mechanism in its Investment Agreements?' (2019) 39 *Nomos*; 'Mapping

Investors' duties in International Investment Law' (2017) 14 *Brazilian Journal of International Law* 50; 'The (mis)use of development in international investment law: understanding the jurist's limits to work with development issues' (2017) 11 *Law and Development Review* 1; and 'Novelty in International Investment Law: The Brazilian Agreement on Cooperation and Facilitation of Investments as a Different International Investment Agreement Model' (2017) 8 *Journal of International Dispute Settlement* 79.

Priscila Pereira de Andrade is a Legal Officer at UNIDROIT, a consultant for the International Institute for Sustainable Development, an Expert for the UNDROIT Working Group on Land Agricultural Investment Contracts, a research fellow (*cultore della materia*) at the Department of International Law of the University of Pisa, and a member of the Brazilian bar. Priscilla was previously Associate Professor and taught Transnational Environmental Law at the University Center of Brasília. Priscilla holds a PhD in International Law from l'Université de Paris 1 (Panthéon-Sorbonne), a MSc in Law of International Relations from the University Center of Brasília, Uniceub, and a Specialization in International Environmental Law from UNITAR International University. Priscilla is the sole author of *Le développement durable des biocarburants: objet d'un droit transnational* (L'Harmattan, 2018) and several articles related to environment law, contract law and private certification schemes for sustainable development.

Nicolás Perrone is Research Associate Professor of International Law at Universidad Andres Bello, Chile. His main research interests are in international economic law, particularly in international investment law and policy. Nicolás has published extensively on local communities and international investment law and is the sole author of *Investment Treaties and the Legal Imagination – How Foreign Investors Play By Their Own Rules* (Oxford University Press, 2021). Nicolás has been a faculty member of the Institute for Global Law and Policy at Harvard Law School and a Visiting Professor at the Universidad Nacional de San Martín, the International University College of Turin, the University of Eastern Piedmont and the Externado University of Colombia. Nicolás has worked and consulted for the Governments of Argentina, Ecuador and Colombia, the OECD, UNCTAD, the International Institute for Sustainable Development and the Friedrich Ebert Stiftung. He is a member of the Editorial Committee of the *Yearbook on International Investment Law and Policy*, and his work has appeared in journals such as the *American Journal of International Law (Unbound)*, *Transnational Legal Theory*, *Journal of International Dispute Settlement*, and the *Journal of World Investment & Trade*.

Prabhash Ranjan is Senior Assistant Professor at the Faculty of Legal Studies at South Asian University. He holds a PhD in law from King's College London. Prabhash was a Visiting Fellow at the Lauterpacht Centre for International Law at the University of Cambridge, and a Visiting Scholar at Brookings India. He teaches and publishes widely in the area of international investment law and international trade law. Prabhash is the sole author of *India and Bilateral Investment Treaties: Refusal, Acceptance and Backlash* (Oxford University Press, 2019).

Lucas Roorda is Assistant Professor and Postdoctoral Researcher at Utrecht University, working with the Utrecht Centre for Accountability and Liability Law. Lucas teaches public international law, human rights and international humanitarian law. He previously worked as a policy advisor for the Netherlands Human Rights Institute, and is currently on the Advisory Committee of the Business and Human Rights project of the European Law Institute. Lucas has published extensively on different aspects of the liability of transnational corporations for human rights violations. His graduate thesis undertaken at Utrecht University in 2012, dealing with the possible implications of the case of *Kiobel v Royal Dutch Petroleum Co*, 133 S Ct 1659 (2013), was awarded the Leo Bouchez thesis prize. The commercial edition of Lucas's doctorate on jurisdiction in foreign direct liability cases in EU Member States will be available in 2021.

Mavluda Sattorova is Reader in International Economic Law at the School of Law & Social Justice and Director of Liverpool Economic Governance Unit, University of Liverpool. Mavluda has published extensively on international investment law and worked in an expert capacity with the UNCTAD Investment Division and the World Health Organization. Lately she has been exploring an empirically driven approach to investigating the interaction between investment treaty rules with national law and policy, in particular in developing countries.

Anil Yilmaz Vastardis is Senior Lecturer at the School of Law at the University of Essex. Her main research interests are in the fields of international investment law and business and human rights. More specifically, Anil examines the nationality of corporate investors under international investment law. Anil leads several projects within the Essex Business and Human Rights Project. Her most recent work with the EBHR focused on improving paths to accountability for human rights and labour violations in global supply chains. This work resulted in a legal guide aimed to assist practitioners and civil society in developing legal claims in this area. Anil is the sole author of *The Nationality of Corporate Investors under International Investment Law* (Hart, 2020) and co-author of 'Overcoming the Corporate Veil Challenge: Could Investment Law Inspire the Propose Business and Human Rights Treaty?' (2018) 67 *International and Comparative Law Quarterly* 389.

Jure Zrilič is Lecturer at the School of Law and Social Justice, University of Liverpool. He gained academic experience at the University of Cambridge, Harvard Law School and Utrecht University. He completed his PhD at Cambridge, focusing on the protection of foreign investors in times of armed conflict. His recent articles include 'International Investment Law in the Context of Jus Post Bellum: Are Investment Treaties Likely to Facilitate or Hinder the Transition to

Peace?' (2015) 16 *Journal of World Investment and Trade* 604, and 'Armed Conflict as Force Majeure in International Investment Law' (2019) 16 *Manchester Journal of International Economic Law* 28. Jure's sole-authored monograph, *The Protection of Foreign Investment in Times of Armed Conflict*, was published by Oxford University Press in 2019.

Introduction

MAVLUDA SATTOROVA AND JEAN HO

On 1 September 1975, Henry Kissinger, then United States Secretary of State, addressed the United Nations General Assembly with a call to agree on the basic rules governing foreign investors:

> [T]he time has come for the international community to articulate standards of conduct for both enterprises and government ... These should apply to transnational enterprises in their relations with governments, and to governments in their relations with enterprises and with other governments.[1]

The speech was prompted by a domestic political crisis in the wake of an exposure of the International Telephone and Telegraph Company's (ITT) involvement in a CIA plot to thwart the election of Salvador Allende following his threats to nationalise ITT's foreign investment in Chile.[2] The revelations triggered investigations by US authorities into bribery and corruption permeating foreign investments overseas, whilst also amplifying a growing disquiet over the wider societal implications of transnational business activities.[3] In response to a complaint filed by Chile concerning ITT, the UN Social and Economic Council admitted that the international community had yet to 'establish effective machinery for dealing with issues raised by the activities of these corporations'.[4]

Elsewhere, under the aegis of the UN, developing countries were pushing for rules governing foreign investors as part of their wider efforts to usher in a New International Economic Order (NIEO). Aside from the ability of foreign investors to interfere in domestic political affairs, developing states shared concerns over a negative impact of foreign investment on 'the distribution of benefits and the ability of indigenous firms to grow and prosper'.[5] Already at a time

[1] HA Kissinger, 'Global Consensus and Economic Development' (Address by US Secretary of State to the Seventh Special Session of the United Nations General Assembly, delivered 1 September 1975 by DP Moynihan, US Representative to the United Nations) 432–33.

[2] See D Lustig, *Veiled Power* (Oxford University Press, 2020) 205–09.

[3] ibid 209.

[4] ECOSOC, 'Summary Record of the 1822nd Meeting of the 53rd Session' 19, 22, UN Doc E/SR.1822 (5 July 1972).

[5] See KP Sauvant, 'Negotiations of the United Nations Code of Conduct on Transnational Corporations: Experience and Lessons Learned' (2015) 16 *Journal of World Investment & Trade* 11, 14, citing ECOSOC, 'Report of the Commission on Transnational Corporations' (1976) 15 ILM 779.

the Abs-Shawcross Convention – a 'Magna Carta for Investment Protection'[6] – was being negotiated, developing states regarded the proposed rules as 'a code of the good debtor' that ought to be complemented with 'a code of the good creditor'.[7] The need to rein in foreign corporate actors and to harness foreign investment to serve the needs of host states was also expressly acknowledged both in the Declaration on the Establishment of a New International Economic Order[8] and the Charter of Economic Rights and Duties of States.[9] Overall, it was recognised that, since foreign investors operated in a global context, any effort at regulation ought to be global as well.[10]

The rest is history: following interminable discussions at the UN,[11] a multilateral Code of Conduct on Transnational Corporations was proposed but eventually abandoned in 1992.[12] In parallel developments, the ascendancy of neoliberal economic policy culminated in the establishment of a treaty-based mechanism for the protection of foreign investors from state interference. By the end of the 1990s, close to 2,000 bilateral treaties on investment protection and promotion were signed[13] and 146 states signed the Convention on the Settlement of Investment Disputes between States and Nationals of Other States (the ICSID Convention).[14] Together, these international instruments constitute the principal tenets of what we call investors' international law.

Have concerns over foreign investors and their accountability died away? Notwithstanding the failure to establish a multilateral instrument governing the conduct of foreign investors, much of the normative content underpinning the debates in the 1970s continue to shape contemporary debates about the relationship between foreign investors, states and societies. International law is currently facing increasingly vocal criticisms for its failure to address corruption, abuse, environmental damage and other forms of investor misconduct.[15] As a recent UNCTAD report highlighted, 'Although (foreign) investment can create positive

[6] T St John, *The Rise of Investor-State Arbitration: Politics, Law, and Unintended Consequences* (Oxford University Press, 2017) 3.

[7] I Seidl-Hohenveldern, 'The Abs-Shawcross Draft Convention to Protect Private Foreign Investment: Comments on the Round Table' (1961) 10 *Journal of Public Law* 100, 109.

[8] Declaration on the Establishment of a New International Economic Order, UNGA Res 3201 (S-V1) (1 May 1974).

[9] Charter of Economic Rights and Duties of States, UNGA Res 3281 (XXIX) (12 December 1974).

[10] Sauvant, 'Negotiations' (2015) 18.

[11] J Faundez, 'International Economic Law and Development before and after Neo-Liberalism' in J Faundez and C Tan (eds), *International Law, Economic Globalization and Development* (Edward Elgar, 2010) 16; see also Sauvant (n 5) 13–27, 38–56.

[12] Lustig, *Veiled Power* (2020) 211.

[13] UNCTAD, *Bilateral Investment Treaties 1959–1999* (United Nations, 2000).

[14] ICSID, '1999 Annual Report', available at icsid.worldbank.org/sites/default/files/publications/annual-report/en/1999-annual-report-english.pdf.

[15] See Erasmus Institute for Public Knowledge, 'Open Letter on the Asymmetry of ISDS' (Erasmus University Rotterdam, 13 February 2019), available at www.eur.nl/en/news/erasmus-institute-public-knowledge, uniting academics in urging states to alter the status quo where 'investors remain largely unaccountable under international law for any misconduct'.

conditions for improving peoples' lives, it can also carry the risk of negatively impacting on the environment, peoples' health and the enjoyment of their human rights'.[16] Policymakers, legal practitioners and civil society groups are variously calling for the dismantling or rewriting of the international law governing foreign investors. Reform initiatives range from the rejection of international law as a governing regime for investors, to the dramatic overhaul of investment treaties that enable investor overprotection, to the creation of a multilateral international instrument that would enable the litigation of claims against errant businesses before an international tribunal. Whether these initiatives succeed in disciplining investors remains to be seen. What these initiatives undeniably show, however, is that change is warranted to counteract this lopsided investors' international law.

Given the title, some might expect this to be a book *on* investors, *for* investors. Yet it is precisely this entrenched, but erroneous, mindset that this volume seeks to change. *Investors' International Law* is indeed a book *on* investors, but it explores how international law can be harnessed to ensure investors' accountability. Despite the sizeable body of literature on the topic of investor accountability that has emerged over the last four decades, from Nye's 'Multinational Corporations in World Politics'[17] to Muchlinski's *Multinational Enterprises and the Law*,[18] some of the discrete and overarching issues of substantive rules and regimes governing investor conduct still remain underexplored. This gap is particularly conspicuous in investment treaty scholarship. In the meantime, significant advances have been made in recent years by scholars of business and human rights, particularly following the publication in 2011 by the UN Special Rapporteur on Business and Human Rights, John Ruggie, of his Guiding Principles on Business and Human Rights (UNGPs).[19] A culmination of extensive discussions with businesses, civil society groups and governments, the UNGPs have been hailed by business groups for their flexible approach, but deplored by civil society actors for their weakness and lack of binding force, thus opening up a new debate about alternative solutions.[20] Besides, much of business and human rights scholarship on investor accountability remains focused on preventing the negative effects of investor misconduct rather than tackling the wider issue of investor obligations towards societies that host them. It is this gap our book seeks to address by widening the debate and dissecting investor responsibilities from multiple thematic angles, zooming in on international investment law as well as its intersections with human rights, international humanitarian law (IHL) and international environmental law.

[16] J Baumgartner et al, 'UNCTAD's Reform Package for the International Investment Regime' (UNCTAD, 18 December 2017) 17, available at investmentpolicy.unctad.org/uploaded-files/document/UNCTAD_Reform_Package_2018.pdf.

[17] JS Nye, 'Multinational Corporations in World Politics' (1974) 53 *Foreign Affairs* 153.

[18] P Muchlinksi, *Multinational Enterprises and the Law* (Oxford University Press, 2007).

[19] OHCHR, 'Guiding Principles on Business and Human Rights: Implementing the United Nations 'Protect, Respect and Remedy' Framework' (2011) UN Doc A/HRC/17/31.

[20] SR Ratner, 'Introduction to the Symposium on Soft and Hard Law on Business and Human Rights' (2020) 114 *American Journal of International Law Unbound* 163.

By doing so, the book seeks to capture the ongoing battles over international regulation of foreign investor conduct – the battles that have not died with the abandonment of the UN draft code, but rather continued in different fora. The overarching message of the book is that change is needed, change is possible and there are numerous precedents from which inspiration can be drawn in efforts to bridge the existing accountability gap.

The issue of investor conduct, often framed as investor obligations, continues to be largely sidelined in the contemporary policy debates about the future of investment treaties and investor-state arbitration. Despite the asymmetry of international investment law having been long criticised in most vocal terms, the recent investment treaty templates of major developed states do not feature legally binding and enforceable obligations of foreign investors. Although lamentable, this silence is hardly surprising – the contemporary investment treaty law has its roots in historical efforts to derail and countenance the NIEO agenda and its aspirations to impose checks and balances on foreign investors. Nonetheless, having morphed into a standalone area of international law with its distinctive and exclusive focus on the protection of foreign investors, investment treaty law has not escaped a growing scrutiny of its resistance to engage with issues of foreign investor accountability. Increasingly, even moderate voices in investment law scholarship are questioning the rationale for granting investors privileges without corresponding responsibilities. To paraphrase one such critique, creating a legal privilege for select groups not only evokes suspicion, but also presents a fundamental challenge to the legitimacy of international investment treaties and their arbitration mechanism.[21] Why should a particular type of economic actor, such as foreign investor, enjoy legal privileges not generally available to other subjects of domestic law and international law?[22] Now that the traditional justification for foreign investor privileges – the contribution of foreign investors to the economic development of host states – is being increasingly contested, the time is ripe to question foreign investors' privileges and their ability to escape responsibilities for the consequences of their conduct.

Interrogating the Normative Underpinnings of the Accountability Gap: Ideas, Norms and Actors

Jean Ho sets the scene by identifying the imperial origins of international law's structural bias for investor protection at the expense of investor accountability. International law governing foreign investment owes its origins to the historical

[21] I Alvik, 'The Justification of Privilege in International Investment Law: Preferential Treatment of Foreign Investors as a Problem of Legitimacy' (2020) 31 *European Journal of International Law* 289, 290–92.

[22] ibid 296.

efforts to legitimise the colonisation and exploitation of the Global South by European nations in the nineteenth century. The principal tenets of investment law continue to bear the trace of its authors' desire to shield colonial trading and commercial interests from interference by host governments. Yet in spite of its imperial origins, Ho argues, there are pockets of possibilities for investor accountability in international law. Chapter one explores three such possibilities – one procedural, one substantive and one institutional. To Ho, multipartite dispute resolution offers the opportunity for those most affected by investor misconduct, including aggrieved local communities, to seek investor responsibility. In a more traditional bipartite setting of investor-state contracts, the opportunity to hold investors accountable is contained within the clauses mandating the use of international law as the law governing the dispute. Although such clauses have been conceived with a view to enabling investors to escape the vagaries of national laws and national courts, they can be utilised by states to demand investors' compliance with international law. At the institutional level, distinct possibilities are presented by the emerging subregional courts as a potential forum for adjudicating certain categories of investor misconduct, such as investor crimes in non-conflict settings.

While Ho views the history of an anti-colonial agenda of NIEO as the missed opportunity to establish an international framework for investor accountability, Mavluda Sattorova (chapter two) views regulatory experiments of the 1970s as a repository of ideas to inform the contemporary efforts to reform international investment law. A momentum was indeed lost when distributive justice concerns, dominant as they were in the NIEO debates, were subsequently redefined in human rights terms and pushed to the margins of discourse on foreign investment. Although the advocates of the contemporary investment treaty regime contend that investment law does not prohibit wealth redistribution,[23] critics have long exposed the structural failures of the existing investment framework to empower the poor and to reduce or otherwise redress inequalities.[24] Some believe that the solution lies in imposing specific responsibility on states to incorporate human rights considerations in their economic decision-making processes,[25] whereas others argue that holding states responsible will not be sufficient to ensure that foreign investors act responsibly.[26] Siding with the latter camp, Sattorova critiques state-centric approaches to investor accountability. The chapter seeks

[23] SW Schill, CJ Tams and R Hofmann, 'International Investment Law and Development: Friends or Foes?' in SW Schill, CJ Tams and R Hofmann (eds), *International Investment Law and Development: Bridging the Gap* (Edward Elgar, 2015) 39.

[24] See KN Schefer, 'The Law of Investment Protection and Poverty Reduction' in Schill, Tams and Hofmann, *International Investment Law* (2015) 369.

[25] DA Desierto, 'The International Mandate for Development: Building Compliant Investment Within the State's Development Decision-Making Process' in Schill, Tams and Hofmann (n 23) 333.

[26] D Davitti, *Investment and Human Rights in Armed Conflict: Charting an Elusive Intersection* (Hart, 2019) 231.

to reorientate the debate by exploring the limits and possibilities international law presents for imposing binding investor obligations to 'do good' for the local communities. Drawing on the emerging empirical data and analysis of investment jurisprudence, she critiques investment treaty law's failure to acknowledge winners and losers of foreign investment activities and explores the opportunities for retooling foreign investment for social inclusion. Sattorova questions what hinders the emergence of a new vision of the relationship between foreign investors and the society and argues that, despite a degree of scepticism, changes in the legal mechanisms governing conduct of foreign investors remain possible.

Social inclusion is also at the heart of chapter three, with Lorenzo Cotula and Nicolás M Perrone interrogating international investment law's asymmetry and its impact on local communities. It is the framing of foreign investment as an investor-state relationship and the ensuing emphasis on state responsibility that render local communities effectively invisible. This, in turn, shapes legal discourse on investor responsibility and constrains the reform agenda. A socially inclusive international investment law, Cotula and Perrone argue, could be a foundation of a more cooperative regime where local communities have a meaningful role throughout the lifetime of an investment project. To Cotula and Perrone, investor accountability towards local communities can be achieved only through a radical overhaul of foreign investment governance, including both substantive and procedural rules of investment protection. Owing to their narrow remit, the ongoing discussions of the reform of international investment law, including those conducted under the aegis of UNCITRAL Working Group III, do not go far enough to redress the existing asymmetries in the relationship between investors and local communities.

In chapter four, Anil Yilmaz Vastardis dissects the normative underpinnings which presently buttress the asymmetry of international law and enable investors to escape liabilities for negative effects of their operations in host state. She uses risk as an analytical lens to interrogate how international law meticulously safeguards investor rights vis-à-vis host governments whilst simultaneously insulating investors from liability for harmful effects of their activities on the environment and human rights in host states. International investment law, with its generous, abstract and far-reaching protections, shields investors from risks of doing business overseas. These protections often safeguard investor interests even in cases where host state interference is justified by legitimate public welfare objectives. At the same time, the idea of derisking that lies at the heart of the corporate law principles of separate legal personality and limited liability allow foreign investors to escape liability for harms they inflicted on the environment and local communities. Crucially, this risk paradigm underpinning foreign investment governance is entirely indifferent to the nature of the risk faced by the investor. International investment law and corporate law are brought together on a shared mission by shifting risks away from the investor to states, local communities and the environment.

Redressing Asymmetries: Between Hard and Soft Laws

'Many players in international law ... define progress based on the promulgation of treaties, the rise in the number of parties, and the ability of treaty implementation bodies to shape behaviour and attitudes.'[27] Yet it has long been argued that the inclusion of binding investor obligations in treaties is likely to remain unfeasible due to trenchant scepticism towards innovation as well as lack of political will. Although these factors indeed continue to shape the ongoing debates concerning investment treaty reform, Prabhash Ranjan strikes a more optimistic note in chapter five, where he examines recent trends in investment treaty practice. The chapter charts the recent innovations in investment treaty texts which, in a departure from the first generation templates, have broken the silence on investor obligations. Ranjan draws attention to the growing number of investment treaty texts containing provisions encouraging a more responsible behaviour by foreign investors in relation to the environment, human rights, anti-corruption and corporate social responsibility. In analysing the utility of the emerging clauses on investor responsibility, Ranjan is cognisant of their shortcomings, including the fact that the relevant provisions are primarily expressed in a hortatory or declaratory, 'best endeavour' language. Does this eviscerate the ability of the newly emerging investment treaties to counter investor misconduct? Ranjan believes that investor obligations, even when couched in weak language, can still be significant in influencing the interpretation by tribunals of investment treaty objectives and thus altering tribunal approaches to instances of investor misconduct. A similar faith in arbitral tribunals can be discerned in his belief that even in treaties that contain no references to investor responsibilities, tribunals can rely on domestic law and human rights instruments to 'import' investor obligations.

Ranjan's overview of the progress with modernising investment treaty texts inevitably circles the debate back to the starting point: what if state signatories to investment agreements are unwilling to go 'beyond the edge of a "commitment curve" in terms of the bite of any duties on themselves and corporations'?[28] Is a binding international framework on investor responsibilities a pipe dream?[29] Again, the recent developments in the field of business and human rights can be instructive. One lesson that can be drawn from the challenges of reaching consensus in negotiating a business and human rights framework is that soft law – complementary and not an alternative to hard law[30] – will remain an

[27] Ratner (n 20) 167.

[28] TL Kirkebø and M Langford, 'Ground-Breaking? An Empirical Assessment of the Draft Business and Human Rights Treaty' (2020) 114 *American Journal of International Law Unbound* 179.

[29] M Krajewski, 'A Nightmare or a Noble Dream? Establishing Investor Obligations Through Treaty-Making and Treaty-Application' (2020) 5 *Business and Human Rights Journal* 105.

[30] Ratner (n 20) 167; JG Ruggie, 'Multinationals as Global Institution: Power, Authority and Relative Autonomy' (2017) 12 *Regulation & Governance* 317, 329–30.

important element of the accountability agenda in investment treaty law. At times, it is precisely the shortcomings of soft law – their lack of legally binding force, a degree of imprecision, and a lack of effective control mechanisms[31] – that have been instrumental in driving changes (however small) in international regulatory frameworks on investor accountability. In chapter six, Barnali Choudhury explores how soft law – norms formulated as rules designed to guide behaviour in areas ranging from human rights to protection of the environment – are generating standards for corporate conduct that permeate many aspects of foreign investor behaviour. Echoing Ranjan's conclusions in chapter five, Choudhury argues that the non-obligatory nature of soft law corporate responsibility initiatives does not detract from their usefulness in shaping the interpretation of investment treaties in concrete cases by clarifying the state parties' intentions and assumptions as well as helping articulate the treaty's object and purpose. Indeed, a glimpse of this effect of referencing international soft law can be found in investment arbitration cases, including *David Aven v Costa Rica*.

Securing Investor Accountability: Arbitrators as Innovators?

While concerns over asymmetry are the shared core of each chapter, the aim of this book is to capture the diversity of scholarly views and responses engendered by the lack of investor accountability in international law. The views presented in this volume vary from those who maintain belief in a reflexive and evolutionary self-correction process[32] through which investment tribunals will gradually respond to the concerns that have been levelled against the legitimacy of international investment law. Some contributions to this volume remain sceptical about such self-corrective possibilities; indeed, where would an impetus come from for an evolutionary interpretation of investor obligations in cases where neither the state nor the investor have shown sufficient concern for those affected by investor activities? Other authors are more optimistic in their faith in incremental changes that both investment treaties and investment arbitration practice can embrace to ensure responsible investor conduct.

In chapter seven, Martin Jarrett turns his eye to disputes that involve misconduct on the part of an investor as well as a host state. Arbitral tribunals have on occasion failed to sanction investor misconduct, instead focusing entirely on the consequences of the wrongful behaviour of the host state. Jarrett questions how this disequilibrium could be rebalanced so as to prevent investor impunity whilst

[31] Ratner (ibid).

[32] See M Langford and D Behn, 'Managing Backlash: The Evolving Investment Treaty Arbitrator' (2018) 29 *European Journal of International Law* 551.

upholding investment treaty norms governing host state behaviour. Two solutions can potentially offer a way forward: investment reprisals (including the use of contributory fault in apportioning liability); and a defence of illegality. Whilst acknowledging that the use of these tools by tribunals has so far been marred by inconsistency, Jarrett places faith in arbitrators' ability to self-correct and adopt a more objective approach to determining the consequences of misconduct by investors and states.

Tomoko Ishikawa strikes a similar tone in chapter eight on counterclaims as a means of holding investors accountable for their deeds. The fact that investment treaty law empowers investors to bring claims directly against host states without the latter being able to initiate counterclaims concerning investor misconduct is yet another example of glaring asymmetry in the ways international investment treaties allocate rights and responsibilities between states and business actors. Chapter eight maps out the current landscape on counterclaims before introducing the doctrine of *parens patriae* as a novel theoretical basis for host states to act as defenders of public interest vis-à-vis foreign investors, by pursuing legal action to hold the investor responsible for the harm done to third parties. Although these proposals might be met with scepticism, particularly from those who argue for a radical overhaul or dismantling of the investment treaty regime, they offer a set of pragmatic solutions that can be put to use now, under investment treaties that remain in force and face a limited prospect of overhaul in the short term.

Locating Investor Obligations Outside Investment Treaties

Despite its growing relevance in the contemporary debates over investor accountability, human rights law is not the only area of international law that could be harnessed in an effort to redress the existing asymmetries and bridge the accountability gap. The concluding chapters of the volume examine specific categories of investor misconduct and explore the possibilities to hold investors responsible by harnessing norms and conventions outside the traditional (narrow) domain of international investment law. Chapter nine charts the application of IHL and international criminal law (ICL) by claimants seeking redress for harm caused by corporate actors. Lucas Roorda and Julian G Ku explore a distinctive strand of jurisprudence generated by national courts of the home state of investors, focusing in particular on the United States Alien Tort Statute (ATS) and its deployment in cases challenging misconduct of investors. The ATS has often been seen as a game changer enabling individual victims to challenge violations of international law by businesses operating overseas. Prior to the emergence of US ATS cases against corporations in the 1990s, no foreign investor was ever held criminally or civilly responsible for violations of international law. While subsequent developments in ATS jurisprudence have sharply diminished the statute's role in holding corporations accountable, it has ushered in a global trend of directly litigating investor behaviour in national courts of home states.

Investors' complicity in human rights violations, particularly in times of armed conflict, is also a subject matter of Jure Zrilič's contribution to the volume in chapter ten. While acknowledging the significance of international human rights law in the development of the normative content of investor obligations, Zrilič also explores the basis for investor responsibility in international criminal law and domestic civil law. Zrilič directs his gaze to the role of investment arbitration in enforcing human rights obligations not only in cases where the investor is a victim, but also those where investor is a contributor to war crimes. The emerging picture yet again consists of a patchwork of soft laws and binding norms, including domestic statutes – from the UK Modern Slavery Act to French Due Diligence Law – which despite their inherent shortcomings, offer an increasingly promising basis for investor accountability.

Investors' environmental obligations are the focus of chapter eleven where Priscila Pereira de Andrade and Nitish Monebhurrun map the sources of investor responsibility across a wide spectrum of international legal instruments. Here too, the lack of legal bases to hold investors accountable stems from their lack of international legal personality. Although this presents a fundamental challenge to identifying (and operationalising) investors environmental obligations, Pereira de Andrade and Monebhurrun draw attention to alternative and less explored possibilities. Aside from corporate social responsibility provisions and other declaratory clauses on the environment protection cropping up in the new generation of investment treaties, attention is drawn to the negotiations within the UN of the Global Pact for the Environment, an initiative aimed at codifying and amplifying a legally binding nature of environmental principles and articulating the role of private actors in ensuring environmental compliance and monitoring. The Pact, the authors concede, is not accompanied by a mechanism to enforce its norms against foreign investors. There is greater scope, arguably, for inducing investor compliance with environmental laws through material incentives, such as those contained in legal frameworks governing the financing of investment projects by international organisations such as the International Finance Corporation.

Investor involvement and complicity in corruption is well recorded, but does international law provide avenues to redress and sanction this form of misconduct? In chapter twelve, José Daniel Amado, Jackson Shaw Kern and Martin Doe Rodriguez question whether corruption can be elevated into an international wrong. Unsurprisingly, the state-centric nature of international norms applicable to investor misconduct is clearly manifested in a plethora of international anti-corruption instruments on corruption, all of which rely entirely upon state parties and their will and capacity to implement the relevant laws in national legislation. If investment arbitration is allegedly 'the only potentially effective mechanism under the international legal order for the control of transnational corruption',[33] why have so few cases resulted in finding the corrupt investor responsible? An overview of seminal investment cases demonstrates that, at best, tribunals have taken account of the investor's involvement in corruption to deny jurisdiction or by apportioning liabilities between the state and the investor. The authors argue that the status quo is unsatisfactory and that the fitting resolution – given the gravity of corruption and its ruinous effect on lives and livelihoods – is to harness investment arbitration as a forum where victims can seek international enforceable remedies for the harmful effects of the investor's corrupt behaviour.

It seems appropriate to conclude this brief introduction with an acknowledgement that, in the manner reminiscent of the debates four decades ago, and arguably despite a burgeoning acceptance of the basic tenets of investor accountability, issues of international regulation of investor conduct continue to attract divergent views among different stakeholders and epistemic communities. *Investors' International Law* has been conceived as a no-filter snapshot of contemporary legal discourse about the relationship between states, investors and society and the role of international law therein. As the history of international pursuit of investor accountability teaches us, the opportunities identified by our authors within the procedural, substantive and normative foundations of international law on foreign investment may not necessarily garner the requisite consensus and be readily operationalised. Yet their very availability – as well as the existence of a plethora of historical antecedents, successful or otherwise – signifies the possibility of change. While the progress of the ongoing efforts to bridge the existing accountability gap illustrated by our authors may variously enthuse, dismay or fail to inspire confidence, the book is intended as a reminder of the need to interrogate investor responsibilities – and other fundamental imbalances of the global economic order – in a pluralised, critical and contextual fashion, by drawing inspiration from the past and seeking change within the narrow constraints of the present.

[33] AP Llamzon, *Corruption in International Investment Arbitration* (Oxford University Press, 2018), para 11.03.

1

International Law's Opportunities for Investor Accountability

JEAN HO

I. Introduction

Does international law exhibit a propensity for investor protection? The prevalence of investors invoking the protection of international law against host state mistreatment, while largely evading accountability for misconduct towards host states and indigenous communities, seems to suggest so. This view of a structural bias (or shortcoming) in international law reflects the imperialist origins of a law developed to legitimise the colonisation and exploitation of South America, large parts of Africa, and Asia by European nations in the nineteenth century.[1] And predominant in the imperial project was the desire to shield colonial trading and commercial interests, held and advanced by individual and corporate investors, from local government interference.

Such calculated use of international law has not gone unchallenged. In the wake of decolonisation in the mid-twentieth century, newly independent and developing nations made concerted efforts to 'create an international law responsive to their needs',[2] relying on their numerical advantage in international fora, such as the United Nations General Assembly, to do so. Of the various documents forging the anticolonial agenda,[3] two of the most important are Resolution 1803 on the Permanent Sovereignty over Natural Resources (PSNR)[4] and the Charter of the Economic Rights and Duties of States, the latter setting out the architecture of the New International Economic Order (NIEO).[5] Drawing on the new doctrine of PSNR, the NIEO advocated the removal of foreign investment from the discipline of international law, relocating it within the purview of domestic law.

[1] A Anghie, Imperialism, Sovereignty and the Making of International Law (Cambridge University Press, 2005) 8.

[2] ibid 198.

[3] Declaration on the Establishment of a New International Economic Order, UNGA Res A/Res/3201 (S-VI) (9 May 1974); Programme of Action on the Establishment of a New International Economic Order, UNGA Res A/Res/3202 (S-VI) (15 May 1974).

[4] UNGA Res 1803 (XVII) (14 December 1962).

[5] Charter of Economic Rights and Duties of States, UNGA Res A/Res/3281(XXIX) (12 December 1974), see especially Report of the Working Party of the Trade and Development Board, TD/B/AC.12/4

And so began an unending, metaphorical tug-of-war between Western neoliberals and their NIEO critics, over an international law that checks sovereign power in the name of investor protection, or an international law that defers to sovereign power in the name of self-determination.

The presence of polarised views, however, does not compel a binary choice. International law can make provision for investor protection as well as investor accountability because it is always susceptible to design and redesign by states and other actors. International law is malleable.[6] The evolution in perception of what international law should stand for, actualised by the writing of newer ideals into existence, creates a dynamic, volatile space where old and new doctrines, competing interests, and shifting agendas co-exist in a constant state of flux.[7] Locating investor accountability in the evolving content of international law may lack the appeal of seeking recourse under the comparatively more stable content of domestic law. However, reflexive gravitation towards the beaten path fosters content stagnation. International law can offer potential solutions to the current investor accountability deficit, but only if one is prepared to leave the comfort of familiarity and venture where many have not sought to venture before.

This chapter argues that, despite the imperial origins of international law, there are pockets of possibilities for investor accountability nestled within the swathes of international law generated by instruments, practice and scholarship for investor protection. These pockets have been obscured by the struggle over the authorship of international law, which began in earnest with the creation of the NIEO in 1974. To situate this chapter's argument in its modern historical context, I first examine how the NIEO proponents, while consciously drafting an anticolonial agenda for international law, left a lacuna with respect to investor accountability. This lacuna remained unfilled until states' subsequent conclusion of bilateral and multilateral investment protection agreements from the 1980s to the present day returned the focus to investor protection (see section II). However, it may be hasty to surmise, without probing further, that the pursuit of investor accountability under international law today is a lost cause. International law's inherent capacity for change and self-correction imbues a lacuna with potential content. Therefore, in order to determine if there are opportunities for investor accountability that have been obscured, but not obliterated, by the extended volleying between the neoliberal and the NIEO camps, I survey the procedures, the substantive law and the institutions that have emerged in the era of investment protection. To the extent that

partially reproduced in J Kuusi, *The Host State and the Transnational Corporation* (Saxon House, 1976) 71, 131–35. The Charter was passed with 120 votes; the 16 states that voted against the Charter or abstained were all developed states, see (1975) 16 ILM 263 for the roll-call vote.

[6] International law's capacity for revision and reinvention has been credited to its 'critical instability' borne from the 'dual quality … [of its] imperial and counter-imperial dimensions', S Pahuja, *Decolonising International Law – Development, Economic Growth and the Politics of Universality* (Cambridge University Press, 2012) 97, also 113, 118, 153, 158.

[7] L Eslava, M Fakhiri and V Nesiah, 'The Spirit of Bandung' in L Eslava, M Fakhiri and V Nesiah (eds), *Bandung, Global History, and International Law – Critical Pasts and Pending Futures* (Cambridge University Press, 2017) 8.

any aspect of these three pillars that prop up the existing system of international investment regulation can be repurposed to secure direct investor accountability, international law is poised for more profound reshaping that will fan the future pursuit of investor accountability (see section III).

Exploratory signs of an international law that at the very least accommodates the pursuit of investor accountability are promising. This chapter identifies and evaluates three opportunities – one procedural, one substantive and one institutional – for securing investor accountability. The first procedural opportunity is the facilitation of multipartite dispute resolution in which not just investors and states, but also affected local communities and other stakeholders, participate in treaty-based adjudication. Currently viewed as a marker of transparency in investor-state dispute settlement, multipartite dispute resolution is not just about letting relevant and interested stakeholders have a say, but also about encouraging those most affected by investor misconduct to call attention to investor accountability (see section III.A). The second substantive opportunity is the stipulation of international law as the governing law in investor-state contracts. Traditionally regarded as a boost for investors who contend that states' contractual breaches amount to international law violations, such a stipulation also permits states to demand investors' compliance with international law during contractual performance (see section III.B). The third institutional opportunity is the positioning of subregional courts as the appropriate forum for adjudicating international crimes committed by investors. Such courts, of which the Court of Community Justice of the Economic Community of West African States is a prime example, can address situations to which the universal jurisdiction of the International Criminal Court and domestic courts do not extend – investor crimes in non-conflict settings (see section III.C). The presence of opportunities for investor accountability in the procedural, substantive *and* institutional pillars on which the international law on investment regulation rests may not be immediately adopted as foolproof ways of securing investor accountability, but their very presence alerts the users of international law to the feasibility and tools of change. Ultimately, the mileage of any opportunity, and its potential for future widespread adoption, will vary in accordance with the vision and flair of its pioneering users.

II. The NIEO and the Struggle for Authorship of International Law

The birth of the NIEO marked the start of a protracted struggle between two opposing factions for control over the content of international law.[8] One faction comprised the proponents of 'classical international law',

[8] J Faundez, 'Between Bandung and Doha' in Eslava, Fakhiri and Nesiah (n 7) 498, 511; J Linarelli, ME Salomon and M Sornarajah, *The Misery of International Law – Confrontations with Injustice in the Global Economy* (Oxford University Press, 2018) 89, 104–05.

crafted by Vitoria, Grotius, Pufendorf and Vattel to justify the act and means of conquering foreign territories by Western traders and nations whose interests they championed. This faction pressed for the safeguarding of foreign private property and capital, at the expense of individual host state development, thereby subscribing to the neoliberal economic school of thought.[9] The other faction comprised developing nations, previously on the receiving end of 'classical international law', determined to throw off the yoke of imperialism and neoliberalism. Through the establishment of the NIEO, this opposing faction announced their firm rejection of the content of 'classical international law'. While such categorical rejection is undeniably significant for the purpose of identifying an ideological shift, it still requires articulation and elaboration of a detailed blueprint for an NIEO-esque international law to replace content-rich 'classical international law'. When the old rules of engagement are rejected, new rules of engagement have to be written.[10] Otherwise, in the absence of alternative content, pre-existing rules may re-emerge as default rules.[11]

It is during the transition from rule-taking to rule-making that the proponents of the NIEO appeared to prioritise broad sketches of the new ideology in the founding documents, seemingly deferring the hard-won authorship of the details of international law to a later occasion. However, 'classical international law' was always more than an abstract ideology,[12] and its critics ought to have articulated the alternatives in greater detail.[13] In the decades leading up to the NIEO, 'classical international law' was applied to disputes arising between foreign investors and developing host states, resulting in the apportionment and quantification of tangible rights and liabilities that was largely detrimental to the latter. The bias vis-à-vis developing states was evident in a quartet of notable arbitral awards involving

[9] Q Slobodian, *Globalists – The End of Empire and the Birth of Neoliberalism* (Harvard University Press, 2018) 124–5.

[10] A Anghie, 'Bandung and the Origins of Third World Sovereignty' in Eslava, Fakhiri and Nesiah (n 7) 535, 540; S Pahuja, 'Letters from Bandung' in Eslava, Fakhiri and Nesiah (n 7) 552, 560.

[11] Eslava, Fakhiri and Nesiah (n 7) 7, 22; Linarelli, Salomon and Sornarajah, *The Misery of International Law* (2018) 64.

[12] For example, Grotius' justification of the use of arms and the right of conquest by the Dutch East India Company (VOC) in the East Indies was detailed in a three-volume manifesto imposingly titled *De Jure Belli Ac Pacis Libri Tres (On the Law of War and Peace: Three Books)* that was first published in 1625. This manifesto purported to clarify and specify when exactly the label of just war could be invoked by the aggressor. For an in-depth study on how Grotius' strategic manifesto, which was commissioned by the VOC to reframe its imperialistic ambitions, gained traction over time as an expression of natural law, see M van Ittersum, *Profit and Principle: Hugo Grotius, Natural Rights Theories and the Rise of Dutch Power in the East Indies, 1595–1615* (Brill, 2006).

[13] To date, scholars chronicling the NIEO cause appear to take the view that its proponents supplied a credible and comprehensive alternative body of law to classical international law; see U Özsu, 'An Anti-Imperialist Universalism? *Jus Cogens* and the Politics of International Law' in M Koskenniemi, W Rech and MJ Fonseca (eds), *International Law and Empire* (Cambridge University Press, 2017) 295, 308; Linarelli, Salomon and Sornarajah (n 8) 94–95.

disputes over oil concessions awarded to Anglo-American investors by Middle Eastern states.

In *Petroleum Development Ltd v The Sheik of Abu Dhabi*,[14] *Ruler of Qatar v International Marine Oil Co*,[15] *Saudi Arabia v Arabian American Oil Co*[16] and *Sapphire International Petroleum Ltd v National Iranian Oil Co*,[17] the tribunals found that the oil concessions in question were governed by international law. This, so the proffered rule mandated, precluded the host state from interfering with the concession, whether by breaching contractual terms or by amending its own laws to the detriment of the foreign investor. Non-compliance with this rule renders the offending state in violation of international law. The phenomenon of identifying international law as the proper law of the oil concession so as to elevate contractual obligations into international obligations, is also known as 'internationalization'.[18] Each and every breach of an internationalized contract is equivalent to a breach of international law. This was an astonishing rule, for it advocated the absolute sanctity of contract, which no legal system in the world recognised. It may not therefore come as a surprise that the way in which the four tribunals achieved internationalization, was to detach the contract from domestic law. The tribunals in the *Abu Dhabi*, *Qatar* and *ARAMCO* arbitrations internationalized to remedy the supposed inadequacies presented by primitive host state laws, while the tribunal in the *Sapphire* arbitration internationalized to counteract the host state changing its own laws to escape its contractual obligations. Internationalization was of grave concern not just to Abu Dhabi, Qatar, Saudi Arabia and Iran, but to all developing capital-importing states. Were it to become a standard protective mantle for all foreign investment contracts, the historic gain on self-determination expressed in the doctrine of PSNR would be lost by the routine ousting of domestic laws, regulations, and policies so as to protect Western capital and commercial interests.

As an ode to newfound sovereignty, the NIEO was necessarily opposed to internationalized contracts. However, the NIEO did not limit itself to staunching the spread of internationalized contracts. The bigger target of the developing states, implicit in the absence of specific reference to contracts in the NIEO's founding documents, was the continued application of classical international law to *both* contract-based and non-contract-based matters, which undermined the right to self-determination. In the context of foreign investment regulation, the proponents of the NIEO sought to shore up sovereign power by laying down the primacy of domestic law as the regulatory law, and in doing so, implicitly

[14] (1951) 18 ILR 144, 149 (Lord Asquith of Bishopstone).
[15] (1953) 20 ILR 534, 544–45 (Sir Alfred Bucknill).
[16] (1958) 27 ILR 117, 168 (Sauser-Hall, Badawi/Hassan, Habachy).
[17] (1963) 35 ILR 136, 172–76 (Cavin).
[18] CL Lim, J Ho and M Paparinskis, *International Investment Law and Arbitration: Commentary, Awards and other Materials* (Cambridge University Press, 2018) 37–50.

rejected any form of sovereign constraint by classical international law. This can be seen in Article 2, arguably the most representative, and also the most contested provision of the Charter of the Economic Rights and Duties of States:[19]

> 1. Every state has and shall freely exercise full permanent sovereignty, including possession, use and disposal, over all its wealth, natural resources and economic activities.
> 2. Each state has the right:
>   (a) To regulate and exercise authority over foreign investment within its national jurisdiction *in accordance with its laws and regulations* and in conformity with its national objectives and priorities. No state shall be compelled to grant preferential treatment to foreign investment;
>   (b) To regulate and supervise the activities of transnational corporations within its national jurisdiction and take measures to ensure that such activities comply *with its laws, rules and regulations* and conform with its economic and social policies. Transnational corporations shall not intervene in the internal affairs of a host state. Every state should, with full regard for its sovereign rights, cooperate with other states in the exercise of the right set forth in this subparagraph;
>   (c) To nationalize, expropriate or transfer ownership of foreign property, in which case appropriate compensation should be paid by the state adopting such measures, taking into account *its relevant laws and regulations* and all circumstances that the state considers pertinent. In any case where the question of compensation gives rise to a controversy, it shall be settled under *the domestic law of the nationalizing state* and by its tribunals, unless it is freely and mutually agreed by all states concerned that other peaceful means be sought on the basis of the sovereign equality of states and in accordance with the principle of free choice of means.

Article 2(1) reiterates the doctrine of PSNR, which was set out in Resolution 1803. Notably, notwithstanding the unequivocal nature of the exercise of sovereign over natural wealth and resources as a corollary of the right to self-determination, the proper exercise of sovereignty is still subject to international law. There are three references to international law in Resolution 1803. The first can be found in the Preamble, where it is stipulated that 'in the conduct of the full survey of the status of the permanent sovereignty of peoples and nations over their natural wealth and resources, due regard shall be paid to the rights and duties of states under international law'. The second can be found in section 3, which provides that 'In cases where authorization [for the exploration, development and disposition of

[19] See (1975) 14 ILM 251, 264 for the roll-call vote on Art 2. Nine countries voted against Art 2(1) (Belgium, Canada, France, Germany, Japan, Luxembourg, Netherlands, UK); 10 countries voted against Art 2(2)(a) (Belgium, Denmark, France, Germany, Ireland, Italy, Japan, Luxembourg, UK and US); 16 countries voted against Art 2(2)(c) (Austria, Belgium, Canada, Denmark, France, Germany, Ireland, Italy, Japan, Luxembourg, Netherlands, Norway, Spain, Sweden, UK and US). The roll-call vote reveals that developed countries objected strongly to the domestic laws of developing countries having a central role in investment regulation, and to the implicit ousting of classical international law.

natural resources] is granted, the capital imported and the earnings on that capital shall be governed by … the national legislation in force, and by international law'. The third reference can be found in section 4, which promises both domestic and foreign investors 'appropriate compensation' in the event of expropriation, 'in accordance with the rules in force in the state taking such measures in the exercise of its sovereignty and in accordance with international law'. There is no elaboration on the content of international law pertaining to the rights and duties of states, the management of inward capital and profits, or the standard or quantification of compensation for expropriation. This presents two distinct possibilities. The first is that the exercise of PSNR is, in some respects, still subject to classical international law whatever the misgivings of newly independent states to its imperial origins. The second is that the exercise of PSNR will be subject to a post-classical international law, whose content will be determined at a later date. If the aim of the proponents of the NIEO was to replace classical international law with an 'international law responsive to their needs', it was incumbent on them to establish the content of a new international law at the earliest opportunity, and especially in an international instrument framing the economic rights and duties of states.[20]

Instead, Article 2(1) is followed by Article 2(2), which subjects foreign investment authorisation (Article 2(2)(a)), transnational corporate activity (Article 2(2)(b)), and the expropriation of foreign investment to domestic law (Article 2(2)(c)). There is no mention of international law, let alone any elaboration of the content of international law governing two out of the three concerns, namely, investment authorisation and expropriation, also found in Resolution 1803. By expressly subjecting foreign investment authorisation, transnational corporate activity and expropriation of foreign investment only to the laws and regulations of the host state, developing states associated self-determination with the self-regulation of foreign investment and investors.[21] However, Article 2(2) does not prohibit reliance on international law to regulate foreign investment, transnational corporations or expropriations. Such a reading of Article 2(2) is consistent with the doctrine of PSNR, which accepts that international law can function as a constraint, albeit undefined in Resolution 1803, on sovereignty. Therefore, the non-reference to international law in Article 2(2), and the resounding silence on the content of a new international law, loops the proponents of the NIEO back to the three undefined references to international law in Resolution 1803. While the NIEO represented an important ideological shift that questioned the legitimacy of classical international law, its proponents, despite successfully reclaiming authorship of international law, did not promptly author sufficiently detailed alternative

[20] Anghie, 'Bandung' (2017) 540.
[21] J Ho, State Responsibility for Breaches of Investment Contracts (Cambridge University Press, 2018) 183–86.

content to displace classical international law. This left the door open for the future reintroduction of classical international law, as well as the further supply of content to substantiate an international law that serves the NIEO. The struggle for authorship of international law was not over.[22] It was soon renewed by the neoliberal camp, riding on intensifying geopolitical tensions of the Cold War, and bent on recovering rule-making ground that was lost amid the nationalistic fervour of self-determination.

In the wake of the creation of the NIEO, where the coalition of 134 developing nations, also known as the Group of 77, sought to rectify the stark inequality between developed and developing states precipitated by a history of colonialism, two movements countering the G-77 victory in the UNGA began to take shape. The first movement was the rejuvenation of the 1947 General Agreement on Tariffs and Trade by neoliberal economists as the foundation for a world economic order that presupposed the formal equality of states.[23] The GATT movement, which sidestepped the NIEO's pursuit of redistributive justice, rested on the conviction that the world economic order is both self-correcting and self-equilibrating, relying on market price signals to stimulate adaptation and change. It sided with the capitalist and free market economic model espoused by the US during the Cold War, which opposed the communist and redistributive economic model of the Soviet Union.[24] Developing states, however, were less free to take sides. With the linking of developmental aid dispensed by the US-led World Bank to international security during the peak of the Cold War in the 1960s and 1970s, recipients of developmental aid were deftly steered to eschew a communist economic model for a capitalist one.[25] The financial strings controlling the economic choices of developing states enabled the GATT movement to gain momentum in the 1980s and 1990s. This was a period of rapid global economic growth followed by financial market volatility, and assumed a concrete form with the establishment of the World Trade Organization in 1995. The NIEO's idealistic vision of redistributive justice had apparently been left behind for an arguably more sophisticated, more egalitarian, and most importantly, more capitalist framework for wealth distribution.

The second movement was a renewed emphasis on foreign investment protection which coincided with a period of significant private capital flows from the countries of the Global North to those of the Global South starting from the 1980s. This movement was foreshadowed by the debt crisis suffered by developing Global South states who borrowed heavily from the largely US-funded World Bank but

[22] Faundez, 'Between Bandung and Doha' (2017) 498, 511; Linarelli, Salomon and Sornarajah (n 8) 89, 104–05.

[23] Slobodian, *Globalists* (2018) 223.

[24] Pahuja, *Decolonising International Law* (2012) 129.

[25] ibid 165; H Shinohara, 'Drift Towards Empire? The Trajectory of American Reformers in the Cold War' in M Koskenniemi, W Rech and MJ Fonseca (eds), *International Law and Empire* (Cambridge University Press, 2017) 316, 324; Faundez (n 8) 506–07, 513.

lacked the means to make repayment once interest rates were hiked by the US Federal Reserve.[26] It also received a boost from the dissolution of the Soviet Union in 1989 and the rush among the newly independent ex-Soviet nations to trade communism for capitalism and welcome all that capitalism had to offer.[27] The outcome was the conclusion of scores of North–South bilateral investment treaties, which developing states were supposedly nudged to accept by their pressing need for foreign capital injection.[28] These treaties are concluded with the objective of reciprocal promotion and protection of investments in Contracting States. However, since it was typically investors from developed states who invested in developing states and not vice versa, the code of host state conduct laid out in investment treaties was really meant for the G-77.[29] The turn to investment treaties for investor protection was an engineered neoliberal response to the NIEO. As Slobodian explains:[30]

> Opposing the world projects of both the NIEO and the global reformists was a formative struggle for neoliberals in the 1970s. Given what they saw as the G-77 misuse of state sovereignty to unsettle world economic order, neoliberals sought ways to circumvent the authority of national governments. By the early 1980s this manifested in renewed attention to modes of investment protection and third-party arbitration alongside the rethinking of criteria for World Bank aid and IMF assistance that would become known as the Washington Consensus. Equally important was the rise of monetarism, culminating in the so-called Volcker Shock in 1979, which dramatically raised U.S. interest rates – and thus debt service payments for Global South nations – initiating the Third World debt crises and dealing the 'death blow to the NIEO movement'.

Undercutting the primacy of domestic law established by the NIEO, investment treaties subject foreign investment regulation and foreign-owned property takings to international law,[31] not domestic law. More importantly, investment treaties, which are often drafted unilaterally by developed states,[32] articulate substantive protection obligations that Contracting States must abide by with respect to

[26] Pahuja (n 6) 167, 169; Linarelli, Salomon and Sornarajah (n 8) 100, for a fuller account of various events that led to the eclipse of the NIEO, see 101–03.

[27] Pahuja (n 6) 129.

[28] Lim, Ho and Paparinskis, *International Investment Law and Arbitration* (2018) 61–66. To date, there is still no definitive answer to the question of whether there is a causal connection between states signing investment treaties and attracting inward FDI flows. One report notes that a 'review of 35 published and unpublished studies on the impact of investment treaties found that the majority suggest that investment treaties do have some positive impact [on] FDI inflows, while a significant minority reach the opposite conclusion', J Bonnitcha, 'Assessing the Impacts of Investment Treaties: Overview of the Evidence' (International Institute of Sustainable Development, September 2017) 3, available at www.iisd.org/sites/default/files/publications/assessing-impacts-investment-treaties.pdf.

[29] M Sornarajah, *The International Law on Foreign Investment*, 4th edn (Cambridge University Press, 2017) 211.

[30] Slobodian (n 9) 227 (footnotes omitted).

[31] Lim, Ho and Paparinskis (n 18) 57–58.

[32] LNS Poulsen, *Bounded Rationality and Economic Diplomacy – The Politics of Investment Treaties in Developing Countries* (Cambridge University Press, 2015) 33–35.

qualifying investments and investors. Common substantive protection obligations in these first-generation investment treaties include the obligation to treat investments and investors fairly and equitably, and the obligation to expropriate only with compensation, for a public purpose, and with respect for due process. A failure to abide by any of these obligations, as determined by an arbitral tribunal constituted in accordance with the terms of the treaty, will amount to a treaty violation, a sanctionable transgression in the eyes of international law. Investment treaties, which are akin to neoliberal constraints on the G-77, thus supplied the content of international law, much of which was new, on foreign investment and investor protection. In retrospect, the NIEO's deferral of the articulation of an international law that best suited its needs was a mistake. The proliferation of investment treaties in the decades after the birth of the NIEO not only allowed international law to gradually eclipse domestic law in setting the baseline for investor protection, but it also meant that authorship of international law had, bit by bit, shifted back to the proponents of neoliberalism.[33]

It did not take long for first generation bilateral investment treaties to facilitate serious incursions into the sovereign right of developing host states to regulate foreign investors. The empowerment of investors to initiate claims in arbitration against states, and the expansive interpretations given by investor-state arbitral tribunals to laconic treaty standards in the name of investor protection,[34] all led some developing state officials to believe that the system favoured investors, contributing to the onset of 'regulatory chill'.[35] The high point (or low point, as the G-77 might prefer) of investor protection through investment treaties was reached when the US imposed trade sanctions on an impecunious Argentina for its failure to satisfy two arbitral awards made in favour of US investors adversely affected by measures introduced to address the collapse of the Argentinian economy in the early 2000s.[36] Punitive in intent and in effect, these sanctions urged compliance with an investor protection regime that was unattuned to the needs and challenges faced by developing states with volatile economies. Argentina was damned if it took no fiscal measures to rescue its ailing economy, and damned if it took

[33] According to David Schneiderman, the neoliberal project relied on investment treaties to 'reduc[e] state functions to behavior that mimics private actors in the marketplace'. Its success works to the eventual detriment of states because it 'renders more difficult the taking up of new measures for societal self-protection'. See D Schneiderman, 'Hayek's Dream: International Investment Law and the Denigration of Politics' (2019) 1–2, available at papers.ssrn.com/sol3/papers.cfm?abstract_id=3397624.

[34] In this regard, Federico Ortino urges tribunals to exercise restraint when reviewing the compatibility of host state measures with their obligations under investment treaties. Tribunals should therefore refrain from applying the most intrusive 'strict balancing or proportionality' test to determine the legality of host state measures. See F Ortino, 'Investment Treaties, Sustainable Development and Reasonableness Review: A Case Against Strict Proportionality Balancing' (2017) 30 *Leiden Journal of International Law* 71, 87–90.

[35] K Tienhaara, 'Regulatory Chill and the Threat of Arbitration: A View from Political Science' in C Brown and K Miles (eds), *Evolution in Investment Treaty Law and Arbitration* (Cambridge University Press, 2011) 611–15.

[36] Presidential Proclamation 8788 of 26 March 2012, 'To Modify Duty-Free Treatment Under the Generalized System of Preferences and For Other Purposes', 77(61) *Federal Register* 18899, 18899.

measures that would invariably interfere with the operation and profitability of its foreign investors.

The prospect of astronomically large pay-outs to affected investors,[37] the numerous forms of investor holdings that qualify as investments eligible for treaty protection,[38] and the apparent ability of investors to pollute the environment and violate human rights in host states without being held accountable under international law, led to pushback from sovereign,[39] civil society[40] and academic quarters.[41] The tide had turned against a successful neoliberal project which appeared to stack the odds against developing states. The rise of China and India, former developing states and NIEO proponents, as capital-exporting economic heavyweights, also poses a challenge to the neoliberal economic worldview which neither country holds.

Mounting disillusionment with the investor regulation regime created by first generation investment treaties fuels the current struggle for the authorship of international law. But unlike previous struggles which had a singular objective (the replacement of imperialism with self-determination, or the replacement of the NIEO with investment treaties), the objective of reform this time around is more nuanced. Investor protection has to be subjected to the proper exercise of the right of states to regulate as well as discipline errant foreign investors, and investor protection through investor-state dispute settlement has to be carried out in a way that minimises systemic error or abuse. Additionally, unlike previous struggles which pit the G-77 against the neoliberals, developed and developing states and other stakeholders converge on some concerns,[42] while diverging on

[37] J Ho, 'Hegemony 101 in International Investment Law', (Afronomicslaw, 9 September 2020), available at www.afronomicslaw.org/2020/09/09/hegemony-101-in-international-investment-law.

[38] One type of investor holding that has been the subject of recent controversy is the 'passive investment', which lacks a meaningful economic connection to the investor bringing the claim. Although investment treaties do not expressly deny protection to 'passive investments', the potential for some claimants to obtain treaty protection without actually making an investment in the host state has been cause for concern. For the implications of recognising passive investments as protected investments, see J Ho, 'Passive Investments' (2020) 35 *ICSID Review – Foreign Investment Law Journal* (advance access) 1–17.

[39] Since 2017, the Working Group III of the United Nations Commission on International Trade Law has engaged Member States in the possible reform of investor-state dispute settlement. The agenda and reports of the Working Group can be perused online at uncitral.un.org/en/working_groups/3/investor-state.

[40] A considerable number of pithy video clips have sprung up on popular hosting platforms in recent years, explaining and denouncing ISDS in lay terms. One such clip is 'ISDS – A corporate system of injustice', available at www.youtube.com/watch?v=dSuIGKSm7z0.

[41] 'An Open Letter to the Chair of the UNCITRAL Working Group III and to all Participating states Concerning the Reform of the Investor-State Dispute Settlement: Addressing the Asymmetry of ISDS', signed by 65 academics critical of the current regime, available at www.eur.nl/en/news/erasmus-institute-public-knowledge.

[42] According to the agenda of UNCITRAL Working Group III which was reached by consensus, Member States agreed to table (i) the inconsistency and incorrectness of arbitral decisions, (ii) the independence, impartiality and diversity of arbitrators deciding investor-state disputes, and (iii) costs and duration of arbitral proceedings; see 'Report of the Working Group III (Investor-State Dispute Settlement Reform) on the work of its thirty-sixth session (Vienna, 29 October–2 November 2018)', UN Doc A/CN.9/964. The areas earmarked for reform are procedural in nature.

others in charting the way forward for investor protection.[43] That said, the general pushback against first generation investment treaties marked the broad rejection of neoliberalism and its possible replacement with neo-NIEO ideals of greater self-determination and sustainability in the rules of engagement applicable to foreign investment and investors.[44] To this end, options for reform ranged from tweaking first generation investment treaty language and content to accommodate ongoing concerns, to doing away with investment treaties altogether and assigning foreign investment and investor regulation to the purview of domestic law or general international law.[45] Whatever the chosen option,[46] it presents the possibility of designing or redesigning the content of international law applicable to investor regulation.[47]

The former option of treaty tweaks combines change in substance with the continuity of a neoliberal form – the investment treaty. This can be seen in investment treaties currently in force, such as the 2009 Association of Southeast Asian Nations (ASEAN) Comprehensive Investment Agreement,[48] as well as Model Bilateral Investment Treaties, such as the 2015 Indian Model BIT[49] and the 2018 Dutch Model BIT.[50] These second generation treaties and treaty templates are noticeably more explicit on the character of investor protection,[51] more restrictive

[43] In response to calls to include more concerns in its agenda for reform, such as investor responsibility as highlighted in the Open Letter, the Working Group responded that its mandate was to 'work on the possible reform of ISDS rather than reform of substantive standards in international investment agreements and that the focus of its work should be on the procedural aspects of ISDS, though taking due note of the interaction with underlying substantive standards'; 'Report of the Working Group III (Investor-State Dispute Settlement Reform) on the work of its thirty-seventh session (New York, 1–5April 2019)', UN Doc A/CN.9/970, 6.

[44] Linarelli, Salomon and Sornarajah (n 8) 97; tangentially Eslava, Fakhiri and Nesiah (n 7) 32.

[45] M Sornarajah, *Resistance and Change in the International Law on Foreign Investment* (Cambridge University Press, 2015) 408.

[46] On the futility of finding a universal solution to investment and investor regulation, see S Puig and G Schaffer, 'Imperfect Alternatives: Institutional Choice and the Reform of Investment Law' (2018) 112 *African Journal of International Law* 361, 362, 379–408, where the authors explain the trade-offs in invoking one institutional option over another or others.

[47] The fact that developing states are speaking up at major forums, such as the UNICTRAL Working Group III on Investor-State Dispute Settlement, contemplating the future of investor regulation is an encouraging sign, see A Roberts and T St John, 'UNCITRAL and ISDS Reforms: The Divided West and the Battle by and for the Rest' (*EJIL: Talk!*, 30 April 2019), available at www.ejiltalk.org/uncitral-and-isds-reforms-the-divided-west-and-the-battle-by-and-for-the-rest/comment-page-1. However, the Table of Contents extent to which they can shape the content of international investment law depends largely on their capacity to transform verbal interventions at global conventions into tangible modifications or revamps of the existing investor regulation regime. Absent the capacity for change, developing states are still no better than grudging users of a dysfunctional system in which they have played and will continue to play a negligible role in constructing and correcting.

[48] Signed 26 February 2009, entered into force 29 March 2012.

[49] Model Text for the Indian Bilateral Investment Treaty (2015), available at investmentpolicy.unctad.org/international-investment-agreements/treaty-files/3560/download.

[50] Netherlands Model Investment Agreement (22 March 2019), available at www.rijksoverheid.nl/ministeries/ministerie-van-buitenlandse-zaken/documenten/publicaties/2019/03/22/nieuwe-modeltekst-investeringsakkoorden.

[51] ACIA, Arts 6, 11, 14, Annex 2; Indian Model BIT, arts 3, 5, 11, 12; Dutch Model BIT, Arts 6, 7, 8, 9, 12, 23.

on the investors' access to arbitration,[52] and more permissive of legitimate host state deviation from treaty obligations,[53] all in a bid to strike the optimal balance between a host state's regulatory freedom and an investor's freedom from undue interference.[54] Some, like the Indian Model BIT even contain provisions on investor obligations towards host states,[55] while the Dutch Model BIT provides for investor accountability in accordance with home state laws when their 'acts or decisions lead to significant damage, personal injuries or loss of life in the host state'.[56] The trend of countries with vastly varying economic statures concluding mega-regional trade agreements containing chapters resembling second generation investment treaties, such as the Comprehensive Economic and Trade Agreement,[57] the Comprehensive and Progressive Agreement for Trans-Pacific Partnership,[58] and the forthcoming Regional Comprehensive Economic Partnership,[59] suggests that when it comes to investor accountability on the international plane, more states still prefer the arguably uneasy alliance of using a neoliberal instrument to showcase or advance distinctly anti-neoliberal goals.

The latter option, which fewer states prefer, advocates starting on a clean slate.[60] Although this does not appear to be on the cards for the current investor

[52] ACIA, Arts 19, 32; Indian Model BIT, Arts 13, 14, 15; Dutch Model BIT, Arts 15, 16, 17.

[53] ACIA, Arts 17, 18; Indian Model BIT, Arts 32, 33, Annex 1; Dutch Model BIT, Art 2.

[54] See also the investment chapter in the Comprehensive Economic and Trade Agreement between Canada and the European Union (signed 30 October 2016, provisional entry into force 21 September 2017). However, as F Ortino rightly points out while proposing a sustainability-oriented paradigm for investment treaty drafters, 'While some treaties have tried to rebalance investment protection and states' right to regulate, this does not appear to have engendered a much higher level of clarity and predictability'; 'Refining the Content and Role of Investment "Rules" and "Standards": A New Approach to International Investment Treaty Making' (2013) 28 *ICSID Review – Foreign Investment Law Journal* 152, 158.

[55] Indian Model BIT, Art 11; Treaty Between the Republic of Belarus and the Republic of India on Investments (signed 24 September 2018, not yet in force), Art 11. Apart from those that India has recently concluded, investment treaties containing provisions on investor obligations are still relatively rare. The Investment Agreement for the COMESA (Common Market for Eastern and Southern Africa) Common Investment Area (signed 23 May 2007, not yet in force), and the Reciprocal Investment Promotion and Protection Agreement Between the Government of the Kingdom of Morocco and the Government of the Federal Republic of Nigeria (signed 3 December 2016, not yet in force), are two known examples. The COMESA Investment Agreement Art 16 provides: 'COMESA investors shall accord a priority to workers who possess the same qualifications and are available in the Member State or any other Member State'. The Morocco–Nigeria investment treaty Arts 14(1) and 18(2) provide respectively: 'Investors or the investment shall conduct a social impact assessment of the potential investment' and 'Investors and investments shall uphold human rights in the host state'. See also chs 2 (Sattorova) and 5 (Ranjan) of this volume.

[56] Dutch Model BIT, Art 7(4).

[57] Signed 30 October 2016, provisional entry into force 21 September 2017. The signatories to the CETA are Canada and the EU.

[58] Signed 8 March 2018, entry into force 30 December 2018. The signatories to the CPTPP are Australia, Brunei, Canada, Chile, Japan, Malaysia, Mexico, New Zealand, Peru, Singapore and Vietnam.

[59] The states negotiating the RCEP are the 10 ASEAN nations of Brunei, Cambodia, Indonesia, Laos, Malaysia, Myanmar, the Philippines, Singapore, Thailand and Vietnam, plus Australia, China, India, Japan, New Zealand and South Korea.

[60] To date, South Africa remains the only country that has terminated all its investment treaties with no plans to negotiate new ones.

protection regime, which is represented by old and new investment treaties, it is currently being tabled for a new corporate investor *accountability* regime taking shape under both UN and private auspices. And although transnational corporations appear to have long occupied the privileged position of being able to violate international law without there being definite means to hold them accountable for committing international wrongs,[61] corporate investors are nonetheless bearers of a growing list of international obligations, such as *jus cogens* and human rights norms. What is missing is a reliable enforcement mechanism for these norms. On 24 June 2014, the United Nations Human Rights Council adopted Resolution 26/9, establishing an intergovernmental working group 'to elaborate an international legally binding instrument to regulate, in international human rights law, the activities of transnational corporations and other business enterprises'.[62] The proposed multilateral treaty was supposed to establish an international tribunal to hear claims brought against transnational corporations. However, the recently published Draft Zero of a Legally Binding Instrument to Regulate, in International Human Rights Law, the Activities of Transnational Corporations and Other Business Enterprises, has not delivered on the promise in Resolution 26/9 of an international tribunal.[63] Instead, victims are directed to seek remedies from domestic courts and under domestic law.[64] The prospect of securing investor accountability under international law may lie in another recently published blueprint – the Hague Rules on Business and Human Rights Arbitration – drafted by academics under the auspices of the Center for International Legal Cooperation, a Dutch non-profit think tank.[65] The Draft Hague Rules set out a detailed procedure where victims of human rights abuses can bring claims in arbitration against offending businesses,[66] and where arbitral tribunals constituted to hear such claims may be empowered to 'have special regard for any business and human rights norms, standards, or instruments that have become part of trade usage or the applicable law'.[67]

[61] J Ho, 'The Creation of Elusive Investor Responsibility' (2019) 113 *American Journal of International Law* (Unbound) 10, 10–5.

[62] UNHRC Res 26/9 'Elaboration of an international legally binding instrument on transnational corporations and other business enterprises with respect to human rights' (24 June 2014) UN Doc A/HRC/26/L.22/Rev.1.

[63] UNHRC Open-Ended Intergovernmental Working Group, 'Legally Binding Instrument to Regulate, in International Human Rights Law, the Activities of Transnational Corporations and other Business Enterprises' (Revised Draft, 16 July 2019), available at www.ohchr.org/Documents/HRBodies/HRCouncil/WGTransCorp/OEIGWG_RevisedDraft_LBI.pdf.

[64] 2019 Draft Zero, Arts 4, 7 and 9.

[65] The Hague Rules on Business and Human Rights Arbitration (December 2019), available at www.cilc.nl/cms/wp-content/uploads/2019/12/The-Hague-Rules-on-Business-and-Human-Rights-Arbitration_CILC-digital-version.pdf. The Draft Hague Rules on Business and Human Rights Arbitration are designed to 'contribute [to] the judicial remedy gap' in the United Guiding Principles on Business and Human Rights; see 'Project Description', available at www.cilc.nl/project/the-hague-rules-on-business-and-human-rights-arbitration.

[66] Draft Hague Rules on Business and Human Rights Arbitration, Preamble and accompanying Commentary.

[67] ibid Art 41(5).

Widespread consensus on the need for reform of the current investor regulation regime, even if reform agendas vary in particulars, has placed the ball firmly back in the court of those who believe that participation in the global economy, especially by Global South states, does not have to be a zero-sum game. Now is the time for the old lacunae on investor accountability, left by the proponents of the NIEO who were preoccupied with the ideological defeat of classical international law, and lit by the cyclical backlash against neoliberalism, to be filled.

III. The Aftermath of the Struggle and the Search for Investor Accountability

The manner in which the content of international law on foreign investor regulation has developed thus far offers three core guiding ideas in the search for investor accountability. First, the principal bone of contention between the neoliberal proponents of classical international law, and the proponents of the NIEO (including its contemporary diffused iteration), is the right to self-determination, later reframed as the right to regulate. Investor accountability does not feature prominently when opportunities for content revision or development arise.[68] Therefore, the search should include solutions or mechanisms devised for other concerns, but with sufficient flexibility to be repurposed for securing investor accountability. Second, despite the reality that investment treaties are less about reciprocity as proclaimed than the renewed subjugation of G-77 developmental needs to the protection of private capital emanating from the Global North, they are arguably so symbolic of investment regulation that the vast majority of states, at present, still prefer to deal with the devil they know. As a result, the search for investor accountability should encompass the dispute settlement regime created by investment treaties.[69] Third, regardless of the impulse states currently exhibit towards the preservation of investment treaties, the fact remains that these treaties were and continue to be tools of foreign policy, whose fates are as unpredictable as the winds of political change.[70] To insure against periodic updates to or even the demise of the investment treaty regime, the search for investor accountability should also exceed the confines of investment treaty-based adjudication, and explore dispute settlement options that will endure in the absence of investment treaties.

Studying the procedural, substantive and institutional pillars of the international law on foreign investor regulation while guided by the core ideas of repurposing, introspection and permanence, reveals three possible avenues for

[68] Pahuja (n 6) 129.

[69] Although investment treaties empower investors to initiate claims against host states, but not vice versa, they accommodate counterclaims against investors in the absence of express treaty language to the contrary. See in particular ch 8 (Ishikawa) of this volume.

[70] Ho, *State Responsibility* (2018) 243–45.

securing investor accountability. The first possible avenue, which can be carved out by parsing and repurposing the common procedure for investor-state dispute settlement in investment treaties, is the replacement of bipartite with multipartite treaty-based adjudication (see section III.A). The second possible avenue, which can be carved out by parsing and repurposing common substantive law provisions in investor-state contracts, is reliance on governing law clauses that apply international law to the merits of the dispute (see section III.B). The third possible avenue, which can be carved out by deploying standing dispute settlement institutions with a higher degree of permanence than ad hoc treaty-based tribunals, is recourse to subregional courts (see section III.C). It is to these previously obscured opportunities for securing investor accountability that the discussion now turns.

A. Multipartite Treaty-Based Adjudication

Multipartite treaty-based adjudication presents an untapped opportunity for securing investor accountability because it encourages and accommodates calls for attention to such accountability, which tend not to originate from one of the disputing parties. In traditionally bipartite treaty-based adjudication which focuses on securing state responsibility for mistreatment of protected investors and investments, disputing investors and states may choose not to raise issues of investor misconduct which can be relevant to legal liability. Their reasons can range from self-preservation to preoccupation with other issues. So when standing to appear and present submissions in an investor-state arbitration is conferred on parties other than investors and states, it enhances the likelihood that otherwise suppressed issues, such as investor misconduct, will be aired by those who are most gravely affected or concerned by such misconduct. Constant suppression of relevant issues from discussion and reflection distorts the content of international law.

Investment treaties are said to enable 'arbitration without privity' because they record the consent of Contracting States to arbitrate future disputes with qualifying investors who are nationals of the other or another Contracting State.[71] Consent is perfected when the investor, who is not a signatory to the treaty, files a request for arbitration in accordance with the procedure laid out in the treaty, thereby 'accepting' the host state's standing 'offer' to arbitrate. This asymmetrical arrangement envisages an investor-state arbitration commencing at the investor's behest, but never the host state's.[72] Participation in treaty-based investor-state

[71] J Paulsson, 'Arbitration Without Privity' (1995) 10 *ICSID Review – Foreign Investment Law Journal* 232, 232.

[72] Whether the applicable investment treaty envisages dispute settlement via ad hoc or institutional arbitration, or via a standing court, the prerogative of initiating a claim still lies with the investor.

arbitration is not strictly limited to the disputing parties. *Amici curiae* submissions by non-governmental organisations, for example, have featured in investment treaty arbitrations.[73]

There is potential for increasing the frequency of third-party participation with the recent entry into force of the United Nations Convention on Transparency in Treaty-based Investor-state Arbitration, which adopts the UNCITRAL Rules on Transparency in Treaty-based Investor-state Arbitration.[74] In Resolution 68/109, the General Assembly declared the necessity for 'provisions on transparency in the settlement of such treaty-based investor-state disputes to take account of the public interest involved in such arbitrations' and that

> rules on transparency in treaty-based in investor-state arbitration would contribute significantly to the establishment of a harmonized legal framework for a fair and efficient settlement of international investment disputes, increase transparency and accountability and promote good governance.

To this end, Article 4(3) permits third-party participation on the following terms:

> In determining whether to allow such a submission, the arbitral tribunal shall take into consideration, among other factors it determines to be relevant:
>
> (a) Whether the third person has a significant interest in the arbitral proceedings; and
> (b) The extent to which the submission would assist the arbitral tribunal in the determination of a factual or legal issue related to the arbitral proceedings by bringing a perspective, particular knowledge or insight that is different from that of the disputing parties.

To date, multipartite investor-state dispute resolution is said to promote 'transparency' in the dispute settlement process, which in turn satisfies the 'public interest' and promotes 'a harmonized legal framework', 'fair and efficient' dispute settlement, 'accountability' and 'good governance'. While few will doubt the desirability these objectives, calling for transparency through multipartite dispute resolution in the context of *treaty-based* investor-state disputes, where investors initiate claims against states but not vice versa, fashions a narrative on public interest in, and accountability of, the nuts and bolts of *state* conduct. In other words, multipartite dispute resolution, a manifestation of transparency, is primarily concerned with illuminating and legitimising the pursuit of state responsibility. This obscures the potential for multipartite dispute resolution for securing, or at the very least raising awareness of, investor accountability.

Notwithstanding the implied contextual bias in the Transparency Rules, there is nothing in earlier practice or in the Transparency Rules concerning

[73] T Ishikawa, 'Third Party Participation in Investment Treaty Arbitration' (2010) 59 *International and Comparative Law Quarterly* 373, 378–84.

[74] Signed 10 December 2014, entered into force 18 October 2017. See also Draft Hague Rules on Business and Human Rights Arbitration, Art 24-*bis*.

third-party submissions which precludes third parties from flagging investor misconduct. Article 4(3) directs an arbitral tribunal to receive third-party submissions when 'the third person has a significant interest in the arbitral proceedings', when 'the submission would assist the arbitral tribunal in the determination of a factual or legal issue' and when any other unspecified 'relevant' factors are present. Article 4(3) reflects and affirms earlier sporadic practice on the admissibility of third-party submissions in treaty-based investor-state arbitrations. With third-party submissions on the rise, it is imperative that the transparency narrative includes an emphasis on the possibility of affected stakeholders in a foreign investment venture, such as local communities, impugning *investor* conduct.[75] One example of a third-party submission going precisely where the host state was unwilling or unable to tread with respect to the investor conduct can be found in *Methanex Corporation v USA*.[76]

The dispute in *Methanex* arose from a ban imposed by the state of California on a gasoline additive known as methyl tertiary-butyl ether (MTBE). Starting from 31 December 2002, gasoline sold or supplied in California, where motorists and gasoline consumers abound, must not contain MTBE. MTBE is a non-biodegradable toxic chemical that is a potential human carcinogen. It is also highly soluble in water, causing substantial groundwater contamination once it is released into the environment. As the majority of Californian residents obtain their drinking water supplies from groundwater, the state of California decided to ban MTBE on the basis that it poses significant risk to the environment and to human health. Methanex is a Canadian company that produces and sells methanol, a component chemical in MTBE. It also markets methanol in the US through two local subsidiaries. Methanex brought a claim against the US under Chapter 11 of the North American Free Trade Agreement,[77] alleging that the ban violated several treaty obligations owed to Methanex's investment in the US gasoline industry,[78] and seeking USD 970 million in damages.[79]

[75] J Kelsey, D Schneiderman and G van Harten, 'Phase 2 of the UNCITRAL ISDS Review: Why "other matters" really matter' (International Institute for Sustainable Development, 23 April 2019), available at iisd.org/itn/2019/04/23/phase-2-of-the-uncitral-isds-review-why-other-matters-really-matter-jane-kelsey-david-schneiderman-gus-van-harten-2. See in particular ch 3 (Cotula and Perrone) of this volume.

[76] *Methanex Corporation v USA*, Final Award of the Tribunal on Jurisdiction and Merits (Veeder, Rowley, Reisman), 3 August 2005 (NAFTA-UNCITRAL).

[77] Signed 17 December 1992, entered into force 1 January 1994, 32 ILM 289. The NAFTA is a trilateral treaty, whose Contracting States are Canada, Mexico and the US. On 30 November 2018, the US, Mexico and Canada signed the United States–Mexico–Canada Agreement (USMCA), which replaces the NAFTA. One area in which the USMCA differs from the NAFTA is differentiated access to investor-state dispute settlement for Canadian and Mexican investors; N Bernasconi-Osterwalder, 'USMCA Curbs How Much Investors Can Sue Countries – Sort Of' (International Institute for Sustainable Development, 2 October 2018), available at www.iisd.org/library/usmca-investors.

[78] Specifically, Methanex alleged the violation of Art 1102 (National Treatment), Art 1105 (Minimum Standard of Treatment) and Art 1110 (Expropriation and Compensation). For the gist of Methanex's argument under each head of claim, see *Methanex Corporation v USA*, Part II para 26-8.

[79] *Methanex Corporation v USA*, Part II para 32.

NAFTA Chapter 11 is an archetype, first generation investment treaty that does not impose any obligations on investors, and only permits claims by investors against host states.[80] The right to potable water has long been recognised as a fundamental human right, and the obligations of states with respect to access to potable water are a part of international human rights law. The continued use of MTBE in gasoline violates a fundamental human right and is incompatible with a state's obligations under international human rights law. The implications of the dispute on the environment and human health mobilised environmental groups and civic bodies to come forward, and the *Methanex* tribunal became the first to admit third-party submissions. The US submitted that Methanex's claim did not satisfy the jurisdictional requirement in Article 1101(1)[81] and, even if it did, Methanex demonstrated neither violation by the US of any Chapter 11 obligation,[82] nor loss occasioned by the MTEB ban.[83] In contrast, the two admitted *amici* submissions focused on the inherent and inalienable right of host states to regulate foreign investment within their territories.[84] Notwithstanding the irony of the Methanex claim,[85] where a corporate investor with a profit-driven interest in the continued manufacture of a harmful chemical sues a host state for taking measures in the public interest to alleviate that harm, it took an *amicus* submission from Earthjustice to call out Methanex's misconduct. In explaining why the ban was warranted, it was submitted that states are under 'an obligation to ensure that *activities under their jurisdiction and control do not violate human rights*'.[86] In explaining why the ban did not discriminate against methanol producers, Earthjustice submitted that 'an investor whose *investment poses a threat to health or the environment* is, for purposes of NAFTA, in a different circumstance from an investor whose investment poses no such threat'.[87]

The tribunal agreed with the US that Methanex failed to establish, as required by Article 1101(1), that the MTEB ban related to methanol-producing investors, thereby removing the Methanex claim from the tribunal's jurisdiction.[88]

[80] See Arts 1116, 1117, 1119, 1120.

[81] Amended Statement of Defense of Respondent United States of America, 5 December 2003, paras 109–212.

[82] ibid paras 281–417.

[83] ibid paras 213–80.

[84] *Amicus Curiae* Submissions by the International Institute for Sustainable Development (IISD Amicus Submission) 9 March 2004, 2–19; Submission of Non-Disputing Parties Bluewater Network, Communities for a Better Environment and Center for International Environmental Law (Earthjustice Amicus Submission), 9 March 2004, 2–19.

[85] Against the weight of early scientific evidence on the hazardous effects of MTBE, summarised in a 2005 WHO report entitled 'Methyl *tertiary*-Butyl Ether (MTBE) in Drinking Water' (2005) WHO/SDE/WSH/05.08/122, 1–14, available at www.who.int/water_sanitation_health/dwq/chemicals/MTBE200605.pdf, Methanex maintains that MTBE is 'a safe, clean and economical gasoline component' whose 'environmentally beneficial characteristics are among the primary factors that have made MTBE the oxygenate of choice in markets where free and fair trade is allowed'; see Claimant Methanex Corporation's Second Amended Statement of Claim, 5 November 2002, paras 12 and 89, also 91–102.

[86] Earthjustice Amicus Submission (n 84) para 18 (emphasis added).

[87] ibid para 32 (emphasis added).

[88] *Methanex Corporation v USA*, Part IV Ch E, para 22.

The tribunal also found, in any event, that the US did not violate any Chapter 11 obligation.[89] Having decided to dismiss the Methanex claim in its entirety, the tribunal then ordered Methanex to bear the legal costs incurred by the US as respondent to the proceedings. This outcome, which the *amici curiae* sought in light of Methanex's strategic claim,[90] may be construed as a veiled acknowledgement and criticism of investor misconduct by the arbitral tribunal. The ruling in *Methanex* strongly suggests that even if the investor's conduct is not a principal point of contention, allowing affected stakeholders to participate in the dispute settlement process, more so than upholding transparency, introduces the important dimension of investor accountability, which may very well have a bearing on the outcome of the dispute.

Repurposing transparency-based multipartite investment treaty arbitration for securing investor accountability provides concrete access to remedy for affected communities and, in time, enables the substantiation of international law on investor regulation, with minimal disruption to the existing investor-state dispute settlement framework of ad hoc adjudication. However, the success of pursuing and securing investor accountability here depends on the receptiveness of tribunals to third-party submissions impugning investor conduct. Whether third-party submissions are admitted will ultimately depend on the circumstances of each case, such as whether allegations of investor misconduct are sufficiently severe and likely to be proved, and whether admitting these submissions will 'disrupt or unduly burden the arbitral proceedings, or unfairly prejudice any disputing party'.[91] It remains to be seen if more tribunals will be inclined to exercise their discretion to admit third-party submissions seeking or alluding to investor accountability.[92] The tentative returns on this route for securing investor accountability calls for the consideration of other options. And given how the vast majority of foreign investment projects originate in a contract or series of contracts concluded between the investor and the state or state entity, investor-state contracts are another potential launchpad for securing investor accountability.

[89] ibid Part IV Ch F, para 6.

[90] IISD Amicus Submission (n 84) para 97; Earthjustice Amicus Submission (n 84) para 43.

[91] UNCITRAL Transparency Rules, Art 5(4).

[92] In this regard, the EU's recent proposal for third-party interventions in investor-state arbitrations conducted under the Energy Charter Treaty (signed 17 December 1994, entered into force 16 April 1998) 2080 UNTS 100 is a step in the direction of flagging investor accountability through multipartite treaty-based adjudication; see proposed new ECT Article in 'EU text proposal for the modernisation of the Energy Charter Treaty (ECT)' (27 May 2020) 19, which provides in part: 'The tribunal shall permit any natural or legal person that can demonstrate a direct and present interest in the result of the dispute (the intervener) to intervene as a third party. The intervention shall be limited to supporting, in whole or in part, the award sought by one of the disputing parties'; available at trade.ec.europa.eu/doclib/docs/2020/may/tradoc_158754.pdf.

B. Governing Law Clauses in Investor-State Contracts

When an investor-state contract contains a governing law clause that identifies international law as a law or the law applicable to the merits of a dispute arising from the contract, it empowers the dispute settlement body constituted according to the terms of the contract to assess the liability of the contracting parties under international law. In the presence of such a clause, and should the circumstances so warrant, the dispute settlement body can pronounce that investor misconduct amounts to a violation of international law.

An investor-state contract, or series of contracts the sum of which constitute the investment project, sets out the rights and obligations of the contracting parties with respect to their venture.[93] Although there is no universal template for an investor-state contract, since specifications necessarily depend on the industry in which the investment will be made, there are certain clauses which guide on contract drafting developed by global policy think tanks recommend including in all investor-state contracts.[94] Standard clauses, which are already found in the majority of investor-state contracts, tend to be those that clearly identify the legal framework for resolving disputes between the contracting parties over performance obligations. Absent such clauses, disputing parties may disagree on the appropriate legal framework or forum for dispute resolution, expending considerable time and expense to find common ground. One such standard clause, which in addition to clarifying the legal framework for dispute resolution, may also serve as a route to securing investor accountability, is the governing law clause.

A governing law clause in an investor-state contract stipulates the body or bodies of law applicable to the substance of any dispute arising from that contract.[95] The law identified in such a clause may be the product of a negotiated agreement, the choice of the more powerful contracting party, or a standard stipulation in an industry boilerplate contract. Governing law clauses come in many forms. Some refer only to national law, which may or may not be host state law; some refer to national law in conjunction with international law; some refer only to international law; and others refer to trade or commercial usages or even *lex mercatoria*.

In investor-state contracts containing arbitration clauses, contracting parties consent to submit an agreed genre of future disputes to arbitration. As consent

[93] The contract may also implicate other stakeholders such as legitimate tenure rights holders, local communities, indigenous peoples and government agencies. For an outline of how an investor-state contract affects both contracting and non-contracting parties in the context of foreign investment in agricultural land, see the UNIDROIT-FAO-IFAD Legal Guide on Agricultural Land Investment Contracts (ALIC) Zero Draft (1 June 2019) 26–55, available at www.unidroit.org/work-in-progress/agricultural-land-investment/online-consultation.

[94] See, for example, L Cotula, 'Investment Contracts and Sustainable Development – How to make Contracts for Fairer and More Sustainable Natural Resource Investments' (International Institute for Environment and Development 2010) 76–82, available at pubs.iied.org/pdfs/17507IIED.pdf.

[95] Lim, Ho and Paparinskis (n 18) 145–46.

to arbitrate cannot be unilaterally withdrawn, disputing parties are bound to arbitrate before a tribunal constituted in accordance with the terms of the arbitration clause, and cannot opt to litigate before national courts. When paired with arbitration clauses, governing law clauses do not self-evidently favour investor protection. They merely direct the arbitral tribunal to the law that should be applied when determining the substance of a dispute. However, claims brought by investors against host states involving a governing law clause that refers to international law present a unique opportunity for some arbitral tribunals. The reference to international law in the governing law clause was once regarded as a feature of an internationalized contract, whereby all contractual obligations by which the host state is bound are converted into international obligations.[96] The notion of an internationalized contract is highly controversial, and finds little to no support today.[97] The clearest assimilation of contractual obligations into international obligations on the authority of a governing law clause referring to international law was attempted in *Texaco Overseas Petroleum Company/California Asiatic Oil Company v The Government of the Libyan Arab Republic*:[98]

> Under what circumstances was the choice of applicable law made and what consequences should be derived therefrom as to the internationalization of the Deeds of Concession in dispute?
>
> In its final version, the clause designating the applicable law or the choice of law established by Clause 28 of the Deeds of Concession reads as follows:
>
> 'This concession shall be governed by and interpreted in accordance with the principles of the law of Libya common to the principles of international law and, in the absence of such common principles, then by and in accordance with the general principles of law, including such of those principles as may have been applied by international tribunals.'
>
> …
>
> As the Tribunal has already observed (see *supra*, para 31, *in fine*), the internationalization of contracts entered into between states and foreign private persons can result in various ways which it is now time to examine.
>
> …
>
> In the present dispute, general principles of law have a subsidiary role in the governing law clause and apply in the case of lack of conformity between the principles of Libyan law and the principles of international law: but precisely the expression 'principles of international law' is of much wider scope than 'general principles of law', because the latter contribute with other elements (international custom and practice which is accepted by the law of nations) to constitute what is called the 'principles of international law'. To take the terms used by the Permanent Court of International Justice in its judgment in the '*Lotus*' case ([1927] P.C.I.J., No. 10, Ser. A, at 16): the meaning of

[96] See also discussion on pre-NIEO arbitral awards in disputes arising from oil concessions in section II above.

[97] Ho (n 21) 181–99.

[98] (1977) 17 ILM 1, paras 36, 40–45.

> the 'words 'principles of international law', as ordinarily used, can only mean international law as it is applied between all nations belonging to the community of states'. Now, these principles of international law must, in the present case, be the standard for the application of Libyan law since it is only if Libyan law is in conformity with international law that it should be applied. Therefore, the reference which is made mainly to the principles of international law and, secondarily, to the general principles of law must have as a consequence the application of international law to the legal relations between the parties.
>
> International arbitration case law confirms that the reference to the general principles of law is always regarded to be a sufficient criterion for the internationalization of a contract. One should remember, in this respect, the awards delivered in *Lena Goldfields v U.S.S.R.* in 1930, *Petroleum Development Ltd. v Sovereign of Abu Dhabi* in 1951, and *International Marine Oil Company v Sovereign of Qatar* in 1953, and in *Sapphire International Petroleum Ltd. v N.I.O.C.*, all cases in which the arbitrators noted a reference to the general principles of law in order to reach their conclusions as to the internationalization of the contract.

The 1978 *Texaco* award, which defended the unpopular notion of internationalization that was completely at odds with the ethos of the NIEO established just four years prior, has been heavily criticised.[99] The apparent ease which an investor-state contract can be internationalized renders a host state extremely vulnerable to sanction by international law, and serves to deter states from reneging on contractual commitments owed to investors. According to pro-internationalization arbitral tribunals, a governing law clause referring to international law is synonymous with investor protection.

More recently, arbitral license with governing law clauses has been taken even further. According to some leading arbitrators, there is room for overriding the contracting parties' express choice of governing law and applying what in the tribunal's view is a more appropriate law to the substance of the dispute.[100] Quite apart from the arguable impropriety of an arbitral tribunal whose powers derive from the consent of the contracting parties to base its decision on matters that the parties did not consent to, such practice allows internationalization to rear its head regardless of whether the governing law clause contains an express reference to international law. If it does not, the arbitral tribunal can, if it sees fit to do so, read such a reference into the clause. The ingrained, if highly controversial, link between a governing law clause and internationalization would dampen states' enthusiasm for contracts where international law is stipulated as governing law.

Thus far, attention devoted to undermining internationalization has also been attention diverted away from using governing law clauses referring to international

[99] One of *Texaco*'s earliest and staunchest critics was M Sornarajah, 'The Myth of International Contract Law' (1981) 15 *Journal of World Trade* 187, 205–06.

[100] G Kaufmann-Kohler, 'Arbitral Precedent: Dream, Necessity or Excuse?' (2007) 23 *Arbitration International* 357, 364; Z Douglas, *The International Law on Investment Claims* (Cambridge University Press, 2012) 40–52 (Rule 3).

law as realistic means to secure investor accountability under international law. Three reasons back the exploration of this untapped opportunity.

First, in investor-state arbitrations stemming from an arbitration clause contained in an investor-state contract, either the investor or the state may initiate a claim in arbitration against the other. This is unlike in investor-state arbitrations stemming from an arbitration clause contained in an investment treaty which empowers only the investor to initiate a claim, leaving the state on the permanent defensive. This means that should the state take issue with the manner in which the investor goes about performing (or failing to perform) its contractual obligations, the state can launch the first strike by invoking the arbitration clause.

Second, investor-state contracts containing arbitration clauses tend to articulate a broad scope of submission to arbitration. This is expressed in wording to the effect that any dispute arising from or connected to the underlying contract falls within the tribunal's jurisdiction. An example of a broadly worded arbitration is Clause 28 in the 14 Deeds of Concession whose satisfactory performance by Libya was under contention in the *Texaco* award:[101]

> If at any time during or after the currency of this Concession any difference or dispute shall arise between the Government and the Company concerning the interpretation or performance hereof, or anything herein contained or in connection herewith, or the rights and liabilities of either of such parties hereunder and if such parties should fail to settle such difference or dispute by agreement, the same shall, failing any agreement to settle it any other way, be referred to … [arbitration].

When paired with a governing law clause that refers to international law, an arbitration clause which generously envisages the resolution of 'any difference or dispute' on the 'interpretation or performance' of the underlying concession, permits disputing parties to bring claims in international law. In concrete terms, an investor can bring a claim against the state alleging state responsibility for a contractual or contract-related violation of international law. Conversely, a state can also bring a claim against the investor, seeking its accountability for contractual or contract-related transgressions under international law. The challenge is identifying the international obligation/s by which an investor performing a contract is bound;[102] the mechanism for obligation enforcement already exists.

Third, as alluded to above, in light of a broadly worded arbitration clause, the governing law clause is likely to be pivotal to the authority of the arbitral tribunal to adjudicate international claims against states or investors. If the governing law clause directs the tribunal to judge disputes in accordance with national law, then, in the absence of arbitral adventurism, the tribunal has no jurisdiction to hear and decide international claims. If, however, the governing law clause directs

[101] *Texaco*, para 23; also RB von Mehren and PN Kourides, 'The Libyan Nationalizations: TOPCO/CALASIATIC v. Libya Arbitration' (1979) 12 *Natural Resources Law* 419, 421.

[102] The challenge is addressed in greater detail at chs 2, 3, 5, 6, 10, 11 and 12 of this volume.

the tribunal to apply, in one way or another, international law to the substance of the dispute between the parties, then the tribunal has jurisdiction to hear and decide international claims. The *Texaco* award is known for its sole arbitrator's views on the viability of internationalization, much to the detriment of host states. Had the facts been altered, such that it was Libya bringing an international claim against Texaco for the commission of human rights abuses in the performance of the 14 Deeds of Concession, a claim which the contractual dispute settlement mechanism accommodates, the *Texaco* award might have had an alternative reputation as a pioneer in securing investor accountability under international law. The demonstrable possibility of a governing law clause containing a reference to international law cutting both ways attests to its untapped potential as an avenue for securing investor accountability.

In investor-state contracts without arbitration clauses and to which no investment treaty providing for ad hoc dispute settlement applies, recourse against investors for internationally wrongful conduct, such as human rights abuses, would have to be sought from the courts. As a later chapter in this volume addresses, the prospect of securing investor accountability from national courts,[103] the following section will focus on the lesser explored category of subregional courts.

C. Subregional Courts

As noted above, the investment treaty regime is susceptible to constant change, making it a potentially unstable platform for pursuing investor accountability in the long run. Although the preferred forum for the settlement of investor-state disputes during the establishment of the NIEO was national courts applying national law, the contemporary landscape for dispute settlement mechanisms is more diverse. National courts are no longer the only alternative to treaty-based or contract-based arbitration. Other judicial fora for investor-state disputes include regional courts, international courts and the mooted multilateral investment court.[104] Unlike national courts, subregional courts, which only appeared in recent decades, were not the designated vehicles for advancing the NIEO agenda.

[103] Ch 9 (Roorda and Ku).

[104] The proposal for a multilateral investment court originated with the European Commission and envisages a standing first instance and appellate court, with state-appointed judges, hearing and deciding investor-state disputes; see Council of the European Union, 'Negotiating directives for a Convention establishing a multilateral court for the settlement of investment disputes' (20 March 2018), available at data.consilium.europa.eu/doc/document/ST-12981-2017-ADD-1-DCL-1/en/pdf. Variants of this dispute settlement model have already appeared in the 2016 CETA, Arts 8.23–8.28, the 2018 European Union–Singapore Investment Protection Agreement (signed 19 October 2018, not yet in force) arts 3.6–3.10, and the 2019 European Union–Vietnam Free Trade Agreement (signed 30 June 2019, not yet in force) arts 3.38–3.39.

However, this section argues that recent vintage does not preclude subregional courts from upholding the neo-NIEO ideal of sustainable economic development through tighter investor regulation. Additionally, subregional courts may fill in for regional and international courts facing certain limitations on securing investor accountability.

Securing investor accountability under international law via human rights litigation requires careful planning. Some domestic courts may be prepared to interpret and apply international law in claims against errant foreign corporate investors,[105] while international and regional courts tend to only entertain claims against respondent states, and not respondent investors. Article 34(1) of the Statute of the International Court of Justice provides that 'Only states may be parties in cases before the Court'.[106] Similarly, Article 61(1) of the American Convention on Human Rights provides that 'Only the states Parties and the Commission shall have the right to submit a case to the Court'. Additionally, the Rules of Procedure of the Inter-American Court of Human Rights only caters for the representation of 'states' and of the 'Commission', affirming that only States Parties to the American Convention, and the Inter-American Commission on Human Rights, have standing to appear before the Court. Although other regional courts like the European Court on Human Rights and the African Court on Human and People's Rights have jurisdiction over claims brought by individuals, these claims are only ever brought against States Parties to the multilateral treaty that these courts are tasked to enforce.[107] When prominent or familiar transnational judicial models do not appear to offer an avenue for securing investor accountability through transnational human rights litigation, one may be forgiven for thinking that such an avenue cannot be found in an existing transnational judicial institution. Yet, this is also how alternative models, like the Community Court of Justice of the Economic Community of West African States, get overlooked.[108]

[105] A leading example of this prospect is US courts applying the Alien Tort Statute. ATS 28 US Code s 1350 provides: 'The district courts shall have original jurisdiction of any civil action by an alien for a tort only, committed in violation of the law of nations or a treaty of the United States'.

[106] Signed 26 June 1945, entered into force 24 October 1945, TS 993.

[107] Rules 46(a) and 47(1)(d) of the Rules of Court of the European Court of Human Rights only envisage proceedings *against* Contracting States to the European Convention on Human Rights, ensuring that claims, regardless of whether they are brought by another Contracting State or an individual, are always brought *against* states. In contrast to the ECtHR, the jurisdiction of the ACHPR does not appear to be limited to claims against states. Article 3 of the Protocol to the African Charter on Human and People's Rights on the Establishment of an African Court on Human and People's Rights provides that '(1) The jurisdiction of the Court shall extend to all cases and disputes submitted to it concerning the interpretation and application of the Charter, this Protocol and any other relevant Human Rights instrument ratified by the states concerned; and (2) In the event of a dispute as to whether the Court has jurisdiction, the Court shall decide'. Article 5 of the Protocol lists the entities entitled to submit cases to the Court, but does not impose express restrictions on the identity of the respondent to a claim. However, because the obligations set out in the African Charter on Human and People's Rights are addressed to Member States (Art 1), the docket of the ACHPR comprises only claims against states.

[108] For an overview of the ECOWAS Community Court and its role in protecting human rights, see KJ Alter, LR Helfer and JR McAllister, 'A New International Human Rights Court for West Africa: The ECOWAS Community Court of Justice' (2013) 107 *African Journal of International Law* 737.

The ECOWAS Community Court was created pursuant to Articles 6 and 15 of the Revised Treaty of the Economic Community of West African States to 'ensure the observance of law and of the principles of equity in the interpretation and application of the provisions of the Treaty'.[109] Judgments of the Community Court are binding on all 'Member States, the Institutions of the Community and on individuals and corporate bodies'.[110] It has broad contentious jurisdiction, including jurisdiction over any dispute relating to 'the interpretation and application of the Treaty, Conventions and Protocols of the Community',[111] over 'cases of violation of human rights that occur in any Member State',[112] and over 'any matter provided for in an agreement where the parties provide that the Court shall settle disputes arising from the agreement'.[113] Additionally, the Community Court is accessible by 'individuals on application for relief for violation of their human rights', without any express restriction on the standing of investors, be they natural or legal persons, before the Community Court as respondents to such individual applications. Specific support for investor accountability before the Community Court can be found in the 2009 Supplementary Act Adopting Community Rules on Investment and the Modalities for their Implementation with ECOWAS. The Supplementary Act on Investment imposes, among other obligations,[114] the obligation on investors to 'not by complicity with, or in assistance with others, including public authorities, violate human rights in times of peace or during social-political upheavals'.[115] Failure to comply exposes the investor to civil actions for liability in both its host and home states,[116] claims for liability brought by the host state before a tribunal established by the Supplementary Act on Investment[117] and, in the event of disagreement over the appropriate forum for settling a dispute over investor misconduct, a referral of the dispute to the Community Court.[118]

Bringing claims against individual or corporate investors for human rights or other stipulated violations before the Community Court on the basis of establishment documents should be a given, but for the 2010 ruling of the Community

Over time, the ECOWAS Community Court has also emerged as an alternative forum to domestic courts for the pursuit of opposition politics, framed in the language of human rights violations of dissidents and disappointed politicians by Member States, indicating the Court's contextual approach to human rights protection, see OD Akinkugbe, 'Towards an Analysis of the Mega-Political Jurisprudence of the ECOWAS Community Court of Justice' in JT Gathii (ed), *The Performance of Africa's International Courts: Using International Litigation for Political, Legal, and Social Change* (Oxford University Press, 2020) 149.

[109] Protocol A/P.1/7/91 on the Community Court of Justice, Art 9(1).

[110] Revised Treaty, art 15(4).

[111] Supplementary Protocol A/SP.1/01/05 relating to the Community Court of Justice, Art 3(1)(a).

[112] ibid Art 3(4).

[113] ibid Art 3(6).

[114] For the full suite of investor obligations, see Supplementary Act on Investment A/SA.3/12/08, Arts 11–16.

[115] Signed 19 December 2008, entered into force 19 January 2009; A/SA.3/12/08, Art 14(3).

[116] Supplementary Act on Investment A/SA.3/12/08, Arts 17 and 29.

[117] ibid Arts 18(3), 33(1) and 33(6).

[118] ibid Art 33(7).

Court in *SERAP v Federal Republic of Nigeria* denying that corporations can be sued for human rights violations.[119] The Community Court missed an excellent opportunity to render what would have been a landmark decision confirming the ECOWAS pledge to 'promote investment that supports sustainable development of the region'.[120] *SERAP v Federal Republic of Nigeria* involved a claim brought by a non-governmental organisation against seven local and foreign oil corporations, whose activities caused oil spills adversely affecting the health and environment of the local community inhabiting the Niger Delta of Nigeria. Despite expressing cognisance of global agitation for corporate investor accountability under international law from the United Nations, national courts and legal scholars,[121] the Community Court nonetheless considered itself bound by an earlier judgment where it held that only Member States and Community Institutions can be sued before the Community Court.[122] There are five reasons why the 2010 *SERAP v Federal Republic of Nigeria* decision must be regarded as an aberration in the Community Court's jurisdictional competence over respondent investors, and not, as some commentators declare, an affirmation that investors cannot be sued before the Community Court.[123]

First, the Community Court made no reference to the 2009 Supplementary Act on Investment, which was already in force at the time the decision was rendered in 2010. Even if the claimant NGO did not frame the dispute as an investment dispute with a human rights dimension, and take the initiative to draw the Court's attention to the Supplementary Act on Investment, the facts clearly triggered the application of the Supplementary Act.[124] And since the Supplementary Act explicitly recognises the jurisdictional competence of the Community Court over investors for disputes involving investor misconduct,[125] the Court should have been guided by the Supplementary Act when determining its jurisdictional competence over the respondent investors. It could have distinguished an earlier decision with a vastly different factual matrix that did not involve any form of investor or investment regulation. Second, the Court's

[119] Suit No ECW/CCJ/APP/08/09; Judgment No ECW/CCJ/APP/07/10 (10 December 2010), para 71.

[120] Supplementary Act on Investment A/SA.3/12/08, Art 3.

[121] *SERAP v Federal Republic of Nigeria* (2010), paras 65–70.

[122] ibid paras 71–73.

[123] M Happold and R Radović, 'The ECOWAS Court of Justice as an Investment Tribunal' (2018) 19 *Journal of World Investment and Trade* 95, 104; M Happold, 'Investor-State Dispute Settlement using the ECOWAS Court of Justice: An Analysis and Some Proposals' (2019) 34 *ICSID Review – Foreign Investment Law Journal* 496, 506.

[124] Supplementary Act on Investment A/SA.3/12/08, Art 4(1) provides: 'This Supplementary Act applies to all investments by an investor, whether the investment is made before or after the entry into force of this Supplementary Act'.

[125] Supplementary Act on Investment A/SA.3/12/08, Art 33(7). As Art 33(7) does not specify by whom the referral must be made, nor lay down conditions for the making of a referral, a claimant may refer its dispute with a respondent investor to the Community Court in the event that neither arbitration under the Act nor litigation before domestic courts are considered viable forums for dispute settlement.

earlier decision in *Peter David v Ambassador Ralph Uwechue*, where it held that individuals cannot be sued before the Community Court for human rights violations because 'the international regime of human rights imposes obligations on states'[126] should not, in contravention of the principle of *effet utile* in treaty interpretation, be used to override the express wording of the Supplementary Act on Investment, which stipulates *investor* obligations,[127] as well as the modes of enforcing those obligations.[128] Third, shortly after its refusal to entertain SERAP's claim against corporate investors on the basis that the latter lacked standing to be sued for human rights violations, the Community Court proceeded to hear a contractual claim involving allegations of bribery brought by one corporation against another,[129] and a claim for an unpaid debt brought by individuals against a corporation.[130] The flexible stance towards the standing of corporate entities as respondents casts serious doubt on the cogency of finding jurisdiction over respondent corporations in garden variety civil matters which can be handled by domestic courts, but not in weightier matters of international concern such as human rights violations. The rapidly diminishing rationale for excluding corporate investor misconduct from the jurisdiction of the Community Court is matched by compelling calls for the Court to reconsider its unwillingness to hear claims against individuals for human rights violations.[131] Fourth, the decisions of the Community Court do not constitute binding precedent and the Court has been known to espouse divergent positions on the same issue.[132] To date, it remains debatable if juridical persons have standing to sue for human rights violations, or whether standing is reserved for natural persons. Therefore, it is entirely possible for the Community Court to depart from its 2010 decision in *SERAP v Federal Republic of Nigeria* on a later occasion.

Fifth and finally, the injustice caused by wrongfully denying investors standing as respondents, which came to light when SERAP resubmitted its claim with a truncated list of respondents before the Community Court, discourages judicial curtailment of the Court's original jurisdictional competence.[133] The 2012 ruling in *SERAP v Federal Republic of Nigeria* highlighted Nigeria's inability to enforce its various laws and compensatory regulations against the polluting investors which ultimately led to the victims' predicament and application for monetary

[126] Suit No ECW/CCJ/APP/04/09; Judgment No ECW/CCJ/RUL/03/10 (11 June 2010), paras 41–43.

[127] Supplementary Act on Investment A/SA.3/12/08, Arts 11–16.

[128] ibid Arts 17, 29, 18(3), 33(1), 33(6) and 33(7).

[129] *Petrostar (Nigeria) Limited v Blackberry Nigeria Limited & Anor*, Suit No ECW/CCJ/APP/08/08, Judgment No ECW/CCJ/JUD/05/11 (18 March 2011).

[130] *Aziablévi Yovo & Ors v Société Togo Telecom & Anor*, Suit No ECW/CCJ/APP/08/11, Judgment No ECW/CCJ/JUG/04/12 (31 January 2012).

[131] ES Nwauche, 'The ECOWAS Community Court of Justice and the Horizontal Application of Human Rights' (2013) 13 *African Human Rights Journal* 30, 31, 46–49.

[132] Happold, 'Investor-State Dispute Settlement' (2019) 502–06.

[133] *SERAP v Federal Republic of Nigeria*, Suit No ECW/CCJ/APP/08/09, Judgment No ECW/CCJ/JUD/18/12 (14 December 2012).

recompense.[134] And yet, the Community Court merely directed Nigeria to step up its monitoring and enforcement efforts.[135] Nigeria was not ordered to pay damages to the victims and it is unclear how Nigeria will, solely at the gentle urging of the ECOWAS Community Court, promptly accomplish what it has consistently failed to do. If the Community Court is reluctant to order Member States to compensate victims of pollution and human rights violations committed by investors out of deference to state dignity and coffers, then it must allow individuals to bring claims against investors. Excluding investors as respondents while declining to order Nigeria to foot the polluting investors' bill leaves the victims with no redress, since the only other avenue for investor accountability is the Nigerian courts, which have proven ineffectual as law enforcers. This is precisely the sort of predicament that the ECOWAS Community Court was set up to preclude, and that the Court itself has vowed to avoid.[136] The Court's misstep in *SERAP v Federal Republic of Nigeria* serves as an important reminder of its mandated jurisdictional competence over respondent investors, and of its greater latitude when ordering compensation from private funds than from state coffers.[137]

An ECOWAS Community Court that embraces its rightful pioneering role in the search for investor accountability by discarding its timid ruling in *SERAP v Federal Republic of Nigeria* may serve as a model for other regional economic blocs like the Mercado Comun del Cono Sur (MERCOSUR)[138] and ASEAN.[139] At present, neither the MERCOSUR nor ASEAN has established a common dispute settlement body.[140] While political will is indispensable to the creation of a subregional court with the competence to hear claims against investors abusing human rights or the environment, and to the enforcement of judgments emanating from such a court, the ECOWAS Community Court offers a realistic

[134] ibid paras 91–112, also 19(j).

[135] ibid para 121.

[136] *Peter David v Ambassador Ralph Uwechue*, paras 41–43.

[137] An order for compensation payable from private funds is very different from one that draws on public funds. In the case of the latter, the state may object to the order on the basis that the sum payable may end up 'depriving the population of a state of its own means of subsistence'. This objection is based on the deleted proviso to the then Art 42(3) of the International Law Commission's Draft Articles on Responsibility of States for Internationally Wrongful Acts which dealt with reparations. Notwithstanding the deletion, the proviso lives on in Art 1(2) of the International Covenant on Civil and Political Rights (signed 16 December 1966, entered into force 23 March 1976) 999 UNTS 171, making its repetition in the ASR in relation to compensation orders directed at states 'unnecessary', see A Gattani, 'The UN Compensation Commission: Old Rules, New Procedures on War Reparations' (2002) 13 *European Journal of International Law* 161, 162.

[138] MERCOSUR comprises Argentina, Bolivia, Brazil, Paraguay, Uruguay and Venezuela (suspended since 2015).

[139] ASEAN comprises Brunei Darussalam, Cambodia, Indonesia, Laos, Malaysia, Myanmar, the Philippines, Singapore, Thailand and Vietnam.

[140] Before more subregional courts come into existence, it is hoped that more frequent recourse to the ECOWAS Community Court and to national courts for securing investor accountability will encourage litigants before investor-state arbitral tribunals, and tribunals themselves, to address rather than avoid issues of investor misconduct.

chance of actual relief for the victims of abuse when diplomatic sparring fails. Disrespect for human rights and the environment is not unique to West Africa. Within the MERCOSUR, Argentina is no stranger to abusive foreign investors, ranging from car manufacturer Daimler in the 1980s[141] to water supplier Urbaser in the 2000s.[142] Within ASEAN, ExxonMobil's complicity in human rights violations in the Aceh province of Indonesia[143] and Unocal's equally brazen conduct in Myanmar, has come to light in lawsuits before US courts.[144] The recent widely condemned Rohingya humanitarian crisis in Myanmar, though not precipitated by errant foreign investors,[145] highlights the urgent need for a subregional dispute settlement body that enables the pursuit of accountability by overcoming the constraints of national courts and the limited jurisdictional reach or practice of regional and international courts.[146]

IV. Conclusion

Understanding the origins and the evolution of the content of international law on foreign investor regulation is the crucial first step to securing investor accountability. Yet, given the various twists and turns in the development of this body of law, its content and caveats are not always easy to discern. The suppression of an imperialistic classical international law focused on investor protection by the idea of an international law more responsive to developmental needs during the establishment of the NIEO was temporary. Broad sketches of a more egalitarian ideology were insufficient to sustain the momentum built up by developing states eager to assert their newfound sovereignty over their natural resources. This enabled the persistent neoliberal objectors to the NIEO, capitalising on the geopolitical tensions during the Cold War and the subsequent sovereign debt crisis, to revive and supplement classical international law through investment treaties,

[141] V Basualdo, TO Quintana and C Varsky, 'The Cases of Ford and Mercedes-Benz' in H Verbitsky and JP Bohoslavsky (eds), *The Economic Accomplices to the Argentine Dictatorship* (Cambridge University Press, 2016) 159, 166–68.

[142] ICSID Case No ARB/07/26, Award (8 December 2016) (Bucher, Martínez-Fraga, McLachlan), paras 56, 62, 479, 483, 487–93, 812–26.

[143] *John Doe et al v Exxon Mobil Corporation et al* (Lamberth J), Civil No 01-1357 (RCL), 1.

[144] *Doe v Unocal Corp*, 395 F.3d 932 (9th Cir 2002).

[145] For a succinct account of the territorial origins of the Rohingya crisis, see M Shahabuddin, 'Postcolonial Boundaries, International Law, and the Making of the Rohingya Crisis in Myanmar' (2019) 9 *Asian Journal of International Law* 334, 347–58.

[146] For illustrations of constraints and limited jurisdictional reach, see J Gilbert, *Natural Resources and Human Rights – An Appraisal* (Oxford University Press, 2018) 58–61, 112–15, 185–88. The Rohingya crisis may supply the critical push that ASEAN needs to reconsider its policy of non-interference vis-à-vis Member States; see E Paulsen, 'ASEAN can no longer turn a blind eye to Myanmar's atrocities' (Al Jazeera, 22 July 2019), available at www.aljazeera.com/indepth/opinion/asean-longer-turn-blind-eye-myanmar-atrocities-190719094526373.html.

tilting the content of international law back in favour of investor protection. The current pushback against the investment treaty regime and, in particular, its facilitation of investor overprotection, is a precursor to yet another period of change in the content of international law. International law now has more to say on investor protection than on investor accountability, but the accountability mechanism proposed by the Draft Hague Rules on Business and Human Rights Arbitration to safeguard human rights from damaging business practices offers hope that the imbalance will be minimised.

Traditional narratives stop here and simply set the robust pursuit of investor accountability as an aspirational goal (usually for someone else to meet). This chapter goes further by arguing that opportunities for investor accountability can nonetheless be found in the existing procedural, substantive and institutional pillars of international law. However, these opportunities have been obscured by decades of emphasis on and efforts to shore up investor protection. As fledgling rebels against entrenched perceptions of an international law wholly oriented towards investor protection, these opportunities will invite more scepticism than speedy endorsement. That said, this chapter has sought to demonstrate how the adoption of multipartite dispute resolution, the reference to international law in the governing law clause of an investor-state contract, and publicised access to subregional courts, enables the pursuit of investor accountability under international law without demanding seismic change. Existing opportunities for investor accountability are the initial blueprint for all future opportunities, because without knowing what is already available, international law content architects risk unnecessary repetition, or worse, reinvention of the wheel.

2

The Foreign Investor as a Good Citizen: Investor Obligations to do Good

MAVLUDA SATTOROVA

I. Background

In 2011, workers and local communities in the Zhanaozen district of the Mangistau Region in Kazakhstan expressed their dissatisfaction over being excluded from the economic benefits generated by oil revenues from foreign investor-led projects operating in the region. The local workers demanded amendments to the collective bargaining agreement, calling for a pay increase and equal rights with foreign workers.[1] Buoyed by the tacit support of the host government, the oil companies were uncompromising and claimed that the disputed take-home pay was already above average.[2] The protests subsequently escalated into violent clashes and led to the declaration of a state of emergency.[3] This had a disruptive effect not only on the foreign investment projects in the region but also on the political stability in Kazakhstan as a whole. From Zhanaozen in Kazakhstan, to Las Bambas in Peru[4] and Oromiya in Ethiopia,[5] growing instances of bottom-up resistance to investment projects are increasingly calling into question the adequacy of the international legal framework governing foreign investment, and in particular, the role of international investment agreements in fostering more inclusive and sustainable relationships between investors and host communities.

[1] P Salmon, 'Repression Intensifies Against Kazakh Oil Workers' Uprising' (2011) 19 *Journal of Contemporary Central and Eastern Europe* 507.

[2] D Satpayev and T Umbertaliyeva, 'The Protests in Zhanaozen and the Kazakh Oil Sector: Conflicting Interests in a Rentier State' (2015) 6 *Journal of Eurasian Studies* 122.

[3] ibid.

[4] WV Diaz, 'Violence, Power and Mining in Peru: How has Las Bambas Worsened Repression?' (Open Democracy, 7 December 2017), available at www.opendemocracy.net/en/las-bambas-mine-peru.

[5] A Maasho, 'Ethiopian Protesters Attack Factories in Africa's Rising Economic Star' (Reuters, 7 October 2016), available at <www.reuters.com/article/us-ethiopia-unrest/ethiopian-protesters-attack-factories-in-africas-rising-economic-star-idUSKCN1270MX.

Elsewhere, a growing discontent over the socio-economic effects of increasingly globalised trade and investment have been linked to major political upheavals, such as the 2016 UK referendum to leave the EU and the Trump presidency in the US. While defending the case for liberalised trade and free enterprise as a vehicle for generating new growth and opportunities, political leaders are increasingly cognisant of the need to address the concerns of those who feel excluded from the benefits of a globalised international economic order.[6] There is a growing acknowledgment that the rules governing international trade and enterprise should become 'more attuned to questions of distribution, more sensitive to other regulatory concerns, and more responsive to the broader public'.[7]

While international trade experts have long acknowledged that international trade redistributes wealth, favouring some over others,[8] such recognition of the unfair distributional effects of investment – and the need for a more inclusive rules framework – is by and large missing in the major discussions of international investment law and its ongoing reform. Although it is relatively uncontested that foreign investment can have a negative impact on the environment and human rights in host states,[9] the idea that investment treaties can be redesigned to maximise the positive contribution that investors can bring to societies, or 'doing good' for the communities that host them,[10] is yet to receive sufficient attention in investment treaty scholarship and policy. This chapter shows that, despite the recent reform efforts, most of the new generation treaties do not contain provisions to address the distributive consequences of foreign investment.[11] Neither does the practice of investment arbitration seem prepared to embrace interpretative approaches promoting a more inclusive and sustainable allocation of benefits and responsibilities of investor-led projects.

The overarching aim of this chapter is to provide novel insights into the hitherto underexplored question of how contemporary international investment law can be redesigned to enable and maximise the positive contribution of foreign investment for the host state. Section II will reveal how traditional narratives constrain regulatory imagination by consistently framing investment protection as a matter of international concern, leaving the wider socio-economic impacts of investment to national policymaking. Contemporary reforms of international investment

[6] See T May, 'PM Speech on the State of Politics', (Prime Minister's Office, 17 July 2019), available at www.gov.uk/government/speeches/pm-speech-on-the-state-of-politics.

[7] HG Cohen, 'What Is International Trade Law For?' (2018) Institute for International Law and Justice Working Paper 2018/6 (MegaReg Series) 5, available at www.iilj.org/wp-content/uploads/2018/12/Cohen-IILJ_2018_6-Megareg.pdf.

[8] G Shaffer, 'Retooling Trade Agreements for Social Inclusion' (2019) 2019 *University of Illinois Law Review* 1.

[9] See for example, K Miles, *The Origins of International Investment Law: Empire, Environment and the Safeguarding of Capital* (Cambridge University Press, 2013).

[10] UNCTAD, 'World Investment Report 2015: Reforming International Investment Governance' (United Nations Publication, 2015) 126.

[11] P Ranjan offers a detailed analysis of investor obligations in the investment treaty landscape in ch 5 of this volume.

law continue to downplay the importance of holding corporations responsible towards local communities, with the newly emerging drafting templates featuring limited provisions on investor obligations. Drawing on emerging empirical data and analysis of the recent trends in investment treaty practice and jurisprudence, section III will examine what needs to change to bridge the existing gap in international investment law. It will expose some of the deeply embedded biases favouring state-centric interpretations of international investment law which enable foreign investors to enjoy extensive privileges and escape liabilities. What hinders the emergence of new visions of the relationship between foreign investors and society? Section IV will seek to answer this question by zooming in on the already entrenched ideas that policymakers are sceptical towards innovation in treaty drafting, and that provisions on investor obligations would be staunchly opposed by industry actors. Turning to the post-colonial history of the international economic order and the more recent developments in business practices, section IV will argue that, despite a degree of resistance, profound changes in the legal mechanisms governing conduct of foreign investors remain possible.

II. Why the Need for Investor Obligations to 'Do Good'?

Investment treaties have long been conceptualised as a means of creating a level playing field and removing the barriers to cross-border flows of capital, technology and know-how. Foreign investors were portrayed as essentially disadvantaged due to their foreign nationality,[12] and any obligations imposed upon them vis-à-vis host states were presented as inefficiencies and thus barriers to investment flows.[13] Far from acknowledging that liberalised investment creates winners and losers, the traditional narratives of international investment law have depicted investors as 'victims of opportunistic politicians' deserving special protection.[14] As a consequence, the investment treaty regime has been functioning as a 'one-way street' system, where investors enjoy a wide array of legal privileges, with no counterbalancing obligations to foster and safeguard responsible business conduct. Furthermore, not only do the bulk of investment treaties feature no express provisions to regulate investor behaviour, but they also limit the capacity of host states to ensure that foreign investments are carried out in a manner that benefits the society.[15]

The asymmetry of the investment treaty regime – its traditional preoccupation with guaranteeing investor rights but not responsibilities – has long been strongly

[12] See A Kulick, *Global Public Interest in International Investment Law* (Cambridge University Press, 2012) 248.

[13] B Legum, 'Understanding Performance Requirement Prohibitions in Investment Treaties' in AW Rovine (ed), *Contemporary Issues in International Arbitration and Mediation* (Brill, 2007) 53, 55–56.

[14] M Sornarajah, *The International Law on Foreign Investment* (Cambridge University Press, 2004) 78.

[15] N Perrone, 'Taking Local Expectations Seriously: A Fresh Start for Foreign Investment Governance?' in JD Haskell and A Rasulov (eds), *European Yearbook of International Economic Law: New Voices and New Perspectives in International Economic Law* (Springer, 2020) 113.

criticised. Equally vociferous and prolific are the existing critiques of the inhibiting effect of investment treaty law on host states' capacity to regulate in the wider public interest. Yet this focus on the host state's right to regulate and the asymmetry in rights and obligations between states and investors somewhat obscures another major problem of the contemporary investment treaty regime: a tendency to view investments as a relational process exclusively between two actors – host states and foreign investors – thus rendering other stakeholders, including local communities, effectively invisible.[16] For decades, concerns about the implications of international investment law on host states were met with a promise of more policy space, and greater freedom to regulate.[17] Yet the language of the 'right to regulate' conveniently shifts the obligation to take care of community interests from investors onto host states. As Schneiderman and Perrone observe, the focus on the sovereign right to regulate 'Elides the fundamental question of what sort of regulatory imagination remains possible under regimes fashioned by a dominant political frame that aspires to unfettered economic freedom'.[18]

Crucially, bringing the need for socially inclusive development under the all-encompassing rubric of the 'right to regulate' creates an illusion of choice and a freedom to act on the part of the host state as a bearer of such a right. The contemporary normative justifications of international investment law frame investment protection and promotion as matters of international concern, while leaving the distributional effects of investments to domestic policymaking.[19] Yet these justifications are not borne out by the evidence of how structural forces shape the global economic order. Foreign investors are able to choose where to invest and how to structure their investments across borders. As host states compete over inward foreign investment, there is a danger they will engage in 'the race to the bottom' by relaxing, or refraining from regulatory policies on key social and environmental issues.[20] Recent empirical studies reveal instances when, driven by the fear of displeasing the prospective investor and losing their investment, senior government officials desisted from the inclusion of public policy-friendly provisions in laws and investment agreements.[21] Just as is the case in international

[16] This theme will be explored further by Cotula and Perrone in ch 3 of this volume. See also NM Perrone, 'The "Invisible" Local Communities: Foreign Investor Obligations, Inclusiveness, and the International Investment Regime' (2019) 113 *American Journal of International Law Unbound* 16.

[17] Cohen, 'What Is International Trade Law For?' (2018) 7.

[18] NM Perrone and D Schneiderman, 'A Critique of International Economic Law: Depoliticization, Inequality, Precarity' in E Christodoulidis, R Dukes and M Goldoni (eds), *Research Handbook on Critical Legal Theory* (Edward Elgar, 2019).

[19] A similar observation is made in the international trade context by Cohen (n 7).

[20] E Aisbett et al, *Rethinking International Investment Governance: Principles for the 21st Century* (Columbia University, 2018) 78.

[21] As one interviewee put it, 'foreign investors are … known for their lobbying and otherwise influencing the government to get the outcome they want, for instance a hands-off regulation of a relevant industry'. See M Sattorova, 'Investor Responsibilities from a Host State Perspective: Qualitative Data and Proposals for Treaty Reform' (2019) 113 *American Journal of International Law Unbound* 22, 23.

trade, structural forces empower capital against host governments in international investment governance.[22] To quote Shaffer:

> Capital plays governments off each other, threatening to invest abroad if taxes on capital are not reduced and if subsidies are not increased. Capital's increased leverage threatens to erode governments' ability to fund social protection and educational and employment policies.[23]

The connection between foreign investment and social outcomes is fraught with controversy, and so are the societal costs and benefits of international investment law.

'The new trade establishment mantra is that trade must be made more inclusive.'[24] While international trade experts are increasingly cognisant of the idea that international trade agreements will only be sustainable if states commit to distribute economic gains broadly,[25] such understanding is still largely missing in international investment law. Investment treaty law, even in its most progressive reform templates, has never expressly concerned itself with domestic social policy and has never acknowledged the existence of winners-losers. Historically, international investment law was preoccupied with safeguarding and maximising investors' wealth, not the well-being of the host state's native population.[26] Investment treaty protections have empowered capital, whilst also – crucially – delimiting host governments' capacity to rebalance the relationship between foreign investors and local communities. Social inclusion is yet to become the regime's new mantra. From its inception, investment law scholarship relegated local communities to a periphery, only as purported beneficiaries that investment treaties were expected to generate and as a source of risk against which investors had to be protected.[27] As Cotula and Perrone observe in their contribution to this volume, 'some investment lawyers may be unaccustomed to the notion of communities in the context of legal scholarship', despite the term having been defined in a number of international treaties and covenants.[28]

Nonetheless, just as is the case with trade, it must be acknowledged that the protection and promotion of investment is not an end in itself, but rather a means

[22] Shaffer, 'Retooling Trade Agreements' (2019) 3.

[23] ibid.

[24] ibid 2.

[25] ibid 25.

[26] KN Schefer, 'The Law of Investment Protection and Poverty Reduction' in SW Schill, CJ Tams and R Hofmann (eds), *International Investment Law and Development: Bridging the Gap* (Edward Elgar, 2015) 380.

[27] GS Akpan, 'Host State Legal and Policy Responses to Resource Control Claims by Host Communities: Implications for Investment in the Natural Resources Sector' in E Bastida, TW Waelde and J Warden-Fernández (eds), *International and Comparative Mineral Law and Policy* (Kluwer Law International, 2005) 284; see also GS Akpan, 'Host Community Hostility to Mining Projects: A New Generation of Risk?' in the same volume, 312.

[28] Ch 3 (Cotula and Perrone) of this volume.

to achieve certain ends.[29] To the extent that investment treaties can catalyse cross-border economic activity, increasing the pay of low income workers or increasing the tax revenue that can be used to redistribute wealth, they could help foster more socially inclusive economic development.[30] This chapter will critically evaluate the role of international investment agreements in allocating economic and social benefits of foreign investment in host states. In doing so, this contribution complements Cotula and Perrone's chapter on local communities and Ranjan's chapter on recent trends in investment treaty practice. The core idea this chapter seeks to explore is how the contemporary international investment framework can be redesigned to move away from its sole focus on investor protection towards a system that compensates, rewards and empowers a much broader range of stakeholders.

III. Foreign Investor as a Good Citizen: What Needs to Change in Investment Treaty Law?

A. Not Enough: Investment Treaty Reform and the (Misplaced) Focus on Negative Effects of Investor Conduct

The importance of addressing the negative impacts of foreign investment on host communities has long been acknowledged. It is uncontested that local communities frequently bear the brunt of the negative effects of foreign investment through physical and economic displacement from land and resources; the degradation of the environment or cultural sites; violence, intimidation, the repression of protests, or inappropriate detentions or arrests.[31] Some investors, for instance, have been known to exploit local labour and natural resources, driving out local businesses, and abusing their market power to extract excess profits.[32] As a recent UNCTAD report highlighted, 'Although (foreign) investment can create positive conditions for improving peoples' lives, it can also carry the risk of negatively impacting on the environment, peoples' health and the enjoyment of their human rights'.[33]

[29] See Shaffer (n 8) highlighting the broader objectives of the WTO Agreement, the principal aim of which is 'raising standards of living, ensuring full employment, and expanding the production of and trade in goods and services, while allowing for the optimal use of the world's resources in accordance with the objective of sustainable development'.

[30] L Sachs and L Johnson, 'Investment Treaties, Investor-State Dispute Settlement and Inequality: How International Rules and Institutions an Exacerbate Domestic Disparities' (2019) Columbia Center on Sustainable Investment Working Paper 4/2019, 2, available at ccsi.columbia.edu/files/2017/11/ISDS-and-Intra-national-inequality.pdf.

[31] See further: KY Cordes, L Johnson and S Szoke-Burke, 'At the Intersection of Land Grievances and Legal Liability: The Need to Reconsider Contract Rights and Expectations at the Supranational Level' (2017) 49 *Loyola University Chicago Law Journal* 515, 524–25.

[32] Aisbett et al, *Rethinking International Investment Governance* (2018) 38.

[33] UNCTAD, 'World Investment Report 2015' (2015) 126.

Since the beginning of the new century, the environmental and social responsibilities of corporations have received much attention in the field of business and human rights, culminating in the endorsement by the United Nations in June 2011 of the Guiding Principles on Business and Human Rights (UNGPs)[34] and the launch of such initiatives as the UN Principles for Responsible Investment.[35] Despite the significant shifts in legal and policy discourse, the need to address distributive consequences of foreign investment has yet to receive full attention in international investment law, which is the principal forum for enforcing the rights (and obligations) of foreign investors. Investment treaties should incorporate not only express provisions to prevent detrimental impacts of investment, but also concrete provisions to boost the positive contribution to host states.

It is almost confounding that at a time when many of the long-criticised aspects of investment treaties and investor-state arbitration are being addressed through systemic treaty reform, the newly emerging treaty models, by and large, still fail to take a strong and effective stance on investor responsibilities towards host states. First, while the bulk of the existing investment treaty stock features no express provisions on investor responsibilities, there is a growing number of treaties which recognise the relevance of investor conduct. Yet this latter category of treaties seeks to address issues arising from investors' (mis)conduct primarily by (1) stipulating host state obligations to fight bribery and corruption, and (2) safeguarding host state rights to protect the environment, human rights and labour standards. For instance, the CARIFORUM–EU Economic Partnership Agreement[36] requires that the contracting state parties cooperate and take any necessary domestic measures to ensure that investors are forbidden from and held liable for bribing public officials. The onus of this obligation is on contracting states, not investors. Other emerging approaches are exemplified by Article 8.18.3 of the EU–Canada Comprehensive Economic and Trade Agreement (CETA),[37] which forecloses an investor's access to investor-state arbitration in cases where its investment agreement was tainted by illegality. Yet the significant shortcoming of this drafting solution is that its scope is limited to the initial period of making investment and does not impose a continuous obligation to act in good faith and refrain from unlawful conduct in *operating* the investment. As the empirical studies reveal, national actors are concerned about the broader influence foreign

[34] United Nations Human Rights Council, 'Guiding Principles on Business and Human Rights: Implementing the United Nations' "Protect, Respect and Remedy" Framework' (21 March 2011) UN Doc A/HRC/17/31.

[35] See 'Why and How Investors Should Act on Human Rights', (United Nations Principles for Responsible Investment, 22 October 2020), available at www.unpri.org/human-rights-and-labour-standards/why-and-how-investors-should-act-on-human-rights/6636.article.

[36] Economic Partnership Agreement between the CARIFORUM States and the European Community (signed 15 October 2008, entry into force 1 January 2009), Art 72.

[37] Signed 30 October 2016, provisional entry into force 21 September 2017.

investors may exercise during the life of an investment project.[38] Investment treaties should provide for investor conduct throughout all stages of investment, not only the entry or dispute settlement stages.

It is also noteworthy that, in contrast with the recently emerged investment treaty templates of developed economies, at least some effort to address investor responsibilities can be found in investment treaties signed between developing states, such as the Slovakia–Iran IIA[39] and the Nigeria–Morocco IIA,[40] as well as the SADC agreement.[41] Even if such formulations are at times not specific, but general and somewhat vague or imprecise in nature, as Ranjan observes in his contribution to this volume, the inclusion of these obligations in South-South IIAs is a significant innovation especially in view of the overwhelming silence on investor obligations in the bulk of investment treaties.[42] The majority of (old and new) investment treaties involving major economic powers such as the US, the EU, Japan and China continue to fall short of providing a meaningful mechanism to address the impact of investor conduct on host states and their communities. As one of the world's largest exporters and importers of foreign direct investment, the EU exercises considerable leverage[43] in the ongoing reform process, but its most recent treaties, as well as negotiating objectives for new mega-regional agreements, do not contain effective and comprehensively framed investor obligations.[44]

The insufficiency of the emerging approaches to incorporating investor obligations in treaties is not limited to the piecemeal nature of the recent reform efforts. Rather, the principal shortcoming of the emerging solutions is that they are rooted in the idea that ultimately, it is the host states, not the corporate actors, that should bear the primary responsibility for controlling the effects of business activities in host states. This core idea lies beneath much of the traditional investment law policy and scholarship and appears to hold sway over what some present as progressive reform efforts. Another critical flaw of the recent reform efforts is that they do not go far enough and tend to focus primarily on preventing investor misconduct. Investment treaties can and should be redesigned not only to avoid detrimental impacts of investment ('doing no harm') but also to maximise the positive contribution that investors can bring to societies ('doing good').[45] This is

[38] See Sattorova, 'Investor Responsibilities' (2019) 23.

[39] Agreement between the Slovak Republic and the Islamic Republic of Iran for the Promotion and Reciprocal Protection of Investments (signed 19 January 2016, entry into force 30 August 2017).

[40] Signed 3 December 2016, not yet in force.

[41] Treaty Establishing the Southern African Development Community (signed 17 August 1992, entry into force 30 September 1993). See also the Investment Agreement for the COMESA Common Investment Area (signed 23 May 2007, not yet in force), which to a certain extent seeks to address investment conduct.

[42] Ch 5 (Ranjan) of this volume.

[43] S Puig and G Shaffer, 'Imperfect Alternatives: Institutional Choice and the Reform of Investment Law' (2018) 112 *American Journal of International Law* 361, 367.

[44] See 'Commission Presents EU Proposal for Modernising Energy Charter Treaty' (European Commission, 27 May 2020), available at trade.ec.europa.eu/doclib/press/index.cfm?id=2148.

[45] UNCTAD (n 10) 126.

particularly important if the international investment regime is to fulfil its promise to foster sustainable development goals. A stronger and more principled approach to foreign investment's contribution to socially inclusive development is necessary at a time when the future of international economic law is being questioned in the face of heightened concerns over the 'denationalization of clusters of political, economic, and social activities that undermine the ability of the sovereign state to control activities on its territory'.[46] The recent backlash against the investment treaty regime is effectively a manifestation of broader concerns about globalisation, in particular its impact on economic dislocation, jobs and livelihoods[47] – something which investment treaties continue to remain silent on.

B. Misplaced Focus on the State as a Sole Bearer of Obligations towards Host Communities

Just as is the case with investment treaty practice, large swathes of investment arbitration practice and scholarship reveal a deeply embedded predisposition towards the idea that it is the host state, and not foreign investors, that should act as the principal bearer of obligations to foster inclusive and sustainable operation of foreign investment in their territory. Consider, for instance, the emerging investment arbitration jurisprudence on social license to operate as a quasi-legal vehicle designed to ensure more equitable participation of local communities in sharing the benefits of foreign investor-led projects. The case of *Bear Creek Mining v Peru* has amply illustrated the pitfalls of the normative idea whereby social and economic inclusion are seen to be outside the remit of investment treaties. The outcome of the case and reasoning of the tribunal expose two principal vehicles commonly deployed by arbitral tribunals in putting that normative idea into practice: the notion that the host state are solely responsible: (1) to design and put in place comprehensive and effective national laws on inclusive and sustainable operation of investment projects; and (2) to utilise approval mechanisms and other screening processes to foresee, forestall and otherwise address any issues that might arise in the case of investor non-compliance with national and international rules governing the process of sharing the benefits of the project with local communities.

The dispute in *Bear Creek* concerned a Canadian investor's operation in Peru, including the Santa Ana silver mining project and the associated legal and contractual rights. From the outset, the investor's projected mining operations in

[46] K Nowrot, 'Legal Consequences of Globalization: The Status of Non-Governmental Organizations Under International Law' (1999) 6 *Indiana Journal of Global Legal Studies* 579, 586.

[47] D Caron and E Shirlow, 'Dissecting Backlash: The Unarticulated Causes of Backlash and Its Unintended Consequences' in G Ulfstein and A Føllesdal (eds), *The Judicialization of International Law – A Mixed Blessing?* (Oxford University Press, forthcoming) 5–6.

Santa Ana met with strong opposition among the local population.[48] The project was expected to affect the territory traditionally occupied by the Aymara people, a group of interconnected indigenous communities.[49] These communities voiced significant concerns over the project's environmental impacts on the natural resources pertaining to their lands, as well as their concerns over the economic benefits of the project. While the numerous indigenous communities covered by the project's mapped area felt entitled to 'participate in the benefits of the investor's activities in the area', the investor's social support commitments were not extended to all concerned groups. The investor was made aware of these grievances as early as 2008, and by 2011 the members of the excluded communities manifested their opposition to the project by rejecting it at a public hearing. This was followed by a series of protests demanding the cancellation of the mining concessions.[50] The protests culminated in the blockades of major roads and violent clashes with police, with the Government having to deploy armed forces to contain the social unrest.[51] To resolve the protests, the Government announced a number of measures, including a decree revoking legal instruments constituting the basis of the investor's mining rights.[52] The investor disputed this decision and claimed that the revocation of its mining rights constituted, among other things, an unlawful expropriation and a breach of fair and equitable treatment.

The investor relied on the fact that at the time of acquiring its mining rights, 'there was no provision of Peruvian law providing any standard by which either the State or local communities could grant "social license" with respect to a mining project'.[53] A similar emphasis on the content of national laws is clearly discernible in the majority's reasoning. Instead of examining whether the investor had sought a meaningful engagement with local communities, the majority merely questioned what actions *were legally required* of the investor in seeking to obtain a social licence, and whether the investor took those actions.[54] The tribunal did not question whether the investor took sufficient steps to obtain social licence from the local communities. Rather, it asked whether the investor 'took the *appropriate and necessary* steps to engage all of the relevant and likely to be affected local communities'.[55] The tribunal acknowledged that, on the evidence, support for the project came from communities that were receiving some form of benefits such as jobs and direct payments for land use, and that social acceptance was missing among the communities that 'were either not receiving benefits, were uninformed,

[48] *Bear Creek Mining v Peru*, ICSID Case No ARB/14/21, Award (30 November 2017), para 152.

[49] See *Bear Creek Mining v Peru*, Award, paras 150–174; *Bear Creek Mining v Peru*, Dissenting Opinion of Phillipe Sands, paras 16–18.

[50] ibid paras 172–201.

[51] ibid paras 189–98.

[52] ibid paras 201–02.

[53] ibid para 238.

[54] ibid para 402.

[55] ibid para 406.

or both'.[56] The tribunal expressly recognised that some communities, including those likely to face the project's negative effects on water and other natural resources, were not brought into the process and offered work or other forms of recompense.[57]

However, despite acknowledging the investor's failure to take 'real and sufficient steps'[58] to engage with all affected local communities, the tribunal denied the existence of a causal link between such failure on the part of the investor and the subsequent social unrest and the revocation of its mining rights.[59] The tribunal instead noted that the investor's local outreach efforts were approved, supported and endorsed by the host government and that no objections had been raised by the authorities.[60] Thus, the majority's reasoning implies that it is the responsibility of the host state to provide and enforce the law requiring that investors meaningfully and effectively engage with local communities. Rather than holding the investor to account for not having gone far enough to secure a social licence,[61] the tribunal preferred to find the host state singularly responsible for the consequences of the local community opposition to the project. The majority's award also places a particular emphasis on the host state's role by questioning what the state authorities' responsibilities were in relation to securing a social licence.[62]

The majority of the tribunal in *Bear Creek* is not alone in endorsing the view that it is the host states, and not the investors, that bear ultimate responsibility for ensuring that investment projects are sustainable and designed so as to maximise their benefits for local community. A recently published treatise on arbitrating mining disputes provides a stark example of contemporary conceptions about investor socio-economic responsibilities. So glaring is the authors' disavowal of corporate obligations towards local communities that the relevant passage warrants quoting in full:

> Mining companies should strive to build realistic expectations on the part of local communities. Owners and operators or mining projects located in underserved areas should be mindful of undertaking social welfare functions that are traditionally better handled by host governments themselves. As the price of minerals and metals continued to rise over the past few years, local stakeholders developed a growing appetite for the benefits associated with mining projects, especially so in emerging economies where national and local governments have struggled to develop the necessary means to meet the needs of their citizens. In some cases, the sustained profits generated by the mining sector have fuelled local expectations (whether at the governmental or communal level) that mining and metal companies undertake community development and social and

[56] ibid para 407.
[57] ibid para 406.
[58] ibid para 19 (in the words of the arbitrator).
[59] ibid para 411.
[60] ibid para 412.
[61] ibid paras 408, 412.
[62] ibid 402.

> logistic infrastructure projects. These expectations also encompass preferred hiring and local procurement policies and redirection of governmental mining profits back into the production area.[63]

The authors conclude that 'The mining company should not be made to shoulder the burden of expansive social programs or infrastructure investments'.[64] A similar dismissal of the need to engage with local communities can be found in an argument which regards social licence as an anathema to the rule of law:

> Thinking of social licence to operate as a new quasi-legal requirement on companies, though, carries with it some extremely dangerous underlying assumptions. These become apparent as soon as one thinks again of what it measures: the risks of legal changes adverse to a business's operations and of extra-legal disruptions of business activities. To say that businesses … should be subjected to a shifting social licence to operate is to say that businesses should face risks of legal changes that damage their business interests and of extra-legal disruption of their business activities by those opposed to them. To put it bluntly, any overly enthusiastic embrace of social licence to operate in its mistakenly transformed senses is actually a rejection of the rule of law.[65]

Investment arbitration case law and large swathes of academic literature on the subject expose a startling absence of binding international norms directing investors to engage with local communities that do not fall under the definition of indigenous people but are nevertheless affected by foreign investment projects, and are excluded from their economic benefits. International investment law is not alone in its state-centric vision of the relationship between foreign investors and local communities. This vision is clearly discernible in other areas of international law governing the relationship between populations and foreign corporations. The idea of empowering peoples, rather than states, had been at the heart of calls for the recognition of developing nations' sovereignty over natural resources in the early years of decolonisation.[66] However, the language of granting the right to permanent sovereignty over resources to the peoples was seen by some states as dangerous and detrimental to the contractual entitlements of foreign companies.[67] It is owing to this opposition from major capital-exporting states that the principal international covenants on human rights acknowledge peoples' rights over natural resources in a limited form: as a right the exercise of which should not prejudice investment protection.[68]

[63] HG Burnett and L-A Bret, *Arbitration of International Mining Disputes: Law and Practice* (Oxford University Press, 2017) 121.

[64] ibid.

[65] D Newman, 'Be Careful What You Wish For: Why Some Versions of 'Social Licence' are Unlicensed and May be Anti-Social' (Macdonald-Laurier Institute Commentary, 2014), available at www.macdonaldlaurier.ca/files/pdf/MLICommentaryNewmansociallicence1114webready.pdf.

[66] J Gilbert, *Natural Resources and Human Rights: An Appraisal* (Oxford University Press, 2018) 17.

[67] ibid 22.

[68] ibid.

Governments are indeed primary bearers of the obligation to protect their populations and to facilitate inclusive and sustainable development. Yet holding national lawmakers singularly responsible for the outcomes enabled by international rules and processes is likely to create problems for both investors and local communities and, in the long run, for the future of the international economic order. As Rodrik has argued, globalisation benefits countries with strong existing institutions while hindering the ability of nations to build institutions to address both regulatory and redistributive issues.[69] Unlike their developed counterparts, developing states frequently lack the economic and institutional capacity to design and implement comprehensive and sophisticated national laws and implementation mechanisms. The fallacy of the prevailing narratives of international investment law is that they often assume parity between developed and developing states. Such narratives disregard the structural factors that impede on the ability of developing states to design and maintain effective laws and institutions to implement them.[70]

The problem of capacity is further exacerbated by corporations that seek to unduly influence national legislators and policy-makers. The emerging qualitative data suggests that foreign investors wield considerable influence over national lawmaking in host states at times. Empirical case studies[71] supply some stark examples. In one recent study, a cross-section of the interviewed government officials recounted the efforts by foreign corporations to influence the extent and rigour of public health, planning and environmental laws.[72] Echoing other empirical studies published to date, interviews with government officials in developing states reveal that, when designing and implementing national regulations, host governments may find themselves facing pressure from foreign investors.[73] Driven by the fear of displeasing the prospective investor or losing the existing investment, government officials may stall the adoption of national laws that had been designed to achieve important public policy objectives.[74]

[69] D Rodrik, 'Globalization for Whom?' (2002) 104 *Harvard Magazine* 29.

[70] See further, MJ Trebilcock and RJ Daniels, *Rule of Law Reform and Development: Charting the Fragile Path of Progress* (Edward Elgar, 2008).

[71] See K Tienhaara, 'Regulatory chill and the threat of arbitration: A view from political science' in C Brown and K Miles (eds), *Evolution in Investment Treaty Law and Arbitration* (Cambridge University Press, 2011) 606; C Côté, 'A Chilling Effect? The Impact of International Investment Agreements on National Regulatory Autonomy in the Areas of Health, Safety and the Environment' (PhD thesis, London School of Economics 2014), available at etheses.lse.ac.uk/897/8/Cote_A_Chilling_%20Effect.pdf.

[72] Sattorova (n 21) 23.

[73] ibid.

[74] ibid. Having learnt about the government plans to introduce health warnings and smoking-free zones, the company condemned the proposed regulations as 'seriously interfering with … commercial freedom' and threatened to withdraw its investment. See further AB Gilmore, J Collin and M McKee, 'British American Tobacco's Erosion of Health Legislation in Uzbekistan' (2006) 332 *British Medical Journal* 355; J Knight and S Chapman, 'Asia is Now the Priority Target for the World Anti-Tobacco Movement: Attempts By the Tobacco Industry to Undermine the Asian Antismoking Movement' (2004) 13 *Tobacco Control* 30.

The emphasis on the state as a sole bearer of obligations towards those who are often left behind by globalised trade and investment is also at odds with the growing acknowledgment that investment treaty law, and in particular its investor-state arbitration mechanism, tends to diminish, rather than enhance, the host government's ability to harness its national laws and regulations to achieve certain economic and public policy objectives. Indeed, one of the major criticisms of the investment treaty regime has been levelled at its proclivity to 'operate with a default bias against change in the regulatory system of the host state which is fundamentally misaligned with the dynamic and unpredictable policy challenges that states face'.[75] The constraining effect of investment treaties on national legislative and regulatory powers has been widely recognised to the extent that one of the major strands of the ongoing investment treaty reform process – including in developed states – has been to introduce safeguards for host governments to legislate and regulate in the wider public interest. Yet such safeguards alone will not redress the systemic factors that presently delimit the capacity of developing states to legislate and regulate in the interest of their populations. Equally, imposing monetary responsibility on developing states for failing to implement international conventions or otherwise legislate in the interests of local communities is likely to divert the already limited financial resources, while depriving investors of an incentive to maximise the societal benefits of their projects.

C. Misplaced Faith in Arbitral Tribunals as Principal Agents of Change

The criticisms of the international investment regime's asymmetry in providing investors with rights but no responsibilities have been dismissed by some authors as conceptually 'rather simplistic and not always accurate'.[76] This is because the national laws of host states and investor-state contracts can impose obligations on investors. Consequently, it is argued, incorporating enforceable investor obligations into treaty texts is unnecessary, and all that is needed is 'a change of mindset' whereby 'reliance on investment treaties is … preserved but as part of a wider array of sources of foreign investment regulation; and one in which these different sources, including treaties, are interpreted in a more balanced manner'.[77] Such a change of mindset would be reflected, among other things, in greater attention paid by tribunals to whether the investor exercised due diligence in making and operating its investment in the territory of the host state.[78]

[75] J Paine, 'On Investment Law and Questions of Change' (2018) 19 *Journal of World Investment and Trade* 173, 186.

[76] JE Viñuales, 'Investor Diligence in Investment Arbitration: Sources and Arguments' (2017) 32 *ICSID Review – Foreign Investment Law Journal* 346, 367.

[77] ibid 367.

[78] ibid.

Although these arguments could indeed prove useful in addressing the consequences of investor misconduct in some cases, they are primarily aimed at deterring negative effects of investor behaviour rather than encouraging socially inclusive investments. The overall long-term effectiveness of such solutions is also likely to be limited due to the lack of binding precedent and the already notorious problems of inconsistency in arbitral jurisprudence. Furthermore, even a cursory overview of investment arbitration practices reveals the reluctance of arbitral tribunals to change their mindset and to use the legal mechanisms at their disposal to interpret investment treaties as vehicles that should benefit host states.[79] Indeed, as shown by Ranjan in his contribution to this volume analysing recent investment arbitration jurisprudence, domestic law could be relied upon by tribunals as a gateway to impose obligations on foreign investors but the trend is far from being uniformly endorsed.

The majority's award in *Bear Creek* neatly exposes the fallacy of placing faith in the arbitral practice as a vehicle for addressing the investment treaty regime's social deficits. The issue of contributory fault was central to the majority's decision to find Peru responsible for social unrest. In its defence, the Government of Peru argued that the social unrest was a direct consequence of the investor's failure to address grievances of the affected communities,[80] and that its contributory fault should be taken into account by the tribunal in determining the party's liabilities. Despite having concluded that the investor had indeed failed to effectively engage with all the concerned communities, the tribunal nevertheless (rather inexplicably) concluded that Peru did not discharge its burden of proof in showing that the local communities' opposition and the ensuing project's collapse had been caused by the investor's acts and omissions.[81] As noted by the dissenting arbitrator, this finding was at odds with the totality of evidence heard by the tribunal as well as the majority's acknowledgement that the investor 'did not do all it could have done to engage with all the affected communities'.[82] In the view of the dissenting arbitrator, the investor's contribution to the events culminating in the protests was significant and warranted the reduction of the amount of damages due.[83] The very fact that the dissenting opinion diverged from the award on the issue of contributory fault – as well as the lack of consensus in arbitral jurisprudence in this area – demonstrate that it is too early to place faith in arbitral tribunals as agents of change. Various interpretative possibilities may indeed be available to arbitral panels, but they do not display a sufficient degree of readiness to embrace a new mindset.

The expectation that investment tribunals would forsake their traditional emphasis on investment protection in favour of promoting responsible investor conduct is also belied by the evidence of arbitrators' inclination to favour legal texts

[79] Z Williams and J Bonnitcha, 'Politically Motivated Conduct in Investment Treaty Arbitration' (Investment Treaty News, 23 April 2019), available at www.iisd.org/itn/en/2019/04/23/politically-motivated-conduct-in-investment-treaty-arbitration-jonathan-bonnitcha-zoe-williams.

[80] *Bear Creek Mining v Peru*, Award (n 48) para 560.

[81] ibid paras 568–69.

[82] ibid para 35.

[83] ibid paras 38–39.

and formalistic reasoning rather than advocating a more balanced interpretation of the totality of legal norms applicable to the dispute. Again, the majority's award in *Bear Creek* is a prime example. The majority had the opportunity to harness the ILO Convention insofar as it safeguards the rights of indigenous communities to 'participate in the use, management and conservation of resources pertaining to their lands' and to 'participate in the benefits of such activities', including 'fair compensation for any damages which they may sustain as a result'.[84] However, the arbitrators opted for a narrower interpretation of the relevant rules. The tribunal's reasoning appears to be based on the understanding of social license to operate solely as an instrument to ensure social acceptability of investment, not as a benefit-sharing arrangement. This, in turn, points to the importance of rethinking the objectives of investment treaty law and creating space for norms incentivising investments that bring benefits to local populations.

The outcomes of other cases involving a disagreement between foreign investors and local communities[85] also strongly suggest that the substantive and procedural norms governing investment arbitration cases do not seem to provide sufficient incentives for arbitral tribunals to embrace a change of mindset, whereby the importance of foreign investment would be seen through its social outcomes and its capacity to promote socially inclusive development in host communities. The usefulness of jurisprudential solutions may also be limited for resource-poor developing states which lack sufficient economic and legal capacity to successfully defend themselves in investor-state arbitration cases. Unlike the cash-strapped developing country governments, large corporations are shown to be more influential in shaping the content and direction of jurisprudential development of international investment norms.[86] Echoing Cotula and Perrone's argument in chapter three, relying on other legal regimes, both domestic and international, could only partly rebalance these asymmetric relations between investors and local communities. These factors make a strong case for amending investment treaties.

D. Outdated Emphasis on Investors' Lack of International Legal Personality

Those who oppose the inclusion of investor obligations in treaties argue that unlike the host state, which can be held to international responsibility, investors cannot be considered to have violated international law. This, it has been argued, stems from the fact that private investors do not have a requisite international legal personality so as to be held responsible for an international wrong.[87]

[84] ibid para 9.

[85] See Williams and Bonnitcha, 'Politically Motivated Conduct' (2019).

[86] J Arato, 'Corporations as Lawmakers' (2015) 56 *Harvard International Law Journal* 301.

[87] Under traditional international law, it is still questionable whether corporations can be held responsible for international law violations. See for example, I Brownlie, *Principles of Public International Law* (Oxford University Press, 2003) 65; P Muchlinski, *Multinational Enterprises and the Law*

Such arguments yet again demonstrate a structural imbalance at the very core of international investment law and certain strands of investment law scholarship: the investor is seen as deserving and indeed needing an international legal standing so to benefit from extensive treaty privileges and protections vis-à-vis host states, but when the issue of investor responsibilities comes to the fore, investors are seen as (conveniently) lacking an international legal personality.

This tension is discernible in the reasoning of arbitral tribunals, the majority award in *Bear Creek* again providing a pertinent example. Whilst recognising that 'social support is fundamental to the successful execution of a mining project',[88] the investor claimed that 'a private company cannot "fail to comply" with ILO Convention 169 because it imposes no direct obligations on them'.[89] By contrast, the dissenting opinion stresses that while the state may indeed be in charge of adopting and enforcing domestic laws to ensure outcomes compliant with the ILO Convention, it is not the function of the host government 'to hold an investor's hand and deliver "social license" out of those processes'.[90]

Using the lack of legal personality as a counter-argument against placing investors under an obligation to conduct their business in a socially inclusive manner may indeed be plausible as a matter of formal legal reasoning. However, such arguments are much less convincing from a wider international investment policy perspective. If national laws fail to retool foreign investment as a mechanism for socio-economic inclusion and international investment agreements similarly remain silent, the lacuna in national law and international legal instruments can ultimately lead host populations to take matters into their own hands,[91] whilst also fuelling the ongoing dissatisfaction with and backlash against the rules and structures of the international economic order.

IV. Countering the Scepticism of the Dominant Frames: Historical Antecedents of Foreign Investor Obligations towards Local Communities

A. Incremental Changes in Investment Treaty Drafting

Even at the more optimistic end of the spectrum, scholars of international investment law argue that the prospect of express recognition of investor obligations,

(Oxford University Press, 2007) 515. This idea is also reflected in Ruggie's Guiding Principles, see United Nations Human Rights Council, 'Guiding Principles on Business and Human Rights: Implementing the United Nations 'Protect, Respect and Remedy' Framework' (21 March 2011) UN Doc HR/PUB/11/04.

[88] ibid para 242.

[89] ibid para 241.

[90] *Bear Creek Mining v Peru*, Partial Dissenting Opinion of Phillipe Sands (n 48) para 37.

[91] See for example, Akpan, 'Host Community Hostility to Mining Projects' (2005) 312.

including obligations towards local communities, in the texts of new and revised investment treaty instruments remains low.[92] It is often argued that the incorporation of sustainable development objectives can redress the existing asymmetry of investment treaties. Yet in those rare instances where an investment treaty features an express reference to sustainable development objectives in its preamble, the usefulness of such provisions is circumscribed by their narrow wording and the often missing acknowledgement of the socio-economic needs of local populations. By way of example, the preamble of the US–Rwanda IIA[93] stipulates that its stated objectives of economic cooperation and the stimulation of private investment should be achieved in a manner consistent with the protection of health, safety and the environment as well as the promotion of internationally recognised labour rights.

Some investment treaties go further and enshrine states' commitment not to derogate from the existing commitments to the detriment of local communities. For instance, the labour clause in the US–Uruguay IIA[94] stipulates that

> the parties recognize that it is inappropriate to encourage investment by weakening or reducing the protections afforded in domestic labour laws. Accordingly, each party shall strive to ensure that it does not waive, or otherwise derogate from, such laws in a manner that weakens or reduces adherence to the internationally recognized labour rights … as an encouragement for the establishment, acquisition, expansion, or retention of an investment in its territory.[95]

However, preambular references, or even the more substantive non-derogation commitments, do not go far enough to address the existing asymmetry of the investment treaty regime and to operationalise it as a vehicle for socially inclusive business practices. A more fundamental rethinking of investment treaty objectives is warranted.

A potentially significant source of inspiration for investor obligations towards local communities could be found in the industrial policies of both developed and developing states. Industrial policy can be defined as

> any type of intervention or government policy that attempts to improve the business environment or to alter the structure of economic activity towards sectors, technologies or tasks that are expected to offer better prospects for economic growth or societal welfare than would occur in the absence of such intervention.[96]

[92] M Gehring and MCC Segger, 'Overcoming Obstacles with Opportunities: Trade and Investment Agreements for Sustainable Development' in SW Schill, CJ Tams and R Hofmann (eds), *International Investment Law and Development: Bridging the Gap* (Edward Elgar, 2015) 109.

[93] Signed 19 February 2008, entry into force 1 January 2012, preamble.

[94] Signed 4 November 2005, entry into force 31 October 2006, Art 12(1).

[95] For a discussion, see V Prislan and R Zandvliet, 'Mainstreaming Sustainable Development into International Investment Agreements: What Role for Labor Provisions?' in SW Schill, CJ Tams and R Hofmann (eds), *International Investment Law and Development: Bridging the Gap* (Edward Elgar, 2015) 390.

[96] K Warwick, *Beyond Industrial Policy: Emerging Issues and New Trends* (OECD Publishing, 2013) 15.

Such interventions can take the shape of, among others, subsidies, job creation targets and training requirements, all geared towards generating economic growth, creating employment and addressing socio-economic inequality within the state.[97]

Contemporary industrial policies are redolent of their historical antecedents in the 1960s and 1970s.[98] As a matter of national policy, during the 1970s a number of developing states resorted to the so-called 'host country operational measures' – a vast array of measures covering all aspects of investment (from ownership and control, to hiring of personnel, procurement of inputs, and sales conditions).[99] Also known as performance requirements, these measures are usually conceived as a means to influence the location and character of foreign investment and, importantly, to increase the benefits of investment for socio-economic development as well as other for non-economic interests within a host state.[100] While recognising that the contribution of foreign investors was not always fully consistent with the needs of host states, developing country governments harnessed performance requirements to modify the behaviour of foreign investors. For instance, local content requirements were deployed to encourage industrialisation or to expand local employment; technology transfer obligations harnessed to develop and diffuse industrial skills; and local training requirements were utilised to foster the creation of skilled cadre at the managerial and professional levels.[101]

Although some of these requirements still feature in carefully negotiated investor-state contracts, the bulk of investment treaties in force today either remain silent on the status of such measures or expressly prohibit them, thus effectively preventing host governments from being able to influence and capture some of the positive spillovers that foreign investment can potentially generate in their territories.[102] The gradual move away from performance requirements was prompted by anti-interventionist sentiment underpinning much of the Washington Consensus prescriptions for economic liberalisation and deregulation in the 1980s and 1990s.[103] There is, nonetheless, a growing number of voices which recognise that, unless equipped with such tools, host states – whether developing or developed – may be unable to ensure that foreign investments generate benefits for a broad range of domestic constituents.[104] This understanding is reflected in

[97] UNCTAD, 'World Investment Report 2018: Investment and New Industrial Policies' (United Nations Publication, 2015) 129.

[98] See S Shadikhodjaev, *Industrial Policy and the World Trade Organization: Between Legal Constraints and Flexibilities* (Cambridge University Press, 2018) 11.

[99] UNCTAD, 'Host Country Operational Measures' 7, UNCTAD/ITE/IIT/26, UN Sales No. E.01.II.D.18 (2001).

[100] ibid 3.

[101] ibid 5.

[102] Aisbett et al (n 20) 58.

[103] Shadikhodjaev, *Industrial Policy and the World Trade Organization* (2018) 11.

[104] ibid 57–58.

some of the more recent investment treaty models which carve out some space for performance requirements pertaining to the important strands of contemporary industrial strategies.[105] This is, however, yet another example of investment treaties remaining silent on direct investor obligations and instead merely providing the state with some regulatory space to do so.

Industrial policies serve as a useful example of how governments, both in developed and developing states, can embrace significant shifts in their relationships with foreign investors. Since governments are increasingly cognisant of the need to harness investment for the benefits of local communities, what is needed is an overhaul of the existing conception of investment treaty objectives. But is such a rethinking of investment treaty objectives possible? What currently hinders the emergence of new visions of the relationship between foreign investors and the local communities is an entrenched belief in (1) the scepticism towards innovations on the part of policymakers, and (2) resistance from the business community. Yet, as this section will argue, evidence from both past regulatory experiments and more recent developments in business practices suggests that, despite a degree of resistance, even fundamental changes in legal mechanisms aimed at retooling investment for social inclusion can be operationalised by governments, business actors and other stakeholders.

B. Drawing Inspiration from the Past: NIEO and Foreign Investor Obligations

Some argue against substantive investor obligations out of the fear of loading too much onto investment treaties and undermining their original mission to protect and promote foreign investment.[106] Others contend that such a reform of investment treaties might not be possible due to 'a lack of political will, scepticism towards respective innovations and probably a so far quite successful resistance from the side of the business community'.[107] Yet the idea of harnessing investments for the benefit of host states in a meaningful way is not entirely new. Regulatory, fiscal and contractual experiments of the NIEO period provide the most pertinent examples. It was during the 1960s and 1970s when traditional concession contracts – a primary instrument governing the relationship between foreign corporations and host governments in the natural resources sector – were profoundly transformed. This transformation was prompted by dissatisfaction on the part of host governments with the terms and structure of

[105] See for example, recent Canadian IIAs that feature public policy exceptions from the prohibition of performance requirements.

[106] Similar arguments have been driving much of international trade scholarship. For a critique, see Shaffer (n 8) 11.

[107] Nowrot, 'Legal Consequences of Globalization' (1999) 631.

early concession contracts through which major US and European corporations had monopolised the exploration and development of natural resources in the countries of the Global South in the first half of the twentieth century.[108] The old concession contracts granted investors extensive privileges: a large concession area; long duration without the possibility of revision; exclusive rights of foreign concession-holder to manage and control all aspects of exploration and development; their right to extracted resources; exemption from all taxes and duties; and modest royalties payable to the government.[109] In the words of Asante, under the old concession contracts, 'what purported to be a royalty … was a provision for the payment of a minute percentage, say 3 to 5 percent of the declared profits of the companies'.[110] The inequities of then-existing patterns of investor-state relations were so obvious that in a seldom historical moment of unanimity, scholars from both developed and developing world converged in acknowledging the impropriety of legal arrangements that had long supported the old concession regimes.[111]

Although foreign companies had exercised inordinate control over national economies across the Global South (the concessions contracts elevated companies to 'a virtual assumption of sovereignty by transnational corporations over the host state's natural resources'[112]), significant strides were made by developing states in their efforts to eliminate the legal, fiscal and financial vestiges of the old economic order. To achieve a meaningful restructuring of relationships between corporations and developing states, a number of governments turned to renegotiating their relationships with foreign investors by altering or replacing the original concession agreements with new legal arrangements featuring considerably different profit sharing, new royalties and taxes and greater participation by the state in management and control of the corporations' operations.[113] Increasingly, revised investor-state contracts came to feature obligations by a concession-holder to train and employ local personnel with a view to benefit the local society and the economy.[114] Other countries went even further and replaced the concession model with production-sharing agreements – an entirely new legal instrument defining the relationship between the government and foreign investors. Not only did production-sharing agreements recentre the state as the owner of natural resources, both in situ and at any phase of exploration and development, but they

[108] Z Gao, *International Petroleum Contracts: Current Trends and New Directions* (Martinus Nijhoff, 1994) 11.

[109] ibid 13.

[110] S Asante, 'Restructuring Transnational Mineral Agreements' (1979) 73 *American Journal of International Law* 335, 339. This description resonates startlingly with contemporary debates over the taxation of profits of multinational corporations.

[111] Gao, *International Petroleum Contracts* (1994) 14.

[112] Asante, 'Restructuring' (1979) 338.

[113] Gao (n 108) 17.

[114] See, for instance, ibid 55 (discussing changes introduced by Thailand into its petroleum concessions).

also attached strong importance to fiscal benefits and to the training and employment of local personnel.[115] In a similar vein, joint ventures and service contracts proliferated from the Middle East to Latin America, heralding a new form of relationship between foreign investors and host states. Unlike the old concession contracts, these arrangements did not confer title to resources on the foreign company; rather, the latter's role was changed to that of a contractor or a business partner performing certain tasks for a fee or consideration in kind.[116]

The profound shift from a regime where foreign companies exercised de facto control over the territory and resources of entire states, to a framework subjecting foreign companies to fiscal, technological and economic obligations, all geared towards the economic development of host states, alludes to the possibility of a similar transformation of the prevailing international rules governing foreign investor obligations. Of course, the historical experiments of the NIEO period have not been uniformly successful, and some legal and political developments heralded during the time failed to achieve their full potential. As captured by a contemporary commentator, 'the formidable difficulties encountered in restructuring the relations between host governments and transnational corporations with respect to the critical areas of control and financial benefits have sometimes engendered despair bordering on cynicism'.[117] Yet, 'the recognition of these sober realities in no way detracts from the value of a continuing and sustained process of revising the legal arrangements with transnational corporations in order to redress the imbalance in the old pattern of relations'.[118]

Most importantly, resistance from the business community and policymakers in capital-exporting states did not deter the lasting changes the NIEO precipitated in the legal frameworks governing the relationships between foreign investors, states and host states. A wave of renegotiations of agreements between host governments and foreign corporations did not result in an exodus of the latter from resource-rich developing countries.[119] Rather, foreign investors adapted to their new historical realities. It must be admitted that this adaption process also spawned the network of international investment instruments that effectively recaptured the developing states' ability to renegotiate and recalibrate their contractual relations with foreign investors. Besides, contractual arrangements ushered in during the decolonisation period did not typically provide a legal basis for investor responsibility that individuals and local communities could rely on.[120] Notwithstanding, the NIEO-era experiments demonstrate both the possibility of transformation and the eventual acceptance by business actors of their changed realities.

[115] ibid 92, discussing Indonesian PSCs.
[116] Asante (n 110) 359.
[117] ibid 369.
[118] ibid 370.
[119] ibid.
[120] J Gathii and IT Odumosu-Ayanu, 'The Turn to Contractual Responsibility in the Global Extractive Industry' (2016) 1 *Business and Human Rights Journal* 69, 85.

C. Echoes of the NIEO Reforms in Contemporary Business Practices

The argument that the introduction of positive investor obligations is a pipe dream and would be impossible due to resistance from the business community is also belied by evidence of the evolving patterns of foreign investor engagement with local communities. Those who oppose the inclusion of express investor obligations in treaty texts ignore the fact that the exclusion of local communities from the benefits of foreign investor-led projects tend to foment not only a dissatisfaction with the regime at a global level but also a resentment against concrete investment projects on the ground. This, in turn, can destabilise and undermine the commercial success of investment projects. Investors may expect the host states to take care of distributive issues and to address socio-economic concerns on the ground, but when the states fail to do so successfully, it is the foreign investor who is exposed to instability, loss of profits, and potentially the need to leave the project as it becomes no longer feasible in the face of local backlash and opposition.[121] Traditional investment treaties contain protections allowing investors to recoup losses when their projects fail due to local community opposition. However, investment treaties do not facilitate the creation of peaceful and stable legal and political environment for the projects to succeed in the long-term.

There is also growing recognition among some in the business community that a successful investment project necessitates the inclusion of local communities in sharing the benefits of the investment. A failure to obtain such license often results in a subsequent frustration of the project due to local community opposition. In many cases investors may frame local community opposition as yet another form of rent-seeking.[122] However, according to emerging case studies, there is growing awareness in the business sector that the local community should be regarded as an actor in its own right. When host governments fail to regulate investment so as to harness its benefits for the society, local communities tend to take matters into their own hands. Foreign investors recognise the need to secure not only a political licence, but also a social licence – even in cases where no express provisions to this effect are contained in legal instruments governing such investments.[123]

[121] There are numerous instances of local community grievances escalating into protests and led to the termination of the project and investors' exit from the country. See for example, D Kemp and JR Owen, 'Community Relations and Mining: Core to Business But Not "Core Business"' (2013) 38 *Resources Policy* 523; G Bridge, 'Contested Terrain: Mining and the Environment' (2004) 29 *Annual Review of Environment and Resources* 205; J Costanza, 'Mining Conflict and the Politics Of Obtaining a Social License: Insight From Guatemala' (2016) 79 *World Development* 97; A Doolotkeldieva, 'Regulating Corporate Social Responsibility (CSR) in the Large-Scale Mining Sector of Kyrgyzstan' (OSCE Academy Policy Brief No 60, 2020), available at osce-academy.net/upload/file/PB_60_May.pdf.

[122] J Heathershaw and A Doolotkeldieva, 'State as Resource, Mediator and Performer: Understanding the Local and Global Politics of Gold Mining in Kyrgyzstan' (2015) 34 *Central Asian Survey* 93.

[123] RW Roeder, 'Applying for the Social License to Operate by Corporate Social Responsibility Policies and Actions' in RW Roeder (ed), *Foreign Mining Investment Law* (Springer, 2016) 145; also JR Owen and D Kemp, 'Social licence and mining: A critical perspective' (2013) 38 *Resources Policy* 29–35.

To obtain a social licence to operate, foreign investors have increasingly been deploying contractual arrangements in their negotiations with local communities. For example, it has been reported that there is 'strong current interest in Impact Benefit Agreements or Community Development Agreements between mining companies and communities'.[124] The idea of benefit-sharing underpinning these agreements is not exclusive to the natural resources sector and is gaining momentum as an important way to maximise the benefits of foreign investment projects for the local communities. Importantly, benefit-sharing arrangements are increasingly negotiated directly between communities and foreign investors.[125] Such agreements are not without considerable flaws – including the asymmetry of bargaining powers between corporations and local communities,[126] and the fact that the concept of benefit-sharing is still understood narrowly as a distribution of financial benefits.[127] However, an uptake in the use of arrangements of this kind exemplifies the burgeoning acceptance by industry actors of the need to engage with the communities that host them. Just like the companies which had to concede to renegotiated terms in the NIEO-inspired revision of agreements in the natural resources sector, contemporary foreign investors are increasingly cognisant of the need to exercise socio-cultural due diligence[128] and undertake specific commitments on sharing the benefits of their projects with the local communities.

V. Conclusion

> Societal opposition to the investment law regime does not stem from hostility to the concept of foreign investment or to the objective of establishing international rules to govern foreign investment per se, but rather from concerns about the non-participatory manner in which the global economy's rules are being written and about restrictions on governments' ability to address the pernicious effects of globalization.[129]

These concerns cannot be addressed by merely reforming procedural norms and safeguarding the host state's right to regulate. It is vital that a diverse range of

[124] H Mann et al, 'IISD Report: Model Mining Development Agreement – Transparency Template' (The International Institute for Sustainable Development 2012) 3; see also L Cotula, *Investment Contracts and Sustainable Development: How to Make Contractors for Fairer and More Sustainable Natural Resource Investments* (International Institute for Environment and Development, 2010).

[125] Gilbert, *Natural Resources and Human Rights* (2018) 82.

[126] For a critique, see Gilbert (n 66) 83; also E Cameron and T Levitan, 'Impact and Benefit Agreements and the Neoliberalization of Resource Governance and Indigenous-State Relations in Northern Canada' (2014) 93 *Studies in Political Economy* 23.

[127] Gilbert (n 66) 80.

[128] J Clark, 'Socio-cultural Due Diligence in the Mining Sector' in E Bastida, TW Waelde and J Warden (eds), *International and Comparative Mineral Law and Policy* (Kluwer Law International, 2005) 331.

[129] IMT Cate, 'International Arbitration and the Ends of Appellate Review' (2012) 44 *New York University Journal of International Law and Politics* 1109, 1111.

stakeholders within host states, especially those left behind by the processes of globalisation, are not only protected against the adverse impacts of foreign investment but are also included in sharing the benefits of foreign investor-led projects. To this end, international investment agreements should start incorporating concrete investor obligations to foster inclusive and sustainable development. Failing to do so is likely to undermine the long-term prospects of individual investment projects, create potential for conflict and instability, and continue to fuel concerns over the already eroding legitimacy of the international investment regime.

Despite significant advances of the recent reform efforts in acknowledging various asymmetries underpinning the investment treaty regime, the scope and promise of such reforms is open to question. There is still a considerable degree of reluctance to acknowledge social deficits of the existing investment treaty framework and in particular, its failure to expressly address the importance of fostering a socially inclusive development in host states. The investment establishment is yet to acknowledge that investments must be made more inclusive. Fundamentally, however, as the distributive implications of corporate business activities are increasingly raising concerns for stakeholders in both developed and developing states, a profound rethinking of investment treaty objectives is warranted in order to address the existing asymmetries and social deficits. As this chapter has demonstrated, investors can and should be placed under an obligation to do good for the societies that host them. Historical precedents of investor obligations can be found in the regulatory, fiscal and contractual arrangements of the NIEO era as well as national industrial policies proliferating across developed and developing economies. While outcomes of the ongoing efforts to rein in corporate actors so far may engender scepticism, cynicism and a degree of despair, governments in both developed and developing states have at various stages in the recent past been able to abandon and renegotiate what was at the time regarded as outdated agreements with foreign investors. To overcome the reluctance to make investor obligations part and parcel of new investment treaties, it is vital to not only address the lack of political will, but also the presently fragmented research agenda whereby discussions on corporate responsibilities towards local communities are held in discrete fora by disparate epistemic communities.

3

Investors' International Law and its Asymmetries: The Case of Local Communities

LORENZO COTULA AND NICOLÁS M PERRONE

I. Introduction

Foreign investment projects involve complex relations not only between governments and investors, but also with a range of other actors, including local communities affected by the investment. Yet, international investment law remains primarily focused on relations between investors and states, both with regards to the substantive standards of treatment it establishes, and in the context of investor-state dispute settlement (ISDS).[1] Investment treaties do not provide effective arrangements to recognise and protect the rights of local communities before, during and after an investment project. This raises questions not only about the extent to which those rights can be upheld in the context of ISDS, but also more general issues about the ability of arbitral tribunals to consider all facts and norms relevant to the investment dispute. In addition, most investment treaties do not elaborate on the obligations investors may hold toward local communities affected by their operations.

This asymmetric structure of international investment law has fuelled public criticism over the years.[2] More recently, new opportunities have arisen to explore possible reform of the investment treaty regime. Several governments have been reviewing their investment treaty policies, and bilateral and regional negotiations have resulted in policy innovations to recalibrate the treaties' substantive standards. At the multilateral level, a working group of the United Nations Commission

[1] NM Perrone, 'The International Investment Regime and Local Populations: Are the Weakest Voices Unheard?' 7 *Transnational Legal Theory* (2016) 383, 384.

[2] See for example, G van Harten, J Kelsey and D Schneiderman, 'Phase 2 of the UNCITRAL ISDS Review: Why 'Other Matters' Really Matter' (2019) All Papers 328, available at digitalcommons.osgoode.yorku.ca/all_papers/328.

on International Trade Law (UNCITRAL) is considering options to reform the procedural dimensions of ISDS.[3] While the ultimate outcomes of these processes are hard to predict, issues concerning the place of local communities in international investment law and ISDS have received little attention. Addressing public concerns about the investment treaty regime would require addressing these asymmetries, exploring ways to strengthen the rights of third parties and affirm effective investor obligations.

This chapter explores these issues and outlines possible ways forward, building on research conducted by the authors over the years. The issues are of general relevance to the field of international investment law, but the analysis focuses particularly on developments concerning the natural resource and infrastructure sectors. More than some other economic sectors, structural features of infrastructure and natural resource investments highlight the impacts, both positive and negative, that investment processes can have on local communities and their rights – for example, in terms of land acquisition, livelihood transformation or environmental degradation. While the themes interrogate global trends, the chapter draws particularly on research concerning developments in Latin American and sub-Saharan Africa.

Throughout the analysis, the generic term 'local community' is used in its broadest sense to mean a group of people who are connected to a particular locality and do not have the power to exercise governmental authority.[4] Some investment lawyers may be unaccustomed to the notion of communities in the context of legal scholarship. But several international instruments use this term, typically without defining it.[5] In some jurisdictions, national law defines the notion of community for particular purposes, for example in connection with land legislation or decentralised governance.[6]

International courts and tribunals have also made extensive references to communities, including in ISDS cases.[7] International tribunals have used the term 'community' to describe diverse groups. Depending on the circumstances, the term can refer to an indigenous people, a number of indigenous peoples or communities

[3] UNCITRAL Working Group III on Investor-State Dispute Settlement Reform, available at uncitral.un.org/en/working_groups/3/investor-state.

[4] L Cotula and M Schröder, 'Community Perspectives in Investor-State Arbitration' (International Institute for Environment and Development, 14 June 2017) 10, available at pubs.iied.org/pdfs/12603IIED.pdf.

[5] See, for example, United Nations Convention on Biological Diversity (adopted 5 June 1992, entered into force 29 December 1992) 1760 UNTS 79 Art 8(j) (referring to 'indigenous and local communities'); Rio Declaration on Environment and Development (adopted 12 August 1992) UN Doc A/CONF.151/26/Rev 1 (Vol I) Annex I, Principle 22 (referring to 'indigenous people and their communities, and other local communities').

[6] See, for example, Mozambique's Lei de Terras, Law No 19/97, Art 1(1) (defining the concept of 'local community').

[7] See, for example, *Copper Mesa Mining Corporation v Republic of Ecuador*, PCA Case No 2012-02, Award (15 March 2016), paras 1.93–1.94, 1.103–1.104; *Bilcon v Canada*, PCA Case No 2009-04, Award on Jurisdiction and Liability (17 March 2015), containing numerous references throughout.

within an indigenous people; to cohesive groups that do not qualify as indigenous peoples under international law; or to local residents united by geographic proximity and the impact of an investment who do not necessarily see the group as a stable source of social identity. In fact, what constitutes a community – who is included and excluded, who speaks on behalf of the group – can itself form the object of contestation. Also, communities typically include diverse interests and visions, partly reflecting social differentiation within and between communities (for example, on the basis of social status, wealth, income, gender, age or ethnicity), and communities are often divided over investment projects.

The purpose of this chapter is to contrast the complexity of foreign investment projects – particularly the situation of local communities – with international investment law as it stands today, and with the reform process at UNCITRAL Working Group III. Section II discusses the multi-actor nature of real-life investment processes, pairing a discussion of broad legal trends with insights from political economy and international relations theory. Section III interrogates the investment treaty regime from the standpoint of local communities' rights and remedies, highlighting the shortcomings of existing arrangements and building the case for reform. Section IV explores possible ways to address the challenges, paying special attention to existing opportunities for policy reform, particularly in connection with ongoing multilateral processes. Finally, section V outlines a few concluding remarks.

II. Complexity of Investment Projects: Foreign Investors, National Elites and Local Communities

Much international investment law literature centres discussions of foreign investment around a binary relationship between foreign investors (particularly multinational corporations, MNCs) and states. Over time, however, legal and socio-political developments have exposed the limitations of this approach. For a start, the approach typically fails to consider the complexity and disaggregation *within* states, assuming that governments can pursue a plurality of diverse and often conflicting interests simultaneously.[8] Cognate disciplines such as political economy, international relations and development studies have long documented this complexity, highlighting that states are not black boxes.[9] Foreign investment

[8] NM Perrone, 'Making Local Communities Visible: A Way to Prevent the Potentially Tragic Consequences of Foreign Investment?' in A Santos, C Thomas and D Trubek (eds), *World Trade and Investment Law Reimagined: A Progressive Agenda for an Inclusive Globalization* (Anthem Press, 2019) 171–82.

[9] See, for example, JT Checkel, 'Review: The Constructivist Turn in International Relations Theory Reviewed Work(s): National Interests in International Society by Martha Finnemore; The Culture of National Security: Norms and Identity in World Politics by Peter Katzenstein; Norms in International Relations: The Struggle Against Apartheid by Audie Klotz' (1998) 50 *World Politics* 324, 326.

projects can establish relations with, or produce reverberations for, a wide range of local and national actors, and state conduct often struggles to reconcile and advance the interests of all these actors, or balance them in mutually satisfactory ways.

Socio-legal research, for example on the construction of a transboundary oil pipeline in sub-Saharan Africa, shows that large-scale investments can involve complex multi-actor relations – including within the oil consortium, between the consortium and its lenders, among government agencies with different institutional mandates (from petroleum development to environment protection), between central and local government bodies, and with a wide range of socially differentiated 'communities' whose land and resource rights are impacted by project construction and/or operation.[10] This more fine-grained understanding of investment relations and state conduct is yet to impact or reshape public understanding of international investment law debates, which – in line with international rules on state responsibility for internationally wrongful acts – continue to consider the state as a unitary actor, typically represented by the federal or national government, and to pay little attention to the plurality of local voices.[11]

This narrow legal framing is changing, however, albeit gradually. Several international legal instruments recognise indigenous communities as human rights holders, and as significant actors in development processes, including with regards to decision-making concerning large-scale investments. For example, International Labour Convention (ILO) 169 establishes free, prior, informed consent (FPIC) as a key concept for any measures capable of affecting indigenous peoples' lands or livelihoods.[12] The special status of indigenous peoples is also acknowledged by the United Nations Declaration on the Rights of Indigenous Peoples.[13] More recently, the United Nations Declaration on the Rights of Peasants and Other People Working in Rural Areas has recognised the status and rights of peasants, including in the context of investment decision-making.[14] Such international instruments show the limitations of traditional conceptions of sovereignty, and the increasing importance of non-state actors in international law.[15] More generally, international human rights treaties create individual and collective rights that can be opposed to states, indicating that – for international law – state action does not automatically align with the interests or the well-being of the entire population, and that

[10] L Cotula, *Human Rights, Natural Resource and Investment Law in a Globalised World: Shades of Grey in the Shadow of the Law* (Routledge, 2012) 27–37.

[11] B Rajagopal, International Law from Below: Development, Social Movements, and Third World Resistance (Cambridge University Press, 2003).

[12] International Labour Organization (ILO) Indigenous and Tribal Peoples Convention (adopted 27 June 1989, entered into force 5 September 1991) 1650 UNTS 384.

[13] UNGA Res 61/295 (2 October 2007) UN Doc A/RES/61/295.

[14] UN Office of the High Commissioner for Human Rights (OHCHR) (28 September 2018) A/HRC/RES/39/12.

[15] L Cotula, 'Reconsidering Sovereignty, Ownership and Consent in Natural Resource Contracts: From Concepts to Practice' in M Bungenberg et al (eds), *European Yearbook of International Economic Law 2018* (Springer, 2018) 143, available at link.springer.com/content/pdf/10.1007%2F8165_2018_23.pdf.

explicit normative standards and effective legal remedies are needed to bind public authorities to protect and advance those interests.

But while this trend has reshaped legal relations between states and human rights holders, it has so far affected relations between foreign investors and local communities only indirectly. ILO Convention 169 and international human rights treaties have primarily been interpreted as creating obligations for states alone. Within the United Nations human rights system, guiding principles have been developed on issues concerning business and human rights, but these create responsibilities rather than legally enforceable obligations. Within a section titled 'The corporate *responsibility* to respect human rights', for example, the UN Guiding Principles on Business and Human Rights affirm that 'Business enterprises *should* respect human rights'.[16] Several ongoing initiatives aim to strengthen the link between foreign investment and human rights obligations, including a proposed binding treaty on business and human rights.[17] However, whether a binding treaty will ultimately be adopted, and in what form, remains to be seen.

There have also been developments within international investment law, with a few recent treaties purporting to create direct obligations for foreign investors.[18] However, ISDS tribunals have generally not been receptive to human rights arguments, particularly those aimed at leveraging investor obligations, although this trend may be changing. Recent awards have recognised that international human rights law *can* create obligations for foreign investors.[19] This legal relationship, however, has been defined as a weak obligation 'on all parts, public and private parties, not to engage in an activity aimed at destroying such rights'.[20] Further, the practical implications of these developments are not yet clear, given the current state of arbitral jurisprudence, as no defences or counterclaims based on investors' human rights obligations have fully succeeded at the merits stage. Also, arbitrators have reached contrasting conclusions on whether investors hold certain human rights obligations, for example in connection with FPIC, and on the consequences of investor conduct violating those obligations.[21]

Overall, international investment law continues to frame foreign investment primarily as a binary relationship between foreign investors and host states.[22] In this view, states are assumed to be well placed to represent the interests of their

[16] OHCHR, 'Guiding Principles on Business and Human Rights. Implementing the United Nations 'Protect, Respect and Remedy' Framework' (June 2011) HR/PUB/11/04 (emphasis added).

[17] OHCHR, 'Open-Ended Intergovernmental Working Group on Transnational Corporations and Other Business Enterprises With Respect to Human Rights', available at www.ohchr.org/en/hrbodies/hrc/wgtranscorp/pages/igwgontnc.aspx.

[18] For example, Morocco–Nigeria BIT 2016. For a broader and more detailed treatment of investor obligations in investment treaties, see ch 5 (Ranjan) of this volume.

[19] *Urbaser v Argentina*, ICSID Case No ARB/07/26, Award (8 December 2016) para 1194; *Bear Creek Mining v Peru*, ICSID Case No ARB/14/2, Partial Dissenting Opinion of Philippe Sands (30 November 2017), paras 10–11.

[20] *Urbaser v Argentina*, Award (ibid) para 1199.

[21] See, for example, *Bear Creek Mining v Peru* (n 19) Partial Dissenting Opinion of Philippe Sands.

[22] NM Perrone, 'The "Invisible" Local Communities: Foreign Investor Obligations, Inclusiveness, and the International Investment Regime' (2019) 113 *American Journal of International Law Unbound* 16.

people, including those most directly impacted by foreign investment projects. The emphasis the investment treaty regime places on protecting investments from adverse state conduct has raised concerns that overly broad investment protections might create a regulatory chill.[23]

For one thing, host states are often concerned about their global economic reputation, as this might affect foreign investment inflows. New ISDS claims can undermine a state's reputation even if, after a long dispute, the state prevails on the merits. For another, arbitral awards have formally recognised states' 'right to regulate', but in many cases they have nonetheless articulated positions that – in practice – create uncertainties about scope for regulatory measures, particularly when these resulted, at least in part, from local mobilisation.[24] A key question in international investment law, from this binary perspective, is how to strike a balance between foreign investor rights and the continued ability of states to regulate for the public interest.[25]

One consequence of this investor-state framing, including in a dispute settlement context, is that it downplays the extent to which, in many real-life investment processes, the investor and the state in fact act in close cooperation. Most large investment projects are only possible with significant governmental support, and establishment requires substantial cooperation and coordination between foreign investors and governments.[26] Government officials often accompany and support investors in community consultations and other activities associated with project set-up. This cooperation is also reflected in the legal structuring of many large-scale foreign investment projects – not only because, at a general level, investments in sectors such as infrastructure and natural resources are often founded on contracts between the investor and the state; but also because, more specifically, the projects often enjoy advantageous legal regimes whereby states grant them special entitlements and privileges, particularly when compared to other domestic actors, whether under national legislation or 'stabilised' contractual arrangements.[27]

This cooperation between states and investors is often driven by the interests and actions of national elites. In many parts of the Global South, some national

[23] K Tienhaara, 'Regulatory Chill and the Threat of Arbitration: A View from Political Science' in C Brown and K Miles (eds), *Evolution in Investment Treaty Law and Arbitration* (Cambridge University Press, 2011) 606–28; J Bonnitcha, L Poulsen and M Waibel, *The Political Economy of the Investment Treaty Regime* (Oxford University Press, 2017) 137–47.

[24] *TecMed v Mexico*, ICSID Case No ARB (AF)/00/2, Award (29 May 2003) paras 127–28, 133; *Bilcon v Canada*, Permanent Court of Arbitration (PCA) Case No 2009–04, Award on Jurisdiction and Liability (17 March 2015) para 548; *Copper Mesa v Ecuador*, PCA Case No 2012-02, Award (15 March 2016) para 5.55.

[25] See, for example, *Saluka v Czech Republic*, PCA – UNCITRAL, Partial Award (17 March 2006) para 263; C Titi, *The Right To Regulate In International Investment Law* (Bloomsbury, 2014) 33.

[26] See, for example, T Lavers, 'Patterns of Agrarian Transformation in Ethiopia: State-Mediated Commercialisation and the "Land Grab"' (2012) 39 *Journal of Peasant Studies* 795; CD Huggins, '"Control Grabbing" and Small-Scale Agricultural Intensification: Emerging Patterns of State-Facilitated "Agricultural Investment" in Rwanda' (2014) 41 *Journal of Peasant Studies* 365.

[27] L Cotula, 'The State of Exception and the Law of the Global Economy: a Conceptual and Empirico-Legal Inquiry' (2017) 8 *Transnational Legal Theory* 424.

elites have historically shown a keen interest in extractivist projects and the infrastructure necessary to make these projects viable. Marxist and postcolonial literatures link this interest to structural processes such as 'accumulation by dispossession'[28] or 'coloniality',[29] whereby post-independence elites did not fundamentally reshape the extractivist model of economic development left behind by the colonial legacy, and instead staked their own economic interests in controlling rent from extractive developments.[30] As a result, the foreign investment imperative, ie, states' need to attract foreign capital, has taken a particular extractive form in the Global South.[31]

This does not imply that national elites have always favoured extractivist projects, or that they will never promote regulation against these projects. In the 1960s and 1970s, national elites in parts of the Global South tried to reduce their country's dependence on natural resource extraction, drawing on the work of economists such as Prebisch, Singer and Sunkel.[32] In international law, these efforts materialised in developing countries' demands for a New International Economic Order.[33] Moreover, national elites may be forced to take measures against certain extractive projects, as social unrest associated with project implementation could ultimately threaten their control over the state and power structures. In these circumstances, national elites may prefer to regulate or terminate a particular project so as to stay in power or maintain the delicate balance between extractivism and social cohesion.[34]

Empirical research also highlights how national elites promoting extractivist projects can appropriate the language of public participation or environmental protection in order to perpetuate the extractivist model in the face of social and environmental challenges.[35] Focusing on the case of Peru, for example, Merino argues that national extractivist elites promote a cynical type of state: at a discursive level, the state purports to promote a delicate balance between conflicting extractive, environmental and social interests, but the extractivist imperative ultimately tends to prevail.[36]

[28] D Harvey, *The New Imperialism* (Oxford University Press, 2003).

[29] A Quijano, 'Coloniality of Power, Eurocentrism, and Latin America' (2000) 1 *Nepantla: Views from South* 533.

[30] See TH Donghi, *The Contemporary History of Latin America* (Macmillan International, 1993), in particular chs IV and V.

[31] R Merino, 'The Cynical State: Forging Extractivism, Neoliberalism and Development in Governmental Spaces' (2020) 41 *Third World Quarterly* 58, 59.

[32] T Sagafi-Nejad, *The UN and Transnational Corporations: From Code of Conduct to Global Compact* (Indiana University Press, 2008) 74–77.

[33] A Anghie, *Imperialism, Sovereignty and the Making of International Law* (Cambridge University Press, 2004) 211.

[34] Perrone, 'The International Investment Regime' (2016) 386.

[35] Merino, 'The Cynical State' (2020); A Valencia, *Human Rights Trade-Offs in Times of Economic Growth: The Long-Term Capability Impacts of Extractive-Led Development* (Palgrave, 2016); D Becker, *The New Bourgeoisie and the Limits of Dependency: Mining, Class, and Power in Revolutionary Peru* (Princeton University Press, 2014).

[36] Merino (n 31) 58. Also, Valencia, *Human Rights Trade-Offs* (2016) 10.

The complexity of large extractive projects, however, also escapes simplified narratives that posit a tension between impossibly monolithic national elites and the rest of the domestic population. Extractive projects often involve tensions between urban middle classes, peasants, artisanal miners or indigenous populations, for example. Depending on the situation, urban middle classes may favour or oppose an investment project – they may appreciate the jobs or public revenues a project may bring, or they may be concerned about potential air or water pollution. Artisanal miners may challenge industrial mining projects or seek to be included into those projects, for example through collaborative, formalised arrangements between small and large-scale miners. Social stratification means that tensions may also emerge within a given group of people: part of a town may react against increasing levels of pollution, while the rest may defend the project to conserve their jobs. These diverse positions may be linked to the unevenly distributed costs and benefits that foreign investment projects often create.

These complexities add distinctive dimensions to prevailing debates about regulatory chill. While some international investment law scholarship casts the state either as a benevolent regulator unduly constrained by international investment law, or as an opportunistic predator requiring international discipline, in practice diverse political economy factors produce complex patterns of state conduct that, depending on the circumstances, may – or may not – advance local or public interests.[37] Pressure from organised citizens, for example in the form of protests, occupations or litigation, can therefore be an important factor in public action. From a regulatory chill perspective, then, one question is whether the investment protections can make it more difficult for citizen groups to obtain what they seek. Methodological challenges constrain systematic evidence, but reports suggest that, on some occasions at least, concerns about costly arbitration proceedings may have been a factor in government responses to public protests.[38]

The case of *La Oroya v Peru*[39] illustrates the multidimensional nature of foreign investment relations. In 1997, the consortium Doe Run Resources Corporation (The Renco Group) acquired La Oroya smelter through a privatisation process. The privatisation contract included an Environmental Mitigation and Management Plan for La Oroya, which contained obligations for the investor and the state to deal with the legacy of pollution problems caused by the smelter dating back to 1922.[40] As Valencia explains, the interests of Doe Run and national elites were closely correlated. The Ministry of Energy and Mines was in charge of both facilitating the project and enforcing the environmental obligations, creating an

[37] L Cotula, 'Democracy and International Investment Law' (2017) 30 *Leiden Journal of International Law* 351, 363.

[38] ibid 364.

[39] *Community of La Oroya v Peru*, Report No 76/09, Resolution (5 August 2009).

[40] Valencia (n 35) 24.

apparent conflict of interest. Valencia adds that 'This conflict of interest would have been, perhaps, less egregious if these bureaucrats had not acted with such leniency with regard to Doe Run's environmental obligations'.[41]

After the ministry extended the deadline to comply with the investors' environmental obligations twice, in 2006 and 2009, the social conflict in La Oroya escalated. Environmental activists and part of the population demanded the termination of the project, while other members of the community defended the project as they feared losing their jobs.[42] This created problems for the project, leading creditors to initiate bankruptcy proceedings against the foreign investor.[43] The intensity of the conflict compromised the support of elites, which had to consider other interests when the dispute escalated and reached the national media.[44] This change of attitude shows that local and national-level support for a project may weaken throughout the life of the investment. After a conflict becomes visible, the Government could no longer ignore the environmental problems related to La Oroya.

At this juncture, the investment treaty regime and the investor-state perspective of the dispute come into play. Doe Run filed an arbitration claim against Peru in 2011. It argued that Peru acted unfairly in the enforcement of its environmental obligations. For the investor, essentially, Peru demanded more environmental obligations than originally agreed, leading to problems in the operation of the project. Doe Run also claimed that Peru had a less demanding approach in relation to a domestic investor, and that it attempted to indirectly expropriate the investment by participating in the bankruptcy process. Further, the investor requested that Peru should be responsible for any lawsuits filed by La Oroya residents concerning the compensation for health issues.[45] Ultimately, Peru prevailed in this case on jurisdictional grounds, but only after litigating the case for almost five years. The tribunal decided that each party should bear its legal costs. Peru spent USD 8.39 million.[46]

The experience in *La Oroya* illustrates the contrast between the complex, contested and multi-actor nature of many investment disputes, and the narrow framing of investor-state dispute settlement. The real-life dispute highlights the multifaceted and evolving political economy of investment relations, including relations between the national elites that control the government administration on the one hand, and local communities and the activists supporting them on the other. Many ISDS cases show that states often regulate in favour of foreign investment projects, and only later – after social mobilisation or litigation – they may address the concerns of local communities. However, these arbitral proceedings

[41] ibid 26.
[42] ibid 29–31.
[43] ibid 34.
[44] ibid 30.
[45] *The Renco Group v Peru*, ICSID Case No UNCT/13/1, Claimants' Notice of Arbitration and Statement of Claim (4 April 2011).
[46] *The Renco Group v Peru*, ICSID Case No UNCT/13/1, Award (9 November 2016) para 28.

are primarily shaped by the arguments developed by the investors and the state, in line with a legal regime that conceptualises foreign investment as involving a fundamentally binary relationship.[47] The next section discusses the ways in which the framing of investment treaties and ISDS sustains this mismatch between social and legal realities.

III. How the Investment Treaty Regime Frames Foreign Investment Relations

Investment treaties aim to promote foreign investment between two or more state parties. The underlying assumption is that ineffective legal protection under domestic legal systems exposes foreign investors to the risk of arbitrary or discriminatory state conduct, and that this constrains cross-border investment flows. To address this issue, the treaties primarily establish standards to govern relations between states and foreign investors. While treaty formulations vary considerably, commonly used provisions require states to uphold certain standards of treatment vis-à-vis foreign investors and investments, and they enable investors to bring alleged breaches to ISDS tribunals. Under most treaties, states cannot discriminate against foreign investors or investments, they cannot directly or indirectly expropriate the investment without paying full compensation, and they must guarantee to foreign investors and investments 'fair and equitable treatment' and 'full protection and security'. The open-ended terminology of fair and equitable treatment provisions has been interpreted as protecting foreign investors' legitimate expectations.[48]

Evidence as to whether these arrangements promote foreign investment is inconclusive, partly due to difficult methodological problems.[49] But as a result of the way the investment treaty regime operates, the arrangements impose obligations on states, reshaping the legal contours of the exercise of their sovereign rights, but not on foreign investors, creating inherent asymmetries in the overall balance of rights and obligations in this legal regime. These imbalances, and the one-way street of ISDS, have been a major concern in public critiques of the investment treaty regime.[50] But while much debate has focused on the relationship between

[47] Perrone, 'Making Local Communities Visible' (2019) 172–73.

[48] R Dolzer and C Schreuer, *Principles of International Investment Law* (Oxford University Press, 2012) 89–194.

[49] J Pohl, 'Societal Benefits and Costs of International Investment Agreements: A Critical Review of Aspects and Available Empirical Evidence' (OECD, 19 January 2018), available at www.oecd-ilibrary.org/finance-and-investment/societal-benefits-and-costs-of-international-investment-agreements_e5f85c3d-en.

[50] For example, A Arcuri, 'The Great Asymmetry and the Rule of Law in International Investment Arbitration' in L Sachs, L Johnson and J Coleman (eds), *Yearbook on International Investment Law & Policy 2018* (Oxford University Press, 2019) 397–416.

investors and states, the asymmetries are in fact more far-reaching, because most investment treaties say little or nothing about the rights and remedies available to local communities affected by investment processes.[51]

Yet, as the example of *La Oroya* illustrates, local actors may be central to the relations underpinning a given investment project, and ultimately to the investment dispute. For example, local communities may claim land or natural resource rights according to customary, state or international law, which may overlap with the investor's concession and which project implementation could undermine.[52] Or they may have advanced legal claims against the investor based on tort law in connection with environmental degradation.[53] Their actions – from protests and public mobilisation, to court litigation – may constitute a key aspect of the factual fabric of the investment dispute.[54] Investment treaties protect the rights of investors but provide neither rights nor remedies to third parties such as local communities affected by investment processes.

In several disputes, arbitral tribunals have had to grapple with issues concerning the interface between investor and community rights, for example with regards to respondent arguments that the investor had failed to obtain FPIC and thus a social licence to operate. While some arbitrators have been sympathetic to this line of argument,[55] these issues are yet to be convincingly resolved in the ISDS context. Most tribunals have focused on legality requirements in the making of the investment (as opposed to the operation phase); or else they considered violations to constitute contributory negligence on the part of the investor, and on this basis, they reduced the amount of damages owed to the investor.[56]

One problem is that the remit of ISDS tribunals is usually limited to the relevant investment treaty. As discussed, these legal instruments focus on setting standards of treatment owed by the state to foreign investors, and they do not affirm or protect the rights of those affected by the investments, or explicit investor obligations towards these actors. International law does require tribunals to take account of any other relevant, applicable norms, including domestic and human rights law, when interpreting investment treaties and settling disputes.[57]

[51] Perrone (n 1) 393–95.

[52] L Cotula, *Human Rights, Natural Resource and Investment Law in a Globalised World: Shades of Grey in the Shadow of the Law* (Routledge, 2012). For an illustrative case involving competing claims to land in connection with an existing commercial operation, see the Inter-American Court of Human Rights case of *Sawhoyamaxa Indigenous Community v Paraguay* (2006) IHRL 1530.

[53] L Johnson, 'Case Note: How Chevron v. Ecuador is Pushing the Boundaries of Arbitral Authority' (Investment Treaty News, 13 April 2012), available at www.iisd.org/itn/2012/04/13/case-note-how-chevron-v-ecuador-is-pushing-the-boundaries-of-arbitral-authority; L Sachs, L Johnson and E Merrill, 'Environmental Injustice: How Treaties Undermine Human Rights Related to the Environment' (2020) 18 *Revue des Juristes de Sciences Po* 90.

[54] See Cotula and Schröder, 'Community Perspectives' (2017).

[55] See *Bear Creek Mining v Peru* (n 19), especially Philippe Sands's dissenting opinion. Further discussion of this award can be found in ch 2 (Sattorova) of this volume.

[56] See, for example, *Copper Mesa Mining Corporation v The Republic of Ecuador* (n 7).

[57] Vienna Convention on the Law of Treaties (adopted 23 May 1969, entered into force 27 Jan 1980) 1155 UNTS 331 Art 31(c); Convention on the Settlement of Investment Disputes Between States and Nationals of Other States (adopted 18 March 1965, entered into force 14 Oct 1966) 575 UNTS Art 42(1).

But tribunals enjoy considerable discretion in determining how consideration of other relevant rules might affect the application of investment treaty standards. And even the relatively few recent investment treaties that explicitly require investors to comply with domestic law and/or uphold international standards of responsible business conduct, for example on human rights, labour or the environment, do not consistently spell out the implications of these provisions in a dispute settlement context. Workers or local residents may be most directly affected by investor non-compliance with these obligations, and could play an important role in holding investors to account for violations. But these aspects are not yet part of the investment treaty regime.[58]

Asymmetries in rights and obligations are compounded when it comes to legal remedies, because ISDS is essentially a one-way street – not only with regards to investor-state relations, but also to local communities. ISDS is primarily designed as a mechanism for foreign investors to bring disputes against states. States can articulate defensive arguments against the investor's claim, whether on jurisdiction, the merits or the amount of damages. Under certain circumstances, states may also be able to make a counterclaim. In ISDS practice, there are many examples of state defences based on investor conduct. Counterclaims are relatively rare but growing in number, and their potential for securing investor accountability is addressed more fully by Tomoko Ishikawa in chapter eight of this volume. They ultimately hinge on the specific wording of the applicable investment treaty: where arbitral tribunals have accepted a counterclaim, as in *Urbaser v Argentina*, the arbitration clause in the relevant treaty was broadly worded, allowing the tribunal to resolve 'any dispute' between the parties related to the investment;[59] while tribunals have been more restrictive where relevant treaty provisions restricted the scope of arbitrable disputes to a 'claim by the investor that a measure taken or not taken by the [host State] is in breach of this Agreement'.[60] Even 'new generation' investment treaties that feature corporate social responsibility or similarly worded clauses do not usually grant tribunals jurisdiction to resolve disputes concerning these clauses.[61]

The above considerations highlight the asymmetries that exist between investors and states in the conduct of ISDS proceedings. For local communities, asymmetries in remedies are even more pronounced. ISDS arrangements are

[58] For a review of recent trends concerning provisions on investor obligations, or responsibilities, in investment treaty-making, see N Bernasconi-Osterwalder, 'Inclusion of Investor Obligations and Corporate Accountability Provisions in Investment Agreements' in J Chaisse et al (eds), *Handbook of International Investment Law and Policy* (Springer Singapore, 2020). See also J Coleman and K Gupta, 'International Investment Agreements, 2015–2016: A Review of Trends and New Approaches' in L Johnson and L Sachs (eds), *Yearbook on International Investment Law and Policy 2015–2016* (Oxford University Press, 2017) paras 2.81–2.88, available at ccsi.columbia.edu/ files/2014/03/YB-2015-16-Chapter-2-Sachs-et-al.pdf.

[59] *Urbaser v Argentina* (n 19) paras 1143–55.

[60] *Rusoro Mining v Venezuela*, ICSID Case No ARB(AF)/12/5, Award, (22 August 2016) paras 623–32.

[61] See, for example, the Pacific Alliance Additional Protocol (adopted 10 February 2014, entered into force 1 May 2016), Art 10.16(1).

structured around disputes between foreign investors and states. This is despite the fact that, in many instances, the investor-state dispute is only one part of a wider dispute, and may have been triggered by tensions between foreign investors and local communities.[62] Local communities cannot bring cases against foreign investors under ISDS arrangements, and do not participate actively in the defence of ISDS cases. Depending on applicable rules, they may be able to submit *amicus curiae* briefs, which would provide the tribunal with an additional perspective on the facts and/or the law. ISDS practice, in this regard, points to some reluctance on the part of arbitral tribunals to accept these submissions and properly consider them. *Amicus* briefs submitted by groups representing or supporting local communities have been rejected on several occasions,[63] and when accepted, the arbitral tribunal did not necessarily engage with the arguments contained in the submissions.[64]

Other legal regimes, both domestic and international, could partly rebalance these asymmetric relations. Depending on the jurisdiction, for example, domestic legal systems may recognise and protect the rights of communities, and they may feature arrangements that enable local communities to seek remedy for violations of their rights. Domestic legal systems may cater for, and provide arrangements for reconciling, multiple competing claims, for example in the form of intervention, joinder or other mechanisms aimed at facilitating multi-actor participation in the proceedings, or through requiring dismissal or reframing of claims where relevant actors cannot be joined.[65]

Depending on the context, however, national law may fail to adequately recognise and protect local resource rights, vesting extensive powers with public authorities and providing limited substantive and procedural rights to those affected by investment decision making.[66] In some contexts, advocates have sought to short-circuit these barriers, or the limitations affecting the enforceability of any decision resulting from domestic litigation, by pursuing transnational litigation

[62] Cotula and Schröder (n 4). For instance, in *Pac Rim Cayman LLC v El Salvador*, ICSID Case No ARB/09/12, a coalition of non-governmental organisations argued that the case was 'fundamentally not a dispute between [the investor] and the Republic, but rather between [the investor] and the independently-organized communities who have risen up against [the investor's] projects': *Pac Rim Cayman LLC v El Salvador*, Application for Permission to Proceed as *Amici Curiae* (2 March 2011) para 2.

[63] See, for example, *Von Pezold & Others v Zimbabwe*, ICSID Case No ARB/10/25, Procedural Order No 2 (26 June 2012) paras 54–60; and *Eco Oro Minerals Corp. v Republic of Colombia*, ICSID Case No ARB/16/41, Procedural Order No 6 – Decision on Non-Disputing Parties' Application (18 February 2019).

[64] See, for example, *Pac Rim Cayman LLC v El Salvador* (n 62) Award, para 3.30.

[65] J Coleman et al, 'Third-Party Rights in Investor–State Dispute Settlement: Options for Reform' Submission to UNCITRAL Working Group III on ISDS Reform in accordance with para 83 of document A/CN.9/970 (Columbia Center on Sustainable Investment, International Institute for Environment and Development and International Institute for Sustainable Development, 15 July 2019), available at ccsi.columbia.edu/files/2019/07/uncitral-submission-third-party-participation-en.pdf.

[66] For an overview, see L Cotula, '(Dis)integration in Global Resource Governance: Extractivism, Rights, and Investment Treaties' (2020) 23 *Journal of International Economic Law* 431.

against foreign investors – either in their home country, or in other relevant jurisdictions. Yet this route also presents difficulties, not least because transnational litigation takes the dispute far from the community, may take several years and often presents low chances of success.[67]

On the international plane, human rights law can provide both substantive protections and legal remedies for the rights of local communities in investment processes. On several occasions, local communities have channelled their claims through international human rights law. As foreign investors have few, if any, obligations under international human rights law, the claims are usually brought against the state. Some of these human rights claims have intersected with the investment treaty regime. In the case of the *Sawhoyamaxa Indigenous Community v Paraguay*, for example, the Government of Paraguay argued that it could not return land to the Sawhoyamaxa community because the land was now registered with a foreign investor protected under an applicable bilateral investment treaty. The Inter-American Court of Human Rights disagreed, reasoning that the Inter-American Convention of Human Rights should prevail over an investment treaty, and found that Paraguay's conduct had violated the rights of the Sawhoyamaxa community.[68]

Arbitral tribunals have taken a different view on the relationship between human rights and investment treaties, finding that the two operate on different planes and that a state must comply with both human rights and investment treaty obligations.[69] More fundamentally, international human rights recourse mechanisms themselves present conceptual, juridical and practical limitations – linked, for example, to normative framings that may contrast with local conceptions of rights, to flexible constructs that grant public authorities extensive discretion on how to reconcile multiple public and private interests, or to ineffective enforcement arrangements in the face of determined non-compliance on the part of the state.[70]

Overall, the legal contours of the investment treaty regime – including its substantive provisions and its dispute settlement arrangements – seem primarily informed by an overriding concern about promoting cross-border investment. On the other hand, promoting quality in investment processes, including in the relations that government agencies and foreign investors develop with local communities, emerges as a secondary consideration – as reflected in the absence of effective provisions on community rights and investor obligations in most

[67] See J Kimerling, 'Indigenous Peoples and the Oil Frontier in Amazonia: The Case of Ecuador, Chevron Texaco, and Aguinda v. Texaco' (2006) 38 *New York University Journal of International Law And Politics* 413. See also T Ferrando, 'Land Rights at the Time of Global Production: Leveraging Multi-Spatiality and "Legal Chokeholds"' (2017) 2 *Business and Human Rights Journal* 275.

[68] *Sawhoyamaxa Indigenous Community v Paraguay* (2006) IHRL 1530, para 140.

[69] For example, *Suez and others v Argentina*, ICSID Case No ARB/03/17, Decision on Liability (30 July 2010), para 240.

[70] Cotula, '(Dis)integration in Global Resource Governance' (2020).

investment treaties. Coordination with other applicable legal norms, whether under domestic law or international human rights treaties, only partly rebalances these asymmetries. The lack of recognition and participation of local communities in ISDS, in effect, 'invisibilises' the rights and perspectives of these communities in international investment law.[71]

IV. Possible Ways Forward

Effectively recognising the rights and interests of local communities requires comprehensive reform of foreign investment governance – starting by clearly identifying its fundamental problems and reforming key aspects of both domestic and international legal frameworks. In other words, the reform of international investment law would benefit from considering the wider context in which this body of international law fits, and its interrelatedness with other areas of both domestic and international law. Indeed, it is often the intersections between different legal instruments that sustain the invisibility of local communities in investment governance.

For example, one key challenge involves strengthening arrangements for local consultation and public participation in investment approval processes – providing a framework for investors, public authorities and local communities to discuss and cooperate before and after investment decisions, so as to prevent rather than quell disputes.[72] Depending on the circumstances, this may entail reforming national laws to integrate local consultation and rigorous impact assessments in investment approval processes – while also reorienting the work of administrative agencies to ensure it supports the implementation of such law reforms, and addressing the structural factors that sustain power imbalances in relations among foreign investors, public authorities and local communities.

At the international level, human rights law provides the main legal arena for local communities to pursue judicial redress arising from the impacts of investment processes. International human rights law contains relevant norms and its recourse institutions are specialised in handling human rights issues. While states are the primary duty bearer under international human rights law, and thus the primary respondent in international human rights litigation, the ongoing negotiation of a proposed binding treaty on business and human rights could transform this area of international law.

In this wider reform context, effective reforms of international investment law could help ensure the rights and interests of local communities are properly considered in settling investment disputes. Most, if not all, ongoing policy reform processes are incrementalist in nature: they take the current system as a given and

[71] Perrone, 'The 'Invisible' Local Communities' (2019).

[72] Perrone (n 8) 175–76.

aim to improve specific aspects of it. This approach presents clear advantages, because there may be greater political space for incremental reforms. Arguably, however, it inherently risks entrenching the traditional investor-state framing of investment relations, and of investment disputes, albeit possibly with new caveats and qualifications. It thus risks limiting the scope and depth of any reforms, and their ability to effectively address public concerns about the asymmetric nature of ISDS.

The more fine-grained understanding of investment relations that other disciplines have developed over the years – including political economy, international relations and development studies – has reconfigured traditional understandings of investment processes and disputes. The complex multi-actor nature of investment processes is one key insight emerging from this work – even more so in economic sectors such as natural resources and infrastructure, where investments can have evident, direct impacts on local communities and their ways of life. These developments beg questions about what an international system for the settlement of investment disputes would look like if it was to be designed from scratch today, based on the empirical evidence that has been generated in the decades since the predominant investor-state framing originally emerged.

A more holistic rethinking of foreign investment governance could result in a more cooperative regime where local communities have a role before, during and after the investment, and in more effective integration of international rules governing foreign investment, sustainable development, environmental protection and human rights.[73] Such comprehensive review is not currently in the cards, at least at a multilateral level. UNCITRAL Working Group III on Investor-State Dispute Settlement Reform provides a space to consider multilateral reforms of the procedural dimensions of ISDS. The limited scope of this process has raised concerns, however, not least due to the difficulty of separating procedural from substantive issues, and the fact that effectively responding to public concerns about ISDS would require rethinking the substantive standards as much as procedural issues.[74] Engaging with these circumscribed reform processes can itself raise difficult questions, because the outcomes might end up legitimising a legal regime, and inhibit more radical change, against only limited reforms that do not address the fundamental issues and asymmetries.

With these caveats, relevant reform options the UNCITRAL Working Group might wish to explore could include requiring that investors exhaust domestic

[73] Perrone (n 8) 177–80.

[74] These points were articulated by the submissions to the UNCITRAL Working Group made by the Governments of Indonesia and South Africa. See 'Possible Reform of Investor-State Dispute Settlement (ISDS): Comments by the Government of Indonesia' (9 November 2018) UN Doc A/CN.9/WG.III/WP.156, paras 2 and 15–16, available at undocs.org/en/A/CN.9/WG.III/WP.156; and 'Possible Reform of Investor-State Dispute Settlement (ISDS): Submission from the Government of South Africa' (17 July 2019) UN Doc A/CN.9/WG.III/WP.176, paras 19–21, available at undocs.org/en/A/CN.9/WG.III/WP.176.

remedies before accessing ISDS, so third parties can use the arrangements national legal systems may provide to intervene in legal proceedings.[75] Some reform proposals also envisage differentiating more clearly between *amicus curiae* submissions made by public-interest bodies and aimed at contributing factual or legal elements that may assist the tribunal, on the one hand; and an actual *legal right* for third parties whose rights are directly at stake to intervene in these arbitrations, so as to protect their rights throughout the proceedings and enforce relevant investor obligations, on the other.[76] The UNCITRAL Working Group could also explore the circumstances under which investor claims should be dismissed, in whole or in part, or suitably reframed, if affected third parties are unable to intervene or be joined in the proceedings.[77] The procedural rules applicable to arrangements such as interventions and joinders under many domestic legal systems might provide some inspiration for exploring these reform options.

It is worth bearing in mind, however, that exhaustion of domestic remedies is resisted by major capital exporters, and that few governments have displayed an explicit interest in addressing issues concerning the rights of local communities in ISDS, partly reflecting a belief that the state is well placed to represent the interests of its people in international legal proceedings.[78] In other words, political support for meaningful reform in this area seems at present very limited. At a deeper level, exploring these reform options is likely to beg complex questions. ISDS tribunals or even a permanent investment court may lack the appropriate expertise to adjudicate disputes where third-party rights – and possibly human rights – are at stake. Local communities may find themselves in an unfavourable dispute settlement forum: far from their locality, expensive and specialising in legal arrangements which protect foreign investors. This raises issues about effective arrangements for communities to participate in ISDS, while also sheltering themselves from the risks that may be associated with complex and costly legal proceedings. In more systemic terms, it also raises issues about possible ways to coordinate the intersections between international investment disputes and domestic and international human rights litigation.

[75] L Cotula and NM Perrone, 'Reforming Investor-State Dispute Settlement: What About Third-Party Rights?' (International Institute for Environment and Development, February 2019), available at pubs.iied.org/pdfs/17638IIED.pdf.

[76] Coleman and Gupta, 'International Investment Agreements, 2015–2016' (2017). This prospect is also alluded to by J Ho's discussion on multipartite treaty-based adjudication in ch1 of this volume.

[77] Coleman and Gupta (n 58).

[78] For exceptions, see for example, the submissions to the UNCITRAL Working Group made by the Governments of Ecuador and South Africa. See Possible Reform of Investor-State Dispute Settlement (ISDS): Submission from the Government of Ecuador (Submission to UNCITRAL Working Group III on Investor-State Dispute Settlement Reform, 17 July 2019, A/CN.9/WG.III/WP.175) paras 23–26, available at undocs.org/en/A/CN.9/WG.III/WP.175; and Possible Reform of Investor-State Dispute Settlement (ISDS): Submission from the Government of South Africa, paras 7–8, 11, 32.

V. Conclusion

This chapter has contrasted the complexity of foreign investment projects, mainly in the extractive and infrastructure sectors, with the substantive rules and procedural arrangements under the investment treaty regime. The analysis has shown that investment treaties are primarily centred on relations between investors and states, including in the context of dispute settlement processes. They do not provide effective mechanisms to recognise or protect the rights and interests of local communities before, during and after an investment project. In other words, the asymmetries that characterise investment treaties refer not only to the imbalance between foreign investor's rights and obligations vis-à-vis the host state, but also to the limited recognition of local communities as a relevant actor in investment relations. In effect, local communities are 'invisibilised' in international investment law.

This situation affects local communities as much as it undermines the ability of ISDS tribunals to consider all the relevant facts and norms involved in a dispute. Addressing these asymmetries poses major theoretical and practical questions. On the one hand, the fact that communities' rights and interests may be directly at stake points to the need to strengthen arrangements for voice and representation in investment and dispute settlement processes. On the other hand, and leaving aside the lack of political support for meaningful reform in this area, at least at this stage, ISDS tribunals or a permanent investment court may not be the appropriate fora to decide over the rights and interests of local communities. In the short term, however, the primary challenge, both for UNCITRAL Working Group III and for the investment law community at large, is to identify this issue, consider its multifaceted implications and inscribe it in the reform agenda – while understanding that any actual reform will require careful thought and consideration.

4

From Risk to Rights: Reorienting the Paradigms at the Heart of Corporate Legal Form and Investment Treaty Standards in Foreign Investment Governance

ANIL YILMAZ VASTARDIS

I. Introduction

International law's disorganised encounter with corporations has typically been concerned with furthering the interests of the market, and in particular, the wealthiest parts of the market.[1] The corporation[2] is the direct beneficiary of legal protection under international investment law (IIL)[3] and benefits indirectly from various international treaties that facilitate the smooth functioning of markets.[4] States have relatively efficiently overcome their differences and cooperated to establish international standards of investment protection that facilitate business and the functioning of markets. Yet, it has been frustratingly difficult to attain international consensus on regulating businesses for their negative impacts on human rights and the environment. The latter type of regulation has typically been viewed by states as a competitive disadvantage, while the former an

[1] Corporations have mostly captured the attention of international law to the extent that they could capture the attention of states as significant economic actors sustaining losses or causing major harms. For international investment law, the protection has been largely available to the wealthier corporate groups. Similarly, diplomatic protection of corporate interests is unlikely to be on the agenda of any state for a small-sized investment.

[2] The term 'corporation' is used here to describe limited liability business forms.

[3] For example, international investment law and international taxation law.

[4] For example, OECD Convention on Combating Bribery of Foreign Public Officials in International Business Transactions (signed 17 December 1997, entry into force 15 February 1999); the World Trade Organization system, and double taxation treaties, to name a few.

enabler of fair competition. This status quo has been described as unjustifiably asymmetrical.[5]

The current legal framework for foreign investment governance is coded[6] to safeguard and privilege capital without placing clear duties on investors to avoid inflicting harm on communities and the environment. The laws are designed to mitigate the risks of business for investors by shifting these on to other actors, such as creditors, taxpayers, local communities and employees. At the centre of the code of foreign investment governance sits a risk paradigm that provides enhanced protection to investor wealth from commercial and political risk, but also from risk of liability from the business's own harmful impacts on the environment and human rights.[7] This chapter deploys risk framing to explain the asymmetrical status quo in foreign investment governance[8] and focuses on two aspects of the legal framework on foreign investment, namely substantive investment treaty standards and corporate personality.[9] The first leg of the legal framework that sustains investor wealth is located in investment treaty 'standards of protection'. These standards offer international protection to investors against the risks of doing business overseas. They are best characterised by their generality and high level of abstraction, minimal exceptions to their application to safeguard investor assets and their

[5] L Pellegrini et al, 'International Investment Agreements, Human Rights, and Environmental Justice: The Texaco/Chevron Case from the Ecuadorian Amazon' (2020) 23 *Journal of International Economic Law* 455; A Arcuri, 'The Great Asymmetry and the Rule of Law in International Investment Arbitration' in L Sachs, L Johnson and J Coleman (eds), *Yearbook on International Investment Law & Policy 2018* (Oxford University Press, 2019) 397–416.

[6] Katharina Pistor explains that the concept of legal coding of capital refers to the way certain assets, such as a property, a share or a claim, are recognised and regulated by law in ways that can turn them into capital and 'increase [their] propensity to create wealth for [their] holder(s)'. K Pistor, *The Code of Capital: How the Law Creates Wealth and Inequality* (Princeton University Press, 2019) 2.

[7] Pistor (ibid) 6 and 13 (the outcome of the coding is that rather than 'the asset itself, … its legal coding, protects the asset holder from the headwinds of ordinary business cycles and gives his wealth longevity, thereby setting the stage for sustained inequality').

[8] Pistor's analysis primarily focuses on domestic laws, with a brief analysis of investment treaties and the availability of choice for business to opt for foreign law in governing their business affairs and revenue streams – I extrapolate from her work on domestic laws to the role of international law and the application of corporate law principles in the international context in coding capital. Investment treaty standards and corporations are not the only enablers of risk avoidance for investors on a global scale. Contracts, too, are tools of risk allocation used by international investors and corporate actors more generally. The focus of this chapter is on the corporate form and IIL in order to expose the risk avoidance functions embedded within these legal fictions. Contracts can be designed by the contracting parties to have similar risk avoidance effects, but the law of contracts do not 'by design' operate as a risk avoidance mechanism. Uses of contracts 'as a device of risk management' in the context of IIL has been fleshed out in S Leader, 'Human Rights, Risks, and New Strategies for Global Investment' (2006) 9 *Journal of International Economic Law* 657.

[9] Foreign investments also benefit from coding in other areas of law such as taxation, property law and contract law, but these go beyond the focus of this chapter – though the conclusions here may be applicable in the application of other fields of law to foreign investments. Not all investors protected by IIL are corporate actors, but the corporate form is the most dominant one used in carrying out domestic or cross-border business.

generous interpretation by arbitral tribunals.[10] Host states have been sanctioned for breaching the standards of protection even when the reason for the state's failure is a legitimate policy goal in the public interest, thus shielding investors from the risks of regulatory reforms or acts of state detrimental to profits.[11] This means that investors can shield against the risk of loss in profits brought by state measures taken to safeguard the environment and human rights of communities. As the corporate form is the most common vehicle used by investors when operating abroad, the second leg of legal coding for foreign investments is embedded in corporate law principles of separate personality and limited liability which benefit foreign investors by insulating them from commercial and political risks faced by the corporate subsidiary operating in host states. They also allow foreign investors to shield against liability for harms they inflicted on the environment and local communities,[12] shifting the risk of loss and damage on aggrieved communities, employees and the environment. Thus, a shared feature of these aspects of the legal framework protecting investments under IIL and corporate law is that both legs aim to promote and facilitate economic activity and sustain investor wealth by shifting risks away from the investor.[13]

Together, they provide enhanced protection to investors to mitigate certain risks involved in cross-border business activity by shielding investors from liability for their own wrongdoings and protecting against regulatory, political and social changes in their operating environment. This risk paradigm at the heart of foreign investment governance is indifferent to the nature of the risk avoided by the investor. In other words, the legal framework treats all risks similarly and the investor is shielded from risk, whether it is a human rights risk, a political risk or a commercial risk. And this approach to risk is a preference embedded in the law that determines how gains and losses should be distributed within the society.[14]

[10] See D Davitti, *Investment and Human Rights in Armed Conflict: Charting an Elusive Intersection* (Hart Publishing, 2019) 55–93.

[11] See, for example, *Bear Creek Mining Corporation v Republic of Peru*, ICSID Case No ARB/14/21, Award (30 November 2017); *South American Silver Limited v Bolivia*, PCA Case No 2013-15, Award (30 August 2018); *Clayton and Bilcon of Delaware Inc. v Government of Canada*, PCA Case No 2009-04, Award on Jurisdiction and Liability (17 March 2015); *Copper Mesa Mining Corporation v Republic of Ecuador*, PCA No 2012-2, Award (15 March 2016).

[12] See for example, *Okpabi v Royal Dutch Shell plc* [2018] EWCA Civ 191; *AAA v Unilever plc and Unilever Tea Kenya Limited* [2018] EWCA Civ 1532; *Aguinda v Texaco, Inc*, 142 F Supp.2d 534 (SDNY 2001).

[13] Pistor, *The Code of Capital* (2019) 9 (the code of capital allows 'gains [to] be made and pocketed anywhere and the losses [to] be left wherever they fall'); G Baars, '"It's Not Me, It's the Corporation": The Value of Corporate Accountability in the Global Political Economy' (2016) 4 *London Review of International Law* 127, 127–63 (describes the corporation as an 'externalising machine'). The 'investor' as used here refers in the corporate context to the shareholders, and in the IIL context to the corporate and individual investor beneficiaries of the law.

[14] C Tan, 'Beyond the "Moments" of Law and Development: Critical Reflections on Law and Development Scholarship in a Globalized Economy' (2019) 12 *Law and Development Review* 285, 298; N Perrone and D Schneiderman, 'Critique of International Economic Law: Depoliticization, Inequality, Precarity' in E Christodoulidis, R Dukes and M Goldoni (eds), *Research Handbook on Critical Legal Theory* (Edward Elgar, 2018) 1.

Calls have been made from a range of state and non-state actors to achieve an equilibrium between rights and obligations of investors in international law.[15] These calls have sometimes been accompanied by reform proposals.[16] Within the IIL and business and human rights (BHR) frameworks, substantive barriers to holding investors accountable for human rights and environmental impacts persist.[17] Both the IIL and BHR literature has tackled the issue from various angles.[18] The notable IIL proposals for progress include introducing direct investor obligations in investment treaties,[19] host states making more effective use of human rights and environmental defences and counter-claims in investment disputes,[20] introducing explicit or stronger terms in treaties on the state's right to regulate[21] and relying on proportionality or balancing exercises when interpreting treaty terms.[22]

In this chapter, I offer a novel perspective to the problem by situating investment treaty standards and corporate personality as components of a risk paradigm that privileges foreign investors and blocks the paths to accountability for harms inflicted by investment activity. To do this, I focus on the context and the subtext

[15] Most recently, 'Symposium on Investor Responsibility: The Next Frontier in International Investment Law' (2019) 13 *American Journal of International Law Unbound*, 1, available at www.cambridge.org/core/journals/american-journal-of-international-law/volume/AED2077F3422BB3F291F651F695CD4FA.

[16] See, for example, the proposals submitted to the 2018 UN Forum on Business and Human Rights, Session 26–28 November 2018, 'Crowd-drafting: Designing a Human Rights-Compatible International Investment Agreement', available at www.ohchr.org/EN/Issues/Business/Pages/IIAs.aspx.

[17] A Marx et al, 'Access to Legal Remedies for Victims of Corporate Human Rights Abuses in Third Countries' (European Parliament Think Tank, 1 February 2019), available at europarl.europa.eu/thinktank/en/document.html?reference=EXPO_STU(2019)603475; G Skinner, R McCorquodale and O de Schutter, 'Third Pillar: Access to Judicial Remedies for Human Rights Violations by Transnational Business' (ICAR-CORE-ECCJ, December 2013), available at corporatejustice.org/documents/publications/eccj/the_third_pillar_access_to_judicial_remedies_for_human_rights_violation.-1-2.pdf; S Baughen, *Human Rights and Corporate Wrongs: Closing the Governance Gap* (Edward Elgar, 2015) 179–90.

[18] Most notably: J Ho, 'The Creation of Elusive Investor Responsibility' (2019) 113 *American Journal of International Law Unbound* 10; M Sattorova, 'Investor Responsibilities From A Host State Perspective: Qualitative Data And Proposals For Treaty Reform' (2019) 113 *American Journal of International Law Unbound* 22; N Bernasconi-Osterwalder, 'Inclusion of Investor Obligations and Corporate Accountability Provisions in Investment Agreements' in J Chaisse et al (eds), *Handbook of International Investment Law and Policy* (Springer, 2020); Davitti, *Investment and Human Rights in Armed Conflict* (2019); LW Mouyal, *International Investment Law and the Right to Regulate: A Human Rights Perspective* (Routledge, 2018); S Leader, 'Human Rights, Risks, and New Strategies for Global Investment' (2006) 9 *Journal of International Economic Law* 657–705; B Simma, 'Foreign Investment Arbitration: A place for human rights?' (2011) 60 *International & Comparative Law Quarterly* 573.

[19] Bernasconi-Osterwalder (ibid); N Monebhurrun, 'Mapping the Duties of Private Companies in International Investment Law' (2017) 14 *Brazilian Journal of International Law* 49.

[20] Ho, 'Elusive Investor Responsibility' (2019).

[21] Mouyal, *International Investment Law* (2018).

[22] G Zarra, 'Right to Regulate, Margin of Appreciation and Proportionality: Current Status in Investment Arbitration in Light of *Philip Morris v Uruguay*' (2017) 14 *Brazilian Journal of International Law* 94; LG Garcia, 'The Role of Human Rights in International Investment Law' in NJ Calamita, D Earnest and M Burgstaller (eds), *The Future of ICSID and the Place of Investment Treaties in International Law* (British Institute of International and Comparative Law, 2013) 29–43.

of the legal standards,[23] analysing them as risk allocation tools that operate at the expense of entrenching inequalities in host state communities. To alleviate the detrimental impacts of this paradigm, I propose reorienting the dominant narratives on risk when applying and interpreting key legal standards on foreign investment protection in order to give greater weight to non-investment interests in interpreting the existing standards. As I will demonstrate in sections II and III below, the risk mitigation rationale of these legal standards are justified on the basis of the ultimate benefits of enhanced economic activity on the wellbeing of communities. I argue that the risk mitigation privileges should no longer apply, when investor activity harms the environment and wellbeing of communities.

In section II, I outline the problem tackled in this chapter, namely the barriers to investor accountability within IIL and BHR, and offer a new framing of this problem focusing on the risk mitigation rationale situated at the heart of foreign investment governance. To do this, I analyse the actors, processes and priorities shaping the development and the interpretation of legal standards in IIL and BHR. In section III, I examine the corporate legal form and IIL as risk allocation tools. I look back to the rationales posited at the initial stages of their gradual development. Based on these early rationales, I categorise both categories of legal protection against risk as a means to create social benefits. I argue that the privileges granted to investors by corporate law and IIL cannot remain justified to the extent that their activities cause or contribute to the worsening of the broader society's well-being. To alleviate damaging impacts of the risk paradigm, I propose an adjustment of the paradigm in section IV by introducing a rights-based approach[24] to establishing limitations on investors' risk mitigation privileges. To unpack this approach, I use two case studies, one BHR and one IIL claim, to demonstrate the current approach to risk and offer an alternative interpretation through those cases.

II. Reframing the Problem: Risk Mitigation at the Heart of Foreign Investment Governance

Barriers to holding foreign investors accountable, both within IIL and BHR, for the impacts of their business on communities and environment, have been well documented in literature.[25] The evolution of IIL in the last three decades has not only vastly improved the legal security offered to investors against risk of loss,

[23] A Perry-Kessaris, 'What Does it Mean to Take a Socio-Legal Approach to International Economic Law?' in A Perry-Kessaris (ed), *Socio-Legal Approaches to International Economic Law: Text, Context and Subtext* (Routledge, 2013) 7.

[24] Including a full catalogue of human rights and environmental rights.

[25] Bernasconi-Osterwalder, 'Inclusion of Investor Obligations' (2020); N Monebhurrun, 'Mapping the Duties of Private Companies in International Investment Law' (2017) 14 *Brazilian Journal of International Law* 49.

but also sharpened the legal tools available to investors to safeguard their wealth against clashing interests of communities and environment. In many instances, IIL allows investors to shield to a greater or a lesser extent from the cost of compliance with regulation needed to safeguard human rights and environment. This coupled with the lack or inaccessibility of robust legal standards imposing obligations on investors to comply with human rights and environmental standards offers investors a double insulation from accountability. As noted in section I, to counteract this problem, arguments have been advanced to balance the scales. Most notably, authors have framed the problem as one of fragmentation of international law and offered solutions on how to reasonably integrate human rights principles into the interpretation of investment law standards under the principles of treaty interpretation under international law.[26] From this lens, several solutions emerged, ranging from the prioritisation of certain rights over IIL standards to applying a proportionality analysis to evaluating the interaction of standards.[27] In the context of treaty reform, explicit clauses on investor obligations and the right to regulate have been proposed and started to be used in investment treaty practice.[28] In the BHR context, the debate at the international level has focused on whether corporations have enforceable human rights responsibilities, the nature of such obligations and possibilities of improving remedies for human rights impacts of businesses.[29] Each of these proposals make a valuable contribution to advancing the discourse on investor accountability.

In this section, I offer an alternative framing of the problem by focusing on the risk mitigation rationale which sits at the heart of foreign investment governance, rather than viewing it from the fragmentation perspective. Though radical reform is desirable, in the meantime investor obligations can be advanced via both IIL and BHR using the existing legal frameworks by reorienting the risk paradigm within the legal framework governing foreign investment. To do this, I start by analysing the key processes, actors and priorities that have shaped the substance of the law governing foreign investments and its interpretation. This allows me to shed light

[26] Mouyal (n 18) 226–31; Simma, 'Foreign Investment Arbitration' (2011).

[27] Ho (n 18); Perry-Kessaris, 'Socio-Legal Approach' (2013).

[28] See, for example, the Comprehensive and Economic Trade Agreement (CETA) between the EU and Canada (signed 30 October 2016, provisional entry into force 21 September 2017) and the reciprocal investment protection and promotion investment agreement between the Government of the Kingdom of Morocco and the Government of the Federal Republic of Nigeria (signed 3 December 2016, not yet in force).

[29] A Ramasastry, 'Corporate Social Responsibility Versus Business and Human Rights: Bridging the Gap Between Responsibility and Accountability' (2015) 1 *Journal of Human Rights* 237; TV Ho, 'International Legal Personality of Corporations: How Investment Law Answers the Supreme Court Question in Jesner' (Just Security, 2 October 2017), available at www.justsecurity.org/45543/international-legal-personality-corporations-investment-law-answers-supreme-court-question-jesner; S Deva, *Regulating Corporate Human Rights Violations: Humanizing Business* (Routledge, 2012); A Clapham, *Human Rights Obligations on Non-State Actors* (Oxford University Press, 2006) 195–201; G Skinner, 'Parent Company Accountability: Ensuring Justice for Human Rights Violations' (International Corporate Accountability Roundtable, November 2015), 14–23, available at www.bhrinlaw.org/documents/pcap-report-2015.pdf.

on the assumptions embedded in the status quo,[30] namely how the risk mitigation objective is at the heart of the law safeguarding the wealth of foreign investors at the expense of local communities and the environment. The ensuing discussion considers the actors, processes and substances in the making of a code on a foreign investment.

In 2019, two multistakeholder intergovernmental working group sessions concerning international business activities took place on the same dates under the auspices of the UN.[31] The first was a meeting in Geneva on the treaty proposal to regulate the human rights impacts of businesses in international law.[32] The second was a meeting in Vienna on reforming the international arbitration system for settling investor-state disputes.[33] The two reform processes seem worlds apart, although they are two sides of the same coin. In essence, the BHR treaty process attempts to regulate, inter alia, the impacts of international investor activity on human rights and the environment.[34] IIL regulates the rights of businesses vis-à-vis host states when operating overseas. While each area may give rise to isolated legal issues and disputes, disputes arising in either context regularly have strong relevance to the other area. Numerous IIL disputes concern state actions reacting to human rights or environmental concerns.[35] BHR disputes can involve investors who have the backing of an IIL treaty to safeguard their business interests in the face of state or community backlash to the impacts of their operations.

It does not come as a surprise that there is an obvious asymmetry between the robust protection investors receive under IIL to safeguard fundamental investor rights and the absence of investor obligations for impacts on the fundamental rights

[30] Davitti (n 10) 229.

[31] First, 38th session of the UNCITRAL Working Group III relating to investor-state dispute settlement reform (14–18 October 2019), available at uncitral.un.org/en/working_groups/3/investor-state. Second, the 5th session of the OEIGWG on transnational corporations and other business enterprises with respect to human rights (14–18 October 2019), available at www.ohchr.org/EN/HRBodies/HRC/WGTransCorp/Session5/Pages/Session5.aspx.

[32] A few states have begun to reform their domestic laws to better regulate corporate impacts on human rights; Most notably, the French Law on the Corporate Duty of Vigilance (Loi No 2017-399 du 27 Mars 2017 relative au devoir de vigilance des sociétés mères et des entreprises donneuses d'ordre), available at www.legifrance.gouv.fr/eli/loi/2017/3/27/2017-399/jo/texte.

[33] Besides the intergovernmental ISDS reform process, many states are working actively on reforming their investment treaties to restrain the scope and extent of IIL protections, most notably, the Dutch Model BIT, and the new EU investment treaty programme.

[34] The current draft of the Legally Binding Instrument to Regulate, in International Human Rights law, the Activities of Transnational Corporations and Other Business Enterprises includes in Art 1(2) environmental rights under the definition of human rights abuse, available at www.ohchr.org/Documents/HRBodies/HRCouncil/WGTransCorp/Session6/OEIGWG_Chair-Rapporteur_second_revised_draft_LBI_on_TNCs_and_OBEs_with_respect_to_Human_Rights.pdf.

[35] See, for example, *Urbaser SA and Consorcio de Aguas Bilbao Biskaia, Bilbao Biskaia Ur Partzuergoa v Argentine Republic*, ICSID Case No ARB/07/26; *Técnicas Medioambientales Tecmed v United Mexican States*, ICSID Case No ARB(AF)/00/2; *The Renco Group, Inc v The Republic of Peru (II)*, PCA Case No 2019-46; *Chevron Corporation and Texaco Petroleum Company v The Republic of Ecuador (I)*, PCA Case No 2007-02/AA277.

of their workers or host communities and on the environment. Internationally protected investor rights have developed and spread around the world at a much faster pace than internationally recognised investor obligations. The first modern investment treaty was signed between Pakistan and West Germany in 1959, and in the 60 years that followed, thousands of investment treaties came into existence throughout the globe to protect investor rights.[36] Although investor obligations have appeared on the international agenda not long after the signing of the first BIT and the establishment of the ICSID in 1965, they never received the support or consensus from the powerful state actors to be internationally recognised and enforceable.[37] Up to this day no bilateral or multilateral binding instrument, comparable to investment treaties in authority and enforceability, on investor obligations for human rights and environmental impacts exists.[38] This gives rise to a de facto prioritisation of investor wealth over the protection of human rights and the environment where investment activity harms or threatens to harm the latter. The latter does not benefit from the kind of robust legal strategies available to investors to protect and enforce their rights.

IIL and BHR evolve highly detached from each other, both on the elements of substantive reform and on active stakeholders dominating/leading the discussion. Only a small number of stakeholders bridge the gap on a small number of issues.[39] Reflecting on the actors influencing the development of the law is an important part of the problem to pay attention to when discussing past and present foreign investment governance.[40] In the context of IIL, global law firms and arbitrators that profit from the existing system of IIL have been exerting influence on the various IIL reform processes.[41] Arbitrators and lawyers involved in investment

[36] Friendship, commerce and navigation treaties were predecessors of modern international investment treaties. They contained guarantees on the treatment of foreign investors, but without giving investors direct standing to enforce the standards.

[37] The appearance of international obligations of investors on the UN agenda can be traced back to 1970s and to the NIEO resolutions, followed by the establishment of a Commission on Transnational Corporations, which presented a draft code of conduct on TNCs in 1983 containing investor obligations and rules on treatment of investors. This code was not endorsed by the General Assembly. Several other non-binding instruments have been developed over the years, most notably the ILO Tripartite Declaration, OECD Guidelines on MNEs, and the UNGPs. For more on this, see KP Sauvant, 'The Negotiations of the United Nations Code of Conduct on Transnational Corporations: Experience and Lessons Learned' (2015) 16 *Journal of World Investment & Trade* 11.

[38] Investment treaty practice is slowly evolving in this area, but these provisions are at their infancy and remain inadequate for offering genuine investor accountability. See Draft Pan-African Investment Code, Arts 19–24; SADC Model Bilateral Investment Treaty, Arts 13–18; Morocco-Nigeria BIT (signed 3 December 2016, not yet in force), Art 18.

[39] From NGOs, IISD, IIED and SOMO are actively engaged in both processes; a few academic experts bridging the gap include Professor Surya Deva and Dr Tara Van Ho.

[40] Pistor (n 6) 19 (argues that law firms have been crucial actors in the evolution of the code of capital and the states' role has been to 'provide the legal tools that lawyers use; and … offer their law enforcement apparatus to enforce the capital that lawyers have crafted').

[41] It has been reported that lawyers and law academics from the arbitration industry have a strong influence over the UNCITRAL ISDS reform agenda; see A Beunder and J Mast, 'As the World Meets to Discuss ISDS, Many Fear Meaningless Reforms' (Transnational Institute, 5 April 2019), available at longreads.tni.org/isds-many-fear-meaningless-reforms; Previously, Corporate

arbitration practice do also significantly influence how the abstract legal standards in investment treaties get to be interpreted. Powerful sovereign actors, most notably the EU, have fully supported investment treaties and have been constructively engaged with recent initiatives for ISDS reforms. By contrast, there has been significantly less support from influential actors for efforts to create binding norms, through the treaty or other efforts, on human rights responsibilities of business.[42] They have instead put their weight behind soft law initiatives in the area of BHR.[43] NGOs and developing states whose populations were harmed by international investor activity such as Brazil, Venezuela, Ecuador and South Africa have constructively engaged with the BHR treaty process while being critical of ISDS and IIL in general, some advocating for its abolition and others demanding substantial reforms.[44] Based on what history tells us, it would not be surprising to see that the IIL reform processes supported by the dominant actors will swiftly produce concrete results to alleviate legitimacy concerns and keep the system functioning.[45] The BHR treaty process is likely to be hindered by the same dominant actors who push for slowing the process down or watering down the text, or even by derailing the process altogether.

Europe Observatory (CEO) reported that leading arbitration law firms provide training to developing country officials on negotiating investment treaties; see CEO, 'Profiting From Injustice' (Transnational Institute, 27 November 2012), available at corporateeurope.org/en/trade/2012/11/chapter-3-legal-vultures-law-firms-driving-demand-investment-arbitration.

[42] The EU even attempted to obstruct the process previously (particularly in the 3rd session): ECCJ, UN Treaty on Business and Human Rights 'Zero Draft' Negotiations Day 1 (Corporate Justice, 16 October 2018), available at corporatejustice.org/news/9757-un-treaty-on-business-human-rights-zero-draft-negotiations-day-1; L Ortiz and A van Schaik, 'Why does the European Union Fear a Binding Human Rights Treaty on Transnational Corporations' (Friends of the Earth International, 11 July 2018), available at www.foei.org/news/why-does-the-european-union-fear-a-binding-human-rights-treaty-on-transnational-corporations. At the domestic level, French Law on Corporate Duty of Vigilance is the most notable achievement so far.

[43] The Hague Rules on Business and Human Rights Arbitration (adopted 12 December 2019), available at www.cilc.nl/cms/wp-content/uploads/2019/12/The-Hague-Rules-on-Business-and-Human-Rights-Arbitration_CILC-digital-version.pdf; OHCHR, 'Guiding Principles on Business and Human Rights: Implementing the United Nations "Protect, Respect and Remedy" Framework' (2011) UN Doc A/HRC/17/31; OECD, 'OECD Guidelines for Multinational Enterprises' (OECD Publishing, 2011), available at www.oecd.org/daf/inv/mne/48004323.pdf.

[44] For the states supporting the work on the BHR treaty, see OEIGWG 'Report on the fifth session of the open-ended intergovernmental working group on transnational corporations and other business enterprises with respect to human rights' (9 January 2020) UN Doc A/HRC/43/55, Annex I. For states demanding substantial reform of ISDS and IIL, see for example: UNGA, 'Possible reform of Investor-State dispute settlement (ISDS): Submission from the Government of South Africa' (17 July 2019) UN Doc A/CN.9/WG.III/WP.176; UNGA 'Possible reform of Investor-State dispute settlement (ISDS): Submission from the Government of Ecuador' (16 July 2019) UN Doc A/CN.9/WG.III/WP.175. For NGOs proposing a move away from the system, see ClientEarth, 'Potential Solutions For Phase 3: Aligning The Objectives Of UNCITRAL Working Group III With States' International Obligations To Combat Climate Change', available at uncitral.un.org/sites/uncitral.un.org/files/media-documents/uncitral/en/wgiii_clientearth.pdf.

[45] S Pahuja, *Decolonising International Law: Development, Economic Growth and the Politics of Universality* (Cambridge University Press, 2011) 2–3; J Linarelli, ME Salomon and M Sornarajah, *The Misery of International Law: Confrontations with Injustice in the Global Economy* (Oxford University Press, 2018); A Anghie, *Imperialism, Sovereignty and the Making of International Law* (Cambridge University Press, 2015).

The legal standards themselves reflect the priorities and values of the groups and the authorities that develop, implement, and reform them. I identified in section I that at the heart of the legal standards on investment protection and corporate personality sits a risk paradigm which minimises the risks of foreign investment. Rules on the functioning of the markets, including IIL and corporate laws have as their purpose facilitation of economic activity and they achieve this by rendering risk-taking less prone to loss for entrepreneurs as well as for ordinary people.[46] These rules are presented as essential in a free-market economy and are promoted by powerful and dominant actors who can effect change efficiently. These rules are often viewed as bringing a competitive advantage. By contrast, social and environmental concerns are perceived as bringing a competitive disadvantage and they must constantly and rigorously justify their importance and urgency to policymakers to even find a place on the agenda. Even when there is overwhelming scientific evidence supporting a new policy in these areas, the progress can be painstakingly slow (eg, climate change and modern slavery). And only when they become to be viewed as a competitive advantage (eg, a business case for human rights),[47] will they start receiving support from key policy makers and lobbyists.

This framing of the interests normalises and legitimises the prioritisation of eliminating the risks involved in doing business[48] whilst those harmed by investment activity lack access to effective legal standards and enforcement to protect themselves from business-induced harm.[49] Investment treaty protections are viewed as offering a competitive advantage as foreign investors can shield from the risk of loss caused by regulatory changes in their operating environment by successfully seeking exorbitant amounts of compensation from host states.[50] The damages paid to the investors is extracted from taxpayers and budgets of host

[46] Pistor (n 6) 134: '[W]hat is good for effective law and democratic self-governance is not necessarily good for capital. The same qualities that make law vibrant and relevant for a polity make it volatile and uncertain in the eyes of foreign traders and investors'.

[47] M Porter and MK Kramer, 'Strategy and society; the link between competitive advantage and corporate social responsibility' (2006) 84 *Harvard Business Law Review* 78.

[48] Tan, 'Beyond the "Moments" of Law and Development' (2019) 25 (the theory and practice of international economic law (IEL) achieves this through its aforementioned culturally productive role, in its function as a system of symbols and signification that creates and attaches meaning to actors, forces and practices, normalising or delegitimising actions, policies, social and economic trajectories and rationales that influence and undergird transactions and relationships in the global economy); see Pistor (n 6) 3 (the way capital is coded legally grants 'important attributes on assets and thereby privilege its holder: Priority, which ranks competing claims to the same assets; durability, which extends priority claims in time, universality, which extends them in space; and convertibility, which operates as an insurance device that allows holders to convert their private credit claims into state money on demand').

[49] Pistor (n 6) 8 (legal coding of capital fosters 'creation of wealth by holders of capital, … but it has also contributed to a highly skewed distribution of wealth for others without access to sophisticated coding strategies').

[50] J Bonnitcha and S Brewin, 'Compensation under Investment Treaties' (IISD Best Practice Series, November 2020), available at www.iisd.org/system/files/publications/compensation-treaties-best-practicies-en.pdf.

states that could have been otherwise, at least partially, invested in the progressive realisation of economic, social and cultural rights.[51] An investment treaty claim or the threat of a claim in response to a regulation or an act of state in the public interest could also give rise to a reversal or watering down of said regulation.[52] Such a reversal could undermine host communities' well-being and access to resources.

The use of corporate form by investors adds a further layer of protection for investors against losses and makes the foreign investment framework even more skewed in favour of investor wealth. The universally adopted basic legal features of corporations that render them unique include separate personality, limited liability, perpetual existence, transferable shares and the ability to acquire shares in other companies.[53] Combined, these features allow corporate groups to be formed and operate on a transnational scale without having an independent legal identity as a group of companies.[54] In other words, the law enables and facilitates the creation of multinational enterprises (MNEs) made up of corporate actors, but fails to recognise or regulate the group of corporations as a distinct entity. As one author describes, the multinational enterprise is an organisation that exists de facto, but it does not exist in law.[55] We can notice here how skewed the legal framework is as it is embedded with features that enable the creation and operation of MNEs as a group but it provides no means by which MNEs can be regulated as a group.[56] In this sense, the MNE exists to the extent it assists in the creation and sustaining of wealth, but it does not exist in the eyes of the law to regulate its activities and assign liabilities to it. The matter is made more challenging by domestic laws being largely unable to regulate cross-border operations.[57]

[51] International Covenant on Economic, Social and Cultural Rights (adopted 16 December 1966, entered into force 3 January 1976) 993 UNTS 3, Art 2(1).

[52] Studies on the regulatory chill caused by threat of investment claims have reached contradicting results on whether the problem is systemic: see TL Berge and A Berger, 'Do Investor–State Dispute Settlement Cases Influence Domestic Environmental Regulation? The Role of Respondent-State Capacity' (2020), available at ssrn.com/abstract=3522366; G van Harten and DN Scott, 'Investment treaties and the internal vetting of regulatory proposals: A case study from Canada' (2016) 7 *Journal of International Dispute Settlement* 92; JL Tobin, 'The Social Cost of International Investment Agreements: The Case of Cigarette Packaging' (2018) 32 *Ethics & International Affairs* 153; whether systemic or not, for the purposes of this paper, I focus on the instances where regulatory chill has happened as a consequence of the code of foreign investment.

[53] Baars, '"It's Not Me, It's the Corporation"' (2013) 134 (states that this Anglo-American conception of the corporation has spread around the globe); P Blumberg, *The Multinational Challenge to Corporation Law* (Oxford University Press, 1993) 56 (notes that New Jersey was the first state in the US to accept acquisition of shares in other companies by a series of acts enacted in 1888, 1889, and 1893).

[54] JP Robe, 'Globalization and Constitutionalization of the World Power System' in JP Robe, A Lyon-Caen and S Vernac (eds), *Multinationals and the Constitutionalization of the World Power System* (Routledge, 2016).

[55] ibid.

[56] Some areas of law, such as EU competition law, allow to some extent for a group of companies to be viewed as a single economic unit for purposes of maintaining fair competition conditions in the market; see C Koenig, 'An Economic Analysis of the Single Economic Entity Doctrine in EU Competition Law' (2017) 13 *Journal of Competition Law & Economics* 281.

[57] To deal with such complex cross-border legal issues and relationships, international law applies domestic legal standards on corporate form designed to govern territorially the corporate person as an individual entity detached from the collective of entities that make a corporate group; Exceptions

The corporate form allows transnational businesses to compartmentalise liabilities by confining liabilities to various subsidiaries located in host states. Where these subsidiaries are left underfunded by the parent company to meet their obligations, the risk of loss is shifted to creditors.[58] By investing through locally incorporated corporate entities in various host states, the investor, which is also likely to be a corporation, can shield itself from liability for harms inflicted in the host state on employees, local communities and the environment. Corporate legal form also facilitates corporate groups to organise their structure to pay the least amount of tax, be subject to the weakest compliance standards and the most advantageous investment protection treaties.[59] The ability of corporations to create countless subsidiary corporations facilitate liabilities to be dissipated further, using combinations of shell corporations located in various offshore and onshore jurisdictions. This territorially and organisationally fragmented legal framework governing the constitutive parts of an MNE provide the loopholes for international investors enabling them to avoid, minimise and shift away risks.[60] The units within an MNE are treated as insulated for purposes of assigning liabilities, but this insulation can be waived or adjusted for sharing and increasing benefits accruing among the parts of the MNE structure. The ability to manipulate risk allocation in this way within an MNE is conducive to investors taking higher risks, intentionally or recklessly.[61]

At the same time, IIL has departed from treating the shareholder (investor) and the corporation (host state entity) separately to protect investors more effectively, recognising the complexities of transnational business enterprises.[62] It allows benefits of IIL to be invoked by any corporation located in the upstream ownership

to territorial application can be found in bribery laws of some countries (for example, the Bribery Act 2010 (UK), c 23, *Foreign Corrupt Practices Act*, 15 USC § 18dd-1).

[58] P Ireland, 'Limited Liability, Shareholder Rights, and the Problem of Corporate Irresponsibility' (2010) 34 *Cambridge Journal of Economics* 837 (describes the corporate legal form as a 'construct that institutionalizes corporate irresponsibility'); H Glasbeek, 'The Corporation as Legally Constructed Site of Irresponsibility' in H Pontell and G Geis (eds), *The International Handbook of White-Collar and Corporate Crime* (Springer, 2010); Pistor (n 6) 59.

[59] Pistor (n 6) 47 ('Corporate Law … can be employed to parcel assets and operations of an integrated economic entity that reduce information costs, thereby lowering the cost of debt finance and minimizing taxes, even regulatory costs').

[60] For an analysis of a different type of risk avoidance by utilising the corporate form with adverse social impacts, see L Talbot, 'Trying to Save the World With Company Law? Some Problems' (2016) 36 *Legal Studies* 513, 519 (explains that another path of risk avoidance for investors in modern capitalism (not the focus of this paper) is the diverting away of investments in productive businesses which have low returns and high risks, and instead channelling investments in financial commodities which bring higher and quicker returns).

[61] Talbot (ibid) 520 (this is analogous to the early uses of limited liability companies that were 'confined to new speculative business with high rates of attrition that sought the protection of limited liability in the expectation of failure').

[62] A Yilmaz Vastardis and R Chambers, 'Overcoming the Corporate Veil Challenge: Could Investment Law Inspire the Proposed Business and Human Rights Treaty?' (2018) 67 *International & Comparative Law Quarterly* 389.

structure of the host state entity.[63] Yet, states have been reluctant to recognise the complexities of transnational business enterprises to regulate investor obligations in international law. An individual or community harmed by the activities of the host state entity is unable to seek remedies from the parent company (investor) when the host state entity lacks the funds to compensate the losses.[64] With domestic legal systems in the host and home states of the investor embracing the principles of separate personality and limited liability as touchstones of business regulation, the risk of irresponsible business conduct passes onto the society to absorb. In other words, the cards are stacked in favour of the investor in both corporate law and in IIL. This is an example of what Tan describes as 'global governance that can and do sustain and perpetuate global economic and geopolitical asymmetries and social hierarchies'.[65]

It is possible to see a shortage of effective legal means available for holding foreign investors accountable for human rights and environmental impacts. Some accountability mechanisms for adverse human rights and environmental impacts of business are available at the national level via civil liability and regulation on the environment, health, etc, but in practice the successful enforcement of these mechanisms rely on the extent to which the risk-mitigating factors in embedded in IIL and corporate law can be pushed back.[66] At the international level, substantive human rights and environmental standards only have theoretical application to international investor conduct, without concrete means to operationalise these theoretical possibilities.[67] The combination of international rights for investors with the limited success of local communities in deploying domestic laws for holding investors accountable and the absence of international accountability mechanisms for human rights and environmental harms inflicted by investors, all create a legal grey zone in which international investors often escape accountability, and even be rewarded despite the damage their business inflicts on communities and the ecosystem.[68]

[63] For instance, IIL has in some cases recognised the influence of the identity of a corporate investor's shareholders to the identity of the corporation, and in other similar cases, it has refused to look behind the corporate veil to take into consideration the shareholders' identity. The only commonality between the two approaches in IIL is that both has resulted in the protection of the investor: see on this, Yilmaz Vastardis and Chambers, 'Overcoming the Corporate Veil Challenge' (2018).

[64] Vastardis and Chambers (n 62) 397.

[65] Tan (n 14) 15.

[66] A good example of this problem can be seen from the string of litigation and arbitration that arose from Chevron's operations in Ecuador: see L Pellegrini et al, 'International Investment Agreements' (2020); Vastardis and Chambers (n 62) 407–11.

[67] Yet, there is every reason to believe, as Pereira de Andrade and Monebhurrun argue in ch 11 of this volume, that the process of extracting investor environmental obligations from international environmental law, investment treaties, international arbitral practice and investment contracts may slowly attune business culture to the social dimension of investor conduct.

[68] For example, *Chevron Corporation and Texaco Petroleum Corporation v The Republic of Ecuador*, UNCITRAL, PCA Case No 2009-23; *Bear Creek Mining Corporation v Republic of Peru*, ICSID Case No ARB/14/21; Crystallex *International Corporation v Bolivarian Republic of Venezuela*, ICSID Case No ARB(AF)/11/2.

A crucial aspect of the laws protecting foreign investment is the interpretation of the legal standards by courts and arbitral tribunals. It is possible to notice that in interpreting investment treaty standards and the rules on corporate personality, courts and tribunals put great emphasis on the risk mitigation rationale of these standards.[69] The risk mitigation rationale is invoked to justify interpretations of standards as if the ultimate and sole objective of IIL and corporate legal form is the protection and promotion of cross-border economic activity. Often, investment treaty standards and corporate personality rules are applied without adjustments in the social and environmental policy contexts, unless their application can be withheld due to extremely abusive investor conduct such as complicity in abuses of *jus cogens* norms[70] or fraudulent behaviour.[71] Yet, the same rules are readily adjusted to further market goals. IIL provides a good example of this in its treatment of the corporate legal form. To the extent that it protects the investor, IIL allows adjustments to be made to the corporate legal form to look behind the corporate veil and identify a 'protected investor'. Yet, when looking behind the veil is requested to hold investors liable for human rights harm, the adjustments are rarely allowed.[72]

I will demonstrate in sections III and IV that while the immediate function of the rules on foreign investments and their risk mitigation features is to facilitate economic activity and achieve economic growth, economic growth itself is merely a means to an end. Economic growth is not the ultimate goal of the legal framework governing foreign investments. The risk mitigation features of these standards find their justification in the promise of the contribution investments will make to the enhancement of welfare and well-being of society. The facilitation of economic activity and growth is often promoted at policy level to increase the welfare and well-being of society. In theory, economic activity and growth are a means to an end. But in practice, economic activity is often invoked or treated as an end in itself. IIL is a prime example of this phenomenon, whereby increased investment flows, in treaty preambles, are described as a means to increase prosperity, but it is common to see arbitral awards interpreting investment treaty standards as if the increased level of investments is an end in itself. If we situate economic activity

[69] M Waibel, 'International Investment Law and Treaty Interpretation' in R Hofmann and CJ Tams (eds), *International Investment Law and General International Law – From Clinical Isolation to Systemic Integration?* (Nomos, 2011) 30 (identifies a pattern and reviews IIL cases that place an excessive reliance on the object and purpose of the investment treaties to protect investments).

[70] See, for example, *Phoenix Action Ltd v The Czech Republic*, ICSID Case No ARB/06/5, Award (15 April 2009), para 78 (the tribunal stated that IIL texts cannot be read in isolation from general international law and stated that limits to the protection of ICSID can be curtailed if an investment is 'made in violation of the most fundamental rules of protection of human rights, like investments made in pursuance of torture or genocide or in support of slavery or trafficking of human organs').

[71] See on exceptions to the corporate veil standard: *Tokios Tokeles v Ukraine*, ICSID Case No ARB/02/18, Decision on Jurisdiction (29 April 2004) paras 54–55 (refers to the *Barcelona Traction* ruling that only situations of fraud, malfeasance or evasion of legal obligations could justify looking behind the corporate veil). See also *David Brian Chandler v Cape Plc* [2011] EWHC 951, paras 66–68.

[72] Vastardis and Chambers (n 62).

and growth as a 'pathway'[73] to improve the welfare and well-being of the society at large, it is possible to find the space within the existing standards of foreign investment protection to be able to restrict the risk mitigation features of both the corporate form and IIL to the extent their use undermines the welfare and well-being of society. One way of translating the welfare and well-being of society into legal terms and re-embedding into the framework of foreign investment governance is to introduce rights-based limitations, which capture both human rights and environmental rights, to the risk paradigm.[74] This approach can alleviate the skewed design of the legal framework in the short term, without having to alter the letter of the law itself.

III. A Closer Look at IIL and Corporate Legal Form as Facilitators of Risk-Taking

Muchlinski observes that 'economic globalisation contains a built-in "bias" in favour of liberalised national economic policies and pro-investor approaches to international business regulation, such as the conclusion of BITs'.[75] IIL and the corporate legal form are among the key tools of this model of economic globalisation. They both fulfil a risk allocation function crucial to the biased model of globalisation.

The corporate legal form insulates the individual or corporate investors from the risk of liability in excess of their initial contribution to the corporation's capital. Investors need not be concerned about having to remedy the wrongdoings of the corporation or to bear losses arising from the failure of the business with their personal wealth. This security provided to investors by the corporate legal form renders what might otherwise be considered excessive risk-taking, such as

[73] Tan (n 14) 21; C Gammage, 'Protecting Human Rights in the Context of Free Trade? The case of the SADC Group Economic Partnership Agreement' (2014) 20 *European Law Journal* 779 ('It is often assumed that, in theory, at least, economic growth and increased foreign direct investment will have a positive impact on human rights standards'); P Muchlinski, 'Holistic Approaches to Development and International Investment Law: The Role of International Investment Agreements' in J Faundez and C Tan (eds), *International Economic Law, Globalization and Developing Countries* (Edward Elgar Publishing, 2010).

[74] Welfare and well-being – also captured by 'development', but the rights-based approach adopted in this paper captures poverty and labour from the lens of economic and social rights; See Tan (n 14) 22 (explains that development is often a proxy for incorporating non-economic values and interests that is insufficiently captured within the traditional ontological lens of IEL, such as poverty, environment, labour and human rights); see also D Alessandrini, S Jivraj and A Zokaiyte, 'Exploring Well-Being and Gross National Happiness in Sustainable Development Policy Making' (2015) 7 *Indian Journal of International Economic Law* 52, 53 ('studies on WBH [well-being and happiness] have been on the agenda of international bodies for quite some time, we see the post-2007 proliferation and transnational convergence of well-being initiatives, particularly those aimed at measuring well-being through indicators, as potentially replacing the development discourse of the post-war period in terms of normative force').

[75] P Muchlinski, *Multinational Enterprises and the Law*, 2nd edn (Oxford University Press, 2007) 89.

investing in a business venture that carries a high risk of adverse social and environmental impact, mildly risky for the individual or corporate shareholders.[76] The risk mitigation features of the corporation have been justified as 'the price of securing efficient capital financing for corporations'.[77]

In a cross-border setting, IIL works in a similar manner minimising the so-called 'political risk'[78] to investors by setting substantive standards of treatment and a delocalised dispute settlement mechanism to secure remedies when substantive standards are breached. With risk-taking made less risky, it is believed that an increasing number of investments will flow across borders and the recipient states will receive economic and even welfare and rule of law benefits from the incoming investments.[79]

Both aspects of the legal framework protecting foreign investment are theoretically expected to provide win-win outcomes whereby the growth in the number of investments enabled by risk mitigation leads to economic growth resulting in economic development and increased welfare.[80] Such economic development is expected to benefit the whole society including investors and their employees, as well as the communities around the business who benefit from increased opportunities, better products and services, and the wider society benefitting indirectly from the taxes and royalties paid by the investor to the host state. While this scenario may materialise, experience and evidence shows that there are many other complex factors influencing the economic and social development of any society.[81] Nevertheless, recognising international investment protection and the corporate legal form, as contributors to development and overall well-being, may provide a justification for reorienting the risk paradigm embedded in the code of foreign investment, and thus create the space within IIL to introduce preconditions to investors benefitting from the risk mitigation features of IIL and corporate legal form within IIL. Before moving on to the discussion of this reconfiguration in section IV, I will provide an overview of the risk allocation rationales posited at the early days of the corporation's history and IIL's gradual development. Even though IIL and the corporate legal form are often posited as necessities for the

[76] H Hansmann and R Kraakman, 'Toward Unlimited Shareholder Liability for Corporate Torts' (1991) 100 *Yale Law Journal* 1879.

[77] ibid.

[78] JW Yackee, 'Political Risk and International Investment Law' (2014) 24 *Duke Journal of Comparative & International Law* 477, 491; G Gertz, S Jandhyala and L Poulsen, 'Legalization, Diplomacy, and Development: Do Investment Treaties De-politicize Investment Disputes?' (2018) 107 *World Development* 239.

[79] For a detailed critique of the good governance function of IIL, see M Sattorova, *The Impact of Investment Treaty Law on Host States: Enabling Good Governance?* (Hart Publishing, 2018).

[80] Alessandrini, Jivraj and Zokaiyte, 'Exploring Well-Being' (2015) 59.

[81] ibid (discusses factors which influence well-being as indicators of development. Among the alternative approaches to the neoclassical economics approach to well-being and development that focuses on income, 'a set of indicators such as health, education, and infant mortality introduced the so-called objective list approach to well-being, which focuses on monitoring the basic needs and rights of the citizens which are essential to enable them to build their capabilities and flourish as individuals').

efficient functioning of the global market and economic growth, an overview of their evolution and current interpretations readily exposes that they are not, in their current form, necessities of a well-functioning market. Their excessive risk avoidance features promote and enable irresponsible business behaviour, cushioning investors not only from the consequences of market failings but also from the consequences of their own irresponsible business decisions.

A. From Partnerships to Corporate Groups: Insulation of Capital from Risk

Businesses without limited liability or full separate personality[82] had been the dominant form for conducting business prior to the corporate form becoming freely accessible to all private businesses in the nineteenth century. In fact, one author has explained that the industrial revolution in Britain took place on the shoulders of partnerships without a dominant corporate presence.[83] Partnerships then and today operate based on trust and accountability. The partners are actively engaged in the business, and have a close working relationship, joint and several unlimited liability, joint asset ownership and the ability to legally bind each other as agents.[84] As such, risk-taking requires very careful consideration.[85]

The corporation operates in a completely different way. The shareholders of a corporation are legally distanced from the corporation. They cannot bind the corporation, do not own its assets, and have limited liability; management is largely separated from ownership and shares are freely transferable.[86] Shareholders are typically only interested in the financial returns, and do not need to actively participate in running the business. As such, the corporation is 'not only for productive activity, but also for rentier investment'.[87] With these features, the corporation does not rely on trust and accountability to operate efficiently. Within such a structure, risky investment can be ventured into more hastily.[88]

[82] For example, sole traders or partnerships.

[83] Ireland, 'Limited Liability' (2010) 839; See also Talbot, 'Trying to Save the World With Company Law? (2016) 520.

[84] P Ireland, 'The Corporation and the New Aristocracy of Finance' in JP Robe, A Lyon-Caen and S Vernac (eds), *Multinationals and the Constitutionalization of the World Power System* (Routledge, 2016) 63.

[85] Talbot (n 60) 520.

[86] Pistor (n 6) 55 (labels these features as enablers of entity shielding and loss shifting).

[87] Ireland, 'The Corporation and the New Aristocracy' (2016) 63. See also Talbot (n 60) 521–22; Pistor (n 6) 47 ('corporate law is increasingly used to maximize financial gains …; it is no longer primarily a legal vehicle for producing goods or offering services but has been transformed into a virtual capital mint').

[88] Pistor (n 6) 51 and 65 (explains the failure of Lehman Brothers in 2008 by the presence of 'too much debt piled on a legal structure [the corporate group] that promised more than it could possibly hold').

The modern corporate form took its current shape incrementally over two centuries. According to Ireland, the emergence of the modern corporate form is owed to the interests of the financial class appearing as rentier investors in the industrial world.[89] In its early years, the corporate legal form that we today consider 'standard' was not welcomed with open arms.[90] The legal community raised serious concerns about how transition from partnerships to limited liability particularly would promote an irresponsible and reckless business climate.[91] The former was owned and directly run by partners who were liable for the losses of the business collectively and as well as benefitting from the successes collectively. Limited liability reversed the risk allocation and the control structures,[92] by shifting the risks of losses ultimately to creditors (voluntary and involuntary) and detaching the ownership from management of the business.[93] Some have considered such a legal intervention to risk allocation contrary to the 'free' market.[94] Limited liability was considered an 'ousting' of the market which 'isolate[es] investors from the full range of market influences' and cocoons them from 'the most fundamental market pressure, fear of personal bankruptcy'.[95] But eventually, it embedded itself firmly into all jurisdictions around the globe, being accepted as a necessity of economic growth and prosperity in a modern economy.

Though the emergence of the modern corporation may be owed to the rentier investment model, all shareholders – rentier or managing – are shielded by the corporation.[96] The shift to the modern corporation from the partnership model gave rise to the transformation of the share from a tool of ownership representing an equitable interest in the company's assets to a property in its own right which gives its owner a right to receive dividends.[97] As shares transformed in this way into property, the market for their sale in the stock exchange developed and expanded. After these changes, share owners were able to gain revenues not only from the company's successful ventures, but also from the trading of the shares themselves.

[89] Ireland (n 84) 63.

[90] Adam Smith in *The Wealth of Nations* considered limited liability a departure from the self-regulation of the free markets, less efficient from an economic viewpoint and a recipe for negligence. See further, Adam Smith on limited liability and the corporation: limited liability should only be available when certain conditions are met, otherwise the corporation would be characterised by negligence and profusion – less efficient than partnerships, etc; Pistor (n 6) 60–61.

[91] E Cox, *The Law and Practice of Joint Stock Companies* (Law Times Office, 1856) i–ii.

[92] Limited liability received statutory recognition in Britain with the *Limited Liability Act 1855* 18 & 19 Vict c 133).

[93] Ireland (n 58) 845.

[94] Most well-known objection was made by Adam Smith, See A Smith, *An Inquiry into the Nature and Causes of Wealth of Nations 1776* (Modern Library, 2000), Book V, Ch I.

[95] D Campbell and S Griffin, 'Enron and the End of Corporate Governance?' in S MacLeod (ed), *Global Governance and the Quest for Justice: Volume II Corporate Governance* (Hart Publishing, 2006).

[96] Talbot (n 60) 523.

[97] P Ireland, 'Capitalism Without the Capitalist: The Joint Stock Company Share and the Emergence of the Modern Doctrine of Separate Corporate Personality' (1996) 17 *Journal of Legal History* 41, 48–49 (explains that in early joint stock companies the number of shares were fixed and the needs of capital increase would not be satisfied by issuance of new shares, but by increasing the value of the existing shares).

These changes allowed companies to raise capital from a much larger audience, which for instance accelerated the construction of railways in nineteenth-century Britain.[98] According to Ireland, this shift towards the development of the modern corporate legal form was owed to political choices which aimed to 'accommodate and protect the *rentier* investor' more than they were owed to the economic rationales and needs.[99] He argues that 'The corporate legal form as presently constituted is not an economic necessity but a political construct developed to further the interests of particular groups'.[100]

The political choices cannot be viewed in isolation from the economic rationales. Prior to the shift from partnerships to corporations, the corporate status and limited liability were granted by the state only for large-scale investments such as those conducted by overseas trading companies. As finance capitalism took hold, the number of larger businesses grew with the emergence of a financial sector, which invested in businesses as silent partners. In such cases, the active partners who were directly running the business were joined by silent partners who would later outnumber the former type of partner. Silent partners were after a return to their investment and not involved in management. Nevertheless, they ran the risk of personal loss from the business's failure at amounts much larger than their investment.[101] The corporate legal form that developed over time eliminated such an eventuality, and thus externalised the risk of failure to voluntary and involuntary creditors, or indirectly to taxpayers (via bailouts),[102] including for the risks of liability arising from human rights and environmental harms.

BHR discourse has so far not been able to overcome the protective shields for investors erected by the legal framework governing foreign investment. While corporate legal form lowers transaction costs for creditors of the corporation by providing legal security that the assets of the corporation are not to be mixed with its owners and prioritising debts to direct creditors of the corporation, growth of corporate groups actually renders it more challenging for creditors to monitor the financial wellbeing of a corporation.[103] Growth of corporate groups and MNEs

[98] ibid 66.

[99] Ireland (n 58) 848; Pistor (n 6) 61 (refers to 'evidence that investments even on the scale required during the process of industrialization are possible without granting shareholders limited liability').

[100] Ireland (n 58) 838; Pistor (n 6) 50 (explains that Lehman Brothers 'had survived in the much more vulnerable legal form of a partnership for more than 130 years (from 1850 to 1983), a period that witnessed the transformation of America from an agricultural into the leading industrial nation, as well as the Civil War, two world wars, several major financial crises, and more than one overhaul of the monetary system in the United States and globally').

[101] D Campbell, 'Marxism, the Market and Corporate Responsibility: A Comment on Paddy Ireland' (2010) 31 *Adelaide Law Review* 229, 231 (in such cases, Campbell explains, 'given the typical size of large companies' working indebtedness, unlimited liability would mean that those investing in large public companies would be exposed to, precisely, a liability which is unlimited in the sense that it is far beyond their ability to absorb it, and they would be loath to invest on this basis').

[102] Prior to the rise of limited liability, investors used other contractual methods to limit their liability, but this was harder to obtain.

[103] Pistor (n 6) 59 ('legal partitioning of assets of an economically fully integrated business organization only pretends to make creditors more secure, when in fact it renders a firm's total debt more opaque and more difficult to monitor for creditors and the parent company alike').

enabled by the legal principle allowing corporations to hold shares in other corporations enhanced the protection from risk for investors even further. As Pistor explains:

> Increasingly, … the corporate form is used to partition assets of the same firm into select asset pools, including receivables for certain types of claims that are shielded from the rest of its operations, with the result that a single firm may comprise of dozens, if not hundreds of legal shells.[104]

Despite all the dangers inherent in it, the immunisation of the shareholders and directors from liability, their legal detachment from the corporation and ability of corporations to be shareholders were, and are still, considered indispensable for growth and progress in our free market economy.[105] It incentivises the risk of pouring resources into businesses by limiting the loss which may result from failure to the amount invested into the company.[106] Today, the risk-takers are not only large financiers or owners of wealth, though they may receive the largest returns, but it also includes ordinary persons who are rentier investors via their pension funds, mortgages or savings.[107] The interests protected by the corporate legal form are so significant that it is considered scandalous to remove or even temper the barrier of corporate personality to hold shareholders liable for the wrongs of the corporation. This first layer of risk mitigation privileges afforded to investors by the corporate form is strengthened further with the risk mitigation features of international investment law.

B. IIL as an Additional Layer of Insulation from Risk for Foreign Investors

IIL originated in the unilateral economic interests of the capital exporting nations and their businesses operating in economically less powerful states.[108] Mitigation of political risk in developing states has been declared among the

[104] ibid 52.

[105] Campbell, 'Marxism, the Market and Corporate Responsibility' (2010) 231.

[106] Ireland (n 58) 844 ('Limited liability, its advocates argued, would not only encourage investment but encourage the creation of outlets for investment – there were frequent references to the abundance of unused capital – for the benefit of the country as a whole'); Pistor (n 6) 48 ('most lawyers agree with economists that the corporate form enhances efficient use of scarce resources by encouraging risk-taking, by broadening the investor base and thereby mobilizing funding for investments, and by creating conditions for deep and liquid markets for the shares and bonds that the corporation issues').

[107] Campbell (n 101) fn 5; Ireland also describes how from the 19th century shares became a device of savings and investment to ordinary citizens, but their investments were too small a portion of the market. Today, pension funds hold significant holdings; see Ireland (n 58).

[108] M Sornarajah, *The Pursuit of Nationalized Property* (Martinus Nijhoff, 1986) 3; See also K Miles, 'International Investment Law: Origins, Imperialism and Conceptualizing the Environment' (2010) 21 *Colorado Journal of International Environmental Law and Policy* 1.

foremost reasons for the promotion of IIL instruments.[109] Though the dichotomy of capital exporting/importing states has recently been losing its longstanding hold on IIL due to increasing flows of capital to and from new directions,[110] the law's defining ideology remains the same. Throughout its evolution, IIL has developed with the single focus of risk mitigation for investors, even if they knowingly invest in politically and/or economically unstable countries or business ventures, without taking due consideration of the rights of host communities and regulatory space of host states.[111] Investment treaty standards offer legal protection, primarily in the form of damages awards, against a wide range of changes in the operating context of the investment that are detrimental to the profits of the investor. Investors have been awarded compensation for losses resulting from direct expropriation of the investor's investment without compensation and due process; cancellation of exploration or operation permits for protection of the environment and indigenous people, changes in regulatory standards in response to financial crises, cancellation of contracts or licences for the investor's own poor business conduct.[112] Investors have not always been successful in claims that arose from the impact of regulatory reform in the public interest or termination of permits/contracts in the interests of protecting human rights and the environment.[113] The risks from which investors are shielded under IIL are extensive. When one views this in conjunction with the lack of explicit investor obligations in treaties that relate to the conduct of the investor vis-à-vis host communities and the environment, it becomes apparent that the legal standards explicitly support the investor and ignore other interests.

Only in the last decade have states begun taking the rights of host communities into account in their investment treaty practice, but progress has been very slow.[114] These 'non-economic' concerns must continuously justify themselves

[109] Yackee, 'Political Risk' (2014) 491; Gertz, Jandhyala and Poulsen, 'Legalization, Diplomacy, and Development' (2018).

[110] For instance, the US is one of the world's largest foreign direct investment recipients as well as the largest source of investment according to the 'World Investment Report 2004: The Shift Towards Services' UN Conference on Trade and Development (New York July, 2004) xix, available at unctad.org/system/files/official-document/wir2004_en.pdf. UNCTAD also found an increasing trend of conclusion of investment protection treaties among developing nations: see UNCTAD, 'South–South Cooperation in International Investment Arrangements' (UNCTAD Series on International Investment Policies for Development United Nations, 13 October 2005), available at unctad.org/system/files/official-document/iteiit20053_en.pdf.

[111] See, KP Sauvant and JE Alvarez, 'International Investment Law in Transition' in KP Sauvant et al (eds), *The Evolving International Investment Regime* (Oxford University Press, 2011) xxxi.

[112] *Bear Creek Mining Corporation v Republic of Peru*, ICSID Case No ARB/14/21, *South American Silver Limited v The Plurinational State of Bolivia*, PCA Case No 2013-15, *Clayton and Bilcon of Delaware Inc v Government of Canada*, PCA Case No. 2009-04, *Copper Mesa Mining Corporation v Republic of Ecuador*, PCA No 2012-2; *Técnicas Medioambientales Tecmed v United Mexican States*, ICSID Case No ARB(AF)/00/2.

[113] See, for example, *Philip Morris Brand Sàrl (Switzerland), Philip Morris Products SA (Switzerland) and Abal Hermanos SA (Uruguay) v Oriental Republic of Uruguay*, ICSID Case No ARB/10/7.

[114] From NGOs, IISD, IIED and SOMO are actively engaged in both processes; a few academic experts bridging the gap include Professor Surya Deva and Dr Tara Van Ho.

as legitimate restrictions of investor rights embodying risk mitigation.[115] When the rights of host communities find their way into an investment treaty, they are usually expressed in watered down language as a result of the compromises made during negotiations.[116] With a few exceptions,[117] this new generation of investment treaties typically encourages the parties to strive to promote sustainable development and socially responsible business behaviour,[118] rather than explicitly requiring investors to act in accordance with environmental and human rights standards. Even the states which ostensibly desire to curb the interference of IIL with their regulatory space[119] continue to sign similar unbalanced treaties because, with some improvements, despite lack of conclusive evidence that BITs increase inward investment, it may be seen as a competitive disadvantage not to sign them.[120] Similarly, the idea of 'investor obligations' in investment treaties are often framed as a competitive disadvantage that would deter investments into the host state.[121]

Skewed legal standards on foreign investment are also reflected in the way arbitral tribunals interpret investment treaty provisions to determine whether a compensable loss was incurred by the investor as a result of host state conduct. Arbitral tribunals typically note the lack of explicit terms in investment treaties on investor obligations and the limited scope of their jurisdiction to determine investment treaty breaches by the host state.[122] The extent to which human rights of communities and environmental rights have (not) been considered in investment treaty awards has been analysed in detail in academic literature and civil society reports.[123] These were outlined in section II above. In this chapter, I offer a reframing of the problem by focusing on the risk paradigm embedded at the heart of IIL with a view to finding an opening within existing standards to operationalise the interests of communities and the environment within the legal frameworks governing foreign investment. As established in section II, IIL aims to secure investors' legally enforceable and broadly formulated commitments from host states via International Investment Agreements (IIA) in order to

[115] A Orford, 'Beyond Harmonization: Trade, Human Rights and the Economy of Sacrifice' (2005) 18 *Leiden Journal of International Law* 179.

[116] See, for example, Art 12 of Argentina–Qatar BIT (signed 6 November 2016, not yet in force), which states that investors 'should make efforts to voluntarily incorporate internationally recognized standards of [CSR] into their business policies and practices'.

[117] Morocco–Nigeria BIT, Art 18.

[118] See CETA, Art 22.3.

[119] Such as Argentina, India and Pakistan.

[120] See Z Elkin, A Guzman and BA Simmons, 'Competing for Capital: the Diffusion of Bilateral Investment Treaties, 1960–2000' (2006) 60 *International Organization* 811–46.

[121] A fuller discussion on the appearance and framing of investor obligations in investment treaties can be found in ch 5 (Ranjan) of this volume.

[122] *Rompetrol Group NV v Romania*, ICSID Case No ARB/06/3, Award (6 May 2013), paras 170–72; *Impregilo SpA v Argentine Republic*, ICSID Case No ARB/07/17, Concurring and Dissenting Opinion of Professor Brigitte Stern (21 June 2011), para 53f.

[123] See above nn 11, 18 and 23.

mitigate the risk of loss for the investor. The risk mitigation rationale appears most prominently within IIL from the frequent reliance by investors on the fair and equitable treatment (FET) standard and its interpretation by arbitral tribunals as a catch-all standard, especially when legitimate expectations of the investor is used as a measure for determining breach of FET.[124] Since investment treaties typically contain standards that are general and brief, their application in individual disputes require significant input from arbitrators who often justify their interpretations by referring to the goal of 'increasing investment flows'.[125] Here, it is not only the IIL legal texts that carry this built-in bias. Arbitral tribunals interpreting them often invoke the risk mitigation rationale when applying the standards. The result of this wide margin of interpretation within a biased system of law is that IIL safeguards investments against a lot more than just political risk.

IIL has been interpreted as requiring host states to shield investors from risk without recognition of the competing obligations of the host state to also protect the interests and rights of other groups in the society. A tribunal noted in a case arising from the Argentina financial crisis that states should uphold both their human rights obligations and their IIL obligations.[126] Indeed, states should in principle uphold all their international obligations, but when this approach is followed in the IIL context it leads to a de facto prioritisation of the investor rights. This is an outcome of the skewed legal frameworks on foreign investment that shields investors from risk but does not offer adequate coding strategies to protect communities and the environment on par with the investors, neither within the IIL framework, nor outside of it as an independent mechanism under BHR. While international human rights law does offer a recourse for communities to enforce their human rights vis-à-vis the host state when the latter fails to protect against impacts of businesses, the wheels of justice turn much slower in enforcing human rights claims.[127] In the aftermath of the Argentina financial crisis, the law on foreign investment translated into shifting the investors' risks of loss caused by the impact of the financial crisis over to the host state communities to absorb. Under the existing legal framework for foreign investment protection, the host state is de facto expected to channel its available resources to first remediating the investor rather than to realising its human rights obligations to its citizens and residents.

[124] See Davitti (n 10) 55.

[125] See, for example, *Guaracachi America, Inc and Rurelec PLC v The Plurinational State of Bolivia*, UNCITRAL, PCA Case No 2011-17, Award (31 January 2014), para 353.

[126] *Suez, Sociedad General de Aguas de Barcelona, SA and Vivendi Universal, SA (formerly Aguas Argentinas, SA, Suez, Sociedad General de Aguas de Barcelona, SA and Vivendi Universal, SA) v Argentine Republic (II)*, ICSID Case No ARB/03/19, Decision on Responsibility (28 July 2010), para 262.

[127] S Joseph, *Blame it on the WTO? A Human Rights Critique* (Oxford University Press, 2011) 50–51; A Yilmaz Vastardis, 'Investment Treaty Arbitration as Justice Bubbles for the Privileged' in T Schultz and F Ortino (eds), *The Oxford Handbook of International Arbitration* (Oxford University Press, 2020).

IV. IIL and Corporate Legal Form as a Means to an End: A Human Rights Based Approach to Risk in Foreign Investment Governance

The legal frameworks protecting foreign investment shields investors from risk without distinguishing the nature of the risks taken by the investor or the types of harms suffered by external actors when shifting the risks of loss and injury onto them, unless the risk-taker is acting with fraudulent or criminal intent.[128] The beneficiaries of an investment made using corporate vehicles and benefitting from IIL protection are not only mitigating the risks of unsuccessful business deals or political turmoil; they are also protected from the failings of the market and consequences of their own harmful impacts on the rights of host communities and the environment through the use of the corporate veil and limited liability.[129] It is notable that in the context of IIL, even when the investor's own irresponsible behaviour impacting human rights and environmental rights gave rise or contributed to an investment treaty dispute, those elements of the investor's behaviour are often made invisible within investment dispute resolution.[130] In cases where tribunals explicitly acknowledge and recount the events relating to the irresponsible behaviour, often these have little or no bearing on the resolution of the dispute. Perrone notes that local communities have neither rights nor remedies within the system to have their grievances acknowledged and repaired. Not only do they lack the means to secure rights directly, but even in cases where the state raises human rights or environmental protection as a defence, such arguments only receive a limited acknowledgement by arbitral tribunals and often do not impact the outcome of the dispute.[131]

One explanation for the blindness of IIA to investment operations' detrimental impacts on third parties and overprotection of investors is the regime's exclusive focus on state responsibility.[132] But the focus on state responsibility alone does not explain the 'overprotection' logic. The equal treatment of different types of risk points to a built-in bias in the legal standards offering protection from risks that

[128] For instance, legal grounds for piercing the corporate veil in most jurisdictions often require members of the company to be acting with fraudulent intent when creating the corporation. See on the corporate veil, K Vandekerckhove, *Piercing the Corporate Veil* (Kluwer Law International, 2007).

[129] This is not to say that the investor will not incur any losses itself, but rather, the losses are mitigated to a lesser or a greater extent depending on the combination of coding strategies used. While the coding strategies shield the investor from losses, these do not evaporate into thin air. Rather, they are shifted onto the creditors or the taxpayer.

[130] N Perrone, 'The "Invisible" Local Communities: Foreign Investor Obligations, Inclusiveness, and the International Investment Regime' (2019) 113 *American Journal of International Law Unbound* 16, 16 (explains that IIA treats local communities as an absent actor).

[131] *Suez and Vivendi v Argentina*, ICSID Case No ARB/03/19, Award (9 April 2015); *EDF International SA, SAUR International SA and León Participaciones Argentinas SA v Argentine Republic*, ICSID Case No ARB/03/23, Award (11 June 2012).

[132] J Gathii and S Puig, 'The introduction to the symposium on investor responsibility: the next frontier in international investment law' (2019) 113 *American Journal of International Law Unbound* 1; Ho (n 18).

prioritise the investor's wealth even where such protection is irreconcilable with the rationale of the risk paradigm embedded into IIL and corporate form. The risk mitigation mechanisms embedded in the IIL and corporate law have been justified 'on their alleged instrumental value in contributing to efficiency, growth and development'.[133] Investment treaty preambles often refer to the welfare-enhancing effects of increasing investment flows as the underlying reason for promoting and protecting foreign investment using the risk mitigation strategies.[134] The standard hypothesis supporting investment liberalisation has been the positive spill-over effects of increased economic activity on the whole society's development.[135] Economic liberalisation policies with their risk avoidance features have also been at the centre of conditionalities or policies set by international finance institutions like the IMF and the World Bank Group, whose stated objectives are to promote high employment and sustainable economic growth, and reduce poverty around the world.[136]

Similarly, the corporate legal form is a tool created by state regulation to increase the volume and scale of economic activity in the marketplace as a means to increased prosperity.[137] Early corporations were viewed as institutions of progress pursuing respectable societal goals. One of the earliest textbooks on corporations describes the corporation as engaged

> in all the varieties of useful pursuit, that we see them directing the concentration of mind and capital to the advancement of religion; to the diffusion of literature, science and the arts; to the prosecution of plans of internal communication and improvement; and to the encouragement and extension of the great interests of commerce, agriculture and manufactures.[138]

In today's economy, corporations 'provide profits without prosperity'.[139]

[133] Ireland (n 58) 852.

[134] For example, the preamble of the Netherlands–Tunisia BIT (signed 23 May 1963, entry into force 19 December 1964): 'Recognizing that the contractual protection of investments is likely to stimulate private economic initiative and increase the prosperity of the two nations'; the preamble of the ASEAN Comprehensive Investment Agreement (signed 26 February 2009, entry into force 24 February 2012): 'Recognising that a conducive investment environment will enhance freer flow of capital, goods and services, technology and human resource and overall economic and social development in ASEAN'.

[135] L Alfaro and J Chauvin, 'Foreign Direct Investment, Finance and Economic Development' in M Spatareanu (ed), *Encyclopedia of International Economics and Global Trade Volume 1: Foreign Direct Investment and the Multinational Enterprise* (World Scientific, 2010) 231–58.

[136] One of the most recent examples of this type of risk shifting is found in The World Bank, 'Guidance on PPP Contractual Provisions' (2017), available at ppp.worldbank.org/public-private-partnership/library/guidance-on-ppp-contractual-provisions-2017-edition, critiqued by H Mann, 'The High Cost of 'De-Risking' Infrastructure Finance' (Project Syndicate, 26 December 2018), available at www.project-syndicate.org/commentary/world-bank-ppp-de-risking-by-howard-mann-2018-12 ('the World Bank's current approach creates moral hazard: the less risk the private party in a PPP assumes, the less it has to lose from poor performance').

[137] Ireland (n 58) 852.

[138] J Angell and S Ames, *Treatise on the Law of Private Corporation Aggregate*, 1st edn (Hilliard, Gray, Little and Wilkins, 1832).

[139] W Lazonick, 'Profits without prosperity' (*Harvard Business Review*, September 2014) 42–55, available at < hbr.org/2014/09/profits-without-prosperity.

If the ultimate objective served by the risk avoidance devices of economic liberalisation is the creation of social and developmental benefits, would it not be justified to restrict the risk privileges of international investors to circumstances when the risks involved undermine the social goals? To do this, I do not propose to assign a social function to corporations or define their formal and immediate purpose as anything other than creating economic benefits.[140] Rather, I suggest that the law should actively intervene when the investor, in pursuing its economic objectives, undermines the social and developmental goals promised by economic liberalisation. Although the law does already intervene in several ways to curb harmful impacts of business on the society and environment, these interventions remain inadequate in their ability to navigate through the grey zones of liability identified in section II above.[141] Pistor argues in this respect that the capital's ability to rule by law is 'dependent on state power yet [has] become dislodged from the social preferences of the citizens of the states that make them'.[142] In this chapter, I argue that the laws protecting foreign investments and their interpretation are not only dislodged from the social preferences of the citizens, but also from the declared justification of these laws themselves to create welfare and prosperity all around.

My argument here is that to effectively navigate through that grey zone, the laws safeguarding foreign investment should move away from their indiscriminate treatment of the risks faced by investors. It is possible to adjust the risk paradigm by removing or reducing certain risk mitigation privileges granted to investors by the corporate legal form and investment treaty standards, where these privileges allow business to avoid human rights and environmental obligations. To establish legal limits to the risk mitigation privileges, I propose considering the respect for and the impact on the full catalogue of human rights and environmental rights as a measure of the economic activity's contribution (or the lack thereof) to well-being and prosperity.[143] With this approach, if a risk mitigation privilege is invoked to avoid the risk of liability from actual or potential harm to human rights or environment, that privilege should be suspended for the purposes of deciding such a claim. A rights-based approach to risk allocation can be embedded in the relevant legal texts, such as investment treaties and domestic and international texts applicable to corporations. This approach can also be adopted by judges and arbitrators when interpreting the legal standards that embody the risk avoidance features.

[140] Baars (n 13) 138–40 (examines throughout the last two centuries the emphasis on the social functions of the corporation after every major corporate crisis as a means to restore its reputation and legitimacy).

[141] I acknowledge here that legal interventions alone cannot tackle global inequalities and adverse social and environmental impacts of business, without changes in the economic and political spheres. But legal interventions can provide important tools to allocate risks more fairly.

[142] Pistor (n 6) 208.

[143] Alessandrini, Jivraj and Zokaiyte (n 74).

As I outlined in section I, there are two strands in the international legal order that focus on foreign investment governance: IIL, which exists as a formal branch of international law to protect investments; and BHR, which may emerge as a formal branch of international law but is to date mostly operationalised through international soft law instruments and domestic litigation. Below I will provide case examples from each strand, embedding the rights-based approach to the risk paradigm dominating the relevant legal standards. The objective is to contextualise the law's approach to risk through these cases.

A. A Rights-based Approach to Risk in Claims against International Investors

One of the primary legal obstacles to international investor accountability for human rights and environmental impacts is the corporate form. Investors organised into MNEs compartmentalise and dissipate liabilities. I will use the *Okpabi v Shell* case[144] to demonstrate how a rights-based approach to risk in interpreting the corporate legal form may provide us with an alternative reading to the one provided in the Court of Appeal's judgment on this case.

The *Okpabi* case concerns a tort claim brought by two Nigerian communities, representing approximately 42,500 individuals, against Royal Dutch Shell (RDS) and its Nigerian subsidiary, Shell Petroleum Development Corporation (SPDC) to remediate the damage suffered by the communities and environment resulting from oil pollution. At the heart of the claim is the question of whether the UK domiciled parent company owes a duty of care to the Nigerian communities who have suffered harm due to the environmental pollution allegedly caused by the SPDC's operations adjacent to the communities. The judgment of the first instance court dealt with the question of whether UK courts can exercise jurisdiction over the claim. The answer to that question is closely tied to the issue of whether there is a real triable issue against the UK parent,[145] and that issue is closely tied to the question of whether the UK parent owes a duty of care to the affected communities.[146] The first instance court and the Court of Appeal held that there was no real triable issue against the UK parent company (and therefore no jurisdiction of UK courts to hear the substance of the claims of damage), as the parent company cannot be held to owe a duty of care to the claimants.

[144] *Okpabi v Royal Dutch Shell Plc* [2018] EWCA Civ 191. This is a domestic litigation which applies English law to determine whether there is an arguable case against the parent company of the Shell group domiciled in London, and whether it owes a duty of care to the Nigerian communities harmed by the environmental devastation caused by the leaks from oil pipelines operated by the Shell subsidiary in Nigeria.

[145] There are other important jurisdictional questions in the case, such as anchor defendants, and the question of access to justice in Nigeria.

[146] *Okpabi v Shell* (n 144) paras 7, 27.

Even though this case did not directly involve an analysis of the corporate form (separate personality or corporate veil), separate personality and limited liability define the viability of these claims. Claimants and their lawyers attempt to side-step the question of corporate veil by framing the legal issue as a direct liability claim under tort of negligence, yet the corporate form sneaks in to undermine the potential success of such investor accountability claims. If it were not for the corporate legal form, we would not be asking whether, or under what conditions, a wholly owning shareholder (ie Royal Dutch Shell (RDS)) of a corporation, (ie Shell Petroleum and Development Corporation (SPDC)) may be liable for the harms inflicted on the communities by the latter. Corporate legal form shifts the consequences of harm away from the shareholders (RDS) exclusively to the corporation (SPDC). If, for any reason (eg, lack of funds, local barriers to justice) the affected persons cannot seek and obtain appropriate remedies from the corporation, the risk of loss remains to be borne by the harmed communities. The argument that, under certain conditions, the shareholder may be directly liable for the harms inflicted by the corporation is an attempt to get around the corporate form. But that attempt is also undermined by the corporate legal form and only succeeds in exceptional circumstances, after a long and protracted legal battle.

The risk mitigation rationale of the corporate legal form is highly relevant to the outcomes of direct liability claims. The Court of Appeal's analysis of the issue was framed around the question of whether the *Okpabi* claim against the shareholder (RDS) was 'bound to fail'.[147] Despite the overwhelming evidence demonstrating the shareholder's role in setting mandatory standards to be followed by the corporation on the health and safety of operations and the mechanisms put in place by the shareholder to monitor compliance of the corporation, the Court of Appeal held that the claim was bound to fail because the claimants were unable to show 'proximity' between the harms they suffered and the shareholder. The claimants' difficulty in convincing the Court to even find that the claim meets the low threshold of not being 'bound to fail' can be explained by the Court's commitment to the corporate legal form when interpreting the notion of 'proximity'. The Court of Appeal set a very high bar to allow the corporate form to be set aside and accept that there is a 'real triable issue' against the shareholder parent company. The risk mitigation function of the corporate form was left intact and the losses were left to remain with the communities.[148]

The existing risk mitigation model benefitting shareholders is applied in the same way regardless of whether the third-party loss results from the corporation's default on a loan or the corporation's failure to comply with safety and environmental standards impacting the human rights of tens of thousands.[149] If, in cases

[147] ibid para 33.

[148] The claimants appealed and the UKSC heard the appeal in June 2020.

[149] The harms complained of in the *Okpabi* claim impact on fundamental rights such as the right to water, right to health and the right to a healthy environment.

such as *Okpabi*, courts apply a rights-based approach to risk mitigation, rather than the current neutral approach, this can transform the interpretation of such concepts as proximity between the parent and the communities, or the question of whether a claim is 'bound to fail'. In *Okpabi*, the claimants presented preponderant evidence demonstrating the standard-setting and supervision by the parent company that its subsidiaries must follow. A neutral approach to risk mitigation tips the balance in favour of the defendants and blocks business accountability for human rights impacts. A rights-based approach to risk would tip the balance, in such a case as *Okpabi*, in favour of the claimants' arguments that the parent must bear its share of liability in the human rights and environmental harms suffered by the communities, especially when it has taken elaborate steps to set the standards of health, safety and security to be followed by its subsidiaries. This could be done by the courts, factoring in the nature of the risk being avoided by the parent company when interpreting the legal concepts pertinent to a duty of care, such as proximity, foreseeability and fairness. Instead of interpreting these concepts in the usual way, courts should assume the presence of proximity and foreseeability to the victims based on the nature of the harm suffered.

The Supreme Court of the United Kingdom (UKSC) took a different approach to the concept of 'real triable issue' in *Vedanta v Lungowe* to claims involving the possibility of a parent company owing a duty of care to the communities harmed by the business of its subsidiary.[150] The UKSC was more willing to temper the risk paradigm where there was prima facie evidence that the parent company had taken steps to intervene in the subsidiary's conduct of the harmful business activity, by setting the standards to be followed by the subsidiary and supervising or monitoring the implementation of these, or at least publicly claiming to do so. While this was a welcome precedent, it still focused on the behaviour of the parent to temper the risk paradigm, rather than doing this on the basis of the nature of the risk the investor is shielded from by shifting the loss to the harmed communities. Here, the essence of the risk paradigm remains alive and kicking. As the UKSC admitted, this was not a special case of parent company liability for harms to communities and did not apply the proximity, foreseeability and fairness standard applied by the *Okpabi* judgment to determine whether the parent owed a duty of care to the affected communities. Rather, the UKSC held that this was merely a case of 'whether A owes a duty of care to C in respect of the harmful activities of B'.[151]

While this approach represents a progress from the *Okpabi* decision, it still remains quite limiting for overcoming the risk paradigm. Instead, the courts should focus on the nature of the risk avoided and the gravity of the harm suffered as a result when determining the parameters of the parent company's insulation from that risk in cases like *Okpabi* and *Vedanta*. To do this, they should depart

[150] *Vedanta Resources Plc and Konkola Copper Mines Plc (Appellants) v Lungowe (Respondents)* [2019] UKSC 20.

[151] ibid para 54.

from the risk mitigation rationale embedded in corporate form when interpreting the jurisdictional and tort law principles applicable in domestic cases seeking investor accountability for human rights and environmental harms. This is necessary to ensure that the risk mitigated by the investor is not one that undermines the very justification of corporate personality to flourish the economy with a view to enhancing well-being of communities.

B. A Rights-based Approach to Risk in Investment Claims against Host States

It is often expressed by IIA tribunals that one of the main reasons why human rights questions cannot be dealt with by an arbitral tribunal established under an investment treaty is the limited scope of the tribunal's jurisdiction.[152] While the limits of the tribunal's competence may restrict its ability to hear and settle claims that fall outside the scope of the investment treaty giving it the powers to exercise jurisdiction, there is no obstacle for international human rights standards to inform the interpretation of investment treaty standards.[153] This argument in itself is not novel.[154] IIA tribunals do refer to human rights standards to inform their interpretation of investment treaty standards[155] or the wrongfulness of the state's behaviour. Rather than unpacking here all types of interactions between IHRL standards and investment treaty standards, I will focus on how international human rights standards impact (and should impact) the extent to which IIL can shield an investor from the risk of loss at the expense of the protection of the affected communities' human rights. The impact on communities' rights may be partially caused by the investor's own obvious failure to respect human rights.[156] In other instances, the detrimental impact on human rights may not be attributable to the investor's behaviour per se, but to the host state's prioritisation of investor rights under investment treaties, thus shifting the risk of loss to be entirely or largely borne by the communities. To unpack the latter example, I will explore the tribunal's approach to the host state's human rights defences in *EDF International v Argentina*.[157]

[152] See, for example, *Rompetrol Group NV v Romania*, ICSID Case No ARB/06/3, Award (6 May 2013) paras 170–72; *Impregilo SpA v Argentine Republic*, ICSID Case No ARB/07/17, Concurring and Dissenting Opinion of Professor Brigitte Stern (21 June 2011) para 53f.

[153] E de Brabandere, 'Human Rights Counterclaims in Investment Treaty Arbitration' (2017) 50 *Revue Belge de Droit International* 591. If the tribunal is constituted under the ICSID Convention (adopted 18 March 1965, entered into force 14 October 1966) 575 UNTS 159, see Art 42.

[154] S Steininger, 'What's Human Rights Got To Do With It?' (2017) 31 *Leiden Journal of International Law* 1, 35.

[155] For example, *Técnicas Medioambientales Tecmed v United Mexican States*, ICSID Case No ARB(AF)/00/2.

[156] For example, *Bear Creek Mining Corporation v Republic of Peru*; *Técnicas Medioambientales Tecmed v United Mexican States*.

[157] *EDF International S.A., SAUR International S.A. and León Participaciones Argentinas SA v Argentine Republic.*

The *EDF* case arose from the emergency measures taken by Argentina in response to the 2001 financial crisis.[158] It is one of the many cases filed against Argentina in this period due to the detrimental impact of the emergency measures on investor profits. Aspects of these cases and the resulting arbitral awards have been analysed in depth in the academic literature and civil society reports.[159] During, and in the aftermath of, the crisis, many businesses (including international investors) suffered losses – but so did host communities and the host state itself. My aim in analysing the *EDF* award is to demonstrate how the current foreign investment governance architecture distributes the potential losses of a crisis among the host communities and investors.

EDF and its co-claimants were investors in an electricity transmission and distribution concession in the Mendoza province of Argentina since 1998. The emergency measures taken by Argentina in response to the financial crisis meant that the tariffs could not be calculated and adjusted as it had been agreed under the concession contract, as continuing to do so would seriously undermine access to electricity for most sections of the community. The IEL framework and, more specifically, the investment treaty system is designed to shield investors from the political risks inherent in overseas investing. But the protection afforded to investors in practice goes beyond political risk, as investment treaty standards have been interpreted in arbitral awards to shield investors from a wide range of risks – from regulatory changes to economic crises – even if the measures impacting the investment's profitability were applied in a non-discriminatory and non-arbitrary manner. Any adverse impact on the investment's value and profitability resulting from host state measures can form the basis of an investment treaty claim for breach of fair and equitable treatment standard or indirect expropriation. As most investment treaty language is framed at a high level of abstraction, it is easy to justify interpretations of these standards as entitling the investors to protection from risk regardless of the reasons giving rise to the investor's loss and the impact of compensating the investor on the host communities' fundamental rights.

[158] F Lapova, 'Crisis, Emergency Measures and the Failure of the ISDS System: The Case of Argentina' (South Centre Investment Policy Brief, July 2015) 2, available at www.southcentre.int/wp-content/uploads/2015/07/IPB2_Crisis-Emergency-Measures-and-the-Failure-of-the-ISDS-System-The-Case-of-Argentina.pdf (lists the relevant measures as (i) the imposition of a 'Corralito' & 'corralón', ie, a temporary bank freeze and rescheduling of term deposits; (ii) the termination of peso convertibility and its pegging to the US dollar at the fixed exchange rate of 1:1 (1 US$ = 4 AR$); (iii) a default on and the unilateral rescheduling of governmental debt; (iv) the termination of right of licensees of public utilities to adjust tariffs according to US PPI; (v) the 'pesification' of tariffs at a rate of AR$ 1 for each US$, as well as the 'pesification' of all contracts denominated in dollars and subject to Argentine law; and (vi) restrictions to transfer funds abroad').

[159] G van Harten, *Investment Treaty Arbitration and Public Law* (Oxford University Press, 2007); Lapova, 'The Case of Argentina' (2015); P di Rosa, 'The Recent Wave of Arbitrations against Argentina under Bilateral Investment Treaties: Background and Principal Legal Issues' (2004) 36 *The University of Miami Inter-American Law Review* 41.

New generation investment treaties contain more detailed provisions on standards of protection to overcome the abstraction problem. For instance, CETA contains provisions that limit the scope of FET and indirect expropriation protections by introducing an explicit 'right to regulate' clause.[160] Some of these more detailed and explicit treaty clauses do limit the interpretive radius of arbitral tribunals by explicitly endorsing the state's right to regulate in the public interest and by clarifying the meaning of standards. These are welcome developments to alleviate some of the problems posed by the risk paradigm, but do not go far enough to shift the law's over-reliance on the risk paradigm that undermines the welfare enhancing potential of foreign investment.[161] It is also yet to be seen how tribunals will interpret these provisions in arbitral awards.

A close reading of many investment treaty awards that impact human rights of host communities and the environment shows that these issues are often excluded or watered down by claimants and tribunals. Instead, the interpretation of standards is centred around the objective of shielding the investor from risk in all circumstances and the issues of human rights and environment are framed either as competing economic interests or issues of sovereignty. For instance, the claimants in the *EDF* case argued that 'it is preposterous to suggest that … Argentine citizens hold a supervening right to consume electricity at certain reduced prices'.[162] This framing of the issue of access to electricity, which is an element of the right to an adequate standard of living, in consumption terms aims to reduce the problem to one of competing economic interests between the investor and consumer. This framing assists the investor to show that its economic interests must be protected against the risk of loss that was caused by the state prioritising the economic interests of consumers. To challenge this argument, Argentina framed the issue in human rights terms:

> [I]t was necessary to enact the Emergency Tariff Measures in order to guarantee the free enjoyment of certain basic human rights – such as, inter alia, the right to life, health, personal integrity, education, the rights of children and political rights which were – directly threatened by the socio-economic institutional collapse suffered by the Argentine Republic, where tens of people lost their lives, the right to health, to personal integrity, to work and safety.[163]

Argentina argued that the investment treaty should be interpreted consistently with international human rights standards,[164] and that the rights of the investor under the investment treaty are not 'absolute to the detriment of the Argentine population's entitlement to universal human rights enshrined in international

[160] CETA, Arts 23.2, 24.3.

[161] See J Ho et al, 'Covid-19 and the Precarity of International Investment Law' (Medium, 6 May 2020), available at medium.com/iel-collective/covid-19-and-the-precarity-of-international-investment-law-c9fc254b3878.

[162] *EDF International v Argentina*, para 191.

[163] ibid para 192.

[164] ibid.

instruments'.[165] Argentina's argument here goes to the opposite extreme from the investor's position, arguing that the basic rights in human rights treaties are non-derogable and are tantamount to *jus cogens*.[166] Argentina further argued that 'measures enacted to safeguard the free enjoyment of human rights should never result in international responsibility'.[167] Here, Argentina seems to suggest eliminating the protection offered to the investor from risk of loss in the treaty, on the grounds that the measures it took aimed to secure the supervening rights of its population.

The tribunal's award failed to address Argentina's human rights arguments in a meaningful way. It acknowledged 'the potential significance and relevance of human rights in connection with international investment law',[168] but was not persuaded that Argentina's 'failure to re-negotiate tariffs in a timely fashion, so as to re-establish the economic equilibrium to which Claimants were entitled under the Concession Agreement's Currency Clause, was necessary to guarantee human rights'.[169] None of these observations were substantiated in any detail in the award. It is not clear from the award that Argentina would need to demonstrate to persuade the tribunal that the host state's actions were necessary to safeguard human rights. The tribunal paid lip service to human rights and avoided a genuine discussion of the severity of the human rights impacts that would have been exacerbated had the respondent not taken measures to stabilise the tariffs to maintain the accessibility of services. The focus of the tribunal remained exclusively on what the state should have done to mitigate the risk of loss to the investor, without evaluating whether renegotiating the tariffs earlier would mean that the risk of loss would be shifted onto the citizens whose access to a fundamental right would be impaired by the increase in tariffs. Without engaging in a serious analysis of what the rights invoked by Argentina demanded from the state under IHRL,[170] the tribunal held that the host state should have re-established the economic equilibrium of the contract 'within a reasonable time following the state of emergency'.[171]

[165] ibid paras 192–93 (Argentina lists the 1948 UN Universal Declaration of Human Rights, the 1966 UN International Covenant on Civil and Political Rights, the 1989 UN Convention on the Rights of the Child, and the 1969 American Convention on Human Rights as examples).

[166] ibid para 193. Argentina's argument here on *jus cogens* fails to distinguish between international human rights norms that have been accepted as *jus cogens*, such as the prohibition of torture, slavery and genocide, from the wider body of human rights norms that are not yet considered *jus cogens* norms. See J Rehman, *International Human Rights Law*, 2nd edn (Pearson, 2010) 25–26.

[167] ibid para 194.

[168] ibid para 912.

[169] ibid para 914.

[170] This type of analysis is suggested by J Harrison, 'Investigative Legal Pluralism in International economic law linkage debates: a strategy for enhancing the value of international legal discourse' (2014) 2 *London Review of International Law* 115, 124–25 ('Human rights should be a mechanism for asking different questions, seeking different information, and ultimately reframing the substantive issues that are at the heart of the case').

[171] *EDF International v Argentina*, para 995.

While the tribunal does not completely dismiss the severity of the situation and its impact on the population, thus allowing some limits to the risk paradigm, it finds such a limitation acceptable only in the most severe situations of emergency. It then expects the investor's protection from loss to be prioritised within a reasonable time after the most severe incursions are alleviated. This detracts attention from the welfare and well-being of the communities impacted, which IIL is supposed to enhance. Here, the tribunal does not offer a discussion of what constitutes a 'reasonable time' in the context of the dispute in a manner that takes into account the IHRL standards that are relevant to the public utility service provided by the investor. For instance, the tribunal fails to discuss the requirements of the right to an adequate standard of living enshrined in Article 11.1 of the ICESCR in relation to access to electricity. Access to affordable energy is a part of the right to an adequate housing, which is a component of an adequate standard of living under Article 11.1.[172] Instead, the tribunal only focuses on the loss suffered by the investor in evaluating the fairness and equity of the investor's treatment by the host state. In protecting the investor from the risk of loss, the tribunal implicitly endorses the view that the risk of loss for communities potentially resulting from a premature return to economic equilibrium for the investor's business is an acceptable compromise. Apart from the superficial analysis of the respondent's human rights defences, human rights play no role in the tribunal's interpretation of the FET protection that shields investors from risk of loss. It is clear from the award that the losses and harms suffered by the host communities played no role in the tribunal's evaluation of FET, as throughout the award the affected communities are referred to as 'users' or 'consumers', and not as rights holders.

Looking at the wider context of this case, the communities whose access to a public utility affect the enjoyment of their rights do not benefit directly or indirectly, via the host state before the tribunal, from effective legal strategies to have their rights considered in determining whether the treatment received by the investor was fair and equitable. Instead of the approach it has taken, the tribunal could have interpreted FET by considering the losses and gains for the actors directly affected by the measures – the investor and the rights holders. If investment law's overarching objective is to contribute to progress and welfare in the host state, the interpretation of the standards needs to capture the impact of the measures or their absence not only on the investor, but also on the communities and the environment. This way of approaching the FET standard would not mean that claims such as the one in EDF would never result in state responsibility when the measures affecting the investment are justified by human rights objectives. Rather, it would require arbitral tribunals to assess the breach of FET taking into account a wider set of rights and interests that are impacted by the state's acts giving rise to the dispute. The focus of the analysis should be on both the state's justification

[172] UN Committee on Economic, Social and Cultural Rights 'General Comment No 4: The Right to Adequate Housing (Art 11(1) of the Covenant)' (13 December 1991) UN Doc E/1992/23.

for taking the measures in dispute and the potential consequences that would have been suffered by the communities and the environment in the immediate and long term, had the state not taken such measures that damage the investor's profits. When tribunals take an approach that exclusively focuses on shielding the investor and dismissing the impact of the measures or their lack thereof as irrelevant to the determination of the IIL claim, they fail to respect the declared objectives of IIL as a means to welfare. If tribunals start taking a more holistic approach in evaluating state acts giving rise to the dispute, these may offer additional considerations to weigh when determining whether, for example, the state's failure to renegotiate tariffs earlier could be considered reasonable in the wider context of a utility service that is essential to the enjoyment of human rights.

The human rights limitation to the risk paradigm in the *EDF* case could allow the tribunal to find that the state's delay in renegotiating the contract was justifiable under the FET standard. The tribunal would also evaluate other elements of FET to decide whether the host state has followed due process in taking the measures and maintaining them for a sustained period. The maintenance of measures in place for safeguarding human rights and the environment does not justify the state acting in an arbitrary manner or breaching due process obligations. The state can still be responsible to the investor for the losses arising from arbitrariness or lack of due process. But this does not mean that the measure *itself* was in breach of FET. This should significantly lower the valuation of the damages awarded, as the loss compensated would focus not on the substantive treatment of the investor, but rather, the process by which the legitimate restriction to the investment was pursued.

V. Conclusion

The legal standards and tools that protect international investors from risk are typically justified on the basis of encouraging overseas investing that will contribute to the growth of the economy and the eventual improvement of wellbeing and prosperity. The developments in the areas of IIL and BHR show that investors are protected from risks of loss even when their activities undermine the wellbeing and prosperity of local communities. In this chapter, I deployed a risk allocation framing to demonstrate how the legal principles central to foreign investment governance within IIL and BHR discourses contain an embedded bias for enhancing investor wealth without offering any legal strategies for other key stakeholders of foreign investment to safeguard their own rights from harms inflicted by investor activity. The problem of barriers to investor accountability are less to do with fragmentation of international law and more to do with the biased distribution of risk within foreign investment governance. The legal frameworks analysed shield investors from risk of loss and liability, even when doing so has an effect of undermining the ultimate objectives of the risk mitigation strategies. While it is more desirable to embark on a complete reimagining of the current model of foreign investment governance, in the short term, tempering the law's risk mitigation features via legal interpretation could alleviate some of the current system's excesses.

To do this, in this chapter I argued in favour of an approach to risk, in the key laws that govern foreign investments, that makes a distinction based on the nature of the risk avoided by the investor. If an investor is hiding behind the corporate veil to avoid the risk of liability for human rights and environmental harms, courts should suspend from the risk mitigation features of the corporate legal form when interpreting the legal principles on jurisdictional and substantive issues applicable in a domestic litigation that pursues investor accountability.

Similarly, the protection against risk afforded by the substantive and procedural standards in IIL must be paused where such protection results in the risk of loss being passed onto communities which suffer human rights and environmental harm as a result. In such cases, the extent to which the investor will be protected should not be determined exclusively by the adverse impacts of the host state measures on the investment's profitability. The evaluation of the investor's rights should take into serious consideration the risks faced by the rights-holders impacted by the investor's operations, and the host state's failure to take the measures that harm the investor's investment and profits.

5

Investor Obligations in Investment Treaties: Missing Text or a Matter of Application?

PRABHASH RANJAN

I. Background and Context

The first modern-day bilateral investment treaty (BIT) was signed in 1959. Between 1959 and 1989, the total number of BITs increased to 385[1] – a modest increase in a three-decade period. However, this number jumped to 1,857 by the end of 1999[2] – a giant leap forward. As of the end of 2019, there are 2,895 BITs in existence.[3] Foreign investors, over the years, have made use of the investor-state dispute settlement (ISDS) mechanism in BITs to invoke the substantive protections promised in the BITs against the host state. The number of such ISDS claims today stands at over 1,000.[4]

A large number of BITs, especially in 1970s to 1990s, were signed between developed or capital exporting countries and developing or capital importing countries. The primary motivation for developed countries to enter into BITs was the desire to protect their investment in developing countries (the countries that had embraced communism or had newly acquired political independence from erstwhile colonial powers).[5] Developed countries were concerned about several communist and other countries expropriating foreign capital without compensation.[6] Thus, BITs were crafted as a new kind of international instruments

[1] UNCTAD, 'Bilateral Investment Treaties: 1959–1999' (United Nations Publications, 2000) UNCTAD/ITE/IIA/2.

[2] ibid.

[3] UNCTAD, 'World Investment Report' (United Nations Publications, 2020) UNCTAD/WIR/2020, 106.

[4] ibid 110.

[5] KJ Vandevelde, *Bilateral Investment Treaties: History, Policy and Interpretation* (Oxford University Press, 2010) 45–60.

[6] ibid.

that would not only overcome the vagaries of customary international law regarding foreign investment, but would also provide substantive protections to foreign investors by imposing binding constraints on the sovereign rights of developing countries. While theoretically BITs were reciprocal in nature, in effect they operate in a mono-directional manner conferring rights on First World investors and imposing obligations on Second and Third World governments.[7]

The proliferating ISDS claims have involved foreign investors challenging a wide array of regulatory measures of the host state such as monetary measures, taxation laws, industrial policies, health and environmental regulations, actions of the judiciary, etc. The expansion of BITs and the corresponding rise in ISDS claims covering such a broad spectrum of regulatory issues considered fundamental to host state governance and exercise of public power, has triggered strong reactions and concerns from many states and non-state actors like academics, civil society organisations and people at large.[8] This contestation has coincided with a backlash against globalisation[9] and against powerful corporations that wield too much power,[10] and whose accountability is challenging to fix under international law.[11] Human rights violations are an important constituent of the demand to hold corporations accountable for their actions internationally.[12] In 2014, the UN Human Rights Council in Geneva established an open-ended working group with the mandate 'to elaborate an international legally binding instrument on Transnational Corporations and Other Business Enterprises with respect to human rights'.[13] Since then, debate and work has begun in all earnest towards developing a business and human rights treaty[14] or finding other ways in which foreign corporations can be made more accountable towards human rights.[15]

In this context, an important critique that has been advanced against the investment treaties is that they are one-sided international law instruments, which

[7] J Kurtz, *The WTO and International Investment Law: Converging Systems* (Cambridge University Press, 2016) 55.

[8] See M Waibel et al (eds), *The Backlash against Investment Treaty Arbitration: Perceptions and Reality* (Kluwer 2010); SD Franck, 'The Legitimacy Crisis in Investment Treaty Arbitration: Privatizing Public International Law through Inconsistent Decisions' (2005) 73 *Fordham Law Review* 1521.

[9] See D Rodrik, *The Globalisation Paradox* (Oxford University Press, 2011); also, A Stein, 'The Great Trilemma: Are Globalization, Democracy, and Sovereignty Compatible?' (2016) 8 *International Theory* 297.

[10] See generally J Tepper and D Hearn, *The Myth of Capitalism* (Wiley, 2018).

[11] B Choudhury, 'Investor Obligations for Human Rights' (2020) *ICSID Review – Foreign Investment Law Journal* (advance access), available at doi.org/10.1093/icsidreview/siaa002.

[12] S Deva, *Regulating Corporate Human Rights Violations: Humanizing Business* (Routledge, 2012).

[13] 'Binding Treaty' (Business and Human Rights Resource Centre), available at www.business-humanrights.org/en/binding-treaty.

[14] S Deva and D Bilchitz (eds), *Building a Treaty on Business and Human Rights: Context and Contours* (Cambridge University Press. 2017).

[15] Also see B Choudhury, 'Balancing Soft and Hard Law for Business and Human Rights' (2018) 67 *International and Comparative Law Quarterly* 961.

impose obligations on host states, thus constraining their right to regulate, but do not impose obligations on foreign investors.[16] Consequently, while foreign investors benefit from protection of international law against a host state's regulatory abuse, it is difficult to fix the accountability of investors or hold them liable for misconduct towards the host states or local communities.[17] It has been argued that an important way to correct the ingrained imbalances in investment treaties so that foreign corporations can be held accountable for their actions under international law is by incorporating provisions on investor's obligations in BITs.[18]

This chapter endeavours to examine the question of investor obligations in two important ways. First, it surveys the recently signed BITs (the second-generation BITs) that contain investor obligations. These second-generation BITs are different from the BITs that were signed earlier, which followed a neoliberal template favouring a minimalist state and containing very broad and substantive guarantees to foreign investors. This appraisal is to critically examine what kinds of investor obligations are found in the new generation of BITs and how effective they would be in holding investors accountable (section II). The chapter then looks closely at some of the ISDS cases involving the question of investor obligations and examines if they provide for a jurisprudential approach to hold investors accountable in those BITs that do not contain investor obligations (section III). Finally, section IV offers some concluding remarks.

II. Obligations on Foreign Investors Incorporated in the Treaty

The new generation investment treaties, unlike the old or the first-generation BITs, contain provisions that impose specific obligations on foreign investors. These obligations range from corporate social responsibility to ensuring that the foreign investor meets the environmental regulations of the host state and does not indulge in any corruption. We study some of the new generation BITs here to enumerate the specific obligations imposed on the foreign investor under the new generations BITs.

[16] See Choudhury, 'Investor Obligations' (2020); J Ho, 'The Creation of Elusive Investor Responsibility' (2019) 113 *American Journal of International Law Unbound* 10; N Bernasconi-Osterwalder, 'Inclusion of Investor Obligations and Corporate Accountability Provisions in Investment Agreements' in J Chaisse et al (eds), *Handbook of International Investment Law and Policy* (Springer, 2020).

[17] J Gathii and S Puig, 'Introduction to the Symposium on Investor Responsibility: The Next Frontier in International Investment Law' (2019) 113 *American Journal of International Law Unbound* 1; Ho (ibid).

[18] Choudhury (n 11); M Sattorova, 'Investor Responsibilities from a Host State Perspective: Qualitative Data and Proposals for Treaty Reform' (2019) 113 *American Journal of International Law Unbound* 22.

A. Corporate Social Responsibility

A common trend among the newer generation BITs is the inclusion of corporate social responsibility (CSR) provisions. According to UNCTAD, there are around 40 investment treaties that contain a CSR clause in the text in some form, excluding those treaties that only talk about CSR in the preamble.[19] For example, Article 12 of the Model Indian BIT provides:

> Investors and their enterprises operating within its territory of each Party shall endeavour to voluntarily incorporate internationally recognized standards of corporate social responsibility in their practices and internal policies, such as statements of principle that have been endorsed or are supported by the Parties. These principles may address issues such as labour, the environment, human rights, community relations and anti-corruption.[20]

Likewise, Article 12 of the recently signed India–Belarus BIT and the India–Taiwan BIT provide the same provision on CSR.[21] Article 10(3) of the Iran–Slovakia BIT provides: 'Investors and their investments should strive to make the maximum feasible contributions to the sustainable development of the Host State and local community through appropriate levels of socially responsible practices'.[22] The use of the words 'shall endeavour to' and 'should strive to' signifies that the obligation on foreign investors to follow CSR standards is part of soft law.

Some treaties put the onus on states to encourage enterprises operating in their jurisdiction to incorporate principles of CSR. For example, Article 5(2) of the investment chapter of the Pacific Agreement on Closer Economic Relations (PACER) plus agreement provides:

> The Parties reaffirm the importance of each Party encouraging enterprises operating within its territory or subject to its jurisdiction to voluntarily incorporate into their internal policies internationally recognised standards, guidelines and principles of corporate social responsibility that have been endorsed or are supported by that Party.[23]

Likewise, Article 17 of the Japan–Argentina BIT provides that:

> [T]he Contracting Parties reaffirm the importance that each of them encourages enterprises operating within its Area or subject to its jurisdiction to voluntarily incorporate into their internal policies those internationally recognised standards, guidelines and

[19] UNCTAD, Mapping of IIA Content, available at investmentpolicy.unctad.org/international-investment-agreements/iia-mapping. Also see Bernasconi-Osterwalder, 'Inclusion of Investor Obligations' (2020).

[20] Model Text for the Indian Bilateral Investment Treaty (adopted 28 December 2015), Art 12.

[21] See Bilateral Investment Agreement Between Indian Taipei Association in Taipei and the Taipei Economic and Cultural Centre in India (signed 18 December 2018, entry into force 14 February 2019), Art 12.

[22] Iran–Slovakia BIT (signed 19 January 2016, entry into force 30 August 2017), Art 10(3).

[23] Pacific Agreement on Closer Economic Relations (PACER) Plus (signed 14 June 2017, entry into force 13 December 2020), Art 5(2).

principles of corporate social responsibility that have been endorsed or are supported by that Contracting Party.[24]

Such language is even softer than that used in the Indian Model BIT, in which the onus is on the investor to incorporate internationally recognised standards and principles of CSR. On the other hand, in treaties like PACER and Japan–Australia BIT, the onus is on the states to encourage investors to do so. Investors themselves are not under an obligation to endeavour to adopt CSR standards.

Somewhat stronger and more elaborate language on CSR is employed in BITs signed by Brazil. These BITs expand the horizon of investor obligations falling within the framework of CSR by coupling it with other responsibilities, such as local capacity building, economic stimulus for sustainable development, non-discrimination amongst employees, maintaining good corporate governance practices, creating employment opportunities and respect for human rights, health, security, the environment, etc.[25] For instance, Article 9 of the Brazil–Malawi BIT[26] provides:

> 1. Investors and their investment shall strive to achieve the highest possible level of contribution to the sustainable development of the Host Party and the local community, through the adoption of a high degree of socially responsible practices, based on the voluntary principles and standards set out in this Article.
> 2. The investors and their investment shall develop their best efforts to comply with the following voluntary principles and standards for a responsible business conduct and consistent with the laws adopted by the Host Party receiving the investment:
>   a) Stimulate the economic, social and environmental progress, aiming at achieving sustainable development;
>   b) Respect the human rights of those involved in the companies' activities, consistent with the international obligations and commitments of the Host Party;
>   c) Encourage the strengthening of local capacities building through close cooperation with the local community;
>   d) Encourage the development of human capital, especially by creating employment opportunities and facilitating access of workers to professional training;
>   e) Refrain from seeking or accepting exemptions that are not established in the legislation of the Host Party, relating to environment, health, security, work or financial incentives, or other issues;

[24] Agreement Between the Argentina Republic and Japan for the Promotion and Protection of Investment (signed 1 December 2018, not yet in force), Art 17.

[25] See Brazil–Mexico Cooperation and Facilitation Investment Agreement (CFIA) (signed 26 May 2015, entry into force 7 October 2018), Art 13(2). Also see the CFIA Between the Federative Republic of Brazil and the United Arab Emirates (Brazil–UAE BIT) (signed 15 March 2019, not yet in force), Art 15. Also see the CFIA Between the Federative Republic of Brazil and the Cooperative Republic of Guyana (Brazil–Guyana BIT) (signed 13 December 2018, not yet in force), Art 15.

[26] Brazil–Malawi BIT (signed 25 June 2015, not yet in force), Art 9.

f) Support and maintain good corporate governance principles, and develop and apply good practices of corporate governance;
g) Develop and apply effective self-regulatory practices and management systems that foster a relationship of mutual trust between the companies and the society in which the operations are conducted;
h) Promote the knowledge of workers about the corporate policy, through appropriate dissemination of this policy, including programs for professional training;
i) Refrain from discriminatory or disciplinary action against the employees who submit grave reports to the board or, whenever appropriate, to the competent public authorities, about practices that violate the law or violate the standards of corporate governance that the company is subject to;
j) Encourage, whenever possible, the business associates, including service providers and outsources, to apply the principles of business conduct consistent with the principles provided in this Article; and
k) Respect local political activities and processes.

While the CSR provisions also occur in the form of best endeavour clauses, non-binding standards or other hortatory language in the Brazil–Malawi BIT, it is stricter and more elaborate in comparison to the language employed in, for example, the Indian Model BIT.

The Nigeria–Morocco BIT, which is often touted as an example of new-age treaty drafting in reforming investment treaties,[27] also employs 'best endeavour' language when it comes to CSR.[28] Article 24(1) of the BIT states that 'investors and their investments should strive to make the maximum feasible contributions to the sustainable development of the Host State and local community through high levels of socially responsible practices'. The presence of words like 'should strive to' clearly point to the hortatory language of the CSR obligation on foreign investors. Likewise, Article 24(3) provides: 'where standards of corporate social responsibility increase, investors should strive to apply and achieve the higher level standards'. Again, the focus is on the words 'should strive to', signalling best endeavour language.

Slightly stronger language is used in Article 22 of the Draft Pan-African Investment Code (PAIC), which provides:

1. Investors shall abide by the laws, regulations, administrative guidelines and policies of the host State.
2. Investors shall, in pursuit of their economic objectives, ensure that they do not conflict with the social and economic development objectives of host States and shall be sensitive to such objectives.

[27] T Gazzini, 'The 2016 Morocco–Nigeria BIT: An Important Contribution to the Reform of Investment Treaties' (2017) 8 *Investment Treaty News* 3.

[28] Reciprocal Investment Promotion and Protection Agreement Between the Government of the Kingdom of Morocco and the Government of the Federal Republic of Nigeria (signed 3 December 2016, not yet in force).

3. Investors shall contribute to the economic, social and environmental progress with a view to achieving sustainable development of the host State.[29]

The use of the word 'shall' signals a slightly stronger formulation in comparison to the language employed in other BITs discussed above. However, even here, the obligations imposed by the treaty are not specific, but general and somewhat vague or imprecise in nature.

Overall, it can be said that while these new generation BITs impose CSR obligations on foreign investors, they do not employ binding language. The CSR obligations on foreign investors exist as best endeavour clauses, thus arguably diluting their significance. This also demonstrates the reluctance of the states to impose binding and enforceable obligations on foreign investors.

B. Environment

The impact of foreign investments on the environment is well known. Several ISDS claims have been brought due to the actions of the host state aimed at protecting the environment. In order to achieve intersectional coherency, many new generation BITs do not merely record the provisions of environment conservation as a part of the state's right to regulate, but also as an obligation on the investors and their investments.[30] Some attempts have been made at imposing environmental obligations on foreign investors through raising counterclaims.[31] Ecuador, in two cases – *Burlington Resources v Ecuador*[32] and *Perenco v Ecuador*[33] – counterclaimed against the investors that they had breached environmental obligations.

In many new-generation BITs, the reference to environment is found in CSR provisions. For example, Article 16 of the Canada–Benin BIT states:

> Each Contracting Party should encourage enterprises operating within its territory or subject to its jurisdiction to voluntarily incorporate internationally recognized standards of corporate social responsibility in their practices and internal policies, such as statements of principle that have been endorsed or are supported by the Contracting Parties. These principle address issues such as labour, the environment, human rights, community relations and anti-corruption.[34]

[29] United Nations Economic and Social Council (ECOSOC) African Union, 'Draft Pan-African Investment Code' (26 March 2016) E/ECA/COE/35/18, Art 22, available at repository.uneca.org/bitstream/handle/10855/23009/b11560526.pdf?sequence=1&isAllowed=y.

[30] Also see *David Aven v Costa Rica*, ICSID Case No UNCT/15/3, Award (18 September 2018).

[31] T Ishikawa discusses counterclaims further in ch 8 of this volume.

[32] *Burlington v Ecuador*, ICSID Case No ARB/08/5, Decision on Counterclaims (7 February 2017).

[33] *Perenco v Ecuador and Empresa Estatal Petroleos del Ecuador (Petroecuador)*, ICSID Case No ARB/08/6, Interim Decision on The Environmental Counterclaim (11 August 2015).

[34] Agreement Between the Government of Canada and the Government of the Republic of Benin for the Promotion and Reciprocal Protection of Investments (signed 9 January 2013, entry into force 12 May 2014), Art 16. See also United States–Mexico–Canada (USMCA) Agreement (signed 30 November 2018, entry into force 1 July 2020), Art 14.17; the Brazil–Mexico CFIA (signed 26 May 2015, entry into force 7 October 2018), Art 13(2), and the Brazil–Colombia CFIA (signed 9 October 2015, not yet in force), Art 13.

Likewise, Article 12 of the India–Belarus BIT provides:

> Investors and their enterprises operating within the territory of each Party shall endeavour to voluntarily incorporate internationally recognized standards of corporate social responsibility in their practices and internal policies, such as statements of principle that have been endorsed or are supported by the Parties. These principles may address issues such as labour, the environment, human rights, community relations and anti-corruption.[35]

This formulation is similar to that of Canada–Benin BIT and is couched in best endeavour language. In the same vein, Article 12.2(a) of the India–Brazil BIT provides that investors and their investments shall 'endeavour' to comply with voluntary principles and standards such as contributing to economic, social and environmental progress, aimed at achieving sustainable development. Same formulation exists in other Brazilian BITs such as Article 15(2) of the Brazil–UAE BIT and Article 15(2) of the Brazil–Guyana BIT.

The Draft PAIC 2016,[36] however, is much more detailed in linking environmental conservation with investor obligations. Article 19(3)(c) of the Draft PAIC states that the 'investor shall ensure that timely and accurate disclosure is made on all material matters regarding a corporation, including … risks related to environmental liabilities'. The use of the word 'shall' here puts the investor under a direct obligation to make timely disclosures regarding environmental risks. Article 23 of the Draft PAIC also imposes environment-related obligations on foreign investors. Article 23(1) provides: 'Investors shall not exploit or use local natural resources to the detriment of the rights and interests of the host State'. Article 23(2) further provides: 'Investors shall respect rights of local populations, and avoid land grabbing practices vis-à-vis local communities'. Thus, the Draft PAIC levies upon the investor the obligation to responsibly use natural resources while keeping in mind the interests of local communities. The use of the word 'shall' shows that the obligation imposed is binding on the foreign investor.

Further, a separate, fully fledged provision on environment is given in Draft PAIC Article 37. Article 37(3) provides that foreign investors, while performing their activities, 'shall' protect the environment, and where such activities cause damages to the environment, take reasonable steps to restore it as far as possible. Further, Article 37(4) puts foreign investors under an obligation to carry out an environmental impact assessment (EIA) in relation to their investments. These obligations too are binding and stronger than those couched in the soft law language in the India–Belarus and Canada–Benin BITs.

The binding requirement to conduct an EIA is also found in Article 14 of the Nigeria–Morocco BIT. Article 14(1) states:

> [I]nvestors or the investment shall comply with environmental assessment screening and assessment processes applicable to their proposed investments prior to their

[35] See also India–Taiwan BIT (signed 18 December 2018, entry into force 14 February 2019), Art 12; India–Kyrgyzstan BIT (signed 14 June 2019, not yet in force), Art 12.

[36] UN ECOSOC African Union, 'Draft Pan-African Investment Code' (n 29).

> establishment, as required by the laws of the host state for such an investment or the laws of the home state for such an investment, whichever is more rigorous in relation to the investment in question.

This provision puts investors under a direct obligation to undertake an EIA as required by the laws of the host state or the home state, whichever is more rigorous. In other words, if the home state laws requiring EIA are more rigorous in comparison to the host state, the investor has to follow the home state standards. Since the obligation on the investor is to follow the EIA standards laid down in the home state or the host state, in case the two states have not laid down EIA norms or have weak EIA norms in their domestic laws, there will be no obligation on the foreign investor to undertake an meaningful assessment of the environmental impact that its investment might have. A case in point here is India's new draft EIA,[37] which significantly dilutes the rigour of undertaking an EIA, and thus constitutes a race to the bottom.[38] In case of such weak domestic laws, if the obligation imposed on the foreign investor were to follow the domestic law, the duty imposed on the foreign investor would be weak.

Article 14(3) of the Nigeria–Morocco BIT states:

> [I]nvestors, their investment and host state authorities shall apply the precautionary principle to their environmental impact assessment and to decisions taken in relation to a proposed investment, including any necessary mitigation or alternative approaches of the precautionary principle by investors and investments shall be described in the environmental impact assessment they undertake.

Thus, it requires not just the host state but also the foreign investor to apply precautionary principle to their EIAs. The use of the word 'shall' means that it is a binding obligation on the investor.

Likewise, another related provision in the Nigeria–Morocco BIT is Article 18(4), which states that: 'investors and investments shall not manage or operate the investments in a manner that circumvents international environmental … obligations to which the host state and/or home state are Parties'. In other words, if the foreign investor does not act in accordance with international environmental obligations that bind both, the host and the home state, the investor will be held liable for not complying with the treaty.

From the point of view of imposing binding environmental obligations on foreign investors, the Draft PAIC and the Nigeria–Morocco BIT have better formulations in comparison to other BITs that contain hortatory language.[39]

[37] J Mazoomdaar, 'Explained: Reading the draft Environment Impact Assessment norms, and finding the red flags' (*The Indian Express*, 10 August 2020), available at indianexpress.com/article/explained/draft-environment-impact-assessment-norms-explained-6482324.

[38] M Mallya, 'India's Race to the Bottom: Bilateral Investment Treaties and the New Draft Environmental Impact Assessment Notification' (*OpinioJuris*, 9 October 2020), available at opiniojuris.org/2020/10/09/indias-race-to-the-bottom-bilateral-investment-treaties-and-the-new-draft-environmental-impact-assessment-notification.

[39] The prospect of imposing binding environmental obligations on foreign investors is considered more fully by P Pereira de Andrade and N Monebhurrun in ch 11 of this volume.

C. Corporate Governance and Practices

Some of the new-generation BITs impose obligations on foreign investors regarding following transparent corporate governance practices. For instance, Article 19(a) of the Draft PAIC provides: 'investments shall meet national and internationally accepted standards of corporate governance for the sector involved, in particular for transparency and accounting practices'. The use of the word 'shall' here means that the obligation is binding on the investor. However, the nature of the obligation is somewhat indefinite since the investor has to meet the corporate governance 'standards' that are nationally and internationally accepted. Article 19(2), the subsequent provision, is couched in best endeavour language. It states that companies are 'encouraged' to improve their legal, institutional and regulatory framework for corporate governance.

Some other corporate governance related obligations imposed on the foreign investors are given in Article 19(3), which states:

> (3) Investors shall:
>
> a. ensure the equitable treatment of all shareholders, in accordance with national laws;
>
> b. encourage active co-operation between corporations and stakeholders in creating wealth, jobs and the sustainability of financially sound enterprises;
>
> c. ensure that timely and accurate disclosure is made on all material matters regarding a corporation, including the financial situation, performance, ownership, and governance of the company, risks related to environmental liabilities, and any other matters in accordance with the relevant regulations and requirements; and
>
> d. provide information relating to human resource policies, such as programs for human resource development.

Following the same structure, Article 19 of Nigeria–Morocco BIT imposes an obligation on foreign investors pertaining to corporate governance and practices. Article 19(1) provides that in accordance with the size and nature of an investment, 'investments shall meet or exceed national and internationally accepted standards of corporate governance for the sector involved, in particular for transparency and accounting practices'. Article 19 also imposes an obligation on investments 'to establish and maintain, where appropriate, local community liaison processes, in accordance with internationally accepted standards when available'. It is interesting to note that the obligation is imposed on investments, not on investors. It is intriguing how 'investments' can be duty-bearers.[40] One possible interpretation of this could be that the investors have to ensure that their investments comply with these obligations. Thus, although the text talks of imposing obligations on

[40] See M Krajewski, 'A Nightmare or a Noble Dream? Establishing Investor Obligations Through Treaty-Making and Treaty Application' (2020) 5 *Business and Human Rights Journal* 105, 114.

'investments', the duty-bearers are 'investors'. These provisions, however, do not find place in other BITs signed in the same year by Nigeria and Morocco such as Nigeria–UAE BIT and Morocco–Russia BIT.[41]

D. Anti-Corruption Provisions

Involvement of foreign investors in corruption has been a significant issue in quite a few ISDS cases.[42] Questions have often arisen on whether investors can be held liable if they are involved in corrupt activities during the making or operation of their investments.[43] An important way to hold foreign investors liable for corruption is by imposing obligations on them in the BIT. Some of the new generation BITs impose obligations on foreign investors pertaining to the issue of corruption. For instance, Article 11(ii) of the 2016 Indian Model BIT provides:

> [I]nvestors and their investments shall not, either prior to or after the establishment of an investment, offer, promise, or give any undue pecuniary advantage, gratification or gift whatsoever, whether directly or indirectly, to a public servant or official of a Party as an inducement or reward for doing or forbearing to do any official act or obtain or maintain other improper advantage nor shall be complicit in inciting, aiding, abetting, or conspiring to commit such acts.[44]

Thus, the investor is under a direct obligation as part of the treaty to refrain from all kinds of corrupt activities. Three recent BITs signed by India with Belarus, Taiwan and Kyrgyzstan have identical provisions.[45]

Article 21 of the Draft PAIC, while similar to the Indian Model BIT, creates a difference by making sure that such pecuniary advantage extending not merely to the public official but also to her family members or business associates is prohibited. Article 21 provides:

> Investors shall not offer, promise or give any unlawful or undue pecuniary or other advantage or present, whether directly or through intermediaries, to a public official

[41] Some other BITs that contain corporate governance related obligations include the Iran–Slovakia BIT (signed 19 January 2016, entry into force 30 August 2017), Art 10(3); see also *SADC Model Bilateral Investment Treaty Template with Commentary* (Southern African Development Community 2012), Art 15(1).

[42] See *World Duty Free v Kenya*, ICSID Case No ARB/00/7, Award (4 October 2006); *Metal-Tech v Uzbekistan*, ICSID Case No ARB/10/3, Award (4 October 2013); *EDF (Services) v Romania*, ICSID Case No ARB/05/13, Award (8 October 2009). The prospect of international obligation against corruption that is binding on foreign investors is explored by JD Amado, JS Kern and M Doe Rodriguez in ch 12 of this volume.

[43] C Vijayvergia and P Belmannu, 'Exploring the Prospects of Host-State Counterclaims in Corruption Disputes' (2020) *Arbitration International* (advance access), available at academic.oup.com/arbitration/advance-article-abstract/doi/10.1093/arbint/aiaa041/5916377?redirectedFrom=fulltext.

[44] Model Text for the Indian Bilateral Investment Treaty (adopted 28 December 2015), Art 11(ii).

[45] See India–Belarus BIT (signed 24 September 2018, not yet in force), Art 11(ii); India–Taiwan BIT (signed 18 December 2018, entry into force 14 February 2019), Art 11(ii); India–Kyrgyzstan BIT (signed 14 June 2019, not yet in force), Art 11(ii).

> of a Member State, or to a member of an official's family or business associate or other person in order that the official or other person act or refrain from acting in relation to the performance of official duties.

Article 17(2) of the Nigeria–Morocco BIT contains a provision on corruption similar to that in Article 21 of the Draft PAIC. However, the Nigeria–Morocco BIT goes a step further. In Article 17(4), it provides that 'a breach of this article by an investor or an investment is deemed to constitute a breach of the domestic law of the Host State Party concerning the establishment and operation of an investment'. Thus, the investor who violates the anti-corruption obligation is in breach of domestic law.

In several new-generation BITs, the anti-corruption obligation is woven into the CSR provisions. For instance, Article 16 of the Canada–Burkina Faso BIT states that countries should 'encourage' enterprises operating within its territory to incorporate internationally recognised CSR standards and 'principles' that address issues such as anti-corruption.[46] Article 11(2) of the Nigeria–Singapore BIT also talks of addressing issues such as anti-corruption by encouraging enterprises to incorporate internationally recognised CSR standards and principles.[47]

The key difference between the treaties like the India–Belarus BIT and Nigeria–Morocco BIT, and other BITs that contain anti-corruption provision as part of CSR, is that the former treaties impose a binding obligation on the foreign investor, whereas, in the latter, the anti-corruption obligation exists in the form of a best endeavour clause. Furthermore, in these latter treaties, the obligation is on the states to 'encourage' foreign investors to incorporate internationally recognised CSR standards, including those on anti-corruption.

Some treaties impose a direct obligation on states to combat corruption without simultaneously expecting best endeavours from foreign investors. For instance, Article 1.7 of the Japan and Mongolia Economic Partnership Agreement provides: 'each party shall, in accordance with its laws and regulations, take appropriate measures to prevent and combat corruption of its public officials regarding matters covered by this Agreement'.

Thus, the obligation to combat corruption is placed squarely on the states without any comparable obligation being imposed on the foreign investor. Likewise, Article 72 of the CARIFORUM–EU Economic Partnership Agreement enunciates that states shall cooperate and take necessary measures to ensure that investors are forbidden from and held liable for bribing public officials.[48] Thus, the obligation is

[46] Agreement between the Government of Canada and the Government of Burkina Faso for the Promotion and Protection of Investments (signed 20 April 2015, entry into force 11 October 2017), Art 16.

[47] Investment Promotion and Protection Agreement Between the Government of the Federal Republic of Nigeria and the Government of the Republic of Singapore (signed 4 November 2016, not yet in force), Art 11(2). Also see Canada–Guinea BIT (signed 27 May 2015, entry into force 27 March 2017), Art 16; Canada–Mali BIT (signed 28 November 2014, entry into force 8 June 2016), Art 15(3).

[48] Economic Partnership Agreement between the CARIFORUM States, of the one part, and the European Community and its Member States, of the other part (signed 15 October 2008, entry into force 1 January 2009), Art 72.

on the states to pursue the liability of investors, and not directly on investors not to indulge in corrupt practices.

E. Human Rights Obligations

One prominent issue in the context of investor obligations is whether or not foreign investors are bound by human rights obligations. This issue has arisen in cases like *Urbaser v Argentina*. Some commentators argue that such human rights obligations can be established through incorporating direct investor obligations in investment treaties.[49] In this regard, the most noteworthy investment treaty is the Nigeria–Morocco BIT. Article 18(2) provides that 'investors and investments shall uphold human rights in the host state'. Interestingly, this provision imposes a direct and binding obligation on both the 'investor' and 'investments'. Krajewski argues that this provision creates three ambiguities.[50] First, it is difficult to conceive how 'investments' can have legal duties, along with the 'investor'.[51] Second, it is not clear what is the meaning of the word 'uphold' in Article 18(2).[52] Presumably, 'uphold' means that the foreign investors are under an obligation to respect protect and fulfil human rights.[53] Third, it is not clear from the text whether 'human rights in the host State' in Article 18(2) includes all international human rights or is it restricted to 'those human rights which are applicable in the host State as a matter of domestic and international law'.[54] Article 18(4) helps in answering this question. As per Article 18(4): 'investors and investments shall not manage or operate the investments in a manner that circumvents international … human rights obligations to which the host state and/or home state are Parties'. In other words, international human rights obligations that are binding on both the home and the host state would fall within the ambit of Article 18(2).

However, apart from the Nigeria–Morocco BIT, no other investment treaty imposes direct and binding obligations on foreign investors related to human rights. At most, BITs reference human rights in CSR provisions. Article 16 of the Canada–Benin BIT and Article 12 of the India–Belarus BIT, discussed above, are two such examples. In these treaties human rights obligations occur as part of the investor's CSR obligations[55] and are expressed in best endeavour language.

[49] B Choudhury, 'Spinning Straw into Gold: Incorporating in Business and Human Rights Agenda into International Investment Agreements' (2017) 38 *University of Pennsylvania Journal of International Law* 425, 469–70; Sattorova, 'Investor Responsibilities' (2019) 24; Krajewski, 'A Nightmare or a Noble Dream?' (2020).

[50] Krajewski (n 40) 114–15.

[51] ibid.

[52] ibid.

[53] ibid.

[54] ibid.

[55] Also see Brazil–UAE BIT (signed 15 March 2019, not yet in force), Art 15(2); Brazil–Guyana BIT (signed 13 December 2018, not yet in force), Art 15(2); Brazil–Chile Free Trade Agreement (signed 21 November 2018, not yet in force), Art 8.15(2); India–Taiwan BIT (signed 18 December 2018, entry into force 14 February 2019), Art 12; India–Kyrgyzstan BIT (signed 14 June 2019, not yet in force), Art 12.

Similar language also exists in BITs signed by Brazil where investors, in respect of CSR obligations, are required to develop best efforts to 'respect the human rights of those involved in the companies' activities, consistent with the international obligations and commitments of the Host Party'.[56] In other words, as long as the foreign investor can show that they endeavoured to address human rights principles, they cannot be held liable for breach of human rights obligations.

A somewhat interesting formulation exists in Article 20 of the Draft PAIC, which although it does not directly impose human rights obligations on the investor, does impose certain socio-political obligations on foreign investors:

> 1. Investors shall adhere to socio-political obligations including, but not exclusively, the following:
>   a. respect for national sovereignty and observance of domestic laws, regulations and administrative practices;
>   b. respect for socio-cultural values;
>   c. non-interference in internal political affairs;
>   d. non-interference in intergovernmental relations; and
>   e. respect for labour rights.
> 2. Investors shall not influence the appointment of persons to public office or finance political parties.
> 3. Investors shall refrain from exercising restrictive practices and from trying to achieve gains through unlawful means.

The non-exhaustive list provided in Article 20 includes respect for socio-cultural values, respect for national sovereignty, non-interference in the internal political affairs of the host State, and respect for labour rights. Interestingly, it also bars foreign investors from financing political parties. This provision is important as often allegations of favouritism to private businesses including to foreign investors is linked to the provision of electoral or other funding to political parties of the country.

Similarly, Article 24 of the Draft PAIC lays down certain principles that govern compliance by investors with business ethics and human rights. One of the principles is the support and respect of the protection of internationally recognised human rights;[57] another is to ensure that the foreign investors are not complicit in human rights abuses.[58]

F. Compliance with Domestic Laws

An important vehicle to impose obligations on foreign investors, apart from imposing direct obligations on them in the treaty or by adopting soft law approaches, is

[56] See Brazil–Malawi BIT (signed 25 June 2015, not yet in force), Art 9(2).
[57] UN ECOSOC African Union, 'Draft Pan-African Investment Code' (n 29) Art 24(a).
[58] ibid, Art 24(b).

to ensure that the treaty requires the foreign investor to comply with domestic laws.[59] Foreign investors are bound by domestic laws. In fact, some ISDS tribunals have concluded that foreign investors have a general obligation to comply with host state laws irrespective of whether the treaty specifies this.[60] However, stipulating this in the treaty can elevate a breach of domestic law by the foreign investor to an issue subject to ISDS.[61]

In several BITs, the requirement that foreign investors should follow domestic laws is given as part of the definition of a protected investment. For instance, Article 1(a) of the India–Netherlands BIT provides: 'investments means every kind of asset invested in accordance with the national laws and regulations of the Contracting Party in the territory of which the investment is made'.[62] Thus, the requirement that foreign investment complies with domestic laws of the host state becomes a jurisdictional issue. Several ISDS tribunals have held that they lack jurisdiction over foreign investment made in contravention of domestic laws.[63]

In other BITs, the requirement to comply with domestic laws is independent of the definition of a protected investment. For example, Article 11 of the 2016 Indian Model BIT, which is part of Chapter III of the treaty titled 'Investor Obligations', provides: 'investors and their investments shall comply with all laws, regulations, administrative guidelines and policies of a Party concerning the establishment, acquisition, management, operation and disposition of investments'. This is a binding obligation on the foreign investors. Similar provisions exist in the India–Belarus BIT,[64] the India–Taiwan BIT,[65] and the India–Kyrgyzstan BIT.[66] Likewise, Article 7(1) of the 2019 Netherlands Model BIT provides: 'investors and their investments shall comply with domestic laws and regulations of the host State, including laws and regulations on human rights, environmental protection and labour laws'.[67] The content of the obligations imposed on foreign investors will depend on the content of domestic laws. If domestic laws contain weak provisions on human rights or environmental protection, for example, then the corresponding obligations on the foreign investors will also be weak.

[59] Krajewski (n 40) 119–20.

[60] *Cortec Mining v Kenya*, ICSID Case No ARB/15/29, Award (22 October 2018), para 333; *Plama Consortium v Bulgaria*, ICSID Case No ARB/03/24, Award (27 August 2008), paras 138–39. Also see Choudhury (n 11).

[61] Krajewski (n 40) 119.

[62] Agreement between the Republic of India and the Kingdom of the Netherlands for the promotion and protection of investments (signed 6 November 1995, entry into force 1 December 1996), Art 1(a).

[63] *Inceysa v El Salvador*, ICSID Case No ARB/03/26, Award (2 August 2006), para 257; *Hamster v Ghana*, ICSID Case No ARB/07/24, Award (18 June 2010), paras 123–24; *Fraport v Philippines*, ICSID Case No ARB/03/25, Award (16 August 2007), paras 394–97.

[64] India–Belarus BIT (signed 24 September 2018, not yet in force), Art 11.

[65] India–Taiwan BIT (signed 18 December 2018, entry into force 14 February 2019), Art 11.

[66] India–Kyrgyzstan BIT (signed 14 June 2019, not yet in force), Art 11.

[67] Netherlands Model Investment Agreement (22 March 2019), available at www.rijksoverheid.nl/ministeries/ministerie-van-buitenlandse-zaken/documenten/publicaties/2019/03/22/nieuwe-modeltekst-investeringsakkoorden.

G. Counterclaims as an Entry Point for Investor Obligations

Some new-generation BITs or investment treaties specifically provide for counterclaims that can be made against foreign investors by host states. These counterclaims could be an entry point for investor obligations.[68] A good example of this is Article 28(9) of the Common Market for Eastern and Southern Africa Investment Agreement 2007 (COMESA),[69] which provides:

> A Member State against whom a claim is brought by a COMESA investor under this Article may assert as a defence, counterclaim, right of set off or other similar claim, that the COMESA investor bringing the claim has not fulfilled its obligations under this Agreement, including the obligations to comply with all applicable domestic measures or that it has not taken all reasonable steps to mitigate possible damages.

Thus, Article 28(9) allows the host state to bring a counterclaim against a foreign investor if the investor has not complied with its obligations under the treaty.

Likewise, Article 43(1) of the Draft Pan African Investment Code, as part of the chapter on ISDS, provides:

> Where an investor or its investment is alleged by a Member State party in a dispute settlement proceeding under this Code to have failed to comply with its obligations under this Code or other relevant rules and principles of domestic and international law, the competent body hearing such a dispute shall consider whether this breach, if proven, is materially relevant to the issues before it, and if so, what mitigating or off-setting effects this may have on the merits of a claim or on any damages awarded in the event of such award.

Article 43(2) of the Draft Pan African Investment Code provides: 'A Member State may initiate a counterclaim against the investor before any competent body dealing with a dispute under this Code for damages or other relief resulting from an alleged breach of the Code'. Thus, it clearly allows the host state to bring a counterclaim against a foreign investor. Article 43(1) provides that in case the foreign investor has failed to comply with the obligations imposed, the ISDS arbitration tribunal shall take such breaches into account to decide whether such breaches have any mitigating or off-setting effects either on the merits of the claim made by the foreign investor or on the damages awarded.

H. Usefulness of BITs Providing Investor Obligations

Some may argue that the utility of providing investor obligations in BITs is limited because most of these obligations, as discussed above, employ soft law or hortatory language, and are not binding on foreign investors. Although some BITs impose

[68] Choudhury (n 11). See also ch 8 (Ishikawa) of this volume.

[69] Investment Agreement for the COMESA Common Investment Area (signed 23 May 2007, not yet in force), Art 28(9).

binding obligations on foreign investors, which can act as a gateway to holding investors accountable, it is true that a majority of them park investor obligations in best endeavour clauses. Hortatory language will not be very effective in holding the foreign investors to account. Thus, one may be sceptical of the proposition that some scholars make, especially vis-à-vis human rights obligations, that the incorporation of human rights obligations on foreign investors amounts to the 'hardening' of the soft law on business and human rights.[70]

However, there is another dimension that should be kept in mind. Investor obligations, even if they are expressed in best endeavour language, can play an important role in altering the manner in which ISDS tribunals have often viewed investment treaties. For instance, ISDS tribunals have looked at BITs largely as instruments for the promoting and protecting foreign investment.[71] In other words, they have given preference to investment protection over other compelling objectives.[72] Thus, the presence of investor obligations, even in non-binding language, would play an important role in being part of the overall context of the investment treaty, thus signalling a reframing of the objectives of the treaty.[73] This could be seen as part of the broader reform project in international investment law, which aims to recalibrate investment treaties into international instruments that go beyond the simplistic goal of providing protection to foreign investors.

The ISDS tribunal shall have to take this new set of objectives into account while interpreting the any BIT provision.[74] In other words, the presence of these investor obligations can be conducive to addressing the asymmetrical design of BITs. They can ensure that ISDS tribunals interpret the key substantive provisions of the BIT while keeping in mind the fact that treaties imposes obligations on foreign investors too (not just states), rendering investor conduct a significant aspect of the interpretative matrix.[75]

III. Investment Treaties that do not Contain Investor Obligations

Barring obligations such as investment shall be made in accordance with the domestic laws of the country, which often occurs as part of the definition of

[70] See for instance the attempts to 'harden' as reviewed in Choudhury, 'Balancing Soft and Hard Law' (2015) 974–79.

[71] *Siemens AG v Argentina*, ICSID Case No ARB/02/8, Decision on Jurisdiction (3 August 2004), para 81. Also see K Gudgeon, 'United States Bilateral Investment Treaties: Comments on their Origin, Purposes, and General Treatment Standards' (1986) 4 *International Tax & Business Lawyer* 105.

[72] For instance, see *Azurix v Argentina*, ICSID Case No ARB/01/12, Award (14 July 2006), para 261.

[73] See Sattorova (n 18).

[74] See JE Viñuales, 'Investor Diligence in Investment Arbitration: Sources and Arguments' (2017) 32 *ICSID Review – Foreign Investment Law Journal* 346, 368; see also, Choudhury (n 11).

[75] For more on how context can play a role in the interpretation of investment treaties see *Adel A Hamidi Al Tamimi v Oman*, ICSID Case No ARB/11/33, Award (3 November 2015), paras 387–90; *David Aven v Costa Rica*, para 412.

investment,[76] most first-generation investment treaties do not contain investor obligations. The question that arises, in the context of investor obligations, is that if a BIT does not provide for investor obligations, can foreign investors be held accountable for violation of human rights[77] or for environmental degradation before an international arbitration tribunal? Or should their accountability be tested only under the domestic laws of the host state before the domestic courts? We discuss this issue by looking at some of the ISDS decisions that have focussed on the issue of investor obligations. Based on the approaches that different ISDS tribunals have adopted, we divide the discussion into three parts; first, we examine whether a reference to other applicable law in a BIT could be used by ISDS tribunals to develop investor obligations (the *Urbaser* approach); second, we consider whether existing BIT provisions be interpreted in a manner that could impose obligations on foreign investors (the *David Aven* approach); third, we examine whether domestic law be used to read investor obligations into BITs.[78]

A. Applicable Laws as the Source of Investor Obligations: The *Urbaser* Approach

A leading case that deals with the issue of investor obligations is *Urbaser v Argentina*.[79] This case primarily examined whether applicable laws that the BIT refers to could be the source of investor obligations, in this case human rights obligations. This case involved a concessionaire that was looking after the supply of water and sewerage services in Argentina, in which *Urbaser* was a shareholder. Argentina adopted a range of emergency measures to ward off a financial crisis. These measures caused losses to the concessionaire, ultimately leading to its insolvency. *Urbaser* brought an ISDS claim against Argentina under the Argentina–Spain BIT. Argentina filed a counterclaim against the concessionaire for failing to ensure the required level of investment in the supply services, thus violating the international human right to water.[80]

The foreign investor contested this claim, arguing that:

> [T]he asymmetric nature of BITs prevents a State from invoking any right based on such a treaty, not even a right to submit a counterclaim against an investor. The main aim of such treaties is, indeed, to protect the investor's rights. BITs neither provide for the procedure for submission of State's counterclaims nor even mention the right of an investor to submit counterclaims. This means that investment Treaties do not impose obligations upon investors and, accordingly, that host States cannot rely on the

[76] See section II.F.

[77] Krajewski (n 40); U Kriebaum, 'Human Rights and International Investment Law' in Y Radi (ed), *Research Handbook on Human Rights and Investment* (Edward Elgar, 2019) 18.

[78] See also Krajewksi (n 40).

[79] *Urbaser v Argentina*, ICSID Case No ARB/07/26 (8 December 2016).

[80] ibid para 36.

> violation of the provision of any such Treaty as basis to sue an investor. Such a right to claim would run counter to the object and purpose of treaty arbitration, which is to grant the investors a one-sided right of quasi-judicial review of national regulatory action.[81]

The tribunal did not agree with the foreign investor. The tribunal held that the language of Article X(1) of the Argentina–Spain BIT – 'Disputes arising between a Party and an investor of the other Party in connection with investments within the meaning of this Agreement shall, as far as possible, be settled amicably between the parties to the dispute' – 'is completely neutral as to the identity of the claimant or respondent in an investment dispute arising 'between the parties. It does not indicate that a State Party could not sue an investor in relation to a dispute concerning an investment'.[82] To bolster its reasoning, the tribunal referred to Article X(2) of the Argentina–Spain BIT, which states that if no settlement has been reached within six months from the date the dispute was brought by one of the parties to the dispute, the dispute shall at the request of either party be submitted to the competent tribunals of the host state.[83] The tribunal held that Article X(2), like Article X(1) of the BIT, does not make any distinction on whether the investor or the host state may be 'one of the parties' or 'either party.'[84]

After establishing that it had the jurisdiction to deal with the counterclaim, the tribunal went on to deal with the merits of the case. First, the tribunal held that the 'BIT system' is not a closed system and those legal sources external to the BIT should be taken into account.[85] The tribunal held that international human rights law were part of the applicable law because they were part of the 'general principles of international law' referred to by the Argentina–Spain BIT.[86] The tribunal then referred to international human rights law – Article 30 of the Universal Declaration of Human Rights (UDHR) and Article 5 of the International Covenant on Civil and Political Rights (ICCPR).[87] The tribunal relied on these conventions to conclude 'that the human right for everyone's dignity and its right for adequate housing and living conditions are complemented by an obligation on all parts, public and private parties, not to engage in activity aimed at destroying such rights'.[88] Thus, these two provisions in the ICCPR and UDHR were relied upon to conclude that there are obligations on corporations such as foreign investors.

Second, the tribunal went on to rule that corporations can be subjects of international law[89] and are under a duty not to engage in activities that harm or

[81] ibid para 1120.
[82] ibid para 1143.
[83] ibid.
[84] ibid.
[85] ibid paras 1182–94.
[86] ibid paras 1182, 1188, 1191, 1192.
[87] ibid paras 1196–98.
[88] ibid para 1199.
[89] ibid para 1194.

destroy human rights.[90] However, as regards the question of whether the foreign investor was under an international law obligation to provide drinking water and sanitation services to the population living on the territory of the Concession, the tribunal held that only states have a positive obligation to meet the human right to water whereas corporations only have a negative obligation in this regard, unless specific human rights obligations are imposed on the foreign investor, say as part of the BIT.[91]

While some argue that the *Urbaser* award has opened up the possibility of holding foreign investors to account for human rights violations,[92] the award has been criticised on doctrinal grounds.[93] Krajewski, for example, argues that the tribunal misinterpreted Article 5 of ICCPR and Article 30 of the UDHR to conclude that they form the legal basis of imposing human rights obligations on individuals and corporations.[94] Nonetheless, the approach of the *Urbaser* tribunal in referring to norms outside the BIT could be used to impose obligations on foreign investors. However, as the *Urbaser v Argentina* case reveals, this is only possible if it can be shown that foreign investors are under an obligation under international law to honour human rights or to protect the environment or etc. The other doctrinal difficulty in this approach will be that it is one thing to refer to a norm outside the treaty, say under Article 31(3)(c) of the VCLT, as an aid to interpret the primary treaty, but quite another to rely on an external norm to create positive obligations on the foreign investor. As the *Urbaser* tribunal (and several others) have held, a BIT does not exist in clinical isolation from the larger body of international law. Thus, external treaty norms and customary norms continue to be relevant. The treaty interpreter (the ISDS tribunal, for instance) can refer to these norms if they satisfy the requirements of Article 31(3)(c) of the VCLT or other rules of treaty interpretation. However, if the BIT is silent and does not impose any obligation, hortatory or otherwise, on the foreign investor, it will be difficult to graft a binding obligation on the investor from external norms. In other words, while the state can bring a counterclaim against the investor provided there is consent and connection (ie, there is a relationship between the claim and the counterclaim),[95] the state's counterclaim in holding the foreign investor liable will be unsuccessful in the absence of an obligation under international law on the investor.

[90] ibid para 1199. For a critique of the reasoning employed by the *Urbaser* tribunal see P Abel, 'Counterclaims Based on International Human Rights Obligations of Investors in International Investment Arbitration' (2018) 1 *Brill Open Law* 61, 84–88.

[91] *Urbaser v Argentina*, paras 1208 and 1210.

[92] N Briercliffe, 'Holding investors to account for human rights violations through counterclaims in investment treaty arbitration' (Practical Law Arbitration Blog, 30 January 2017), available at arbitrationblog.practicallaw.com/holding-investors-to-account-for-human-rights-violations-through-counterclaims-in-investment-treaty-arbitration.

[93] K Crow and LL Escobar, 'International Corporate Obligations, Human Rights, and the Urbaser Standard: Breaking New Ground?' (2018) 35 *Boston University International Law Journal* 87, 116–17; Krajewski (n 40) 123–24.

[94] Krajewski (n 40) 124.

[95] Choudhury (n 11).

B. Interpreting Existing BIT Provisions in a Manner that Imposes Obligations on Foreign Investors: The *David Aven* Approach

Another recent case that dealt with the issue of investor obligations is *David Aven v Costa Rica*.[96] This case was decided under the Free Trade Agreement between Central America, the Dominican Republic and the USA (DR-CAFTA),[97] and concerned a real estate project where US citizens invested in several parcels of land and a concession site in 2002 on Costa Rica's Pacific coast. Costa Rica shut down the project on environmental grounds, which, in turn, triggered the claims of violation of DR-CAFTA by the foreign investors. Costa Rica filed a counterclaim against the foreign investors for breaching mandatory rules of environmental protection.

In order to decide whether the foreign investor had any obligations under the DR-CAFTA investment chapter, the tribunal looked at Articles 10.9(3)(c) and 10.11. Article 10.9(3)(c) provides:

> Provided that such measures are not applied in an arbitrary or unjustifiable manner, and provided that such measures do not constitute a disguised restriction on international trade or investment, paragraphs 1(b), (c), and (f), and 2(a) and (b), shall not be construed to prevent a Party from adopting or maintaining measures, including environmental measures:
>
> (i) necessary to secure compliance with laws and regulations that are not inconsistent with this Agreement;
> (ii) necessary to protect human, animal, or plant life or health; or
> (iii) related to the conservation of living or non-living exhaustible natural resources.

Article 10.11 provides:

> Nothing in this Chapter shall be construed to prevent a Party from adopting, maintaining, or enforcing any measure otherwise consistent with this Chapter that it considers appropriate to ensure that investment activity in its territory is undertaken in a manner sensitive to environmental concerns.

Article 10.9(3)(c) of DR-CAFTA is like a general exception clause that recognises the right of the host states to deviate from their treaty obligations, subject to certain conditions, when adopting measures to achieve compelling objectives such as environmental protection. The tribunal looked at this provision, along with Article 10.11 of DR-CAFTA and held that:

> [A] logical effect of Article 10.11 could be that the 'measures' adopted by the host State for the protection of the environment should be deemed to be compulsory for everybody under the jurisdiction of the State, particularly the foreign investors. Therefore,

[96] *David Aven v Costa Rica*.
[97] Signed 5 August 2004, entry into force 1 January 2009 (2004) 43 ILM 514.

> following said interpretation the investors have the obligation, not only under domestic law but also under Section A of Chapter 10 of DR-CAFTA to abide and comply the environmental domestic laws and regulations, including the measures adopted by the host State to protect human, animal, or plant life or health. No investor can ignore or breach such measures and its breach is a violation of both domestic and international law, so that the perpetrator cannot be exempt of liability for the damages caused.[98]

The tribunal concluded that these provisions impose affirmative obligations on foreign investors. Therefore, if an investor breaches domestic environmental law, it would qualify as a violation of the international treaty.[99]

The tribunal also endorsed the view of the *Urbaser* tribunal that investors operating internationally are not immune from becoming subjects of international law.[100] The tribunal further held that this view is particularly cogent when it comes to rights and obligations in which all states have an interest such as those pertaining to the protection of the environment.[101] In light of this, the tribunal referred to the idea of *erga omnes* obligations (ie, obligations that states have towards the international community as a whole).[102] The tribunal concluded that treaty provisions allowing host states to adopt measures for the protection of the environment place an international obligation on the foreign investors to abide by and comply with the domestic environmental laws and regulations,[103] so that foreign investors breaching these laws and regulations would not only violate domestic law but also international law.[104]

However, the tribunal ended up dismissing Costa Rica's counterclaims against the foreign investors on a technicality. According to the tribunal, counterclaims were inconsistent with Articles 20 and 21 of UNCITRAL Arbitration Rules, under which the foreign investor brought the case.[105] The tribunal arrived at this decision because the counterclaim was not precise or accurate enough as regards the damages claimed; and also failed to follow any proper method of valuation for remedies as required under Articles 20 and 21 of UNCITRAL Arbitration Rules.[106]

An important takeaway from the *David Aven* approach is the possibility of imposing international obligations on foreign investors through the interpretation of provisions like general exception clauses. Let us assume that a BIT contains a general exception clause allowing the host state to deviate from treaty obligations in order to protect environment or public health. Let us further assume that the

[98] *David Aven v Costa Rica*, para 734.
[99] ibid para 735.
[100] ibid para 738.
[101] ibid para 738.
[102] ibid.
[103] *David Aven v Costa Rica*, para 741.
[104] ibid.
[105] ibid paras 744–45.
[106] ibid para 745. Also see D Bose, 'David R Aven v Costa Rica: The Confluence of Corporations, Public International Law and International Investment Law' (2020) *ICSID Review – Foreign Investment Law Journal* (advance access), available at doi.org/10.1093/icsidreview/siaa010.

concerned host state enacts a domestic law for the same, imposing obligations on the foreign investor. While these obligations are part of the domestic law, the *David Aven* tribunal allows such a domestic legal obligation to be also read as an obligation under the BIT. Such an interpretation would open up dramatically the ability of host states to impose obligations on foreign investors, and consequently bring counterclaims against the foreign investor, even if the BIT does not specifically impose obligations on the foreign investor. Of course, the host state will still have to satisfy any jurisdictional requirements laid down in the arbitration rules under which the ISDS claim has been brought.

Finally, the approach of the *David Aven* tribunal is not without its problems. The purpose of a general exception or a non-precluded measures provision of the kind given in Articles 10.9(3)(c) and 10.11 is to provide sufficient regulatory latitude to host states to adopt measures for the pursuit of objectives that may otherwise be inconsistent with the treaty. To read these provisions in a manner that imposes obligations on foreign investors is to take it too far and give it an interpretation, which the text does not quite support. While it does deliver the desirable outcome of holding foreign investors to account, it does violence to the ordinary meaning of the text and the purpose of general exception clauses.

C. Domestic Law Imposing Obligations on the Investor

We have already discussed how reference to domestic laws in the BIT could be the basis of imposing obligations on the investor, including specifically referring to compliance with domestic laws as part of the BIT. However, even if the BIT does not contain a specific reference to compliance with domestic laws, investors have a general obligation to comply with the domestic laws of the host state. This point was elucidated in *Cortec v Kenya*, where the tribunal held that:

> [T]he text and purpose of the BIT and the ICSID Convention are not consistent with holding host governments financially responsible for investments created in defiance of their laws fundamental protecting public interests such as the environment. The explicit language to the effect that protected investments must be made 'in accordance with the laws of Kenya' is therefore unnecessary to secure the objects and purpose of the BIT.[107]

The investor, in this case, had failed to obtain an EIA licence for its investment activities and thus violated the Kenyan law.[108] In the view of the tribunal, denying the errant investor protection under the BIT and the ICSID Convention was a proportionate response to its non-compliance with Kenyan law.[109]

[107] *Cortec Mining v Kenya*, para 333.
[108] ibid para 365.
[109] ibid.

In *Burlington v Ecuador*,[110] Ecuador brought a counterclaim against Burlington for harming the environment and part of the related infrastructure through its activities. In this case, the tribunal concluded that it had jurisdiction to hear counterclaims because the parties had entered into an agreement in May 2011 conferring jurisdiction on the tribunal to decide the counterclaim. Thus, there was no need for the tribunal to look at the ISDS provision in the applicable BIT to determine its jurisdiction over the counterclaim. The tribunal applied both Ecuadorian law and international law to conclude that Burlington had indeed caused harm to the environment and to the infrastructure and awarded Ecuador USD 41 million in damages.[111]

These cases are significant because they show how domestic law could be used by ISDS tribunals as a gateway to impose obligations on foreign investors. *Cortec v Kenya* and several other cases show that if the host state is able to demonstrate a violation of domestic law by the foreign investor, treaty protection will be denied to the foreign investor. In other cases, such as *Burlington v Ecuador*, the tribunal could look at the violation of domestic law at the merits stage, and award damages to the state when the investor is found to be in violation of domestic law.

IV. Conclusion

There are two ways to theorise the presence of investor obligations in BITs – either as part of the recalibration project aimed at balancing investment protection and host states' right to regulate in BITs; or as part of a project that aims to make foreign or transnational corporations accountable for their actions under international law and not just as part of the domestic legal systems in which they operate, where recalibrating treaties is a side point.

If the recalibration theorisation is accepted, where the objective is to strike a balance between investment protection and host state's right to regulate, then the provisions on investor obligations could be seen as the normativity of embedded liberalism, something which has been missing in the first generation BITs.[112] John Gerard Ruggie, an American political scientist, conceptualised the post-World War II international economic order as a case of 'embedded liberalism'[113] – a

[110] *Burlington v Republic of Ecuador*, ICSID Case No ARB/08/5, Decision on Counterclaims (7 February 2017).

[111] Also see *Perenco v Ecuador*, ICSID Case No ARB/08/6, Interim Decision on the Environmental Counterclaim (11 August 2015); *Perenco v Ecuador*, ICSID Case No ARB/08/6, Award (27 September 2019).

[112] See D Kalderimis, 'Investment Treaties and Public Goods' (2010) 7 *Transnational Dispute Management Journal* 1; C Titi, *The Right to Regulate in International Investment Law* (Hart Publishing, 2014) 56.

[113] JG Ruggie, 'International Regimes, Transactions, and Change: Embedded Liberalism and the Postwar Economic Order' (1982) 36 *International Organization* 379. Also see ATF Lang, 'Reconstructing Embedded Liberalism: John Gerard Ruggie and Constructivist Approaches to the Study of the International Trade Regime' (2006) 9 *Journal of International Economic Law* 81; ATF Lang, *World Trade Law after Neoliberalism: Re-imagining the Global Economic Order* (Oxford University Press, 2011).

multilateral economic order predicated upon domestic interventionism.[114] Ruggie argued that the post-World War II international economic order shows how 'power and legitimate social objectives become fused to project political authority into the international system'.[115] 'Embedded liberalism' represented compromise between free market and the state intervening in favour of political and social stability.[116] Thus, imposing specific obligations on foreign investors can be seen as part of building a new BIT template premised on embedded liberalism.

The discussion in this chapter shows that while states have started inserting investor obligation provisions in the newly signed BITs, provisions in most BITs employ soft law or hortatory language, thus framing investor obligations as non-binding best endeavours. These provisions appear to be more a part of the recalibration project than of holding transnational corporations accountable under international law. They also reveal a certain degree of reluctance among states to impose binding obligations on foreign investors. States appear to be more comfortable with imposing best endeavour clauses on investors. Consequently, the criticism that many make that BITs are essentially neoliberal instruments that are resistant to tweaks has merit. The discussion in this chapter demonstrates that while BITs have definitely undergone an adjustment to their neoliberal character of the 1990s, a certain degree of continuity of the neoliberal design continues.

Investors can be held accountable, especially in those BITs that do not contain investor obligations even in a soft-law language, through innovative treaty interpretation, as the tribunals in *Urbaser v Argentina* and *David Aven v Costa Rica* have demonstrated. However, as the above discussion shows, these interpretative approaches are not without problems and labour under certain doctrinal limitations. For instance, using general exceptions or a non-precluded measures provision to impose obligations on foreign investors, as the *David Aven* tribunal did, stretches the ordinary meaning of the general exception clauses a little too far.

In sum, it can be said that the surest way of holding foreign investors accountable is by imposing direct and binding obligations on investors as part of the text of the treaty. The Nigeria–Morocco BIT, the Draft PAIC and a few other BITs provide promising templates in this regard. It is critical that countries undertake these treaty reforms, not just as an important step in recalibrating investment treaties, but also to address the concern that corporations wield too much power without accountability under international law. These reforms are doable. The incorporation of the best endeavour clauses on investor obligations is a progressive step, which should lead to the next logical step of binding obligations on foreign investors. These reforms are critical to build, what Joseph Stiglitz describes as 'progressive capitalism'.[117]

[114] ibid 393.

[115] ibid 382.

[116] D Harvey, *A Brief History of Neoliberalism* (Oxford University Press, 2007). Also see Ruggie, 'International Regimes' (1982).

[117] J Stiglitz, *People, Power and Profits: Progressive Capitalism for an Age of Discontent* (Penguin Random House, 2019).

6

The Role of Soft Law Corporate Responsibilities in Defining Investor Obligations in International Investment Agreements

BARNALI CHOUDHURY

I. Introduction

Do multinational corporations, particularly when acting as foreign investors, bear any obligations under international law? For the most part, the answer to this question must be answered in the negative since international law applies only to state and other international actors, and not to corporations.[1] Certainly, that is the approach embodied in most international investment agreements (IIAs) which, despite offering multinational corporations numerous benefits, are reluctant, in most instances, to impose obligations on foreign investors. Indeed, state efforts to specify investor obligations in IIAs[2] seem to suggest that without the inclusion of these new treaty provisions, multinational corporations and other foreign investor are free to act with impunity.

However, while IIAs take a cautious approach to imposing investor obligations, soft law – norms formulated as rules designed to guide behaviour – is defining the expected standard of conduct for multinational corporations at the international level, particularly in the context of social responsibilities. Ranging from the protection of human rights to protection of the environment, soft law initiatives are creating norms for corporate conduct that permeate many aspects of multinational corporate activity, including in relation to foreign investment. Although these responsibilities are not legally enforceable, they define the minimum

[1] See generally JE Alvarez, 'Are Corporations 'Subjects' of International Law?' (2011) 9 *Santa Clara Journal of International Law* 1. Although, international treaties that directly apply to corporations or include corporations within their ambit can impose international obligations.

[2] See for example, Morocco–Nigeria BIT (signed 3 December 2016, not yet in force), Art 18.

standard of conduct states can expect from foreign investors and can also work to contextualise and inform the interpretation of host state obligations under IIAs. As a result, multinational corporations acting as foreign investors are expected under soft law to bear particular social responsibilities even in the face of IIA silence on the issue.

This chapter makes this argument in three sections. In section II, it begins by outlining the impact of multinational corporations on social issues. It describes the detrimental effects that these entities can have on human rights and the environment generally, as well as within the particular arena of international investment law. In this latter context, section II explores the characteristics of IIAs that particularly empower multinational corporations and other foreign investors to be in a position of having adverse impacts on social issues. Section III moves to look at developments in soft law that, in response to the negative impacts of corporations, are gradually beginning to define norms of corporate conduct at the international level. This section begins by defining soft law and describing its elements before turning to examine some of the most influential initiatives emerging in this area. Section III concludes by examining the norms for corporate conduct that soft law has defined for human rights and environmental issues. Finally, section IV explores how soft law norms defining corporate conduct at the international level also influence international investment law. It finds that these soft law norms can condition investment obligations, whether or not they are explicitly included in the text of IIAs, and concludes that they should join the already ample soft law toolkit of investment arbitrators.

II. The Impact of Multinational Corporations on Social Issues

Today the idea that multinational corporations can have an impact on social issues, such as the environment or human rights, is well accepted. In the last couple of years, the world has borne witness to high-profile corporate disasters such as the collapse of the Rana Plaza building, leading to the death and injuries of over 3,000 garment factory workers,[3] and the Deepwater Horizon oil spill, the largest marine oil spill history that resulted in extensive damage to marine and wildlife habitats.[4] Well-known corporations – such as Nestlé, Facebook, and Apple, among others – have been accused of corporate abuse including engaging in modern slavery and bad labour practices, refraining from paying sufficient tax, making corrupt payments

[3] T Hoskins, 'Reliving the Rana Plaza factory collapse: a history of cities in 50 buildings, day 22' (*The Guardian*, 23 April 2015), available at www.theguardian.com/cities/2015/apr/23/rana-plaza-factory-collapse-history-cities-50-buildings.

[4] United States Environmental Protection Agency, 'Deepwater Horizon – BP Gulf of Mexico Oil Spill', available at www.epa.gov/enforcement/deepwater-horizon-bp-gulf-mexico-oil-spill.

and contributing to climate change.[5] As John Ruggie, the former UN Special Rapporteur for Business and Human Rights has observed, the increasing instances of corporate abuses 'are the canary in the coal mine, signalling that all is not well'.[6]

The impact of corporations on social issues is also evident in the international investment arena. Commentators have shown that corporations and other foreign investors have affected a number of social issues including those relating to culture, the environment, human rights, health and corruption.[7] These impacts have been further highlighted in high-profile arbitrations such as *Philip Morris v Uruguay*,[8] *Methanex v USA*,[9] *CMS v Argentina*,[10] *Bilcon v Canada*[11] and *Urbaser v Argentina*,[12] among others.

In all of these instances, the unique features of IIAs have contributed to the ability of corporations to impact social issues. For instance, the ability of corporations and other foreign investors to *directly* initiate arbitration against a state challenging its regulation has empowered corporations/foreign investors vis-à-vis the state.[13] As Reisman has argued, investment arbitration guarantees the foreign investor's bargaining power against the state in a fundamentally asymmetrical context,[14] in which the investor faces the arsenal of the state's executive, police and judicial powers. Yet while it is undoubtedly true that corporate and foreign investor power is strengthened with the use of investment arbitration, it is unclear whether these entities are always operating in a 'fundamentally asymmetrical' context that requires their power to be augmented. Thus, it seems trite to suggest that Philip Morris – whose 2017 revenue outstripped Uruguay's GDP – needs a further basis of power to challenge the developing country's anti-smoking regulations.

[5] For an overview of corporate impacts on public issues see generally B Choudhury and M Petrin, *Corporate Duties to the Public* (Cambridge University Press, 2019).

[6] United Nations Human Rights Council, 'Protect, Respect and Remedy: a Framework for Business and Human Rights – Report of the Special Representative of the Secretary-General on the issue of human rights and transnational corporations and other business enterprises, John Ruggie' (7 April 2008) UN Doc No A/HRC/8/5, para 2.

[7] See for example, V Vadi, *Cultural Heritage in International Investment Law and Arbitration* (Cambridge University Press, 2014); JE Viñuales, *Foreign Investment and the Environment in International Law* (Cambridge University Press, 2012); Filip Balcerzak, *Investor – State Arbitration and Human Rights* (Brill, 2017); V Vadi, *Public Health in International Investment Law and Arbitration* (Routledge, 2013); AP Llamzon, *Corruption in International Investment Arbitration* (Oxford University Press, 2014).

[8] *Philip Morris Brands Sàrl et al v Uruguay*, ICSID Case No ARB/10/7, Award (8 July 2016).

[9] *Methanex v USA*, Final Award on Jurisdiction and Merits (3 August 2005) 44 ILM 1345, avalailable at www.italaw.com/sites/default/files/case-documents/ita0529.pdf.

[10] *CMS Gas Transmission Co. v Argentina*, ICSID Case No. ARB/01/8, Award (12 May 2005).

[11] *Bilcon of Delaware et al v Canada*, UNCITRAL, PCA Case No 2009-04, Award (17 March 2015).

[12] *Urbaser SA and Consorcio de Aguas Bilbao Bizkaia, Bilbao Biskaia Ur Partzuergoa v Argentina*, ICSID Case No ARB/07/26, Award (8 December 2016).

[13] See, for example, US–Rwanda BIT (signed 19 February 2008, entry into force 1 January 2012), Art 24; Comprehensive Economic and Trade Agreement (CETA) Between Canada And the European Union (signed 30 October 2016, provisional entry into force 21 September 2017), Art 8.23.

[14] WM Reisman, 'International Investment Arbitration and ADR: Married but Best Living Apart' (2009) 24 *ICSID Review – Foreign Investment Law Journal* 185.

A second characteristic of IIAs that have enabled corporations to have an impact on social issues is the imprecise and open-ended nature of the standards of treatment found in the treaties.[15] Because of the abstract nature of the IIA standards of treatments, arbitral tribunals are afforded significant interpretive discretion. A recent survey found that in over three-quarters of investment arbitrations, tribunals have engaged in expansive interpretations of the terms indirect expropriation and fair and equitable treatment.[16] Not surprisingly, the commentator concluded that investment arbitration has been turned into more like 'painting a picture than doing a sum'.[17]

These expansive interpretations of IIA standards of treatment can pose particular problems for state efforts to regulate in the public interest.[18] They can result in states being found liable to foreign investors despite acting to protect the public interest.[19] Moreover, because such interpretations are dependent on judicial discretion, states must legislate social issues in the face of unpredictability as to which situations may trigger an IIA breach as well as in the face of an indeterminacy of the threshold of liability for an IIA breach.[20] This can result in states striking an inadequate balance between preserving investor rights and regulating public interest issues.[21]

Finally, corporations affect social issues in the international investment arena because investment arbitrations have become powerful tools in their own right. For instance, investment arbitrations can inspire regulatory chill in states.[22] That is, states may refrain from enacting regulations to protect certain social issues out of fear of becoming a target of an investment arbitration. Thus, Indonesia prevented its environmental laws banning open-pit mining from applying to foreign investors when they threatened to initiate an investment arbitration against the state.[23]

[15] S Montt, *State Liability in Investment Treaty Arbitration – Global Constitutional and Administrative Law in the BIT Generation* (Hart, 2012) 3; UN Conference on Trade and Development (UNCTAD), 'Fair and Equitable Treatment– UNCTAD Series on Issues in International Investment Agreements II' (3 May 2012) UN Doc UNCTAD/DIAE/IA/2011/5, 1, 11.

[16] G van Harten, 'Leaders in the Expansive and Restrictive Interpretation of Investment Treaties: A Descriptive Study of ISDS Awards to 2010' (2018) 29 *European Journal of International Law* 507, 518–19.

[17] ibid 508.

[18] UNCTAD, 'Fair and Equitable Treatment – UNCTAD Series on Issues in International Investment Agreements II', 11–5.

[19] See, for example, *Bilcon v Canada*; *Enron Corporation and Ponderosa Assets v Argentina*, ICSID Case No ARB/01/3, Award (22 May 2007); *Suez, Sociedad General de Aguas de Barcelona, SA and Vivendi Universal, SA v Argentina*, ICSID Case No ARB/03/19, Decision on Liability (30 July 2010).

[20] UNCTAD, 'Fair and Equitable Treatment II' (n 15) 11–2.

[21] ibid 12.

[22] See K Tienhaara, 'Regulatory Chill and the Threat of Arbitration: A View from Political Science' in C Brown and K Miles (eds), *Evolution in Investment Treaty Law And Arbitration* (Cambridge University Press, 2011) 606.

[23] SG Gross, 'Inordinate chill: BITS, Non-NAFTA MITS, and Host-State Regulatory Freedom: An Indonesian Case Study' (2003) 24 *Michigan Journal of International Law* 893; K Tienhaara, 'What You Don't Know Can Hurt You: Investor-State Disputes and the Protection of the Environment in Developing Countries' (2006) 6 *Global Environmental Politics* 73.

Similarly, New Zealand refrained from introducing its tobacco plain packaging laws until Philip Morris's arbitration on the same issue with Australia was decided.[24]

Corporations have also been using investment arbitrations as a tool to delay or discourage regulation either in the defendant state or in a third state.[25] In other instances, they have been using them to prompt undisclosed settlements.[26] One commentator has even suggested that corporations are using investment arbitrations to thwart government regulatory efforts in secret.[27]

In short, corporations – emboldened by IIAs – are able to affect social issues in states in a variety of different ways. Yet, despite the noticeable impact corporations and foreign investors can have on human rights and the environment in the international investment arena, IIAs are mainly silent on the expected conduct of corporations/foreign investors in this regard.

There are, of course, a handful of exceptions. For instance, some states have included provisions in their IIAs specifying that states should 'encourage' enterprises to voluntarily incorporate corporate social responsibility (CSR) standards.[28] The Brazil–Malawi BIT uses stronger language stipulating that investors '*shall* strive to achieve the highest possible level of contribution to the sustainable development of the Host Party' and outlines methods by which this responsibility can be met.[29]

Some IIAs have also made attempts at imposing binding obligations on foreign investors. Thus, the Morocco–Nigeria BIT articulates a specific provision establishing investor obligations.[30] Under this provision, investors are required to, among others, uphold human rights, act in accordance with internationally recognised labour standards, and maintain an environmental management system.[31] Enforcement appears to be through a provision enabling the home state to hold a foreign investor liable for any investment-related acts in the host state that causes significant damage, injuries or loss of life.[32]

[24] E Crosbie and G Thomson, 'Why did it take 53 months for NZ to introduce plain cigarette packs?' (*Noted*, 14 June 2018); J Bonnitcha, LNS Poulsen and M Waibel, *The Political Economy of the Investment Treaty Regime* (Oxford University Press, 2017) 241.

[25] KJ Pelc, 'What Explains the Low Success Rate of Investor-State Disputes?' (2017) 71 *International Organization* 559; J Pohl, 'Societal Benefits and Costs of International Investment Agreements: A Critical Review of Aspects and Available Empirical Evidence' (2018) OECD Working Papers on International Investment 1/2018, 65, available at doi.org/10.1787/e5f85c3d-en.

[26] EM Hafner-Burton, S Puig and DG Victor, 'Against Secrecy? The Social Cost of International Dispute Settlement' (2017) 42 *Yale Journal of International Law* 280, 319.

[27] Pohl, 'Societal Benefits' (2018) 65.

[28] See, for example, Canada–Mongolia BIT (signed 8 September 2016, entry into force 24 February 2017), Art 14; Chile–Hong Kong, China SAR BIT (signed 18 November 2016, entry into force 14 July 2019), Art 16; Argentina–Qatar BIT (signed 6 November 2016, not yet in force), Art 12; Morocco–Nigeria BIT (signed 3 December 2016, not yet in force), Art 18.

[29] Brazil–Malawi BIT (signed 25 June 2015, not yet in force), Art 9. See also Brazil–Mozambique BIT (signed 30 March 2010, not yet in force), Art 10.

[30] Morocco–Nigeria BIT (signed 3 December 2016, not yet in force), Art 18.

[31] ibid.

[32] ibid Art 20.

Still, these provisions remain the exception, not the norm. Consequently, IIAs continue to be primarily defined by the host state's obligations to the foreign investor, leaving the foreign investor without any responsibilities.

III. Responsible Conduct for Business – Standards in Soft Law

While international investment law remains reticent to impose obligations on foreign investors, the movement to impose responsibilities on business outside of the international investment law sphere continues to increase. In particular, the business and human rights movement has continued to impose more exacting responsibilities on business, albeit only in soft law. While soft law responsibilities are hardly akin to the legally enforceable obligations one finds in IIAs, this section argues that the soft law responsibilities imposed on business have begun to set norms for the expected conduct of business in all fields, including international investment law.

The section[33] begins by examining what is meant by soft law, how it can be distinguished from hard law, and explores its utility before moving to examine the soft law responsibilities being imposed on business in both the human rights and environment contexts. It concludes by finding that soft law initiatives, despite their non-binding status, are establishing norms for corporate conduct in these areas, which are at best influencing corporate actions and, at the very least, focusing corporate managers' attention to these issues.

A. Soft Law

Although hard law is widely thought of as consisting of legally binding obligations that create enforceable rights and duties, soft law does not have a universally accepted definition.[34] It may refer to 'principles, norms, standards or other statements of expected behaviour' that do not create enforceable rights and duties.[35] Alternatively, it may be defined in the negative; that is, as lacking one or more of the properties normally ascribed to law – normative content, formal legal status,

[33] For a more thorough examination of soft law in the business and human rights context see B Choudhury, 'Balancing Soft and Hard Law for Business and Human Rights' (2018) 67 *International & Comparative Law Quarterly* 961. Section III of this chapter is based on sections of that article.

[34] RR Baxter, 'International Law in "Her Infinite Variety"' (1980) 29 *International & Comparative Law Quarterly* 549; C Brummer, *Soft Law and the Global Financial System: Rule Making in the 21st Century* (Cambridge University Press, 2011) 2.

[35] DL Shelton, 'Normative Hierarchy in International Law' (2006) 100 *American Journal of International Law* 291, 319–20; Baxter, '"Her Infinite Variety"' (1980) 549.

and enforceability.[36] Soft law can also be thought of in terms of the legal impact it can have, whether by helping to interpret or informing the understanding of legal rules or by constituting a representation that elicits a legitimate expectation by another.[37]

One reason for the impreciseness of the definition of soft law may be because soft and hard law are not dichotomies.[38] Rather, they may simply represent two ends of a continuum,[39] with a sliding scale of normativity and behaviour-influencing capacity.[40] Still, it may be considered a type of law since the norms in soft law are formulated as rules and are designed to guide behaviour.[41]

Soft law may further be identified by the outcomes that flow from the performance or breach of the norm it represents. Where legal consequences of both performance and breach can be ascertained with precision, a norm is considered to have hardened.[42] Conversely, soft law norms are more likely to be represented by vague or uncertain outcomes flowing from either the performance or breach of that norm.

Despite this uncertainty, states and other international actors often turn to soft law because it possesses a number of advantages over hard law. Soft law, for instance, can be more flexible for states to use because it enables them to respond to problems or changing circumstances on an as needed basis.[43] This can be particularly advantageous for issues that are developing or changing quickly since states can swiftly adopt soft law instruments or easily alter them. Their utility is also especially high for areas marked by a lack of consensus or in which states are reluctant to make binding commitments.[44]

One of soft law's additional advantages is that it is not law, meaning that it will not be subject to the normal legal enactment processes, but it can still influence

[36] T Gammeltoft-Hansen, S Lagoutte and J Cerone, 'Introduction: Tracing the Roles of Soft Law in Human Rights' in S Lagoutte, T Gammeltoft-Hansen and J Cerone (eds), *Tracing the Roles of Soft Law in Human Rights* (Oxford University Press, 2016) 3.

[37] JE Alvarez, 'Reviewing the Use of 'Soft Law' in Investment Arbitration' (2018) Public Law & Legal Theory Research Paper Series Working Paper No 18-46, 12, available at ssrn.com/abstract=3258737; AT Guzman and TL Meyer, 'International Soft Law' (2010) 2 *Journal of Legal Analysis* 171, 174. See also M Jacob and SW Schill, 'Going Soft: Towards a New Age of Soft Law in International Law?' (2014) 8 *World Arbitration and Mediation Review* 1, 3.

[38] J d'Aspremont, 'Softness in International Law: A Self-Serving Quest for New Legal Materials' (2009) 19 *European Journal of International Law* 5; J Cerone, 'A Taxonomy of Soft Law: Stipulating a Definition' in S Lagoutte, T Gammeltoft-Hansen and J Cerone (eds), *Tracing the Roles of Soft Law in Human Rights* (Oxford University Press, 2016) 16–17.

[39] Shelton, 'Normative Hierarchy' (2006) 320; CM Chinkin, 'Normative Development' in D Shelton (ed), *Commitment and Compliance: The Role of Non-Binding Norms in the International Legal System* (Oxford University Press, 2003) 37.

[40] G Kaufmann-Kohler, 'Soft Law in International Arbitration: Codification and Normativity' (2010) *Journal of International Dispute Settlement* 1, 3; Cerone, 'A Taxonomy of Soft Law' (2016) 16.

[41] Cerone (n 38) 6.

[42] Chinkin, 'Normative Development' (2003) 859.

[43] ibid 852; Shelton (n 35) 322; KW Abbott and D Snidal, 'Hard and Soft Law in International Governance' (2000) 54 *International Organization* 421, 423.

[44] Shelton (n 35) 322; Abbott and Snidal (ibid) 423.

conduct in a desired manner.[45] By fostering dominant norms, soft law acts as a behaviour-coordinating tool between actors.[46] Its function is to shape and share values and to create a standard of expectations. It can thus mould the behaviour of actors subject to it, including corporations.[47]

Finally, soft law can act as a complement to hard law. It can help codify the norms in an area or supplement existing hard law.[48] Soft law can thus resolve ambiguities, provide detailed rules or technical standards necessary for interpretation, or fill voids.[49]

B. Corporate Responsibilities for Human Rights and the Environment

Today there are a number of different international initiatives detailing the responsibilities of corporations. While these instruments take different approaches to outlining these responsibilities or focus on different issues, what they all have in common is that they represent soft law initiatives. That is, the leading initiatives detailing corporate responsibilities for social issues foster norms or standards of expected behaviour for corporations but are generally non-binding and unenforceable.

For instance, in the business and human rights area, there are four leading international initiatives: the OECD Guidelines for Multinational Enterprises, the ILO Tripartite Declaration, the UN Global Compact and the UN Guiding Principles on Business and Human Rights. Similarly, in the business and environment arena, both the OECD Guidelines and the UN Global Compact outline corporate responsibilities vis-à-vis the environment. There are also a number of other international instruments, which devote aspects of their contents to outlining corporate responsibilities to the environment.

i. Business and Human Rights Initiatives

One of the earliest soft law initiatives outlining corporate responsibilities for human rights is the OECD Guidelines for Multinational Enterprises. The OECD Guidelines were first developed in 1976 and last revised in 2011. Among other

[45] Shelton (n 35) 322; P Weil, 'Towards Relative Normativity in International Law' (1983) 77 *American Journal of International Law* 413, 415.

[46] Brummer, *Soft Law and the Global Financial System* (2011) 132.

[47] Chinkin (n 39) 865; Shelton (n 35) 322; Weil, 'Towards Relative Normativity' (1983) 415.

[48] S Lagoutte, T Gammeltoft-Hansen and J Cerone (eds), *Tracing the Roles of Soft Law in Human Rights* (Oxford University Press, 2016) 1; Shelton (n 35) 320-1; Abbott and Snidal, 'Hard and Soft Law' (2000) 423.

[49] Shelton (n 35) 320; Lagoutte, Gammeltoft-Hansen and Cerone (ibid) 1.

issues, the Guidelines contain a section outlining expected conduct for corporations vis-à-vis human rights. These include recommendations that corporations avoid infringing on the human rights of others, address adverse human rights impacts with which they are involved, and seek ways to prevent or mitigate adverse human rights impacts that are directly linked to their business operations.[50] While the OECD Guidelines are non-binding, they delegate their interpretation to third parties or reviewing bodies set up in individual countries known as National Contact Points, which are tasked with enforcement.[51] However, the National Contact Points can only suggest recommendations to corporations to align their conduct with the Guidelines; they cannot impose binding consequences for breach of the Guidelines.[52]

A second initiative is the 1978 International Labour Organization's (ILO) Tripartite Declaration of Principles Concerning Multinational Enterprises and Social Policy.[53] The Tripartite Declaration provides voluntary standards for corporate practices in relation to labour and employment issues. For instance, it provides detailed policies on employment promotion, child and forced labour, and safety and health standards, among other issues. The ILO delegates interpretation of the Tripartite Declaration to the Officers of the Committee on Multinational Enterprises[54] and imposes reporting obligations on governments.[55] However, the Declaration neither specifies the consequences of breach of its provisions nor provides for an enforcement mechanism.[56]

A third initiative is the UN Global Compact, a policy instrument that advocates good corporate practices in several areas, including human rights.[57] The UN Global Compact delineates its voluntary standards for corporate conduct in 10 broadly worded principles.[58] Among these 10 principles are two devoted to human rights. They recommend that businesses support and respect human rights and not be complicit in human rights abuses.[59] In addition, the UN Global

[50] Organization for Economic Co-Operation and Development (OECD), *Guidelines for Multinational Enterprises* (OECD Publishing 2011) 31.

[51] OECD, 'National Contact Points for the OECD Guidelines for Multinational Enterprises', available at mneguidelines.oecd.org/ncps.

[52] JL Cernic, 'Corporate Responsibility for Human Rights: A Critical Analysis of the OECD Guidelines for Multinational Enterprises' (2008) 3 *Hanse Law Review* 71; O de Schutter, *Transnational Corporations and Human Rights* (Hart, 2006) 8–9.

[53] *Tripartite Declaration of Principles Concerning Multinational Enterprises and Social Policy*, 5th edn (International Labour Organization, 2017) 4.

[54] ibid 24.

[55] For a full overview of the process see de Schutter, *Transnational Corporations* (2006) 6–8.

[56] O Amao, *Corporate Social Responsibility, Human Rights and the Law: Multinational Corporations in Developing Countries* (Routledge, 2011) 30.

[57] See A Rasche, 'A Necessary Supplement – What the United Nations Global Compact Is and Is Not' (2009) 48 *Business Society* 511.

[58] D Weissbrodt, 'Business and Human Rights' (2005) 74 *University of Cincinnati Law Review* 55, 66; S Deva, 'Global Compact: A Critique of UN's Public-Private Partnership for Promoting Corporate Citizenship' (2006) 34 *Syracuse Journal International Law & Commerce* 107, 129.

[59] UN Global Compact, 'The Ten Principles of the UN Global Compact', Principles 1 and 2, available at www.unglobalcompact.org/what-is-gc/mission/principles.

Compact reiterates the main principles of the ILO Tripartite Declaration, namely that businesses should uphold the right to freedom of association and collective bargaining, abolish forced and compulsory labour as well as child labour, and eliminate discrimination in employment.[60] As a purely soft law initiative, the UN Global Compact neither specifies the consequences of its breach nor provides any third-party oversight over its principles. However, corporate members are required to file annual communication on progress reports and, in case of failure, risk dismissal from the Global Compact.[61]

Finally, the latest international standard for corporate responsibility for human rights is found in the United Nations Guiding Principles on Business and Human Rights (the UNGPs).[62] The UNGPs flow from an earlier report by UN Human Rights Special Representative, John Ruggie, which established the 'Protect, Respect and Remedy' Framework.[63] The Framework concluded that business and human rights responsibility rested on three differentiated but complementary pillars: the state duty to protect against human rights abuses; the corporate responsibility to respect human rights; and the need for more effective access by victims to remedies.[64] Ruggie expanded on the corporate responsibility to respect in the UNGPs, noting that corporations should refrain from infringing on the human rights of others as well as 'address adverse human rights impacts with which they are involved'.[65] Moreover, he advised that corporations should not cause or contribute 'to adverse human rights impacts through their own activities' and should 'prevent or mitigate adverse human rights impacts that are directly linked to their operations' by engaging in a process of human rights due diligence.[66]

While the UNGPs were deliberately framed as soft law – since Ruggie found that business responsibility for human rights was derived from social norms or expectations[67] – the corporate responsibility to respect human rights is not

[60] ibid Principles 3–6.

[61] UN Global Compact, 'The Communication on Progress (COP) in Brief', available at www.unglobalcompact.org/participation/report/cop.

[62] UN Human Rights Council, 'Guiding Principles on Business and Human Rights: Implementing the United Nations 'Protect, Respect and Remedy' Framework' (2011) UN Doc No HR/PUB/11/04.

[63] UN Human Rights Council, 'Protect, Respect and Remedy: a Framework for Business and Human Rights – Report of the Special Representative of the Secretary-General on the issue of human rights and transnational corporations and other business enterprises, John Ruggie' (7 April 2008) UN Doc No A/HRC/8/5.

[64] UN Human Rights Council, 'Guiding Principles on Business and Human Rights: Implementing the United Nations 'Protect, Respect and Remedy' Framework' (2011) UN Doc No HR/PUB/11/04.

[65] ibid Guiding Principle 11.

[66] ibid Guiding Principle 13; UN Human Rights Council, 'Protect, Respect and Remedy: a Framework for Business and Human Rights – Report of the Special Representative of the Secretary-General on the issue of human rights and transnational corporations and other business enterprises, John Ruggie' (7 April 2008) UN Doc No A/HRC/8/5, paras 25, 56–64.

[67] UN Commission on Human Rights, 'Report of the United Nations High Commissioner on Human Rights on the Responsibilities of Transnational Corporations and Related Business Enterprises with regard to Human Rights – Business and Human Rights: Towards Operationalizing the "Protect, Respect and Remedy" Framework' (2009) UN Doc No A/HRC/11/13, para 46.

voluntary. Rather, as the UN Office of High Commission explains, the corporate responsibility to respect human rights is 'a global expectation of all companies',[68] despite the fact that is not a legal obligation unless a domestic government imposes such a duty.[69] Accordingly, corporations are expected to adhere to this responsibility as if it was a legal obligation even though the UNGPs do not specify any consequences for breaching this corporate responsibility to respect or provide any type of third party oversight.[70]

Soft law initiatives therefore set the norms for corporate responsibility for human rights as being: refraining from infringing on the human rights of others; not causing or contributing to adverse human rights impacts; addressing adverse human rights impacts with which corporations are involved; and preventing adverse human rights impacts directly linked to business operations by engaging in human rights due diligence. Corporations are, further, expected to refrain from adverse labour practices such as using forced or child labour or engaging in employment discrimination.

ii. Business and Environment Initiatives

As with business and human rights initiatives, two of the leading soft law initiatives outlining business responsibility for the environment are found in the OECD Guidelines and the UN Global Compact. The OECD Guidelines, for instance, encourage corporations to 'take due account of the need to protect the environment' by having, among other things, a sound environmental management system in place. Such a system helps control a corporation's environmental impacts and integrates environmental considerations into business operations.[71] The Guidelines further recommend that corporations should act, 'in a proactive way, to avoid … serious or irreversible environmental damages resulting from their activities'.[72]

The Global Compact similarly outlines environmental responsibilities for corporations, basing three of its 10 principles on the Rio Declaration.[73] It recommends that businesses assess environmental risks, promote environmental responsibility and encourage the development and diffusion of environmentally friendly technologies.[74]

Apart from these two initiatives, soft law does not delineate corporate responsibilities for the environment as well as human rights issues. In some instances,

[68] UN Human Rights Office of the High Commissioner, 'Frequently Asked Questions about The Guiding Principles on Business and Human Rights' (2014) UN Doc No HR/PUB/14/3, 10.

[69] ibid 29.

[70] GG Brenkert, 'Business Ethics and Human Rights: An Overview' (2016) 1 *Business and Human Rights Journal* 277, 294.

[71] OECD, Guidelines for Multinational Enterprises (2011) para 61.

[72] ibid para 69.

[73] Report of the United Nations Conference on Environment and Development (Rio de Janeiro, 3–14 June 1992), UN Doc No A/CONF.151/26 (Vol. I) (Rio Declaration on Environment and Development).

[74] UN Global Compact, Principles 7–9.

international environmental instruments directed at states may provide for indirect or derivative responsibilities for corporations. For instance, the UN's Voluntary Action Plan on Sustainable Development encouraged corporations to employ environmentally sound technologies while the Paris Climate Change Agreement invited corporations to 'scale up their efforts and support actions to reduce emissions'.[75] However, more recently, efforts have been made to outline corporate responsibilities more directly. Thus, the Convention on Biological Diversity encourages corporations to monitor and assess impacts on biodiversity and to develop and apply processes that minimise or avoid negative impacts on biodiversity,[76] while the UN Sustainable Development Goals encourage companies to adopt 'sustainable practices'.[77] The UN Special Rapporteur on the Situation of Human Rights and Fundamental Freedoms of Indigenous People also outlined corporate responsibilities to the environment.[78] He noted that corporations should conduct environmental impact studies before engaging in corporate activities and concluded that corporations should 'seek technically feasible solutions to mitigate or limit' environmental impacts as well as impacts on indigenous peoples.[79]

Therefore, although the norms for corporate responsibilities to the environment are not as well developed as they are in relation to human rights responsibilities, they suggest that, at a minimum, corporations should seek to minimise their impact on the environment and to engage in processes or technologies that will reduce adverse environmental impacts relating to their business operations.

iii. Soft Law Corporate Responsibilities

As the discussion on soft law at the outset of this section suggested, soft and hard law are not dichotomous entities, but rather represent only two ends of a spectrum with a shifting scale of norm formation. While the UN Global Compact, the ILO Tripartite Declaration and the OECD Guidelines for Multinational Enterprises have begun the process of establishing corporate responsibilities for human rights, it is clear that promulgation of the UNGPs has helped to shift the

[75] UN Conference on Environment and Development, 'Earth Summit: Agenda 21 – The United Nations Programme of Action from Rio' (United Nations, 1993) para 30; UN Framework Convention on Climate Change, 'Adoption of the Paris Agreement Proposal by the President, Draft decision -/CP.21' (12 December 2015) UN Doc No FCCC/CP/2015/L.9/Rev.1, para 134.

[76] UN Conference of the Parties to the Convention on Biological Diversity, 'Decision Adopted by the Conference of the Parties to the Convention on Biological Diversity at Its Tenth Meeting – X/21 – Business Engagement', UN Doc No UNEP/CBD/COP/DEC/X/21 (29 October 2010), s 2.

[77] UN Sustainable Development Goals (2016), Target 12.6, available at www.un.org/sustainabledevelopment/sustainable-consumption-production.

[78] Special Rapporteur on the Situation of Human Rights and Fundamental Freedoms of Indigenous People, James Anaya, 'Summary of activities, corporate responsibility with respect to indigenous peoples' (2010) UN Doc No A/HRC/15/37, Section III.

[79] ibid para 74.

norm of expected corporate conduct for human rights just short of hard law. Indeed, the UNGPs have had a transformative effect on the expected conduct of corporations in relation to human rights. This can be seen by their implementation into existing initiatives, such as the UN Global Compact[80] and the OECD Guidelines. It can also be seen in their impact in other areas such as on the EU's strategy for CSR and its forthcoming human rights due diligence legislation,[81] the National Action Plans of several states[82] and on a number of other international initiatives including the International Finance Corporation Performance Standards on Environmental and Social Sustainability,[83] among others. In part, this may be because the UNGPs had the authority of the United Nations behind it, or because they were developed in consultation with business ensuring their buy-in was secured from the outset. In any case, while not encompassing a binding legal obligation, the corporate responsibility to respect human rights has become a well-established norm.

The impact of soft law, particularly the UNGPs, on shaping norms of corporate responsibility has been particularly noteworthy despite the fact that the UNGPs, themselves, do not impose consequences for corporations that fail to adhere to the expected conduct. To some, this failure to impose penalties on corporations suggests that soft law does not influence the actual conduct of corporations.[84] However, the value of soft law, and especially the UNGPs, has been in crystallising the norm of the corporate responsibility to respect human rights, which previously remained elusive. Once established, the norm has been allowed to flourish in, or used as the basis for numerous other instruments, many of which are better designed to hold corporations accountable for failures. For example, the new EU human rights due diligence law will impose sanctions on corporations for failures to respect human rights or the environment while the Equator Principles impose human rights requirements on corporations as conditions of obtaining financing. Both of these instruments, in addition to countless others, have been influenced

[80] United Nations Global Compact and Office of the High Commissioner for Human Rights (OHCHR), 'The UN Guiding Principles on Business and Human Rights: Relationship to UN Global Compact Commitments' (1 July 2011) Joint note by the UN Global Compact and OHCHR.

[81] European Commission, 'A Renewed EU Strategy 2011–14 for Corporate Social Responsibility' (2011) COM(2011) 681 final; European Parliament Working Group on Responsible Business Conduct, 'EP RBC Working Group: EU Is Well Placed To Show Leadership With Its Future Due Diligence Legislation' (27 May 2020), available at responsiblebusinessconduct.eu/wp/2020/05/27/ep-rbc-working-group-eu-is-well-placed-to-show-leadership-with-its-future-due-diligence-legislation.

[82] See generally EU Directorate-General for External Policies Policy Department, 'Implementation of the UN Guiding Principles on Business and Human Rights' (2017) EP/EXPO/B/COMMITTEE/FWC/2013-08/Lot8/09.

[83] International Finance Corporation (IFC), 'UN Guiding Principles on Business and Human Rights and IFC Sustainability Framework' (2012), available at www.ifc.org/wps/wcm/connect/topics_ext_content/ifc_external_corporate_site/sustainability-at-ifc/publications/un_guidingprinciplesbusinesshumanrights.

[84] See, for example, the criticisms expressed in J Ho, 'The Creation of Elusive Investor Responsibility' (2019) 113 *American Journal of International Law Unbound* 10.

by norms set by the UNGPs.[85] Soft law has thus been particularly adept at helping to establish the norm of the corporate responsibility to respect human rights and influencing its use in other instruments.

Conversely, corporate responsibilities to the environment are not as well developed. Although both the OECD and the UN Global Compact, alongside other initiatives, recommend corporations pay heed to the environmental impacts of their activities, it is not clear what precisely is expected of corporations in relation to the environment. However, while a clear norm for corporate responsibility for the environment has not yet emerged, what is clear is that soft law initiatives in this area suggest that, at a minimum, corporations cannot ignore their impact on the environment. This is particularly true when it comes to climate change as there is an emerging norm that corporations should disclose, and accordingly manage, climate change risks.[86]

IV. Soft Law Corporate Responsibilities and International Investment Law

Given the well-established norm of the corporate responsibility to respect human rights and the less well-established, but emerging norm, of the corporate responsibility to minimise harm to the environment, international investment law should be read in conjunction with these norms. The aim in doing so is to promote consistency in international law, which serves to strengthen its overall legitimacy and normative power.[87] However, the question remains how these norms, drafted in soft law and without binding effect, can infiltrate the decidedly legal obligation-based sphere of international investment law.

One way would be to include such norms in IIA themselves. Already several IIAs include specific references to the OECD Guidelines for Multinational Enterprises,[88] the UN Global Compact,[89] the ILO Tripartite Declaration[90] and the

[85] European Parliament Working Group on Responsible Business Conduct, 'The Equator Principles' (2020), available at equator-principles.com/wp-content/uploads/2020/05/The-Equator-Principles-July-2020-v2.pdf.

[86] See B Choudhury, 'The Grey Rhino: Climate Change as Systemic Risk' (2021, forthcoming), available at papers.ssrn.com/sol3/papers.cfm?abstract_id=3704962.

[87] A Peters, 'The Refinement Of International Law: From Fragmentation To Regime Interaction And Politicization' (2017) 15 *International Journal of Constitutional Law* 671, 680; G Abi-Saab, 'Fragmentation or Unification: Some Concluding Remarks' (1999) 31 *New York University Journal of International Law & Policy* 919, 926.

[88] See, for example, CETA, Preamble and Art 22.3; Netherlands–United Arab Emirates BIT (signed 26 November 2013, not yet in force), Art 2(3).

[89] See, for example, Austria–Nigeria BIT (signed 8 April 2013, not yet in force), Preamble; Free Trade Agreement Between the EFTA States and Georgia (signed 27 June 2016, entry into force 1 September 2017), Preamble.

[90] See, for example, EU–Ukraine BIT (signed 27 June 2014, entry into force 1 January 2016), Art 422; EU–Moldova BIT (signed 27 June 2014, entry into force 1 July 2016), Art 35.

Rio Declaration.[91] Even the newest soft law initiative, the UNGPs, is being referenced in a new model treaty.[92] Several IIAs also contain references to CSR, which generally encourage investors to incorporate international standards of CSR and which are sometimes defined with specific reference to soft law initiatives such as the OECD Guidelines.[93]

However, the references in IIAs to either soft law initiatives or the general concept of CSR tend not to take a consistent form. In some instances, the initiatives or the notion of CSR can be found in the preambles of agreements, while in others it can form parts of individual treaty provisions. Yet even when the references appear in the treaties' preambles, they can entail different levels of commitment. For instance, the Austria–Nigeria BIT's preamble 'takes note' of the UN Global Compact, while the Netherlands–UAE BIT's preamble asks that the contracting parties promote the application of the OECD Guidelines for Multinational Enterprises in their domestic laws.[94] Conversely, state use of CSR provisions has taken somewhat of a more consistent approach. Thus, whether the reference is made in the IIA's preamble or as a separate provision, the references generally 'encourage' investors to observe internationally recognised guidelines on CSR or engage in responsible business practices.[95] Moreover, although the wording for the references to CSR in IIAs may differ slightly from one agreement to the next, state practice in this area is generally consistent in relying on non-obligatory language. Thus, investors are only 'encouraged' or asked to 'strive' – not required – to adopt good corporate practices.

Despite the non-obligatory nature of soft law corporate responsibility initiatives, they can influence the interpretation of IIAs. For instance, references to soft law initiatives or the importance of CSR can provide 'normative background'.[96] The references can help clarify the state parties' intentions and assumptions[97] as well as enlighten arbitrators on the IIA's object and purpose.[98] In addition,

[91] CETA, Art 22.1; EU–Vietnam Free Trade Agreement (signed 30 June 2019, not yet in force), art 13.1.

[92] See, for example, the Dutch Model BIT (22 March 2019), Art 7, available at www.rijksoverheid.nl/ministeries/ministerie-van-buitenlandse-zaken/documenten/publicaties/2019/03/22/nieuwe-modeltekst-investeringsakkoorden.

[93] See, for example, Argentina–Qatar BIT (signed 6 November 2016, not yet in force), Art 12; Benin–Canada BIT (signed 9 January 2013, entry into force 12 May 2014), Art 16; Brazil–Chile BIT (signed 24 November 2015, not yet in force), Art 15; China–Switzerland FTA (signed 6 July 2013, entry into force 1 July 2014), Preamble.

[94] Austria–Nigeria BIT (signed 8 April 2013, not yet in force), Preamble; Netherlands–United Arab Emirates BIT (signed 26 November 2013, not yet in force), Art 2(3).

[95] See, for example, China–Switzerland FTA (signed 6 July 2013, entry into force 1 July 2014), Preamble; EU–Moldova BIT (signed 27 June 2014, entry into force 1 July 2016), Art 35.

[96] SW Schill, 'The OECD Guidelines for Multinational Enterprises and International Investment Agreements: Converging Universes' in N Bonucci and C Kessedjan (eds), 40 Years of the OECD Guidelines for Multinational Enterprises (Pedone, 2018) 66. This view is also shared by P Ranjan in ch 5 of this volume.

[97] ibid.

[98] Vienna Convention on the Law of Treaties (1969) 1155 UNTS 331, Art 31.

they can 'shape or condition the understanding of investment obligations'.[99] For instance, the Dutch Model BIT provides that an arbitral tribunal may consider non-compliance with the UNGPs or the OECD Guidelines for Multinational Enterprises in determining the amount of compensation owed to an investor.[100]

Yet apart from specific provisions requiring tribunals to consider these references, in general, IIA references to CSR or soft law corporate responsibility initiatives should factor into the interpretation of the IIA. After all, these references form part of the treaty's 'ordinary meaning' and context. Pursuant to the Vienna Convention on the Law of Treaties, they must therefore form part of the interpretive toolkit used by arbitrators to interpret every aspect of the IIA, including obligations owed by the state to the investor.[101]

In short, the norms embodied in these soft law initiatives and CSR provisions should colour the state's obligations to the investor, pushing interpretations of IIAs to a less investor-friendly stance. We have already seen glimpses of this 'colouring' in several arbitrations where tribunals drew from soft law provisions in international treaties or in other parts of the treaty to interpret standards of treatment.[102] Moreover, as the EU has observed, inserting these norms into IIAs is one means of balancing 'the rights and responsibilities of investors'.[103] Thus beyond the conditioning of investment obligations, inclusion of soft law initiatives or CSR provisions may also be a veiled attempt by states to have corporations adhere to the norms of corporate responsibility espoused in these provisions, despite their non-binding nature.

However, the role for soft law corporate responsibility norms in international investment law is trickier to discern when the IIAs are silent on either references to the initiatives themselves or related concepts such as CSR or sustainable development. As a 2014 OECD study confirms, most (88 per cent) treaties do not contain any references to a state's sustainable development agenda and promotion of responsible business conduct.[104] Thus, in most instances, soft law corporate responsibility initiatives will not form part of the primary tools used to interpret IIAs. Still, these initiatives can form part of the subsidiary means of interpreting IIAs. For example, one of the parties to the dispute can introduce these initiatives by including it in their pleadings. Moreover, once a party has included such an

[99] Jacob and Schill, 'Going Soft' (2014) 17.

[100] Dutch Model BIT, Art 23.

[101] Vienna Convention on the Law of Treaties, Art 31(1).

[102] See, for example, *World Duty Free Company Limited v Republic of Kenya*, ICSID Case No ARB/00/7, Award (4 October 2006); *David R Aven v Republic of Costa Rica*, ICSID Case No UNCT/15/3, Award (18 September 2018). For a more thorough discussion of this topic see B Choudhury, 'Investor Obligations for Human Rights' (2020) *ICSID Review – Foreign Investment Law Journal* (advance access), available at doi.org/10.1093/icsidreview/siaa002.

[103] European Commission, 'Towards A Comprehensive European International Investment Policy' (7 July 2010) COM(2010)343 final, 9.

[104] K Gordon, J Pohl and M Bouchard, 'Investment Treaty Law, Sustainable Development and Responsible Business Conduct: A Fact Finding Survey' (2014) OECD Working Papers on International Investment 2014/01, available at dx.doi.org/10.1787/5jz0xvgx1zlt-en.

initiative in their pleadings, the parties have arguably consented to its use.[105] It is then up to the arbitrator to consider the initiative and either incorporate it into their analysis or dismiss it.

Moreover, the soft law nature of these initiatives does not detract from their utility. As commentators have shown, there is ample evidence of investment tribunals relying on soft law as part of their efforts to interpret IIAs.[106] For instance, arbitral tribunals have looked to IBA Rules on the Taking of Evidence in International Arbitration and other soft law instruments relating to procedural issues;[107] and norms emanating out of international trade law.[108] More to the point, at least one arbitral tribunal has also referred to soft law corporate responsibility initiatives. In *Urbaser v Argentina*, the tribunal cited the UNGPs as evidence that 'international law accepts CSR as a standard of crucial importance for companies'[109] and the ILO Tripartite Declaration, among other soft law initiatives, to note that private parties should not engage in activities that destroy human rights.[110]

One of the reasons for the increased utility of soft law in international investment law is because IIA provisions leave a number of interpretive gaps. Ambiguously worded standards of treatment, such as fair and equitable treatment, do not have a long history of application.[111] Comparatively speaking, international investment law is a relatively new specialised regime of law that contains interpretive questions to which answers are still being provided. Soft law is therefore useful in international investment law as a means of answering these interpretive questions, whether that is by suggesting changes to the current system, addressing issues of uncertainty, or by helping to adapt legal rules to changed circumstances.[112]

Given the benefits of using soft law in investment arbitration and the prevalence of its use by arbitrators (including in instances where it is the arbitrators and not the parties that have introduced the soft law in question),[113] it is unclear

[105] Alvarez, '"Soft Law" in Investment Arbitration' (2018) 18. See also TW Wälde, 'International Standards in Transnational Investment & Commercial Disputes: The Role of International standards, Soft Law, Guidelines, Voluntary and Self-regulation in International Adjudication, Negotiation and Other Forms of Dispute Management' (2004) 1 *Transnational Dispute Management* 1 (arguing that arbitrators can without the consent of parties resort to soft law).

[106] See generally Alvarez (n 37). See also Jacob and Schill (n 37); DB King and R Moloo, 'International Arbitrators as Lawmakers' (2014) 46 *New York University Journal of International Law & Politics* 875, 883.

[107] See the discussion in Kaufmann-Kohler, 'Soft Law in International Arbitration' (2016) 5–9.

[108] G Marceau, A Izaguerri and V Lanovoy, 'The WTO's Influence on Other Dispute Settlement Mechanisms: A Lighthouse in the Storm of Fragmentation' (2013) 47 *Journal of World Trade* 481; J Kurtz, *The WTO and International Investment Law: Converging Systems* (Cambridge University Press, 2016).

[109] *Urbaser v Argentina*, para 1195.

[110] ibid paras 1196–99.

[111] Alvarez (n 37) 17; Wälde, 'International Standards in Transnational Investment & Commercial Disputes' (2004).

[112] Jacob and Schill (n 37) 5–6.

[113] See the analysis in Alvarez (n 37), wherein he demonstrates that arbitrators often introduce soft law without prompting from the parties.

why soft law corporate responsibility initiatives cannot find an equally hospitable home in international investment law. Not only do these initiatives provide nuance to interpretive questions on IIA obligations, but they may also help international investment law adapt to the changed circumstances of the increasingly powerful multinational corporation without having to change the IIA's legal rules.

In any case, several *amicus curiae* and states have already included these initiatives within their pleadings, suggesting an increasing reliance on their use.[114] Certainly, if future tribunals rely on the *Urbaser* judgment, soft law corporate responsibility initiatives are primed to join the already well stocked soft law toolkit of international investment law.

V. Conclusion

At the international level, the corporate responsibility to respect human rights is well established in soft law. The corporate responsibility to minimise environmental impact is also slowly becoming an established norm. In light of these international expectations of corporations, it is unreasonable to assume that international investment law is immune to these developments.

Regardless of whether states have included references to the UNGPs or CSR in their IIAs, the norm of the corporate responsibility to respect human rights, and to a lesser extent, corporate responsibilities to the environment, operate as normative background, influencing the expectations society has of corporations, even when they act as foreign investors.

In an age where international investment law continues to face criticisms about its lack of legitimacy, public participation and democratic deficits, it cannot be immune to societal expectations of corporations. Rather, international investment law must allow these norms to enter the IIA sphere, preferably via party submissions, and arbitrators must interpret obligations owed to investors in light of these norms. Of course, this does not suggest that soft law CSR norms should be used to trump state obligations to investors, since they remain soft law compared to the hard law of IIAs. Rather, the purpose of recognising the corporate responsibility to respect human rights and to minimise impacts on the environment is simply to ensure that IIAs cannot, indirectly, contribute to the long history of corporate harms to human rights and the environment.

[114] See, for example, *Bear Creek Mining v Peru*, ISCID Case No ARB/14/21, Amicus Curiae Brief Submitted By The Association Of Human Rights and the Environment-Puno and Mr Carlos Lopez (9 June 2016); *Glamis Gold v United States Of America*, Submission of the Quechan Indian Nation (16 October 2006) 13; *South American Silver v Bolivia*, UNCITRAL, PCA Case No 2013-15, Respondent Counter-Memorial (31 March 2015) para 220; *Mobil Investments v Canada*, ICSID Case No ARB(AF)/07/4, Canada's Counter-memorial (30 June 2016) para 170.

7

Responding to Investor Misconduct: The Line between Lawful and Unlawful Responses and Apportionment in Cases of Unlawful Responses

MARTIN JARRETT

I. Introduction: The Problem of Balancing the Exercise of Domestic Rights against Respect for International Obligations

When a state becomes aware of investor misconduct, which has been performed by an investor with investor status under an investment treaty that the state is party to, it faces a dilemma. Considerations of the rule of law mean that it has to act against the investor – the requirement of equality before the law demands that all persons must face the wrath of the law if they have breached it.[1] Typically, its action will take the form of the imposition of some sanction against the investor. Invariably, that sanction will cause some kind of devaluation of its investment or, in serious cases, the loss of the investment. Given that investment valuation or investment loss is the trigger event for claims under investment treaties, the state thereby opens the door for the investor to make a claim against it, a claim which could potentially lift the sanction and see the investor receive compensation.

The now-settled case of *Gazprom v Ukraine* offers a recent example of how this situation can play out.[2] After its investigations of the investor, Ukraine concluded that it had engaged in anti-competitive practices and fined it approximately

[1] T Bingham, *The Rule of Law* (Penguin, 2011) 55.

[2] This summary of *Gazprom v Ukraine*, UNCITRAL, PCA Case No 2019-10 draws from V Djanic, 'Ukraine's Deputy Justice Minister Announces Settlement of Multi-Billion Dollar BIT Arbitration with Gazprom' (IAReporter, 30 December 2019), available at www.iareporter.com/articles/ukraines-deputy-justice-minister-announces-settlement-of-multi-billion-dollar-bit-arbitration-with-gazprom.

USD 6.5 billion.[3] Using the Russia–Ukraine BIT,[4] the investor filed a claim in arbitration in which it alleged that the imposition of this fine constituted a treaty breach. This move on the part of the investor was seemingly successful. According to media reports,[5] Ukraine agreed to waive the investor's payment of the fine in the settlement between it and the investor.

Whether Ukraine was justified in imposing this fine or whether it amounted to illegal conduct deserving of international responsibility is not in focus. The point is that investors can play the investment-treaty card to challenge state responses to their misconduct. Whatever the rights and wrongs of the investor having this option are, that is the legal reality. It means that, in some cases, a state's response to an investor's misconduct will give rise to international responsibility for it under an investment treaty. Accepting that reality, this chapter examines the following questions: when both the investor and the state, because of its response, are guilty of misconduct, how have arbitral tribunals balanced out their respective degrees of misconduct, and what improvements can be made to the current balancing act?

Answering these questions begins with understanding how a state incurs international responsibility for responding to investor misconduct. Two investment protection standards are likely to be in play: expropriation and fair and equitable treatment, particularly that strain of this investment protection standard called 'denial of justice'. How states' responses to investor misconduct can lead them to breach these investment protection standards is the focus of section III. When they are found in breach, arbitral tribunals usually order that states pay compensation to investors.[6] This is apparently paradoxical. What starts off as a matter of investor misconduct eventually turns into a situation where the state compensates the investor. This outcome should provoke the question: what about the investor's misconduct and are there not some consequences for it? Arbitral tribunals have developed some novel answers to this question. They are examined in section IV. In combination with the analysis of section III, these examinations show the balance that arbitral tribunals have struck between holding states accountable to their international obligations under investment treaties, while also ensuring that the matter of the investor's misconduct does not go unresolved. This lays the foundation for section V, which critically appraises the balancing act

[3] In other media reports, the fine was valued at USD 7.2 billion. See for example, D Krasnolutska, 'Ukraine Approves Settlement with Gazprom Over Antitrust Claim' (Bloomberg, 28 December 2019), available at www.bloomberg.com/news/articles/2019-12-28/ukraine-approves-settlement-with-gazprom-over-antitrust-claim.

[4] Signed 27 November 1998, entry into force 27 January 2000.

[5] V Soldatkin et al, 'Russia's Gazprom to Pay Ukraine $2.9 Billion Before December 29 to Settle Row' (Reuters, 21 December 2019), available at www.reuters.com/article/us-russia-ukraine-gas-payment/russias-gazprom-to-pay-ukraine-2-9-billion-before-december-29-to-settle-row-idUSKBN1YP08M.

[6] In international law, the primary remedy to cure breaches of international obligations is restitution. See R Kolb, *The International Law of State Responsibility: An Introduction* (Elgar, 2017) 154–55. But in investor-state arbitrations, this primary remedy has been largely replaced by compensation. See B Sabahi, *Compensation and Restitution in Investor-State Arbitration: Principles and Practice* (Oxford University Press, 2011) 91.

that arbitral tribunals have performed when adjudicating cases involving investor misconduct and unlawful state responses to that misconduct, particularly focusing on the shortcomings of the main tool that is used for the balancing act: 'investment reprisal'. Before tackling those questions, however, some preliminary matters need to be dealt with, specifically the meaning of 'merits-relevant investor misconduct' and why this chapter exclusively focuses on it.

II. Distinguishing Jurisdiction-Relevant Investor Misconduct from Merits-Relevant Investor Misconduct

A. The Importance of the Distinction between Jurisdiction-Relevant Investor Misconduct and Merits-Relevant Investor Misconduct

As indicated above, this chapter is concerned with investor misconduct that is labelled as such because the relevant conduct of the investor is illegal under the domestic law of the state hosting its investment. This domestic investor misconduct can be contrasted with international investor misconduct. Most particularly, in cases where the investor misconduct takes the form of corruption,[7] arbitral tribunals have held that such conduct assumes the status of misconduct not only because it is contrary to domestic law, but also because it is contrary international public policy.[8]

[7] Some exceptions are *Churchill Mining and Planet Mining v Indonesia* and *Inceysa v El Salvador*. There, the investors' misconduct took the form of fraud. The arbitral tribunal held such fraudulent activity was contrary to international public policy; see *Churchill Mining PLC and Planet Mining Pty Ltd v Republic of Indonesia*, ICSID Case No ARB/12/14 and 12/40, Award (6 December 2016) (*Churchill v Indonesia*) para 508; *Inceysa Vallisoletana SL v Republic of El Salvador*, ICSID Case No ARB/03/26, Award (2 August 2006) (*Inceysa v El Salvador*) para 252. See also ch 12 (Amado, Kern and Rodriguez) of this volume, where the authors discuss the prospect of transforming an international public policy against corruption into an international obligation that is binding on investors.

[8] See, for example, *Churchill v Indonesia*, para 508; *Inceysa v El Salvador*, para 252; *World Duty Free v Republic of Kenya*, ICSID Case No ARB/00/7, Award (4 October 2006) para 139 (this is contract-based investor-state arbitration, as opposed to a treaty-based investor-state arbitration); *Vladislav Kim and others v Republic of Uzbekistan*, ICSID Case No ARB/13/6, Decision on Jurisdiction (8 March 2017) (*Kim v Uzbekistan*) para 593; *Metal-Tech Ltd v Republic of Uzbekistan*, ICSID Case No ARB/10/3, Award (4 October 2013) (*Metal-Tech v Uzbekistan*) para 292. Additionally, it has been reported in the case of *Spentex Netherlands BV v Uzbekistan*, ICSID Case No ARB/13/26, Award (27 December 2016), where the arbitral tribunal ruled that corruption amounted to a breach of international public policy: see K Betz, *Proving Bribery, Fraud and Money Laundering in International Arbitration: On Applicable Criminal Law and Evidence* (Cambridge University Press, 2017) 130–31; V Djanic, 'In Newly Unearthed Uzbekistan Ruling, Exorbitant Fees Promised to Consultants on Eve of Tender Process are Viewed by Tribunal as Evidence of Corruption, Leading to Dismissal of All Claims Under the Dutch BIT' (IAReporter, 22 June 2017) Amado, JS Kern and MD Rodriguez, available at www.iareporter.com/articles/in-newly-unearthed-uzbekistan-ruling-exorbitant-fees-promised-to-consultants-on-eve-of-tender-process-are-viewed-by-tribunal-as-evidence-of-corruption-leading-to-dismissal-of-all-claims-under-dutch.

The focus here is not only on domestic investor misconduct, but specifically, investor misconduct relevant at the merits stage of an investor-state arbitration. This is called 'merits-relevant investor misconduct'. Merits-relevant investor misconduct must be distinguished from jurisdiction-relevant investor misconduct. If investor misconduct is relevant to the arbitral tribunal's jurisdiction and the arbitral tribunal declines jurisdiction on account of it, then the international legality of the state's response to that misconduct will not be reviewed.[9] Practically, such a decision terminates the investor's claim.[10] If investor misconduct is relevant to the merits of the investor's claim, then the international legality of the state's response will be reviewed. If that review concludes that the state's response was in breach of one of the investment protection standards of the applicable investment treaty, then the state will accrue international responsibility for its response.[11] But that is not the end of the matter. There is still the lingering issue of the investor's misconduct. Taking the investor's misconduct, the state has the possibility to mount a defence. If its defence is successfully pleaded, then the state's international responsibility will typically be reduced[12] or, in exceptional cases,[13] eliminated.[14]

This explains the focus on merits-relevant investor misconduct. As noted in section I, one goal of this chapter is to find out where the pendulum of international responsibility lies in cases involving investor misconduct and unlawful state responses to that misconduct. The spectre of that pendulum only comes into view during the merits phase of an investor-state arbitration.

B. The Substantive Distinction between Jurisdiction-Relevant Investor Misconduct and Merits-Relevant Investor Misconduct

Given this focus on merits-relevant investor misconduct, the question is now: how is merits-relevant investor misconduct substantively distinguished from jurisdiction-relevant investor misconduct? This question can be answered with a

[9] CA Miles, 'Corruption, Jurisdiction, Admissibility and Competence in Investment Treaty Arbitration' (2014) 3 *Journal of International Dispute Settlement* 329, 334, 338.

[10] The other adjudicative body with potential jurisdiction over the investor's claim is the local courts in the host state, but it is unlikely to file a claim there. See R Dolzer and C Schreuer, *Principles of International Investment Law*, 2nd edn (Oxford University Press 2012) 231–32.

[11] See ILC, 'Responsibility of States for Internationally Wrongful Acts' (2001) *Yearbook of the International Law Commission*, VolulI, Pt 2, 32 (Art 1).

[12] See further section 4.A below.

[13] See further section 4.B below. As described there, the illegality defence has the potential to eliminate the state's international responsibility that it has accrued for breaching an international obligation.

[14] S Rosenne (ed), *The International Law Commission's Draft Articles on State Responsibility (Part 1, Articles 1–35)* (Nijhoff, 1991) 311; S Szurek, 'The Notion of Circumstances Precluding Wrongfulness' in J Crawford, A Pellet and S Olleson (eds), *The Law of International Responsibility* (Oxford University Press, 2012) 427. Although this view has been challenged, see J Crawford, *State Responsibility: The General Part* (Cambridge University Press, 2013) 275.

syllogism: investor misconduct is either merits-relevant or jurisdiction-relevant;[15] if it is not jurisdiction-relevant, then it can only be merits-relevant.[16] Accordingly, to understand what merits-relevant investor misconduct is, it must first be understood what jurisdiction-relevant investor misconduct is.

Investor misconduct becomes relevant to the arbitral tribunal's jurisdiction if, one, a state's consent to arbitration is conditioned on investment legality[17] and, two, the investor misconduct in question falls within the scope of that condition. In short, a condition of investment legality arises if the applicable investment treaty contains words to the effect that the investment must be established,[18] invested,[19] made,[20] or permitted[21] 'in accordance with host state law' and those words relate to the state's offer to arbitrate investor-state disputes,[22] as opposed to appearing the treaty provision on admission of investments.[23] 'In-accordance-with-host-state-law' clauses create explicit conditions of investment legality. For those investment treaties that do not explicitly condition the state's consent on the legality of the investment, which will sometimes be the case for older generation investment treaties, there is a doctrinal debate whether they might arise by implication.[24] It is beyond the remit of this chapter to attempt to resolve this debate, but it can be noted that in the absence of an 'in accordance with host state law' clause conditioning the state's consent to arbitration, there will be a question mark whether any investor misconduct can assume jurisdictional relevance.

If the state's consent is conditioned on investment legality, the next step to make any investor misconduct relevant to the jurisdiction is to bring such

[15] Although some arbitral tribunals have held that investor misconduct might also be a point of admissibility, this view is erroneous. The question of a claim's admissibility looks at whether the claim is mature enough for adjudication and, in making that determination, the relevant factors are matters pertaining to the claim *itself*, as opposed to issues of substantive investor misconduct, see further M Waibel, 'Investment Arbitration: Jurisdiction and Admissibility' in M Bungenberg et al (eds), *International Investment Law: A Handbook* (Hart, 2015) 1212.

[16] *Abaclat and others v Argentine Republic*, ICSID Case No. ARB/07/5, Decision on Jurisdiction and Admissibility (4 August 2011) (*Abaclat v Argentina*) para 648(i).

[17] ibid paras 648(i) and 649(i).

[18] See, for example, Agreement between the Government of the Republic of Finland and the Government of Mongolia on the Promotion and Protection of Investments (signed 15 May 2007, entry into force 19 June 2008), Art 1(1).

[19] See, for example, Agreement between the Republic of San Marino and Bosnia and Herzegovina on the Promotion and Reciprocal Protection of Investments (signed 2 August 2011, entry into force 24 May 2012), Art 1(1).

[20] See, for example, Agreement between Australia and the Oriental Republic of Uruguay on the Promotion and Protection of Investments (signed 5 April 2019, not yet in force), Art 1(1)(a).

[21] See, for example, Agreement between the Government of the Republic of Singapore and the Government of the People's Republic of Bangladesh for the Promotion and Protection of Investments (signed 24 June 2004, entry into force 19 November 2004), Art 1(a).

[22] *Gustav F W Hamester GmbH & Co KG v Republic of Ghana*, ICSID Case No ARB/07/24, Award (18 June 2010) para 125.

[23] A Reinisch, 'How to Distinguish "In Accordance with Host State Law" Clauses from Similar International Investment Agreement Provisions?' (2018) 7 *Indian Journal of Arbitration Law* 70, 80–82.

[24] For an overview of the jurisprudence, see M Polkinghorne and SM Volkmer, 'The Legality Requirement in Investment Arbitration' (2017) 34 *Journal of International Arbitration* 149, 155–58.

misconduct within the notion of investment 'illegality'; in other words, to show that the investor conduct is contrary to host state law. What amounts to investor conduct contrary to host state law has been interpreted narrowly on account of two factors. Firstly, the investor misconduct must be performed during the initial stages of the life of the investment, as dictated by the requirement that the investment must be either *established*, *invested*, *made*, or *permitted* in accordance with the state law.[25] This same limitation has also been held to arise in respect of implicit conditions of investment legality.[26] Because of this first factor, investor misconduct performed during the operating life of the investment will not have jurisdictional relevance.[27] The second factor narrowing the scope of any condition of investment legality is the seriousness criterion. The seriousness criterion is a short-hand expression for the requirement that any investor misconduct must be sufficiently grave before it will fall foul of the condition. Although this requirement is generally not mentioned in any 'in accordance with the state law' clause, arbitral tribunals have consistently read this requirement into them.[28] It has also been included as an element of implicit conditions of investment legality.[29] Effectively, this seriousness criterion means that investors rarely fall foul of conditions for investment legality. Out of approximately 1,000 publicly known treaty-based investor-state arbitrations,[30] there have only been six cases in which an arbitral tribunal has ruled that the investor's misconduct[31] has amounted to the non-fulfilment of this condition.[32]

Because of the narrow scope of conditions of investment legality, instances of investor misconduct will only sometimes assume jurisdictional relevance. Accordingly, investor misconduct will generally assume relevance to the merits of the dispute, thereby giving it a role to play in the determination of the state's international responsibility. This prompts the question: what is that role?

[25] Sometimes referred to as the 'temporal scope of the legality requirement'. See Polkinghorne and Volkmer (ibid) 158.

[26] *Gustav F W Hamester GmbH & Co KG v Republic of Ghana*, para 127.

[27] ibid.

[28] J Hepburn, 'In Accordance with *Which* Host State Laws? Restoring the 'Defence' of Investor Illegality in Investment Arbitration' (2014) 5 *Journal of International Dispute Settlement* 531, 545.

[29] See *Phoenix Action, Ltd. v The Czech Republic*, ICSID Case No ARB/06/5, Award (15 April 2009) (*Phoenix v Czechia*) para 102.

[30] As of 31 December 2019, see UNCTAD, 'Investment Dispute Settlement Navigator' (Investment Policy Hub, 31 December 2019), available at investmentpolicy.unctad.org/investment-dispute-settlement.

[31] As opposed to misconduct performed by a government officer. In *Cortec Mining v Kenya*, for example, a 'rogue' official granted a permit in defiance of Kenyan law, leading the arbitral tribunal to conclude that it lacked jurisdiction. See *Cortec Mining Kenya Limited, Cortec (Pty) Limited and Stirling Capital Limited v Republic of Kenya*, ICSID Case No ARB/15/29, Award (22 October 2018).

[32] *Spentex v Uzbekistan; Fraport AG Frankfurt Airport Services Worldwide v Republic of the Philippines*, ICSID Case No ARB/11/12, Award (10 December 2014); *Metal-Tech v Uzbekistan; Inceysa v El Salvador; Alasdair Ross Anderson v Republic of Costa Rica*, ICSID Case No ARB(AF)/07/3, Award (19 May 2010); *Fraport AG Frankfurt Airport Services Worldwide v The Republic of the Philippines*, ICSID Case No ARB/03/25, Award (16 August 2007). Note that this list does not include contract-based investor-state arbitrations.

III. Accruing International Responsibility for Responding to Investor Misconduct

It is best described as a contingent role. As mentioned in section II.A, the determination of international responsibility consists of two phases, namely the breach phase and the defence phase. In the breach phase, the basic question is: has the state's response to the investor misconduct breached one of the investment protection standards in the applicable investment treaty? Although the investor's misconduct features in this phase, it will not be the main feature. As this question indicates, the main role in the breach phase goes to the state's conduct. This changes in the defence phase. There, the investor's misconduct takes the lead role. However, unless the state's response is held to be in breach of one of the investment protection standards, the defence phase does not happen. This explains why the investor's misconduct is described as contingent – if there is a breach, only then will this misconduct enter the stage. Because the investor's conduct only has a role after the state has been found to be in breach, it is logical to first examine the question of breach, before then turning to the defence phase in section IV.

A. State Responses to Investor Misconduct and the Standard on Expropriation

A state's response to an instance of investor misconduct might potentially amount to a breach of any of the investment protection standards (primary rules)[33] usually found in investment treaties, but two rules are standout candidates: expropriation and fair and equitable treatment. Expropriation fundamentally prohibits state-mandated deprivations of investments belonging to foreign investors.[34] An example of the standard formulation of the provision reads as follows:[35]

> Investments shall not be expropriated, nationalized or subject, directly or indirectly, to measures of similar effects except for a public purpose, in a non-discriminatory manner, upon payment of prompt, adequate and effective compensation, and in accordance with due process of law.

[33] Because investment protection standards regulate state conduct, they are primary rules, see E David, 'Primary and Secondary Rules' in J Crawford, A Pellet and S Olleson (eds), *The Law of International Responsibility* (Oxford University Press, 2010) 27.

[34] C McLachlan, L Shore and M Weiniger, *International Investment Arbitration: Substantive Principles*, 2nd edn (Oxford University Press, 2017) paras 8.01–8.02.

[35] Agreement between the Republic of Turkey and the Transitional Islamic State of Afghanistan concerning the Reciprocal Promotion and Protection of Investments (signed 10 July 2004, entry into force 19 July 2005), Art 4(1).

In a number of cases,[36] states have fallen foul of the standard on expropriation in their reactions to investor misconduct. *Occidental v Ecuador* offers an example. There,[37] the investor had a production-sharing contract with the Ecuadorian state-owned oil company.[38] It subcontracted some of its rights and obligations under this contract to another company.[39] Under the production-sharing contract, the investor had to obtain Ecuador's consent prior to such subcontracting.[40] The arbitral tribunal[41] determined that it never obtained that consent.[42] Under the production-sharing contract, Ecuador had the right to declare '*caducidad*' (forfeiture)[43] of the contract for this breach,[44] the exercise of which was subject to certain procedural requirements,[45] such as giving the investor an opportunity to remedy the defect. Ecuador followed these procedural prerequisites. It subsequently made a declaration of *caducidad*.[46] Additionally, it confiscated the investor's physical assets for oil production,[47] allegedly with the investor's consent.[48] Among other causes of action,[49] the investor claimed that Ecuador's conduct breached the standard on expropriation.[50] This claim was successful.[51] The legal reasoning supporting this conclusion is light, but the arbitral tribunal held that its more substantive legal reasoning[52] in respect of its finding that Ecuador breached the standard on fair and equitable treatment also applied to its finding of expropriation.[53] On fair and equitable treatment, the arbitral tribunal concluded that although the investor was guilty of misconduct

[36] *Gemplus SA, SLP SA, Gemplus Industrial SA de C v The United Mexican States*, ICSID Case No ARB(AF)/04/3, Award (16 June 2010) (*Gemplus v Mexico*); *Bear Creek Mining Corporation v Republic of Peru*, ICSID Case No ARB/14/21, Award (30 November 2017) (*Bear Creek v Peru*); *Copper Mesa Mining Corporation v Republic of Ecuador*, PCA No 2012-2, Award (15 March 2016) (*Copper Mesa v Ecuador*).

[37] For a more detailed overview of the facts of this case, see B Sabahi and K Duggal, '*Occidental Petroleum v Ecuador* (2012): Observations on Proportionality, Assessment of Damages and Contributory Fault' (2013) 28 *ICSID Review – Foreign Investment Law Journal* 279, 280.

[38] *Occidental Petroleum Corporation and Occidental Exploration and Production Company v The Republic of Ecuador*, ICSID Case No ARB/06/11, Award (5 October 2012) (*Oxy v Ecuador*) para 105. The production-sharing contract was called the 'participation contract' in the arbitral award, although the arbitral tribunal clarified that it was best described as a production-sharing contract (see para 114).

[39] *Oxy v Ecuador*, para 129.

[40] ibid para 119.

[41] This finding was contested by the investor, ibid paras 147–60.

[42] ibid para 381.

[43] Sabahi and Duggal, '*Occidental Petroleum v Ecuador*' (2013) 80.

[44] *Oxy v Ecuador*, paras 120–21.

[45] See further, ibid para 179.

[46] ibid para 199.

[47] ibid para 199.

[48] ibid para 252.

[49] ibid para 456.

[50] For the details of the investor's arguments, see ibid 453.

[51] ibid para 455.

[52] ibid paras 384–453.

[53] ibid para 455.

described as 'imprudent and ill advised',[54] Ecuador's response was disproportionate,[55] as explained in the following extract:[56]

> The overriding principle of proportionality requires that any such administrative goal must be balanced against the Claimants' own interests and against the true nature and effect of the conduct being censured. The Tribunal finds that the price paid by the Claimants – total loss of an investment worth many hundreds of millions of dollars – was out of proportion to the wrongdoing alleged against [the investor], and similarly out of proportion to the importance and effectiveness of the 'deterrence message' which the Respondent might have wished to send to the wider oil and gas community.

This case can be compared with the outcome in *Yukos v Russia*. As in *Occidental v Ecuador*, the investor had engaged in investor misconduct, specifically it established a 'tax optimisation scheme'[57] among its local operating companies, although it might be have been characterised as a tax avoidance/evasion scheme.[58] The scheme was such that the arbitral tribunal characterised it as 'abusive'.[59] Its full extent was allegedly discovered by Russia through audits of the investor's local companies.[60] After the completion of these audits, the investor was ordered to pay approximately USD 24,180,000[61] in back taxes and fines for tax fraud.[62] The investor sought to pay this amount,[63] but various measures imposed by Russia blocked its path,[64] including the freezing of its bank accounts. Russia initiated the auction of the investor's main income-generating subsidiary.[65] A private company submitted the winning bid – a price that was far below the fair market value of the asset.[66] This private company was subsequently acquired by Russia's state-owned oil company immediately after the auction.[67]

Again, the investor succeeded in proving expropriation,[68] but the concept of disproportionality did not figure in the arbitral tribunal's reasoning. It centred its analysis on Russia's motivations for its response. After finding that Russia's response was not primarily motivated by reasons of tax collection,[69] but rather

[54] ibid para 384.
[55] ibid para 452.
[56] ibid para 450.
[57] *Yukos Universal Limited (Isle of Man) v The Russian Federation*, PCA Case No. 2005-04/AA227, Final Award (18 June 2014) (*Yukos v Russia*) para 75.
[58] ibid para 1614.
[59] The arbitral tribunal characterised the tax optimisation scheme as an 'abuse' of the relevant tax laws, see ibid para 1615.
[60] ibid para 109.
[61] ibid para 517.
[62] ibid para 95.
[63] ibid para 94.
[64] ibid para 95.
[65] ibid para 98.
[66] ibid para 1020.
[67] ibid para 1006.
[68] ibid para 1585.
[69] ibid para 1579.

the elimination of a political rival, the arbitral tribunal went on to conclude that the response was expropriatory.[70]

B. State Responses to Investor Misconduct and the Standard on Fair and Equitable Treatment (Denial of Justice)

In both *Occidental v Ecuador* and *Yukos v Russia*, the facts giving rise to international responsibility were primarily performed by the executive arm.[71] This will not be the case in all situations involving state responses to investor misconduct. In other cases, the relevant state response will be performed by the judicial arm. Typically, the state will become aware of some investor misconduct, activate some form of prosecution against the investor and, if the state's prosecution is successful, the judiciary will impose the response on the investor. Judicial conduct can also be expropriatory.[72] But owing to the difficulty of proving it,[73] most investors will complain about judicial conduct that takes the form of a response to their misconduct via a claim of denial of justice. Denial of justice is an outgrowth of the multifaceted standard on fair and equitable treatment.[74] An ancient cause of action, denial of justice is the vehicle through which arbitral tribunals review the propriety of the procedure in a particular adjudication involving the investor. Applied to cases involving investor misconduct, this means that the examination focuses on the procedural fairness of the trial where the investor is prosecuted for its misconduct.[75] Because adjudicative action is mostly performed by a state's judicial arm,[76] this explains why this rule of international investment law is most commonly used to complain about judicial conduct.[77]

A classic case where the investor used denial of justice to complain about the state's response to its misconduct was *Al-Warraq v Indonesia*. There, the investor

[70] ibid para 1585.

[71] In *Yukos v Russia*, the Russian courts were involved in various ways in the dispute, but it is apparent from the facts that the conduct of the Russian state was being orchestrated by the executive arm.

[72] For an overview of the jurisprudence on judicial expropriation, see generally JM Cox, *Expropriation in Investment Treaty Arbitration* (Oxford University, Press 2019) ch 9.

[73] The explanation for this is that many arbitral tribunals have insisted that judicial expropriation not only involve an expropriatory decision by the local court, but also require that the processes of the court amount to denial of justice, see HG Gharavi, 'Discord Over Judicial Expropriation' (2018) 33 *ICSID Review – Foreign Investment Law Journal* 349, 351–52.

[74] McLachlan, Shore & Weiniger, *International Investment Arbitration* (2017) para 7.103.

[75] J Paulsson, *Denial of Justice in International Law* (Cambridge University Press, 2005) 82.

[76] Although both the legislative and executive arms are also capable of performing adjudicative functions, thereby meaning their (improper) adjudicative conduct can fall within the scope of denial of justice, see ibid 44.

[77] Although judicial conduct comes within the purview of the other investment protection standards commonly featuring in investment treaties, see M Sattorova, 'Denial of Justice Disguised? Investment Arbitration and the Protection of Foreign Investors from Judicial Misconduct' (2012) 61 *International & Comparative Law Quarterly* 223, 243.

had a shareholding in a local bank, and he was one its officers.[78] In that capacity, he was found to have committed six instances of investor misconduct,[79] all of which could be described as financial crimes. In the midst of the financial crisis of 2008/09, the local bank was given a bailout loan.[80] After the bailout, Indonesia began to investigate the investor.[81] Those investigations led to his prosecution for financial crimes.[82] He was tried in absentia and convicted.[83] His punishment consisted of the confiscation of his assets, the value of which exceeded approximately EUR 174,000.[84] Citing human rights conventions,[85] the arbitral tribunal ruled that trials held in absentia would generally be viewed as a denial of justice, save in exceptional circumstances.[86] This was not a case involving exceptional circumstances. Accordingly, Indonesia was held to have breached the standard on fair and equitable treatment.[87]

In keeping with the core of denial of justice, specifically that it will be found in cases involve procedural failings by the presiding adjudicative body, the arbitral tribunal in *Al-Warraq v Indonesia* found that Indonesia's trial processes were unfair because the investor was not adequately informed about his trial, he could not appoint a lawyer to represent him, and he had no opportunity to appeal his conviction.[88] This failing to afford investors their rights to fair trials has been the explanation for other cases[89] where states have breached the standard on fair and equitable treatment when responding to (alleged) investor misconduct. The point is that if the adjudicative processes that investors are subject to reach the minimum standards of due process, then a claim of denial of justice cannot be made out. Some emphasis needs to be placed on the fact that these are *minimum* standards of due process. An example of how far a state can go before it falls below these minimum standards can be seen in *Genin v Estonia*.[90]

[78] *Hesham Talaat M Al-Warraq v Republic of Indonesia*, UNCITRAL, Final Award (15 December 2014) (*Al-Warraq v Indonesia*) paras 73–78.

[79] ibid para 634.

[80] ibid para 96.

[81] ibid para 108.

[82] ibid para 124.

[83] ibid para 141.

[84] ibid para 141.

[85] See particularly ibid para 588.

[86] ibid para 595.

[87] ibid para 621.

[88] ibid para 621.

[89] *Ibrahim Abou Khalil v Senegal* (at the time of writing, the arbitral award for this case had not been made public, but media reports indicated that the investor prevailed using denial of justice as his cause of action. See D Charlotin, 'UNCITRAL tribunal upholds denial of justice claim against Senegal' (IAReporter, 22 July 2020), available at www.iareporter.com/articles/uncitral-tribunal-upholds-denial-of-justice-claim-against-senegal. See also, *Mohamed Abdel Raouf Bahgat v Arab Republic of Egypt*, PCA Case No 2012-07, Final Award (23 December 2019).

[90] *Alex Genin, Eastern Credit Limited, Inc. and A.S. Baltoil v The Republic of Estonia*, ICSID Case No ARB/99/2, Award (25 June 2001) (*Genin v Estonia*). In *Genin v Estonia*, the relevant process affecting the investor was performed by Estonia's executive arm, not its courts. Nonetheless, the arbitral tribunal still referred to the investor's claim as one of 'denial of justice'; see para 357. As for why adjudicative action performed by the executive arm can amount to denial of justice, see Paulsson, *Denial of Justice* (2005) 44.

Again, this case involved investor misconduct in respect of a local bank that the investor had purchased in an auction.[91] There were three distinct instances of investor misconduct: various occasions when share capital in the local bank fell below minimum levels, a lack of transparency regarding the identity of the shareholders, and other conduct concerning transactions with related parties.[92] But these instances of investor misconduct were not the direct cause of the main event which gave rise to the investor's claim, which was Estonia's revocation of the local bank's permit.[93] That revocation was based on what the arbitral tribunal described as an 'exceedingly formal ground':[94] the investor indicated that 'Eurocapital Group *Limited*' was a shareholder in the local bank, whereas Estonia had only given permission to 'Eurocapital Group *Company*' to have a shareholding in the local bank.[95] There was confusion regarding whether these companies were the same.[96] Estonia concluded that they were not. The result was that the share capital of Eurocapital Group Limited, which was the company listed as having a shareholding in the local bank, was discounted from its capital reserves, meaning that the local bank then had a large capital deficiency.[97] This large capital deficiency then entailed the revocation of the local bank's permit. The arbitral tribunal held that this process was lawful under the applicable investment treaty, with the critical extract in the arbitral award reading as follows:[98]

> Can the revocation of [the local bank's] license be justified on grounds that, at first blush, appear extremely technical? It is the opinion of this Tribunal that the decision taken by the Bank of Estonia must be considered in its proper context – a context comprised of serious and entirely reasonable misgivings regarding [the local bank's] management, its operations, its investments and, ultimately, its soundness as a financial institution.

Notwithstanding the fact that Estonia afforded the investor no possibility to contest the revocation of the local bank's permit,[99] the arbitral tribunal found that there was no denial of justice.[100] This decision is ostensibly difficult to reconcile with the decision in *Al-Warraq v Indonesia*. But what the arbitral tribunal emphasised was that while Estonia's conduct 'invited criticism'[101] and it hoped that Estonia would act with greater caution in the future,[102] Estonia's actions did not shock its sense of judicial propriety because Estonia acted out of justified concerns about the

[91] ibid para 43.
[92] ibid paras 352 and 353.
[93] ibid para 348.
[94] ibid paras 352 and 359.
[95] ibid para 351.
[96] ibid.
[97] ibid para 360.
[98] ibid para 361.
[99] ibid paras 358 and 364.
[100] ibid para 367.
[101] ibid para 365.
[102] ibid para 372.

investor's misconduct,[103] not arbitrariness.[104] The arbitral tribunal for *Al-Warraq v Indonesia* held that Indonesia's conduct did shock its judicial propriety.[105] This illustrates the point that not only must the state's response to investor misconduct involve procedural impropriety for it to be classified as a denial of justice, but such impropriety must be shocking.[106] This 'shocking' element is vague.[107] Although arbitral tribunals are inclined to interpret it in such a way to offer some latitude to states,[108] the line is not clearly drawn and states will, on occasion, step over it. In that circumstance, what options does the state have to defend itself?

To answer that question, it is helpful to revert back to the balancing metaphor. If a state's response breaches the applicable investment treaty, the pendulum swings towards the investor's favour. It stands to benefit from an order of compensation to remedy the state's breach.[109] But in cases of proven investor misconduct, arbitral tribunals are loath to make such orders. There are certain defences in international investment law that can push the pendulum back in favour of the state. How far the pendulum can be pushed back is considered in the next section.

IV. Eliminating or Reducing International Responsibility for Unlawfully Responding to Investor Misconduct

A. Contributory Fault (Investment Reprisal)

One defence[110] pleaded with increasing frequency is contributory fault. It finds its doctrinal foundations in Article 39 of the Articles on State Responsibility:[111] 'In the determination of reparation, account shall be taken of the contribution

[103] ibid para 371.
[104] ibid paras 369–70.
[105] See *Al-Warraq v Indonesia*, para 621.
[106] *Case Concerning Elettronica Sicula SpA (ELSI) (United States of America v Italy)* (Judgment) [1989] ICJ Rep 15, para 128.
[107] Paulsson (n 75) 66.
[108] As explained by the arbitral tribunal for *Al-Warraq v Indonesia*: 'The Tribunal also stresses that the threshold to establish a claim of denial of justice is high' (see para 620). See further SW Schill, 'Deference in Investment Treaty Arbitration: Re-Conceptualizing the Standard of Review' (2012) 3 *Journal of International Dispute Settlement* 577, 584.
[109] See further Kolb, *The International Law of State Responsibility* (2017) 154–55; Sabahi, *Compensation and Restitution in Investor-State Arbitration* (2011) 91.
[110] Although contributory fault is described as a defence in this chapter, it appears under the heading 'Reparations for Injury' in the ILC, 'Draft articles on Responsibility of States for Internationally Wrongful Acts, with commentaries' (2001) *Yearbook of the International Law Commission*, Vol II Pt Two (Articles on State Responsibility), thereby indicating that it functions as a remedy rule. For the explanation on why this characterisation is erroneous, see M Jarrett, *Contributory Fault and Investor Misconduct in Investment Arbitration* (Cambridge University Press, 2018) ch 2.
[111] Articles on State Responsibility, 29 (Art 39), discussed in *MTD Equity Sdn Bhd and MTD Chile SA v Republic of Chile*, ICSID Case No ARB/01/7, Decision on Annulment (21 March 2007) (*MTD v Chile*, Annulment) para 99.

to the injury by wilful or negligent action or omission of the injured State or any person or entity in relation to whom reparation is sought'.

Although this provision indicates that contributory fault is a solitary concept, it is better understood as comprising two forms: 'investment mismanagement' and 'investment reprisal'. As the name suggests, investment reprisal can be pleaded where the state takes (internationally illegal) measures of reprisal (responses) in reaction to investor misconduct.[112] It is more in focus in this chapter because it can be pleaded by states in cases involving investor misconduct, but, to properly understand how it is distinguishable from investment mismanagement, it is worth briefly describing investment mismanagement.

In cases of investment mismanagement, the investor's contribution to its investment loss does not take the form of a provocation of the state, but rather a direct contribution to the investment loss. Such a contribution becomes mismanagement when, at the time of its performance, there is a risk that the state might breach the applicable investment treaty. The paradigm case is *MTD v Chile*. Despite signs that it would not get the permit it needed,[113] the investor ploughed ahead with its investment plan by purchasing the land for its investment activity.[114] Its application for this permit was rejected.[115] Because this rejection was inconsistent with other Chilean conduct,[116] Chile was found to have breached the applicable investment treaty.[117] But the investor did not escape condemnation. After concluding that the investor's management of the initial stages of its investment was plagued by a lack of due diligence,[118] the arbitral tribunal apportioned 50 per cent of the international responsibility to the investor.[119] Because investment mismanagement cannot be pleaded as a defence in situations where the state has reacted to investor misconduct, it is not in focus here.

Investment reprisal was successfully pleaded in *Occidental v Ecuador* and *Yukos v Russia*. In both cases, the result was the same: the investors had to accept 25 per cent of the international responsibility for their investment losses.[120] In *Occidental v Ecuador*, the dissenting arbitrator concluded that the investor should have been apportioned 50 per cent,[121] although she noted that apportionment largely turned on

[112] At the time writing, this concept had not been recognised in the jurisprudence of international investment law. The arbitral tribunal for *Yukos v Russia*, however, recognised that in some cases of contributory fault, the investor had provoked the state's wrongful conduct and then this indirect contribution nonetheless constituted a cause for the purposes of Art 39 of the Articles on State Responsibility. See *Yukos v Russia*, para 1605.

[113] *MTD Equity Sdn Bhd and MTD Chile SA v Republic of Chile*, ICSID Case No ARB/01/7, Award (25 May 2004) (*MTD v Chile*, Award) para 169.

[114] For further details, see ibid para 49.

[115] ibid paras 80–81.

[116] ibid para 166.

[117] ibid para 253(1).

[118] ibid para 177.

[119] ibid para 246.

[120] *Yukos v Russia*, para 1637; and *Oxy v Ecuador*, para 687.

[121] *Occidental Petroleum Corporation and Occidental Exploration and Production Company v The Republic of Ecuador*, ICSID Case No ARB/06/11, Dissenting Opinion (20 September 2012) (*Oxy v Ecuador*, Dissenting) para 8.

an adjudicator's appreciation of the factual situation.[122] In reaching these decisions, the arbitral tribunals did not explicitly define the content of investment reprisal, but synthesising from their reasoning, it is apparent that it consists of two elements.

First, there must be some form of investor misconduct. As the investors' conduct was illegal under the states' domestic law, this element was satisfied in both *Occidental v Ecuador*[123] and *Yukos v Russia*.[124] In another case where investment reprisal was successfully pleaded, namely *Copper Mesa v Ecuador*, this element was satisfied by the investor's planning and directing violent acts against the local population in the vicinity of the investment activities.[125]

An open question is whether investor misconduct that is not contrary to domestic law, but otherwise objectively offensive, can satisfy this element. There are two cases[126] where the state pleaded investment reprisal and the investor's 'misconduct' was formally legal,[127] but was (arguably) wrongful when viewed from an objective perspective. The arbitral tribunals ruled in those cases that the pleas of investment reprisal failed for other reasons[128] and did not continue to comment on this question. One of these cases was *Bear Creek v Peru*. There, Peru failed to establish that the investor's (alleged) misconduct caused its response.[129] This is the second element: the investor misconduct must have provoked the state's response. Arbitral tribunals have insisted that the degree of provocation must be 'material'[130] – their findings, however, defy this insistence. In *Occidental v Ecuador*, for example, the arbitral tribunal held that this element was satisfied,[131] notwithstanding evidence that Ecuador's response was primarily motivated by political considerations, specifically the ill will towards the investor on account of an arbitral award in its favour and against Ecuador.[132] The arbitral tribunal for *Yukos v Russia* adopted an even weaker interpretation. It held that even though Russia used the investor's misconduct as a 'pretext' for its expropriated reaction, this element was nonetheless satisfied.[133] According to this jurisprudence, the investor's misconduct need not have any actual causal effect, but rather must be a good reason for reacting.

[122] ibid para 7.

[123] *Oxy v Ecuador*, para 680.

[124] *Yukos v Russia*, para 1611.

[125] *Copper Mesa v Ecuador*, para 6.100.

[126] *Gemplus v Mexico*; *Bear Creek v Peru*.

[127] In *Gemplus v Mexico*, this investor 'misconduct' was hiring a director who had previously committed serious crimes. Because the investor had no knowledge of his past, nor could have obtained that knowledge, Mexico's plea failed, see *Gemplus v Mexico*, para 11.14. In the other case, *Bear Creek v Peru*, Peru argued that the investor's use of its Peruvian legal representative to obtain its permit was illegal because the arrangement between them managed to circumvent Peruvian law on foreign ownership of mining permits. The arbitral tribunal concluded that it was not illegal, see *Bear Creek v Peru*, para 126.

[128] In *Gemplus v Mexico*, the investor had no knowledge of the prior criminal activities of its directors; see *Gemplus v Mexico*, para 11.14.

[129] *Bear Creek v Peru*, para 567.

[130] *Copper Mesa v Ecuador*, para 6.88; *Yukos v Russia*, para 1600; and *Oxy v Ecuador*, para 670.

[131] *Oxy v Ecuador*, para 680.

[132] ibid para 684.

[133] *Yukos v Russia*, para 1615.

Once these legal elements have been established, the apportionment of international responsibility can begin. Arbitral tribunals have repeatedly emphasised that they enjoy some discretion when apportioning international responsibility between investors and states.[134] This explains the varying percentages that the investors have had to accept as representing their contributions to their losses. As noted above, the percentages were 25 per cent for the investors in *Occidental v Ecuador*[135] and *Yukos v Russia*.[136] In *Copper Mesa v Ecuador*, the arbitral tribunal went to 30 per cent,[137] while in *Bear Creek v Peru*, the dissenting arbitrator measured the investor's contribution at 50 per cent.[138]

Two things stand out about investment reprisal. First, it has not been successfully pleaded as a defence in respect of a finding of denial of justice. In all the cases mentioned above, the arbitral tribunals made findings of expropriation.[139] The explanation for this inapplicability of investment reprisal in respect of findings of denial of justice is that proving the causation element is nigh impossible. Particular instances of procedural impropriety in the context of adjudicative proceedings are the founding facts of a claim of denial of justice. It is difficult to imagine how investor misconduct could specifically provoke such improprieties. A second stand-out feature is that no arbitrator or arbitral tribunal has been willing to apportion more than 50 per cent of the international responsibility to the investor. Effectively, this implicit limitation means that a finding of investment reprisal can only bring the pendulum back to the halfway point between investors and states. To swing the pendulum all the way back in the state's favour, something stronger is needed.

B. Illegality Defences

That something is the illegality defence. The imprecise expression of the 'illegality defence' is used because the jurisprudence of international investment law has not settled on a description for the defence under consideration, with various descriptors being used, such as 'unclean hands',[140] the *ex turpi causa* defence,[141] and

[134] *Copper Mesa v Ecuador*, paras 6.94 and 6.96; *Yukos v Russia*, paras 1600 and 1637; *Oxy v Ecuador*, paras 670 and 686; *MTD v Chile*, Annulment, para 101.

[135] *Oxy v Ecuador*, para 687.

[136] *Yukos v Russia*, para 1637.

[137] *Copper Mesa v Ecuador*, para 6.102.

[138] *Bear Creek Mining Corporation v Republic of Peru*, ICSID Case No ARB/14/21, Partial Dissenting Opinion of Professor Philippe Sands (12 September 2017) para 39.

[139] *Bear Creek v Peru*, para 415; *Copper Mesa v Ecuador*, para 11.4; *Yukos v Russia*, para 1888(e); and *Oxy v Ecuador*, para 876(iii).

[140] For an overview of clean hands in international investment law, see generally P Dumberry, 'State of Confusion: The Doctrine of 'Clean Hands' in Investment Arbitration after the Yukos Award' (2016) 17 *Journal of World Investment & Trade* 229.

[141] See, for example, *Plama Consortium Limited v Republic of Bulgaria*, ICSID Case No ARB/03/24, Award (27 August 2008) (*Plama v Bulgaria*) para 146.

'post-establishment illegality'.[142] What binds all of these concepts together is that merely on account of its illegal conduct, an investor cannot recover from the state, which reflects how the illegality defence operates in domestic tort law.[143] This also reveals what makes the illegality defence stronger in comparison to investment reprisal: it is a complete defence that operates to *eliminate* the state's international responsibility. Additionally, it has been pleaded as a defence in respect of a finding of denial of justice, as demonstrated in *Al-Warraq v Indonesia*.

As recounted in section III.B above, Indonesia's trial of the investor amounted to denial of justice. The fact of the investor's misconduct still lingered. To bring into it into consideration, the arbitral tribunal relied on an unusual provision in the applicable investment treaty which reads as follows:

> The investor shall be bound by the laws and regulations in force in the host state and shall refrain from all acts that may disturb public order or morals or that may be prejudicial to the public interest. He is also to refrain from exercising restrictive practices and from trying to achieve gains through unlawful means.[144]

As the arbitral tribunal found that he had breached Indonesian law and Indonesian 'public order',[145] on multiple occasions,[146] the investor was simultaneously in breach of this provision. Drawing inspiration from the 'unclean hands' doctrine, the arbitral tribunal ruled that this treaty breach rendered the investor's claim inadmissible.[147] A finding of inadmissibility is legally distinct from a rejection of the investor's claim on the merits on account of a successful plea of a defence,[148] but the practical outcomes are the same:[149] no international responsibility for the state.[150]

This makes the illegality defence a more powerful defence than investment reprisal. Because the triggering event for the illegality defence and investment reprisal are the same, namely the investor's illegal conduct under the state's domestic law, it will be queried why states in the cases where they successfully pleaded investment reprisal did not plead the illegality defence instead, given that it offers a better outcome for the state. In *Yukos v Russia*, Russia did plead the illegality

[142] See generally Jarrett, *Contributory Fault* (2018) 149–55.

[143] For an overview, see generally M Fordham, 'The Role of *Ex Turpi Causa* in Tort Law' (1998) *Singapore Journal of Legal Studies* 238.

[144] Agreement on Promotion, Protection and Guarantee of Investments Among Member States of the Organisation of the Islamic Conference (signed 5 June 1981, entry into force 1 February 1988) Art 9.

[145] *Al-Warraq v Indonesia*, para 645.

[146] For details of this misconduct, see ibid paras 635–42.

[147] ibid paras 646–47.

[148] Articles on State Responsibility, 72 (Ch V, Commentary 7).

[149] For this reason, some arbitral tribunals have had difficulty making the distinction, see CN Brower and J Ahmad, 'The State's Corruption Defence, Prosecutorial Efforts, and Anti-Corruption Norms in Investment Treaty Arbitration' in K Yannaca-Small (ed), *Arbitration under International Investment Agreements: A Guide to the Key Issues*, 2nd edn (Oxford University Press, 2018) para 18.16. For a brief explanation of the concept of admissibility, see Waibel, 'Investment Arbitration' (2015) 1212.

[150] *Al-Warraq v Indonesia*, para 648.

defence,[151] or what it called the Unclean Hands Doctrine,[152] in preference to investment reprisal. It listed many instances of alleged investor misconduct,[153] including the misconduct that formed the foundation of its successful plea of investment reprisal.[154] Russia's plea of the illegality defence failed. In a devastating[155] blow to the existence of the Unclean Hands Doctrine, the arbitral tribunal opined as follows:[156]

> The Tribunal is not persuaded that there exists a 'general principle of law recognized by civilized nations' within the meaning of Article 38(1)(c) of the ICJ Statute that would bar an investor from making a claim before an arbitral tribunal under an investment treaty because it has so-called 'unclean hands.'
>
> General principles of law require a certain level of recognition and consensus. However, on the basis of the cases cited by the Parties, the Tribunal has formed the view that there is a significant amount of controversy as to the existence of an 'unclean hands' principle in international law.

What this extract reveals is that there should be serious doubts about the doctrinal foundations of the Unclean Hands Doctrine,[157] and by extension the illegality defence in international investment law. In *Al-Warraq v Indonesia*, the arbitral tribunal had the benefit of pointing to a treaty clause providing that the investor had to respect local law to shore up its reasoning. Most arbitral tribunals will not have this luxury. Rather, they will have to ground the illegality defence that they apply in a general principle of law. Only one arbitral tribunal[158] has been willing to go down this path, specifically the arbitral tribunal for *Plama v Bulgaria*.[159] In sum, a body of jurisprudence on the illegality defence has not been built, thereby making it difficult for states to plead.

It is considered that these features have engendered a preference for investment reprisal over the illegality defence among arbitral tribunals.[160] And because of

[151] For the arbitral tribunal's recount of its arguments, see *Yukos v Russia*, paras 1281–90.

[152] ibid para 1273.

[153] ibid para 1281.

[154] ibid para 1307.

[155] What makes this dictum particularly devastating is that Stephen Schwebel served on the arbitral tribunal for *Yukos v Russia*. In the *Nicaragua v United States*, he wrote a dissenting opinion in which he advocated for the existence of the clean hands doctrine in international law, see *Military and Paramilitary Activities in and against Nicaragua (Nicaragua v United States of America)* (Dissenting Opinion of Judge Schwebel) [1986] ICJ Rep 259, paras 269–71.

[156] *Yukos v Russia*, para 1358.

[157] S Schwebel, 'Clean Hands, Principle' in R Wolfrum (ed), *Max Planck Encyclopedia of Public International Law* (Oxford University Press, 2013) para 3.

[158] Although in *Fraport v Philippines (I)*, the dissenting arbitrator held that the investor's misconduct was relevant to the merits and The Philippines should have used the misconduct as the basis for a plea of illegality: see *Fraport AG Frankfurt Airport Services Worldwide v The Republic of the Philippines*, ICSID Case No ARB/03/25, Dissenting Opinion of Mr BM Cremades (19 July 2007) para 38.

[159] *Plama v Bulgaria*, para 146.

[160] See particularly *Copper Mesa v Ecuador*, para 6.97 and *Yukos v Russia*, paras 1307–08 (where the arbitral tribunal lists the instances of investor misconduct but concludes that it will discuss these instances as a matter of contributory fault, without offering any reasoning in support of that conclusion).

this preference, investment reprisal will be the default tool when arbitral tribunals seek to balance out the state's unlawful response to the investor's misconduct. Because it has assumed this status, it is worth critically examining the jurisprudence on investment reprisal in view of answering the question: can this tool be better crafted to carry out this balancing role?

V. A Critical Appraisal of the Jurisprudence on Investment Reprisal

A. Investment Reprisal as a Self-Help Remedy

A number of faults can be identified with the current approach. First, by accepting investment reprisal as part of international investment law, arbitral tribunals have legitimised states' recourse to self-help to deal with instances of investor misconduct. Law rarely endorses self-help remedies. Law rather encourages recourse to adjudicative bodies for the resolution of legal disputes. When law does recognise a self-help remedy, it strictly controls its use. An example in international law is countermeasures. It is recognised as a defence in the Articles on State Responsibility, but a full chapter of six Articles regulate how this defence might be used.[161] By contrast, the other defences codified in the Articles on State Responsibility only have one article explaining their application.[162] The jurisprudence on investment reprisal currently places no conditions on the circumstances when it may be used. To repair this problem, one idea would be to give states access to international justice to complain about investor misconduct. But turning this idea into reality would be a long-term venture. There is currently no possibility for a state to take a direct action against an investor in investment treaty arbitration.[163] Making such a possibility a reality would involve considerable investments in law reform, assuming that there was sufficient political will behind such a reform idea. Moreover, there are already adjudicative bodies where states can bring actions in respect of investor misconduct: their own domestic courts.

Various factors support pushing states towards domestic adjudication for resolving their disputes with investors. First, domestic courts will have the most expertise on the law that the investor has (allegedly) breached. Second, using domestic courts to prosecute investor misconduct constitutes a win for the rule of law in the state. A functional judiciary is a key plank of a state governed by

[161] Articles on State Responsibility, 26, 30 (Arts 49–54).

[162] ibid 27–28 (Arts 20–25).

[163] For a discussion of this issue, see G Laborde, 'The Case for Host State Claims in Investment Arbitration' (2010) 1 *Journal of International Dispute Settlement* 97, 102–07.

the rule of law. When misconduct under domestic law leads to judicial proceedings, this is the epitome of a functional judiciary. Third, if the investor is subject to maltreatment in the domestic courts, then it still has the option of filing a claim in investor-state arbitration alleging denial of justice. In light of these reasons, the question is therefore: how should states be pushed towards domestic adjudication?

One option would be to exclude pleas of investment reprisal. It is doubtful whether this option would be realistically accepted into the jurisprudence. Through the various cases mentioned in this chapter, investment reprisal has become a settled part of international investment law. If an arbitral tribunal denied its existence, then it would be denying itself the use of a tool that can be flexed to do justice between the parties. Another option with a softer edge is possible. It involves arbitral tribunals giving deference to local courts when they adjudicate on cases of investor misconduct. If these local courts enjoy the deference from arbitral tribunals, then their procedures are less likely to amount to a denial of justice. This practically means that the state's (judicial) response is less likely to give rise to international responsibility, thereby gently encouraging the use of local courts. Fortunately, this option is already in operation. As detailed in section III.B above, arbitral tribunals already follow a policy of showing deference to domestic courts. Proof of this policy can be seen in *GPF v Poland*. There, the investor had a contract with the City of Warsaw for the redevelopment of some historic buildings.[164] However, the investor demolished these buildings.[165] Via an application to the relevant local courts, the City of Warsaw sought to terminate its contract with the investor.[166] Its application was successful.[167] The appellate courts upheld this decision.[168] The investor filed a claim in investment treaty arbitration, with one its causes of action being expropriation by the Polish courts.[169] This claim failed.[170] In making its case for expropriation, the investor argued that the Polish courts had misapplied Polish law. In dismissing this argument, the arbitral tribunals held that investor-state arbitration was not a venue for the substantive review of domestic decisions given that arbitral tribunals must unconditionally defer to domestic courts on matters of substantive law.[171] This outcome was not surprising. It should be contrasted with the likely decision if the City of Warsaw had immediately

[164] *GPF GP Sàrl v Republic of Poland*, SCC Case No V 2014/168, Final Award (29 April 2020) (*GPF v Poland*) para 10.
[165] ibid para 86.
[166] ibid para 93.
[167] ibid para 95.
[168] ibid paras 96–97.
[169] ibid para 189.
[170] ibid para 607.
[171] ibid para 474. Although admittedly in some parts of its reasoning, the arbitral tribunal is seemingly engaging in a substantive review of the Polish courts' decision, see particularly *GPF v Poland*, paras 480–83.

terminated the contract. In this situation, notwithstanding the legality of such action under Polish law, the investor would have had a far better chance of succeeding.

B. Arbitrariness in the Apportionment of International Responsibility

A second point of criticism is that the process of apportionment is apparently characterised by its arbitrariness. The case in point is *Occidental v Ecuador*, although other cases where the arbitral tribunal or arbitrator made a finding of investment reprisal can equally be criticised on account of the arbitrariness of their decision-making on apportionment.[172] The investor in *Occidental v Ecuador* was initially awarded approximately USD 2,359,000,000 in compensation, but this amount was cut to approximately USD 1,769,000,000 on account of the finding of investment reprisal.[173] Effectively, the investor was handed a formal punishment of USD 590,000,000 for its misconduct. The dissenting arbitrator's penalty came to USD 1,179,500,000.[174] To give these figures some perspective, if they were paid as penalties under the Foreign Corrupt Practices Act, they would put the investor inside the top 10 list for the highest penalties paid under this legislation.[175] But the investor's misconduct barely met the description of misconduct.[176] Admittedly, it denied Ecuador the chance to vet the subcontractor,[177] but this was the absolute extent of the wrongfulness of its conduct. Ecuador suffered no material harm.[178] The investor remained legally liable to Ecuador for the misconduct of the subcontractor.[179] The subcontractor had already received authorisation by Ecuador to act as a subcontractor in respect of another investment in the upstream oil sector.[180] The authorisation almost certainly would have been forthcoming to the investor if it had sought it.[181]

[172] See, for example, *Copper Mesa v Ecuador* where the arbitral tribunal recounted some of pertinent facts, before it simply concluded: 'Taking all these factors into account … the Tribunal assesses the [investor's] contribution … at 30 per cent. On the facts of this case, it could not be less': see *Copper Mesa v Ecuador*, para 6.102.

[173] These amounts are exclusive of interest, see *Oxy v Ecuador*, para 825. Although the investor later settled its claim for enforcement of this arbitral award for USD 980,000,000, see E Hoffmann, 'Ecuador is paying Occidental $980M to settle its lawsuit' (Seeking Alpha, 10 Jan. 2016), available at seekingalpha.com/news/3022556-ecuador-paying-occidental-980m-settle-lawsuit.

[174] *Oxy v Ecuador*, Dissenting, para 8.

[175] H Cassin, 'Airbus shatters the FCPA top ten' (The FCPA Blog, 3 February 2020), available at fcpablog.com/2020/02/03/airbus-shatters-the-fcpa-top-ten.

[176] Also remembering that there was considerable evidence that Ecuador had authorised the subcontracting, *Oxy v Ecuador*, para 683.

[177] ibid para 679.

[178] ibid para 447.

[179] ibid para 333.

[180] ibid para 445.

[181] ibid para 445.

Finally, as the arbitral tribunal ruled that the investor's negligence was the explanation for not obtaining the authorisation, the investor misconduct was more in the form of an oversight, as opposed to a malicious act.[182]

This problem of arbitrary apportionment is not beyond repair. The process of reparation begins with jettisoning the idea that apportionment can be based on the causal potency of the investor's contribution, an idea most clearly exhibited in the arbitral tribunal's reasoning in *Occidental v Ecuador*:[183]

> The Tribunal recalls that the violation of the law by [the investor] was invoked by Ecuador as the principal legal basis for the [response]. On the other hand, [other factors] were also causes which ... contributed in a material and significant way to [Ecuador's response]. In other words, it is a conjunction of different factors which ... were the causes ... of the Respondent's [response]. *The difficult task of the Tribunal in this case is to weight the relative causal link of this series of causes.*

As this extract indicates, apportionment based on causal potency examines the degree to which a contribution causes a consequence and then values that degree.[184] But the idea that the degree to which a contribution causes a particular outcome can be accurately valued is fanciful.[185] Consequences always have a multitude of causes,[186] but the idea that some are more potent than others is nonsensical because causality is a binary concept – either an event is a cause or it is not.[187] And even if it is accepted that some causes could be more causally potent than others, there is no reason-grounded method to measure a cause's degree of potency. As the dissenting arbitrator in *Occidental v Ecuador* implicitly admitted, the valuation of the degree of causal potency is a matter of how an adjudicator 'appreciates' the case; in other words, this is primarily a subjective process.[188] This explains why the process of apportionment is defined more by arbitrariness than objectivity. A more objective approach is possible.

The first step towards that new approach is discarding the notion that international responsibility apportioned to the investor should correspond to the degree to which the investor's misconduct provoked the state's wrongful international conduct. Not only is the valuation of this degree impossible, but it also constitutes an erosion of individual responsibility. Embracing that principle is the second step. It provides that the person performing an act is solely responsible for

[182] ibid para 380.

[183] ibid para 685 (emphasis added).

[184] See also *Copper Mesa v Ecuador*, paras 6.97–6.98.

[185] The same observation has also been made in respect of apportionment in Anglo-American tort law; see J Goudkamp and L Klar, 'Apportionment of Damages for Contributory Negligence: The Causal Potency Criterion' (2016) 53 *Alberta Law Review* 849, 861.

[186] JS Mill, *A System of Logic, Ratiocinative and Inductive* (Cambridge University Press, 2011) 506.

[187] RW Wright, 'Allocating Liability Among Multiple Responsible Causes: A Principled Defence of Joint and Several Liability for Actual Harm and Risk Exposure' (1988) 21 *UC Davis Law Review* 1141, 1146.

[188] This attitude is also apparent among the arbitral tribunal for *Copper Mesa v Ecuador* given its emphasis on how apportionment centred on its assessment of the facts: see particularly *Copper Mesa v Ecuador*, paras 6.98–6.102.

the consequences causally related thereto, as opposed to the conduct of persons causing that act. Because of this principle, it is the state that has to bear sole responsibility for the consequences that it causes. But this does not mean that the investor misconduct should be overlooked. If a person is solely responsible for the consequences of his or her conduct, then the investor must be responsible for the harm caused by its misconduct. Accordingly, the investor should be apportioned international responsibility corresponding to the extent of this harm. For example, if the investor has its investment expropriated and that investment has a value of 3,000,000 ducats, but the investor's misconduct causes environmental damage that will cost 2,200,000 ducats to repair, then the investor should be apportioned 73.3 per cent of the international responsibility.

VI. Conclusion

Returning to the first question posed in section I on what balance arbitral tribunals have struck in cases involving state responses to investor misconduct, the first point is that such responses can breach investment protection standards found in investment treaties. It could not be any other way. If state responses to investor misconduct could not breach these primary rules, they would lose much of their legal value because states could routinely disguise their otherwise unlawful conduct as responses to investor misconduct. But investor misconduct still figures prominently in the final determination of the offending state's international responsibility. It assumes this prominence via certain defences, namely investment reprisal and the illegality defence. The illegality defence is the more powerful of the two. It can act to eliminate the state's international responsibility. But its doctrinal foundations are very unstable. Moreover, there is an apparent preference among arbitral tribunals for investment reprisal. A successful plea of investment reprisal reduces the state's international responsibility according to the degree to which its response was provoked by the investor's misconduct.

Because of its flexibility, investment reprisal is an apt tool to strike the balance between holding the state accountable for its misconduct, while simultaneously sanctioning the investor's misconduct. This tool, however, is being improperly used at present. Starting from the erroneous foundation that it is possible to accurately value the degree to which an investor's misconduct causes the state's response, it has been used in an arbitrary fashion. The proper way to use this tool is to apportion to the investor a percentage of the international responsibility reflecting the harm that its misconduct causes. Coming back to the second question posed in section I on how arbitral tribunals can strike a better balance, adopting this more objective approach counts as the main recommendation.

8

Counterclaims in Investment Arbitration: Is the Host State the Right Claimant?

TOMOKO ISHIKAWA

I. Introduction: Rise of the Notion of Counterclaims

The proliferation of international investment agreements (IIAs) and investor-state disputes has given rise to concerns about the one-sidedness of investment arbitration.[1] Barring a handful of exceptions,[2] IIAs specify obligations for host states with respect to investment promotion and protection, while remaining silent on investor obligations.[3] Likewise, access to IIA-based investment arbitration is generally limited to investors, despite the fact that neither the Convention on the Settlement of Investment Disputes between States and Nationals of other States (ICSID Convention) nor the United Nations Commission on International Trade Law (UNCITRAL) arbitration rules restrict access to investment arbitration by host states.[4] This one-sidedness in investment arbitration is largely

[1] M Toral and T Schultz, 'The State, a Perpetual Respondent in Investment Arbitration? Some Unorthodox Considerations' in M Waibel et al (eds), *The Backlash Against Investment Arbitration* (Kluwer, 2009) 578; G Laborde, 'The Case for Host State Claims in Investment Arbitration' (2010) 1 *Journal of International Dispute Settlement* 97, 100.

[2] For example, the Nigeria–Morocco BIT (signed 3 December 2016, not yet in force) Art 19, the Agreement on Promotion, Protection and Guarantee of Investments among Member States of the Organization of the Islamic Conference (OIC Agreement) (signed 5 June 1981, entry into force February 1988) Art 5, the Unified Agreement for the Investment of Arab Capital in the Arab States (signed 26 November 1980, entry into force 22 February 1988) Art 14.

[3] MM Mbengue, <<Les obligations des investisseurs étrangers>>, in L Dubin et al (eds), *L'entreprise multinationale et le droit international* (Pedone, 2017) 297; AK Bjorklund, 'The Role of Counterclaims in Rebalancing Investment Law' (2013) 17 *Lewis & Clark Law Review* 461, 463.

[4] The drafters of the ICSID Convention did consider that both investors and the states should have access to arbitration under the Convention. See the report of the World Bank Executive Directors, para 13: 'the Convention permits the institution of proceedings by host States as well as by investors and the Executive Directors have constantly had in mind that the provisions of the Convention should be equally adapted to the requirements of both cases', available at icsidfiles.worldbank.org/icsid/ICSID/StaticFiles/basicdoc/basic-en.htm.

attributed to the way in which an arbitration agreement is concluded through an IIA. The host state expresses its consent to arbitrate investment disputes through the dispute settlement clause of the IIA. This constitutes an offer to arbitrate, which is addressed to (potential) investors of the other contracting party (or parties) to the IIA, and an arbitration agreement is concluded when the investor accepts the offer by submitting its request for arbitration.[5] By contrast, the submission of a request for arbitration by the host state needs separate consent from the investor. It follows that an arbitration agreement cannot be concluded as long as the investor withholds its consent to the specific request for arbitration made by the host state.[6]

The one-sidedness of the IIA-based dispute settlement mechanism, along with the imbalance between the state's investment protection obligations and the lack of means to hold investors responsible in the IIA regime, has been facing growing criticism.[7] Several countries raised this issue in their submissions at the investor-state dispute settlement (ISDS) reform discussions at the UNCITRAL Working Group III sessions.[8] The Moroccan Government criticised the 'legal imbalance' in the current IIA-based arbitration system in the following terms:

> Only the investor can resort to this arbitration mechanism, and it can determine the timing and arbitration regime that best suit it. It enjoys something of a monopoly on recourse to an arbitral tribunal, whereas the State has no such power.[9]

One way to address, at least to a certain extent, this procedural inequality between the investor and the host state is through counterclaims. A note

[5] Z Douglas, *The International Law of Investment Claims* (Cambridge University Press, 2009) 258; AK Hoffmann, 'Counterclaims in Investment Arbitration' (2013) 28 *ICSID Review – Foreign Investment Law Journal* 438, 446.

[6] Laborde, 'The Case for Host State Claims' (2010) 109.

[7] See, for example, JD Amado, JS Kern and MD Rodriguez, *Arbitrating the Conduct of International Investors* (Cambridge University Press, 2018) 10–19; IC Popova and F Poon, 'From Perpetual Respondent to Aspiring Counterclaimant? State Counterclaims in the New Wave of Investment Treaties' (2015) 2 *Bahrain Chamber for Dispute Resolution International Arbitration Review* 223, 223–24; H Bubrowski, 'Balancing IIA arbitration through the use of counterclaims' in A de Mestral and C Lévesque (eds), *Improving International Investment Agreements* (Routledge 2013) 214–15; JE Kalicki, 'Counterclaims by States in Investment Arbitration' (2013) *Investment Treaty News*, available at cf.iisd.net/itn/en/2013/01/14/counterclaims-by-states-in-investment-arbitration-2; C Schreuer, 'Why Still ICSID?' (2013) 9 *Transnational Dispute Management* 1, 1; J Wouters and L Chanet, 'Corporate Human Rights Responsibility: A European Perspective' (2008) 6 *Northwestern Journal of International Human Rights* 262, 263–65.

[8] References to counterclaims as one of the reform options are found in, eg, UNGA 'Possible reform of Investor-State dispute settlement (ISDS): Submission from the Government of Costa Rica' (31 July 2019) UN Doc A/CN.9/WG.III/WP.178; UNGA 'Possible reform of Investor-State dispute settlement (ISDS): Submission from the Government of Morocco' (4 March 2019) UN Doc A/CN.9/WG.III/WP.161); UNGA 'Possible reform of Investor-State dispute settlement (ISDS): Submission from the Government of South Africa' (17 July 2019) UN Doc A/CN.9/WG.III/WP.176.

[9] UNGA 'Possible reform of Investor-State dispute settlement (ISDS): Submission from the Government of Morocco', Annex II, para 4.

by the UNCITRAL Secretariat titled 'Possible reform of investor-State dispute settlement (ISDS) – Multiple proceedings and counterclaims' stated that:

> The Working Group may wish to consider devising a framework in which States could raise counterclaims in ISDS, which would reduce uncertainty, promote fairness and rule of law, and ultimately ensure a balance between respondent States and claimant investors.[10]

Many scholars also underscore the host state's right to raise counterclaims in investment arbitration.[11]

Certainly, the host state has 'avenues of relief' other than investment arbitration, mainly its own courts.[12] However, even if the host government successfully obtained relief against a foreign investor through its national courts, such relief would have little practical benefit in situations where the investor has already withdrawn from the state. This is because of the absence of a widely accepted international mechanism concerning the recognition and enforcement of domestic court judgments by other states. Although the recent Hague Conference on Private International Law adopted the Convention on the Recognition and Enforcement of Foreign Judgments in Civil or Commercial Matters,[13] as of the date of this writing, Uruguay, Ukraine and Israel were the only signatories to the Convention, which has not yet entered into force.[14] By contrast, in investment arbitration, the winning party benefits from the strong enforcement mechanism for pecuniary

[10] UNGA 'Possible reform of investor-State dispute settlement (ISDS) – Multiple proceedings and counterclaims' (22 January 2020) UN Doc A/CN.9/WG.III/WP.193, para 38.

[11] J Burda, <<Le Consentement aux demandes reconventionnelles dans le cadre du CIRDI à la lumière de la sentence Spyridon Roussalis contre Roumanie>> (2003) 3 *Revue d'arbitrage et de médiation* 25, 29–30; WB Hamida, <<L'arbitrage État-investisseur cherche son équilibre perdu: Dans quelle mesure l'État peut introduire des demandes reconventionnelles contre l'investisseur prive'?>> (2005) 7 *International Law Forum du droit international* 261, 262–63; HE Kjos, *Applicable Law in Investor-State Arbitration: The Interplay Between National and International Law* (Oxford University Press, 2013) 130–31; S Dudas, 'Treaty Counterclaims under the ICSID Convention' in C Baltag (ed), *ICSID Convention after Fifty Years: Unsettled Issues* (Wolters Kluwer, 2017) 405; Popova and Poon, 'From Perpetual Respondent to Aspiring Counterclaimant?' (2015) 225; Bjorklund, 'The Role of Counterclaims' (2013) 463–64.

[12] Dudas (ibid) 386.

[13] The text of the Convention is available at assets.hcch.net/docs/f55fc0a1-1a3c-4368-9199-48e8df11ff3e.pdf.

[14] See 'Status Table' available at www.hcch.net/en/instruments/conventions/status-table/?cid=137. It should be noted that the scope of its application is limited to 'the recognition and enforcement of judgments in civil or commercial matters' (Art 1). Also relevant is the Convention of 30 June 2005 on Choice of Court Agreements which entered into force on 1 October 2015. The Convention provides the obligation of member states to recognise and enforce 'a judgment given by a court of a Contracting State designated in an exclusive choice of court agreement', subject to certain grounds for refusal of recognition or enforcement (Arts 8–9). This Convention applies to the situation where a state is a party to the agreement (Art 2(5)). However, the Convention applies only to foreign judgments in civil or commercial matters and excludes, for example, 'tort or delict claims for damage to tangible property that do not arise from a contractual relationship' (Art 2(2)(k)) from the scope of its application. Also, as of the date of writing, its membership is limited to the EU, the Member States of the EU, the UK, Mexico, Singapore and Montenegro. See also Amado, Kern & Rodriguez, *Arbitrating* (2018) 7–8.

damages under the ICSID Convention[15] or the Convention on the Recognition and Enforcement of Foreign Arbitral Awards (New York Convention).[16] The host state may well consider the enforceability of investment arbitral awards as an advantage over domestic litigation.[17] Moreover, in host states where the independence[18] and legitimacy of domestic judicial authorities[19] are not guaranteed, determining the responsibility of the investor at an international tribunal, rather than at local courts will also enhance the rule of law in the investor-state dispute settlement system.[20]

Therefore, in many cases, raising counterclaims in an IIA-based dispute settlement mechanism has comparative benefits over domestic litigation. Counterclaims also bring the oft-cited benefits of procedural economy, consistency[21] and judicial economy[22] to investment arbitration. Moreover, as discussed above, counterclaims serve as a way of addressing the existing imbalance in procedural rights between disputing parties in investment arbitration. Accordingly, there is the expectation that counterclaims 'enhance the general acceptance of international investment arbitration and increase the legitimacy of the international investment law regime'.[23]

II. Counterclaims as a Way to Hold the Investor Accountable for its Conduct

In addition to the above-mentioned benefits and functions, counterclaims also serve as a potentially effective means to hold an investor accountable for its

[15] The Convention on the Settlement of Investment Disputes Between States and Nationals of Other States – International Centre for Settlement of Investment Disputes, Washington 1965 (signed 18 March 1965, entered into force 14 October 1966) 17 UST 1270.

[16] The Convention on the Recognition and Enforcement of Foreign Arbitral Awards (signed 10 June 1958, entered into force 7 June 1959) 330 UNTS 38. It is observed that 'virtually all other awards (than ICSID awards) are enforceable under the New York Convention on Recognition': Bjorklund, 'The Role of Counterclaims' (2013) 475–76.

[17] JE Viñuales, *Foreign Investment and the Environment in International Law* (Cambridge University Press, 2012) 92.

[18] Relying on Polity IV Project, Political Regime Characteristics and Transitions, 1800–2014 (Polity5 Project, Political Regime Characteristics and Transitions, 1800–2018 is available at www.systemicpeace.org/inscrdata.html, Sloss and van Alstine conclude that 'Roughly one-third of the countries in the world lack an independent judiciary': D Sloss and M van Alstine, 'International Law in Domestic Courts' in W Sandholtz and CA Whytock (eds), *Research Handbook on the Politics of International Law* (Edward Elgar, 2017) 80.

[19] DI Márquez, 'Legal Avenues for Holding Multinational Corporations Liable for Environmental Damages in a Globalized World' (2015) 2 *ARACÊ – Direitos Humanos em Revista* 58, 65; E Morgera, *Corporate Accountability in International Environmental Law* (Oxford University Press, 2009) 29.

[20] Bjorklund, 'The Role of Counterclaims' (2013) 477.

[21] See, for example, *Application of the Convention on the Prevention and Punishment of the Crime of Genocide (Bosnia and Herzegovina v Yugoslavia)* (Counter-Claims) [1997] ICJ Rep 243, para 30.

[22] See, for example, *David R Aven v Republic of Costa Rica*, ICSID Case No UNCT/15/3, Award (18 September 2018) para 741.

[23] Bubrowski, 'Balancing IIA arbitration' (2013) 215. See also Hamida, <<L'arbitrage État-investisseur cherche son équilibre perdu>> (2005) 271. See also Y Kryvoi, 'Counterclaims in Investor-State Arbitration' (2012) 21 *Minnesota Journal of International Law* 216, 218.

conduct in the context of investor-state disputes. For the reasons discussed in the following sections, this function is particularly important in situations where the investor's activities undermine the interests of third parties to the dispute such as the local people in the host state.

A. Impact of Foreign Investors' Activities

Inasmuch as activities of foreign investors bring economic, social and environmental benefits to the host state,[24] there are situations where their activities have significant negative implications for the public interest in the concerned host state,[25] as demonstrated by the ample number of publicised cases about the actions of transnational corporations (TNCs) that resulted in serious environmental degradation and/or violation of human and labour rights in host states.[26] In the context of investor-state disputes, the dramatic increase in the number of investment arbitration cases, including some high-profile cases involving environmental and human rights issues,[27] has produced concern over the impact of IIAs and investment arbitration on the public interest of the host states. This concern has been exacerbated by the following factors. First, TNCs have been increasingly involved in activities that were once in the public domain,[28] including the

[24] See, for example, P Kusek and A Silva, 'What Matters to Investors in Developing Countries: Findings from the Global Investment Competitiveness Survey' in *Global Investment Competitiveness Report 2017/2018: Foreign Investor Perspectives and Policy Implications* (The World Bank, 2017); M Kordos and S Vojtovic, 'Transnational Corporations in the Global World Economic Environment' (2016) 230 *Procedia – Social and Behavioural Sciences* 150; O de Schutter, 'Transnational Corporations as Instrument of Human Development' in P Alston and M Robinson (eds), *Human Rights and Development: Towards Mutual Reinforcement* (Oxford University Press, 2005).

[25] See, for example, N Jägers, *Corporate Human Rights Obligations: In Search of Accountability* (Intersentia, 2002) ch I; T Weiler, 'Balancing Human Rights and Investor Protection: a New Approach for a Different Legal Order' (2004) 27 *Boston College International & Comparative Law Review* 429, 433; J Cazala, <<Le respect des droits de l'homme comme justification de la violation d'un traité d'investissement>>, in WB Hamida and F Coulée (eds), *Convergences et contradictions du droit des investissements et des droits de l'homme: une approche contentieuse* (Pedone, 2017) 333, 334; Márquez, 'Legal Avenues' (2015) 59–60.

[26] To mention a few, the toxic gas leak at the Union Carbide pesticide plant in Bhopal (India), the dumping of chemical waste at the port of Abidjan (Cote d'Ivoire), oil spills and related human rights violations concerning Royal Dutch/Shell and its subsidiary's operations in the Niger Delta (Nigeria), alleged environmental damages, forced labour and other human rights violations concerning the construction of a gas pipeline by Total and Unocal in Myanmar. See, for example, A Pigrau et al, 'Legal Avenues for EJOs to Claim Environmental Liability' (29 May 2012) 'Environmental Justice Organizations, Liabilities and Trade Report No 4'; JA Zerk, *Multinationals and Corporate Social Responsibility: Limitations and Opportunities in International Law* (Cambridge University Press, 2006); Jägers, *Corporate Human Rights Obligations* (2002); C Kaeb, 'Emerging Issues of Human Rights Responsibility in the Extractive and Manufacturing Industries: Patterns and Liability Risks' (2008) 6 *Northwestern Journal of International Human Rights* 327.

[27] See, for example, *Metalclad Corporation v The United Mexican States*, ICSID Case No ARB(AF)/97/1; *Chevron Corporation v Ecuador*, UNCITRAL, PCA Case No 2009-23; *Philip Morris Brands Sàrl v Uruguay*, ICSID Case No ARB/10/7; *Vattenfall v Germany*, ICSID Case No ARB/09/6.

[28] MK Addo, 'Human Rights and Transnational Corporations – an Introduction' in MK Addo (ed), *Human Rights Standards and the Responsibility of Transnational Corporations* (Kluwer, 1999) 7.

provision of essential infrastructure systems (such as electricity and gas, communication systems, and water and sewage management). Second, TNCs often invest in large-scale projects that have grave environmental implications such as waste management, exploration and exploitation of natural resources, and mining. Therefore, there remains a genuine risk that an investor's activities would have negative effects on the host state's society, including environmental degradation and a violation of human and labour rights.

B. Difficulties in Holding TNCs Accountable in International and Domestic Fora

The risk of negative effects underscores the importance of a mechanism to hold TNCs accountable for their conduct in an effective manner. However, it is often difficult to pursue legal recourse against TNCs in international or domestic fora.

First, no effective international law mechanisms are available yet to hold TNCs accountable for any detrimental effects of their operations on host societies. Notably, the UN's attempts to develop the Norms on Business and Human Rights as rules that directly bind corporations and to create 'a global network of human rights obligations enforceable against multinational corporations' failed due to oppositions from certain, mostly developed, states.[29] Instead, the then UN Commission on Human Rights (now the Human Rights Council) decided to develop the norms as non-binding principles – the UN Guiding Principles on Business and Human Rights – which set out the duties of states and the social responsibilities of corporations.[30] Certainly, in recent years, there have been important developments towards establishing binding international obligations on businesses. The drafting of an 'international legally binding instrument on transnational corporations and other business enterprises with respect to human rights' has been in process[31] since the UN Human Rights Council adopted the

[29] LC Backer, 'On the Evolution of the United Nations 'Protect-Respect-Remedy Project': The State, the Corporation and Human Rights in a Global Governance Context' (2011) 9 *Santa Clara Journal of International Law* (2011) 37, 45–46; D Augenstein and D Kinley, 'Beyond the 100 Acre Wood: in which international human rights law finds new ways to tame global corporate power' (2015) 19 *The International Journal of Human Rights* 828, 831–33.

[30] OHCHR, 'Guiding Principles on Business and Human Rights: Implementing the United Nations "Protect, Respect and Remedy" Framework' (2011) UN Doc A/HRC/17/31 (UN Guiding Principles on Business and Human Rights). See also J Clapp, 'Transnational Corporations and Global Environmental Governance' in P Dauvergne (ed), *Handbook of Global Environmental Politics* (Edward Elgar, 2005) 294–95; A Bonfanti, 'Applying Corporate Social Responsibility to Foreign Investment: Failures and Prospects' in T Treves, F Seatzu and S Trevisanut (eds), *Foreign Investment, International Law and Common Concerns* (Routledge, 2014) 234–36.

[31] The UN Human Rights Council's open-ended intergovernmental working group on transnational corporations and other business enterprises with respect to human rights published the 'zero draft' in July 2018 and issued its revised versions in July 2019 and August 2020. The text of the second revised zero draft is available at www.ohchr.org/en/hrbodies/hrc/wgtranscorp/pages/igwgontnc.aspx.

resolution in its elaboration in 2014.[32] Nevertheless, it remains to be seen if this project will gain wide support from the international community. So far, it has lacked support from developed countries[33] as well as the international business community.[34] Outside international human rights law, international agreements that provide obligations of juridical persons do exist, but they remain extremely rare.[35] The existence of customary international law that applies to corporations remains controversial.[36] In addition, except in situations where an international arbitration agreement exists, international courts and tribunals do not generally have jurisdiction to enforce TNC's obligations.[37] Therefore, together with the paucity of provisions on investor obligations in IIAs and the 'one-sidedness' of investment arbitration, there is also a general lack of substantive obligations that are directly binding on foreign investors and mechanisms to enforce such obligations.

When it comes to domestic legal systems, parties that have incurred damages due to a foreign investor's conduct ('the victims') face a number of difficulties in seeking legal recourse in national courts, that is, courts of the host state, the investor's home state or third countries. Litigation in the host state would be the most immediate path for victims to hold the perpetrators accountable.[38] However, in developing countries in particular, there are a variety of practical barriers to

[32] UNHRC 'Elaboration of an International Legally Binding Instrument on Transnational Corporations and Other Business Enterprises with Respect to Human Rights' (14 July 2014) UN Doc No A/HRC Res. 26/9. Another development in this regard is the drafting of arbitration rules for business and human rights disputes, available at www.cilc.nl/cms/wp-content/uploads/2019/06/Draft-BHR-Rules-Final-version-for-Public-consultation.pdf.

[33] Fourteen members of the Human Rights Council, including the US, Japan and the Member States of the EU opposed the adoption of the resolution.

[34] International Chamber of Commerce et al, 'Response of the international business community to the "elements" for a draft legally binding instrument on transnational corporations and other business enterprises with respect to human rights' (20 October 2017), available at www.ohchr.org/Documents/HRBodies/HRCouncil/WGTransCorp/Session3/BIAC-FTA-BSCI-ICC-IOE.pdf.

[35] V Chetail, 'The Legal Personality of Multinational Corporations, State Responsibility and Due Diligence: The Way Forward' in D Alland et al (eds), *Unity and Diversity of International Law. Essays in Honour of Prof. Pierre-Marie Dupuy* (Martinus Nijhoff, 2014) 115. Exceptions include Arts 137(1) and (3) of the United Nations Convention on the Law of the Sea (adopted 16 November 1973, entered into force 16 November 1994) 1833 UNTS 397 (UNCLOS) and International Seabed Authority's exploration regulations (for example, the Regulations on Prospecting and Exploration for Polymetallic Nodules in the Area (22 July 2013) Doc No ISBA/191C/17, Regs 3–8). It should be noted that international environmental agreements concerning the 'civil liability' of juridical persons do not actually provide private entities' obligations on specific behaviour concerning environmental protection but provide contracting states' obligations to establish the necessary mechanisms to materialise the responsibility of corporations.

[36] Contrasting views have been presented in cases such as *Kiobel v Royal Dutch Petroleum*, 569 US 108 (2013); *Presbyterian Church of Sudan v Talisman Energy, Inc*, 244 F.Supp 2d 289 (SDNY 2003); and *Nevsun Resources Ltd. v Araya* (2020) SCC 5.

[37] An exception (albeit of a limited scope) is the compulsory jurisdiction of the Seabed Disputes Chamber over certain 'disputes between parties to a contract, being States Parties, the Authority or the Enterprise, state enterprises and natural or juridical persons': UNCLOS, Art 187(c).

[38] Márquez, 'Legal Avenues' (2015) 62; Morgera, *Corporate Accountability* (2009) 25.

effective judicial remedy, including the lack of financial and other resources in order to have access to information and legal services[39] and the lack of institutional capacity.[40] In addition, as noted in section I, the independence and legitimacy of domestic judicial authorities are not guaranteed in many jurisdictions.[41] Pursuing legal action against foreign investors in their home states through transterritorial tort claims[42] also involves a number of barriers and limitations.[43] Important legal obstacles are as follows. First, the principle of limited liability may shield a parent company from liability for the torts committed by its subsidiary companies.[44] Secondly, the *forum non conveniens* doctrine may be applied in certain jurisdictions outside the EU.[45] Thirdly, if the home state's court decides to apply the law

[39] G Skinner, 'Parent Company Accountability: Ensuring Justice for Human Rights Violations' (2015) 'International Corporate Accountability Roundtable 11/2015', 10–11, available at www.bhrinlaw.org/documents/pcap-report-2015.pdf.

[40] Márquez 'Legal Avenues' (2015) 65.

[41] See UNHRC, 'Report of the Special Rapporteur on the independence of judges and lawyers: Classifications of the situations addressed by the Special Rapporteur 1994–2006 by Leandro Despouy' (18 January 2007) UN Doc No A/HRC/4/25, para 22: 'Serious interference by the executive branch in the composition and functioning of the Supreme Court and corruption within the Court itself are recurrent themes in the complaints received'.

[42] On transnational tort cases and home states' duty to regulate TNCs, see, for example, JA Zerk, *Multinationals and Corporate Social Responsibility: Limitations and Opportunities in International Law* (Cambridge University Press, 2006) chs 4 and 5; de Schutter, 'Transnational Corporations' (2005) 19–100; C van Dam, 'Tort Law and Human Rights: Brothers in Arms on the Role of Tort Law in the Area of Business and Human Rights' (2011) 2 *Journal of European Tort Law* 221; MD Goldhaber, 'Corporate Human Rights Litigation in Non-U.S. Courts: A Comparative Scorecard' (2013) 3 *University of California Irvine Law Review* 126; A Ramasastry, 'Corporate Social Responsibility Versus Business and Human Rights: Bridging the Gap Between Responsibility and Accountability' (2015) 14 *Journal of Human Rights* 237; M McVey, 'A powerful Re*tort*: Foreign Direct Liability as an Essential Mechanism of Redress for Victims of Human Rights Violations by Multinational Extractive Corporations' (2015) Postgraduate HRC 2015 Working Paper No. 1, available at www.academia.edu/29712093/A_powerful_Retort_Foreign_direct_liability_as_an_essential_mechanism_of_redress_for_victims_of_human_rights_violations_by_multinational_extractive_corporations.

[43] See G Skinner, R McCorquodale and O de Schutter, 'The Third Pillar. Access to Judicial Remedies for Human Rights Violations by Transnational Business' (ICAR-CORE-ECCJ, December 2013), available at corporatejustice.org/documents/publications/eccj/the_third_pillar_-access_to_judicial_remedies_for_human_rights_violation.-1-2.pdf. See also SL Seck and A Ogunranti, 'Accountability: Legal Risks and Remedies' in R Lindsay and R Martella (eds), *Corporate Responsibility, Sustainable Business: Environmental, Social and Governance Frameworks for the 21st Century* (Kluwer Law International, 2020) 597–600.

[44] There is an observable tendency in some domestic jurisdictions to set a high threshold for piercing the 'corporate veil', although there are important developments that suggest otherwise, such as the adoption of the French Corporate Duty of Vigilance Law in 2017 (Article L 225-102-4 Code de commerce, modifié par Ordonnance n° 2017-1162 du 12 juillet 2017 – Art 11). For recent cases on parent company liability, see S Spears, 'Corporate Responsibility and National and International Legal Frameworks' in R Lindsay and R Martella (eds), *Corporate Responsibility, Sustainable Business: Environmental, Social and Governance Frameworks for the 21st Century* (Kluwer Law International, 2020) 575–79.

[45] For example, *Re: Union Carbide Corporation Gas Plant Disaster at Bhopal, India in December, 1984*, 634 F Supp 842 (SDNY 1986) and *Re: Union Carbide Corporation Gas Plant Disaster at Bhopal, India in December, 1984*, 809 F.2d 195 (2d Cir 1987); *Aguinda v Texaco, Inc*, 142 F Supp 2d 534 (SDNY 2001); *Aguinda v Texaco, Inc*, 303 F.3d 470 (2d Cir 2002). By contrast, in the EU, Art 4 of the Brussels I Regulation (recast) precludes the application of the doctrine of *forum non conveniens* for cases brought

of the host state, this may well mean various limitations in the pursuit of remedies such as a significantly lower amount of damages.[46] In any event, the success of transterritorial tort claims primarily depends on the legal systems and the existence or absence of willingness to advance such cases in the concerned state,[47] factors that vary widely among countries.[48] As a forum for transnational tort litigation in third countries, the US Alien Tort Statute (ATS) has been employed by *foreign* plaintiffs to sue *non-US (foreign)* nationals and corporations in US courts for alleged international law violations committed in other nations.[49] However, the US Supreme Court has limited the scope of international law that can serve as the basis for jurisdiction under the ATS (*Sosa v Alvarez*),[50] as well as the territorial scope of permissible claims (*Kiobel v Royal Dutch Petroleum*).[51] The most restrictive view was presented by the Court of Appeals for the Second Circuit in *Kiobel v Royal Dutch Petroleum*, in which Judge Cabranes (writing for the majority) held that corporate liability cannot be grounds for ATS claims.[52] Recently, in *Jesner v Arab Bank*, the Supreme Court concluded (by a majority of 5:4) that 'foreign corporations may not be defendants in suits brought under the ATS'.[53] This has, at least so far, put significant limitations on the scope of the ATS as a cause of action.[54]

against a company which is domiciled in a Member State (where 'domiciled' is described in Art 63): Regulation (EU) No 1215/2012 of the European Parliament and of the Council of 12 December 2012 on jurisdiction and the recognition and enforcement of judgments in civil and commercial matters [2012] OJ L 351/1.

[46] Skinner, McCorquodale & De Schutter, 'The Third Pillar' (2013) 41–43; Goldhaber, 'Corporate Human Rights Litigation in Non-U.S. Courts' (2013) 132.

[47] LFH Enneking, 'Crossing the Atlantic? The Political and Legal Feasibility of European Foreign Direct Liability Cases' (2009) 40 *George Washington International Law Review* 903, 912–13; Morgera, Corporate Accountability (2009) 31.

[48] B Stephens, 'Translating Filártiga: A Comparative and International Law Analysis of Domestic Remedies for International Human Rights Violations' (2002) 27 *Yale Journal of International Law* 1, 34.

[49] For example, *Kadic v Karadzic*, 70 F.3d 232 (2d Cir 1995); *Doe v Unocal*, 395 F.3d 932 (9th Cir 2002).

[50] *Sosa v Alvarez-Machain*, 542 US 692 (2004). This is the case in which the Supreme Court interpreted the ATS for the first time. The court, while assuming that 'the First Congress understood that the district courts would recognize private causes of action for certain torts in violation of the law of nations', limited the scope of international law norms to those 'accepted by the civilized world and defined with a specificity comparable to the features of the18th-century' torts', such as the violation of safe conducts, infringement of the rights of ambassadors, and piracy (at 725).

[51] *Kiobel v Royal Dutch Petroleum*, 569 US 108 (2013). In this case, the Supreme Court applied the presumption against extraterritoriality to the case and held that plaintiffs' 'case seeking relief for violations of the law of nations occurring outside the United States is barred' (at 14). On this case, see for example, S Davis and CA Whytock, 'State Remedies for Human Rights' (2018) 98 *Boston University Law Review* 397, 409–11; RP Alford, 'Human Rights After Kiobel: Choice of Law and the Rise of Transnational Tort Litigation' (2014) 63 *Emory Law Journal* 1089, 1097–98; CR Knight, 'International Human Rights Litigation after Bauman: The Viability of Veil Piercing to Hale Foreign Parent Corporations into U.S. Courts' (2016) 41 *University of Dayton Law Review* 214.

[52] *Kiobel v Royal Dutch Petroleum*, No. 06-4800-cv, 06-4876-cv, 2010 WL 3611392 (2d Cir 2010).

[53] *Jesner v Arab Bank*, 138 S Ct 1386 (2018), 27.

[54] For additional discussion, see ch 9 (Roorda and Ku) of this volume; A Sanger, 'Transnational Corporate Responsibility in Domestic Courts: Still Out of Reach?' (2019) 113 *American Journal of*

Therefore, in addition to the lack of an international mechanism to hold foreign investors accountable for their conduct, it is often difficult to seek recourse in domestic legal systems. This speaks to the potentially corrective function of counterclaims in the investment arbitration system.

C. Is the Host State the Right Claimant?

Raising counterclaims therefore has genuine potential to not only address procedural inequality but also require the investor to redress the harm caused to the society of the host state. A case in point is *Urbaser v Argentina*, in which the counterclaim was based on the allegation that 'the Claimants' alleged failure to provide the necessary investment into the Concession' amounted to a violation of 'its obligations under international law based on the human right to water'.[55] Such situations and resulting counterclaims always involve the interests of third parties to the dispute, or people that were actually affected.

As the principal purpose of pursuing investor accountability in such contexts should be to redress the harm suffered by the victims, there arises the question of whether or not the host state is the right party to receive compensation for such damage.

This chapter addresses this fundamental yet relatively unexplored question. The following sections argue that there are circumstances where the host state should be allowed to pursue such claims in its own right and/or on behalf of the victims as *parens patriae*, and examine the factors to be considered in assessing when such counterclaims should be justified.

III. Pursuing Counterclaims in the Host State's Own Interest

It is now widely recognised that a state is responsible not only for its own human rights violations but also for human rights abuses by private entities that occurred in its territory. Principle 1 of the Guiding Principles on Business and Human Rights states the following: 'States must protect against human rights abuse within their territory and/or jurisdiction by third parties, including business enterprises.

International Law Unbound 4. It should be noted that the conclusion of the Supreme Court in *Jesner* is 'expressly limited to suits against *foreign* [as opposed to US] corporations'. WS Dodge, 'Jesner v. Arab Bank: The Supreme Court Preserves the Possibility of Human Rights Suits Against U.S. Corporations' (*University of California Davis School of Law Faculty Blogs*, 26 April 2018), available at facultyblog.law.ucdavis.edu/post/jesner-v-arab-bank-the-supreme-court-preserves-the-possibility-of-human-rights-suits-against-us-corporations.aspx (emphasis in original).

[55] *Urbaser SA and Consorcio de Aguas Bilbao Bizkaia, Bilbao Biskaia Ur Partzuergoa v The Argentine Republic* (*Urbaser v Argentina*), ICSID Case No ARB/07/26, Award (8 December 2016) para 36.

This requires taking appropriate steps to prevent, investigate, punish and redress such abuse through effective policies, legislation, regulations and adjudication'.[56]

Foreign investors are subject to the sovereignty of the host state, and as such must comply with the state's legal and administrative requirements in order to establish and operate their businesses. This being so, in authorising and monitoring business operations as well as adopting and applying legislation and regulations concerning such operations, the host state is required to pay due diligence to protect against possible human rights violations by private parties.[57] In *Social and Economic Rights Action Center for Economic and Social Rights v Nigeria*,[58] a case based on the African Charter of Human and Peoples' Rights, the African Commission on Human and Peoples' Rights explicitly acknowledged the following: 'Governments have a duty to protect their citizens, not only through appropriate legislation and effective enforcement but also by protecting them from damaging acts that may be perpetrated by private parties'.[59] The Commission then concluded that Nigeria, by giving 'the green light to private actors, and the oil Companies in particular, to devastatingly affect the wellbeing of the Ogonis', breached its obligation to protect its people against interferences in the enjoyment of their rights.[60]

It is also widely recognised that the state's duty to protect includes the obligation to provide effective remedies in the case of failures to fulfill the obligation to protect.[61] In *Social and Economic Rights Action Center for Economic and Social Rights v Nigeria*, the Commission thus appealed to the Government of Nigeria

[56] UN Guiding Principles on Business and Human Rights, Principle 1. See also CA Sevilla Albornoz, 'Can Foreign Investors Be Held Liable for Human Rights Violations? International Human Rights Law and Beyond' (2017) 8 *Investment Treaty News* 10–11.

[57] M Nowak and KM Januszewski, 'Non-State Actors and Human Rights' in M Noortmann, A Reinisch and C Ryngaert (eds), *Non-State Actors in International Law* (Hart Publishing, 2017) 142; International Council on Human Rights and Policy, 'Beyond Voluntarism: Human Rights and the Developing International Legal Obligations of Companies' (2002) 52, available at papers.ssrn.com/sol3/papers.cfm?abstract_id=1551200.

[58] *The Social and Economic Rights Action Center & the Center for Economic and Social Rights v Nigeria* (2001) Comm No 155/96.

[59] ibid para 57 (citing 74/92 *Commission nationale des droits de l'Homme et des libertés / Chad*).

[60] ibid. See also A Adeyeye, 'Corporate Responsibility in International Law: Which Way to Go?' (2007) 11 *Singapore Yearbook of International Law* 141, 144–45.

[61] See, for example, B Stephans, 'Translating Filartiga: A Comparative and International Law Analysis of Domestic Remedies For International Human Rights Violations' (2002) 27 *Yale Journal International Law* 1, 46; H Shue, *Basic Rights*, 2nd edn (Princeton University Press 1996) 60; F Francioni, 'International Human Rights in an Environmental Horizon' (2010) 21 *European Journal of International Law* 41, 52; R McCorquodale and L Smit, 'Human Rights, Responsibilities and Due Diligence' in S Deva and D Bilchitz (eds), *Building a Treaty on Business and Human Rights: Context and Contours* (Cambridge University Press, 2017) 216, 225–26; The Committee on Economic, Social and Cultural Rights, Statement on the Obligations of States Parties Regarding the Corporate Sector and Economic, Social and Cultural Rights, E/C.12/2011/1, para 3; International Covenant on Civil and Political Rights (open for signature 16 December 1966, effective 23 March 1976) 999 UNTS 171, Art 2(3); Human Rights Committee 'General Comment No. 31: The Nature of the General Legal Obligation Imposed on States Parties to the Covenant' (26 May 2004) UN Doc CCPR/C/21/Rev. 1/Add. 13, para 8. See also JG Ruggie, 'Business and Human Rights: The Evolving International Agenda' (2007) 101 *American Journal of International Law* 819, 829; Morgera, Corporate Accountability (2009) 28–29; Sevilla Albornoz, 'Can Foreign Investors Be Held Liable for Human Rights Violations?' (2017) 11.

'to ensure protection of the environment, health and livelihood of the people of Ogoniland' by, inter alia, 'Ensuring adequate compensation to victims of the human rights violations, including relief and resettlement assistance to victims of government sponsored raids, and undertaking a comprehensive cleanup of lands and rivers damaged by oil operations'.[62]

Likewise, the Inter-American Court of Human Rights held the state liable for damages caused by private parties in *Kichwa Indigenous People of Sarayaku v Ecuador*.[63] This case concerned Ecuador's granting of a permit to a private oil company to carry out oil exploration and exploitation activities in the territory of the Kichwa Indigenous People of Sarayaku. The Court found that several rights under the American Convention on Human Rights were violated, including the rights to consultation (Article 21)[64] and the rights to life and to personal integrity (Articles 4(1) and 5(1)). The Court first found that 'the oil company, with the state's acquiescence and protection, cleared trails and planted nearly 1400 kilograms of pentolite explosives in Block 23, which includes the Sarayaku territory'. It then concluded that the state was 'responsible for having put at grave risk the rights to life and physical integrity of the Sarayaku People' on the grounds that

> the State's non-compliance with its obligation to guarantee the Sarayaku People's right to communal property by allowing explosives to be placed on its territory, has created a permanent situation of risk and threat to the life and physical integrity of its members.[65]

Accordingly, the Court ordered, inter alia, that Ecuador must pay USD 90,000 and USD 1,250,000 to the Sarayaku People as compensation for pecuniary and non-pecuniary damages, respectively.[66] The Court also ordered Ecuador to 'neutralize, deactivate and, if applicable, remove all pentolite left on the surface and buried in the territory of the Sarayaku People'.[67]

[62] *The Social and Economic Rights Action Center & the Center for Economic and Social Rights v Nigeria* (2001), Holding.

[63] *Case of the Kichwa Indigenous People of Sarayaku v Ecuador (Merits and Reparations)*, Inter-American Court of Human Rights, Judgment (27 June 2012). For an analysis of this case, see C Binder and JA Hofbauer, 'Case Study: Burlington Resources Inc. v Ecuador/Kichwa Indigenous People of Sarayaku v Ecuador' (15 July 2016), available at ssrn.com/abstract=2810062.

[64] In reaching this conclusion, the Court stated that 'the planning and executing of the consultation process is not an obligation that can be avoided by delegating it to a private company or to third parties': ibid para 187.

[65] ibid para 248.

[66] ibid paras 317, 323 and operative para 8.

[67] ibid operative para 1. Other Inter-American Human Rights Court cases in which the liability of states based on the duty to protect was found include: *Mayagma Sumo Awas Tigni Community v Nicaragua*, IACHR Series C No 79, Judgment (31 August 2001); *Community of La Oroya v Peru*, Petition 1473-06, IACHR, Report No 76/09, OEA/Series L/V/II, Doc 51, corr 1 (2009), available at www.cidh.oas.org/annualrep/2009eng/Peru1473.06eng.htm; *Yanomami v Brazil*, Case No. 7615, Resolution No 12/85 of 5 March 1985, available at www.cidh.org/annualrep/84.85eng/Brazil7615.htm; *Maya Indigenous Community of the Toledo District v Belize* [2004] IACHR Case 12.053, Report No 40/04, OEA/Series L/V/II.122 Doc 5 rev 1, 727; *Case of the Mayagna (Sumo) Awas Tingni Community v Nicaragua, Mayagna (Sumo) Awas Tingni Community v Nicaragua*, Merits, reparations and costs, IACHR Series C No 79, [2001] IACHR 9, IHRL 1462 (IACHR 2001) (31 August 2001).

In addition, when the state is found to have been negligent in authorising or monitoring the operations of private business, which has resulted in environmental and human rights damage, the state may be held responsible for the harm done by private parties via its own domestic legal framework, by the application of its domestic laws such as tort law or even the constitution.[68] Pigrau et al observed that:

> [I]t is more typical that victims start out by appealing to the appropriate government entities responsible for authorising and overseeing the activities causing the damages, and if this proves ineffective, appealing to the administrative, civil, or criminal courts, or even to environmental courts, if they exist. All of this must take place, for each case, according to the possibilities offered by national legislation. This is what has occurred in most cases, though with variable results.[69]

The assessment of the circumstances under which the state's liability is established requires a context-specific analysis that takes account various factors including the severity and nature of the harm, the relationship between the state and the abuser and the reasonableness of the measures taken by the state. As discussed above, if the state is found liable for damage caused by private parties, it assumes the obligation to effect payment in satisfaction of a claim of the victims. It means that it does have the financial interest in pursuing the investor's responsibility to the extent appropriate,[70] and therefore should be allowed to raise counterclaims in its own right.

IV. The Host State as *Parens Patriae*

A. Development of the *Parens Patriae* Doctrine

It is argued that a host state should be allowed to bring counterclaims on behalf of victims in certain circumstances. As discussed below, the *parens patriae* doctrine, which has its origin in English law, provides normative support to this proposition.

The *parens patriae* doctrine is traced back to the time of King Edward I (1272–1307). The doctrine was first founded on the concept of royal prerogative, that is, the King's power of wardship derives from his duty 'to take care of his subjects as are legally unable' to care for themselves such as those who were termed idiots. The power of wardship later extended to cover minor heirs in the feudal tenurial system, and this power became a source of profit for the crown.[71]

[68] See, for example, L Abramchayev, 'A Social Contract Argument for the State's Duty to Protect from Private Violence' (2004) 18 *Journal of Civil Rights and Economic Development* 849.

[69] A Pigrau et al, 'Legal avenues for EJOs to claim environmental liability' (June 2012) Environmental Justice Organisation, Liabilities and Trade Report No 4, 39.

[70] See also Amado, Kern and Rodriguez, Arbitrating (2018) 52–54.

[71] For the historical origin of the *parens patriae* doctrine, see LB Custer, 'The Origins of the Doctrine of Parens Patriae' (1978) 27 *Emory Law Journal* 195; MS Thomas, '*Parens Patriae* and the States' Historic Police Power', (2016) 69 *Southern Methodist University Law Review* 759.

However, subsequently in the US, the doctrine of *parens patriae* developed in a very different context. That is, in the beginning of the twentieth century, this doctrine was relied on by states as a basis of exercising police power to protect their 'quasi-sovereign' interests such as 'the general comfort, health, or property rights of its inhabitants',[72] before it further developed into an alternative to class actions for antitrust and other economic claims.[73] Subsequently, in *New Jersey, Department of Environmental Protection v Jersey Central Power and Light Co*, in which the state sued a power plant operator for the killing of fish in tidal waters by pollution and through a sharp reduction in water temperature, the New Jersey Superior Court agreed with the trial judge's conclusion that 'The State has not only the right but also the affirmative fiduciary obligation to … seek compensation for any diminution in that trust corpus', because 'absent some special interest in some private citizen, it is questionable whether anyone but the State can be considered the proper party to sue for recovery of damages to the environment'.[74] In Canada, in *British Columbia v Canadian Forest Products Ltd*, the Attorney-General sought compensation for environmental damage caused by a forest fire for which Canfor was partially responsible. The majority of the Supreme Court of Canada (opinion delivered by Binnie J), after citing US cases in which 'a common law *parens patriae* jurisdiction to represent the collective interests of the public' was acknowledged, concluded as follows:

> It seems to me there is no legal barrier to the Crown suing for compensation as well as injunctive relief in a proper case on account of public nuisance, or negligence causing environmental damage to public lands, and perhaps other torts such as trespass.[75]

In these cases, the states were allowed in a *parens patriae* capacity to litigate on behalf of its citizens, without proving specific injury to the affected states.[76]

In the context of transnational tort claims, on 29 March 1985, three months after the Bhopal gas leak incident, the Indian Government adopted the Bhopal Gas Leak Disaster (Processing of Claims) Act[77] by which it empowered itself

[72] *North Dakota v Minnesota*, 263 US 365 (1923) 375. See also WR MacKay, '*Parens Patriae* as Basis for Provincial Standing in Judicial Review of Federal Decisions' (2008) 45 *Alberta Law Review* 961, 977–79.

[73] LF Butler, '*Parens Patriae* Representation in Transnational Crisis: The Bhopal Tragedy' (1987) 17 *California Western International Law Journal* 175, 179. Early cases based on *parens patriae* causes of action in which environmental and public health concerns were discussed include *Georgia v Tennessee Copper Co*, 206 US 230 (1907); *Missouri v Illinois*, 180 US 208 (1901) and *Kansas v Colorado*, 206 US 46 (1907).

[74] *State v Jersey Central Power & Light Co*, 336 A.2d 750 (New Jersey Superior Court Appellate Division 1975) 392.

[75] *British Columbia v Canadian Forest Products Ltd* [2004] 2 SCR 74, Judgment of McLachlin CJ and Iacobucci, Major, Binnie, Arbour and Deschamps JJ, para 81.

[76] TW Merrill, 'Golden Rules for Transboundary Pollution' (1997) 46 *Duke Law Journal* 931, 937.

[77] Available at legislative.gov.in/actsofparliamentfromtheyear/bhopal-gas-leak-disaster-processing-claims-act-1985.

as the exclusive legal representative for all claimants under the doctrine of *parens patriae*. In particular, section 3 of the Act states the following:

> Subject to the other provisions of this Act, the Central Government shall, and shall have the exclusive right to, represent, and act in place of (whether within or outside India) every person who has made, or is entitled to make, a claim for all purposes connected with such claim in the same manner and to the same effect as such person.

One month after the adoption of the Act, the Indian Government filed a case against Union Carbide Corporation in the US, acting in a *parens patriae* capacity for the victims of the incident. This claim was however dismissed by the US courts by the application of the *forum non conveniens* doctrine based on the consideration that Indian courts 'have the proven capacity to mete out fair and equal justice'.[78]

Indeed, the *Bhopal* case was not an exception, as the US Courts of Appeal have consistently denied *parens patriae* jurisdiction in US courts to foreign governments.[79] In *Estados Unidos Mexicanos v Decoster*, the US Court of Appeal (1st Circuit) explained the reasons for this rejection that a foreign nation has no 'cognizable interests in our system of federalism', which are 'a critical element of *parens patriae* standing'.[80] However, this consideration does not apply to the question of the appropriateness of the state's representing its citizens' interests by raising counterclaims in investment arbitration.

Several cases heard by international courts and tribunals have invoked the *parens patriae* doctrine.[81] For example, in the *Genocide Convention Case (Croatia v Serbia)*, Croatia requested the Court to adjudge and declare, inter alia, the following:

> [T]he Federal Republic of Yugoslavia has an obligation to pay to the Republic of Croatia, in its own right and as *parens patriae* for its citizens, reparations for damages to persons

[78] *In re Union Carbide Corp. Gas Plant Disaster at Bhopal in India*, 634 F Supp 842 (SDNY 1986) 867. This order was affirmed by the Court of Appeals (Second Circuit): see *In re Union Carbide Corp. Gas Plant Disaster at Bhopal in India*, 809 F.2d 195 (2nd Cir 1987). For a discussion of this case, see U Baxi, 'Geographies of Injustice: Human Rights at the Alter of Convenience' in CM Scott (ed), *Torture as Tort: Comparative Perspectives on the Development of Transnational Human Rights Litigation* (Hart, Publishing 2001); Butler, '*Parens Patriae*' (1987).

[79] *Pfizer, Inc v Lord*, (522 F.2d 612 (8th Cir 1975)); *Estados Unidos Mexicanos v Decoster*, 229 F.3d 332 (1st Cir 2000).

[80] *Estados Unidos Mexicanos v Decoster*.

[81] *Military and Paramilitary Activities (Nicaragua v US)* (Judgment, Merits) [1986] ICJ Rep 14, 19; *Case Concerning Application of the Convention on the Prevention and Punishment of the Crime of Genocide (Bosnia & Herzegovina v Yugoslavia (Serbia & Montenegro)* (Order, Provisional measures) [1993] ICJ Rep 3, 7; *Application of the Convention on the Prevention and Punishment of the Crime of Genocide (Croatia v Serbia)* (Judgment, Preliminary Objections) [2008] ICJ Rep 412 and (Judgment, Merits) [2015] ICJ Rep 3; *Application of the International Convention on the Elimination of All Forms of Racial Discrimination (Qatar v United Arab Emirates)*, Order, Request for the indication of provisional measures (23 July 2018); Case 86 of the Iran–US Claims Tribunal (in which the US presented the statement of claim 'in continuance of the exercise of diplomatic protection of its nationals, acting as *parens patriae*, trustee, guardian and representative on their behalf'). See DD Caron, 'The Nature of the Iran–United States Claims Tribunal and the Evolving Structure of International Dispute Resolution' (1990) 84 *American Journal of International Law* 104, 133–34. See also D Sloss, 'Using International Court of Justice Advisory Opinions to Adjudicate Secessionist Claims' (2001) 42 *Santa Clara Law Review* 357.

> and property, as well as to the Croatian economy and environment caused by the foregoing violations of international law in a sum to be determined by the Court.[82]

Borchard identified the *parens patriae* doctrine as one of the normative bases that justify the exercise of the right of diplomatic protection.[83] In addition, Orrego Vicuña observes that the reliance on the *parens patriae* doctrine in the *Genocide Convention Case (Croatia v Serbia)* demonstrated a shift away from the 'traditional' interpretation of diplomatic protection. That is, the classical theory of diplomatic protection is that 'a State is in reality asserting its own rights – its right to ensure, in the person of its subjects, respect for the rules of international law'.[84] However, with changes in international law, in particular given that the state is no longer the sole subject of international law, he argues that: 'While the transition from a legal fiction to a different reality takes place, the interesting thought that a claim may actually have a "dual nature" and represent the interest of both the individual and the state has been advanced'.[85]

Certainly, as observed by the US Court of Appeal (1st Circuit) in *Estados Unidos Mexicanos v Decoster*,[86] the *parens patriae* doctrine, in itself, has not acquired the status of customary international law.[87] Nor can it be qualified as 'the general principles of law recognized by civilized nations' within the meaning of Article 38(1)(c) of the Statute of the International Court of Justice.[88] This is because, while the consent of the majority (if not all) of states is necessary for a principle existing in domestic legal orders to be elevated to the level of a general principle of international law,[89] the *parens patriae* doctrine, which has been developed and practised

[82] *Application of the Convention on the Prevention and Punishment of the Crime of Genocide (Croatia v Serbia)*, Judgment, Preliminary Objections; Judgment, Merits, 24–32. It should be noted that Croatia's claim was rejected on the merits. *Application of the Convention on the Prevention and Punishment of the Crime of Genocide (Croatia v Serbia)*, Judgment, Merits, 154.

[83] E Borchard, 'Protection of Citizens Abroad and Change of Original Nationality' 3472 *Yale Law School Faculty Scholarship Series* (1934), available at digitalcommons.law.yale.edu/fss_papers/3472, 371. Professor Lee describes the doctrine of *parens patriae* in the domestic context as 'a weaker, domestic cousin' of the international law doctrine of espousal. TH Lee, 'The Supreme Court of the United States as Quasi-International Tribunal: Reclaiming the Court's Original and Exclusive Jurisdiction over Treaty-Based Suits by Foreign States Against States' (2004) 104 *Columbia Law Review* 1765, 1855 (at fn 393).

[84] *Mavrommatis Palestine Concessions*, PCIJ, Series A, No 2. See also *Factory at Chorzów (Germany v Poland)* 1928 PCIJ, Series A, No 9, 27–28; Borchard (ibid) 363–66.

[85] F Orrego Vicuña, 'Interim Report on "The Changing Law of Nationality of Claims"', Report of the Sixty-Ninth Conference held in London (25–29 July 2000), International Law Association 631, 633–64.

[86] *Estados Unidos Mexicanos v Decoster*.

[87] ibid 399.

[88] By contrast, Sloss acknowledges the possibility that a state may pursue the right of self-determination (secessionist claims) of the people on behalf of them before the ICJ, by arguing that the *parens patriae* doctrine is a general principle of law recognized by civilized nations. Sloss, 'Using International Court of Justice Advisory Opinions' (2001) 375.

[89] See in particular MC Bassiouni, 'A Functional Approach to 'General Principles of International Law" (1990) 11 *Michigan Journal of International Law* 768; R Yotova, 'Challenges in the Identification of the "General Principles of Law Recognized by Civilized Nations": The Approach of the International Court' (2017) University of Cambridge Faculty of Law Research Paper No 38/2017, available at ssrn.com/abstract=3020190.

in common law countries, lacks this requirement of a certain degree of recognition and consensus.[90]

However, in assessing the question of the appropriateness of allowing the defendant state to file counterclaims on behalf of its citizens, there is no need to *apply* the *parens patriae* doctrine to establish jurisdiction over counterclaims in investment arbitration. The rationale of the *parens patriae* doctrine that it would bring satisfaction and protection for the affected citizens in an effective manner will provide normative support to the admissibility of such counterclaims.

B. Factors that Support the Host State's Right to Counterclaim as *Parens Patriae*

Although there are normative rationales for counterclaims by a host state as *parens patriae*, they also raise various concerns that largely overlap with those raised over the state's exercise of the right of diplomatic protection. For instance, it is often contended that the defendant state, which has full control over the claims, may compromise the case for political or other public policy considerations in a way that undermines the interests of the victims;[91] that there might be conflicts between the victims and the defendant state over 'issues of settlement, appropriate relief, and the like';[92] the victims may be barred from subsequently bringing claims in different forums;[93] and due to the absence of international guarantees that the victims will actually receive satisfaction from the state, there remains the possibility that the victims are left without proper compensation.[94]

The *Bhopal* case might well illustrate some of these concerns. After the US Court of Appeal rejected the US courts' jurisdiction over the Bhopal case, the Indian Government brought the case to its national courts. In 1989, the Supreme Court of India ordered the Union Carbide Corporation to pay USD 470 million to the Indian Government in 'full settlement of all claims, rights and liabilities related to and

[90] On this requirement, for example, the 'clean hands' doctrine was found not to qualify as general principle of law by several investment arbitration tribunals. A tribunal observed that while general principles of law 'require a certain level of recognition and consensus', 'there is a significant amount of controversy as to the existence of an 'unclean hands' principle in international law'. *Veteran Petroleum Limited (Cyprus) v The Russian Federation*, UNCITRAL, PCA Case No 2005-05/AA228, Final Award (18 July 2014); *Hulley Enterprises Limited (Cyprus) v The Russian Federation*, UNCITRAL, PCA Case No 2005-03/AA226, Final Award (18 July 2014); and *Yukos Universal Limited (Isle of Man) v The Russian Federation*, UNCITRAL, PCA Case No 2005-04/AA227, Final Award (18 July 2014) para 1359. See also *South American Silver Limited v Bolivia*, PCA Case No 2013-15, Award (22 November 2018) para 445.

[91] Borchard, 'Protection of Citizens Abroad' (1934) 363–36.

[92] *Estados Unidos Mexicanos v Decoster*, 399 (on the *parens patriae* doctrine in the US). See also Orrego Vicuña, 'Interim Report' (2000) 632 (on diplomatic protection).

[93] ibid.

[94] Butler, 'Parens Patriae' (1987) 193.

arising out of the Bhopal Gas disaster'.[95] Following this judgment, various groups challenged the settlement for a higher amount of compensation, but the Court confirmed the 1989 orders as 'fair, reasonable and adequate'.[96] Attempts to challenge the settlement were made in various jurisdictions in India, all of which were rejected.[97]

Against these considerations, it is argued that the following factors would support a host state's counterclaims as *parens patriae*. First, there are cases where the victims have insufficient access to an effective, fair and equal judicial forum in the domestic legal system. As discussed in section I, in certain jurisdictions, the rule of law remains weak and the independence and legitimacy of domestic judicial authorities cannot be taken for granted. Victims may also find it difficult to pursue their claims due to practical obstacles, including the difficulty to gain access to information. Seck and Ogunranti identify 'information asymmetry' between individual claimants and TNCs as an obstacle to pursuing retroactive justice, because 'Corporations may conceal or manipulate the nature and extent of harm because survivors have little or no resources to investigate it'.[98] Likewise, van Dam observes that, lawsuits against TNCs 'are complex, risky, hard-fought by the TNCs, resource-intensive, of uncertain duration and outcome, and have significant cash flow implications for the lawyers', and that victims have fewer 'opportunities for legal aid' in developing countries.[99] Pursuing judicial remedy in the home country of the investor or third countries also faces legal and practical barriers, as discussed in section II.B. When domestic dispute settlement mechanisms are an unrealistic option for victims, there is a greater need for the host state's intervention. Second, if the host state provides an administrative mechanism that enables the efficient and fair distribution of the award the host state may receive by, for example, the passing of a law to that effect, then this provides support for the admissibility of a counterclaim raised by the host state on behalf of the victims.

An additional consideration is required in a situation where the defendant state was also involved in the activities that caused damage, in particular environmental and human rights damage. In the worst cases, there may be collusion between the government and a TNC in causing damage, as exemplified by cases such as Shell in Nigeria, BP Amoco in Colombia and Unocal and Total in Myanmar.[100] Where

[95] *Union Carbide Corporation v Union of India* (1990) AIR 273.

[96] *Union Carbide Corporation v Union of India* (1991) 4 SCC 584.

[97] A Uff, <<La Réparation du dommage et la place du règlement transactionnel, point de vue des praticiens>>, in L Dubin et al, *L'entreprise multinationale et le droit international* (Pedone, 2017) 496.

[98] SL Seck and A Ogunranti, 'Accountability: Legal Risks and Remedies' in R Lindsay and R Martella (eds), *Corporate Responsibility, Sustainable Business: Environmental, Social and Governance Frameworks for the 21st Century* (Kluwer Law International, 2020) 587, 605.

[99] van Dam, 'Tort Law and Human Rights' (2011) 228.

[100] For different types of direct and indirect corporate complicity and cases, see F Wettstein, *Multinational Corporations and Global Justice: Human Rights Obligations of a Quasi-Governmental Institution* (Stanford University Press, 2009) 295–305. See also L Zarsky, 'Global Reach: Human Rights and Environment in the Framework of Corporate Accountability' in L Zarsky (ed), *Human Rights and the Environment: Conflicts and Norms in a Globalizing World* (Earthscan Publications, 2012) 31, 44–45; R McCorquodale, 'Corporate Social Responsibility and International Human Rights Law' (2009) 87 *Journal of Business Ethics* 385, 388–89.

such damage is attributable to not only the investor but also the state, the appropriateness of the state's counterclaim against the investor is called into question. However, even in such circumstances, the host state should be allowed to pursue legal action to hold investor accountable to the extent that the liability is apportioned to the investor. In this regard, the case of *British Columbia v Canadian Forest Products Ltd*, in which *parens patriae* jurisdiction was granted by the Supreme Court of Canada (see above), is highly instructive. In this case, the trial judge found that the Crown's inadequate firefighting efforts contributed to the losses resulting from the fire caused by Canfor's negligence, and divided the responsibility evenly between them. The Court of Appeal varied this decision and allocated 70 per cent of the responsibility to Canfor and 30 per cent to the Crown.[101] The Supreme Court upheld the Court of Appeal's order awarding compensation for diminution of the value of the non-harvestable trees at a figure equivalent to one-third of their commercial value. In such circumstances, the host state indeed fails to fulfil its obligation to protect against harms done by private persons, and thus assumes the responsibility to provide effective remedies to victims. In certain cases, allowing the host state to claim compensation from the investor to the extent of the latter's responsibility would be necessary for the state to fulfil this obligation.

To conclude, in the circumstances described above, the host state should be allowed to pursue legal action to hold the investor responsible for the harm done to third parties to the dispute by raising a counterclaim on its own interest and/or on behalf of those who actually suffered damage.

V. Conclusion

Amidst growing concerns over the IIA regime and greater recognition of the potentially grave impact of investors' activities on the public interest of the host state, counterclaims have received increasing attention. In investment arbitration, counterclaims serve to not only address the procedural inequality between the investor and the host state in investment arbitration but also hold the claimant investor accountable for the damage they allegedly caused in the territory of the host state.[102] In the current investment arbitration framework, raising counterclaims is effectively the only means to seek pecuniary damages from a claimant investor, and it does have certain comparative benefits over domestic litigation.

[101] *British Columbia v Canadian Forest Products Ltd*, para 2.

[102] In the current discussions on the Investor-State Dispute Settlement Reform at UNCITRAL, the issue of counterclaims has been considered by the Working Group (UNGA 'Report of Working Group III (Investor-State Dispute Settlement Reform) on the work of its thirty-fourth session' (Vienna, 27 November–1 December 2017) UN Doc A/CN.9/930/Add.1/Rev.1, paras 3–7) and may be considered further (UNGA 'Possible reform of investor-State dispute settlement (ISDS) Note by the Secretariat' (30 July 2019) UN Doc A/CN.9/WG.III/WP.166, para 50).

Nevertheless, when the alleged damage caused by the investor's conduct affected third parties to the dispute such as the local people, a question regarding the appropriateness of the use of counterclaims in investment arbitration arises: whether or not the host state is in the right position to receive compensation for such damage. This chapter has examined this relatively underexplored question. It is argued that in certain circumstances, the host state has the right to pursue legal action against investors in its own right and/or on behalf of victims, with the latter supported by the doctrine of *parens patriae*.

Certainly, active use of counterclaims in appropriate cases has a great potential to serve 'the overall integrity and legitimacy of international investment law by infusing balance into the dispute settlement mechanism'.[103] However, in situations described above, the principal aim of counterclaims against investors should be to redress the loss and injury suffered by those who were affected by their activities. If this is so, assessment of normative grounds for the host state's counterclaims should be based not only on 'correcting the asymmetry in investment arbitration', but also on the consideration of whether a counterclaim may help provide relief to victims. This chapter has sought to clarify the situations in which counterclaims by the host state may indeed fulfil this function.

[103] Bubrowski, 'Balancing IIA arbitration' (2013) 229.

9

Applying International Law to Corporations: The Limits to the Lessons Offered by the United States Experience with the Alien Tort Statute

LUCAS ROORDA AND JULIAN G KU

I. Introduction

The relationship of private corporations with public international law has been the subject of broad interest among scholars worldwide. One important branch of this scholarship has sought to explore ways in which businesses, that are usually organised as corporations, could be regulated or held accountable for violations of international law; in particular violations of human rights law. One avenue that has been explored is whether regulation and accountability mechanisms can be improved through new international treaties or other international mechanisms. Some familiar mechanisms specifically geared towards improving respect of businesses for international law and human rights are the UN Guiding Principles on Business and Human Rights (UNGPs)[1] and the OECD Guidelines for Multinational Enterprises.[2]

There have also been endeavours to create binding international instruments addressing business conduct and international law. In 2014, a United Nations intergovernmental working group was created with a mandate to 'elaborate an international legally binding instrument to regulate, in international human rights law, the activities of transnational corporations and other business enterprises'.[3]

[1] OHCHR, 'Guiding Principles on Business and Human Rights: Implementing the United Nations 'Protect, Respect and Remedy' Framework' (2011) UN Doc A/HRC/17/31.

[2] OECD, 'OECD Guidelines for Multinational Enterprises' (OECD Publishing, 2011), available at www.oecd.org/daf/inv/mne/48004323.pdf.

[3] UNHRC, 'Elaboration of an international legally binding instrument on transnational corporations and other business enterprises with respect to human rights' (14 July 2014) UN Doc A/HRC/RES/26/9, Art 1.

The working group has thus far released several drafts of what could become a legally binding treaty, generally requiring states to impose international human rights obligations on private businesses, including corporations, and organise accountability and remedies when these businesses do not live up to those obligations.[4]

The development of these international instruments, both binding and non-binding, is partially informed by experience from national jurisdictions. This is the case in particular when it comes to questions of accountability and legal liability. In the absence of an international tribunal that has jurisdiction over business entities, national courts are still the most important mechanism for litigating negative impacts on human rights and other norms of international law by businesses. The focus thus turns to national jurisdictions and their handling of lawsuits against businesses.

No national jurisdiction has had more experience with litigating business liability for international law violations than the US. Beginning in the 1990s, US courts issued numerous opinions allowing lawsuits under the Alien Tort Statute (ATS)[5] to proceed against business corporations for violations of customary international law. The ATS has often been cited in literature as kickstarting the trend of directly litigating possible violations of international (human rights) law by businesses, a trend which is now increasingly global. In that respect, the ATS has become an important point of comparison for developing legal regimes concerning the accountability and liability of corporations, both international as to the proposed binding treaty, and national as in other jurisdictions.

What is less well known and thus less understood, however, is that US courts have relied heavily, and sometimes exclusively, upon doctrines emerging from international humanitarian law (IHL) and conversely, international criminal law (ICL) to shape its jurisprudence on business liability for international law violations. This importance of IHL and ICL to the development of ATS jurisprudence on business corporations is somewhat surprising. While IHL is somewhat unique in international law in that it can impose duties on individuals, the leading IHL conventions do not mention corporate entities. Moreover, neither *ad hoc* international criminal tribunals, nor the International Criminal Court (ICC) have jurisdiction over corporate entities. Prior to the rise of ATS litigation against corporations in the 1990s, no corporate entity was ever held criminally or civilly responsible for violations of IHL.[6] Yet, US courts have extensively relied on

[4] See for an overview of the Draft documents and their annexes, OHCHR, 'Open-ended intergovernmental working group on transnational corporations and other business enterprises with respect to human rights', available at www.ohchr.org/EN/HRBodies/HRC/WGTransCorp/Pages/IGWGOnTNC.aspx.

[5] Alien Tort Claims Act, 28 USC § 1350 (ATS).

[6] Some cases, including the trials of German industrialists at Nuremberg, did concern corporate activities, but only involved individual defendants – often senior executives of German companies. See the United States Military Tribunal's various cases: *United States v Friedrich Flick et al* (20 April–22 December 1947) Case No 48; *United States v Carl Krauch, et al* (14 August 1947–29 July 1948) Case No 57 and *United States v Alfred Felix Alwyn Krupp von Bohlen und Halbach* (17 November 1947–30 June 1948) Case No 58.

doctrines originating from IHL and ICL to establish standards for liability under the ATS, sometimes explicitly, often implicitly. While the ATS may now for all intents and purposes have lost its place at the foreground of corporate liability for violations of international law, its rich history may still be informative for future developments.

This chapter will review the role of IHL and ICL in the first wave of ATS lawsuits imposing liability on corporations for international law violations. It will discuss how US courts adapted IHL concepts developed for private individuals and applied them to corporate entities despite the lack of international authority for them to do so. Indeed, US courts' reliance on IHL in corporate litigation could have created important precedents for how such doctrines might be adapted in other jurisdictions against corporations or in a new international treaty. But because US courts did not acknowledge the distinct origins of these doctrines, the importance of these precedents for ongoing efforts to create a formal international legal regime to regulate and impose liability on private businesses is more limited than is generally realised. To put it another way, US courts would have been innovators in the application of IHL and ICL to corporations if they had known that they were doing so.

II. The United States, Businesses and the Alien Tort Statute: Rising and Falling

Almost accidentally, the US became – at least temporarily – a world leader in using its domestic courts to develop international law norms for private business entities. But this leadership role did not emerge as a result of a considered decision by the US Government. Rather, it was a result of innovative litigation brought by private individuals invoking the ATS, an obscure two-and-a-half-century-old US statute that had laid dormant for most of its history. The statute's text simply gives federal courts jurisdiction over 'any civil action by an alien for a tort only, committed in violation of the law of nations or a treaty of the United States'.

The ATS was mostly forgotten since its inception,[7] but in the late 1970s US-based NGOs and private law firms began filing lawsuits under the ATS seeking to impose civil liability for violations of international law.[8] Such lawsuits initially focused on private individuals living in the US who had allegedly committed such violations against foreign nationals. The first (and paradigmatic) case for this first

[7] Only one case has been recorded prior to the 'rediscovery' of the ATS, concerning the doctrine of seaworthiness under international maritime law; see *Lopes v Reederei Richard Schroder*, 225 F Supp 292 (ED Pa 1963).

[8] See JG Ku, 'The Third Wave: The Alien Tort Statute and the War on Terrorism' (2005) 19 *Emory International Law Review* 105, 107–10 (discussing three waves of ATS litigation), and TH Lee, 'The Three Lives of the Alien Tort Statute: The Evolving Role of the Judiciary in U.S. Foreign Relations Judiciary in U.S. Foreign Relations' (2014) 89 *Notre Dame Law Review* 1645, 1646–47.

wave of ATS lawsuits is *Filartiga v Peña-Irala*, brought in New York federal courts against a Paraguayan government official living in the US by two other Paraguayan nationals for alleged torture that occurred in Paraguay.[9] Most early ATS lawsuits followed this fact pattern by focusing on foreign government officials who were alleged to have committed (or ordered) state-sanctioned violence against other foreign nationals in a foreign country.

The ATS is only open to lawsuits brought by aliens and the targets of these aliens in this first wave of lawsuits was almost exclusively other aliens because US defendants were more easily sued under domestic US law. Some of these aliens were residents of the US at the time the lawsuits were filed, such as in *Filartiga*; others were only temporarily present in the US, such as in the lawsuit filed against Radovan Karadzic, leader of the Republika Srpska during the Bosnian genocide.[10] The latter case was also groundbreaking, as this was the first case where provisions of international law were applied to an individual acting in private capacity and not formally on behalf of a state.[11] By the mid-1990s, however, a second 'wave' of ATS cases emerged as increasingly plaintiffs started bringing such lawsuits against private corporations, both US and foreign. Most of these lawsuits concerned alleged complicity in the actions of foreign governments outside of the US. These corporate liability lawsuits became the focus of much of US litigation. This wave of litigation also generated significant pushback from corporate defendants, who were much more organised and well-funded than individual defendants of the first wave. Moreover, many corporations had at least some presence in the US, and strongly contested the lawsuits brought against them.

The corporate counter-revolution against ATS claims has relied significantly on the Supreme Court's 2004 decision *Sosa v Álvarez-Machain*.[12] *Sosa* was the first ATS case to be granted *certiorari* by the Supreme Court, and its first entry into the then rapidly developing body of ATS case law. The case concerned the abduction and extrajudicial rendition to the US of a Mexican national by other Mexican nationals, allegedly working for the DEA. It did not involve a corporate defendant, but the business community was well aware of its potential impact on ATS litigation against businesses and the corporate defense bar was heavily involved in the case in several instances.[13]

The question at the heart of *Sosa* was *which* norms of international law could be actionable under the ATS. As noted above, lower courts had recognised a

[9] *Filartiga v Peña-Irala*, 630 F.2d 876 (2nd Cir 1980).

[10] *Kadic v Karadzic*, 70 F.3d 232 (3rd Cir 1996). The summons was served when Karadzic was visiting New York on invitation of the UN. For commentaries, see TR Posner, 'Kadic v. Karadzic. 70 F.3d 232' (1996) 90 *American Journal of International Law* 658; M Koebele, *Corporate Responsibility under the Alien Tort Statute: Enforcement of International Law through US Torts Law* (Brill, 2009) 55–56.

[11] Note that the Republica Srpska at the time was not recognised as an independent state, meaning that Karadzic acted on behalf of a non-state entity.

[12] *Sosa v Álvarez-Machain*, 542 US 692 (2004), 732.

[13] See, for example, Brief of Amici Curiae in support of Petitioner by National Association of Manufacturers in *Sosa v Alvarez-Machain*. This was also cited in Ku, 'The Third Wave' (2005) 110 (fn 22).

plethora of international rules as potential causes of action under the ATS. The Court did validate to a certain extent that developing body of ATS case law,[14] noting that while the ATS was in principle a jurisdictional statute, courts could accept a limited number of causes of action under their common law powers. Those causes of action should however meet a strict 'specific, universal and obligatory' standard.[15] The Court did not provide much elaboration as to when a norm would meet that standard, but it did note that it should be as accepted as those norms the ATS was originally intended to cover at the time the statute was drafted – such as the prohibition of piracy in the eighteenth century.[16] This standard has since been used by courts to determine whether particular causes of action are indeed universally accepted in customary international law.

Sosa may have limited the actionable norms under the ATS, but was not fatal to the wave of lawsuits against businesses entirely; indeed, after *Sosa*, courts still found a diverse array of international law norms to be 'specific, universal and obligatory' enough to meet the *Sosa* standard. The Supreme Court further limited the possibilities to litigate against foreign persons under the ATS. In *Kiobel v Royal Dutch Shell*,[17] it applied a presumption against extraterritoriality to the ATS, meaning that a statute should not be read to have extraterritorial effect without a clear indication that Congress intended it to do so.[18] According to the Court's majority decision written by Chief Justice Roberts, the presumption exists to prevent unintended clashes with foreign laws and limit potential diplomatic conflict, echoing the need for judicial caution in *Sosa*.[19] The Court then found that neither the text, nor the history or purpose of the ATS could overcome the presumption. It thus ruled out so-called 'foreign-cubed' lawsuits, where there is a foreign plaintiff suing a foreign defendant for acts committed on foreign soil; only cases where the alleged wrongful conduct 'touched and concerned' US territory could be brought under the ATS. As the plaintiffs could not demonstrate a sufficient connection to satisfy that test, their case was dismissed.

Finally, in the 2017 decision *Jesner v Arab Bank*, the Court addressed a question that was also raised before the lower courts in *Kiobel* but had not been ruled on by the Supreme Court, namely whether norms of international law – in particular, international human rights law – could be applied to corporate entities at all. *Jesner* concerned the alleged complicity of defendant Arab Bank in the financing of terrorist activities. While not going as far as ruling out lawsuits against corporate entities entirely, it held that at least foreign corporations could never be subject to such claims, whether or not the norm was universal and whether or not the conduct involved had significant connections to US territory.[20]

[14] *Sosa v Álvarez-Machain*, 3–6.
[15] ibid 38.
[16] ibid 30–31.
[17] *Kiobel v Royal Dutch Shell*, 569 US 108 (2013).
[18] *Morrison v National Australia Bank Ltd*, 561 US 247 (2010).
[19] *Kiobel v Royal Dutch Shell*, 5.
[20] *Jesner v Arab Bank, PLC*, 138 S Ct 1386 (2018).

The Court's plurality opinion written by Justice Kennedy, with partial concurrences by Justice Alito, Justice Gorsuch and Justice Thomas, and a strong dissent by Justice Sotomayor, relied significantly on *Sosa*. First, the Court held that whether or not corporations can be liable for breaches of international law under the ATS is a question of international law itself and subject to the *Sosa* test – not a question of US domestic law.[21] The Court held that there was insufficient support that corporate liability was sufficiently accepted in international law and practice to meet the *Sosa* standard, emphasising the lack of international tribunals with jurisdiction over corporations. It then considered that nevertheless recognising the liability of foreign corporations under the ATS would be an imprudent exercise in judicial discretion and that such should be left to Congress. It further noted that recognising foreign corporate liability could impair foreign relations of the US and possibly have repercussions for US companies too. The Court thus rejected that foreign corporations could be held liable under the ATS.

These decisions suggest that the proliferation of ATS lawsuits against corporations has mostly come to an end.[22] During the 'ATS era', however, US courts served on the frontlines of the jurisprudential wars over direct corporate responsibility for international law. In particular, US courts were almost the only national courts in the world to directly consider two areas of central importance to corporate responsibility for international law violations. First, US courts are unique in having considered the problem of whether international law imposes duties directly on corporations in the context of actual lawsuits. While there have also been lawsuits in European and Canadian courts that were factually similar to ATS lawsuits,[23] these have almost exclusively been based on causes of action under domestic tort or wrongful act laws and thus have not had to consider the direct application of international law to corporate legal persons. Second, and as a consequence of this, US courts have wrestled with whether and how international law concepts of complicity could be applied to corporations. While in some ATS cases corporations have been alleged to have violated international law on their own accord, in many other cases corporations were alleged to have aided, abetted or profited from violations of international law by foreign governments.

To develop doctrinal solutions in both these areas, US courts have relied significantly on sources of IHL and the case law of international criminal tribunals.

[21] ibid 1399–1400, citing *Sosa v Álvarez-Machain*.

[22] At the time of writing, the case of *Doe v Nestlé* is pending before the Court. In this case, the Court may decide whether or not lawsuits against US corporations are still possible under the ATS, or whether the ATS does not allow lawsuits against corporations at all.

[23] Cf *Nevsun Resources Ltd. v Araya* (2020) SCC 5 and *Lungowe v Vedanta Resources plc* [2019] UKSC 20. The European cases have thus far mostly concerned the question of whether courts could even exercise jurisdiction: see L Roorda, 'Jurisdiction in Foreign Direct Liability Cases in Europe' (2019) 113 *Proceedings of the ASIL Annual Meeting* 161; E Aristova, 'Tort Litigation against Transnational Corporations in the English Courts: The Challenge of Jurisdiction' (2018) 14 *Utrecht Law Review* 6; and generally C Ryngaert and J Wouters, 'Litigation for Overseas Corporate Human Rights Abuses in the European Union: the Challenge of Jurisdiction' (2009) 40 *George Washington International Law Review* 101.

They have conceptualised ways and applied doctrines of secondary liability not principally intended to be applied to corporate behaviour or outside of the IHL/ICL paradigm. The role of US courts in directly applying substantive norms of international law to legal entities has been extensively studied and the *Kiobel* and *Jesner* decisions in particular has been the subject of domestic and international critique, but the application of secondary liability doctrines prior to those cases is less discussed. And yet, now that corporate criminal liability and accessory liability is in focus pursuant to the negotiations on the proposed business and human rights treaty, it is worthwhile to revisit the ATS and US jurisprudence on secondary liability for international crimes and violations of IHL.

III. International Humanitarian Law, International Criminal Law and Corporations

Traditional public international law limited its applicability to sovereign states and generally excluded individuals and other collective groups from its ambit. Non-state actors, including natural persons and corporations, had neither rights nor duties under traditional international law. That does not mean individuals were completely outside the purview of international law at all: both the law of state responsibility and the law of diplomatic protection were engaged with the conduct and protection of non-state actors, albeit indirectly. The law of diplomatic protection, which also provided an important background to the adoption of the ATS,[24] allowed states to take action on behalf of their nationals present in foreign states. The law of state responsibility conversely, conceptualised ways in which states could be held accountable for the conduct of private individuals, not formally acting as organs of the state.

IHL does not fall neatly within this tradition because it prescribes numerous rules and duties directly upon individual actors. Traditional IHL, which included the 1907 Hague Convention IV and its accompanying Regulations, was still a state-centered form of international law that imposed duties on states to regulate the activities of non-state actors. Gradually, however, IHL has come to recognise the importance of individuals. Modern IHL, while still emanating from treaties and custom created by states, is principally aimed at individuals in the field, in particular military commanders. Such commanders may be organs of the state, but the principle of command responsibility at the heart of modern IHL emphasises the individual responsibility of commanders, distinct from state responsibility. IHL as applied in non-international armed conflict (NIAC), such as the Additional Protocol II to the Geneva Conventions of 1977, also contains similar duties to individuals not acting on behalf of states but on behalf of non-state actors such as organised armed groups.

[24] *Sosa v Álvarez-Machain*, 29.

The obligation to hold those accountable is however mostly the duty of states themselves. Even the 1949 Geneva Conventions, which were agreed to in the aftermath of the Nuremberg and Tokyo criminal trials, made it clear that states had to 'undertake to enact any legislation necessary to provide effective penal sanctions' for persons violating the Conventions.[25]

The post-World War II trials of German and Japanese war criminals at Nuremberg did, however, mark a shift in general international law by, for the first time, punishing natural persons directly for violations of international law through an international mechanism.[26] These landmark trials are often described as the beginning of the shift toward modern international law's direct applicability to individual natural persons.

The establishment of the International Criminal Tribunal for the Former Yugoslavia and the International Criminal Tribunal for Rwanda in the 1990s, and the ICC in 2003 definitively cemented the place of individual accountability for violations of IHL in international law. These tribunals are specifically authorised to apply IHL in the criminal prosecution of individuals – just as they could apply norms not directly derived from IHL, such as the prosecution of genocide and more recently the crime of aggression. Indeed, such has been the importance of the international criminal tribunals that some consider them to inhibit a separate, IHL-adjacent realm of international law: international criminal law.

Despite this evolution, neither general international law nor IHL has as of yet been directly applied to corporate entities by international criminal tribunals. That does not mean that the corporate role in the commission of atrocities during the Second World War was entirely ignored. Businesses were named in the post-WWII trials and evidence of their activities was used against individual defendants, outlining how major German industrial corporations were aligned with the Nazi regime and how German industrial production materially contributed to the Holocaust.[27] But no legal persons were directly charged during those trials, or trials taking place later in the Allied zones for violating international law or IHL in particular,[28] although some companies were later dissolved through measures taken by the Allied Control Council.[29]

[25] Geneva Convention (IV) relative to the Protection of Civilian Persons in Time of War (signed 12 August 1949, entered into force 21 October 1950) 75 UNTS 287, Art 146.

[26] T Giannini and S Farbstein, 'Corporate Accountability in Conflict Zones: How *Kiobel* Undermines the Nuremberg Legacy and Modern Human Rights' (2010) 52 *Harvard International Law Journal* 119, 127–29.

[27] J Kyriakis, 'Corporations Before International Criminal Courts: Implications for the International Criminal Justice Project' (2017) 30 *Leiden Journal of International Law* 221, 223.

[28] See the trial of German industrialists in *re Tesch and Others* (1 March 1946–8 March 1946) Case No 9, available at www.worldcourts.com/ildc/eng/decisions/1946.03.08_United_Kingdom_v_Tesch.pdf. See generally, OK Fauchald and J Stigen, 'Corporate Responsibility Before International Institutions' (2009) 40 *George Washington International Law Review* 1025, 1035–36.

[29] Control Council Law No 9 Preamble, 'Seizure of Property Owned by I.G. Farben industrie and the Control Thereof' (30 November 1945), available at www.loc.gov/rr/frd/Military_Law/Enactments/01LAW06.pdf.

Similarly, neither the ad hoc tribunals nor the ICC ever applied IHL to corporate entities in their decisions. The charters establishing both the International Criminal Tribunal for the former Yugoslavia (ICTY) and the International Criminal Tribunal for Rwanda (ICTR) expressly confined the tribunals' jurisdiction to 'natural persons'.[30] As the Secretary-General's report for the ICTY noted, 'the ordinary meaning of the term "persons responsible for serious violations of international humanitarian law" would be *natural persons to the exclusion of juridical persons*'.[31] Indeed, like the Nuremberg courts, the ICTR did consider a case concerning incitement to genocide by the now-infamous radio station known as Radio Télévision Libre des Milles Collines, but it only charged individuals working for the radio station – not the station itself.[32]

The ICC's jurisdiction is also limited to natural persons.[33] During the drafting of the Rome Statute, a proposal was considered that would have granted the ICC jurisdiction over legal persons,[34] if the crimes were committed 'on behalf of such legal persons or by their agents or representatives'.[35] While the proposal was met with sympathy from state representatives, it was eventually voted down. Thus, no international criminal tribunal has jurisdiction over legal persons. The only exception has been a decision by the Special Tribunal for Lebanon, which accepted jurisdiction over a radio station for a contempt of court charge; however, this decision did not involve IHL or other norms of public international law.[36]

[30] See UNSC Res 827 (25 May 1993) UN Doc S/RES/827 (Statute of the International Criminal Tribunal for the former Yugoslavia), adopting UNSC 'Report of the Secretary-General Pursuant to Paragraph 2 of Security Council Resolution 808' (3 May 1993) UN Doc S/25704, Art 6 ('The International Tribunal shall have jurisdiction over *natural persons*'); UNSC Res 955 (8 November 1994) UN Doc S/RES/955, Art 5 (Statute of the International Tribunal for Rwanda).

[31] UNSC 'Report of the Secretary-General Pursuant to Paragraph 2 of Security Council Resolution 808', Art 50, cited in *Kiobel v Royal Dutch Petroleum Co*, 621 F.3d 111 (2nd Cir 2010), 136, affirmed in *Kiobel v Royal Dutch Shell.*

[32] See *Prosecutor v Nahimana*, Case No ICTR-99-52-T, Judgment and Sentence (3 December 2003), paras 99–101.

[33] Rome Statute of the International Criminal Court (adopted 17 July 1998, entered into force 1 July 2002) 2187 UNTS 38544, Art 25(1).

[34] See 'Proposal Submitted by France' UN Diplomatic Conference of Plenipotentiaries on the Establishment of an International Criminal Court (Rome 15 June–17 July 1998) (16 June 1998) UN Doc A/CONF.183/C.1/L.3, 'Working Paper on Article 23, Paragraphs 5 and 6' UN Diplomatic Conference of Plenipotentiaries on the Establishment of an International Criminal Court (Rome, 15 June–17 July 1998) (3 July 1998) UN Doc A/CONF.183/C.1/WGGP/L.5/Rev.2 and 'Summary Records of the Meetings of the Committee as a Whole' UN Diplomatic Conference of Plenipotentiaries on the Establishment of an International Criminal Court (Rome, 15 June–17 July 1998) (8 July 1998) UN Doc A/CONF.183/C.1/SR.26, para 10.

[35] 'Report of the Preparatory Committee on the Establishment of an International Criminal Court Volume II' UN Diplomatic Conference of Plenipotentiaries on the Establishment of an International Criminal Court (Rome, 15 June–17 July 1998) (14 April 1998) UN Doc A/CONF.183/2/Add.1, 49.

[36] *Al Jadeed SAL & Ms Khayat*, STL-14-05 (8 March 2016). See N Bernaz, 'Corporate Criminal Liability under International Law: The *New TV S.A.L.* and *Akhbar Beirut S.A.L.* Cases at the Special Tribunal for Lebanon' (2015) 13 *Journal of International Criminal Justice* 313.

On the one hand, that international criminal tribunals do not exercise jurisdiction over legal persons fits within the general tendency of international law to steer clear of direct duties on businesses under international law. International human rights law, developed parallel to modern IHL and ICL and sometimes intersecting with it, created rights but not direct duties for corporate entities. International investment law similarly has imbued businesses with rights in their capacity as investors, but not with direct, enforceable duties.[37]

On the other hand, one should be careful not to overstate the relevance of international tribunals' lack of jurisdiction over legal persons. It has already been mentioned that the Allied Control Council took specific measures against German companies involved with crimes against humanity in WWII after the Nuremberg trials, even while those companies were not prosecuted.[38] Similarly, the ICC's lack of jurisdiction over corporations need not signal a wholesale rejection of corporate criminal liability under international law. As evidenced by the negotiations on the French proposal during the drafting of the Rome Statute, few representatives had conceptual problems with applying ICL and IHL to corporations. Their reasons for eventually rejecting the proposal were generally of a more practical nature. Some feared introducing corporate criminal liability would have extended already difficult negotiations; not all domestic legal systems recognise the criminal liability of corporations, giving rise to potential conflicts with the ICC's principle of complementarity; corporate liability might have led to complex evidentiary problems; and more generally, some representatives questioned the morality of states applying norms of ICL to every actor in international law but themselves.[39]

And to be sure, some international instruments do mention some form of direct liability for corporate entities, including for international crimes. Most notably, the International Convention on the Suppression and Punishment of the Crime of Apartheid named 'organisations' as liable for apartheid crimes.[40] Similarly, the Basel Convention on the Control of Transboundary Movements of Hazardous Wastes and their Disposal defined persons liable for improper disposal of hazardous waste as 'any natural or legal person'.[41] Legal persons were

[37] Although such duties are contemplated in the negotiations on a proposed treaty on business and human rights; see UNHRC, 'Report on the fifth session of the open-ended intergovernmental working group on transnational corporations and other business enterprises with respect to human rights', UN Doc A/HRC/43/55 (9 January 2020).

[38] Giannini and Farbstein, 'Corporate Accountability in Conflict Zones' (2010) 129.

[39] Fauchald and Stigen, 'Corporate Responsibility' (2009) 1038–39; WA Schabas, 'General Principles of Criminal Law in the International Criminal Court Statute (Part III)' (1998) 6 *European Journal of Crime, Criminal Law and Criminal Justice* 84.

[40] International Convention on the Suppression and Punishment of the Crime of Apartheid (entered into force 18 July 1976) 1015 UNTS 243, Art I, para 2: 'The States Parties to the present Convention declare criminal those organisations, institutions and individuals committing the crime of apartheid'.

[41] Basel Convention on the Control of Transboundary Movements of Hazardous Wastes and their Disposal (signed 22 March 1989, entered into force 5 May 1992), Art 2 ('Person means any natural or legal person') contains a provision to the effect that the Parties shall prohibit 'all persons' from transporting or disposing of hazardous waste unless authorised or allowed to do so.

also clearly designated as liable in Article 10 of the United Nations Convention against Transnational Organised Crime. The latest draft of the proposed treaty on business and human rights also implores states to prosecute corporate entities for the commission of international crimes.[42] But none of these instruments purported to change or alter customary international law, nor do they include a mechanism for holding legal persons liable; enforcement is left to state parties under domestic criminal law.

This quagmire on corporate liability for international crimes and the dearth of authoritative international judgments reminds us how US jurisprudence on IHL and the case law of international criminal tribunals on corporations broke new ground. Prior to the ATS cases applying IHL to corporations in the 1990s, no court (domestic or international) had ever applied IHL principles or rules to corporate entities, nor any other norm of international law. Even in recent years, courts have only very rarely applied IHL or equivalent provisions of domestic criminal law to corporations – either in a criminal or civil context. That leaves ATS case law of US courts as one of the few sources for exploring corporate complicity for international crimes, and this is explored in the next section.

IV. The ATS and Corporate Complicity Standards

The first reported ATS case against a private corporation was brought as early as 1985, but it was dismissed on other grounds and the court never considered any legal questions specially applicable to corporations.[43] Other cases were also brought and dismissed,[44] but the first major US decision allowing an ATS lawsuit to proceed against a business corporation occurred in the 1997 decision of *Doe v Unocal*.[45] *Unocal* represented a landmark decision, not just because it ultimately ended in a settlement which paid out substantial funds to the plaintiffs. Jurisprudentially, the litigation over the case highlighted the way in which international law would

[42] The first full draft included a list of international crimes that mostly mirrored the Rome Statute of the International Criminal Court, but the latest revision of the draft has dropped such a list and only refers to 'most serious crimes of concern to the international community as a whole'. See OEIGWG '2nd revised draft legally binding instrument to regulate, in international human rights law, the activities of transnational corporations and other business enterprises' (6 August 2020), draft Art 10, available at www.ohchr.org/Documents/HRBodies/HRCouncil/WGTransCorp/Session6/OEIGWG_Chair-Rapporteur_second_revised_draft_LBI_on_TNCs_and_OBEs_with_respect_to_Human_Rights.pdf.

[43] *Jaffe v Boyles*, 616 F Supp 1371 (WDNY 1985), 1381 (transferring case because of improper venue).

[44] See, for example, *Carmichael v United Techs. Corp*, 835 F.2d 109 (5th Cir 1988), 112 (dismissing a case against a corporation for lack of personal jurisdiction (service) and lack of subject matter jurisdiction (no cause of action for aiding and abetting)); *Beanal v Freeport-McMoRan, Inc*, 969 F Supp 362 (ED La 1997) 365–66 (dismissing a case brought under ATS for lack of cause of action and dismissing the case under TVPA for, among other things, corporation not an 'individual' who can be held liable).

[45] 963 F Supp 880 (CD Cal 1997).

be applied to develop legal theories of liability for corporations in ATS suits. The lawsuit was filed against Unocal, a US-based oil exploration company now owned by Chevron Corporation. The plaintiffs, who were residents of Myanmar, alleged a wide variety of wrongful acts including forced labour, wrongful death, false imprisonment and assault, perpetrated by the Myanmar Government in relation to the Yadana gas pipeline project and by Unocal in allowing or supporting this misconduct, Unocal also being the main operator of the pipeline.

The Myanmar Government defendants successfully invoked a foreign sovereign immunity defence, and the suit against it was dismissed. Unocal raised a number of defences including that, as a non-state actor, it could not be held liable for directly violating international law since international law applied only to state actors. This defence was rejected by the district court, which held that private actors could be liable directly under international law for certain egregious acts such as slavery and forced labour.[46] The court did not address, in part because parties did not raise, any questions about whether a legal entity like Unocal could be liable under international law for slavery as opposed to natural persons.

The 1997 decision (referred to as *Unocal I*)[47] allowed the *Unocal* plaintiffs to present their facts to the court. Subsequent court proceedings fleshed out the legal theories that would be employed against corporate entities under the ATS. In 2000, Unocal filed a motion for summary judgment, arguing that the evidence showed it should not be responsible for the forced labour practices of the Myanmar Government because it was not an active participant in those practices and lacked full knowledge that those practices were occurring. Judge Lew writing for the district court reviewed the post-WWII cases against industrialists on how international law might impose liability and held that active participation, rather than mere knowledge, was needed to impute liability to Unocal.[48] Because the district court found that there was no evidence that Unocal actively participated in the alleged forced labour, it dismissed the case (*Unocal II*).

On appeal against the district court's judgment,[49] the 9th Circuit agreed with the district court that the relevant source for any complicity standard was international rather than domestic law, declaring at the outset that international criminal law standards were applicable to determining standards for civil liability.[50]

[46] *Doe I v Unocal Corp*, 67 F Supp.2d 1140 (CD Cal 1999); *Doe I v Unocal Corp*, 27 F Supp.2d 1174 (CD Cal 1998) affirmed in 248 F.3d 915 (9th Cir 2001).

[47] A Rosencrantz and D Louk, 'Doe v. Unocal: Holding Corporations Liable for Human Rights Abuses on Their Watch' (2005) 8 *Chapman Law Review* 135, 139.

[48] *Doe v Unocal Corp*, 110 F Supp 2d 1294, 1310 (CD Cal 2000), affirmed in part and revised in part sub nom. *Doe I v Unocal Corp*, 395 F.3d 932 (9th Cir 2002) (on reh'g en banc sub nom). Subsequently, in *John Doe I v Unocal Corp*, 403 F.3d 708 (9th Cir 2005), the opinion was vacated, and the appeal dismissed sub nom.

[49] Note that the plaintiffs also refiled the case in California state courts, splitting the case in two. This chapter further only examines the federal case against Unocal.

[50] *Doe I v Unocal Corp*, 395 F.3d 932 (9th Cir 2002) 950 (on reh'g en banc sub nom). *John Doe I v Unocal Corp*, 403 F.3d 708 (9th Cir 2005), noting that decisions of the ICTY and ICTR were 'especially helpful for ascertaining the current standard for aiding and abetting under international law as it pertains to the [ATS]'.

But it disagreed with the lower court's application of the standards of complicity to Unocal.

The court rejected the district court's 'active participation' requirement as a misapplication of precedents from the post-WWII military tribunals. That standard for complicity, the court held, was only invoked in the WWII cases to overcome a necessity defence and not indicative of the internationally accepted standards for aiding and abetting. Instead, and drawing directly on the ICTY's decision in *Furundzijia*,[51] the Unocal appeals court held that the standard 'requires practical assistance, encouragement, or moral support which has a substantial effect on the perpetration of the crime'.[52] But, quoting the ICTY again, the court also adopted its view that 'assistance need not constitute an indispensable element' to incur liability. The court further cited the ICTR's holding in *Musema* that even 'moral support' that 'substantially contribute[d] to the commission of the crime' could constitute the *actus reus* for a corporation's complicity liability.[53]

The *Unocal* appeals court also drew directly upon both the ICTY and ICTR to develop a *mens rea* standard for aiding and abetting. Citing both the ICTY and the ICTR again, the court concluded that liability may be imposed as long as there is 'actual or constructive' knowledge that the actions will assist in the commission of the crime. The corporation accused of complicity need not even have the knowledge of the precise crime the principal criminal intended to commit, as long as it was aware there are a number of crimes that the principal intended to commit.[54] It ultimately considered there to be sufficient evidence presented by the plaintiffs that the criteria for both the *actus reus* and *mens rea* were met, for the case to move forward.

In sum, the *Unocal* appeals court decided upon an aiding and abetting standard that imposes liability on a corporation for 'knowing practical assistance, encouragement or moral support which has a substantial effect on the perpetration of the crime'.[55] It left aside the question of whether mere moral support could also be the basis for complicity liability.[56] For our purposes, it is worth noting that it did not draw upon international human rights law, domestic US law, or general principles of international law in order to develop a complicity standard. Instead, it drew directly upon the precedents developed by the ICTY and ICTR.

[51] *Prosecutor v Furundzija* (1999) 38 ILM 317.

[52] *Prosecutor v Furundzjia*, para 235, cited in *Doe I v Unocal Corp*, 395 F.3d 932 (9th Ci. 2002), 950 (on reh'g en banc sub nom).

[53] *Prosecutor v Musema* (Judgment and Sentence), ICTR-96-13-T (27 January 2000), para 126, cited in *Doe I v Unocal Corp*, 395 F.3d 932 (9th Cir 2002), 951 (on reh'g en banc sub nom) and *John Doe I v Unocal Corp*, 403 F.3d 708 (9th Cir 2005), 58.

[54] ibid.

[55] *Doe I v Unocal Corp*, 395 F.3d 932 (9th Cir 2002), 951 (on reh'g en banc sub nom). *John Doe I v Unocal Corp*, 403 F.3d 708 (9th Cir 2005).

[56] ibid.

Although this *Unocal* decision was subsequently vacated and the case settled, other US courts subsequently followed the same aiding and abetting approach and adopted the same complicity standard.[57] Indeed, standards for corporate complicity became the crucial legal doctrine for almost all cases involving corporate liability in the ATS context.[58] As noted, in contrast to the early cases – including *Filartiga*, *Kadic* and *Sosa* – almost none of the corporate entities sued in US courts under the ATS were alleged to have directly committed violations of international law themselves. Rather, like Unocal those companies were almost always involved in a large infrastructure project in cooperation with governments allegedly involved in international crimes.[59]

While courts in several ATS cases have thus relied principally on the standards developed by the ICTY and ICTR, some US courts have also drawn upon a different source of international law: the Rome Statute of the ICC. The ICC's jurisdictional mandate largely draws from IHL as well and could draw on the existing case law of the ad hoc tribunals, but it is also the product of a separate and distinct negotiation between a majority of the world's nations, as discussed more extensively above. This is especially notable given that the US ultimately never ratified the Rome Statute, and has even taken a hostile stance towards the ICC on several occasions. Nevertheless, some ATS cases have explicitly relied on the Rome Statute in their considerations of the appropriate legal standards, specifically the standards for complicity and other forms of secondary liability, creating a split in ATS case law.

There are some important differences between the standards adopted by the ICTY and ICTR on the one hand, and the ICC on the other. Importantly for the purposes of this chapter, Article 25(c) of the Rome Statute defined a distinct standard of aiding and abetting liability only where the individual, 'For the purpose of facilitating the commission of such a crime, aids, abets or otherwise assists in its commission or its attempted commission'.[60] This standard is distinct because

[57] See, for example, *Romero v Drummond Co, Inc*, 552 F.3d 1303 (11th Cir 2008); *Doe v Exxon Mobil Corp*, 654 F.3d 11, 38 (DC Cir 2011), vacated; *Doe v Exxon Mobil Corp*, 527 F Appendix 7 (DC Cir 2013) ('Accordingly, we hold that aiding and abetting liability is available under the ATS because it involves a norm established by customary international law and that the mens rea and actus reus requirements are those established by the ICTY, the ICTR, and the Nuremberg tribunals').

[58] See *Bigio v Coca-Cola Co*, 239 F.3d 440 (2nd Cir 2001); *Sarei v Rio Tinto PLC*, 221 F Supp.2d 1116 (CD Cal 2002), *Aguinda v Texaco, Inc*, 303 F.3d 470 (2nd Cir 2002); *Presbyterian Church of Sudan v Talisman Energy, Inc*, 244 F Supp.2d 289 (SDNY 2003), vacated; *Presbyterian Church Of Sudan v Talisman Energy, Inc*, 582 F.3d 244 (2d Cir 2009) 259; *Almog v Arab Bank*, 471 F Supp. 2d 257 (EDNY 2007) 285; *Vietnam Association for Victims of Agent Orange v Dow Chemical Co*, 517 F.3d 104 (2d Cir 2008).

[59] See HY Liu, *Law's Impunity: Responsibility and the Modern Private Military Company* (Bloomsbury 2017) 275–77; C Keitner, 'Conceptualizing Complicity in Alien Tort Cases' (2008) 60 *Hastings Law Journal* 61, 63; TF Maassarani, 'Four Counts of Corporate Complicity: Alternative Forms of Accomplice Liability Under the Alien Tort Claims Act' (2006) 38 *New York University Journal of International Law and Politics* 39, 43–45; D Diskin, 'The Historical and Modern Foundations for Aiding and Abetting Liability Under the Alien Tort Statute' (2005) 47 *Arizona Law Review* 805, 807–10. See also UNHRC 'Report of the Special Representative of the Secretary-General, Business and Human Rights: Mapping International Standards of Responsibility and Accountability for Corporate Acts' (19 February 2007) UN Doc A/HRC/4/35, 30.

[60] Rome Statute of the International Criminal Court,A 25(c) (emphasis added).

it requires a showing that the defendant's acts were 'for the purpose of facilitating' the wrongful act. Under the more expansive standard drawn from the ad hoc tribunals and adopted by the Unocal appeals court, a corporate defendant could be liable for acting with mere knowledge of a possible criminal act by its principal, even if there was no explicit purpose to facilitate that act. Thus, a corporate defendant that had information or news reports about the government's use of forced labour could be held complicit. Under the more demanding Article 25 standard, that corporate defendant would have to be shown to have acted 'for the purpose' of furthering the said government's use of forced labour.

The significance of this disagreement on aiding and abetting standards is most dramatically illustrated by the 2007 US Court of Appeals for the Second Circuit's plurality decision in *Khulumani v Barclays Bank*, a case concerning the involvement of Barclays Bank and other companies with the South African Apartheid regime. The district court had originally dismissed the claim, arguing that there was no aiding and abetting liability under the ATS.[61] Two judges on the appeals court concurred in their decision to remand the claim to allow a lower court to apply the aiding and abetting standard.[62] But they could not agree on which international standard to apply for assessing corporate defendant's complicity.

Judge Hall endorsed US federal law as the appropriate standard, in particular the Second Restatement of Torts,[63] arguing that international law does not 'set its own means for domestic enforcement'. Judge Katzmann, drawing heavily on footnote 20 in *Sosa*, favoured international law.[64] While Judge Katzmann did extensively cite the military tribunals as well as ICTR and ICTY case law to argue that international law did recognise aiding and abetting liability, he concluded that the most recent and thus appropriate standard was that of the Rome Statute.[65] Interestingly, in his reasoning he concluded that the Rome Statute was consistent with the ICTR and ICTY, without engaging with the differences as to the *mens rea* requirements.[66]

Upon remand, Judge Scheindlin writing the lower court returned to the ICTY/ICTR standard for aiding and abetting liability rather than Article 25 of

[61] *In re South African Apartheid Litigation*, 346 F Supp.2d 538 (SDNY 2004) 550. See also 'Khulumani v. Barclay National Bank Ltd. – Second Circuit Holds that Human Rights Plaintiffs May Plead Aiding and Abetting Theory of Liability' (2008) 121 *Harvard Law Review* 1953; K Hutchens, 'International Law in the American Courts – Khulumani v. Barclay National Bank Ltd.: The Decision Heard 'Round the Corporate World' (2008) 9 *German Law Journal* 639.

[62] *Khulumani v Barclay National Bank Ltd*, 504 F.3d 254, 260 (2nd Cir 2007), affirmed sub nom. *American Isuzu Motors, Inc v Ntsebeza*, 553 US 1028 (2008). Judge Korman dissented but did argue *per curiam* that federal common law should be the appropriate standard.

[63] Restatement (Second) of Torts § 876(b) (1977).

[64] ibid 269 (citing *Sosa v Álvarez-Machain*, 732).

[65] ibid 36 ('The Rome Statute is particularly significant for the present inquiry because, unlike other sources of international legislation, it articulates the mens rea required for aiding and abetting liability').

[66] ibid 37.

the Rome Statute. In an extensive examination of the standards for aiding and abetting liability, she rejected the application of the purpose standard supposedly derived from Article 25 as a requirement for aiding and abetting. Noting its apparent deviance from the ICTY and ICTR case law, the judge considered that it was uncertain whether Article 25 was intended to modify customary international law or create a specific rule for the ICC alone. Moreover, she reflected on to the paucity of ICC case law at the time, noting that the contours and content of Article 25 and the precise meaning of 'purpose' in the Rome Statute still had to be construed by the ICC.

Indeed, judge Scheindlin found that Article 25 was 'ambiguous' and could just as easily be interpreted to be closer to the ICTY and ICTR's 'knowledge' requirement, as to create a separate 'purpose' standard. This could be the case when purpose is inferred from knowledge that certain actions contribute to ongoing crimes. The court noted that such an interpretation of 'purpose' in Article 25 might actually apply to a corporate entity that provides materials for profit to a foreign government committing crimes. For example, 'it may reasonably be inferred that an arms dealer providing weapons to perpetrators of a genocide tacitly supports the genocide, as it creates demand for that increases profit' – even if that arms dealer did not have an explicit purpose of contributing to the genocide itself.[67] In any event, the district court concluded that the ICTR and ICTY cases had a more established basis in international law for determining a complicity standard. Applying that standard, it found that some – but not all – of the plaintiffs' allegations were sufficient to allow the case to move forward on this basis.

While the NY district court reverted back to the ICTY and ICTR standards, the Second Circuit endorsed the 'purpose' standard in *Presbyterian Church v Talisman*.[68] This case concerned the alleged complicity of energy company Talisman in crimes against humanity including displacement, rape and killings. The majority opinion looked towards Judge Katzmann's concurring opinion in *Khulumani* to determine that international law required that the defendant acted with purpose, as the requisite *mens rea* for aiding and abetting liability.[69] It noted that no consensus existed in international law to hold that knowledge of a criminal act alone is sufficient to establish liability. Because it found that the plaintiffs had not put forward sufficient evidence that the defendants had indeed acted with purpose, it dismissed the case.

The question of what the appropriate standard is for aiding and abetting could have been definitively decided by the Supreme Court, given that the *Kiobel* case initially also concerned similar issues of aiding and abetting. However, instead of ruling on those issues the Court of Appeals for the Second Circuit ruled that

[67] *In re South African Apartheid Litigation*, 617 F Supp 2d 228 (SDNY 2009).

[68] *Presbyterian Church of Sudan v Talisman Energy, Inc*, 259; see also *Aziz v Alcolac, Inc*, 658 F.3d 388, 398 (4th Cir 2011).

[69] *Presbyterian Church of Sudan v Talisman Energy, Inc*, 257–59.

corporations could not be liable under the ATS at all,[70] whereas the Supreme Court dismissed the case on its lack of territorial connections to the US as noted above.[71] That has left the matter unresolved, and given the Supreme Court's decisions in *Kiobel* and *Jesner*, it may remain so in the foreseeable future.[72]

V. Lessons from United States' Judicial Adoption of ICL, IHL and Corporate Liability

That US courts (sometimes unknowingly) have drawn largely from IHL and ICL sources for developing complicity standards is significant for three reasons. First, it calls into the question whether the complicity standards developed by US courts should be applied to corporate defendants outside of situations involving armed conflicts or international crimes. Second, it leaves open the question of how such standards relate to other conceptions of complicity and contribution that have been developed with regard to corporations, especially in international human rights law. Third, it serves as a warning for drawing too much on ATS case law or US law in general for further developments, as it may say more about US domestic views of corporate liability than about the state of international law.

The first issue with the ATS cases discussed here is that they have relied on standards developed for international crimes, and specifically international crimes committed during armed conflict, and taken them to represent standards of accountability for violations of international law in general. Whether it concerns the application of jurisprudence of the military tribunals at Nuremberg, the *ad hoc* tribunals or the ICC, the modes of liability derived from that jurisprudence were intended to apply to a very specific set of norms, in a very specific institutional context. While this was groundbreaking work, it can be questioned whether these standards were intended to create international customary standards applicable beyond that institutional context and even more so whether they can be analogously applied to domestic civil liability questions, especially when they involve human rights standards rather than international criminal law standards.

It should be reiterated that corporate liability for complicity in international crimes and violations of IHL is still underdeveloped. As the international criminal tribunals lack jurisdiction over corporate entities, few courts have considered accessory liability for corporations in international crimes in depth; even in

[70] *Kiobel v Royal Dutch Petroleum Co*, 621 F.3d 111 (2nd Cir 2010), affirmed in part, reviewed in part in *Kiobel v Royal Dutch Petroleum Co*, 569 US 108 (2013).

[71] *Kiobel v Royal Dutch Petroleum Co*, 569 US 108 (2013).

[72] At the time of writing, the Court has granted *certiorari* in *Doe I v Nestlé*, 929 F.3d 623 (9th Cir 2019), and oral argument is currently planned for December 2020. Note that Justice Kavanaugh, currently on the Supreme Court, wrote a dissenting opinion in *Doe v Exxon Mobil Corp* arguing that corporations could not be the subject of ATS suits at all: *Doe v Exxon Mobil Corp*, 654 F.3d 11, 38 (DC Cir 2011) (Kavanaugh J dissenting), vacated.

jurisdictions that recognise corporate criminal liability, prosecutions of corporate entities for international crimes are exceedingly rare. As corporate complicity in international crimes is still a topic of interest,[73] the body of ATS case law discussed in this chapter can still be an important source of inspiration and be informative of the types of problems other courts may face. It should thus not be easily discarded, just because the ATS may no longer be the most popular avenue for bringing international lawsuits against corporations.

At the same time, this application has its limitations, which have already become implicit during the 'ATS era'. These limitations firstly follow from the self-imposed restrictions to which international norms are considered relevant under the ATS. Under the *Sosa* standard, US courts are supposed to look for standards that are 'specific, universal and obligatory'. As may be clear from the discussion in the previous section, however, jurisprudence in international criminal law has not been a matter of consistent precedent and gradual evolution towards such 'specific' standards, let alone 'universal'. Instead, the applicable standards follow from separate frameworks and decisions of institutions that are not in hierarchical relations to one another, and that need not follow each other's precedents.[74] This alone may make a determination of what constitutes *the* proper standard in international criminal law for secondary liability (that meets the *Sosa* standard) close to meaningless.

Moreover, even if one could distinguish a clear line in the case law of international criminal tribunals on aiding and abetting and find such norms, those norms would arguably only be applicable to liability for international crimes recognised by the statutes of these tribunals. Setting aside the discussion of whether these statutes represent customary international law to the extent required by *Sosa*, it is questionable whether the standards for aiding and abetting liability were ever intended to be applied beyond the specific field of international criminal law. And indeed, whereas some of the cases discussed in this contribution did concern complicity in international crimes as defined in the statutes of the respective international criminal courts – genocide[75] and the crime of Apartheid[76] – other

[73] Recent scholarship includes Kyriakis, 'Corporations Before International Criminal Courts' (2017); Bernaz, 'Corporate Criminal Liability under International Law' (2015); Fauchald and Stigen (n 28); Giannini and Farbstein (n 26). See also generally C Ryngaert, 'Accountability for Corporate Human Rights Abuses: Lessons from Possible Exercise of Dutch National Criminal Jurisdiction Over Multinational Corporations' (2018) 29 *Criminal Law Forum* 1, D Scheffer, 'Corporate Liability under the Rome Statute' (2016) 57 *Harvard International Law Journal* 35; J Kyriakakis, 'Corporate Criminal Liability and the ICC Statute: The Comparative Law Challenge' (2009) 56 *Netherlands International Law Review* 333.

[74] Similar debates exist with regard to the development of the 'joint criminal enterprise' doctrine for determining the applicable standards, which was developed by the ICTY but not adopted in the Rome Statute, where separate standards were developed in Art 25(3). See S Ranieri, 'Extended Joint Criminal Enterprise in International Criminal Law: From Foreseeability, to Intention, to Control over the Crime' (2016) 80 *Journal of Criminal Law* 436; M Cupido, 'Common Purpose Liability versus Joint Enterprise: A Practical View on the ICC's Hierarchy of Liability Theories' (2016) 29 *Leiden Journal of International Law* 897; JD Ohlin, 'Three Conceptual Problems with the Doctrine of Joint Criminal Enterprise' (2007) 5 *Journal of International Criminal Justice* 69.

[75] *Presbyterian Church of Sudan v Talisman Energy*.

[76] *Khulumani v Barclay National Bank Ltd.*, affirmed sub nom.

allegations were more based in human rights law, such as allegations of forced labour,[77] and torture and extrajudicial killings.[78] Indeed, US courts have often referred to the alleged violations as 'human rights abuses' rather than 'international crimes',[79] without further discussing whether liability for such abuses could also be determined by applying standards from international criminal law.

There is an additional problem regarding the application of ICTY and ICTR jurisprudence specifically. Both *ad hoc* tribunals were designated with applying IHL through individual criminal liability, as noted above. IHL is in principle only applicable in situations of armed conflict. Moreover, IHL distinguishes between international[80] and non-international conflict,[81] and not all provisions of IHL applicable to the former are also applicable in the latter. In fact, while both the ICTY and the ICTR were erected as a response to (specific) armed conflicts, whether or not certain provisions of IHL – such as individual liability for war crimes – actually applied in those respective, non-international conflicts were a major point of contention in the early days of the *ad hoc* tribunals.[82]

None of the cases discussed earlier in this chapter involved an armed conflict of any kind, whether of an international or of a non-international character. Other ATS cases against corporate defendants also often involve allegations of illegal activities during peacetime.[83] Substantive norms of IHL would therefore not be applicable to the conduct of the defendant corporations in these cases. Remarkably, none of the US courts wrestling with the aiding and abetting standard in ATS cases addressed the IHL origins of the doctrines they drew upon. This is surprising because US courts heavily considered the scope of the law of armed conflict in its development of military commissions for the prosecution of alleged terrorists.[84]

[77] *Doe I v Unocal Corp*, 67 F.Supp.2d 1140 (CD Cal 1999); *Doe I v Unocal Corp*, 27 F Supp.2d 1174 (CD Cal 1998), affirmed in 248 F.3d 915 (9th Cir 2001).

[78] *Doe v Exxon Mobil Corp*, 393 F Supp.2d 20 (DC Cir 2005); *Kiobel v Royal Dutch Petroleum Co*, 569 US 108 (2013). Note that torture and extrajudicial killings can constitute international crimes when committed as part of genocide, as a crime against humanity or as a war crime pursuant to the Rome Statute. In such cases, however, other elements are required to be present, such as genocidal intent for genocide (Rome Statute, Art 6(1)), a 'widespread or systematic attack against any civilian population' (Rome Statute, Art 7(1)) or an armed conflict for war crimes (Rome Statute, Art 8(1)).

[79] See *Presbyterian Church of Sudan v Talisman Energy, Inc*; *Jesner v Arab Bank, PLC* (classifying the alleged acts consistently as actions that 'contravene fundamental human rights').

[80] Art 1, common to the four Geneva Conventions of 1949.

[81] Either as determined by Art 1, Protocol (II) Additional to the Geneva Conventions of 12 August 1949, and relating to the Protection of Victims of Non-International Armed Conflicts (signed 8 June 1977, entry into force 7 December 1978) or *Prosecutor v Duško Tadić* (Judgment) IT-94-1-T (7 May 1997), 561–68 for non-international conflicts where AP II is not applicable.

[82] *The Prosecutor v Duško Tadić* (Decision on the Defense Motion for Interlocutory Appeal on Jurisdiction) IT-94-1-AR72 (2 October 1995).

[83] For instance, a 2008 compilation of corporate ATS lawsuits identified numerous cases but none involve an armed conflict. See D Cassel, 'Corporate Aiding and Abetting of Human Rights Violations: Confusion in the Courts' (2008) 6 *Northwestern University Journal of International Human Rights* 304, 6 (listing ATS corporate defendants).

[84] *Hamdan v Rumsfeld*, 548 US 557 (2006), although this case has been criticised as a misapplication of IHL. See JC Dehn, 'The *Hamdan* Case and the Application of a Municipal Offence: The Common Law Origins of 'Murder in Violation of the Law of War' (2009) 7 *Journal of International Criminal Justice* 63.

A further exploration of how IHL applies to corporations would of course be useful in cases that *do* concern corporate conduct during armed conflict.[85] It is plausible, for instance, that an aiding and abetting standard developed for determining the liability of a commander of a paramilitary groups like in *Furundija* may not fit as well for determining the liability of a corporate entity. After all, the former is governed by principles of command responsibility under IHL, whereas the latter is governed by corporate law. The Supreme Court's restrictions to the liability of corporations under the ATS have, however, made such a determination unlikely in the near future.

The second issue is that the focus on ICL, IHL and aiding and abetting standards by the US court has somewhat obscured the fact that a whole body of norms and scholarship has been developed around the corporate complicity in human rights abuses – which is addressed in several other contributions in this volume.[86] While this development also has some provenance in ATS jurisprudence,[87] it mainly draws from other areas of international and domestic law: indirect obligations and responsibilities under human rights law, but also domestic law of other states and private international law. This development has occurred partially parallel and partially after the 'second wave' of ATS cases and is still very much ongoing; while it has thus not been the main focus of this chapter, it is worth mentioning because it contextualises some of the findings from US case law discussed above.

There has been a marked evolution in understanding the different ways in which business enterprises can impact human rights. The UN Guiding Principles on Business and Human Rights and subsequent scholarship have been instrumental to this evolution. Principle 13 in particular discusses how businesses can be involved with human rights abuses through its own actions, by contributing to human rights abuses committed by others, or by being directly linked through its business relationships to the abuses.[88]

[85] For example, there have been ATS cases against US private military companies over alleged torture and war crimes in the Abu Ghraib facility in occupied Iraq; see *Saleh v Titan Corp*, 580 F.3d 1 (DC Cir 2009) and *Al Shimari v CACI Premier Tech, Inc*, 119 F Supp.3d 434 (ED Va 2015) 444–47 (vacated); *Al Shimari v CACI Premier Tech, Inc (Al Shimari IV)*, 840 F.3d 147 (4th Cir 2016), 151 (on remand); *Al Shimari v CACI Premier Tech, Inc*, 263 F Supp. 3d 595 (ED Va 2017).

[86] See especially ch 10 (Zrilič) and also ch 5 (Ranjan), ch 6 (Choudhury) and ch 4 (Yilmaz Vastardis) of this volume.

[87] The ATS was extensively discussed in preparatory reports by the Special Representative of the Secretary-General (SRSG) John Ruggie for what eventually resulted in the UNGPs, see UNHRC 'Business and Human Rights: Representative of the Secretary-General (SRSG) on the issue of human rights and transnational corporations and other business enterprises' (9 February 2007) UN Doc A/HRC/4/035. SRSG Ruggie also co-submitted an *amicus* brief to the US Supreme Court in *Kiobel v Royal Dutch Petroleum*: *Amicus Curiae* of John Ruggie, Philip Alston and the Global Justice Clinic at NYU School of Law (12 June 2012) 3.

[88] See also JG Ruggie, 'Comments on Thun Group of Banks – Discussion Paper on the Implications of UN Guiding Principles 13 & 17 In a Corporate and Investment Banking Context' (Harvard Kennedy School of Government, 21 February 2017), available at www.ihrb.org/uploads/submissions/John_Ruggie_Comments_Thun_Banks_Feb_2017.pdf.

To be sure, these 'modes' of contributing to human rights abuses by corporations are not meant to directly result in liability and are not direct alternatives to the standards employed in ATS cases. They are also unlikely to have met the *Sosa* standard of being 'specific, universal and obligatory' – in fact, nothing in the UNGPs nor in subsequent instruments is 'obligatory', and neither are these principles considered customary international law. Yet they show an important counter-perspective to the somewhat myopic focus of US courts on standards of international criminal law, without paying due regard to debates in international human rights law. This is of course understandable for earlier ATS cases, having been decided before work was even started on the UNGPs, but later cases too failed to recognise these developments – neither in *Kiobel*, nor in *Jesner* does the Supreme Court make any mention of the UNGPs or any of the preceding reports.

This failure to recognise the broader context of these lawsuits is even more poignant when considering that the ATS is not a criminal statute and can only lead to compensation and damages – not punishment. In that respect, it fits better within the human rights doctrine of a 'right to remedy',[89] as in reparations for harms suffered from human rights abuses, and with 'traditional' tort cases and other forms of civil liability, than it does within the doctrines of (secondary) criminal liability of the international criminal tribunals. The respective purposes of these mechanisms are different, as are the consequences; one could therefore question why the US has resorted so strongly to the relatively strict standards employed by the international criminal tribunals, instead of looking towards more general tort law doctrines – as even suggested by the concurring opinions in *Khulumani*.[90]

None of this is to say that there is a strict bar to analogously applying standards of ICL, even if derived from IHL, to questions outside the international crimes and armed conflict paradigms; especially when human rights violations and international crimes intersect. But it does serve as a caution for expanding legal norms across areas of specialisation since rules developed in one area – ICL and IHL – may not be appropriate to conceptualise corporate complicity in other areas such as human rights and civil liability. And even if such norms are 'transplanted', due regard needs to be paid to what other doctrines these norms intersect with.

In the end, it could be argued that through the (selective) use of international law and exclusive reliance on international criminal law, US courts created a distinct set of liability standards within the microcosm of the ATS. Just as their European counterparts have struggled with accountability and liability of corporations under their own tort and wrongful act laws, so have US courts created a

[89] See GL Skinner, *Transnational Corporations and Human Rights: Overcoming Barriers to Judicial Remedy* (Cambridge University Press, 2020); GL Skinner, 'Beyond *Kiobel*: Providing Access to Judicial Remedies for Violations of International Human Rights Norms by Transnational Business in a New (Post-*Kiobel*) World' (2014) 46 *Columbia Human Rights Law Review* 158.

[90] *Khulumani v Barclay National Bank Ltd* (Judge Hall concurring and Judge Korman dissenting).

particular American 'brand' of corporate liability under the ATS. They have been clear groundbreakers and innovators in that regard, but their conclusions are not without their limitations and should not be taken to represent the general state of international law on secondary liability.[91] This is important to keep in mind in the development of new instruments that take the ATS as a source of inspiration, as well as for companies wishing to avoid liability.

VI. Conclusion – The Limitations of the United States' Corporate Liability Experience

Quite inadvertently, the US became the first and most active jurisdiction in the world when it came to developing civil litigation against corporations for violations of international law. Over a period of nearly 40 years, private plaintiffs brought lawsuits against multinational corporations alleging complicity and support for foreign government atrocities and violations of international law.

Just as inadvertently, the US also became the first jurisdiction to apply IHL and ICL concepts and rules to those same private corporate entities, in the context of civil liability. This can be most clearly seen in the development of the aiding and abetting standard for complicity liability. Because almost all corporate defendants were accused of complicity instead of direct commission of illegal acts, this standard became crucial for any effort to win judgments against corporations under the ATS. Without acknowledging its origins, many US courts ended up drawing on ICL and indirectly on IHL to fashion a complicity standard for adjudicating corporate liability under international law.

Since other doctrinal developments have sharply limited the ability of plaintiffs to bring any ATS claims in US courts, whether or not they involved corporate defendants, those distinct origins of the aiding and abetting standard may not be litigated or acknowledged by US courts. However, this does not mean it remains a meaningless historical anomaly.

As international efforts to develop international conventions to regulate transnational corporations develop, those looking for lessons in the US can draw at least two lessons. First, the IHL origins of the US aiding and abetting complicity standard should be recognised in any efforts to cite or duplicate the US standard. Second, the IHL origins of the aiding and abetting standard could also be used to justify the application of IHL to corporate entities. Although US courts did not consider the significance of the IHL basis for its legal concepts, any lingering concerns about whether IHL should be applied to corporations can be partially rebutted by the US experience.

[91] See also B Thompson, 'Was Kiobel Detrimental to Corporate Social Responsibility? Applying Lessons Learnt from American Exceptionalism' (2014) 30 *Utrecht Journal of International and European Law* 78.

10

Investor Obligations Amid Armed Conflict

JURE ZRILIČ

I. Introduction

Foreign investors commonly conduct business in conflict-affected areas. While the presence of some companies in such countries precedes the outbreak of armed conflict,[1] others may be attracted to such areas due to business opportunities and higher gains associated with a higher risk,[2] yet some may be the actual cause of a violent conflict. From the perspective of legal accountability, foreign investors can play a twofold role in conflict-ridden states.[3] On the one hand, they can sustain economic and human losses as a victim of violence at the hands of either state or non-state forces. I have explored this aspect of investor protection law in a monograph.[4] On the other hand, conflict can emerge in response to an investor's activity, or investors can contribute to human rights abuses and other atrocities that are common in times of armed conflict either directly or, more commonly, by being complicit in commission of such violations by other actors.

Traditionally, foreign investors have paid little attention to the risk of their complicity in human rights abuses amid armed conflict. One reason for this is the

[1] This chapter follows the definition of armed conflict articulated in international humanitarian law sources, most prominently by International Criminal Tribunal for the Former Yugoslavia (ICTY) in the *Tadić* case. According to the tribunal, an armed conflict exists whenever 'there is resort to armed force between States or protracted armed violence between governmental authorities and organized armed groups or between such groups within a State': *Prosecutor v Tadić* (Decision on Defence Motion for Interlocutory Appeal on Jurisdiction) IT-94-1-T (2 October 1995) para 70. For different approaches to defining armed conflict, especially in investment law, see J Zrilič, *The Protection of Foreign Investment in Times of Armed Conflict* (Oxford University Press, 2019) 7.

[2] J Bennett, 'Multinational Corporations, Social Responsibility and Conflict' (2002) 55 *Journal of International Affairs* 393.

[3] For a more detailed typology of different roles that business performs in war, see H Slim, 'Business Actors in Armed Conflict: Towards a New Humanitarian Agenda' (2012) 94 *International Review of the Red Cross* 903, 911.

[4] Zrilič, *The Protection of Foreign Investment* (2019).

state-centric nature of the international human rights law (IHRL), which does not impose enforceable obligations on corporations.[5] While there are ongoing negotiations at the United Nations (UN) level to adopt an international human rights instrument, which would bind business entities directly,[6] so far most global initiatives addressing specifically the role of corporations in conflict-related human rights violations have been developed at the level of soft law.[7] While those non-binding instruments elaborate on the responsibilities that corporations should exercise in the context of conflict, they often highlight that by not following the outlined recommendations, corporations could become legally liable for breaches of international obligations in the field of law specifically regulating conduct in armed conflict, namely international humanitarian law (IHL).

In contrast to IHRL, IHL obligations directly bind both state and non-state actors, including businesses.[8] Over the recent decades, the avenues to hold corporations accountable for their contribution to conflict-related abuses have been expanding. Investor misconduct can thus lead to criminal prosecution of corporations and/or individual staff members under domestic and international criminal law,[9] as well as give rise to litigation based on extraterritorial civil claims brought to domestic courts by the victims of the corporate abuse.[10] The past examples of such liabilities have importantly contributed to the evolution of the relevant standards of corporate accountability,[11] and further reaffirmed that prudent investors can no longer afford to pay nominal consideration to the adverse role their operations can play in the areas of conflict.

While this problematic aspect of economic activity in armed conflicts has been widely acknowledged and discussed within the framework of business and human rights,[12] up until recently the topic has not attracted much attention in investment

[5] This view is contested by some academics. See, for example, N Jägers, *Corporate Human Rights Obligations: In Search of Accountability* (Intersentia, 2002); J Zerk, *Multinationals and Corporate Social Responsibility: Limitations and Opportunities in International Law* (Cambridge University Press, 2006); S Deva, *Regulating Corporate Human Rights Violations: Humanizing Business* (Routledge, 2012).

[6] Negotiations opened in 2015 following the resolution of the UN Human Rights Council (UNHRC), 'Elaboration of an International Legally Binding Instrument on Transnational Corporations and other Business Enterprises with Respect to Human Rights' (14 July 2014) UN Doc A/HRC/RES/26/9.

[7] See section II.A.

[8] International Committee of the Red Cross, 'Business and International Humanitarian Law: An Introduction to the Rights and Obligations of Business Enterprises under International Humanitarian Law' (ReliefWeb, 1 December 2006), available at reliefweb.int/sites/reliefweb.int/files/resources/543048595E265015C125723A003766EB-ICRC-Dec2006.pdf.

[9] For examples, see sections II and III.

[10] ibid.

[11] ibid.

[12] See, for example, Slim, 'Business Actors' (2012); S Tripathi, 'Business in Armed Conflict Zones: How to Avoid Complicity and Comply with International Standards' (2010) 50 *Politorbis* 131; A Graf and A Iff, 'Respecting Human Rights in Conflict Regions: How to Avoid the "Conflict Spiral"' (2017) 2 *Business and Human Rights Journal* 109; N Lubell, 'Challenges in Applying Human Rights Law to Armed Conflict' (2005) 87 *International Review of the Red Cross* 737; D Olson, 'Corporate Complicity In Human Rights Violations Under International Criminal Law' (2015) 1 *DePaul International Human Rights Law Journal* article 5; Z Hassan, '"When Caterpillars® Kill": Holding US Corporations Accountable for

law scholarship.[13] This can be explained by investment law's inherent focus on the responsibility of host states for injuries to foreign investors: the regime has been created with an aim to effectively protect foreign investors and provide them with remedies when a host state fails to meet relevant protection standards. Yet, some of the recent practices in investment treaty-making and case law have started to reflect awareness of the investors' negative impact in volatile times as well as a willingness to account for such investor misconduct within the investment treaty framework.[14] Overall, however, the progress has been slow and insufficient.

This chapter argues that for better understanding and further advancement of these developments, investment law should not be observed in isolation, but in the context of wider regulatory efforts to hold corporations to account for their contributions to conflict-related violations. The standards of responsibility developed in voluntary codes of conduct and obligations codified in IHL, can thus become an important reference point in the negotiation of new, more balanced investment treaties, as well as in the pleadings of parties and in the reasoning of arbitral awards under the existent investment treaty framework. The embedding of mechanisms for investor accountability more firmly in the investment treaties and decision-making presents a necessary step towards a more symmetrical investment law, which would effectively discourage investors from contributing to abuses in armed conflict.

The chapter is structured as follows. Section II outlines IHL obligations binding investors and soft law obligations in voluntary initiatives specifically addressing corporate responsibility in times of conflict and explains how they relate. Section III provides an overview of avenues of investor accountability, especially in the sphere of international criminal law and domestic civil law. Lastly, section IV discusses the potential of investment law as a tool for enforcing IHL from the perspective of an investor as both a victim of, and a contributor to, war crimes. It further identifies different ways in which investor misconduct in times of armed conflict can be taken into account in investment law. Drawing on examples from case law

Knowingly Selling Equipment to Countries for the Commission of Human Rights Abuses Abroad' (2004) 6 *San Diego International Law Journal* 341; J Oetzel et al, 'Business and Peace: Sketching the Terrain' (2009) 89 *Journal of Business Ethics* 351; A Ramasastry, 'Corporate Complicity: From Nuremberg to Rangoon – An Examination of Forced Labor Cases and Their Impact on the Liability of Multinational Corporations' (2002) 20 *Berkeley Journal of International Law* 91.

[13] For recent contributions, see D Davitti, *Investment and Human Rights in Armed Conflict: Charting an Elusive Intersection* (Hart, 2019); J Gilbert, *Natural Resources and Human Rights: An Appraisal* (Oxford University Press, 2018) ch 4; P Ambach, 'International Criminal Responsibility of Transnational Corporate Actors in Doing Business in Zones of Armed Conflict' in F Baetens (ed), *Investment Law within International Law: Integrational Perspectives* (Cambridge University Press, 2014); K Crow, 'Corporations and Crimes against Humanity: Financial Liability through ISDS?' in KF Gómez, A Gourgourinis and C Titi (eds), *International Investment Law and the Law of Armed Conflict* (Springer, 2019) 459; L Vanhonnaeker, 'The Recourse to Private Military and Security Companies by Foreign Investors in Conflict-Affected Countries: Dangers, Opportunities and the Need to Regulate' in Gómez, Gourgourinis and Titi (ibid) 487.

[14] See section IV.

and treaty-making, it argues that investment law should engage better and more expressly with the legal frameworks addressing the role of business in conflict-affected areas. This, in turn, could incentivise investors to adjust more prudently the manner in which they conduct business in conflict-affected areas.

II. Do Investors have Obligations in Armed Conflict?

A discussion about the obligations investors have on the international plane inevitably starts with the question of whether corporations are capable of being bound by international law at all.[15] The traditional view that only states are subjects and addressees of international law has been increasingly contested, in particular by human rights scholars,[16] who argued that given their significant economic power and influence, corporations too are capable of being holders of human rights obligations.[17] While this debate is far from settled, it becomes somewhat less problematic when it is centred on corporate misconduct in times of armed conflict, with both IHL and international criminal law (ICL) imposing obligations on non-state actors.

IHL is a branch of international law that regulates conduct during armed conflict with an aim to minimise the suffering that it causes. The rules of IHL apply only once a violent situation crosses the threshold of armed conflict as defined by the IHL sources.[18] Regardless of which set of IHL rules applies, depending on the characteristics of the conflict (international or non-international),[19] IHL must be respected not only by states, but also by non-state actors such as organised armed groups and other entities, including companies and individuals whose actions are closely associated with armed conflict.[20] The International Committee of the Red

[15] See, for example, A Clapham, *Human Rights Obligations of Non-state Actors* (Oxford University Press, 2006) 25.

[16] ibid; P Alston (ed), *Non-State Actors and Human Rights* (Oxford University Press, 2006); O De Schutter (ed), *Transnational Corporations and Human Rights* (Hart, 2006).

[17] See, for example, Clapham, *Human Rights* Obligations (2006) 266–70; Jägers, *Corporate Human Rights Obligations* (2002) 75–95; P Muchlinski, *Multinational Enterprises and the Law* (Oxford University Press, 2007) 520; D Weissbrodt and M Kruger, 'Current Developments: Norms on the Responsibilities of Transnational Corporations and Other Business Enterprises with Regard to Human Rights' (2013) 97 *American Journal of International Law* 901, 913; D Kinley and J Tadaki, 'From Talk to Walk: The Emergence of Human Rights Responsibilities for Corporations at International Law' (2004) 44 *Virginia Journal of International Law* 931, 962.

[18] See *Prosecutor v Tadić*, para 70; Zrilič (n 1) 7.

[19] International conflicts (including struggles for national liberation against 'alien occupation' or 'colonial domination') are governed by the Hague Regulations, the four Geneva Conventions and Additional Protocol I, while non-international armed conflicts are regulated by Common Article 3 to the four Geneva Conventions (regarding less-intense conflicts) and Additional Protocol II (regarding high-intensity conflicts).

[20] International Committee of the Red Cross, 'Business and International Humanitarian Law' (2006) 11, 13–14. This means that serious IHL violations like war crimes can be committed without involvement of state agents or agents of any other belligerent party. See *Prosecutor v Akayesu*, ICTR-96-4, Judgment (1 June 2001) 425.

Cross (ICRC) recognised that determining 'which activities are closely linked to an armed conflict' may be complicated (a clear example would be providing direct support to a party to the hostilities); however, companies operating in zones of armed conflict should exercise great caution to avoid their involvement in IHL violations.[21]

The fact that some IHL prohibitions are binding on business actors has already been indicated by the post-World War II criminal tribunals,[22] and in domestic civil law cases,[23] asserted in scholarship,[24] and even acknowledged by the Special Representative on Business and Human Rights, John Ruggie, who observed that while the main human rights instruments do not seem to impose direct responsibilities on companies,[25] there are certain international obligations that indeed are directly binding on corporate actors, notably prohibitions of war crimes and crimes against humanity.[26] Recently, an investment tribunal in *Urbaser v Argentina* made a similar pronouncement that investors have an obligation to abstain from violations of general international law (including IHL),[27] and that 'Such an obligation can be of immediate application, not only upon States, but equally to individuals and other private parties'.[28] As indicated by the tribunal, this would be the case in particular when the investor was involved in *jus cogens* violations, such as war crimes.[29] War crimes are serious violations of IHL (conventional and customary) that incur direct criminal responsibility under international law (such as murder, inhuman treatment and torture, pillage, the unlawful transfer of civilians during armed conflict, intentionally directing attack against civilian population or civilian

[21] ibid 14.

[22] The International Military Tribunal at Nuremberg prosecuted German businessmen for their complicity with the Nazi regime. While those cases focused on individual criminal liability, some judgments show how closely intertwined that was with the liability of corporations. See, for example, 'The Farben Case' in *Trials of War Criminals Before the Nuernberg Military Tribunals Under Control Council Law No 10* (United States Government Printing Office, 1952) vols VII and VIII. See also K Priemel, 'Tales of Totalitarianism: Conflicting Narratives in the Industrialist Cases at Nuremberg' in K Priemel and A Stiller (eds), *Reassessing the Nuremberg Military Tribunals: Transitional Justice, Trial Narratives, and Historiography* (Berghahn Books, 2012) 170.

[23] See, for example, *In re Agent Orange Product Liability Litigation*, 373 F Supp.2d 7 (EDNY 2005) 59; *Presbyterian Church of Sudan v Talisman Energy, Inc*, 244 F Supp.2d 289 (SDNY 2003) 305–14.

[24] See, for example, V Nerlich, 'Core Crimes and Transnational Business Corporations' (2010) 8 *Journal of International Criminal Justice* 895, 899; Ramasastry, 'Corporate Complicity' (2002) 100–18; S Ratner, 'Corporations and Human Rights: A Theory of Corporate Responsibility' (2001) 111 *Yale Law Journal* 443, 504.

[25] UNHRC 'Business and Human Rights: Mapping International Standards of Responsibility and Accountability for Corporate Acts: Report of the Special Representative of the Secretary-General (SRSG) on the Issue of Human Rights and Transnational Corporations and Other Business Enterprises' (9 February 2007) UN Doc A/HRC/4/035, 44.

[26] UNHRC, 'Interim Report of the Special Representative of the Secretary-General on the Issue of Human Rights and Transnational Corporations and Other Business Enterprises' (22 February 2006) UN Doc E/CN.4/2006/97, 60.

[27] *Urbaser SA v The Argentine Republic*, ICSID Case No ARB/07/26, Award (8 December 2016), para 1210.

[28] ibid.

[29] ibid fn 446 (citing the ATCA case *Filartiga v Pena-IRala*, 630 F.2d 876 (2nd Cir 1980)).

property, etc), and are identified in the IHL treaties,[30] the ICL treaties,[31] and international customary law.[32] Practice, legislation and case law confirm that war crimes can be committed not only by members of armed forces, but also by any other person, including civilians.[33]

Investors can contribute to grave violations of IHL in different ways. For example, an investor's acquisition of assets (natural resources, property, shares, etc), which is based on 'threats, intimidation, pressure, or a position of power derived from the surrounding armed conflict',[34] can constitute pillage which is prohibited under IHL.[35] Furthermore, if the investment acquired during armed conflict or occupation results in the forceful eviction of residents by the belligerent forces (eg, with a view to secure land or resources for investment), this can amount to the violations of the IHL prohibition against the displacement of civilians.[36] For example, internal conflict in Colombia was characterised by land usurpation and forcible displacement of the local community, with some land subsequently resold or rented out to investors.[37] A similar situation transpired recently in Myanmar, where the Rohingya people were forcibly displaced, which was preceded by land-grabbing at the hands of the military forces, with the land often being sold off to foreign investors for their development projects.[38] Should the armed conflict threshold in these situations be met, foreign investors benefitting from violence and forcible displacement could be potentially implicated in grave violations of IHL.

[30] See, for example, Geneva Convention (IV) relative to the Protection of Civilian Persons in Time of War (signed 12 August 1949, entered into force 21 October 1950) 75 UNTS 287 (GC IV), Art 147; Protocol (I) Additional to the Geneva Conventions of 12 August 1949, and relating to the Protection of Victims of International Armed Conflicts (signed 12 December 1977, entered into force 7 December 1978) 1125 UNTS 3 (AP I), Art 85.

[31] Rome Statute of the International Criminal Court (adopted 17 July 1998, entered into force 1 July 2002) 2187 UNTS 90, Art 8.

[32] J-M Henckaerts and L Doswald-Beck, *Customary International Humanitarian Law* (Cambridge University Press, 2005) Rule 156, Vol II, Ch 44, Section A.

[33] ibid, referring to the military manuals of Australia, the UK, the US, New Zealand and Ecuador, among others.

[34] International Committee of the Red Cross (n 8) 22.

[35] GC IV, Art 33; AP II, Art 4.2; Hague Convention (IV) respecting the Laws and Customs of War on Land and its annex: Regulations concerning the Laws and Customs of War on Land (Hague Regulations) (signed 18 October 1907, entry into force 26 January 1910), Arts 28 and 47.

[36] Under IHL, civilians cannot be forcibly relocated unless 'security of the population or imperative military reasons so demand'. GC IV, Art 49; AP II, Art 17(1).

[37] See, for example, Inter-American Commission on Human Rights, Truth, Justice and Reparation: Fourth Report on Human Rights Situation in Colombia (31 December 2013) OEA/Series L/V/II Doc 49/13; Oxfam, 'Divide and Purchase, How Land Ownership is Being Concentrated in Colombia' (Oxfam Research Report, 2013); MA Velasquez-Ruiz, 'Foreign Investment-Induced Migration in Colombia: Rethinking the Legal Schemes of Protection and Accountability' (2013) 22 *International Law: Revista Colombiana Derecho Internacional Bogotá (Colombia)* 147; R Tamayo-Alvarez, 'Colombia's Land Restitution Programme and International Investment Law: Normative Tensions and Possible Convergences Concerning Investor Diligence' (2018) 15 *Manchester Journal of International Economic Law* 114.

[38] See S Sassen, 'Is Rohingya Persecution Caused by Business Interests Rather than Religion?' (*The Guardian*, 4 January 2017), available at www.theguardian.com/global-development-professionals-network/2017/jan/04/is-rohingya-persecution-caused-by-business-interests-rather-than-religion. On response of corporations to being called out for complicity in the Rohingya crisis,

Investors benefitting from the labour of civilians and prisoners of war that does not meet the standards laid down by the IHL,[39] or investors supplying the warring parties with weapons and tools to inflict harm also run risks of contributing to violations of IHL.[40] The former scenario factually transpired in *Unocal* case, in which the Myanmar military used forced labour from local villagers to provide support for construction of the foreign investor's pipeline.[41] The latter situation, on the other hand, was at the heart of the *Van Anraat* case, in which the Dutch criminal court found the Dutch investor criminally liable for aiding and abetting war crimes by supplying Saddam Hussein with chemicals that were instrumental for the production of mustard gas, which was used for the murder of the Kurdish minority in Iraq.[42]

The risk of liability is particularly high when investors contract security services to protect their personnel and assets,[43] and the hired security forces violate IHL while engaging in hostilities (for example, by committing torture or murder of local residents and activists protesting the investment).[44] As stressed by the ICRC, this could give rise to legal liability of investors, 'even if they did not intend the violations to occur and if the offences were not perpetrated on their behalf'.[45] Investors could incur liability by relying either on state or non-state security providers. For example, in *Wiwa v Shell*, Royal Dutch/Shell was accused of working with Nigerian military to suppress demonstrations carried out against the investor's oil activities that were causing environmental damage in the Niger Delta.[46] In the analogous case,

see Business and Human Rights Resource Centre, 'Myanmar: Business and Investor Responses to the Rohingya Crisis', available at www.business-humanrights.org/en/latest-news/myanmar-business-investor-responses-to-the-rohingya-crisis.

[39] GC IV, Arts 40, 51, 95; GC III, Arts 49–55; AP II, Art 5(1)(e).

[40] International Committee of the Red Cross (n 8) 25.

[41] *Doe v Unocal Corp*, 395 F.3d 932 (9th Cir 2002) (*Unocal*), 940.

[42] See judgment of the Hague District Court: *Public Prosecutor v Van Anraat* (2005) LJN AU8685, para 14; appealed to the Hague Court of Appeal: (2007) LJN BA6734, 2200050906-2. For a civil law case involving investor complicity through supply of provisions to the military regime, see, for example, *In re South African Apartheid Litigation*, 3 Civ 4524 (SDNY 2009), 57 (in this case, several corporations were accused of aiding and abetting human rights abuses committed by the apartheid regime by supplying weapons, vehicles with specific military equipment and computer systems designed to implement a racist passport system and segregation).

[43] Investors who have funded public or private military companies to ensure security of their facilities and pipelines include Shell, Chevron and British Petroleum. See D Avant, 'The Privatization of Security and Change in the Control of Force' (2004) 5 *International Studies Perspective* 153, 154; S Percy, 'Regulating the Private Security Industry: a Story of Regulating the Last War' (2012) 94 *International Review of the Red Cross* 941; Vanhonnaeker, 'The Recourse to Private Military and Security Companies' (2019).

[44] Arbitrary killings of environmental activists resisting investment projects in natural resources area has been in particular common. For an overview, see Gilbert, *Natural Resources and Human Rights* (2018) 108; UNHRC 'Report of the Special Rapporteur on the Rights to Freedom of Peaceful Assembly and of Association' (28 April 2015) UN Doc A/HRC/29/25.

[45] International Committee of the Red Cross (n 8) 21.

[46] *Wiwa v Royal Dutch Petroleum*, 96 Civ 8386 (SDNY 2002); *Wiwa v Anderson*, 1 Civ 1909 (SDNY 2002); *Wiwa v Shell, Petroleum Development Company*, 4 Civ 2665 (SDNY 2009). For an overview, see Center for Constitutional Rights, 'Wiwa v Royal Dutch Petroleum', available at ccrjustice.org/home/what-we-do/our-cases/wiwa-et-al-v-royal-dutch-petroleum-et-al.

Bowoto v Chevron,[47] the investor allegedly paid the Nigerian military to intervene against the protestors, which resulted in the killing of civilians and the destruction of villages. Similar violations have occurred when investors procured security from non-state actors. For example, a Dutch businessman, Guus Kouwenhoven, whose timber companies made an investment in Liberia, was convicted for aiding and abetting war crimes by hiring Liberian militias (and supplying them with weapons), which then participated in the massacre of civilians.[48]

While these IHL violations are defined in the IHL and ICL instruments, there is nonetheless a lack of clarity as to what the content of such obligations with respect to investors is. In other words, while it is clear how state forces and organised armed groups can commit murder, torture, destruction of civilian property and pillaging, it is less clear how such prohibitions can be operationalised with respect to corporate conduct. To an extent, this gap has been filled by the voluntary initiatives that emerged in response to the increasing involvement of corporations in conflict-related atrocities. The next section turns the focus to them.

A. Investor Obligations under Soft Law

Most corporate social responsibility (CSR) initiatives that specify soft obligations that corporations hold in volatile contexts, started developing at the beginning of the twenty-first century, and reached a peak with the official adoption of the UN Guiding Principles on Business and Human Rights (UNGP) in 2011.[49] What is common to these initiatives is that they highlight that companies should adjust the manner in which they conduct business to the conflict-sensitive environment by, for example, carrying out continued and enhanced due diligence in order to avoid or mitigate negative impacts of their operation on human rights, or by promoting positive impacts on the society affected by their operation.[50]

Broadly speaking, these initiatives have focused on two types of overlapping businesses most likely to contribute to conflicts and be involved in large scale

[47] *Bowoto v Chevron*, 312 F Supp.2d 1229 (ND Cal 2006). For a factually similar case, see also pending *Doe v Exxon Mobile Corp* (a lawsuit brought to the US federal court by Indonesian villagers alleging that the investor was complicit in human rights abuses at the hands of the government security forces).

[48] *The Public Prosecutor v Guus Kouwenhoven* (2017) ECLI:NL:GHSHE:2017:1760 (Dutch Court of Appeal). For civil law cases involving complicity in violence at the hands of security providers, see *Doe v Chiquita Brands International* (alleging that American investor made payments to the paramilitary organisation, which murdered hundreds of civilians, especially trade unionist and social activists working at the investor's plantations; the case was settled); *Saleh v Titan* (concerning allegation of torture at the hands of a security provider hired by the US Government to provide services at detention facilities in Iraq; the case was dismissed).

[49] Guiding Principles on Business and Human Rights: Implementing the United Nations 'Protect, Respect and Remedy' Framework, A/HRC/17/31 (UNGP).

[50] See Graf and Iff, 'Respecting Human Rights in Conflict Regions' (2017) 119 (distinguishing between two approaches followed in the CSR initiatives: human rights due diligence and conflict sensitivity); Tripathi, 'Business in Armed Conflict Zones' (2010) 139 (summarising responsibilities of companies operating in armed conflict zones).

abuses of human rights: extractive industries, and private military and security companies. The former mostly aims to prevent corporations from fuelling conflict and conflict-related atrocities through trade of minerals,[51] or to prevent and mitigate natural resources-related conflicts with local communities.[52] The latter, on the other hand, emerged in response to the growing number of cases in which atrocities were committed by the investors' public and private security providers.[53] These voluntary codes articulate standards that assist governments and private companies in implementing their IHL and human rights obligations, with a view to prevent, mitigate and efficiently respond to human rights abuses.

The fact that most of the relevant voluntary initiatives adopted human rights as the main reference framework, rather than IHL and ICL, is not surprising. It is widely accepted that IHRL continues to apply during armed conflict.[54] Most of the time, this will not be problematic as human rights law is similar in its objective, values and terminology to IHL and ICL and, in the context of armed conflict, purports to prevent and minimise the suffering of innocent people.[55] There are, however, advantages to adopting a human rights approach in voluntary initiatives, reflecting the reality in which corporate misconduct often takes place. First, IHL and ICL are rather narrow and rigid in scope: the conduct will amount to war crimes only if it was committed in the context of armed conflict, with ICL extending its scope of application to other core crimes: genocide, crimes against humanity and the crime of aggression.[56] In contrast, IHRL is broader in its scope and addresses violations of civil, political, economic, social, cultural and group rights.[57]

[51] See, for example, Kimberley Process (2003), available at www.kimberleyprocess.com/en/what-kp; 'OECD Due Diligence Guidance for Responsible Supply Chains of Minerals from Conflict-Affected and High-Risk Areas', 2nd edn (OECD Guidance on Conflict Minerals, 2013) available at www.oecd.org/daf/inv/mne/mining.htm.

[52] See United Nations' and European Union's Toolkit and Guidance for Preventing Conflict and Managing Land and Natural Resources Conflicts, available at www.un.org/en/land-natural-resources-conflict/pdfs/Resource%20Rich%20Economies.pdf; International Council on Mining & Metals (ICMM) Guidance, available at guidance.miningwithprinciples.com; IPIECA (the oil and gas industry association for environmental and social issues) Guidelines, available at www.ipieca.org/our-work/social/indigenous-peoples. See also, United Nations Declaration on Indigenous People (adopted 13 September 2007) UN Doc No. A/61/295, Art 10; International Labour Conference (76th Session) Convention C169: Indigenous and Tribal Peoples Convention (Geneva, 7 June 1989), Art 6.

[53] Most important initiatives are The Montreux Document On Pertinent International Legal Obligations and Good Practices for States Related to Operations of Private Military and Security Companies during Armed Conflict (2008), available at www.icrc.org/en/download/file/135841/montreux_document_en.pdf, and International Code of Conduct for Private Security Service Providers, available at icoca.ch/the-code. See also, The Voluntary Principles on Security and Human Rights, available at www.voluntaryprinciples.org/what-are-the-voluntary-principles.

[54] *Legal Consequences of the Construction of a Wall in the Occupied Palestinian Territory* (Advisory Opinion) [2004] ICJ Rep 136, 178. The relationship between two bodies of law has been subject to much doctrinal discussion; see, for example, O Ben-Naftali (ed), *International Humanitarian Law and International Human Rights Law* (Oxford University Press 2011).

[55] *Kunarac and others*, IT-96-23-T, Judgment (22 February 2001), para 467.

[56] In contrast to war crimes, the contextual element of armed conflict is not required for other core crimes.

[57] L van der Herik and JL Černič, 'Regulating Corporations under International Law: From Human Rights to International Criminal Law and Back Again' (2010) 8 *Journal of International Criminal Justice* 725, 741.

Second, the IHRL's area of application is much wider as it also applies outside the narrow IHL definition of armed conflict, including violent situations that are expressly excluded from the IHL and the ICL sources, namely 'internal disturbances and tensions, such as riots, isolated and sporadic acts of violence or other acts of a similar nature'.[58] As such, it has greater potential to effectively address corporate misconduct in volatile situations. The CSR initiatives have recognised that by expressly extending their application beyond the IHL definition of armed conflict so as to encompass other types of violent situations.[59] This is important because it is notoriously difficult to ascertain whether the threshold for application of the IHL rules has been met, especially with regard to non-international armed conflicts. This is due to the difficulties in determining the beginning or the end of an armed conflict, the fluctuating nature of a conflict's characteristics, and the fact that states often downplay the intensity of conflicts in order to avoid the application of IHL rules, as this would impose on a belligerent state certain obligations, confer on rebels certain rights, and potentially invite interventions from foreign forces.[60] Constraining the debate on corporate responsibilities to IHL-defined armed conflicts would thus create unnecessary, and indeed, harmful limitations in designing and applying incentives for investors' responsible conduct as well as sanctions for investor misconduct. Overcoming these definitional boundaries does not only bring more clarity to investors' expectations as to how they should act in volatile contexts, but also prevents potential strategic limitations in taking necessary measures in only certain arbitrarily created categories of conflict.

Having explained the advantages of the human rights approach, the question that needs to be answered next is what the relationship is between the human rights-based soft obligations and IHL and ICL hard prohibitions. The answer can be found in the UNGP, which operationalised the 'Protect, Respect and Remedy' framework developed under the leadership of John Ruggie, and which states that companies are under a responsibility to respect human rights, ie, to undertake 'human rights due diligence' to identify, prevent, mitigate and account for adverse impacts on human rights.[61] Crucially, in conflict-affected areas companies are expected to exercise greater care. The UNGP stresses that in situations when abuses of human rights are gross (Principles 7, 23) and human rights impact is

[58] Rome Statute of the International Criminal Court, Art 8(2)(f).

[59] See, for example, UNGP (Commentary to Principle 7) 10; 'Guidance on Responsible Business in Conflict-Affected and High-Risk Areas: A Resource for Companies and Investors' (UN Global Compact–PRI, 2010) 7; OECD Guidance on Conflict Minerals (n 51) 13.

[60] Zrilič (n 1) 182; A Cullen, *The Concept of Non-International Armed Conflict in International Humanitarian Law* (Cambridge University Press 2010); W Abresch, 'A Human Rights Law of International Armed Conflict: The European Court of Human Rights in Chechnya' (2005) 16 *European Journal of International Law* 741, 756.

[61] UNGP, Principle 15. See also, IRHB and Shift, 'Oil and Gas Sector Guide on Implementing the UN Guiding Principles on Business and Human Rights, European Commission' (IRHB, 2013); R Mares, 'Corporate and State Responsibilities in Conflict-Affected Areas' (2014) 83 *Nordic Journal of International Law* 293.

severe (Principles 14, 17),[62] which is likelier in conflict-affected areas, the companies' response should be quicker, and more proactive and attentive (Principles 14, 24).[63] The UNGP also emphasise that companies' contributions to gross human rights abuses could be penalised under relevant national and international rules. Thus, Principle 23 recommends to 'Treat the risk of causing or contributing to gross human rights abuses as a legal compliance issue wherever they operate'.[64] In other words, the UNGP highlights the complementary nature of the relevant legal frameworks: adhering to the human rights due diligence could help investors avoid the risk of legal liability, including that arising from the violations of the IHL and ICL rules.[65] Since the CSR instruments are voluntary and impose no sanctions for non-compliance, the synergy with binding obligations will be successful only if there are effective avenues for enforcing them. The next section looks into the relevant accountability mechanisms.

III. How Can Investors be Held to Account?

In the previous section, it was argued that international law imposes certain substantive obligations on investors in times of armed conflict; for example, an obligation to abstain from violating IHL rules that give rise to international crimes. A separate question is whether and where such obligations can be enforced against investors who participated in violations. Pursuing a claim before municipal courts in host states, where such violations typically occur, does not inspire confidence, as such states, which are still immersed in, or emerging from, conflict often lack institutional infrastructure and resources needed for an efficient trial and investigation. In addition, in situations where a foreign investor was complicit in the atrocities committed by a government itself, the impartiality of a host state's prosecutorial and judicial institutions is questionable. Alternatively, investor accountability could be sought in the investor's home states or, at the international level and inasmuch as investors are natural persons, before the International Criminal Court (ICC). Both of these options, however, are fraught with legal and practical obstacles, some of which are outlined below.

A. Accountability under International Criminal Law

Under IHL, states are obliged to criminalise grave violations of IHL, and investigate and prosecute war crimes regardless of the location of the offences or the

[62] For example, Ruggie linked gross abuses to international crimes. SRSG, 'Recommendations on Follow-Up to the Mandate' (11 February 2011).

[63] UN Office of the High Commissioner for Human Rights, 'The Corporate Responsibility to Respect Human Rights – An Interpretive Guide' (2012) HR/PUB/12/02, 80.

[64] UNGP, Principle 23.

[65] ibid 26 (see in particular the commentary).

identity of the perpetrators.[66] War crimes have thus become part of national legislation of most countries and some jurisdictions even provide for the option to hold corporations, rather than only natural persons (eg, managers), responsible for the commission of, and complicity in, war crimes.[67] Corporate officials and investor employees have thus been prosecuted for their complicity in war crimes before courts in investors' home as well host states.[68]

The latter example transpired in the case involving an Australian corporation, Anvil Mining, accused of providing logistical assistance to Congolese military forces in a violent reprisal resulting in murder, rape, torture of civilians, pillaging and other atrocities.[69] While Anvil argued that their support to the military operation was in compliance with the Congolese law, the pressure from the NGOs and general public resulted in a criminal trial against military commanders as well as three Anvil employees for, among others, aiding and abetting war crimes and other violations of the IHL.[70] The Congolese military court acquitted all defendants, finding that the investor's employees provided support under duress and were thus not liable. Interestingly, investigations against Anvil also commenced in Australia, the investor's home state, but was ultimately discontinued due to insufficient evidence.[71] Had it proceeded, the outcome of the proceedings would have been much more interesting and potentially set an important precedent, since Australian criminal law enables the prosecution of corporations, rather than just individuals, for such international crimes.

At the international level, an investor's involvement in international crimes could potentially be adjudicated by the ICC. While the Court, or any other international criminal tribunal, does not have jurisdiction to prosecute corporations,[72] this does not mean that an investor's activities are outside the realm of international

[66] See, for example, GC I, Art 49; Rome Statute of the International Criminal Court, Preamble; Henckaerts and Doswald-Beck, *Customary International Humanitarian Law* (2005) Rule 158, Vol II, Ch 44, Section C.

[67] International Committee of the Red Cross (n 8) 26; 'Report of the ICJ Expert Legal Panel on Corporate Complicity in International Crimes', Vol II (2008) 57 (ICJ Panel Report). Some municipal jurisdictions provide for corporate criminal liability, for example, Australia, the Netherlands, France, Belgium and Switzerland.

[68] For criminal cases in home states, see, for example, *Public Prosecutor v Guus Kouwenhoven*; *Public Prosecutor v Van Anraat.*

[69] See Business & Human Rights Resource Centre, Anvil Mining Lawsuit, available at www.business-humanrights.org/en/latest-news/anvil-mining-lawsuit-re-dem-rep-of-congo; A McBeth, 'Crushed by Anvil: A Case Study on Responsibility for Human Rights in the Extractive Sector' (2008) 11 *Yale Human Rights and Development Law Journal* 127.

[70] ibid.

[71] ibid 150.

[72] Rome Statute of the International Criminal Court, Art 25(1). While during the negotiation of the Rome Statute, the French delegation proposed to expand the jurisdiction of the ICC so as to cover corporate criminal liability, the proposal gained little political support and was deemed to dilute the core goals of the Rome conference. See 1995 Report of the Ad Hoc Committee on the Establishment of an International Criminal Court, UN Doc. A/50/22, 58. See also DE Stoitchkova, *Towards Corporate Liability in International Criminal Law* (Intersentia, 2010) 16–17.

criminal law. As the Nuremberg Trials have shown, investors who are natural persons and corporate officials who, in the course of their business activities, become involved in war crimes perpetrated by a belligerent party, can be prosecuted and held criminally accountable.[73] In the aftermath of World War II, a number of German industrialists were tried for conducting business with the Nazi regime and being complicit in the Nazi slave labouring system.[74]

So far, however, the ICC has yet to decide to prosecute officials with respect to business-related crimes. This could be explained by the fact that in view of the Court's limited capacity, priority is given to the prosecution of direct perpetrators, namely those who bear the greatest responsibility for the crimes,[75] and whose criminal responsibility is easier to prove.[76]

Although criminal responsibility of aiders and abettors (which is the most likely mode of responsibility for investors), is possible under the Rome Statute,[77] the prosecutor is required to be selective in starting investigations and prosecutions.[78] Despite these limitations, the 2016 Policy Paper of the ICC Office of the Prosecutor (OTP) may signal a wind of change in the ICC's willingness to prosecute business-related crimes. The Paper states that the OTP 'will give particular consideration to prosecuting Rome Statute crimes that are committed by means of, or that result in … the destruction of the environment, the illegal exploitation of natural resources or the illegal dispossession of land'.[79] As mentioned in the previous section, pillage of natural resources and land-grabbing, accompanied with dispossession of marginalised communities, have been highlighted by the ICRC as the crimes where the risk of corporate complicity is particularly high.[80] It is thus not surprising that human rights NGOs and academics have welcomed the Policy Paper as a step towards effective prosecution of business-related abuses of human rights.[81] Recently authorised investigations of the ICC into the situation

[73] ICJ Panel Report (n 67) 6.

[74] See, for example, 'The Farben Case', 'The Flick Case' and 'The Krupp Case' in *Trials of War Criminals Before the Nuernberg Military Tribunals Under Control Council Law No. 10* (United States Government Printing Office, 1952) vols VI and IX.

[75] 'Understanding the International Criminal Court', 5, available at www.icc-cpi.int/iccdocs/PIDS/publications/UICCEng.pdf.

[76] N Bernaz, 'An Analysis of the ICC Office of the Prosecutor's Policy Paper on Case Selection and Prioritization from the Perspective of Business and Human Rights' (2017) 15 *Journal of International Criminal Justice* 527, 533; Tripathi (n 12).

[77] Rome Statute of the International Criminal Court, Art 25(3)(c).

[78] Office of the Prosecutor (OTP), 'Prosecutorial Strategy: 2009–2012' (1 February 2010) 19, available at www.icc-cpi.int/NR/rdonlyres/66A8DCDC-3650-4514-AA62-D229D1128F65/281506/OTPProsecutorialStrategy20092013.pdf.

[79] OTP, 'Policy Paper on Case Selection and Prioritisation' (15 September 2016) 41, available at www.icc-cpi.int/itemsdocuments/20160915_otp-policy_case-selection_eng.pdf.

[80] See also Gilbert (n 13) 106 (discussing how pillage of natural resources can amount to international crimes).

[81] See 'Company Executives Could Now Be Tried for Land Grabs and Environmental Destruction' (Global Witness press release, 15 September 2016), available at www.globalwitness.org/en/press-releases/company-executives-could-now-be-tried-land-grabbing-and-environmentaldestruction-historic-move-international-criminal-court-prosecutor; Bernaz, 'An Analysis of the ICC Office of the Prosecutor's Policy Paper' (2017) 533, 542; Gilbert (n 13) 106.

of Myanmar, involving forcible displacement of Rohingya people, could provide the first opportunity to scrutinise the complicity of corporate actors in alleged crimes.[82] However, given the ongoing backlash the Court has been experiencing,[83] and in view of the general reticence regarding the investigation of business-related crimes, the expectations about the ICC becoming an effective avenue for holding investors to account, are best kept low.

B. Accountability under Civil Law

In view of the challenges concerning the criminal liability of companies and the paucity in prosecution of business officials in international criminal fora, other accountability mechanisms may present a viable and more appealing route for addressing investors' involvement in war crimes and gross human rights violations in conflicts. In particular, victims of the investors' wrongdoing can seek damages from domestic courts on the basis of the domestic law of tort in common law systems and the law of non-contractual obligations in civil law jurisdictions.[84] On the one hand, civil prosecution gives victims more control over the process as the commencement of proceedings no longer depends on the discretion of public authorities like in criminal cases. On the other hand, establishing civil liability is met with various legal obstacles, not least by complex corporate structures and separate legal personalities of companies forming multinational enterprise, and jurisdictional problems related to extraterritoriality.

The most important contribution to the development of legal standards for civil liability of businesses has been made by the claims for violations of international law brought against multinational corporations in the United States under the 1789 Alien Tort Claims Act (ATCA), considered in more detail in chapter 9 of this volume by Lucas Roorda and Julian Ku.[85] ATCA provides non-US nationals with an opportunity for a civil tort suit before the US federal courts for actions 'committed in violation of the law of nations and the treaties of the US',[86] which includes the most egregious human rights violations, war crimes, crimes against humanity, etc.[87] Although no claim has been successful on the merits, the cases

[82] 'ICC judges authorise opening of an investigation into the situation in Bangladesh/Myanmar' (ICC press release, 14 November 2019), available at www.icc-cpi.int/Pages/item.aspx?name=pr1495.

[83] L Helfer and A Showalter, 'Opposing International Justice: Kenya's Integrated Backlash Strategy against the ICC' (2017) 17 *International Criminal Law Review* 1.

[84] ICJ Panel Report (n 67) 6; International Committee of the Red Cross (n 8) 26.

[85] Alien Tort Claims Act, 28 USC § 1350.

[86] ibid.

[87] *Sarei v Rio Tinto*, 487 F.3d 1193, 1202 (9th Cir 2007). As cited above, many claims were brought on the ground that corporations were complicit in war crimes, crimes against humanity and human rights abuses by military regimes. See, for example, *Unocal*; *Presbyterian Church of Sudan* (the claim concerned alleged corporate aiding and abetting to acts of genocide of the president of Sudan); *In Re South African Apartheid Litigation*; *Khulumani v BarclayNat Bank ltd*, 509 F.3d (2nd Cir 2007).

brought public attention to corporate involvement in human rights abuses and atrocities.[88] ATCA used to be celebrated by human rights lawyers for its extensive extraterritorial application – for American courts to hear civil claims it used to suffice for the sued corporation to have a form of business activity or financial holdings in the US.[89] Recent decisions, however, have tightened the jurisdictional threshold,[90] signalling the decline of ATCA's popularity.

Most national legal systems require the company to be domiciled or incorporated in the jurisdiction where the claim is brought.[91] While in some common law jurisdictions, courts may exercise discretion to refuse jurisdiction on the basis that there is a more appropriate forum for adjudicating the case elsewhere (*forum non conveniens*),[92] this is no longer an option for national courts in the EU, which must permit proceedings to commence against companies domiciled in EU,[93] even if the harm occurred outside the EU,[94] or the victim seeking civil remedies is not an EU resident or national.[95] Rather than contemplating a European version of ATCA, the focus in the EU has been on strengthening the direct liability of the parent company and the establishment of a duty of vigilance.[96]

It is thus unsurprising that, following the CSR initiatives outlined in the preceding section, some countries have taken further steps to specifically legislate the companies' duty of vigilance. While some domestic laws, like the UK Modern Slavery Act,[97]

[88] Bernaz (n 76) 537; MD Goldhaber, 'Corporate Human Rights Litigation in Non-US Courts – A Comparative Scorecard' (2013) 3 *University of California Irvine Law Review* 127, 129.

[89] See B Stephens, *US Litigation Against Companies for Gross Violations of Human Rights*, written in 2007 for the ICJ Expert Legal Panel on Corporate Complicity in International Crimes.

[90] ATCA's potential has been undermined in light of the US Supreme Court decisions in *Kiobel v Royal Dutch Petroleum Co*, 569 US 108 (2013) (which limited its extraterritorial reach and decided that claims brought under ATCA must 'touch and concern the territory of the United States … with sufficient force to displace the presumption against extraterritorial application'), and *Jesner v Arab Bank, plc*, 138 S Ct 1386 (2018) (deciding that foreign corporations cannot be sued under ATCA).

[91] ICJ Panel Report (n 67) Civil Remedies, Vol III, 49. Outside the US, victims are increasingly bringing claims on the ground of corporate complicity in human rights violations abroad. For an overview of recent cases, see Business and Human Rights Resource Centre, 'Briefing Note: Latin America Briefing Focus on Human Rights Defenders under Threat & Attack' (January 2017).

[92] ICJ Expert Panel Report, Civil Remedies, Volume III, 51; International Law Association Conference Committee on International Civil and Commercial Litigation, 'Third Interim Report: Declining and Referring Jurisdiction in International Litigation' (London, 2000).

[93] Regulation (EU) No 1215/2012 of the European Parliament and of the Council on Jurisdiction and the Recognition and Enforcement of Judgments in Civil and Commercial Matters (adopted 12 December 2012, entered into force 10 January 2015) OJ L 351, Art 4.

[94] Case C-281/02 *Andrew Owusu v NB Jackson* [2005] ECR I-1445.

[95] Case C-412/98 *Group Josi Reinsurance Company SA v Universal General Insurance Company (UGIC)* [2000] ECR I-5925.

[96] See W Kaleck and M Saage-Mass, 'Corporate Accountability for Human Rights Violations Amounting to International Crimes: The Status Quo and Its Challenges' (2010) 8 *Journal of International Criminal Justice* 699, 723; referring to F Gregor and H Ellis, 'Fair Law: Legal Proposals to Improve Corporate Accountability for Environmental and Human Rights Violations, European Coalition for Corporate Justice' (Ritimo, May 2008), available at www.ritimo.org/Fair-law-legal-proposals-to-improve-corporate-accountability-for-environmental.

[97] Modern Slavery Act 2015. For similar duty of vigilance with respect to reporting see also the California Transparency in Supply Chains Act, SB 657 § 2 (2010); and Section 1502 of the Dodd-Frank Act of 2010, Pub L 111-203, 124 Stat 1376 (concerning trade in conflict minerals).

limit such a duty to a disclosure and reporting stage only, the recently adopted French Due Diligence Law requires the companies[98] to develop and implement mechanisms for the prevention of human rights abuses throughout their chain of production, including their subsidiaries, companies under its control, suppliers and subcontractors.[99] If the company's failure to establish and implement their due diligence plan results in harm (eg, in the form of contribution to a war crime), the company can be liable to pay damages for corporate negligence.[100] More specifically to the context of companies operating in conflict-affected and high-risk areas, the EU recently adopted Regulation 2017/821 laying down supply chain due diligence obligations for EU importers of conflict minerals.[101] While the EU Regulation closely follows the due diligence measures enumerated in the OECD Guidance on Conflict Minerals, it has transformed the hortatory language of 'recommendations' into binding 'obligations', the breach of which can result in remedial action as defined by the EU Member States.[102]

These developments are reflective of the UNGP regime which addresses the conflict-affected zones within the state's duty to protect human rights. More specifically, the UNGP in Principle 7 recommends that home states and neighbouring states have responsibilities to ensure that companies operating in such volatile contexts are not involved in gross human rights abuses, by providing requisite assistance to companies, denying access to public support and services to companies that are engaged in such abuses or refuse to cooperate, and ensuring that their regulatory and enforcement framework is effective in dealing with such situations.[103] This drafting innovation was driven by two considerations: first, the acknowledgment that most voluntary initiatives that address the role of businesses in conflict-affected zone focus only on the due diligence responsibility for business but fail to provide any guidance for states;[104] and second, the recognition that host states 'may be unable to protect human rights adequately due to the lack of effective control'.[105] In view of the heightened risk of gross human rights abuses, the burden thus shifts to home states who are advised to act 'at the earliest stage possible' and, in addition, explore avenues for 'civil,

[98] The law covers large companies headquartered in France and foreign companies headquartered outside France with French subsidiaries that employ at least 5,000 employees in France.

[99] Available at www.assemblee-nationale.fr/14/ta/ta0924.asp.

[100] ibid. A similar initiative making the human rights due diligence mandatory for Swiss companies has been proposed, but ultimately rejected, in Switzerland. See E Umlas, 'Human Rights Due Diligence: Swiss Civil Society Pushes the Envelope' (Business & Human Rights Resource Centre, 13 March 2015), available at www.business-humanrights.org/en/human-rights-due-diligence-swiss-civil-society-pushes-the-envelope.

[101] Council Regulation (EU) 2017/821 of 17 May 2017 laying down supply chain due diligence obligations for Union importers of tin, tantalum and tungsten, their ores, and gold originating from conflict-affected and high-risk areas, OJ L130, 19.5.2017.

[102] Council Regulation (EU) 2017/821, Art 16.

[103] UNGP, Principle 7.

[104] UNHRC 'Business and human rights in conflict-affected regions: challenges and option towards State responses, Companion report' (27 May 2011) UN Doc A/HRC/17/32, paras 7–8.

[105] UNGP, Principle 7 and its accompanying commentary, 9.

administrative or criminal liability for enterprises domiciled or operating in their territory and/or jurisdiction that commit or contribute to gross human rights abuses'.[106] This shows that while the voluntary initiatives like the UNGP may assist investors in complying with the relevant obligations and thereby minimise the risk of legal liability, they can be also used as a source of inspiration for domestic legislators, as seen in France with regard to the Due Diligence Law, and in the EU with regard to the Regulation 2017/821.

Despite the progress described above, the reality remains that the mechanisms for implementing obligations against investors are deeply flawed, especially on the international level with only the ICC having some unutilised capacity to scrutinise investor misconduct. It is clear that a more proactive approach is needed in developing an effective enforcement framework. Could international investment law provide an alternative accountability venue? The next section takes a closer look at this question.

IV. Investor Obligations under Investment Law: Limitations, Opportunities and Strategies

It is widely accepted that investment protection law can be applied in the context of armed conflict.[107] This is not surprising as the international customary law on the protection of aliens, which has importantly influenced modern international investment law and continues to be applied by investment tribunals, was often clarified in the jurisprudence of post-conflict arbitrations and mixed claims commissions in the late nineteenth and early twentieth century.[108] While throughout the twentieth century such conflict-related cases became less common due to the popularity of other remedial regimes,[109] the expansion of the modern investment treaty regime in the 1990s has been followed by a number of investment arbitrations emerging from violent conflicts.[110] At the centre of those cases has

[106] ibid 10.

[107] See, for example, C Schreuer, 'The Protection of Investments in Armed Conflicts' and G Hernández, 'The Interaction between Investment Law and the Law of Armed Conflict in the Interpretation of Full Protection and Security Clauses' in F Baetens (ed), *Investment Law Within International Law: Integrationist Perspectives* (Cambridge University Press, 2013); Zrilič (n 1).

[108] For these developments, see Zrilič (n 1) ch 2.

[109] ibid ch 7.

[110] While initially, such cases have been sporadic, the number has increased over the past few years in light of the conflicts in North Africa and Ukraine. See, for example, *Asian Agricultural Products Ltd (AAPL) v Republic of Sri Lanka*, ICSID Case No ARB/87/3, Award (21 June 1990); *American Manufacturing & Trading, Inc (AMT) v Republic of Zaire*, ICSID Case No ARB/93/1, Award (21 February 1997); *Patrick Mitchell v Democratic Republic of Congo*, ICSID Case No ARB/99/7, Award (9 February 2004); *LESI SpA and ASTALDI SpA v People's Democratic Republic of Algeria*, ICSID Case No ARB/05/3, Award (12 November 2008); *Ampal v Arab Republic of Egypt*, ICSID Case No ARB/12/11, Decision on Liability and Heads of Loss (21 February 2017); *Aeroport Belbek LLC and Kolomoisky v Russian Federation*, UNCITRAL, PCA Case No 2015-07 (pending); *JSC CB PrivatBank and Finilon LLC v Russian Federation*, UNCITRAL, PCA Case No 2015-21 (pending). *Strabag SE v Libya*, ICSID Case No ARB(AF)/15/1, Award (29 June 2020); *Cengiz Sanayi v Libya*, ICC Case No 21537/ZF/AYZ, Award (7 November 2018); *Oztas Construction v Libya*, ICC Case No 21603/ZF/AYZ, Award (14 June 2018).

been the determination of state responsibility for mistreating investors or not providing them with adequate protections in conflict situations, rather than the accountability of investors for the consequences of their own misconduct. This is a corollary of the in-built asymmetry of international investment law, one of its most criticised features.[111] In the words of one investment tribunal, an investment treaty 'imposes no obligations on investors, only on contracting States'.[112] In addition, only investors are empowered to pursue procedural remedies under investment law; host states can do so only under very limited conditions,[113] while other actors (such as local communities affected adversely by investment) have no right at present to initiate proceedings against investors.[114]

This does not mean that investor misconduct has never been accounted for in conflict-related cases, or moreover, that investment law does not provide for legal options for arbitral tribunals to inspect investor's diligence amidst armed conflict and factor that into their decisions. While investment treaties do not create an independent avenue in establishing investors' liability for their complicity in conflict-related violations of international law, such investors' contribution could be a legal basis for presenting a counterclaim and thus a finding of financial liability or, more commonly, a justification for depriving investors of procedural and substantive privileges they enjoy under investment treaties.[115]

The major disadvantage of these accountability avenues is obvious: the legal scrutiny of investor misconduct and determination of its consequences will depend on the action within investors' control, namely their decision to initiate arbitration under the relevant investment treaty. In other words, an investor would have to sustain losses as a consequence of a host state's measure which could qualify as a breach of the investment treaty provision (eg, full protection and security, expropriation, fair and equitable standard). Such state measures could, for example, target investors due to their involvement in the conflict and complicity in atrocities committed by the opposite party in the conflict (eg, rebels or terrorists). On the other hand, the room for accounting investor misconduct will be significantly limited if investors are 'partnering' with a host state in commission of conflict-related abuses. In such cases, the investment treaty framework could come into play if the new government (especially in the context of transition) 'penalises'

[111] See, for example, A Arcuri, 'The Great Asymmetry and the Rule of Law in International Investment Arbitration' in L Sachs, L Johnson and J Coleman (eds), *Yearbook on International Investment Law and Policy 2018* (Oxford University Press, 2019).

[112] *Spyridion Roussalis v Romania*, ICSID Case No ARB/06/1, Award (7 December 2011), para 871.

[113] In a few cases, tribunals have confirmed they have jurisdiction to hear counterclaims. See, for example, *Occidental Petroleum Corp v Republic of Ecuador*, ICSID Case No ARB/06/11, Award (5 October 2012); *Antoine Goetz & Consorts v Burundi*, ICSID Case No ARB/01/2, Award (21 June 2012); *Burlington Resources Inc v Republic of Ecuador*, ICSID Case No ARB/08/5, Decision on Ecuador's Counterclaims (7 February 2017); *Perenco Ecuador Ltd v Republic of Ecuador*, ICSID Case No ARB/08/6, Award (27 September 2019).

[114] The prospect of and ways to enable local community representation in investor-state dispute settlement proceedings is given fuller treatment in ch 1 (Ho) and ch 3 (Cotula and Perrone) of this volume.

[115] See section IV.B.

investors for their complicity in abuses committed by the previous regimes or attempts to restore the situation that existed before such abuses had occurred (eg, by redistributing 'pillaged' assets from investors to original owners).[116] Beyond these examples, investors will have no need to avail themselves of investment law protections and thus the potential of investment treaties as an avenue for addressing conflict-related investor misconduct will be diminished.

These limitations notwithstanding, the legal risk of losing investment treaty protections or even incurring financial liability as a result of an investor's actions or omissions in the context of armed conflict, creates an additional incentive for investors to avoid or minimise their contribution to conflicts and related adverse impact on human rights. In addition, investors could be discouraged from bringing a claim against a host state due to the risk that their alleged complicity in gross human rights violations or conflict-related atrocities will be discussed in increasingly transparent investment proceedings, exposed to the wider public and thus result in reputational damage.[117] As often highlighted by the business and human rights lawyers, and illustrated by the ATCA cases,[118] the impact of bringing details of such investor misconduct to the public fora should not be neglected.

The following sections investigate what happens when investment claims emerging from war crimes and similar conflict-related violations reach investment arbitrations. Should tribunals start applying IHL, and would that affect the outcome of a case? This question can be observed from two perspectives: first, when an investor bringing a claim is a victim of a war crime or similar atrocity; and second, when the investor was implicated in such a crime or contributed to violent conflict.

A. Investor as a Victim of War Crimes

Foreign investors and their property, qualifying as civilians and civilian objects, enjoy certain protections under IHL.[119] Such protections are not limitless, however. Investors and their property can be lawfully attacked by parties to the conflict if

[116] Arguably, a similar situation transpired in Egypt in 2011, with national courts ordering the post-revolution Government to renationalise natural resources that were sold to foreign investors by Mubarak administration in conditions of corruption. See J Bonnitcha, 'Investment Treaties and Transition from Authoritarian Rule' (2015) 15 *Journal of World Investment & Trade* 965; J Zrilič, 'International Investment Law in the Context of Jus Post Bellum: Are Investment Treaties Likely to Facilitate or Hinder the Transition to Peace?' (2015) 16 *Journal of World Investment & Trade* 604.

[117] The 'deterring' potential that a risk of reputational damage bears will depend on a number of factors, including the degree of transparency of arbitration, the nature and type of alleged investor misconduct, as well as the tribunal's willingness to account for such misconduct. See below, section IV.B.

[118] See Bernaz (n 76); Kaleck and Saage-Mass, 'Corporate Accountability' (2010) 724.

[119] International Committee of the Red Cross, *Commentary on the Additional Protocols* (Kluwer, 1987) 1909. See also Y Dinstein, *The Conduct of Hostilities under the Law of International Armed Conflict*, 3rd edn (Cambridge University Press, 2016) 142; I Henderson, *The Contemporary Law of Targeting* (Martinus Nijhoff, 2009) 227–29.

they have directly participated in hostilities or their property has been used for military purposes.[120] For example, investors' premises that accommodate the troops of a belligerent party, or investor oil pipelines that carry oil mainly used by the military, can become legitimate military targets.[121] By getting directly involved in armed conflict, investors thus run a risk of sustaining lawful losses that cannot be remedied. Similarly, they cannot expect to be compensated when the losses are incurred during the combat and are due to military necessity.[122]

While investors enjoy protections in IHL as well as IHRL, they will prefer to litigate their conflict-related losses before investment tribunals, since investment treaties grant them direct access to justice and have been traditionally interpreted in investors' favour.[123] When such claims are made, normative intuition would dictate respondent states to invoke IHL to justify their actions that inflicted injuries on investors. In one case emerging from a violent situation that had arguably met the threshold of IHL definition of armed conflict, *AAPL v Sri Lanka*,[124] the host state did not do so. Instead, it defended its actions by relying on the provisions of investment treaties. While this strategic litigation choice may not be ideal for clarifying the relationship between IHL and investment law, it can be explained by two reasons. First, and as mentioned above, states experiencing internal conflicts tend to be apprehensive about invoking IHL and thereby acknowledging that they are in a civil war, as that could have unwanted political and legal repercussions.[125] Second, investment treaties are capable of being applied and interpreted in the same way as IHL. Many investment treaties include defences mirroring IHL language, namely so-called armed conflict clauses and general security exceptions.[126] Even in the absence of such exceptions, the provisions can still be interpreted in line with the IHL and its values. Have they been in that case?

In *AAPL v Sri Lanka*, the state security forces launched the military attack against the investor's prawn farm on the ground that the investor's facility was used by the Tamil terrorists.[127] The attack resulted in the death of more than 20 staff working on the farm, the destruction of the property, as well as the death of the nearby villagers. Although IHL was never invoked or relied on in that case, the investor's claim, the state's defence and the tribunal's reasoning were permeated

[120] See AP I, Arts 51(3) and 52(2).

[121] International Committee of the Red Cross, *Commentary on the Additional Protocols* (Kluwer, 1987) 632, 636, paras 2021–23.

[122] See, for example, Hague Convention IV Respecting the Laws and Customs of War on Land (signed 18 October 1907, entered into force 26 January 1910) 187 Consol T S 227, Art 23(g).

[123] Zrilič (n 1) chs 1 and 7.

[124] *Asian Agricultural Products Ltd (AAPL) v Republic of Sri Lanka.*

[125] Zrilič (n 1) 182; A Cullen, *The Concept of Non-International Armed Conflict in International Humanitarian Law* (Cambridge University Press, 2010); W Abresch, 'A Human Rights Law of International Armed Conflict: The European Court of Human Rights in Chechnya' (2005) 16 *European Journal of International Law* 741, 756.

[126] Zrilič (n 1) chs 4 and 5.

[127] *Asian Agricultural Products Ltd (AAPL) v Republic of Sri Lanka.*

with the IHL terminology. While the investor argued that the state forces committed wanton destruction and murder (war crimes) and thus violated investment treaty standard full protection and security,[128] the state argued that the investor facility was the base of the enemy forces (thus a military target) and tried to justify the losses by relying on the necessity exception in the armed conflict clause of the investment treaty (military necessity).[129] The tribunal found the state responsible for breaching its due diligence duty for not taking precautions in the military attack, which could have prevented death of innocent civilians and destruction of the property.[130]

The award has been criticised by the dissenting arbitrator and in scholarship for interfering with the state's prerogative to protect its security interests and for applying standards not appropriate for armed conflict.[131] Some commentators suggested that applying IHL in that case would have led to a different outcome.[132] As I have argued in greater detail elsewhere,[133] a close reading of the award does not withstand this claim. The tribunal's reasoning is evocative of the IHL obligation to take precautions in military attack, which is measured against a due diligence standard,[134] and has been reaffirmed by regional human rights courts many years later.[135] The tribunal applied investment treaty standards in line with the IHL values and reached the same conclusion it would have had, had it applied IHL directly.

The case demonstrates how investment arbitration could potentially be used to effectively enforce IHL obligations in limited circumstances, namely when victims of war crimes are investors. This could have a spillover beneficial effect on other victims of state war crimes. For example, in the *AAPL* case, the benefits for the local Tamil community were twofold. First, the arbitration established the international responsibility of the state for the atrocities against the villagers. In this way, it filled the enforcement gap that exists in IHL and IHRL.[136] Second, the investor was also said to share its award with the affected victims, thus generating some material benefits for them.[137]

[128] ibid paras 28, 79.

[129] ibid para 82.

[130] ibid para 85(b).

[131] *Asian Agricultural Products Ltd (AAPL) v Republic of Sri Lanka*, Dissenting Opinion of S Asante (15 June 1990), 590; O Mayorga, 'Arbitrating War: Military Necessity as a Defence to the Breach of Investment Treaty Obligations' (Harvard University Program on Humanitarian Policy and Conflict Research Policy Brief, August 2013), available at www.hpcrresearch.org/sites/default/files/publications/081213%20ARBITRATING%20WAR%20%28final%29.pdf; J Gathii, 'War's Legacy in International Investment Law' (2009) 11 *International Community Law Review* 353, 370.

[132] ibid.

[133] Zrilič (n 1) ch 6.

[134] AP I, Art 57(1). See also Dinstein, *The Conduct of Hostilities* (2016) 165; W Boothby, *The Law of Targeting* (Oxford University Press, 2012) 122, 177.

[135] See, for example, *McCann and Others v The United Kingdom* App no 18984/ 91 (ECtHR, 27 September 1995); *Isayeva v Russia* App no 57950/00 (ECtHR, 24 February 2005).

[136] There is no regional human rights court in Asia.

[137] M Trawick, 'Lessons from Kokkadichcholai' (Tamilnation, 21–22 May 1999), available at tamilnation.org/conferences/tamil_eelam/99_canada/trawick.html.

This is not to suggest that investment arbitration provides a systemic solution for inadequate enforcement mechanisms in IHL. There is no guarantee that tribunals will interpret and apply investment treaty standards in line with the IHL, and in fact, in some other cases they have arguably not.[138] Similarly, sharing the awarded damages with those who do not have similar access to justice is not based on any international obligation, but merely on investors' goodwill. Moreover, the enforcement potential of investment arbitration is hampered when investors are complicit in war crimes. If, in such cases, they decide to pursue a claim against a state, investor misconduct can still be accounted for. The next section explains how.

B. Investor as a Contributor to War Crimes

When an investor bringing an arbitration claim is implicated in a war crime or other atrocity (eg, perpetrated it directly through its private security service, or aided and abetted the rebel forces or the previous regime), respondent states should not shy away from invoking the above-discussed IHL obligations and voluntary codes in structuring their defence. This would not only compel tribunals to engage better with IHL sources and clarify obligations investors have amid armed conflict, but could potentially provide for an investor accountability mechanism inasmuch as a state would initiate a counterclaim. To my knowledge, a case emerging from armed conflict where this could have been an option has not yet been arbitrated. Many other cases, however, suggest that tribunals have considered investor misconduct on four different levels of an investment dispute: counterclaims, jurisdiction and admissibility, merits, and quantum.[139]

First, a state could file a counterclaim and base it on the investor's violation of IHL.[140] The *Urbaser* case is particularly instructive because of the tribunal's recognition that investors have certain obligations under international law and the suggestion that that the company's compliance with the CSR standards could potentially serve as a measure for assessing an investor's misconduct.[141] States would thus be encouraged to rely in their pleadings not only on relevant international law obligations, but also on soft law obligations specified in voluntary codes, and draw on civil law and criminal law cases in which standards for corporate complicity, and aiding and abetting liability have been applied.[142]

[138] *Patrick Mitchell v Democratic Republic of Congo*. See also section IV.B.

[139] See, for example, JE Viñuales, 'Investor Diligence in Investor Arbitration: Sources and Arguments' (2017) 32 *ICSID Review – Foreign Investment Law Journal* 346; P Muchlinski, 'Caveat Investor? The Relevance of the Conduct of the Investor under the Fair & Equitable Treatment Standard' (2006) 55 *International & Comparative Law Quarterly* 527.

[140] For more on counterclaims, see ch 8 (Ishikawa) of this volume.

[141] *Urbaser v Argentina*, para 1195. See also K Crow and LL Escobar, 'International Corporate Obligations and the Urbaser Standard: Breaking New Ground?' (2018) 36 *Boston University International Law Journal* 87.

[142] ATCA cases and judgment of international criminal tribunals could provide helpful source for inspiration and analogies. See Crow; ICJ Panel Report (n 67) Vol I, 21–22.

Second, an investor's contribution to conflict-related abuses can be a basis for precluding the tribunal to entertain the claim on jurisdictional and admissibility grounds, provided that such violations of international law were made at the stage of acquiring the investment.[143] So far, this line of defence, based on legality requirements and a clean hands doctrine, was mostly used with respect to investor's involvement in fraud and corruption.[144] In the context of armed conflict, the illegality of investments could be invoked in order to bar jurisdiction when investors acquire assets (eg, land rights, natural resources) without genuine consent from the title-holders. As mentioned above, such acquisitions constitute pillage, which is prohibited under IHL. One could argue that such a defence would be available, even when the rights were obtained through ostensibly legal channels, if such acquisitions were accompanied by violent practices such as the forceful displacement of the local community that the investor actively participated in (eg, through the contracted security agents),[145] or was or should have been aware of.

Third, investors' failure to abide by IHL norms could contextualise state measures and inform the determination of state (non)-liability at the merits stage.[146] Relying on IHL provisions could help the tribunal better contextualise a state's actions against an investor acting in bad faith. The state could thus invoke investor's contribution to the conflict-related atrocity (either deliberate or due to investor's lack of diligence) to justify its intervention and to argue that its measures were reasonable or that the investor's legitimate expectations were not breached.[147] For example, in *Mitchell v Congo*, the Government seized the investor's property and detained its employees for allegedly assisting the rebels in wartime.[148] The tribunal paid little deference to the state's decision-making in volatile times and decided in favour of the investor. Had the IHL rules been applied, notably the standard of military necessity assessed in view of information available to the military commander at the time when the state measures had been taken,[149] the outcome would have likely been different.

[143] See generally, S Schill, 'Illegal Investments' (2012) 11 *The Law and Practice of International Courts and Tribunals* 281; A Newcombe, 'Investor Misconduct: Jurisdiction, Admissibility, or Merits?' in C Brown and K Miles (eds), *Evolution in Investment Treaty Law and Arbitration* (Cambridge University Press, 2011) 187–200.

[144] See, for example, *World Duty Free Company Limited v Republic of Kenya*, ICSID Case No ARB/00/7, Award (4 October 2006), paras 148, 157; *Liman Caspian Oil BV and NCL Dutch Investment BV v Republic of Kazakhstan*, ICSID Case No ARB/07/14, Award (22 June 2010), para 194; *Hesham Talaat M Al-Warraq v Republic of Indonesia*, UNCITRAL, Award (15 December 2014), para 647.

[145] See the decision of the Colombian tribunal in *Resguardo Indigena Embera Katio de Alto Andagueda*, Tribunal Superior, Judgment No 1007 (23 September 2014) (arguing that the investor should have been aware of the violence that prompted forcible displacement of the indigenous community from the concession area) cited and analysed in Tamayo-Alvarez, 'Colombia's Land Restitution Programme' (2018) and Velasquez-Ruiz, 'Foreign Investment-Induced Migration in Colombia' (2013).

[146] See, for example, *Fraport AG Frankfurt Airport Services Worldwide v Republic of Philippines*, ICSID Case No ARB/03/25 Award (16 August 2007), para 354.

[147] Viñuales 361; Zrilič (n 1) 188.

[148] *Patrick Mitchell v Democratic Republic of Congo*. Ultimately, the award was annulled and holds little precedential value.

[149] See, for example, Hague Regulations, Art 23(g); Zrilič (n 1) 42, 128.

Lastly, the host state can argue that the investor misconduct was a contributing factor to its injury and should thus result in reduced quantum of awarded damages.[150] The principle of contributory fault has been invoked when the investor's contribution was in the form of their lack of caution that should be reasonably exercised in conditions of hostilities,[151] or their indirect,[152] or direct contribution to a violent conflict.[153] The latter example transpired in the *Copper Mesa* case where the mining company planned and induced violent acts (by recruiting and using armed men) against the local residents who opposed the investment, which exacerbated the conflict situation.[154] Had those events occurred amid armed conflict, the Government could have argued that the investor violated relevant IHL prohibitions,[155] which could then present a basis for one of the defence options listed above. Beyond IHL, states should also substantiate their arguments by referencing relevant voluntary codes concerning private and military security and CSR initiatives on prevention of conflict in natural resources, which recommend procedures for investors' early and authentic cooperation with the affected communities.[156]

The success of these defence strategies will depend on the wording of applicable investment treaties as well as a tribunal's willingness to account investor misconduct under available rules of international law. Since different interpretations of the above principles have yielded different outcomes in different cases,[157] respondent states should be careful in selecting an arbitrator, who has good knowledge of IHL and other relevant fields of international law and is more likely to engage

[150] UNGA 'Articles on Responsibility of State for Internationally Wrongful Acts' UN GAOR 53rd Session Supp No 10 UN Doc A/RES56/83 (2001), Art 39. For the limitations of the doctrine of contributory fault as a marker of and penalty for investor wrongdoing, see ch 12 (Amado, Kern and Rodriguez) of this volume.

[151] See *Lillie Kling v Mexico* (1930) RIAA Vol IV 575, 585.

[152] In *Bear Creek* case, the respondent (ultimately unsuccessfully) argued that the investor contributed to the social unrest by failing to conduct responsible community outreach: *Bear Creek Mining Corporation v Peru*, ICSID Case No ARB/14/21, Award (30 November 2017), paras 560, 569; Dissenting Opinion, para 39. For a similar case, with a different outcome see *KWP v Kenya*, ICC Award (the tribunal held that the investor's insufficient outreach efforts was at the root of the violent protests and thus investor could not rely on the investment protections), reported in D Charlotin, 'Investigation: Newly-Unearthed ICC Award Analyses whether Local Community Opposition to Project is a Political Risk for which African State had Pledged to Indemnify Investors' (*IA Reporter*, 30 November 2018), available at www.iareporter.com/articles/investigation-newly-unearthed-icc-award-analyses-whether-local-community-opposition-to-project-is-a-political-risk-for-which-african-state-had-pledged-to-indemnify-investors.

[153] *Copper Mesa Mining v Republic of Ecuador*, PCA No 2012-2, Award (15 March 2016), paras 6.99–6.102.

[154] ibid.

[155] See section II.

[156] *Bear Creek Mining Corporation v Peru*, para 258 (see specifically fn 296, which makes a reference to standards like ILO Convention 196, ICMM Good Practice Guide, etc). See section II.A.

[157] For example, in *Copper Mesa*, the tribunal treated the principle of contributory fault and the clean hands doctrine as the same, while in *Bear Creek* case, disagreement existed between arbitrators as to the applicability of the principle of contributory fault. *Copper Mesa v Ecuador*, para 6.84; *Bear Creek v Peru*, Dissenting Opinion, para 39.

with them in the interpretation and application of investment treaty standards.[158] Such a task is made easier if the mandate to do so is spelt out expressly in investment treaties. How this can be achieved is explained in the next section.

C. Changes in Investment Treaties

The previous section outlined how tribunals can account investors' involvement in, or contribution to, the conflict situation when deciding whether and to what extent they are entitled to investment treaty protections. In view of the inconsistent jurisprudence and fragmented nature of investment arbitration, the approach more conducive to certainty would be to introduce requisite changes in the text of investment treaties, reasserting the consequences of the investor misconduct in explicit terms. The rebalancing of investment law would be achieved most optimally if investment treaties stipulated enforceable investor obligations in investment treaties, including the right of victims of investor misconduct to bring claims against them. As commendable as this normative objective is, it still does not seem to be politically viable, notwithstanding the ongoing backlash against the investment treaty regime. Thus, none of the reforms currently being undertaken by the UNCITRAL and the ICSID contemplate such changes.[159]

Regardless, some model investment treaties have started including investor obligations in investment treaties,[160] sometimes expressly referencing conflict situations. For example, closely mirroring Ruggie's framework, Article 15(1) of the 2012 SADC Model BIT states that:

> Investors and their investments have a duty to respect human rights in the workplace and in the community and State in which they are located. Investors and their investments shall not undertake or cause to be undertaken acts that breach such human rights. Investors and their investments *shall not assist* in, or be *complicit* in, the violation of the human rights by others in the Host State, including by public authorities or *during civil strife*.[161]

The explicit reference to complicity of investors, either with private actors (for example, private security companies, rebel groups, etc) or public authorities in violent conflicts, leaves little doubt that such activity can give rise to an investment treaty violation. While the model treaty limits the consequences of such investor contribution only to the merits of the claim and damages,[162] it also provides for

[158] Tribunals can engage with the IHL sources on the basis of the applicable law clauses and rules on treaty interpretation. See *Asian Agricultural Products Ltd (AAPL) v Republic of Sri Lanka*, para 12; Zrilič (n 1) 184.

[159] The ongoing reforms at UNCITRAL and ICSID are mostly focusing on procedural aspects.

[160] See 2015 Indian Model Bilateral Investment Treaty (BIT), Art 12; 2012 SADC Model BIT, Art 15; 2016 Nigeria-Morocco BIT, Arts 18–20.

[161] 2012 SADC Model BIT, Art 15.1 (emphasis added).

[162] ibid Art 17.1.

the obligation of the investor home state to 'ensure that their legal systems … allow for … the bringing of court actions on their merits before domestic courts relating to the civil liability of investors …' stemming from investor misconduct on the territory of the host state.[163]

Other textual changes can concern the loosening of the conditions under which counterclaims can be brought against investors,[164] and references to voluntary initiatives,[165] giving tribunals an explicit mandate to consider the compliance with the CSR standards when applying investment treaties. For example, the 2019 Dutch Model BIT stipulates that the investor's non-compliance with the UNGP will be taken into account when deciding the amount of compensation.[166] Even more specific is the 2017 Colombian Model BIT, which stipulates that the Government's measures in compliance with the Peace Agreements between the Government and armed groups does not constitute a breach of the investment treaty, and that investors must participate in 'successful implementation of the Peace Agreements and the achievement of full reparation to victims affected by the Colombia Armed Conflict'.[167] Following this addendum, the Colombian Land Restitution programme involving the forfeiture of investors' land rights over a property previously taken from the victims of armed conflict, could not give rise to successful investment treaty claims.

Such drafting solutions affirm that investors should exercise heightened due diligence in turbulent times, as they could otherwise run the risk of losing legal protections and potentially sustain considerable financial losses. Future drafting innovations could see strengthening the obligation of home states to create effective avenues for holding investors to account and introducing similar situation-specific provisions like that in the Colombia Model BIT. Furthermore, they could extend the provisions dealing with investor behaviour as to encompass other sector- or issue-specific CSR initiatives, such as guides on prevention of natural resources conflicts and principles addressing conduct of private security service providers, as well as extend the consequences of non-compliance beyond the quantum stage. While such voluntary codes are largely based on human rights framework and thus also applicable outside of armed conflict, adhering to them will help investors avoid IHL violations. Arguably, this could incentivise corporations to plan and implement measures required from them in these instruments, and consequently improve their compliance with international obligations in times of armed conflict.

[163] 2012 SADC Model BIT, Art 17.2. For similar provision see 2015 Indian Model BIT 2015, Art 13.2; 2016 Nigeria-Morocco BIT, Art 20.

[164] 2012 SADC Model BIT, Art 19.2; 2015 Indian Model BIT, Art 14.11(i).

[165] See, for example, Canada–Cameroon BIT (signed 3 March 2014, entry into force 16 December 2016), Art 15(2); Canada–Senegal BIT (signed 27 November 2014, entry into force 5 August 2016), Art 16; 2013 Canada–Panama FTA (signed 14 May 2010, entry into force 1 April 2013), Art 9(17); 2015 Norway Model BIT, Art 31.

[166] 2019 Dutch Model BIT, Art 23.

[167] 2017 Colombia Model BIT, Annex 6.

V. Conclusion

This chapter has set out to review investor responsibilities and obligations amid armed conflict. It has argued that certain IHL rules are directly binding on investors and this is becoming increasingly accepted in doctrine and case law. It has been further observed that the most notable progress in detailing investor responsibilities in conflict-affected zones has occurred in the CSR sphere. While soft law initiatives largely draw on the human rights framework, which transcends the narrow area of IHL application, they aim to help corporations bring their operations in line with international obligations and thus minimise the risk of legal liability.

So far, investor accountability for violation of IHL obligations has been mostly sought in domestic criminal and civil fora, with the CSR initiatives advancing development in this area. On the international level, despite ICL being capable of prosecuting business-related crimes, the enforcement potential is small since the ICC only has jurisdiction over individuals and is generally reluctant to investigate corporate crimes. Given its limited capacity, the ongoing backlash and the general preference to prosecute direct perpetrators of the most serious crimes, the Court is unlikely to become a productive avenue for holding investors to account.

The chapter's main argument was that investment law presents another, underutilised and unexplored mechanism for enforcing IHL obligations. Due to the asymmetric nature of the investment regime, the enforcement potential is stronger when investors are victims of violence than when they participate in it. Despite this limitation, the chapter has outlined strategies, highlighting the potential of investment treaties to financially sanction investors involved in conflict-related violations, by either permitting claims for damages against them, or by depriving them of investment treaty protections. It has been argued that maximising this potential would require changes in investment treaties and the establishment of a clearer connection with the legal frameworks that address the interplay between business and conflict.

11

Mapping Investors' Environmental Commitments and Obligations

PRISCILA PEREIRA DE ANDRADE AND NITISH MONEBHURRUN

I. Introduction

Private investors have an indisputable role to play in the mitigation of business-adverse environmental impacts and in the attainment of sustainable development goals (SDGs).[1] While international investors are considered partners in building a sustainable development, their activities in various fields like agriculture, mining, construction and energy often cause negative environmental impacts in host states. Depending on the way these activities take place, these investments may have negative consequences not only on the environment per se, but may also affect human rights related to a safe, clean and healthy environment.[2]

The increasing list of environmental lawsuits[3] illustrates the need to rebalance the environmental obligations of foreign investors and the protection guaranteed to them vis-à-vis their host states and their respective populations. Domestic law has been the dominant framework for the regulation of investors' environmental

[1] See Rio +20 United Nations Conference on Sustainable Development, 'Outcome of the Conference: The future we want' (22 June 2012) UN Doc A/CONF.216/L.1, para 69.

[2] A number of international human rights treaties indirectly protect the right to safe water. The International Covenant on Economic, Social and Cultural Rights provides for the human right to water under Art 11(1) (right to adequate standard of living) and Art 12(1) (right to health). In the Inter-American Human Rights system, the right to a healthy environment is expressly enshrined in Art 11 of the Protocol of San Salvador. For some examples of cases that addressed human rights see: the *Bhopal* case in India; the *Trafigura* case in Ivory Coast; the *Chisso Corporation* case in Minamata, Japan; the *AngloGold Ashanti silicosis* case in South Africa; the *Rana Plaza* case in Bangladesh; the *Comilog* case in Gabon; the *Nestlé, Archer Daniels Midland and Gargill* case in Ivory Coast; the *Bolivian immigrant workers in the Sweatshops* cases in Argentina; the *Chevron* case in Ecuador; the *Thomson Safaris* case in Tanzania; the *Vedanta Alumina Ltd and the Dongria tribe* case in Orissa, India.

[3] For some examples, see the *Doe Run/Renco* case in Peru, the *Pacific Rim* case in El Salvador, the *Chevron* case in Ecuador, the *Glencore* case in Gambia, the *Shell* case in Nigeria, the *Grupo México chemical spill* case in Mexico. See generally: W Miles and M Lawry-White, 'Arbitral Institutions and the Enforcement of Climate Change Obligations for the Benefit of all Stakeholders: The Role of ICSID' (2019) 34 *ICSID Review – Foreign Investment Law Journal* 1, 7ff.

obligations and plays a key role in establishing rules, institutions and processes for the protection of the environment. For example, each state establishes its own environmental impact assessment requirements and terms of environmental liabilities. However, the establishment of environmental obligations should not be exclusively centred within the sole realm of domestic law considering that such laws may contain some lacunae or fall short of an expected minimum international standard of environmental protection. While the domestic legal system is the main source of environmental obligations for investors, other legal fields should be calibrated in a way to fill any existing gaps. Accordingly, international and transnational laws can also have a significant and innovative regulatory role when it comes to defining investors' substantive environmental obligations and the minimum environmental standards of conduct with which they should comply when investing abroad.[4]

Although normative instruments adopted under public international law regulate the activities of individuals and enterprises to a very limited extent and, in general, depend on domestic legislation for their implementation,[5] there seems to be a positive trend leaning towards incorporating some patterns of behaviour expected from the investors in various public international law fields. For instance, human rights instruments can be used for the purpose of environmental protection. This point was made by the Inter-American Court of Human Rights in its advisory opinion on the environment and human rights.[6] The European Court of Human Rights has likewise engaged in linking human rights to the environment.[7] Similarly, the World Bank has adopted environmental and social safeguard policies in order to mitigate the impacts of its financial activities on the environment and on the host society of the states in which its projects are implemented.[8] The Law of the Sea equally juxtaposes the regulation of the sea, the exploration and

[4] A Nollkaemper, 'Responsibility of Transnational Corporations in International Environmental Law: Three Perspectives' in G Winter (ed), *Multilevel Governance of Global Environmental Change. Perspectives from Science, Sociology and the Law* (Cambridge University Press, 2006).

[5] A number of different opinions have been expressed in the literature on the possibility of directly applying international law to private actors, see for example: W Friedmann, *The Changing Structure of International Law* (Columbia University Press, 1964); JE Alvarez, 'Are Corporations 'Subjects' of International Law' (2011) 9 *Santa Clara Journal of International Law*; M Karavias, *Corporate obligations under international law* (Oxford University Press, 2013).

[6] 'The Environment and Human Rights (State Obligations in Relation to the Environment in the Context of the Protection and Guarantee of the Rights to Life and Personal Integrity: Interpretation and Scope of Articles 4(1) and 5(1) in Relation to Articles 1(1) and 2 of the American Convention on Human Rights', Advisory Opinion OC-23/17, Inter-American Court of Human Rights Series A No 23 (15 November 2017).

[7] In March 2020, the European Court of Human Rights published a 30-page factsheet that listed its case law in environmental matters, thereby affirming the intrinsic link between human rights principles and environmental protection. 'Factsheet – Environment and the European Convention on Human Rights', European Court of Human Rights, available at www.echr.coe.int/Documents/FS_Environment_ENG.pdf.

[8] World Bank, 'OP 4.00 – Piloting the Use of Borrower Systems to Address Environmental and Social Safeguard Issues in Bank-Supported Projects', World Bank Operational Manual (March 2005, updated in April 2013), available at ppfdocuments.azureedge.net/1564.pdf.

exploitation of its resources, and the protection and preservation of the marine environment.[9]

Practice therefore shows that environmental protection can also be tentatively achieved through a network of legal instruments situated outside the sphere of environmental law. Indeed, environmental governance is a multilayered structure. One such layer is composed of legal regulation tools which are structured in various strata amongst which some instruments of international investment law do serve an environmental purpose.

International investment agreements (IIAs) mainly focus on the legal protection of foreign investors and typically do not establish investors' obligations. However, some of these agreements provide for corporate social responsibility (CSR), which often include an environmental dimension. Private foreign investment contracts may also nudge parties towards more responsible investments and more appropriate environmental conduct. The foreign investment contract, as one of the three primary sources of applicable law to international investments,[10] may contribute to 'harden' voluntary environmental commitments.

Thus, investors have the freedom of choice to incorporate voluntary environmental commitments into their business practices. This trend of incorporating minimum environmental standards of behaviour for investors through CSR provisions highlights that transnational corporations and other business enterprises are increasingly required to be more transparent about the impacts of their economic activities abroad.[11] The International Labour Organization (ILO) defines CSR as:

> [A] way in which enterprises give consideration to the impact of their operations on society and affirm their principles and values both in their own internal methods and processes and in their interaction with other actors. CSR is a voluntary, enterprise-driven initiative and refers to activities that are considered to exceed compliance with the law.[12]

As a form of environmental and social voluntary self-regulation by private actors,[13] CSR provisions represent a grid within which business activities can be read as going beyond shareholders' interests towards stakeholders in general.[14] CSR thus regroups a set of expected behaviours from companies in the states

[9] See: United Nations Convention on the Law of the Sea (adopted 10 December 1982, entered into force 16 November 1994) 1833 UNTS 397, Pt XII.

[10] H Mann, 'Foreign Investment in Agriculture: Some Critical Contract Issues' (2012) 17 *Uniform Law Review* 129.

[11] Such a reporting duty is, for instance, provided for by the Free Trade Agreement between Canada and Colombia (27 May 2010). This agreement is accompanied by an Agreement concerning Annual Reports on Human Rights and Free Trade between Canada and Colombia.

[12] ILO, 'Infocus Initiative for Corporate Social Responsibility (CSR)' ILO Subcommittee on Multinational Enterprises, Document No GB.295/MNE/2/1 (2006).

[13] UN Environment Programme, 'Corporate Social Responsibility and Regional Trade and Investment Agreements' (2011) UN Doc DTI/1429/GE, 13.

[14] UNCTAD, 'Social Responsibility', UNCTAD Series on issues in international investment agreements, UNCTAD/ITE/IIT/22 (2001), 3.

where they have their business activities[15] and is often dressed as a series of commitments – which sometimes have a relative effectiveness in practice.[16]

A commitment can be understood as an agreed norm generally found in a non-binding instrument.[17] Despite not being mandatory, it has a normative intent, as it aims at guiding or influencing the behaviour of those actors to which it is addressed.[18] Even if not accompanied by effective enforcement mechanisms, it may be argued that these commitments have been purposefully inserted into IIAs, as well as in other types of international instruments. It belongs to the legal scholarship to decipher the rationale of such arrangements and not let these sit as a 'pathological phenomenon of international normativity',[19] to borrow the expression from Professor Prosper Weil. Therefore, the non-mandatory character of some environmental commitments developed by international instruments does not constitute sufficient ground to rule out the study of the legal purpose they might – even minimally – have.

In this context, guiding instruments elaborated by international organisations, IIAs, arbitral decisions and foreign investment contracts may acquire an innovative and supplementary role in filling the gaps of domestic and international environmental law. As a result, while the environmental conduct of foreign investors in the past was rarely regulated by international investment law[20] and roughly considered in arbitral awards,[21] recent trends show that through cross-referencing to other international treaties and non-legally binding instruments,[22] IIAs and foreign investment contracts, not only environmental issues but also human rights are increasingly considered.[23]

[15] See generally P Muchlinski, 'Corporate Social Responsibility' in P Muchlinski, F Ortino and C Schreuer (eds), *The Oxford Handbook of International Investment Law* (Oxford University Press, 2008) 641; S Tully, *International Corporate Legal Responsibility* (Kluwer, 2012) 21; M Capron and F Quairel-Lanoizelée, *La responsabilité sociale d'entreprise*, 3rd edn (La Découverte, 2016); J Gond and J Igalens, *La responsabilité sociale d'entreprise* (Presses Universitaires de France, 2010).

[16] For a recent critical work, see J Bakan, *The New Corporation: How 'Good Corporations' are Bad for Democracy* (Vintage, 2020).

[17] D Shelton, 'Law, Non-Law and the Problem of Soft-Law' in D Shelton (ed), *Commitment and Compliance: The Role of Non-Binding Norms in the International Legal System* (Oxford University Press, 2003). CC de Oliveira, 'Sustainable Development Partnerships as a Bridge between Commitments and their National Implementation' in M Fitzmaurice, S Maljean-Dubois and S Negri (eds), *Environmental Protection and Sustainable Development from Rio to Rio+20* (Brill, 2014).

[18] D Bodansky, *The Art and Craft of International Environmental Law* (Harvard University Press, 2011) 99.

[19] P Weil, 'Towards Relative Normativity in International Law' (1983) 77 *American Journal of International Law* 413, 416.

[20] K Tienhaara, 'Foreign Investment Contracts in the Oil and Gas Sector: A Survey of Environmental Relevant Clauses' (2011) 11 *Sustainable Development Law and Policy* 15.

[21] S Schacherer, *International Investment Law and Sustainable Development: Key cases from the 2010s* (International Institute for Sustainable Development, 2018).

[22] P Dupuy, 'Unification rather than Fragmentation of International Law? The Case of International Investment Law and Human Rights' in P Dupuy and F Francioni (eds), *Human Rights in International Investment Law and Arbitration* (Oxford University Press, 2009).

[23] B Choudhury, 'Investor Obligations for Human Rights' (2020) ICSID Review – Foreign Investment Law Journal (advance access), available at doi.org/10.1093/icsidreview/siaa002.

Therefore, while at a first glance it may seem difficult to identify investors' substantive environmental obligations, this chapter argues that alternative and typically unattended venues for the establishment of investors' environmental obligations already exist in the realm of international investment law. This chapter aims to map the opportunities and challenges to extract investors' non-binding environmental commitments and mandatory obligations from four sources of law: international environmental law (section II), international investment agreements (section III), international investment arbitration (section IV); and foreign investment contracts (section V).

II. Extracting Investors' Environmental Commitments from International Environmental Law

Apart from some rare international instruments which establish direct obligations or liability for private actors,[24] international environmental law typically follows a state-centric approach and defines substantive obligations only for states. The regulation of responsible business conduct by international environmental law requires the intermediation of domestic law which defines the environmental obligations that investors need to comply with, as well as the liabilities they would eventually incur in cases of non-compliance.[25]

However, while international environmental law has not yet successfully established investors' mandatory environmental obligations (section II.A) it has nonetheless found ways to establish environmental commitments, through non-legally binding instruments, which establish minimum environmental standards and gradually delineate the duty of corporate environmental accountability (section II.B).

A. The Lack of Investors' Mandatory Environmental Obligations in International Environmental Law

Private actors are subjects of international law only to a limited extent.[26] Further, legally binding instruments such as treaties adopted under international

[24] See, for instance, International Convention on Civil Liability for Oil Pollution Damage (CLC) (adopted 29 November 1969, entry into force 30 May 1996), Art 3(1): 'Except as provided in paragraphs 2 and 3 of this Article, the owner of a ship at the time of an incident, or where the incident consists of a series of occurrences at the time of the first such occurrence, shall be liable for any pollution damage caused by oil which has escaped or been discharged from the ship as a result of the incident'.

[25] S Maljean-Dubois, 'The Applicability of International Environmental Law to Private Enterprises' in P Dupuy and J Vinuales (eds), *Harnessing Foreign Investment to Promote Environmental Protection: Incentives and Safeguards* (Cambridge University Press, 2013) 69.

[26] See generally J d'Aspremont (ed), *Participants in the International Legal Systems – Multiple Perspectives on Non-State Actors in International Law* (Routledge, 2011); JE Alvarez, 'Are Corporations 'Subjects' of International Law?' (2011) 9 *Santa Clara Journal of International Law* 1. The arbitral

environmental law typically do not impose binding obligations on investors. However, they may encourage private actors to adopt certain voluntary actions, such as reducing greenhouse gas emissions and the use of ozone-depleting substances, as well as adopting specific production methods to avoid biodiversity loss. Despite the current lack of investors' mandatory environmental obligations in international environmental law, there are a few normative initiatives which deserve to be mentioned as attempts to change this scenario and which seek to define direct international obligations, including environmental obligations for corporations in legally binding instruments.

The debate on the need to include environmental concerns in corporate decision-making has existed since at least the United Nations (UN) Conference on the Human Environment, held in Stockholm in 1972.[27] During the late 1970s and the early 1990s, there was a parallel attempt to directly impose international obligations for corporations at the international level through the UN draft code of conduct for transnational corporations.[28] Even though this instrument was not eventually adopted, the negotiations that took place reflected the need to consider international law when regulating the impact of corporate activities investing abroad. The UN draft code aimed at promoting corporations' contribution to national developmental goals and world economic growth while also controlling any negative impacts of their activities.[29] Under this framework, environmental protection was one of several obligations that transnational corporations would have been called to comply with.

According to the UN draft code, transnational corporations would have an obligation to carry out their activities in accordance with national laws, regulations, administrative practices and policies related to the preservation of the environment of the countries in which they operate and with due regard to relevant international standards.[30] In addition, the UN draft code proposed that corporations would have to take steps to restore the environment in cases of environmental damage. They are also obliged to cooperate with international organisations to

awards in *David Aven v Costa Rica* and *Urbaser v Argentina* have highlighted that 'it can no longer be admitted that investors operating internationally are immune from becoming subjects of international law'. *Urbaser v Argentina*, ICSID Case No ARB/07/26, Award (8 December 2018), para 1195; *David Aven v Costa Rica*, ICSID Case No UNCT/15/3, Award (18 September 2018), para 738. The Tribunal in *David Aven* quoted the *Urbaser* award *ipsis litteris.*

[27] United Nations Commission on Transnational Corporations, 'Report of the Secretary-General on the follow-up to the United Nations Conference on Environment and Development as related to transnational corporations' (1993), UN Doc E/C.10/1993/7.

[28] United Nations Economic and Social Council, 'Report of the Intergovernmental Working Group on a Code of Conduct on its fifteenth, sixteenth and seventeenth sessions' (5 June 1982), UN Doc E/C.10/1982/6.

[29] KP Sauvant, 'The Negotiations of the United Nations Code of Conduct on Transnational Corporations: experiences and lessons learned' (2015) 16 *The Journal of World Investment & Trade* 11; N Bernaz, *Business and Human Rights. History, Law and Policy – Bridging the Accountability Gap* (Routledge, 2017) 164ff.

[30] See paras 41–43 of the United Nations Draft Code of Conduct on Transnational Corporations, UN Doc E/C.10/1982/6 (5 June 1982).

develop international environmental standards. Unfortunately, despite being an important issue, the host states' lack of political will and the opposition of corporations towards binding international obligations led to the closure of the UN draft code negotiations in 1992.[31]

Nevertheless, there are other international initiatives which may succeed in directly regulating the environmental obligations of transnational corporations. Some of them are currently under negotiations, including the 'Legally binding instrument to regulate, in international human rights law, the activities of transnational corporations and other business enterprises and the global pact for the environment'. Relating to the former, the second revised draft of the legally binding instrument (which has been submitted for further intergovernmental negotiations in October 2020) makes at least eight references to the environment. Article 1(2) of the draft instrument defines human rights violation or abuse as:

> [A]ny harm committed by a State or a business enterprise, through acts or omissions in the context of business activities, against any person or group of persons, individually or collectively, including physical or mental injury, emotional suffering, economic loss or substantial impairment of their human rights, including environmental rights.[32]

Correspondingly, the remedies made available for the victims by the draft instrument include 'environmental remediation and ecological restoration'.[33] One of the limits of this legally binding instrument, however, is that it only binds states, and not transnational corporations, in its current version.

In addition, the process of negotiation of the Global Pact for the Environment began in 2018 with the UN General Assembly establishing an Ad Hoc Open-ended Working Group[34] tasked with analysing the gaps in international environmental law as identified by the UN Secretary-General[35] and to propose ways to strengthen its implementation. The main objective of this initiative is to induce uniformity in environmental laws and to address the fragmented and inconsistent implementation of international environmental law. It also aims at codifying and giving a legally binding nature to environmental principles. Based on a report prepared by a group of international environmental lawyers – the *Club des Juristes*[36] – the draft

[31] E Morgera, 'The UN and Corporate Environmental Responsibility: Between International Regulation and Partnerships', (2006) 15 *Review of European Community & International Environmental Law* 93.

[32] UNHRC Open-Ended Intergovernmental Working Group, 'Legally Binding Instrument to Regulate, in International Human Rights Law, the Activities of Transnational Corporations and other Business Enterprises' (Revised Draft, 16 July 2019), available at www.ohchr.org/Documents/HRBodies/HRCouncil/WGTransCorp/OEIGWG_RevisedDraft_LBI.pdf.

[33] Legally binding instrument to regulate, in international human rights law, the activities of transnational corporations and other business enterprises (Revised Draft as of July 2019), Art 4(5)(b).

[34] United Nations General Assembly Resolution, 'Towards a Global Pact for the Environment' (10 May 2018) UN Doc A/RES/72/277.

[35] UN Secretary-General Antonio Guterres issued a report titled, 'Gaps in International Environmental Law and Environment-Related Instruments: Towards a Global Pact for the Environment' (30 November 2018) UN Doc A/73/419.

[36] Environmental Commission of *Le Club des Juristes* (CDJ), 'Increasing the Effectiveness of International Environmental Law: Duties of States, Rights of Individuals' (Le Club des Juristes, 2015).

proposal for a legally binding global pact clearly identifies the need to enhance the role of the private sector for more effective international environmental law making, implementation and monitoring.

If adopted as originally drafted,[37] the Global Pact will have 26 Articles and will establish the 'duty to take care of the environment' according to which 'every person, natural or legal, public or private' will be required to contribute to the conservation, protection and restoration of the integrity of the Earth's ecosystem. However, this initiative has not yet established, at least not for the moment, an enforcement mechanism to ensure compliance by private actors.[38] Therefore, despite being a worthy initiative it does not appear that this treaty would directly establish substantial and enforceable environmental obligations for investors. Nonetheless, it may further encourage non-binding environmental commitments.

Consequently, on the one hand, if treaty-based investors' environmental obligations seem to be lacking in international environmental law, on the other hand, non-legally binding instruments adopted in the context of the CSR movement tend to gradually establish minimum environmental standards which outline non-mandatory environmental commitments for investors.

B. The Gradual Definition of Non-Mandatory Environmental Commitments in Corporate Social Responsibility Instruments

Non-mandatory environmental commitments for private actors have been defined in several international instruments which regulate CSR, such as the UN Global Compact, the Organization for Economic Co-operation and Development (OECD) Guidelines for Multinational Enterprises, the UN Guiding Principles on Business and Human Rights, as well as the International Finance Corporation (IFC) Performance Standards, just to name a few.[39] There is a normative convergence among all these CSR instruments as they seek to translate international obligations established for states into voluntary standards for private actors. To illustrate, the UN Global Compact contains three principles on environmental protection which encourage private actors to: support a precautionary approach when dealing with an environmental challenge (Principle 7); undertake initiatives to promote greater environmental responsibility (Principle 8); and to develop and diffuse environmentally friendly technologies (Principle 9).

[37] Le Club des Juristes, 'Towards a Global Pact for the Environment' (White Paper, 2017).

[38] L Kotzé and D French, 'A Critique of the Global Pact for the Environment: a Stillborn Initiative or the Foundation for *Lex Anthropocenae*?' (2018) 18 *International Environmental Agreements: Politics, Law and Economics* 811.

[39] It should be noted that private standards also encourage environmental protection through corporate social responsibility. See for instance the development under the International Organization for Standardization (ISO), in particular the ISO 26000.

The OECD Guidelines, for their part, provide that:

> [E]nterprises should, within the framework of laws, regulations and administrative practices in the countries in which they operate, and in consideration of relevant international agreements, principles, objectives, and standards, *take due account of the need to protect the environment*, public health and safety, and generally to conduct their activities in a manner contributing to the wider goal of sustainable development[40] (emphasis added).

According to these Guidelines, in order to fulfil the obligation of protecting the environment, enterprises should do three things: establish a system of environmental management to keep track of all data regarding the environmental impacts of their activities; define measurable objectives to improve the environmental performance of their activities; and adopt mechanisms to monitor and verify their environmental impacts.

Moreover, the investment projects financed by the IFC must follow the Performance Standards on environmental and social sustainability, which 'recognize that protecting and conserving biodiversity, maintaining ecosystem services and sustainability managing living natural resources are fundamental to sustainable development'.[41] Overall, these converging CSR international initiatives have contributed to the definition of minimum environmental standards that investors should consider for the implementation of sustainable development in host states.

Based on these CSR instruments, the minimum environmental standards include: the undertaking of environmental impact assessments and establishment of environmental management systems; compliance with the prevention principle, especially when investments may cause transboundary environmental harm; compliance with the precautionary principle; disclosure of environmental information; public involvement through consultations and grievance mechanisms; the sustainable use of natural resources; and the respect for internationally protected environmental sites and species.

The normative convergence of the CSR instruments permits investors and other stakeholders to identify the minimum environmental standards that they should respect and incorporate into their business activities. This process is undoubtedly a step in the right direction towards establishing binding obligations in the future. We do not claim, however, that these minimum environmental standards are the best solution to prevent investors' environmental misconduct. Nevertheless, they represent the current practice and 'state of law', at least in the context of international environmental law. They offer a point of departure from which the conundrum of investors' environmental duties and accountability can be reflected upon and eventually enlightened. Through these environmental

[40] OECD, 'OECD Guidelines for Multinational Enterprises' (OECD Publishing, 2011) 42 (emphasis added).

[41] International Finance Corporation, 'Performance Standard 6 – Biodiversity Conservation and Sustainable Management of Living Natural Resources' (1 January 2012).

minimum standards, corporate environmental accountability has been proposed as a tool to engage private actors in reporting their environmental decisions.[42]

Therefore, investors are expected to take environmental protection into account as a precondition for all their activities. However, notwithstanding the progress made by these international CSR initiatives in establishing direct non-binding environmental commitments for corporations, the effectiveness of their implementation still remains limited and difficult to assess since their adoption and enforcement basically depend on the willingness of companies, to engage in environmental self-regulation.[43] In addition, no compulsory enforcement mechanisms have been adopted by any of these CSR instruments to promote compliance. All these voluntary normative initiatives require a mere reporting for the monitoring of implementation, and in cases of non-compliance, some organisations have at best established quasi-adjudicatory mechanisms to provide adversely affected stakeholders an opportunity for redress.[44]

Besides risks to brand image and reputation, no legal sanctions can be applied. Therefore, it is necessary to search for alternative means to implement the minimum environmental standards proposed by CSR instruments in other sources of law. As mentioned in the introduction, these alternative means may exist beyond international environmental law. The second part of this chapter discusses how international investment law can be one of the sources for (other) investors' environmental commitments.

III. Extracting Investors' Environmental Commitments and Obligations from International Investment Agreements

In international investment law, investors' environmental commitments also stem from the CSR provisions found in IIAs. These CSR provisions may regroup a set of expected behaviours from companies in the states where they undertake their business activities. Generally speaking, CSR is often dressed as a series of commitments which can emanate at three levels: a micro level through self-imposed commitments in codes of conducts; a meso level where the commitments are jointly discussed with the civil society; and a macro level with commitments proposed and recommended by the public authority.[45] This third macro level is the most relevant to international

[42] E Morgera, *Corporate Environmental Accountability in International Law* (Oxford University Press, 2020).

[43] On self-regulation, see R van Gestel, 'Self-regulation and Environmental Law', (2005) 9 *Electronic Journal of Comparative Law* 1. See also more generally: J Braithwaite and P Drahos, *Global Business Regulation* (Cambridge University Press, 2000).

[44] See, for example, the OECD national contact point.

[45] A Kolk, R van Tulder and C Welters, 'International Codes of Conduct and Corporate Social Responsibility: Can Transnational Corporations Regulate Themselves?' (1999) 8 *Transnational Corporations* 143, 152.

investment law given that the CSR provisions are addressed in a top-down fashion. These commitments can be classified in at least four categories: non-mandatory commitments addressed indirectly to investors via the states (section III.A); environmental obligations imposed on states but aimed at investors (section III.B); non-mandatory commitments directed to investors (section III.C); and mandatory obligations addressed to investors (section III.D).

A. Non-Mandatory Environmental Commitments Addressed to States but Aimed at Investors

In one category of IIAs containing CSR provisions, states are expected to encourage investors to comply with CSR standards while conducting business.[46] These provisions contain double non-mandatory commitments: first, they address a mere CSR recommendation to the states' parties; second, if these states decide to give effect to the recommendation, they can only propose the incorporation of CSR standards into the investors' activities. For example, Article 14.17 of the Australia–Indonesia Comprehensive Economic Partnership Agreement's Investment Chapter reads:

> Each Party reaffirms the importance of encouraging enterprises operating within its territory or subject to its jurisdiction to voluntarily incorporate into their internal policies those internationally recognised standards, guidelines and principles of corporate social responsibility that have been endorsed or are supported by that Party.[47]

Similarly, the Comprehensive and Progressive Agreement for Trans-Pacific Partnership (CPTPP)[48] and the United States–Mexico–Canada Agreement (USMCA)[49] specifically refers to the OECD Guidelines for Multinational Enterprises, while the Armenia–European Union Comprehensive and Enhanced

[46] See, for example, the Canada–Senegal Foreign Investment Promotion and Protection Agreement (signed 27 November 2014, entry into force 5 August 2016), Art 16; the Australia–Hong Kong Investment Agreement (signed 26 March 2019, entry into force 17 January 2020), Art 16; the Argentina–Japan BIT (signed 1 December 2018, not yet in force), Art 17; the EU–Japan Economic Partnership Agreement (signed 17 July 2018, entry into force 1 February 2019), Art 16.12(e); the Australia–Peru FTA (signed 12 February 2018, entry into force 11 February 2020), Art 8.17; the Singapore–Sri Lanka FTA (signed 23 January 2018, entry into force 1 May 2018), Art 10.26; the Chile–Hong Kong, China SAR BIT (signed 18 November 2016, entry into force 14 July 2019), Art 16; the Argentina–Qatar BIT (signed 6 November 2016, not yet in force), Art 12; the Nigeria–Singapore BIT (signed 4 November 2016, not yet in force), Art 11; the EU–Georgia Association Agreement (signed 27 June 2014, entry into force 1 July 2017), Art 352; the EU–Moldova Association Agreement (signed 27 June 2014, entry into force 1 July 2016), Art 35; the CARIFORUM–EC EPA (signed 15 October 2008, entry into force 1 January 2009), Art 196 (2)(d).

[47] Investment Chapter of the Australia–Indonesia CEPA (signed 4 March 2019, entry into force 5 July 2020), Art 14.17.

[48] Comprehensive and Progressive Agreement for Trans-Pacific Partnership (CPTPP) (signed 8 March 2018, entry into force 30 December 2018), Art 9.17.

[49] United States, Mexico, Canada Agreement (USMCA) (signed 30 November 2018, entry into force 1 July 2020), Art 14.7. Specific reference to the OECD Guidelines is also found in the Argentina–United Arab Emirates BIT (signed 16 April 2018, not yet in force), Art 17.

Partnership Agreement (CEPA) mentions not only the OECD Guidelines, but also the UN Global Compact, the ILO tripartite declaration of principles concerning multinational enterprises and social policy, and ISO 26000.[50] As seen in the first part of this chapter, most of these CSR instruments refer to minimum environmental standards.

The CSR provisions of other IIAs directly provide for environmental commitments, but again addressed to states, and only indirectly to investors. The USMCA states, for example, that CSR 'standards, guidelines, and principles may address areas such as labour, environment, gender equality, human rights, indigenous and aboriginal peoples' rights, and corruption'.[51] This is also a trend shown by some Canadian investment agreements.[52] Obviously, the main difficulty here rests on the existence of a double good will: that of the state to voluntarily encourage investors operating under its jurisdiction to incorporate the CSR standards and that of the investor to accept and implement the commitments.

B. Environmental Obligations Indirectly Addressed to Investors

One IIA is particularly interesting here: The Economic Partnership Agreement between the CARIFORUM[53] and the UK. While yet to be in force, one provision deserves further reflection. Article 72 of the Agreement on the Behaviour of Investors' states:

> 72. The United Kingdom and the Signatory CARIFORUM States shall cooperate and take, within their own respective territories, such measures as may be necessary, inter alia, through domestic legislation, to ensure that:
>
> [...]
>
> (c) Investors do not manage or operate their investments in a manner that circumvents international environmental or labour obligations arising from agreements to which the United Kingdom and the Signatory CARIFORUM States are parties.[54]

[50] Armenia–EU CEPA (signed 24 November 2017, not yet in force). For a similar CSR provision, see the EU–Moldova Association Agreement (signed 27 June 2014, entry into force 1 July 2016), Art 367 (e).

[51] USMCA (signed 30 November 2018, entry into force 1 July 2020), Art 14.7.

[52] The Canada–Senegal Foreign Investment Promotion and Protection Agreement (signed 27 November 2014, entry into force 5 August 2016), Art 16; Canada–Mali Foreign Investment Promotion and Protection Agreement (signed 28 November 2014, entry into force 8 June 2016), Art 15.3; Foreign Investment Promotion and Protection Agreement (Canada–Guinea) (signed 27 May 2015, entry into force 27 Mach 2017), Art 16; Canada–Mongolia BIT (signed 8 September 2016, entry into force 24 February 2017), Art 14. For another example, see also Ecuador–EFTA FTA (signed 25 June 2018, not yet in force), Art 8.7.

[53] The Caribbean Forum (CARIFORUM) is composed of the following sates: Antigua and Barbuda, The Bahamas, Barbados, Belize, Dominica, Grenada, Guyana, Jamaica, Saint Lucia, Saint Vincent and the Grenadines, Saint Kitts and Nevis, Suriname, Trinidad and Tobago, and the Dominican Republic.

[54] Economic Partnership Agreement between the CARIFORUM states, of the one part, and the United Kingdom of Great Britain and Northern Ireland, of the other part (signed 22 March 2019, not yet in force), Art 72.

Thus, an environmental obligation initially aimed at the state and included in the investment chapter of the agreement might ultimately translate into an obligation binding upon the investor by the means of a domestic legislation. Calling on host states to incorporate environmental norms directed to foreign investors in their domestic laws might be a more effective means to guarantee an environment-friendly investment.

In the *David Aven v Costa Rica* case, a discussion arose on the scope of Article 10.11 of the Free Trade Agreement between Central America, the Dominican Republic and the United States of America (CAFTA-DR)[55] which provides that the state parties can adopt appropriate measures to ensure that foreign investments are respectful of the local environment. Although the article is aimed at the signatory states, the arbitral tribunal ruled that it also contained an 'affirmative' obligation addressed to the investors.[56] To quote the tribunal:

> A logical effect of article 10.11 could be that the measures adopted by the host State for the protection of the environment should be deemed to be compulsory for everybody under the jurisdiction of the State, particularly the foreign investors. Therefore, following said interpretation the investors have the obligation, not only under domestic law but also under Section A of Chapter 10 of the CAFTA-DR agreement to abide and comply with the environmental domestic laws and regulations, including the measures adopted by the host State to protect human, animal, plant life or health. No investor can ignore or breach such measures and its breach is a violation of both domestic and international law, so that the perpetrator cannot be exempt of liability for the damages caused.[57]

Indeed, Article 10.11[58] clearly does not refer to any investors' affirmative, let alone implicit obligation. In fact, the word 'investor' is not even mentioned. At best, the provision recognises a margin of environmental regulatory power to the states. Still, this case bears relevance in showing how international investment law does not always keep pace with reality and with the current forms of environmental misconduct, namely when it comes to the need for more investors' environmental obligations and liabilities, forcing some tribunals to read far and deep between the lines while interpreting the existing texts.

C. Non-Mandatory Environmental Commitments Directly Addressed at Investors

A new generation of IIAs is characterised by CSR provisions directly addressed to investors. The Brazilian investment agreements entitled Agreements on

[55] Signed 5 August 2004, entry into force 1 January 2009.

[56] *David Aven v Costa Rica*, UNCITRAL, Award (18 September 2018), para 735.

[57] ibid para 734. For a critique of this holding, see ch 5 (Ranjan) of this volume.

[58] Art 10.11 of the CAFTA-DR states: 'Nothing in this Chapter shall be construed to prevent a Party from adopting, maintaining, or enforcing any measure otherwise consistent with this Chapter that it considers appropriate to ensure that investment activity in its territory is undertaken in a manner sensitive to environmental concerns.'

Cooperation and Facilitation of Investments (ACFIs) are a noteworthy example.[59] Since 2015, the ACFIs contain a chapter or an annex on CSR describing how investors are expected to conduct their investment activities in an environmentally friendly manner. Consequently, amongst other CSR considerations, investors are encouraged not to seek exemptions which would soften the applicable environmental norms and regulations.[60]

For example, the CSR provision included in Article 12 of the Brazil–India ACFI states:

> Investors and their investments shall strive to achieve the highest possible level of contribution to the sustainable development of the Host State and the local community, through the adoption of a high degree of socially responsible practices, based on the voluntary principles and standards set out in this article and internal policies, such as statements of principle that have been endorsed or are supported by the Parties.

In addition, the same article mentions:

> The investors and their investments shall endeavour to comply with the following voluntary principles and standards for a responsible business conduct and consistent with the laws adopted by the Host State:
>
> a) contribute to the economic, social and environmental progress, aiming at achieving sustainable development;
>
> [...]
>
> e) refrain from seeking or accepting exemptions that are not established in the legal or regulatory framework relating to human rights, environment, health, security, work, tax system, financial incentives, or other issues.[61]

Commitments of this nature, addressed directly to investors, can also be found in the IIA signed between Argentina and Qatar which states that 'Investors operating in the territory of the host contracting party should make efforts to voluntarily incorporate internationally recognised standards of corporate social responsibility into their business policies and practices'.[62] Similar provisions also exist in the India–Belarus IIA,[63] as well as in the India–Kyrgyzstan IIA.[64]

[59] See generally N Monebhurrun, 'Novelty in International Investment Law: The Brazilian Agreement on Cooperation and Facilitation of Investments as a Different International Investment Agreement Model' (2017) 8 *Journal of International Dispute Settlement* 79.

[60] See, for instance, Brazil–Ecuador BIT (signed 25 September 2019, not yet in force), Art 14(2)(a),(e); Brazil–Morocco BIT (signed 13 June 2019, not yet in force), Art 13(2)(a),(e); Brazil–United Arab Emirates BIT (signed 15 March 2019, not yet in force), Art 15(3)(a),(e).

[61] ACFI between Brazil and India (signed 25 January 2020, not yet in force), Art 12.

[62] Argentina–Qatar BIT (signed 6 November 2016, not yet in force), Art 12.

[63] Belarus–ndia BIT (signed 24 September 2018, not yet in force), Art 12: 'Investors and their enterprises operating within the territory of each Party shall endeavour to voluntarily incorporate internationally recognized standards of corporate social responsibility in their practices and internal policies, such as statements of principle that have been endorsed or are supported by the Parties. These principles may address issues such as labour, the environment, human rights, community relations and anticorruption'.

[64] India–Kyrgyzstan BIT (signed 14 June 2019, not yet in force), Art 12.

However, as the drafting language shows, these CSR provisions are not mandatory, let alone enforceable. Furthermore, some agreements expressly exclude CSR provisions from the ambit of arbitration. For example, the agreement signed between Canada and Mongolia for the promotion and protection of investments states in Article 20 that 'an investor of a party may submit to arbitration a claim that the other party has breached an obligation under Section B (substantives obligations), other than an obligation under … article 14 (Corporate Social Responsibility)'.[65]

It can be worthy to note, however, that in terms of prospective enforceability, the ACFI between Brazil and Morocco established a Joint Committee, which can examine issues regarding CSR, as well as environmental commitments whilst supervising the agreement's implementation.[66]

D. Mandatory Environmental Obligations Directly Addressed at Investors

These obligations are twofold: they may be explicitly included in a provision or implicitly addressed at investors, through the concept of sustainable development. In the first category, the bilateral investment agreement between Morocco and Nigeria constitutes a good, maybe an *avant-gardist* example.[67] For instance, it states that investors must undertake an environmental impact assessment (EIA) of their activities before their establishment in the host states. This assessment must be carried out as per the law of the home or of the host state 'whichever is more rigorous in relation to the investment in question'.[68] In conducting the EIA, the investors are expected to apply the precautionary principle.[69] This agreement also imposes the use of an environmental management system such as the ISO 14001[70]

[65] Canada–Mongolia BIT (signed 8 September 2016, entry into force 24 February 2017), Art 20(1.a). Other IIAs which also include a similar provision to exclude CSR provisions from the ambit of arbitration include: Brazil–United Arab Emirates BIT (signed 15 March 2019, not yet in force), Art 25.3; Argentina–United Arab Emirates BIT (signed 16 April 2018, not yet in force), Art 21(1)(b)(i); Belarus–India BIT (signed 24 September 2018, not yet in force), Art 13.1; Foreign Investment Promotion and Protection Agreement (Canada-Guinea) (signed 27 May 2015, entry into force 27 March 2017), Art 21(1); Brazil–Chile BIT (signed 24 November 2015, not yet in force), Annex 1, Art 1(2); Brazil–Colombia BIT (signed 9 October 2015, not yet in force), Art 23(3); Chile–Hong Kong, China SAR Investment Agreement (signed 18 November 2016, entry into force 14 July 2019), Art 21[1](a)(i); Intra-Mercosur Cooperation and Facilitation Investment Protocol (signed 7 April 2017, entry into force 30 July 2019), Art 24(3); and Model Text for the Indian Bilateral Investment Treaty (2015), Art 14.2.

[66] Brazil–Morocco BIT (signed 13 June 2019, not yet in force), Art 14(4)(a).

[67] See generally: O Ejims, 'The 2016 Morocco–Nigeria Bilateral Investment Treaty: More Practical Reality in Providing a Balanced Investment Treaty?' (2019) 34 *ICSID Review – Foreign Investment Law Journal* 62.

[68] Morocco–Nigeria BIT (signed 3 December 2016, not yet in force), Art 14.1.

[69] ibid Art 14.3.

[70] ibid Art 18.1.

and it requires that the investors' activities must not be exercised to the detriment of international environmental agreements to which its home or its host state is a party.[71] Furthermore, in case of an environmental damage caused by the investor in the host state, its civil liability can be engaged before the tribunals of its home state.[72]

Although this IIA is not yet in force, it surely represents, to date, one of the most interesting and advanced agreements which combines investors' protection and investors' obligations.[73] It could serve as a model for other states, more specifically for developing states when signing IIAs between themselves, as well as with more developed countries.

The African continent, therefore, seems to lead the way when it comes to drafting models of investment agreements and investment codes with direct investors' environmental obligations.[74] The Pan African Investment Code, for instance, contains a whole chapter on investors' obligations, with a specific mention of their expected contributions to environmental progress[75] and the non-depletion of natural resources to the detriment of the host state and its population.[76] While non-binding, the Pan African Investment Code serves as a treaty model for the region.[77] It is interesting because it proposes a core set of minimum standards of investors' obligations and commitments which the African states can use while drafting their investment agreements or even their domestic investment law or codes. Even if it may be too early to measure the Pan African Investment Code's impact on treaty drafting in practice, this initiative unveils the ambition to establish what could be called a regional minimum standard of investors' duties. Similarly, under the Southern African Development Community IIA model, where investors have the obligation to conduct prior environmental and social impact assessments,[78] they must keep an environmental management and improvement system[79] and must abide by those international environmental obligations binding upon either the home or the host state, whichever offers the highest protection standard.[80]

In addition, three recent agreements signed by India, namely with Brazil, Belarus and Kyrgyzstan contain a chapter on investors' obligations. One of the

[71] ibid Art 18.4.

[72] ibid Art 20.

[73] For more information see N Zugliani, 'Human Rights in International Investment Law: the 2016 Morocco–Nigeria Bilateral Investment Treaty' (2019) 68 *International and Comparative Law Quarterly* 761.

[74] MM Mbengue, 'Les Obligations des Investisseurs étrangers' in L Dubin et al (eds), *L'Entreprise multinationale et le droit international* (Pédone, 2017) 329.

[75] Draft Pan-African Investment Code (2016), see Ch 4 and Art 22(3).

[76] ibid Art 23. For a general comment, see W Kidane, 'Contemporary International Investment Law and Africa's Dilemmas in the Draft Pan-African Investment Code' (2018) 50 *George Washington International Law Review* 523, 567; MM Mbengue, 'Africa's Voice in the Formation, Shaping and Redesign of International Investment Law' (2019) 34 *ICSID Review – Foreign Investment Law Journal* 455, 471.

[77] Mbengue (ibid) 472.

[78] SADC Model Bilateral Investment Treaty Template (2012), Art 13.

[79] ibid Art 14.

[80] ibid Art 15.3.

agreements' provisions is on non-mandatory CSR commitments whilst the other refers to compliance with local laws. For example, two parts of the provision which can correspondingly be useful are drafted in the following way:

> a) Investors and their investments shall comply with all laws, regulations, administrative guidelines and policies of a Party concerning the establishment, acquisition, management, operation and disposition of investments. …
>
> d) An investor shall provide such information as the Parties may require concerning the investment in question and the corporate history and practices of the investor, for purposes of decision making in relation to that investment or solely for statistical purposes.[81]

As previously discussed, the effectiveness of paragraph (a) will depend upon the availability, content and rigor of the domestic environmental laws. As for paragraph (d), it provides for a duty of corporate transparency which can, by extension, contain a duty of environmental transparency which may be triggered by a request from the host state to the investor.

Moreover, it should also be noted that there are examples of obligations directly addressed to investors in some older IIAs, but these remain rare. For instance, the investment agreement of the Organisation of the Islamic Conference states that investors: 'shall refrain from all acts that may disturb public order or morals or that may be prejudicial to the public interest. He is also to refrain from exercising restrictive practices and from trying to achieve gains through unlawful means'.[82] This provision was used by an arbitral tribunal in *Hesham Talaat M Al-Waraaq v Indonesia*, where an investor from Saudi Arabia was denied protection under the investment agreement for having indulged in acts of corruption and of money laundering. The arbitral tribunal applied the above-mentioned provision to conclude that the investor had 'unclean hands' and could not, for this reason, receive a legal protection from the investment agreement.[83] The provision is rather generic – with words like 'public order', 'morals' or 'public interest' – but imposes a direct obligation on the investor.[84] This could by extension encompass environmental protection. Article 9 of the above-mentioned agreement generally holds that the investor must 'refrain from exercising restrictive practices and from trying to achieve gains through unlawful means'. These 'practices' and 'means' could include domestic environmental laws. The aim here would not be to hold the investor accountable for environmental misconduct during a main investment arbitration but to ensure that such misconduct acts as a bar to its claims against the host state. This statement is not a mere hypothesis: interestingly, in the

[81] India–Kyrgyzstan BIT (signed 14 June 2019, not yet in force), Art 11; Belarus–India BIT (signed 24 September 2018, not yet in force), Art 11; Brazil–India BIT (signed 25 January 2020, not yet in force), Art 11.

[82] Agreement on Promotion, Protection and Guarantee of Investments among Member States of the Organization of the Islamic Conference (signed 5 June 1981, entered into force February 1988), Art 9.

[83] *Hesham Talaat M. Al-Warraq v Indonesia*, UNCITRAL, Award (15 December 2014), paras 645 and 647.

[84] The verb tenses show the mandatory nature of the provision.

Cortec v Kenya case, the investor had failed to obtain an EIA licence as required by the local law and the arbitral tribunal ruled that such conduct 'constituted violations of Kenyan law that, in terms of international law, warrant the proportionate response of a denial of treaty protection under the BIT and the ICSID Convention'.[85]

In the second category, an indirect environmental obligation is set in the very definition of 'investment' via the concept of sustainable development. The IIA between Morocco and the Democratic Republic of Congo specifically states that a given economic activity must contribute to the sustainable development of the host state to be qualified as an investment.[86] A similar provision can be found in the Morocco–Nigeria IIA.[87] The investor must subsequently incorporate this parameter of sustainability in its economic activity to benefit from the agreement's legal protection.[88]

Therefore, the protection of the environment might influence both the investors' decision to invest as well as its subsequent ability to take advantage of the IIA protections. If the investor does not have a direct and explicit obligation to contribute to sustainable development and to protect the environment in a specific provision, there may exist a corresponding implied duty incumbent upon it. One of the problems which can arise in this case is the lack of a clear (legal) methodology to measure a contribution to sustainable development. Would a prospective investor which plans prima facie to make substantial economic and social contributions, but which cannot sustain evidence of a similar environmental commitment still be contributing to the host state's sustainable development?

Such challenges might ultimately have to be settled by arbitral tribunals whose technical competences in environmental and sustainable development problems are questionable.[89] In any case, for the moment, these sustainable development provisions currently feature in only a small number of IIAs. That said, they do represent a drafting technique which may pressure investors to duly consider environmental concerns in their investment activities.

Mapping investors' environmental commitments and obligations in IIAs reveals at least one main difficulty. As most of these are non-mandatory commitments, their very *raison d'être* – their legal purpose within IIAs – can be questioned, thus bringing up an old subject regarding the purpose of soft norms and their alleged ineffectiveness. In the next part of this chapter, we propose a discussion on the

[85] *Cortec Mining Kenya Limited, Cortec (Pty) Limited and Stirling Capital Limited v Republic of Kenya*, para 365.

[86] Congo–Morocco BIT (signed 30 April 2018, not yet in force), Art 1.1.

[87] Morocco–Nigeria BIT (signed 3 December 2016, not yet in force), Art 1.

[88] See also: Economic Partnership Agreement between the CARIFORUM States, of the one part, and the United Kingdom of Great Britain and Northern Ireland, of the other part (signed 22 March 2019, not yet in force), Arts 3, 183. These Articles provide that the whole agreement must be implemented towards the realisation of sustainable development.

[89] N Monebhurrun, 'The (Mis)use of Development in International Investment Law: Understanding the Jurist's Limits to Work with Development Issues' (2017) 10 *Law and Development Review* 451.

practical purposes of these investors' environmental commitments by analysing how they may be interpreted to further understand if there is an alternative way to draw their normative effects from investment agreements.

IV. Extracting the Legal Purpose of Investors' Environmental Commitments and Obligations from the International Arbitral Practice

International investment tribunals may find investors accountable for environmental misconduct, but they may also find that such misconduct acts as a bar to guaranteeing the protection they typically claim against the host state. In both cases, the environmental argument can serve as a warning to non-diligent foreign investors and encourage more environmentally friendly investments. Therefore, this section defines investors' environmental obligations in counterclaim cases (section IV.A) before discussing how environmental commitments, even though non-binding, can act as a tool for interpreting provisions on investment protection in IIAs (section IV.B).

A. Defining Investors' Environmental Obligations in Counterclaim Cases

Counterclaims, which receive fuller treatment by Tomoko Ishikawa in chapter eight of this volume, have enabled states to directly engage investors' liability at the international level. A counterclaim procedure is characterised by an inversion of the claimant's and of the defendant's role, in the same case. The original defendant may thus become the claimant regarding other legal questions.[90] As described by case law, the counterclaim is 'a separate claim, autonomous with respect to the respondent's statement of defence, although it is usual that materially it is a part of that statement'.[91] In the case of the International Centre for Settlement of Investment Disputes (ICSID) arbitration, Article 46 of the Washington Convention states that the

> Tribunal shall, if requested by a party, determine any incidental or additional claims or counterclaims arising directly out of the subject-matter of the dispute provided that they are within the scope of the consent of the parties and are otherwise within the jurisdiction of the Centre.

[90] HE Veenstra-Kjos, 'Counterclaims by Host States in Investment Treaty Arbitration', (2007) 4 *Transnational Dispute Management* 1, 5; N Monebhurrun, 'La Demande Reconventionnelle comme Procédure Permettant d'Engager la Responsabilité Environnementale des Investisseurs: l'Exemple du Droit International des Investissements' (2020) 45 *Revue Juridique de l'Environnement* 526.

[91] *David Aven v Costa Rica* (ICSID, 18 September 2018), para 745.

In the *Perenco v Ecuador* environmental counterclaim case, the arbitral tribunal had underpinned as a principle

> that if a legal relationship between an investor and the State permits the filing of a claim by the State for environmental damage caused by the investor's activities and such a claim is substantiated, the State is entitled to full reparation in accordance with the requirements of the applicable law.[92]

In the *Burlington v Ecuador* counterclaim case,[93] the arbitral tribunal condemned the investor by enforcing the host state's environmental constitutional norms. After having reviewed the environmental norms entrenched in the Ecuadorian Constitution, the arbitral tribunal concluded that 'environmental protection is one of the 2008 Constitution's fundamental pillars and that environmental stewardship has taken on a new dimension in Ecuador's society, where nature (or Pacha Mama) is itself bearer of constitutional rights'.[94] Moreover, Article 396, third paragraph, of the same Constitution mentions that the environmental stewardship applies to all public or private actors[95] – which therefore binds the foreign investor. In this case, the arbitral tribunal not only considered that the counterclaim was admissible, but also condemned the private investor after having recognised its liability.[96]

The *Burlington* counterclaim was successful because of the existence of a clear environmental obligation incumbent upon the investor. That obligation was, however, not entrenched in an international agreement but in the host state's domestic law. It may indeed be easier for states to set mandatory environmental obligations as well as secondary rules of responsibility[97] for investors – and not mere commitments or recommendations – through their local laws. Some states have already adopted this practice.[98] The IIAs could accordingly underscore the investors' general obligation to abide by the local laws while establishing and conducting their activities.

Some arbitral tribunals have upheld that any investment should be made legally and in good faith, even when these requirements are not expressly written in an IIA.[99] In the *Cortec v Kenya* case, the arbitral tribunal held that the 'text and

[92] *Perenco v Ecuador*, ICSID Case No ARB/08/6, Interim Decision on Environmental Counterclaim (11 August 2015), para 34. For a comment, see J Harrison, 'Environmental Counterclaims in Investor-State Arbitration' (2016) 17 *Journal of World Investment & Trade* 479.

[93] *Burlington v Ecuador*, ICSID Case No ARB/08/5, Counterclaims (7 February 2017).

[94] ibid para 216.

[95] Constitution of Ecuador (2008), Art 396, para 3.

[96] *Burlington v Ecuador*.

[97] L Dubin, 'RSE et Droits des Investissements, les Prémisses d'une Rencontre' (2018) 122 *Revue Générale de Droit International Public* 867, 888.

[98] For a small sample, see the investment laws/codes of: Angola (Art 18e, h), Algeria (Art 3), Belarus (Art 5), Burkina Faso (Art 7, Art 20), Cuba (Art 54, Art 56.2), Egypt (Art 2.2, Art 15.1), Ethiopia (Art 38), Guinea (Art 21), Indonesia (Art 16d, Art 17), Iraq (Art 14.5), Kosovo (Art 13.2), Lao (Art 44c, Art 74), Mali (Art 27, Art 28), Mauritania (Art 28), Senegal (Art 14, Art 25), South Sudan (Sch C), Tunisia (Art 10).

[99] See for instance: *Saluka v Czech Republic*, UNCITRAL, Partial Award (17 March 2006), para 204; *SAUR International SA v Argentina*, ICSID Case No 04/4, Decision on Jurisdiction and Liability (6 June 2012), para 308; *Gustav F W Hamester GmbH & Co KG v Ghana*, ICSID Case No ARB/07/24, Award (18 June 2010), paras 123–24; *Mamidoil Jetoil Greek Petroleum Products Société SA v Albania*,

purpose of the Bilateral Investment Treaty (BIT) and the ICSID Convention are not consistent with holding host governments financially responsible for investments created in defiance of their laws fundamentally protecting public interests such as the environment'.[100] Any state can indeed have legitimate expectations that its domestic environmental laws will be duly respected by foreign investors as the possibility of picking and choosing the domestic laws with which investors wish to be subject to does not exist.

This reasoning was taken further by the arbitral tribunal in the *Inceysa v El Salvador* case, which ruled that disrespecting domestic laws would fall short of what it called a principle of international public policy. In the tribunal's words, 'It is not possible to recognize the existence of rights arising from illegal acts, because it would violate the respect for the law which, as already indicated, is a principle of international public policy'.[101] In practice, a report elaborated by the OECD indicates that 68 per cent of the codes of conduct of the studied companies include a commitment to comply with the domestic laws.[102] As a principle, investors themselves do not plan their activities in a way to confront the national laws. However, one arbitral tribunal, in the *Bear Creek v Peru* case, did conclude that given that the applicable IIA (the investment chapter of the Peru–Canada Free Trade Agreement) did not contain a specific requirement for the investment to be constituted as per the local laws, the investor's claim consequently could not be barred on jurisdiction nor on admissibility,[103] even though the investment had been made in breach of the domestic laws. For this reason, a prudential measure would consist of systematically including an obligation of respecting domestic laws in IIAs, leaving these local laws the task of establishing environmental obligations and liability. This connection between national and international law would ultimately benefit the host state in cases of counterclaims.

Through this method, however, one cannot always guarantee a high standard of environmental protection. Many states do agree that there exists a minimum standard of treatment of foreign investors[104] but it is still unclear whether investors

ICSID Case No ARB/11/24, Award (30 March 2015), para 359; *Phoenix Action, Ltd v Czech Republic*, ICSID Case No ARB/06/5, Award (15 April 2009), para 106. See generally H Ascensio, 'La légalité de l'investissement devant l'arbitre international: à la recherche d'un point d'équilibre' (2017) 14 *Brazilian Journal of International Law* 72; Mbengue, 'Les obligations des investisseurs étrangers' (2017).

[100] *Cortec Mining Kenya Limited, Cortec (Pty) Limited and Stirling Capital Limited v Republic of Kenya*, para 333(a).

[101] *Inceysa Vallisoletaba v El Salvador*, ICSID Case No ARB/03/26, Award (2 August 2006), para 249. In a similar sense see *David Minnotte and Robert Lewis v Poland*, ICSID Case No ARB(AF)/10/1, Award (16 May 2014), para 131.

[102] OECD (Working Party of the Trade Committee), 'Codes of Conduct. An Expanded Review of their Content' (9 June 2000) TD/TC/WP (99)56/FINAL, 11.

[103] *Bear Creek Mining Corporation v Republic of Peru*, ICSID Case No ARB14/21 para 319 (for jurisdiction), para 335 (for admissibility).

[104] See generally CL Lim, J Ho and M Paparinskis, *International Investment Law and Arbitration. Commentary, Awards and other Materials* (Cambridge University Press, 2018) 259. For a more nuanced position, see M Sornarajah, *The International Law on Foreign Investment* (Cambridge University Press, 2017) 405.

must correspondingly follow a minimum standard of commitments or obligations, for environmental protection. It is therefore challenging to know if the local environmental laws fall short of an expected international minimum environmental standard, as set in CSR instruments. Still, when they exist, these domestic environmental laws may have some relevant impact in enabling, if need be, a successful counterclaim. A counterclaim can also be convincingly contended when the IIAs provide for investors' (environmental) obligations, like the Morocco–Nigeria IIA. Yet, when it comes to the other environmental commitments referred to in section II of this chapter, their effectiveness will be limited, even though they may have an interpretative function.

B. The Interpretative Function of Environmental Commitments

Environmental commitments may serve a technical purpose as they can act as a yardstick to interpret the level of protection effectively due to foreign investors in international arbitrations. When states juxtapose investment protection provisions and CSR commitments in one same agreement, they intend to give at least a minimum legal purpose to this combination. These provisions enable arbitral tribunals to interpret how 'clean the investors' hands are'[105] when examining their claims against their host states. According to the clean hands doctrine, 'a party cannot seek equitable relief or assert an equitable defence if that party has violated an equitable principle'.[106] A claimant's illegal or fraudulent act or conduct does act as a parameter of his/her access to justice.[107]

In international investment law, some tribunals have declined jurisdiction because of a fraudulent behaviour of the investor[108] whilst others have barred the claims as inadmissible.[109] However, these cases did not concern environmental questions per se and the investors' conduct was deemed illegal on the basis of a binding national or international norm[110] and not on non-mandatory commitments.

[105] R Kreindler, 'Corruption in International Investment Arbitration: Jurisdiction and the Unclean Hands Doctrine' in K Hobér, A Magnusson and M Öhrstörm (eds), *Between East and West: Essay in the Honour of Elf Franke* (Juris, 2010) 309, 317–18; P Dumberry and G Dumas-Aubin, 'How to Impose Human Rights Obligations on Corporations Under Investment Treaties?' (2012) 4 *Yearbook of International Investment Law and Policy* 568, 589–91.

[106] *Black's Law Dictionary* West, 9th edn (2009) 286. See also J Salmon, 'Des mains propres comme conditions de recevabilité des réclamations internationales' (1964) 10 *Annuaire Français de Droit International* 225, 232.

[107] Sornarajah, *Foreign Investment* (2017) 182–83.

[108] *Inceysa Vallisoletaba v El Salvador*, paras 247–52.

[109] *Hesham Talaat M. Al-Warraq v Indonesia*, paras 647–48. In a similar sense: *Plama Consortium Ltd v Bulgaria*, ICSID Case No ARB/03/24, Award (27 August 2008), para 143. See generally J Viñuales, 'Invest Diligence in Investment Arbitration: Sources and Arguments' (2017) 32 *ICSID Review – Foreign Investment Law Journal* 355ff.

[110] In the *Hesham Talaat* case, for instance, the investor violated Art 9 of the Agreement on Promotion, Protection and Guarantee of Investments among Member States of the Organisation of the Islamic

The investors' environmental commitments provided in IIAs can, nonetheless, be a means to assess such behaviour. These commitments express what the signatory states consider as minimally important in terms of environmental conduct. Therefore, the investment agreements can be interpreted as implying that falling short of this minimum level is a prospective bar to seeking treaty protection. This argument can be placed at three levels. Firstly, at the jurisdictional level if the environmental commitments were disregarded when the investment was made. Secondly, at the admissibility level, to claim that the investment agreement only applies to environmentally committed investors. Thirdly, at the compensation level, to contend that even though the arbitral tribunal decided to grant protection to the investor, the compensation should be calculated in consideration of its environmental misbehaviour.[111]

This type of interpretation contributes to give a practical meaning to the investors' environmental commitments which would otherwise be tantamount to window dressing. This approach is certainly not revolutionary in that it will not trigger a major contribution in terms of environmental protection. However, it is still an indirect, albeit minor, step in screening and regulating environmentally friendly investors who might be willing to demonstrate more diligence, once acknowledging that this can determine their level of protection by the investment agreement.

Interestingly, the Southern African Development Community Investment Agreement Model has a specific provision whereby the infringement of investors' obligations and the dispute settlement procedure are paired together. It states that if the investor fails 'to comply with its obligations under this Agreement, the tribunal hearing such a dispute shall consider whether this breach, if proven, is materially relevant to the issues before it, and if so, what mitigating or off-setting effects this may have on the merits of a claim or on any damages awarded in the event of such award'.[112] This reasoning is also in line with an older arbitral practice which has acknowledged that IIAs are not supposed to act as insurance policies covering international investments in absolute terms.[113]

Besides these interpretative functions of environmental commitments, some international investment tribunals have also recognised the role of contracts as

Conference which states: 'The investor shall be bound by the laws and regulations in force in the host state and shall refrain from all acts that may disturb public order or morals or that may be prejudicial to the public interest. He is also to refrain from exercising restrictive practices and from trying to achieve gains through unlawful means'.

[111] By analogy, in this partial dissenting opinion in the *Bear Creek* case, arbitrator Philippe Sands considered that the investor's project had failed because of its inability to obtain a social licence to operate and to gain the local Aymara indigenous community's trust and support. This, according to the arbitrator, justified a reduction in the value of damages due to the investor. See *Bear Creek Mining Corporation v Republic of Peru*, ICSID Case No ARB14/21, Partial Dissenting Opinion (Philippe Sands) (30 November 2017), para 39.

[112] SADC Model Bilateral Investment Treaty Template (2012), Art 19.1.

[113] *Emilio Agustín Maffezini v Spain*, ICSID Case No ARB/97/7, Award (13 November 2000), para 64; *MTD Equity Sdn. Bhd. & MTD Chile SA v Chile*, ICSID Case No ARB/01/7, Award (25 May 2004), para 178.

a source of investors' environmental obligations. For instance, as demonstrated in some arbitral decisions regarding environmental counterclaims, the investor's environmental obligations may be found in investment contracts (*Burlington v Ecuador*).[114] Moreover, in the *Urbaser v Argentina* case, while recognising that the investor's obligation to ensure the population's access to drinking water could not be based on international law, the tribunal observed that this type of obligation could, however, be applicable to a particular investor via a contract or similar legal relationship of a civil or commercial law nature.[115] Therefore, foreign investment contracts should also be considered when mapping the sources of the investors' environmental obligations.

V. Extracting Investors' Environmental Obligations from Foreign Investment Contracts

As mentioned in section I of this chapter, international instruments that address CSR (such as the OECD guidelines for multinational enterprises, the UN Global Compact, the UN Guiding Principles on Business and Human Rights, the Principles for Responsible Contracts, and the IFC Performance Standards) all recognise and encourage the use of contracts for environmental protection.[116] The scope of environmental contractual obligations can be very different from one contract to the other and environmental clauses may be introduced through a variety of strategies and contractual arrangements. The inclusion of environmental clauses in contractual investment arrangements can be explicit or implicit with reference to other normative instruments such as codes of conduct. In other words, both express and implied contractual environmental obligations may be adopted. Very often, environmental clauses reiterate domestic legislations, regulations, standards and certification requirements.[117] These environmental clauses can also be drafted in a way that leads investors beyond what is imposed on them by law, in a manner that maximises the investment's contribution to sustainable development.[118]

[114] *Burlington v Ecuador*, para 93.

[115] *Urbaser v Argentina*, paras 1208–10.

[116] See, for example, OECD Guidelines for Multinational Enterprises (2011), Ch VI (Environment). Reference to use of contract on para 21 of the Commentary on General Policies. See also the efforts made by the ISO, specially ISO 26000:2010, 'Guidance on social responsibility', para 6.6.6.2, which mentions that 'to promote social responsibility in its value chain, an organization should: integrate ethical, social, environmental and gender equality criteria, and health and safety, in its purchasing, distribution and contracting'.

[117] N Affolder, 'Beyond Law as Tools: Foreign Investment Projects and the Contractualisation of Environmental Protection', in P Dupuy and J Viñuales (eds), *Harnessing Foreign Investment to Promote Environmental Protection: Incentives and Safeguards* (Cambridge University Press, 2013).

[118] L Cotula, 'Rethinking Investor-State Contracts Through a Sustainable Development Lens' in E Blanco and J Razzaque (eds), *Natural Resources and the Green Economy: Redefining the Challenges for People, States and Corporations* (Brill, 2012) 13.

Based on some samples of environmental clauses adopted under foreign investment contracts in the field of agriculture, forestry and other land-based investment contracts which are made available online, through websites such as the openland.org and resourcecontracts.org, it is possible to identify some typical categories of contractual environmental obligations. It is worth noting that the content of the environmental obligations varies throughout the lifetime of the contract (before, during and after the investment takes place) and may create cumulative contractual obligations for the investors.

Contractual environmental clauses may mention the findings of EIAs and management plans and may clarify and quantify the environmental issues that need to be monitored and reviewed during the investment project. Contractual terms may emphasise, for instance, that the investors' right to water is subject to the requirement that its activities does 'not interfere with the rights of third parties or the government and does not deprive water from any tribes, villages, towns, houses or watering places for animals'.[119] Open clauses that mention that 'there will be no restriction on the volume of water extracted from rivers, other water courses, wells and boreholes'[120] should not be used when seeking environmentally friendly investments. Therefore, water access can be addressed as an ancillary right of the investor subject to review during the lifetime of the contract, according to present and future environmental and water laws and regulations that the host state may decide to adopt.

While contractual references to the need to protect biodiversity do not yet seem to be a common practice in foreign investment contracts (at least not in the contracts analysed and available on the Open Land Contract database), it is possible to identify that some contracts address this issue by recognising that investors are 'obliged to not make any harm to any fragile ecological system defined by Ministry of Environment and not to hunt wild animals'.[121] Foreign investment contracts may also be the source of investors' obligations regarding climate change.[122]

In cases of environmental non-performance by the investors, these contractual provisions may be drafted in different levels, according to the extent of non-compliance. Usually, the termination of the contract is considered the last solution in cases of non-performance. Therefore, clauses on environmental non-performance should reflect different stages of non-performance to progressively permit the cure

[119] As it was done in the Concession Agreement between Golden Veroleum Liberia and the Government of the Republic of Liberia (signed 16 August 2010), Art 4.4(e).

[120] 'Water and Utilities' of the Concession Agreement between Sierra Leone and Sierra Akker Agricultural Company Limited (signed 2 December 2013), Appendix topic 9, available at openlandcontracts.org/contract/ocds-591adf-6185563903/download/pdf.

[121] Concession Agreement between Cambodia and HLH Agriculture (Cambodia) Co Ltd (signed 27 March 2009).

[122] Many authors have been recognising the role contracts play in the regulation of climate change. See, for example, B Fauvarque-Cosson, 'L'enterprise, le Droit des Contrats et la Lutte Contre le Changement Climatique' (2016) *Recueil Dalloz* 324; K Mitkidis 'Using Private Contracts for Climate Change Mitigation' (2014) 2 *Groningen Journal of International Law* 54; M Hautereau-Boutonnet, 'Le Risque Climatique en Droit des Contrats' (2016) 2 *Revue des Contrats* 312.

of environmental failure instead of immediately ending the contract. The right to terminate the contract due to a breach of one of the obligations provided in the environmental clauses requires some circumstances to be fulfilled in order to certify that the non-performance is essential and substantially affects the legitimate expectations of one of the parties. The proof of fault is generally not essential for a contractor to be able to demand the termination of the contract in the event of non-performance, although the damage needs to be proven. Eventually, if environmental damage occurs, the investor may be held liable based on the contract. However, the type of environmental liability will depend on the law selected by the contracting parties to govern the contract. Therefore, contractors should consider including a clause that stipulates explicitly 'who is liable for what and to whom'.[123]

VI. Conclusion

When discussing the relationship between international investment and environmental protection, some commentators have noted that 'it is concerning that the majority of these agreements do not refer to sustainable development, promotion of public policy, or environmental protection'.[124] To this we could add, as demonstrated in this chapter, that when IIAs do provide for environmental protection, this is normally done in a non-mandatory way, thereby becoming grist to the mill of the common belief that the social and environmental externalities generated by investment activities cannot be effectively regulated[125] or that regulation, in such cases, only acts as a friendly pressure.

However, even if investors' environmental obligations mainly remain established on a voluntary basis, corporations have been increasingly encouraged to adapt their investments accordingly to attain the SDGs. The motivation for complying with environmental obligations derives mainly from reputational risks of consumer protests, negative media publicity, home or host state environmental regulations, and eventual liability in case of environmental damages.

Overall, it is in the (rational) investors' own interest to comply with environmental commitments. Investors cannot be expected to be fully and permanently covered irrespective of their behaviour vis-à-vis the host state. Just like companies' codes of conduct, these environmental and, more generally, CSR commitments might be non-binding, but they are now part of the game and of its rules.[126] Some

[123] K Tienhaara, 'Foreign Investment Contracts in the Oil and Gas Sector: A Survey of Environmental Relevant Clauses' (2011) 11 *Sustainable Development Law and Policy* 15.

[124] K Miles, *The Origins of International Investment Law. Empire, Environment and the Safeguarding of Capital* (Cambridge University Press, 2015) 131.

[125] JA Zerk, *Multinational Companies and Corporate Social Responsibility. Limitations and Opportunities in International Law* (Cambridge University Press, 2006) 1; J Bakan, *The Corporation. The Pathological Pursuit of Profit and Power* (Free Press, 2004) 79–80.

[126] A Kolk and R van Tulder, 'Setting New Global Rules? TNCs and Codes of Conduct' (2005) 14 *Transnational Corporations* 1, 10, 19.

studies show that even if soft law may suffer from a low compliance, it does have a high influence on behaviour.[127] This means that commitments, as an inherent part of soft law, do have a normative value.[128] As put by Richard Baxter, 'there are norms of various degrees of cogency, persuasiveness, and consensus which are incorporated in agreements between States but do not create enforceable rights and duties'.[129] The jurist should learn how to play in this field where soft and hard norms interact 'with the common purpose of regulating behaviour within a rule of law framework'.[130]

This influence of non-mandatory commitments, especially CSR ones, on corporate behaviour may be explained by various factors, such as market access,[131] social pressure and social acceptability,[132] reputation[133] or even competitiveness.[134] It is on this basis that in this chapter we have argued that environmental commitments have a prospective behavioural and educative purpose. They provide a learning opportunity[135] to investors whose environmental diligence might change. Of course, to this argument one could oppose the fact that such CSR soft law instruments and environmental commitments have existed for some time now,[136] and that the inclusion of CSR provisions in IIA and environmental clauses in foreign investment contracts does not bring novelty. However, even if such commitments already exist elsewhere, their inclusion – as directly addressed to investors – is a new trend that deserves new interpretation. As mentioned earlier, equally balancing investment protection standards and environmental commitments enables the latter to pressure the former and this might help accelerate or force the learning process.

[127] DG Victor, 'The Use and Effectiveness of Nonbinding Instruments in the Management of Complex International Environmental Problems' (1997) 91 *American Society of International Law Proceedings* 241.

[128] J Pauwelyn, 'Is It International Law or Not, and Does It Even Matter?' in J Pauwelyn, R Wessel and J Wouters (eds), *Informal International Lawmaking* (Oxford University Press, 2012) 130.

[129] RR Baxter, 'International Law in Her Infinite Variety' (1980) 29 *International and Comparative Law Quarterly* 549.

[130] D Shelton, 'Law, Non-Law and the Problem of Soft-Law' in D Shelton (ed), *Commitment and Compliance. The Role of Non-Binding Norms in the International Legal System* (Oxford University Press, 2003) 10.

[131] D Vogel 'Private Global Business Regulation' (2008) 11 *American Review of Political Science* 261, 271.

[132] Kolk, van Tulder and Welters, 'International Codes of Conduct and Corporate Social Responsibility' (1999) 150.

[133] RW Grant and RO Keohane, 'Accountability and Abuses in World Politics' (2005) 99 *American Political Science Review* 29, 35.

[134] JA Zerk, *Multinational Companies and Corporate Social Responsibility* (2006) 24.

[135] The 'learning' and corporate education is not new. It was addressed by John Ruggie when discussing the United Nations Global Compact in J Ruggie, 'The Global Compact as a Learning Network' (2001) 7 *Global Governance* 371. See also N Monebhurrun, 'Mapping the Duties of Private Companies in International Investment Law' (2017) 14 *Brazilian Journal of International Law* 50, 57.

[136] J Ho, 'The Creation of Elusive Investor Responsibility' (2019) 113 *American Journal of International Law Unbound* 10.

Moreover, environmental commitments aim at changing a whole business culture and mindset, something which is done step-by-step and over a long period of time. It should therefore be considered that CSR does not operate against but alongside investors' interest. For this reason, their abidance to CSR commitments goes hand-in-hand with their CSR education, in particular when their home state's law adopts due diligence legislations which tend to require more transparency and non-financial reporting of economic activities held abroad[137] and also when national courts have begun to recognise that parent companies have a 'duty of care' and may be held liable for operations of their subsidiaries abroad.[138] Therefore, it seems we are most probably at the first and not the last stages of this corporate cultural change.

[137] See, at the regional level, the Directive 2014/95/EU of the European Parliament and of the Council of 22 October 2014 amending Directive 2013/34/EU as regards disclosure of non-financial and diversity information by certain large undertakings and groups. At the national level, France Corporate Duty of Vigilance Law adopted on 21 February 2017 and the Italian *Piano d'Azione Nazionale su Impresa e Diritti Umani* 2016–21.

[138] See the case brought in the English Supreme Court: *Vedanta Resources Plc v Lungowe* [2019] UKSC 20. See also M Hautereau-Boutonnet, 'The Duty of Care of Parent Companies: A Tool for Establishing a Transnational Environmental Civil Liability' (2019) 16 *Brazilian Journal of International Law* 289.

12

Elevating Corruption to an International Tort

JOSE DANIEL AMADO, JACKSON SHAW KERN
AND MARTIN DOE RODRIGUEZ

I. Introduction

The posture of nations toward the scourge of corruption in international commerce and investment has undergone dramatic advancement with an alacrity seldom seen in international law. This revolution has seen the enlistment of nearly all internationally recognised governments on the face of the earth in a coordinated anti-corruption campaign, and has caused civil society across the globe to look auspiciously upon the promise of a new landscape at the turn of the twenty-first century. By this time, apologists were in retreat, and a previously prevalent view that corrupt practices were a sort of necessary evil in the ongoing endeavour of international economic development ceased to be spoken.

In a co-authored piece appearing in the *Foreign Affairs* magazine in 2006, the former long-time general counsel to General Electric and a co-founder of Transparency International jointly wrote as follows:

> Underlying these changes in rules, rhetoric, and awareness is the growing recognition that bribery and extortion have demonstrably deleterious consequences. Gone is the day when some pundits seriously argued that corruption was an efficient corrective for overregulated economies or that it should be tolerated as an inevitable by-product of intractable forces. The true impact of corruption is now widely acknowledged: corruption distorts markets and competition, breeds cynicism among citizens, undermines the rule of law, damages government legitimacy, and corrodes the integrity of the private sector. It is also a major barrier to international development – systemic misappropriation by kleptocratic governments harms the poor.[1]

[1] BW Heineman Jr and F Heimann, 'The Long War Against Corruption' (2006) 85 *Foreign Affairs* 75, 75. In an indication that the struggle continues, the President Emeritus of the World Peace Foundation has echoed them as follows more than 10 years onward: 'The insidious practice of corruption cripples institutions, consumes communities, and cuts deeply into the very structure of people's lives. It destroys nations and saps their moral fiber. Corruption is invasive and unforgiving, degrading governance,

Declaring the death of a more cynical era in which governments engaging in 'international trade battles on behalf of their national champions' were often 'reluctant to crack down on the bribery of foreign officials',[2] the tone of the authors was transcendental. They projected the ascendant narrative in writing that 'Ultimately, the most potent force for change is the idea that corruption is morally repugnant and inimical to competition, globalization, the rule of law, international development, and the welfare of citizens around the world'.[3] In this narrative, the world chose to focus not only upon the scandal and outrage of individual acts of corruption, but to frame the matter magnanimously in the terms of a universal battle for the rule of law that strikes at the very core of human decency and aspiration. Corruption was to be regarded not merely as a depraved criminal conduct, but as a deplorable phenomenon that afflicts the economic, social and moral foundations of peoples and nations.

Ten years earlier, the then-President of the World Bank James Wolfensohn, stating a desire not to 'mince words', had invoked a need 'to deal with the cancer of corruption' as the centrepiece of his address to the Bank's 1996 annual meeting.[4] On 29 March of that year, the 34 members of the Organization of American States had adopted the text of an Inter-American Convention Against Corruption (the IACAC), which entered into force on 6 March 1997, marking the emergence of the first international convention dedicated to combatting corruption.[5] In November 1997, the Organisation for Economic Co-operation and Development adopted a Convention on Combating Bribery of Foreign Public Officials in International Business Transactions (the 'OECD Convention') which entered into force on 15 February 1999, thus becoming the second international anti-corruption instrument.[6] A draft African Union Convention on Preventing and Combating Corruption (the 'AU Convention') was adopted by the Assembly of the African Union in July 2003 and, on 31 October 2003, the General Assembly of the United Nations adopted its own Convention Against Corruption (UNCAC).

distorting and criminalizing national priorities, and privileging acquisitive rent-seeking, patrimonial theft, and personal gains over concern for the commonweal. It also costs an estimated $1 trillion annually – roughly a loss of 2 percent of global GDP–and disproportionally affects the most needy countries and their peoples'. RI Rotberg, 'Accomplishing Anticorruption: Propositions and Methods' (2018) 147 *Daedalus: Journal of the American Academy of Arts & Sciences* 5.

[2] ibid 79.

[3] ibid 80.

[4] 'Biography of James David Wolfensohn, 9th President of the World Bank Group, 1995–2005' (The World Bank), available at www.worldbank.org/en/about/archives/history/past-presidents/james-david-wolfensohn.

[5] Organization of American States, 'Inter-American Convention Against Corruption' (IACAC) (29 March 1996) 35 ILM 724.

[6] OECD Convention on Combating Bribery of Foreign Public Officials in International Business Transactions (signed 18 December 1997, entry into force 15 February 1999) 37 ILM 1. See also OECD Working Group on Bribery in International Business Transactions, 'Recommendation of the Council for Further Combating Bribery of Foreign Public Officials in International Business Transactions' (26 November 2009) (with amendments adopted by Council 18 February 2010 to reflect the inclusion of Annex II, 'Good Practice Guidance on Internal Controls, Ethics and Compliance').

The UNCAC entered into force on 14 December 2005 following ratification by the thirtieth signatory state,[7] while the AU Convention entered into force on 5 August 2006 following ratification by the fifteenth African state.[8] Thus, in the space of barely 10 years, the legal foundation of a global anti-corruption regime was entered firmly into place.[9]

This chapter proceeds in a brief comparative survey of these four instruments, including a cursory examination of their core operative provisions. Second, the question of whether or not 'corruption' now rises to the level of a truly international wrong is considered. Third, the prospects of international investment arbitration as a forum for redress to victims of corrupt acts are presented in order to narrow an enduring gap in access to justice.

II. The Anti-Corruption Conventions

The substantive provisions of the key international anti-corruption conventions are inspired by an item of national legislation that emerged fully two decades prior to the entering into force of the IACAC, namely the United States Foreign Corrupt Practices Act (FCPA). Congressional corruption investigations that had begun during the presidency of Richard M Nixon as well as parallel actions across law enforcement cut a wide swath through corporate America and revealed striking findings. The United States Securities and Exchange Commission ultimately 'gathered admissions from four hundred US multinational corporations that they made payments amounting to $300 million in bribing foreign officials', with 'One hundred and seventy-seven of the multinationals that admitted corrupt practices or bribery' being Fortune 500 companies, including such names as Exxon and Lockheed Martin, while 'The recipient foreign public officials included Japanese Prime Minister Tanaka Kakuei, Prince Bernhard of the Netherlands, and Italian Prime Minister Giovanni Leone'.[10]

These findings demanded a response, and the FCPA became law in 1977.[11] It was the first national law to aggressively criminalise foreign bribery, and the very

[7] United Nations Convention Against Corruption (UNCAC) (adopted 31 October 2003, entry into force 14 December 2005) 2349 UNTS 41.

[8] African Union Convention on Preventing and Combating Corruption (adopted 1 July 2003, entry into force 5 August 2006) 43 ILM 5.

[9] Another significant instrument not discussed in this chapter is the League of Arab States' Arab Convention Against Corruption of 2010.

[10] TR Snider and W Kidane, 'Combating Corruption through International Law in Africa: A Comparative Analysis' (2007) 40 *Cornell International Law Journal* 691, 697 (citing PW Schroth, 'The United States and International Bribery Conventions' (2002) 50 *American Journal of Comparative Law* 593, 595–96).

[11] Foreign Corrupt Practices Act of 1977, Pub L No 95-213, 91 Stat 1494, amended by Omnibus Trade and Competitiveness Act of 1988, Pub L No 100-418, 102 Stat 1415 and the International Anti-Bribery and Fair Competition Act of 1988, Pub L No 105-366, 112 Stat 3302 (codified as amended at 15 USC §§ 78m(b), 78dd-1 to -3, 78ff (1998)).

first in any major capital-exporting nation.[12] It is noteworthy that the international anti-corruption conventions (in particular the OECD Convention) would emerge following intensive lobbying efforts by the US,[13] which viewed its enterprises as being disadvantaged vis-à-vis those of other nations that did not face any similar constraint.[14]

A. 1996 Inter-American Convention against Corruption

The IACAC broke ground as the first international anti-corruption convention. In defining principal acts of corruption, the IACAC sets forth that it is applicable to

[12] Sweden had in fact earlier enacted a law to criminalise certain instances of foreign bribery. See M Bogdan, 'International Trade and the New Swedish Provisions on Corruption' (1979) 27 *American Journal of Comparative Law* 665 passim (discussing the Swedish Penal Code (1997) SFS § 103). However, that law has been described as 'weak almost to the point of nonexistence' in PM Nichols, 'The Myth of Anti-Bribery Laws as Transnational Intrusion' (2000) 33 *Cornell International Law Journal* 627, 638 (see fn 60). More recently, the Bribery Act 2010 (UK) has assumed a place alongside the FCPA as the second municipal instrument of truly global influence in the anticorruption space.

[13] These efforts appear to have begun concurrently with the drafting and passage of the FCPA itself, achieving in 1979 the adoption of a UN Recommendation of a draft convention to combat bribery in international business transactions. United Nations Economic and Social Council, 'Report of the Ad Hoc Intergovernmental Working Group on the Problem of Corrupt Practices' (5 July 1977) UN Doc E/6006; United Nations Economic and Social Council, 'Report of the Committee on An International Agreement on Illicit Payments on its 1st and 2nd sessions' (25 May 1979) UN Doc E/1979/104. This initiative would never reach treaty status. Nearly 10 years later, a 1988 amendment to the FCPA would require the president to 'pursue international accord' on the criminalisation of bribery. See LH Randall, 'Multilateralization of the Foreign Corrupt Practices Act' (1997) 6 *Minnesota Journal of Global Trade* 657. It would take nearly another 10 years for the IACAC and the OECD Convention to emerge.

[14] In a vivid and oft-cited example of the discrepancy, expenses incurred in bribery often remained tax-deductible in European jurisdictions. Thus, foreign bribery was not only *not* outlawed but was, in a sense, government-sponsored or government-incentivised. American prosecutors have adopted expansive interpretations of the jurisdictional bases that are afforded under the FCPA in order to pursue non-US persons and entities for conduct believed to be corrupt (perhaps the most common example is the passage of illicit funds through US banks), with the result that the differential may be sometimes more apparent than real. Some observers have opined that this practice ultimately undermines the goals of justice, in language that would seem sentimental about sovereignty. See, for example, 'Tackling Corruption: Judge Dread' (2019) 430 *The Economist* 12; 'America and Extraterritoriality' (2019) 430 *The Economist* 61; and 'The GE and Alstom affair' (2019) 430 *The Economist* 63. Meanwhile, the FCPA has been amended to include an oft-litigated exception to the rule of liability in those cases where a payment rendered is not a 'bribe,' but merely a 'facilitating or expediting payment … the purpose of which is to expedite or to secure the performance of a routine governmental action.' FCPA, § 78dd-1(b). This exception was adopted in 1998 in order to loosen US law in alignment with the OECD Convention. See Commentaries on the Convention on Combating Bribery of Foreign Public Officials in International Business Transactions, Adopted by the Negotiating Conference on 21 November 1997, para 9 ('Small "facilitation" payments do not constitute payments made "to obtain or retain business or other improper advantage" within the meaning of [the Convention] and, accordingly, are also not an offence. Such payments, which, in some countries, are made to induce public officials to perform their functions, such as issuing licenses or permits, are generally illegal in the foreign country concerned. Other countries can and should address this corrosive phenomenon by such means as support for programmes of good governance. However, criminalisation by other countries does not seem a practical or effective complementary action'). See www.oecd.org/daf/anti-bribery/ConvCombatBribery_ENG.pdf.

'The solicitation or acceptance, directly or indirectly, *by* a government official or a person who performs public functions' as well as 'The offering or granting, directly or indirectly, *to* a government official or a person who performs public functions' of 'any article of monetary value, or other benefit, such as a gift, favor, promise or advantage for himself or for another person or entity, in exchange for any act or omission in the performance of his public function'.[15] The IACAC requires that its states party 'shall adopt the necessary legislative or other measures to establish as criminal offenses under their domestic law' these acts of corruption, and 'to facilitate cooperation among themselves pursuant to [the] Convention'.[16] As for its general jurisdictional principles, the IACAC establishes a mandatory prescription upon each state party to establish the corruption offences where committed in its territory,[17] and a permissive one where committed by its nationals.[18]

The IACAC sets forth a separate offence of transnational bribery, imposing upon its states parties the obligation to:

> [P]rohibit and punish the offering or granting, directly or indirectly, by its nationals, persons having their habitual residence in its territory, and businesses domiciled there, to a government official of another state, of any article of monetary value, or other benefit, such as a gift, favor, promise or advantage, in connection with any economic or commercial transaction in exchange for any act or omission in the performance of that official's public functions.[19]

B. 1997 OECD Convention on Combating Bribery of Foreign Public Officials in International Business Transactions

In a manner similar to the transnational bribery offence set out in the IACAC, the OECD Convention targets only the supply side of bribery, in the following language:

> Each Party shall take such measures as may be necessary to establish that it is a criminal offence under its law for any person intentionally to offer, promise or give any undue pecuniary or other advantage, whether directly or through intermediaries, to a foreign public official, for that official or for a third party, in order that the official act or refrain from acting in relation to the performance of official duties, in order to obtain or retain business or other improper advantage in the conduct of international business.[20]

[15] IACAC, Art VI(1)(a)–(b) (emphasis added).
[16] ibid Art VII.
[17] ibid Art V(1).
[18] ibid Art V(2).
[19] ibid Art VIII. Thus, it would seem that States party to the IACAC are obliged to establish jurisdiction over the crime of transnational bribery on the basis of nationality or residency principles only.
[20] OECD Convention, Art 1(1). See also the Commentaries on the Convention on Combating Bribery of Foreign Public Officials in International Business Transactions, Adopted by the Negotiating Conference on 21 November 1997, at para 1 ('This Convention deals with what, in the law of some countries, is called "active corruption" or "active bribery", meaning the offence committed by the person who promises or gives the bribe, as contrasted with "passive bribery", the offence committed by

The OECD Convention does not require its states parties to criminalise demand-side bribery in international business, namely the solicitation or acceptance of bribes by public officials. The OECD Convention obliges its states parties to establish jurisdiction over the offence on the basis of the territorial principle[21] as well as the nationality principle, but only insofar as the relevant state party exercises 'jurisdiction to prosecute its nationals for offences committed abroad' generally.[22]

C. 2003 African Union Convention on Preventing and Combating Corruption

Perhaps more so than the IACAC or the OECD Convention, the AU Convention endorses the magnanimous view of the anti-corruption campaign in framing it as part and parcel of a broader battle, stating as its first fundamental principle a 'respect for democratic principles and institutions, popular participation, the rule of law and good governance'.[23]

The AU Convention seeks to criminalise both supply and demand-side bribery in language that recalls the IACAC, with notable deviations. In seeking to extend its ambit to the private sector, the AU Convention refers not to 'a government official or a person who performs public functions'[24] but rather to 'a public official or any other person'.[25] In contrast to the OECD Convention (whose very object is the criminalisation of transnational bribery) and the IACAC (which specifically mandates the criminalisation of transnational bribery), the AU Convention does not expressly differentiate between the bribery of foreign versus domestic persons.

The AU Convention prescribes only that its states parties 'undertake' to 'Adopt legislative and other measures that are required to establish as offences' the acts of corruption defined therein.[26] Furthermore, in setting out its jurisdictional principles, the AU Convention does not prescribe any particular exercise of jurisdiction by the states parties, but rather states only that 'Each State Party *has* jurisdiction over acts of corruption' in accordance with principles of territoriality and nationality.[27] As these two bases of jurisdiction are long recognised by international law, the statement may be little more than a truism.[28]

the official who receives the bribe. The Convention does not utilise the term "active bribery" simply to avoid it being misread by the non-technical reader as implying that the briber has taken the initiative and the recipient is a passive victim. In fact, in a number of situations, the recipient will have induced or pressured the briber and will have been, in that sense, the more active').

[21] ibid Art 4(1).

[22] ibid Art 4(2).

[23] AU Convention, Art 3(1).

[24] IACAC, Art VI(1)(a).

[25] AU Convention, Art 4(1)(a)–(b).

[26] ibid Art 5(1).

[27] ibid Art 13(1)(a)–(b) (emphasis added).

[28] The AU Convention also states, more adventurously, that each State party 'has' jurisdiction 'when the offence, although committed outside its jurisdiction, affects, in the view of the State concerned, its

On balance, the obligations of the AU Convention may thus fairly be said to be softer than those of the IACAC or the OECD Convention.

D. 2003 United Nations Convention against Corruption

In its scope of application, the UNCAC provides that it 'shall apply, in accordance with its terms, to the prevention, investigation and prosecution of corruption and to the freezing, seizure, confiscation and return of the proceeds of offences established in accordance' therewith.[29] In language again reminiscent of the IACAC, the UNCAC seeks to criminalise both supply- and demand-side bribery of national public officials in the following mandatory terms:

> Each State Party shall adopt such legislative and other measures as may be necessary to establish as criminal offences, when committed intentionally:
>
> (a) The promise, offering or giving, to a public official, directly or indirectly, of an undue advantage, for the official himself or herself or another person or entity, in order that the official act or refrain from acting in the exercise of his or her official duties;
>
> (b) The solicitation or acceptance by a public official, directly or indirectly, of an undue advantage, for the official himself or herself or another person or entity, in order that the official act or refrain from acting in the exercise of his or her official duties.[30]

In a manner also akin to the IACAC, the UNCAC sets forth a separate offence upon the supply side of transnational bribery, imposing upon states parties the obligation to:

> [A]dopt such legislative and other measures as may be necessary to establish as a criminal offence, when committed intentionally, the promise, offering or giving to a foreign public official or an official of a public international organization, directly or indirectly, of an undue advantage, for the official himself or herself or another person or entity, in order that the official act or refrain from acting in the exercise of his or her official duties, in order to obtain or retain business or other undue advantage in relation to the conduct of international business.[31]

vital interests or the deleterious or harmful consequences or effects of such offences impact on the State Party'. AU Convention, Art 13(1)(d).

[29] UNCAC, Art 3(1).

[30] ibid Art 15. The UNCAC also contains provisions with regard to anti-corruption measures in the private sector, but these do not include mandatory criminal penalties. See UNCAC, Art 12.

[31] ibid Art 16(1). Llamzon has observed 'the more tentative tenor of the [UNCAC] regarding the solicitation or acceptance of bribes *by* foreign public officials', which is to say the demand side of transnational bribery. AP Llamzon, *Corruption in International Investment Arbitration* (Oxford University Press, 2018) para 4.62 (emphasis in original) (citing UNCAC, Art 16(2)) ('Each State Party *shall consider* adopting such legislative and other measures as may be necessary to establish as a criminal offence, when committed intentionally, the solicitation or acceptance by a foreign public official or an official of a public international organization, directly or indirectly, of an undue advantage, for the official himself or herself or another person or entity, in order that the official act or refrain from acting in the exercise of his or

Lastly, and once again in manner similar to the IACAC, in setting out its general jurisdictional principles, the UNCAC mandatorily prescribes each state party to establish the corruption offences where committed in its territory,[32] and permissively where committed by its nationals.[33]

In reaching beyond the narrower participation of the prior conventions, the community of nations has yielded in the UNCAC a nearly universal instrument embodying a truly global achievement. As of February 2020, it has attained no fewer than 187 states parties.[34] Only Syria and Barbados have signed but not ratified, with there being only a handful of states that have done neither, amongst them North Korea, Eritrea and Suriname.[35]

In sum, it is seen that the anti-corruption conventions rely entirely upon their states parties to be operationalised. Their provisions are notable for the absence of self-execution, in respect of sovereignty. The instruments thus require implementing legislation to be enacted within the states parties in order to establish and prosecute the corruption offences.

III. Is Corruption an International Wrong?

One may now pose the question as to whether corruption is contemporarily elevated to the status of an international wrong. To present day, there does not seem to exist any jurisdiction or forum for the prosecution of anti-corruption norms in international law. As has been seen, the conventions adopt the approach of reliance upon their states parties for implementation of the anti-corruption proscriptions via municipal machineries.[36]

her official duties') (emphasis added). The drafters of the UNCAC may have had their eyes turned toward a likely limited practical usage, for municipal criminalisation of solicitation or acceptance by a *foreign* public official would only obtain where (i) the act of solicitation or acceptance occurred while the foreign official was present within the territory of the criminalising State; or, perhaps, (ii) the soliciting or accepting foreign public official were a dual national who also held the nationality of the criminalising State; or (iii) the criminalising State sought to exercise a more expansive jurisdiction, perhaps in emulating practices such as those pioneered by the United States under the FCPA.

[32] UNCAC, Art 42(1)(a). The UNCAC also contains a mandatory prescription with regard to offences 'committed on board a vessel that is flying the flag of that State Party or an aircraft that is registered under the laws of that State Party' at the time of commission: ibid Art 42(1)(b). This too is a basis of jurisdiction that is well established in international law, often known as the flag principle.

[33] ibid Art 42(2)(b). In an acknowledgement of corruption's victims, the UNCAC also includes a permissive basis of jurisdiction where the offence is committed not by but against a national of the relevant state party, sometimes known as the passive personality principle: ibid Art 42(2)(a).

[34] United Nations Office on Drugs and Crime, 'UNCAC Signature and Ratification Status', available at www.unodc.org/unodc/en/corruption/ratification-status.html.

[35] ibid.

[36] Llamzon has observed that 'international conventions have mostly been confined to the level of general principles and proscriptions, arrogating unto individual States sole responsibility for enacting and enforcing anti-bribery legislation': Llamzon, *Corruption in International Investment Arbitration* (2018), para 1.05. It has also been observed that 'the primary shortcoming of current international anti-corruption treaties has precisely been the abdication of the control function to domestic institutions': ibid para 4.121.

Voices have been raised in favour of a notable alternative to the anti-corruption conventions, namely the prosecution of grand-scale corruption as a crime against humanity. As early as 2006, it was written that corruption might constitute such a crime 'where it culminates in famine, disease and lack of medical care that leads to death', as 'It is no longer necessary to establish a nexus between crimes against humanity and armed conflict'.[37] Further, it was written, 'International law has already responded in the affirmative on whether non-state actors are capable of committing crimes against humanity'.[38] Thus, in this view, 'there is no reason why a crime against humanity cannot be perpetrated against a civilian population by means of corruption', with such an approach 'do[ing] away with the jurisdictional limitations encountered in anti-corruption treaties' and 'paving the way for universal jurisdiction, as well as access to the International Criminal Court'.[39]

Turning first to the International Criminal Court, in remarks given in July 2018 on the occasion of the twentieth anniversary of its foundational Rome Statute, the President of the Court acknowledged a 'desire expressed by [the President of Nigeria] for expansion of the Rome Statute to … cover … serious cases of corruption', and further informed the audience that the President of Ecuador had 'expressed the same desire that the [Court] should … prosecute cases of corruption executed at a scale the effects of which are capable of approximating the human costs of violent crimes against humanity'.[40] He then affirmed that 'The decision to amend the Rome Statute in order to allow that manner of jurisdiction belongs to States'.[41] This statement may be read as a strong and reliable indicator that the Court presently views crimes of corruption as falling outside its mandate. Furthermore, even if the Court were to exercise such jurisdiction (whether resulting from amendment of the Rome Statute or not), the inherent limitations (both in terms of jurisdiction and prosecutorial capacity) would likely be such that it

[37] I Bantekas, 'Corruption as an International Crime and Crime against Humanity: An Outline of Supplementary Criminal Justice Policies' (2006) 4 *Journal of International Criminal Justice* 466. In support of this assertion, Bantekas cites *Prosecutor v Tadić* (Decision on Defence Motion for Interlocutory Appeal on Jurisdiction) IT-94-1-T (2 October 1995), paras 140–41.

[38] ibid 11. In support of this assertion, Bantekas cites, as regards guerrilla groups, ILC 'Report of the International Law Commission on the Work of its 48th Session' (6 May–26 July 1996) UN Doc A/51/10/ Supp No 10, 94 (regarding the Draft Code of Crimes Against the Peace and Security of Mankind), and *Karadžić and Mladić* (Review of the Indictments Pursuant to Rule 61 of the Rules of Procedure and Evidence) IT-95-5-R61/IT-95-18-R61 (11 July 1996).

[39] ibid 19.

[40] Judge Chile Eboe-Osuji, 'Remarks of Judge Chile Eboe-Osuji, President of the International Criminal Court, at the Solemn Hearing in Commemoration of the 20th Anniversary of the Adoption of the Rome Statute of the International Criminal Court' (ICC, 17 July 2018) 7, available at www.icc-cpi.int/itemsDocuments/20180717-pres-speech.pdf.

[41] ibid. Judge Chile further stated that the judges of the Court were 'ready and willing to exercise any jurisdiction which the States confer on [them]' (ibid). In the meantime, a proposal has been put forth for the establishment of an international anti-corruption court that would exercise criminal jurisdiction separately from the ICC. See B Roach and E Mortensen, 'An International Anti-Corruption Court' (2019) LXII *Bulletin of the American Academy of Arts & Sciences*. Such seems unlikely to be realised in the near future.

could not act as an effective counter to any but the most massive and egregious acts of corruption causing, for example, widespread deprivation of food or medicine to a civilian population over a prolonged period of time.[42] This restriction is not in keeping with the expansive scope of the anti-corruption conventions. It seems evident that national judiciaries will remain the workhorses of criminal penalties for corruption.

With regard to the exercise of universal jurisdiction to prosecute grand corruption in national courts, such would seem, once again, to run against the grain of the anti-corruption conventions, which openly rely upon more traditional bases of internationally accepted criminal jurisdiction, namely territoriality and nationality.[43] Further, by compliance with the obligations of the anti-corruption conventions (in particular those of the UNCAC with its near-exhaustive geographical reach), states would establish jurisdiction to prosecute all manner of corrupt acts (the overwhelming majority of which fall far short of the high threshold of a crime against humanity), thus rendering it unnecessary to reach toward a more controversial jurisdictional basis.[44]

This point returns one squarely to the theme of the conventions' reliance upon their states parties for establishment and enforcement of the anti-corruption norms. A common core may be distilled across the conventions in order to elucidate an international conception of the corruption offence. However, this conception is entirely left to be actualised in the municipal laws, in tandem with efforts to increase and enhance international cooperation in matters such as investigation and extradition.[45] The national laws are the implementing tools of the international instruments, and states may be relied upon to embody the treaty directives in divergent form and manner where imposing the international norms onto the national plane via their various (and varying) legislative processes.[46]

[42] See, for example, Rome Statute of the International Criminal Court (signed 17 July 1998, entry into force 1 July 2002) 2187 UNTS 38544, Art 7(1);UNSC Res 827 (1993) Statute of the International Criminal Tribunal for the Former Yugoslavia, Art 5; UNSC Res 955 (1994) Statute of the International Criminal Tribunal for Rwanda, Art 3.

[43] The AU Convention seemingly reaches beyond traditional territoriality to allow for jurisdiction where *effects* of the corrupt act are felt in the exercising State. See AU Convention, Art 13(1)(d). However, even this more expansive basis requires a factual connection to the event of corruption, and is thus by definition distinct from (and more restrictive than) an exercise of universal jurisdiction.

[44] An exercise of universal jurisdiction may nonetheless prove useful where given states fail to establish or enforce the criminal offences as stipulated under the UNCAC or are not party to it.

[45] See, for example, UNCAC, Ch IV; IACAC, Arts XIII and XIV; AU Convention, Arts 15, 18–19; and OECD Convention, Arts 9–10.

[46] The primacy of municipal law is beyond doubt. In this regard, see for example UNCAC, Art 30(9) ('Nothing contained in this Convention shall affect the principle that the description of the offences established in accordance with this Convention and of the applicable legal defences or other legal principles controlling the lawfulness of conduct is reserved to the domestic law of a State Party and that such offences shall be prosecuted and punished in accordance with that law'). Such is witnessed in, for example, the arbitral award in the case of *Hesham TM Al Warraq v Indonesia*. There, the tribunal found that 'The Claimant failed to demonstrate how the offences of corruption and money laundering under Indonesian law do not accord with internationally recognised principles of criminal law,' and that '[t]he Claimant's reliance on Articles 15 and 21 of the UNCAC is misplaced because these provisions do

States parties must translate the treaties' international prescriptions into the national rules of diverse criminal codes or other statute books, all within the context of their own legal traditions and constitutional philosophies. This reality, while aspiring for harmony, militates against unison, despite the common core from which the municipal manifestations emerge.

The inevitability of regional and national variation was openly acknowledged ex ante in, for example, the official commentary to the OECD Convention, where it is written that the Convention 'seeks to assure a functional equivalence among the measures taken by the Parties to sanction bribery of foreign public officials, without requiring uniformity or changes in fundamental principles of a Party's legal system'.[47] In the context of the UNCAC, it has been observed ex post in a 2017 report to review the state of implementation that 'substantial challenges remain', including 'technical issues in the formulation of criminalization provisions' and 'the incorporation of particular elements' of the Convention into 'complex procedural structures'.[48] The divergence is further illustrated in an overview of regional trends within the same report.[49] A diversity of sausage-makers yields a diversity of sausages.

Despite the common core of the anti-corruption conventions, defining the contemporary landscape are: (i) the absence of international jurisdiction for the prosecution of the anti-corruption norms; and, furthermore, (ii) a high degree of variation in the embodiment of those international norms within the correspondingly emergent municipal laws. While a campaign against corruption is firmly established as a matter of international or transnational public policy, these phenomena foreclose any identifiable status of corruption as an internationally justiciable wrong at present. By calibrated engineering of international investment instruments, the UNCAC's proscription of corruption may be rendered directly applicable in international arbitration, and thereby requisitioned into the service of corruption's many victims.

not set out the elements of corruption and/or money laundering, but instead impose a general obligation on State Parties to adopt legislation which criminalises the bribery of public officials': UNCITRAL, Final Award (15 December 2014), para 607.

[47] Commentaries on the Convention on Combating Bribery of Foreign Public Officials in International Business Transactions, Adopted by the Negotiating Conference on 21 November 1997, para 2.

[48] UN Office on Drugs and Crime, 'State of implementation of the United Nations Convention against Corruption: Criminalization, Law Enforcement and International Cooperation', 2nd edn (United Nations, 2017) vii.

[49] As examples, the authors of the review note that 'countries in the [Group of African States] are likely to have not established the offence of bribery of foreign public officials and officials of public international organizations, perhaps in part as a result of the fact that the follow-up mechanism of the African Union Convention on Preventing and Combating Corruption does not involve monitoring assessments,' that countries in the Group of Asia-Pacific States 'adhere to a strict territoriality principle, in a way that deviates from the possibilities envisaged in the Convention', and that some countries in the Group of Western European and other States 'have concerns about the offence of illicit enrichment ... often because of constitutional limitations and the perceived breach of the presumption of innocence': ibid.

IV. Arbitration as an International Anti-Corruption Jurisdiction

Arbitration is firmly established as the predominant mechanism for resolution of disputes in international commerce and investment. As Aloysius Llamzon observes in his seminal work on corruption in international investment law, the anti-corruption conventions 'continue to arrogate the prerogatives of curbing and prosecuting corruption to national authorities, thus depriving these instruments and the international legal order of any real control function for combating transnational corruption'.[50] He thus concludes that 'the only potentially effective mechanism under the international legal order for the control of transnational corruption currently available is international investment arbitration'.[51] Meanwhile, further diverse constituencies urge that, in addition to the historical role of treaty-born arbitration as a forum for the foreign investor to enforce obligations of investment protection that fall upon the host state, the regime might impose a reciprocal responsibility upon the investor,[52] thereby restoring the mutuality that is arbitration's essence.

The impact of corrupt acts upon arbitral proceedings has long been an object of lively debate. The prevailing view is that use of corrupt practices will operate to

[50] Llamzon (n 31) para 11.03. He further notes that 'Plans for effective anti-corruption monitoring and dedicated dispute settlement mechanisms to decide cases of transnational corruption (including a U.N. proposal for an arbitral framework) have not borne fruit' (ibid). For more on the unavailing UN initiative, see ibid, paras 4.77–4.79.

[51] ibid. He has also written that 'Given the lack of any concerted international mechanism to enforce anti-corruption norms, investor-State arbitration has, almost by default, emerged as one of the few areas in the international legal order where the infrastructure is already in place to regulate foreign investment, including those tainted with corruption, in an authoritative and controlling manner' (ibid, para 1.05), and that 'this key public issue will for the foreseeable future have to be addressed through existing international systems; and investment arbitration is currently the closest thing the international legal order has to a standing system able to extract direct accountability from those who engage in corruption' (ibid, para 11.47).

[52] See, for example, United Nations Economic Commission for Africa, African Union and UNCTAD, 'Next Steps for the African Continental Free Trade Area: Assessing Regional Integration in Africa IX' (July 2019) 198 ('The international investment regime historically imposed obligations only on host States, not on private investors (Paulsson, 1995). However, as underscored by the [Pan-African Investment Code], [international investment agreements] may serve as vehicles for investor rights and also for their obligations, which could rebalance the regime. Investor obligations can be a source for claims against transgressing investors and for counterclaims by defending States. The right to initiate proceeding may be bestowed upon the [host] State, its nationals or both (Amado, Kern & Rodriguez, 2017)') (citations omitted); see also UNGA 'Possible reform of investor-State dispute settlement (ISDS): Multiple proceedings and counterclaims' (22 January 2020) UN Doc A/CN.9/WG.III/WP.193, para 41 (stating that the Working Group III on Investor-State Dispute Settlement Reform 'may wish to consider formulating provisions on investor obligations which would form the basis for a State's counterclaims' and that such obligations 'may relate to the protection of human rights and the environment, compliance with domestic law, measures against corruption and the promotion of sustainable development') and fn 26 (stating that the Working Group 'may wish to consider whether the framework for counterclaims by respondent States could be expanded to allow for claims by third parties against investors') and UNGA 'Report of Working Group III (Investor-State Dispute Settlement Reform) on the work of its thirty-seventh session' (New York, 1–5 April 2019) UN Doc A/CN.9/970, paras 31, 34–35.

foreclose any access to arbitral remedies. As Judge Gunnar Lagergren famously held in a 1963 award regarding the matter, 'Parties who ally themselves in [such] an enterprise … must realise that they have forfeited any right to ask for assistance of the machinery of justice (national courts or arbitral tribunals) in settling their disputes'.[53] As seen in the award, the status of international public policy *contra* corruption was achieved long prior to the emergence of the anti-corruption conventions.[54] In the years following their entering into force, an arbitral tribunal reaffirmed the international public policy in the case of *World Duty Free v Kenya*, which it described as 'an international consensus as to universal standards and accepted norms of conduct'[55] while similarly dismissing the claimant's claim.

The result of dismissal has subsequently been reached in treaty-born arbitrations. For example, in the case of *Metal-Tech Ltd v Uzbekistan*, in acknowledging a seeming 'unfair advantage' to the shielded respondent state, the tribunal nonetheless found that

> the idea … is not to punish one party at the cost of the other, but rather to ensure the promotion of the rule of law, which entails that a court or tribunal cannot grant assistance to a party that has engaged in a corrupt act.[56]

Certain nuances amongst these cases must be identified. In *World Duty Free*, the tribunal applied principles of separability to 'examine the relative evidence of corruption in the underlying contract in order to determine its enforceability',[57] ultimately concluding in the negative.[58] This marks a distinction from Judge Lagergren's case, which concerned not corruption in the *making* of the contract, but rather corruption as the *object* of the contract. Meanwhile, in a treaty case, corruption in the making of the investment may vitiate a tribunal's jurisdiction by operation of a legality clause requiring investments to be established in accordance with law, a defect which no separability presumption may cure.[59] In any case, the

[53] Award in ICC Case No 1110 of 1963, 21 *Yearbook Commercial Arbitration* (1996) 47.

[54] See ibid 56, where Judge Lagergren recorded as follows: 'there exists a general principle of law recognized by civilized nations that contracts which seriously violate *bonos mores* or international public policy are invalid or at least unenforceable and that they cannot be sanctioned by the courts or arbitrators … such corruption is an international evil; it is contrary to the good morals and to an international public policy common to the community of nations'.

[55] (2007) 46 ILM 339, para 139. Although more than 10 years have elapsed since the *World Duty Free* decision, this remains an accurate appraisal, owing to the inherent limitation where the norms of the anti-corruption conventions are imposed only indirectly via the lenses of the municipal laws. See, for example, *Plama Consortium Limited v Bulgaria*, ICSID Case No ARB/03/24, Award (27 August 2008), para 143; *Chevron Corporation & Texaco Petroleum Company v Ecuador*, PCA Case No 2009-23, Second Partial Award on Track II (30 August 2018), para 9.16.

[56] *Metal-Tech Ltd v Uzbekistan*, ICSID Case No ARB/10/3, Award (4 October 2013), para 389.

[57] RZ Torres-Fowler, 'Undermining ICSID: How the Global Antibribery Regime Impairs Investor-State Arbitration' (2012) 52 *Virginia Journal of International Law* 995, 1012.

[58] For a recent perspective on the case, see W Kidane, 'The Culture of Investment Arbitration: An African Perspective' (2019) 34 *ICSID Review – Foreign Investment Law Journal* 411.

[59] Tribunals have also ruled that an illegal acquisition of an investment renders the investor's claim inadmissible even in the absence of an express legality clause. See, for example, *Plama Consortium Ltd v Bulgaria*, ICSID Case No ARB/03/24, Award (27 August 2008), para 135 and *Phoenix Action Ltd v Czech Republic*, ICSID Case No ARB/06/5, Award (15 April 2009), para 101.

barring of an investor's affirmative claims marks the extent of any mechanism to directly confront corruption in international investment law.[60]

Judge Lagergren's holding, applied as it was in a case of commercial bribery (it was a dispute over a contract as between two private parties the object of which, Judge Lagergren came to be convinced, included the paying of bribes to Argentine officials),[61] may not serve very well in investor-state arbitration.[62] It is difficult to escape the notion that behind the treaty case dismissals may lie a fear that any other result would be seen to punish innocent peoples following corrupt acts of their ruling élites, in a time when investor-state arbitration has fallen under great scrutiny. This dilemma has produced a position in the law that is deeply perverse. As observed by Llamzon, 'Current case law suggests that host states can only be held responsible for bribe solicitations or attempts at extortion' committed by their officials,[63] but 'when corruption is "successfully" consummated such that the public action or inaction purchased by the bribe has occurred, host states are *not* internationally responsible for such corruption'.[64] Further than this, not only is the state not internationally responsible for the corruption, but the corrupt act may give rise to the unpalatable spectre of a penalty shield to be raised against responsibility for *other* state conduct that is alleged to be internationally wrongful, thus raising a considerable moral hazard.[65] Equally, the extent of the asymmetry

[60] In the event of investor misconduct that falls short of the threshold of corruption, it has been observed that 'In some cases, tribunals have ruled that there was an implicit requirement of "clean hands" to benefit from treaty protection', but that 'In other cases, tribunals concluded that the "clean hands" doctrine had not crystallised into a general principle of international law which would bar a claim by an investor in the absence of treaty provisions'. Y Kryvoi, 'Economic Crimes in International Investment Law' (2018) 67 *International and Comparative Law Quarterly* 1, 5–6 (citing *Yukos Universal Limited (Isle of Man) v The Russian Federation*, UNCITRAL, PCA Case No 2005-04, Award (18 July 2014)).

[61] The respondent conceded that its sole reason for retaining the claimant was 'the quite remarkable degree of influence which he had with the political appointees of the Peronista Government'; Torres-Fowler, 'Undermining ICSID' (2012) 1011, fn 71.

[62] For an elaboration of the argument, see AB Spalding, 'Deconstructing *Duty-Free*: Investor-State Arbitration as Private Anti-Bribery Enforcement' (2016) 49 *University of California Davis Law Review* 443, 488–93.

[63] Llamzon (n 31) para 11.07. Such might constitute a breach of, for example, a treaty guarantee of fair and equitable treatment of investments. See for example, *EDF (Services) Ltd v Romania*, ICSID Case No ARB/05/13, Award (8 October 2009).

[64] ibid (emphasis in original). One observer has, however, opined that any fairness objection may be misguided where 'The "state" derives no benefit from corruption. Bribes are not paid into the public revenue. Rather, the "state" suffers a significant loss when assets or other valuable legal entitlements are transferred into private hands for less than their real value through corrupt transactions. The actors that benefit from corruption are the particular individuals or groups exercising state authority corruptly and the individuals or groups with which they corruptly transact'. See J Bonnitcha, 'Investment Treaties and Transition from Authoritarian Rule' (2014) 15 *Journal of World Investment & Trade* 965, 1000.

[65] While acknowledging this current state of affairs, Llamzon has himself questioned and criticised it, suggesting that the holding in *World Duty Free* may be inconsistent with the law of state responsibility. A Llamzon and A Sinclair, 'Investor Wrongdoing in Investment Arbitration: Standards Governing Issues of Corruption, Fraud, Misrepresentation and Other Investor Misconduct' in AJ van den Berg (ed), *Legitimacy: Myths, Realities, Challenges* (Kluwer, 2015), 466.

in consequences as between an investor and a host state has been deemed a factor in tribunals' general reluctance to make findings of corruption, as well as their application (transparently or not) of a much more rigid standard of proof to such allegations.[66]

Numerous observers have put forth proposals intended to resolve this current contradiction in the law, primarily by the imposition of a regime of contributory fault as between investor and host state.[67] These proposals miss the mark, for they would seek to apportion fault without attaching a remedy to the true victims of the offence. Liability as between host state and investor (as may flow from, for example, a breach of a state's obligation of investment protection or an investor's obligation of environmental stewardship) is often distinct from the injury or entitlement that may arise from an act of corruption. It is inapposite to suggest a mere adjustment of liabilities as between state and investor for *other* ostensible wrongs where the fitting resolution lies in access to justice for any victims of the corrupt acts. In other words, there must be a match between wrong and remedy.

The key may lie in shifting away from the conventions' fixation upon criminal penalties – which, for reasons earlier examined, are likely to remain the province of national courts – and turning instead toward the realm of internationally enforceable civil remedies to victims.[68] In the latter, one might see an emerging role for international arbitration. Where jurisdiction is properly conferred, a tribunal might serve to order monetary compensation or other relief for injury. Acts of corruption by a foreign investor or by a public official of the host state may lay a basis for liability to those who would bring claims for injury flowing from the corrupt acts. By establishing an international forum to adjudicate such liability, we might elevate corruption toward the status of an international tort.[69]

[66] Llamzon and Sinclair (ibid) 468, 496.

[67] See for example, Kryvoi, 'Economic Crimes' (2018) 18–21. See also Torres-Fowler (n 57) 1010 (stating that 'no arbitral tribunal facing this argument to date has found the recipient of the bribe to be contributorily responsible') and 1031 (suggesting that 'Determining the relative levels of culpability between the claimant and host state should be a fact-based inquiry whereby the tribunal will assess a number of factors that will ultimately place the host state on a spectrum ranging from low-culpability to high-culpability', with possible factors to include '(i) the number of government officials involved in the bribery scheme; (ii) levels of government involved in the bribery scheme; (iii) the frequency to which bribes were paid; (iv) the amount of money exchanged; and (v) the degree to which the host state engaged in extortive measures to [elicit] the bribes').

[68] The notion of imposing criminal liability upon juridical persons remains problematic in some legal traditions, recalling the 18th century pronouncement by a Lord Chancellor of England that corporations have 'no soul to damn, no body to kick.' JC Coffee, '"No Soul to Damn, No Body to Kick": An Unscandalized Inquiry into the Problem of Corporate Punishment' (1981) 79 *Michigan Law Review* 386. Their civil liability for damages is less controversial.

[69] Llamzon has written that 'investment arbitration remains one of the rare international tools already available to the international community to combat corruption in a manner that goes beyond rhetoric and empty crusade, and into true international law.' Llamzon (n 31) para 11.54.

An obligation to establish a private right of action in the national courts is seen in the UNCAC, but not in the other instruments surveyed.[70] Article 35 of the UNCAC, entitled 'Compensation for damage', provides in full as follows:

> Each State Party shall take such measures as may be necessary, in accordance with principles of its domestic law, to ensure that entities or persons who have suffered damage as a result of an act of corruption have the right to initiate legal proceedings against those responsible for that damage in order to obtain compensation.[71]

A note from the time of the UNCAC's negotiation states that:

> While article 35 does not restrict the right of each State Party to determine the circumstances under which it will make its courts available in such cases, it is also not intended to require or endorse the particular choice made by a State Party in doing so.[72]

In contrast to the detailed prescriptions regarding criminalisation, Article 35 thus appears to grant to the states parties a much broader discretion in determining the particulars of their respective private rights of action.[73] Beyond the mandatory prescription to ensure the *existence* of a private right of action, the UNCAC appears entirely devoid of any dictation (or even any guidance) as to its form. The 2017 report on implementation of the UNCAC offers an apparently contradictory appraisal, stating in its article-by-article review that 'All but a few of the reviewed States Parties have adopted measures to fully or partly implement [Article 35]'[74]

[70] The OECD Convention does provide that 'Each Party shall consider the imposition of additional civil or administrative sanctions upon a person subject to sanctions for the bribery of a foreign public official'. OECD Convention, Art 3(4).

[71] UNCAC, Art 35. In addition to the private right of action for monetary compensation, the UNCAC also contains detailed provisions regarding the recovery of actual proceeds of corrupt practices, known as asset recovery (UNCAC, Ch V). While it may be problematic to vest arbitral jurisdiction in such matters due to difficulties in arbitral tribunals adjudicating upon title or ownership of property (particularly where bona fide non-parties may be interested in the objects of dispute), one provision within the UNCAC's chapter on asset recovery must be noted. The UNCAC provides that, in certain cases, States party shall 'give priority consideration to … compensating the victims of the crime'. UNCAC, Art 57(3)(c). This provision seems to envision the possibility that recovered assets might be used to establish a fund against which victims could then claim, including in international arbitration or before an international claims commission. See also, in this regard, the Commentaries on the Convention on Combating Bribery of Foreign Public Officials in International Business Transactions, Adopted by the Negotiating Conference on 21 November 1997, at para 22 (stating that a provision for confiscation, forfeiture, or other deprivation of property is 'without prejudice to rights of victims').

[72] Ad Hoc Committee for the Negotiation of a Convention Against Corruption, 'Report of the Ad Hoc Committee for the Negotiation of a Convention Against Corruption on the Work of Its First to Seventh Sessions: Addendum' (7 October 2003) UN Doc A/58/422/Add 1, para 38.

[73] In the US, for example, in an official recommendation of the American Bar Association in favor of ratification of the UNCAC, it was noted that 'Although U.S. courts do not recognize a private right of action under the [FCPA], they do [already] recognize private remedies in certain circumstances for corruption-related actions. Corruption related activities have, for example, served as predicate acts for civil RICO [Racketeer Influenced and Corrupt Organizations Act] claims … and for claims of tortious interference with prospective economic advantage … Cases have also been brought in tort under the theory of conversion, for example, as in the cases against the former Philippine President Ferdinand Marcos and the former leader of Haiti, "Baby Doc" Duvalier'. Recommendation of the American Bar Association, Adopted by the House of Delegates (8–9 August 2005) 10–11 (citations omitted).

[74] UN Office on Drugs and Crime, 'State of implementation of the United Nations Convention against Corruption' (2017) 160.

but then recording in its concluding observations that the 'essentially non-criminal provisions of article … 35' were 'comparatively underrepresented [in states' reporting] and do not appear to have attracted the same degree of attention as provisions that are considered to be more important'.[75]

The text of Article 35 is, in any event, rather sparse. As always in formulating civil remedies, at the core of the matter are the twin questions of what is the appropriate remedy, and to whom does it belong. The list of items for consideration is varied and includes (i) the proscription of the offence (including any accompanying evidentiary rules regarding, for example, the standard and burden of proof); (ii) the types of qualifying injury; (iii) the types of remedies available; and (iv) *locus standi* to bring a claim.

With regard to definition and proscription of the offence, reference to Article 16 of the UNCAC, with its near-universal reach, is suggested as the preferred approach.[76] In setting out the elements of civil liability, drafters might find a textual aid in, for example, Article 4 of the Council of Europe's Civil Law Convention on Corruption (the 'Civil Law Convention'):

> i. the defendant has committed or authorised the act of corruption, or failed to take reasonable steps to prevent the act of corruption;
> ii. the plaintiff has suffered damage; and
> iii. there is a causal link between the act of corruption and the damage.[77]

One might question whether arbitration is well suited to the adjudication of corruption in view of inherent evidentiary challenges that arbitral tribunals face. Tribunals do not enjoy investigative powers and generally face an inability to compel the production of evidence in the absence of judicial assistance. Llamzon has put forth a proposal for an evidentiary regime that he describes as 'equal to the task of unearthing inherently clandestine corruption' by addressing 'the various evidentiary matters that have led to difficulties in proving corruption, including the burdens of proof, standards of proof, and the use of inferences, presumptions, and "red flag" indicia of corruption'.[78] Another observer has similarly examined in great detail five possible solutions to ease the evidentiary challenges, namely: (i) drawing adverse inferences; (ii) placing greater reliance on circumstantial

[75] ibid 272.

[76] Thus, 'when committed intentionally, the promise, offering or giving to a foreign public official or an official of a public international organization, directly or indirectly, of an undue advantage, for the official himself or herself or another person or entity, in order that the official act or refrain from acting in the exercise of his or her official duties, in order to obtain or retain business or other undue advantage in relation to the conduct of international business' may be established as tortious: UNCAC, Art 16(1). As for demand-side bribery, the 'tentative tenor' of Art 16(2) may be cast away in the emergence of a truly international jurisdiction.

[77] Council of Europe: Civil Law Convention on Corruption (4 November 1999) ETS 174, Art 4(1). It may be said that these elements form the common core of extra-contractual liability across diverse legal traditions. If desired, drafters might opt for a higher degree of specificity, such as might be found in, for example, a regime of civil liability for corruption within an existing body of national law.

[78] Llamzon (n 31) para 1.41 (referencing Ch 9, 'Proving Corruption').

evidence; (iii) lowering the standard of proof; (iv) shifting the burden of proof; and (v) drawing on factual findings in domestic proceedings.[79] All are worthy of consideration where adjudicating civil liability only. Further, where allegations of corruption are concurrently examined in domestic court proceedings, the parties may gain access to a rich body of evidence. Quite aside from the ultimate findings of any court, evidence introduced before such court may, to the extent it is public, be useful in examining allegedly corrupt conduct under a newly applicable treaty standard. Another valuable source of evidence lies in whistle-blower colleagues of the briber or bribee.[80]

The liable party (or parties) may include: (i) the briber, who may come in the form of a natural person (or persons) found to have committed a corrupt act and/or a business entity or other principal on whose behalf this person purported to act; or (ii) the bribee, who may come in the form of a public official (ie a natural person) and/or his state.[81] The underlying rationale with regard to an offending natural person is that, although the agent of a principal, the agent might act ultra vires where he conducts himself corruptly and illegally, thus incurring personal liability. The countervailing rationale is that it is suitable to impose a sort of vicarious liability upon the briber's employer and/or upon the bribee's state, which bear responsibility to properly train and monitor their personnel and are uniquely situated to do so.[82]

For motives of simplicity, imposing vicarious liability of: (i) the briber's employer (or other principal, if one exists) for the corrupt acts of its employee; and (ii) the host state for the corrupt acts of its official may be the preferred approach,[83]

[79] C Rose, 'Questioning the Role of International Arbitration in the Fight against Corruption' (2014) 31 *Journal of International Arbitration* 183.

[80] Prospects of whistleblowing may be improved by the use of incentivising features. See, for example, OECD, 'G20 Anti-Corruption Action Plan: Protection of Whistleblowers – Study on Whistleblower Protection Frameworks, Compendium of Best Practices and Guiding Principles for Legislation' (OECD Publishing, 2012).

[81] For simplicity, bribery is here used as a catch-all term for the various corrupt acts that might be defined as giving rise to liability. For a more elaborate typology, see Llamzon (n 31) Ch 3.

[82] Furthermore, the briber (and, in some cases, the bribee) will often have acted under instruction in committing the corrupt act.

[83] Llamzon has written that 'The question of the extent to which States can, if at all, be held responsible for the corruption of their public officials is fundamental to the inquiry because the very idea of bilaterality – that both the "supply" and "demand" sides of bribery bear the attendant legal consequences – hinges on the idea that public officials motivated by corruption nonetheless exercise State power and in so doing can at least in principle engage the responsibility of the State': see Llamzon (n 31) para 1.41 (referencing Ch 10, 'State Responsibility for Corruption: The Attribution Asymmetry'). It is noted that in the law of attribution, the commentary to the International Law Commission's Draft Articles on Responsibility of States for Internationally Wrongful Acts provides as follows: 'It is irrelevant … that the person concerned may have had ulterior or improper motives or may be abusing public power. Where such a person acts in an apparently official capacity, or under colour of authority, the actions in question will be attributable to the State': ILC, 'Report of the International Law Commission on the Work of Its 53rd Session' (23 April–1 June 2001 and 2 July–10 August 2001) UN Doc A/56/10 (regarding Draft Articles on Responsibility of States for Internationally Wrongful Acts, with Commentaries), Ch IV.E.1, 42, 13. Such a result would seem to be contrary to the position reached in *World Duty Free*, where the tribunal found that the claimant's payment 'was received corruptly by the Kenyan head

within a regime of contributory fault.[84] In setting out the bounds of qualifying injury in instances of corruption, a useful guide is found once more in the Civil Law Convention, which provides that categories of compensable harm shall include 'material damage, loss of profits and non-pecuniary loss'.[85] With regard to remedy, victims may seek judgment (in the form of an arbitral award that declares a finding of corrupt acts) and accompanying compensation for damage.

Finally, with regard to access, the evident candidates for standing are those nationals of the host state who suffer injury flowing from the corrupt acts.[86] Jurisdiction may be attained by the crafting of calibrated treaty text such that investor consent is obtained as a condition to admission or establishment of an investment (Option I in Figure 12.1)[87] or by the simple fact of such admission or

of state; it was a covert bribe; and accordingly its receipt is not legally to be imputed to Kenya itself': *World Duty Free Company Limited v Kenya*, ICSID Case No ARB/00/7, Award (4 October 2006), para 169. However, the Draft Articles are arguably inapplicable where the claimant in that (contract) case did not contend that it had been harmed by an internationally wrongful act. In any event, separate and apart from any debate over the precise state of the law of attribution, vicarious liability of the state for corrupt acts of its officials may be imposed by treaty as *lex specialis*. Readily adaptable language suitable for this purpose may be found once again in the Civil Law Convention. See CLC, at Art 5 ('State Responsibility') ('Each Party shall provide in its internal law for appropriate procedures for persons who have suffered damage as a result of an act of corruption by its public officials in the exercise of their functions to claim for compensation from the State').

[84] If wished, the assessment of contributory fault may be accompanied by the institution of joint and several liability. See for example, CLC, Art 4(2) ('Each Party shall provide ... that, if several defendants are liable for damage for the same corrupt activity, they shall be jointly and severally liable'). In addition to procedural efficiency, there are further grounds of both policy and practicality underpinning this approach. A proportional finding of contributory fault would impose a powerful incentive equally upon the investor and the state in ensuring preventative measures against corruption, and also serve to better ensure that victims will not be left without redress in the event of offending natural persons that might be judgment-proof for lack of sufficient assets to satisfy an award for damages. Llamzon has written that 'fairness demanded not least by the populace of poor States requires arbitrators to look intently at the asymmetry of obligation that is currently in place, and in so looking, to realize perhaps that accountability must be extracted from all malefactors: foreign investors, their agents and employees, certainly, but also public officials and indeed, even host States themselves'. Llamzon (n 31) para 11.54. A finding of proportional liability under principles of contributory fault would of course require that indeed both the investor *and* the state are liable in the given instance. The UNCAC, as the suggested model, defines offering or soliciting a bribe to be offences even where there is ultimately no giving or acceptance of the same. UNCAC, Arts 15–16. Where a bribe is unconsummated it might be solely the offeror or solicitor that is liable, with the claimant bearing the burden to prove causation of a compensable injury.

[85] CLC, Art 3(2).

[86] Llamzon has written that 'payers of bribes will do one of two things to recoup this additional cost: either build the bribe into the price, or provide shortcuts to the quality of the project or product delivered. In either case, the immediate participants in corruption are enriched at the ultimate expense of the public'. Llamzon (n 31) para 1.10. Further, in some cases, corruption may be used to 'immuniz[e] the investment not only from political upheaval and changes in government policy, but indeed even from the uncertainties of the business cycle itself by purchasing a contractually guaranteed return on the investment, all of which is underwritten by an unsuspecting populace'; ibid para 1.12.

[87] In this model, the investor must give his express consent to arbitration of the anti-corruption norms as a condition to issuance of a requisite investment licence or authorization. See JD Amado, JS Kern and MD Rodriguez, *Arbitrating the Conduct of International Investors* (Cambridge University Press, 2018) 87–90 and Annex, Model 6 ('Contingent Consent Clause').

establishment *ab initio* (Option II),[88] and an offer of arbitration may thereby be extended to host state nationals as beneficiaries of the instrument.[89]

Figure 12.1

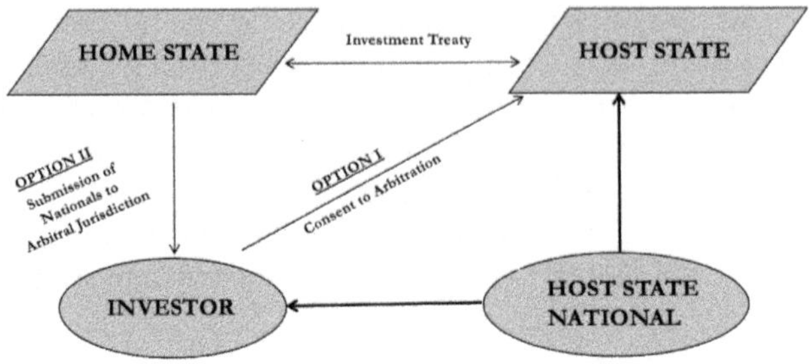

In order to strive for a uniform proscription establishing corruption as a widely justiciable international wrong, the definition might be formulated within a single multilateral convention which alters the effect of prior investment treaties of its contracting states, or might serve as one component of a multilateral convention engineered to achieve broader reforms of investor-state dispute settlement.[90] Another opportunity may exist in the present European initiative

[88] See ibid 90–93 and Model 7 ('Jurisdiction without Privity'); see also the Netherlands–Indonesia Agreement on Economic Cooperation (with Protocol and Exchanges of Letters dated 17 June 1968) (signed 7 July 1968, entered into force on 17 July 1971) 799 UNTS 13, Art 11 ('The Contracting Party in the territory of which a national of the other Contracting Party makes or intends to make an investment, shall assent to any demand on the part of such national and any such national shall comply with any request of the former Contracting Party, to submit, for conciliation or arbitration, to [ICSID] any dispute that may arise in connection with the investment') and Declaration of the Government of the Democratic and Popular Republic of Algeria concerning the settlement of claims by the Government of the United States of America and the Government of the Islamic Republic of Iran (19 January 1981) Art II. By according to such a treaty, the investor's home state exercises a sovereign power to compel its nationals to the jurisdiction of an international tribunal.

[89] The recently adopted Hague Rules on Business and Human Rights Arbitration, substantially derived from the UNCITRAL Arbitration Rules, offer a thoroughly modern and progressive body of procedural rules well suited to this purpose. City of The Hague and Center for International Legal Cooperation, 'The Hague Rules On Business and Human Rights Arbitration' (launched 12 December 2019). It is noted that 'The characterization of the dispute as relating to business and human rights is not necessary for jurisdiction where all the parties to the arbitration have agreed to settle a dispute under [the Hague] Rules'; ibid Art 1. Claims might be advanced by a designated representative acting to prosecute mass or collective claims on behalf of all victims. See Amado, Kern and Doe Rodriguez (n 87) ch 4.

[90] The Republic of Colombia has put forth a worthy proposal for such an opt-in mechanism based upon the Organisation for Economic Co-operation and Development's 'Multilateral Convention to Implement Tax Treaty Related Measures to Prevent Base Erosion and Profit Shifting' in the context of UNCITRAL's Working Group III for Investor-State Dispute Settlement Reform. See UNGA 'Possible reform of Investor-State dispute settlement (ISDS): Submission from the Government of Colombia' (13 July 2019) UN Doc A/CN.9/WG.III/WP.173 (14 June 2019). In so doing, Colombia refers positively to a prior joint submission by Chile, Israel and Japan, and in particular to their call for 'sufficient flexibility to develop a menu of possible solutions, which may vary in form, and that member States can choose to adopt, based on their specific needs and interests', all to be effected within 'a unique

to establish a permanent investment court.[91] If either comes to life, its drafters might craft language to elevate corruption toward the status of an internationally justiciable tort.

Any emergent investment court is unlikely, in any event, to entirely displace the multitude of existing international investment agreements providing for arbitration and presently numbering in their thousands. The advantages of the arbitral forum for the bringing of claims by victims of corruption are evident. In the absence of such a forum, and as presumed under the UNCAC and the Civil Law Convention, victims are left to navigate the world of transnational remedies, seeking to establish jurisdiction in either the courts of the host state, the courts of the investor's home state, or, more remote still, some third state. Even where jurisdiction lies, a court might dismiss the claim on grounds of *forum non conveniens* or other similar doctrine existing in the civil law traditions.[92] There are numerous barriers in constraining both the allegedly corrupted investor and state to be defendants in the same court, and in winning an enforceable judgment. Some of these difficulties are captured in an explanatory note to the Civil Law Convention:

> [D]ifficulties may relate, for instance, to the transmission of judicial and extra-judicial acts, to the choice of jurisdiction to seek redress, the uncertainties of the applicable law in a situation where several different alternatives may be possible, the obligation for the company to advance security for legal costs if the law suit is filed with the courts of another country and difficulties in having the judgement recognised and executed in a foreign country.[93]

In arbitration, victims might find a unitary forum serving to overcome many of the obstacles of the international judicial cooperation upon which the anti-corruption

multilateral instrument common to all countries'; ibid, paras 19, 8. The referenced document is the Proposal for Work Plan of Working Group III Submitted by the Delegations of Chile, Israel and Japan: UNGA 'Submission from the Governments of Chile, Israel and Japan' (14 March 2019) UN Doc A/CN.9/WG.III/WP.163 (15 March 2019) (in which those delegations refer to solutions that may form 'a "suite" of options, which Member States could adopt either individually, in combination or in their entirety as a package'). The Colombian proposal has received a considered response in subsequent sessions of the Working Group. See, for example, UNCITRAL, 'Possible Reform of Investor-State Dispute Settlement (ISDS): Multilateral instrument on ISDS reform, Note by the Secretariat' (16 January 2020) UN Doc A/CN.9/WG.III/WP.194, para 38 (noting that 'it is feasible to develop a multilateral instrument that would apply the reforms in a coherent and flexible manner').

[91] See European Commission, 'Commission Proposes New Investment Court System for TTIP and Other EU Trade and Investment Negotiations' (European Commission press release, 16 September 2015), available at ec.europa.eu/commission/presscorner/detail/en/IP_15_5651.

[92] See generally R Brand and S Jablonski, *Forum Non Conveniens: History, Global Practice, and Future Under the Hague Convention on Choice of Court Agreements* (Oxford University Press, 2007). See also Z Douglas, *The International Law of Investment Claims* (Cambridge University Press 2009) 395–96 (noting that 'Although the doctrine of *forum non conveniens* is a creature of the common law, some commentators have observed that the flexibility built into jurisdictional rules in civilian systems is such that the gulf between the two legal traditions in the respect is more apparent than real'), citing AS Bell, *Forum Shopping and Venue in Transnational Litigation* (Oxford University Press, 2003) 72.

[93] Council of Europe: Civil Law Convention on Corruption (4 November 1999) ETS 174, Explanatory Report, para 87.

conventions so heavily rely,[94] and one that is better suited to the pursuit of effective remedies.[95] These realities call for the establishment of an international jurisdiction in which claims for compensation for the injuries of corruption may be finally resolved.[96] The 'uncertainties of the applicable law' are dispelled where the governing law emerges directly from the treaty instrument itself, and 'difficulties in having the judgement recognised and executed in a foreign country' are lessened where arbitral awards enjoy broader international enforceability than national court judgments.[97]

V. Conclusion

The anti-corruption conventions that began to emerge in the 1990s and culminated in the nearly universal UNCAC embody swift and impressive achievements in international law. Nonetheless, their success is constrained at the will or whim of diverse states parties in enacting and enforcing the anti-corruption norms. A vigorous anti-corruption campaign is undoubtedly established as a matter of international or transnational public policy. However, the fact that the conventions' norms are, by design, applied only indirectly, via the lenses of disparate municipal laws, weighs against any identifiable status of corruption as an internationally justiciable wrong at present. In the meantime, victims who seek redress are condemned to the trials and tribulations of transnational litigation.

These austere limitations may be overcome by establishing in arbitration an international jurisdiction for the direct application of an investment treaty's substantive anti-corruption norms, with accompanying international remedies to victims. In so doing, we might elevate corruption toward the status of an international tort, thus better ensuring that corrupt conduct ceases to be viewed as victimless, and that victims of corruption do not hold a right without remedy.

[94] See, for example, UNCAC, Ch IV. Furthermore, these extensive provisions regarding international cooperation are all but exclusively targeted toward purposes of criminal penalties. For a treaty provision regarding international cooperation toward civil remedies, see CLC, Art 13.

[95] Effectiveness of remedy is the ultimate objective. As noted by one commentator, remedies to implement the Council of Europe's Civil Law Convention on Corruption must aspire to be 'effective': F Haugeneder and C Liebscher, 'Corruption and Investment Arbitration: Substantive Standards of Proof' (2009) *Austrian Arbitration Yearbook* 539, 544. See also, in this regard, CLC, Art 1 ('Each Party shall provide in its internal law for effective remedies for persons who have suffered damage as a result of acts of corruption, to enable them to defend their rights and interests, including the possibility of obtaining compensation for damage'). Pursuit of international enforceability laudably serves this end.

[96] The arbitration mechanism may need to include a fork-in-the-road or waiver provision in order to ensure its proper effect. For an overview of the operation of these provisions, see H Wehland, *The Coordination of Multiple Proceedings in Investment Treaty Arbitration* (Oxford University Press, 2013) 86–98. A fork-in-the-road or waiver provision suitably serves the premise that the emergence of an international jurisdiction need not diminish the right of victims to choose their own national courts (or indeed any forum that might accept jurisdiction) for the litigation of their claims should they wish to do so. However, where they elect arbitration, they must accept and abide by an obligation to respect the exclusivity of the tribunal's jurisdiction.

[97] See, in this regard, Amado, Kern and Doe Rodriguez (n 87) ch 6.

Conclusion: Investors' International Law: Beyond the Present

SURYA DEVA

I. Introduction

There are growing calls – as well as ongoing processes[1] – to reform or rebalance international investment law (IIL).[2] For example, in a 2018 report, UNCTAD observed: 'In the last ten years, the need for systematic reform of the global international investment agreements (IIAs) regime has become increasingly evident. Heated public debate, parliamentary hearing processes and demonstrations on the streets have been taking place in many countries and regions'.[3] Such calls for reform have only become louder in times of COVID-19.[4]

However, there is lesser consensus among various stakeholders on what such reform or rebalancing should look like. There is a risk that this uncertainty about the substance of IIL reforms may be used to introduce symbolic or superficial changes, rather than addressing deep-rooted problems. In this context, I will argue in this concluding chapter that transformative changes are required in IIL, as any minor

[1] See. for example, UNCITRAL Working Group III relating to investor-state dispute settlement reform, available at uncitral.un.org/en/working_groups/3/investor-state. Reforming international investment agreements is also a key component of the ongoing process at the UN Human Rights Council to negotiate a legally binding international instrument: see the OEIWG on transnational corporations and other business enterprises with respect to human rights, available at www.ohchr.org/EN/HRBodies/HRC/WGTransCorp/Pages/IGWGOnTNC.aspx.

[2] See, for example, UNCTAD, 'UNCTAD's Reform Package for the International Investment Regime' (UNCTAD, 2018); J Coleman et al, 'Human Rights Law and the Investment Treaty Regimes' in S Deva and D Birchall (eds), *Research Handbook on Human Rights and Business* (Edward Elgar, 2020) 290. For some of the reasons triggering these reform calls, see M Khor, 'A Summary of Public Concerns on Investment Treaties and Investor-State Dispute Settlement' in K Mohamadieh et al (eds), *Investment Treaties: Views and Experiences from developing Countries* (South Centre, 2015) 1.

[3] UNCTAD, 'Reform Package' (2018) 7.

[4] D Davitti et al, 'COVID-19 and the Precarity of International Investment Law' (Medium, 6 May 2020), available at medium.com/iel-collective/covid-19-and-the-precarity-of-international-investment-law-c9fc254b3878; APWLD, 'Open Letter to Governments on ISDS and COVID-19' (APWLD, 30 June 2020), available at apwld.org/open-letter-to-governments-on-isds-and-covid-19. For a contrary view, see P Ranjan, 'Covid-19 and ISDS Moratorium – An Indiscreet Proposal' (Opinio Juris, 15 June 2020), available at opiniojuris.org/2020/06/15/covid-19-and-isds-moratorium-an-indiscreet-proposal.

tweaks will only reinforce and further entrench existing asymmetries[5] and unfairness consciously built in the system to mostly benefit investors.[6] As a way of thinking through this transformation process, I propose six pathways that will take the current IIL beyond its present status. These pathways are aimed at making transformative changes not only to the nature and purpose of the current IIL, but also to the types of investment-related disputes that are settled, and how these disputes are settled.

II. Beyond the Present

This section outlines six 'beyond pathways' to rescue IIL from historical wrong turns and reorient it to the needs of society – not merely investors – in the twenty-first century: beyond economic development, beyond window-dressing, beyond investors, beyond compartments, beyond obligations, and beyond investor-state dispute settlement (ISDS).

A. Pathway 1: Beyond Economic Development

The debate about whether BITs facilitate foreign investment – much needed for economic development – may remain inconclusive. What is more certain is that BITs alone are insufficient to attract foreign investment.[7] Nevertheless, many states perceive BITs to be an important tool to attract investment. Even if this perception about the relationship between BITs and foreign investment is true, states should not pursue any type of development.

Instead of treating investment attraction as an end in itself, states should pay more 'attention to "investment for *what*" and "investment for *whom*" aspects'.[8]

[5] For an analysis of how IIL shifts risks of doing business from investors to states, local communities and the environment, see ch 4 (Vastardis) of this volume.

[6] BITs create or reinforce many asymmetries. For example, the ISDS system allows parent investors as shareholders to claim damages as reflective loss, while parent companies are generally treated as separate legal persons and not responsible for the conduct of their subsidiaries under corporate laws. See D Gaukrodger, 'Investment Treaties as Corporate Law: Shareholder Claims and Issues of Consistency', OECD Working Papers on International Investment, 2013/03 (OECD Publishing, 2013). BITs also increase corporate power in the agri-food system. AC Bull, J Plahe and L Gregory, 'International Investment Agreements and the Escalation of Private Power in the Global Agri-Food System' (2019) *Journal of Business Ethics* (advance access), available at doi.org/10.1007/s10551-019-04333-2.

[7] Akyüz concludes: 'Evidence suggest that BITs are neither necessary nor sufficient to bring significant amounts of FDI'. Y Akyüz, 'Foreign Direct Investment, Investment Agreements and Economic Development: Myths and Realities' in K Mohamadieh et al (eds), *Investment Treaties: Views and Experiences from developing Countries* (South Centre, 2015) 17, 30. See also UNCTAD, 'The Role of International Investment Agreements in Attracting Foreign Direct Investment to Developing Countries' (UNCTAD, 2009); Asian Development Bank, 'Asian Economic Integration Report: What Drives Foreign Direct Investment in Asia and the Pacific' (ADB, 2016).

[8] S Deva, 'Managing States' "Fatal Attraction" to International Investment Agreements' (Investment Policy Blog, 13 August 2018), available at investmentpolicy.unctad.org/blogs/75/managing-states-fatal-attraction-to-international-investment-agreements-.

States should first develop – through bottom-up meaningful consultations – an investment policy which identifies the 'for what' and 'for whom' aspects of foreign investment. Such a policy should go beyond the sole focus of attracting investment and look at achieving inclusive, humane and sustainable development. BITs should then be negotiated to operationalise such a policy.[9] For example, before negotiating BITs, states should conduct a comprehensive human rights impact assessment to investigate how expected investment will impact existing situation of poverty, (gender) inequality, rights of indigenous peoples, civil space and climate change.[10]

It seems that states – even those with a public commitment for human rights and sustainability – do not always act coherently when negotiating investment agreements. Let us consider the recent Comprehensive Agreement on Investment (CAI) concluded in principle between the European Union (EU) and China.[11] The CAI, which opens access to the Chinese market for European businesses on an equal footing, 'includes a commitment by both sides to try to complete negotiations on investment protection and investment dispute settlement within two years of the signature of the CAI'.[12] What is relevant for our purpose is the claim made by the European Commission that the CAI embeds sustainability:

> The CAI will bind the parties into a values-based investment relationship underpinned by sustainable development principles … China is undertaking commitments in the areas of labour and environment such as not to lower the standards of protection in order to attract investment, to respect its international obligations, as well as to promote responsible business conduct by its companies. China has also agreed to effectively implement the Paris Agreement on climate change as well as to effectively implement the International Labour Organisation Conventions (ILO) it has ratified. China has also agreed to make continued and sustained efforts to ratify the ILO fundamental Conventions on forced labour.[13]

Although the official text of CAI is not yet publicly available, it seems that the Chinese Government has successfully sold empty promises to the EU. Considering how much is well-known about China's human rights record generally and under President Xi in particular,[14] the EU can hardly be a naïve negotiator: rather, it must

[9] BITs should 'be harmonized with, and made conducive to, the broader goal of sustainable development'. UNCTAD (n 2) 15. See also NM Perrone, 'The ISDS Reform Process: The Missing Development Agenda' (South Centre Investment Policy Brief No 19, March 2020), available at www.southcentre.int/wp-content/uploads/2020/03/IPB19_The-ISDS-Reform-Process-The-missing-development-agenda_EN-2.pdf.

[10] See Committee on Economic, Social, and Cultural Rights, 'General Comment No 24 (2017) on State obligations under the International Covenant on Economic, Social and Cultural Rights in the context of business activities' (10 August 2017) UN Doc E/C.12/GC/24, para 13.

[11] European Commission, 'EU and China Reach Agreement in Principle on Investment' (30 December 2020), available at ec.europa.eu/commission/presscorner/detail/en/ip_20_2541.

[12] ibid.

[13] ibid.

[14] See, for example, H Davidson, 'China in Darkest Period for Human Rights Since Tiananmen, Says Rights Group' (*The Guardian*, 13 January 2021), available at www.theguardian.com/world/2021/jan/13/china-in-darkest-period-for-human-rights-since-tiananmen-says-rights-group; K Roth, 'China's Global Threat to Human Rights' (Human Rights Watch, 5 July 2020), available at www.hrw.org/world-report/2020/country-chapters/global.

be putting first the economic interests of EU investors. Krajewski, who considers the CAI to be a *sui generis* agreement,[15] notes: 'It appears that there has been only a limited assessment of the CAI from a human rights perspective, which is especially problematic in light of recent political developments in China'.[16] He rightly predicts that 'the obligations on sustainable development and labour in the CAI may not change anything on the ground'.[17] While the EU did conduct a sustainability impact assessment of the CAI, serious doubts have been expressed about its value in ascertaining the human rights implications of the CAI.[18] A research study had in fact cautioned:

> The EU should also consider whether it is wise to conclude such an agreement without a commitment on the part of China to protect human rights – including in Hong Kong and within Uyghur and other ethnic and religious minority communities – and should ensure the CAI includes binding and enforceable commitments with respect to upholding international human rights, labour rights, and environmental protections.[19]

Despite such caution, it seems that the EU did not consult a range of voices; it should have consulted civil society actors not just in the EU, but also in China (including Chinese dissidents based outside China). It remains to be seen whether the European Parliament will approve of the CAI. The European Commission's claim that the CAI will provide for 'a transparent resolution of disagreements with the involvement of civil society'[20] should be taken with a pinch of salt.

B. Pathway 2: Beyond Window Dressing

As Ranjan in his chapter for this volume[21] and others highlight,[22] the second-generation BITs (2.0 version) have started taking baby steps to recognise investors' responsibility towards contributing to sustainable development or having certain social responsibilities, such as those regarding human rights and the environment. For example, most of the BITs concluded in 2019 contain reform features: from

[15] M Krajewski, 'Dancing with the Dragon: The new EU-China Investment Agreement' (Verfassungsblog, 5 January 2021), available at verfassungsblog.de/dancing-with-the-dragon (the 'CAI is neither a typical free trade agreement as it lacks any rules on trade in goods (tariffs, non-tariff barriers, technical standards, trade remedies) and on trade-related intellectual property rights (TRIPS) nor is it a classical investment agreement as it does not contain any rules on investment protection').

[16] ibid.

[17] ibid.

[18] J Lawrence, T van Ho and A Yilmaz Vastardis, 'EU-China Comprehensive Agreement on Investment – A Scoping Study' (December 2020), available at www.boell.de/sites/default/files/2020-12/Endf%20EU-China%20Investment%20Agreement-korr.pdf?dimension1=division_ip.

[19] ibid 7–8.

[20] European Commission, 'EU and China' (2020).

[21] Ch 5.

[22] See, for example, I Seif, 'Business and Human Rights in International Investment Law: Empirical Evidence' in J Chaisse et al (eds), *Handbook of International Investment Law and Policy* (Springer, 2021).

preserving states' regulatory space, to adopting a sustainable development orientation, and modifying the investor-state dispute settlement mechanism.[23] It is also 'expected that the post-pandemic period will witness an acceleration of countries' efforts to reform their IIAs to ensure their right to regulate in the public interest, while maintaining effective levels of investment protection'.[24] In addition, arbitration tribunals are also developing investors' human rights obligations, including with reference to international human rights law.[25]

This shift is a direct response to the growing recognition that states should preserve regulatory space when negotiating BITs. Principle 9 of the UNGPs, for example, provides:[26] 'States should maintain adequate domestic policy space to meet their human rights obligations when pursuing business-related policy objectives with other States or business enterprises, for instance through investment treaties or contracts'. The commentary to Principle 9 further explains:

> [T]he terms of international investment agreements may constrain States from fully implementing new human rights legislation, or put them at risk of binding international arbitration if they do so. Therefore, States should ensure that they retain adequate policy and regulatory ability to protect human rights under the terms of such agreements, while providing the necessary investor protection.[27]

It is critical, though, that the current trend of reforming BITs does not end up becoming a window dressing exercise. First, merely mentioning investors' human rights obligations in the Preamble or in a vague hortatory manner will not go far. Nor will a preambular reference to a BIT's objective being to promote sustainable development suffice. Rather, the human rights obligations of investors and sustainability provisions in BITs should be on an equal footing to the rights of investors. Let us take the Regional Comprehensive Economic Partnership Agreement (RCEP) signed by ASEAN (Association of Southeast Asian Nations), Australia, China, Japan, the Republic of Korea and New Zealand as an example.[28] The Preamble to the RCEP recognises that 'the three pillars of sustainable development are interdependent and mutually reinforcing, and that economic partnership can play an important role in promoting sustainable development'.[29] This recognition is not, however, translated into a tangible action agenda in substantive

[23] UNCTAD, 'The Changing Landscape: New Treaties and Recent Policy Developments' (July 2020) 6–8, available at unctad.org/en/PublicationsLibrary/diaepcbinf2020d4.pdf.

[24] ibid 5.

[25] *Urbaser SA and Consorcio de Aguas Bilboa Bizkaia, Bilbao Biskaia Ur Partzuergoa v The Argentine Republic*, ICSID Case No ARB/07/26, Award (8 December 2016). See also M Krajewski, 'A Nightmare or a Noble Dream? Establishing Investor Obligations Through Treaty-Making and Treaty-Application' (2020) 5 *Business and Human Rights Journal* 105, 121–28.

[26] OHCHR, 'Guiding Principles on Business and Human Rights: Implementing the United Nations "Protect, Respect and Remedy" Framework' (2011) UN Doc A/HRC/17/31 (UNGP).

[27] UNGP, Commentary to Principle 9.

[28] Regional Comprehensive Economic Partnership Agreement (signed 15 November 2020, not yet in force), available at investmentpolicy.unctad.org/international-investment-agreements/treaty-files/6032/download.

[29] ibid 2.

provisions: it is proposed to establish a Committee on Sustainable Growth, but the sustainable development goals (SDGs) are not part of its mandate.[30] Moreover, there is no provision at all about the human rights obligations or social responsibilities of investors.

Second, the debate about the need for states to preserve regulatory space in BITs misses a crucial point: states do not merely have a *right* (or power) to regulate investors, they have a non-negotiable and non-delegable *obligation* under international human rights law to do so. This distinction is critical from the perspective of international human rights law. For example, an exception to expropriation included in the RCEP – ie, non-discriminatory regulatory actions by a Party that 'are designed and applied to achieve legitimate public welfare objectives, such as the protection of public health, safety, public morals, the environment, and real estate price stabilisation, do not constitute expropriation'[31] – merely empowers state parties to intervene, rather than obliging them to act to protect human rights.

Third, a more ambitious 3.0 version of BITs might need to go beyond managing the negative impact of investment projects on people or the planet: it should harness the potential of BITs to encourage investors to contribute to realising human rights and achieving the SDGs for everyone.[32] It is worrying that private sector investment in developing and transition economies in sectors relevant for the SDGs was on course to fall by about one-third in 2020 because of the COVID-19 pandemic.[33] Reversing this trend would require a fundamental change in conceiving both investment and IIL as a means to create global public good – earning profits for investors should only be part of an overarching goal of building a just and inclusive society. Sattorova in her chapter for this volume rightly reminds us why and how to move beyond the dominant discourse of IIL which see states as the sole bearer of obligations 'to do good'.[34]

A proposal to make such radical changes to BITs is likely to raise questions about whether IIL is the right tool to promote human rights and whether doing so will burden BITs. As I discuss below, these concerns are based on a historical misconceptualisation of IIL being a compartmentalised international law subfield that safeguards only the interests of investors.

C. Pathway 3: Beyond Investors

The current IIL is primarily geared to serve investors and their economic interests. It is literally 'investors' international law': created and adjudicated *by* investors'

[30] ibid, Art 18.6(1)(c); Annexure 18A, paras 12–14.

[31] ibid, Annexure 10B, para 4.

[32] Deva, 'Fatal Attraction' (2018).

[33] UNCTAD, 'SDG Investment Trends Monitor: International SDG Investment Flows to Developing Economies Down by One Third Due to COVID-19' (December 2020) 1, available at unctad.org/system/files/official-document/diaemisc2020d3_en.pdf.

[34] Ch 2.

agents *for* investors. However, this was not always meant to be so. As I have argued elsewhere,[35] at least since the early 1970s the regulatory intent at the UN level was to develop international standards which deal with *both* rights and responsibilities of foreign investors. The failure of this ambition resulted in a decoupling of the rights and responsibilities of investors with the abandonment of negotiations for the 1990 UN Code of Conduct on Transnational Corporations in 1992.[36]

In terms of investors' rights, the 1990 Draft Code had, for example, provided that transnational corporations (TNCs) 'shall receive fair and equitable treatment in the countries in which they operate' (para 49) and that entities of TNCs 'should be entitled to treatment no less favourable than that accorded to domestic enterprise in similar circumstances' (para 50). Moreover, while para 55 of the Code acknowledged the right of states to 'nationalize or expropriate the assets of a transnational corporation operating in their territory', it had provided that 'adequate compensation is to be paid by the State concerned, in accordance with the applicable legal rules and principles'. The 1990 Draft Code also contained a provision about the settlement of disputes between states and investors: if disputes are not amicably settled, they 'shall be submitted to competent national courts or authorities', but if the parties agree, the disputes could also be 'referred to other mutually acceptable or accepted dispute settlement procedures' (para 57). One can therefore see glimpses of investor-protection provisions commonly found in BITs.

At the same time, para 13 of the 1990 Draft Code had stipulated that TNCs 'shall respect human rights and fundamental freedoms in the countries in which they operate'. TNCs were also expected to refrain from supporting or sustaining the apartheid regime in South Africa (para 15), abstain from indulging in corrupt practices (para 20), respect labour rights in accordance with the ILO Tripartite Declaration (para 25), respect consumer rights and the environment (para 37–43), and disclose non-financial information (para 44).[37]

This attempt to marry rights and responsibilities of investors failed. And this failure resulted in a bifurcated evolution of 'soft' responsibilities and 'hard' rights of investors: investors' soft responsibilities were outlined in the OECD Guidelines for Multinational Enterprises in 1976 and in the ILO Tripartite Declaration of Principles concerning Multinational Enterprises in 1977, while their hard

[35] S Deva, 'International Investment Agreements and Human Rights: Assessing the Role of the UN's Business and Human Rights Regulatory Initiatives' in J Chaisse et al (eds), *Handbook of International Investment Law and Policy* (Springer, 2021).

[36] For an analysis, see KP Sauvant, 'The Negotiations of the United Nations Code of Conduct on Transnational Corporations: Experience and Lessons Learned' (2015) 16 *Journal of World Investment & Trade* 11; K Hamdani and L Ruffing (eds), *The United Nations Centre on Transnational Corporations: Corporate Conduct and the Public Interest* (Routledge, 2015).

[37] Considering these provisions, Ruggie was not correct in suggesting that human rights did not feature in the formation of this Code: J Ruggie, 'Business and Human Rights: The Evolving International Agenda' (2007) 101 *American Journal of International Law* 819.

rights got included in BITs (especially during 1990–2009).[38] The subsequent UN initiatives – in particular the UN Guiding Principles on Business and Human Rights (UNGPs) and the proposed business and human rights (BHR) treaty – have tried to address the side-effects of this decoupling failure since then.

Investors have a legitimate expectation to protect their investment. Foreign investors may also have a fear of arbitrary, discriminatory or unpredictable policies of host states. One may also concede that governments are not always the most benevolent actors. Having said this, even local investors or people in host states are subject to capricious actions by the same governments, and international law in most cases does not come to the rescue of such people. The special protection of foreign investors, in comparison to local investors or people, against state actions seems unjustified.[39] Moreover, one should keep in mind that investment alone is never enough for development or profit. Rather, a number of other societal actors (eg, workers, consumers) have to add their *investment* to make an investment project successful.[40]

Therefore, BITs should protect the legitimate interests of both investors and non-investors.[41] Such protection should include both rights and obligations of investors as well as the adjudication of investment-related disputes between various parties (eg, state vs state, investor vs state, community vs investor).[42] Doing so would be in line with going beyond the existing investor-state binary approach articulated by Cotula and Perrone in their chapter for this volume.[43]

D. Pathway 4: Beyond Compartments

International law remains fragmented[44] with little hope of a cohesive evolution in the near future. Nor does an agreement on hierarchy within different strands of

[38] Out of 3,224 BITs concluded during 1950–2019, 2,511 (about 78%) were signed during 1990–2009: Deva, 'International Investment Agreements and Human Rights' (2021) 8.

[39] See also J Ho, 'Passive Investments' (2020) 35 *ICSID Review – Foreign Investment Law Journal* (advance access) 1, available at doi.org/10.1093/icsidreview/siaa045.

[40] Rajan has argued that investors of a firm should be broadened to include those who make 'non-financial investment': R Rajan, '"50 Years Later, It's Time to Reassess": Raghuram Rajan on Milton Friedman and Maximizing Shareholder Value' (ProMarket, 18 September 2020), available at promarket.org/2020/09/18/50-years-later-its-time-to-reassess-raghuram-rajan-on-milton-friedman-and-maximizing-shareholder-value.

[41] UNCTAD (n 2) 7 ('A shared view has emerged on the necessity to ensure that the international investment regime works for all stakeholders'). See also ch 3 (Cotula and Perrone) of this volume.

[42] A study of 20 arbitrations involving some form of community action highlights that there is 'a need for systemic reform to ensure the rights, interests and perspectives of communities receive fuller consideration in investment processes'. L Cotula and M Schröder, *Community Perspectives in Investor-State Arbitration* (IIED, 2017) 31.

[43] Ch 3 (Cotula and Perrone) of this volume.

[44] See M Young (ed), *Regime Interaction in International Law: Facing Fragmentation* (Cambridge University Press, 2012).

international law seem likely, despite arguments,[45] calls[46] and attempts[47] to assert the primacy of international human rights law over IIL. Considering the continued divergence in different branches of international law,[48] what should be the way forward? Although the primacy of international human rights law is desirable at the normative level, three practical steps could be taken in the interim to start denting the current compartmentalised approach towards IIL. First, international human rights should, at a minimum, be regarded as *primus inter pares* (first among equals) among different branches of international law. In other words, it should not be assumed by states or arbitrators that obligations flowing from international human rights law would have to operate only within the space left or provided by obligations created under IIL.[49] Rather, human rights obligations of states and investors should be fully integrated in interpreting IIL, even if the former are not expressly part of the latter.

Second, states, investors, arbitrators and scholars should not operate within solo compartments of IIL, international human rights law, or international environmental law.[50] Rather, they should adopt a more holistic approach to international law.[51] Adopting such an approach would mean that states – or more precisely government officials from trade, finance and investment ministries – should not negotiate BITs as if international human rights law ceased to exist temporarily. Nor should investors or arbitrators assume that investors have no human rights responsibilities merely because old generation BITs did not include these.[52] Investors as business enterprises have a responsibility, at a minimum, to

[45] For example, reliance can be placed on Art 103 of the UN Charter, which provides: 'In the event of a conflict between the obligations of the Members of the United Nations under the present Charter and their obligations under any other international agreement, their obligations under the present Charter shall prevail'. See also A Guterres, 'Marking 75 Years of the Charter of the United Nations' (*UN Chronicle*, 25 June 2020), available at www.un.org/en/un-chronicle/marking-75-years-charter-united-nations.

[46] See, for example, submissions made by Amnesty International, APWLD, CIDSE, ESCR-Net, FIDH and ITUC. OHCHR, Written contributions in 'Third session of the open-ended intergovernmental working group on transnational corporations and other business enterprises with respect to human rights', available at www.ohchr.org/EN/HRBodies/HRC/WGTransCorp/Session3/Pages/WrittenContributions.aspx.

[47] See, for example, OHCHR, 'Elements for the Draft Legally Binding Instrument on Transnational Corporations and other Business Enterprises with Respect to Human Rights' (2017) paras 1.2, 1.4 and 10, available at www.ohchr.org/Documents/HRBodies/HRCouncil/WGTransCorp/Session3/LegallyBindingInstrumentTNCs_OBEs.pdf.

[48] For divergence even within international economic law, see S Gáspár-Szilágyi, D Behn and M Langford (eds), *Adjudicating Trade and Investment Disputes Convergence or Divergence?* (Cambridge University Press, 2020).

[49] For example, Viñuales argues that 'as a matter of principle there is no pre-determined hierarchy between an international environmental obligation and an investment discipline arising from an IIA'. JE Viñuales, *Foreign Investment and the Environment in International Law* (Cambridge University Press, 2012) 392.

[50] For an analysis of interactions between IIL and international environmental law, see Viñuales (ibid)

[51] The integration of international environmental law into investor regulation is considered and urged in ch 11 (Pereira de Andrade and Monebhurrun) of this volume.

[52] Choudhury argues that even if BITs are silent, TNCs as foreign investors are expected under soft international law to respect human rights and the environment; see ch 6 (Choudhury) of this volume.

respect all internationally recognised human rights[53] as well as norms of international humanitarian law which directly bind non-state actors like investors.[54] Their human rights responsibility is increasingly hardening at the national level because of mandatory human rights due diligence laws[55] or judicial decisions recognising a direct duty of care of parent companies towards affected communities in certain situations.[56] Because of these developments, it 'may soon be unsustainable for large multinational corporations to refuse to meet the responsibilities established by the Guiding Principles throughout their corporate group'.[57]

Third, BITs too have a role in turning responsibilities of investors into obligations.[58] Doing so will be consistent with the original regulatory intent highlighted above. It will also contribute to fixing an unjust asymmetry created by IIL. While a 'soft vs hard' or 'voluntary vs obligatory' debate is not very illuminating (as there is a role for both in a regulatory ecosystem), the battle between two unequal variables – hard rights of investors and soft human rights responsibilities of investors[59] – is inherently unfair and indefensible. Either investors' rights should become soft, or else investors' human rights responsibilities should become hard. BITs are both part of the problem and solution in this respect.

E. Pathway 5: Beyond Obligations

Including investors' human rights obligations in BITs – explicitly and in non-hortatory manner – is required, but this alone will not suffice. Rights require remedies. If investment-related projects breach human rights of community members,

[53] UNGPs, Principles 11 and 12; OECD Guidelines for Multinational Enterprises, Ch IV. For an analysis of emerging norms in this field, see D Gaukrodger, *Business Responsibilities and Investment Treaties – Consultation Paper by the OECD Secretariat* (OECD, 2020).

[54] See J Zrilič's analysis in ch 10 of this volume. See also discussion by Roorda and Ku in ch 9 of this volume, on how US courts used – without an explicit acknowledgment – doctrines under international humanitarian law and international criminal law to hold businesses accountable under the Alien Tort Statute.

[55] Mandatory human rights due diligence legislation in Europe are a prominent example of this. Business & Human Rights Resource Centre, 'National & Regional Developments on Mandatory Human Rights Due Diligence', available at www.business-humanrights.org/en/mandatory-due-diligence/national-regional-developments-on-mandatory-human-rights-due-diligence.

[56] See, for example, *Vedanta Resources PLC v Lungowe* [2019] UKSC 20; *Nevsun Resources Ltd v Araya* [2020] SCC 5.

[57] T van Ho, 'Vedanta Resources Plc and Another v. Lungowe and Others' (2020) 114 *American Journal of International Law* 110, 115.

[58] 'The best method to ensure that human rights obligations and responsibilities of businesses are taken into account is to have an express human rights clause in the IIA that makes the observance of human rights by the investor a precondition for the enjoyment of protection.' P Muchlinski, 'The Impact of a Business and Human Rights Treaty on Investment Law and Arbitration' in S Deva and D Bilchitz (eds), *Building a Treaty on Business and Human Rights: Context and Contours* (Cambridge University Press, 2017) 373. See also B Choudhury, 'Investor Obligations for Human Rights' (2020) *ICSID Review – Foreign Investment Law Journal* (advance access), available at doi.org/10.1093/icsidreview/siaa002.

[59] 'IIAs are legally binding instruments and not 'harmless' political declarations.' UNCTAD (n 2) 16. It seems that many human rights instruments lack teeth and are generally harmless for investors even if they breach them.

they must have *effective remedies* – not merely *effective mechanisms* that may provide some remedies – against the relevant investors.[60]

BITs raise at least three sets of issues concerning access to remedy.[61] The first relates to one of the asymmetries that they create: while investors are able to seek redress for their grievances before a fairly effective and functional arbitration system, no such recourse is available to people affected by investment projects. Second, investors often use BITs and the ISDS process to deny remedies to communities even before regular courts in both host and home states. Third, investors' arbitration claims – or even threats of bringing such claims – creates a regulatory chill in that states may hesitate to introduce effective regulatory frameworks or mechanisms to provide remedy for human rights abuses or environmental pollution.

BITs have a role to play in ensuring accountability of investors for human rights abuses. There are several possibilities as to how this reform could take place. For example, permanent tribunals could be established at national, regional or international levels to deal with all investment-related disputes.[62] The jurisdiction of such tribunals could be expanded to include claims brought by affected communities against investors.[63] Alternatively, as neither the arbitration process nor the arbitrators are eminently suitable to address human rights issues, remediation may be sought before courts in home states of investors and BITs may include provisions to this effect as a pre-condition of making investment.[64]

F. Pathway 6: Beyond ISDS

The ISDS system provides privileged justice to investors by creating special 'justice bubbles' for them.[65] It allows investors – third parties to BITs – to protect their

[60] In the vein of moving beyond any fixation on investor obligations, the available responses of states to investor wrongdoing, as well as the effectiveness of both mechanisms and remedies in this context, are explored in ch 7 (Jarrett) of this volume.

[61] See Columbia Centre on Sustainable Investment and UN Working Group on Business and Human Rights, 'Impacts of the International Investment Regime on Access to Justice' (September 2018), available at www.ohchr.org/Documents/Issues/Business/CCSI_UNWGBHR_InternationalInvestmentRegime.pdf.

[62] The EU, for example, has proposed to establish a multilateral investment court to replace ISDS. European Commission, 'The Multilateral Investment Court project' (21 December 2016), available at trade.ec.europa.eu/doclib/press/index.cfm?id=1608. Butler and Subedi have argued for the establishment of a world organisation as a standing mechanism for settlement of investment disputes: N Butler and S Subedi, 'The Future of International Investment Regulation: Towards a World Investment Organisation' (2017) 64 *Netherlands International Law Review* 43. See also discussion on the potential for sub-regional courts to play a larger role in investor regulation in ch 1 (Ho) of this volume, section III.C.

[63] See E George and E Thomas, 'Bringing Human Rights into Bilateral Investment Treaties: South Africa and a Different Approach to International Investment Disputes' (2018) 27 *Transnational Law & Contemporary Problems* 403, 446–49.

[64] See B Choudhury, 'Spinning Straw into Gold: Incorporating the Business and Human Rights Agenda into International Investment Agreements' (2017) 38 *University of Pennsylvania Journal of International Law* 425, 472–74.

[65] A Yilmaz Vastardis, 'Justice Bubbles for the Privileged: A Critique of the Investor-State Dispute Settlement Proposals for the EU's Investment Agreements' (2018) 6 *London Review of International*

business interests and claim millions of dollars in damages from states. On the other hand, states have very limited space to lodge counterclaims against investors for polluting the environment or causing human rights abuses.[66] Moreover, the opportunity for affected communities, as another set of third parties, to seek redress for investment-related human rights abuses or environmental pollution is marginalised to the submission of amicus briefs. Then there are concerns related to inconsistent arbitral awards, claims by indirect or remote owners, non-transparency, regulatory chill, and the independence of arbitrators.[67]

In view of these concerns, some states in recent times have started to find alternatives to ISDS, as minor or superficial reforms may not overcome fundamental or structural problems. A state-to-state dispute settlement process or establishing a permanent arbitration tribunal are two prominent alternatives being considered.[68] While it is unlikely that all states will embrace the same reform option for settling investment-related disputes, any new mechanism should address the several problems with the ISDS. Marceddu and Ortolani contend that from the perspective of the public, 'it is unclear what the main problem is (or is perceived to be) and where it originates'.[69] The perspectives of different stakeholders are likely to vary as to the nature and extent of problems with the ISDS as well as the proposed solutions. In my view, any alternative tribunal to the ISDS, in order to be normatively sound from a human rights perspective, should satisfy at least the following seven principles:

Principle 1: Equality. While one may justify establishing a specialised non-judicial tribunal to resolve special types of disputes,[70] providing access to such a tribunal only to investors is unjustifiable. Consequently, any alternative tribunal should have jurisdiction to all hear all investment-related disputes raised by states, investors, and communities.

Law 279. On how the treatment of allegations of corruption on the part of investors reinforces these 'justice bubbles' and should be revisited in order to pierce the bubbles, see ch 12 (Amado, Kern and Rodriguez) of this volume.

[66] T Ishikawa examines the right of host states to pursue counterclaims, which have some advantages over domestic litigation, against investors in their own right and/or on behalf of victims, in ch 8 of this volume. However, the practical efficacy of such counterclaims to hold investors accountable may be undermined by several factors, eg, corporate capture of the state.

[67] UNCTAD (n 2) 23, 43 and 48. On the uptick of and dilemmas posed by claims presented against states by indirect/remote owners, see especially Ho, 'Passive Investments' (2020).

[68] See UNCTAD (n 2) 55–58.

[69] ML Marceddu and P Ortolani, 'What Is Wrong with Investment Arbitration? Evidence from a Set of Behavioural Experiments' (2020) 31 *European Journal of International Law* 405, 407. They pose the following possibilities: (i) is it because investment arbitration offers a special channel for foreign investors, as compared with the citizens of the host state; (ii) is the problem the fact that arbitral tribunals are not a 'court-like', standing system with tenured adjudicators; (iii) is the main point of friction attributable to the nature of the rights protected by investment arbitration; or (iv) is it, more radically, because ISDS is an international jurisdiction, existing outside of the institutional architecture of any single state?

[70] ibid 426. Based on behavioural experiments of public concerning ISDS, Marceddu and Ortolani conclude that 'there is no proof of any a priori aversion to the creation of an international system for the resolution of investor-state disputes, as opposed to exclusive reliance on domestic courts'.

Principle 2: Accessibility. Any alternative arbitration tribunal should be accessible, especially to weaker or vulnerable parties to disputes.[71] To address inherent power asymmetries between investors and communities (or even investors and states in some cases), procedures should be in place to establish an equality of arms by overcoming barriers related to language, cost, and expertise, etc.

Principle 3: Coherence. To ensure coherence, the alternative tribunal should interpret a BIT in the light of its objectives (including those specified in the Preamble) and other relevant international law instruments such as those related to human rights, labour rights, the environment, climate change and sustainable development.[72]

Principle 4: Consistency. The current ad hoc system of selecting arbitrators is a recipe for inconsistent and unpredictable arbitration awards. The selection process also nurtures potential conflicts of interests. These concerns could be addressed by establishing a permanent tribunal whose arbitrators are selected in a transparent manner and for a long duration.[73]

Principle 5: Competence. Members of the tribunal should be drawn from a range of expert domains such as IIL, international human rights law and international environmental law.

Principle 6: Diversity. Members of the tribunal should be reflective of societal diversity in terms of gender, race, and geographical region.

Principle 7: Reviewability. The awards delivered by the alternative tribunal should be reviewable by an appellate panel before enforcement.

III. The Way Forward

This volume challenges the current 'business as usual' approach of IIL. While it may be tempting (due to political considerations and preserving the vested economic interests of a select privileged few) to be content with tweaks in IIL, transformative and systemic reforms are required to create a new economic order which does not leave behind a significant number of people as a matter of design.[74] For now, IIL is part of the problem. However, there is no reason that it cannot be part of the solution, provided IIL is reformed to respond to the current socio-economic context as well as existing needs and challenges.[75]

[71] Accessibility is a key component for access to justice under international human rights law.

[72] See Vienna Convention on the Law of Treaties (1969) 1155 UNTS 331, Art 31.

[73] One may draw inspiration here from international norms regarding independence of judges from both external and internal pressures. See, for example, Basic Principles on the Independence of the Judiciary (endorsed by UNGA Res 40/32 (29 November 1985) UN Doc A/RES/40/32).

[74] S Deva, 'A Just Recovery for Whom? And How to Achieve it?' (Business & Human Rights Resource Centre, 8 January 2021), available at www.business-humanrights.org/en/blog/a-just-recovery-for-whom-and-how-to-achieve-it.

[75] UNCTAD (n 2) 14–15.

Various contributions in this volume (including this concluding chapter) shed light not only on *why* such a transformation is required but also on *how* to do this. For example, Ho in her chapter shows that some opportunities for investor accountability can be found even under 'the existing procedural, substantive, and institutional pillars of international law'.[76] More opportunities could be created by reorienting the nature and purpose of IIL by following the six 'beyond pathways' articulated above.

Lack of political will is often cited as a reason for non-transformative reforms of IIL. However, instead of accepting the currents deficits in political will, multiple strategies should be employed to build the necessary political will, as 'Political and economic constraints can be overcome' to boost up the commitment of states.[77] Scholars have a key role in articulating these strategies, especially if a 'healthy regulatory climate for trade and investment requires that businesses and investors act responsibly'.[78] This volume is reflective of this desire to harness the power of IIL to contribute to creating a just global order, not merely for investors but also for hundreds of millions of intended beneficiaries of investment.

[76] Ch 1 (Ho) of this volume, section IV.

[77] TL Kirkebo and M Langford, 'The Commitment Curve: Global Regulation of Business and Human Rights' (2018) 3 *Business and Human Rights Journal* 157, 182.

[78] Gaukrodger, 'Business Responsibilities and Investment Treaties' (2013) 9.

INDEX

Lightning Source UK Ltd.
Milton Keynes UK
UKHW020101290621
386327UK00002B/80